MOTOR LEARNING
CONCEPTS AND APPLICATIONS

SIXTH EDITION

Richard A. Magill

Louisiana State University

Boston   Burr Ridge, IL   Dubuque, IA   Madison, WI   New York   San Francisco   St. Louis
Bangkok   Bogotá   Caracas   Lisbon   London   Madrid
Mexico City   Milan   New Delhi   Seoul   Singapore   Sydney   Taipei   Toronto

McGraw-Hill Higher Education

*A Division of The **McGraw-Hill** Companies*

MOTOR LEARNING: CONCEPTS AND APPLICATIONS
SIXTH EDITION

Published by McGraw-Hill, an imprint of The McGraw-Hill Companies, Inc., 1221 Avenue of the Americas, New York, NY 10020. Copyright © 2001, 1998, 1993, 1989, 1985, 1980 by The McGraw-Hill Companies, Inc. All rights reserved. No part of this publication may be reproduced or distributed in any form or by any means, or stored in a database or retrieval system, without the prior written consent of The McGraw-Hill Companies, Inc., including, but not limited to, in any network or other electronic storage or transmission, or broadcast for distance learning.

Some ancillaries, including electronic and print components, may not be available to customers outside the United States.

This book is printed on acid-free paper.

1 2 3 4 5 6 7 8 9 0 QPF/QPF 0 9 8 7 6 5 4 3 2 1 0

ISBN 0–07–232936–X

Vice president and editor-in-chief: *Kevin T. Kane*
Executive editor: *Vicki Malinee*
Developmental editor: *Carlotta Seely*
Senior marketing manager: *Pamela S. Cooper*
Project managers: *Rose Koos/Richard H. Hecker*
Media technology associate producer: *Judi David*
Senior production supervisor: *Sandy Ludovissy*
Coordinator of freelance design: *David W. Hash*
Interior designer: *Sheilah Barrett*
Cover designer: *Sarin Creative*
Cover image: © *The Stock Market/Pete Saloutus*
Senior photo research coordinator: *Carrie K. Burger*
Supplement coordinator: *Tammy Juran*
Compositor: *Shepherd, Inc.*
Typeface: *10/12 Times Roman*
Printer: *Quebecor Printing Book Group/Fairfield, PA*

Unit Openers: 1: © Sports: The Competitive Spirit/PhotoDisc; **2, 4:** © Competitive Sports/Corbis CD; **3, 6:** Active Lifestyles 2/Corbis CD; **5:** Arts & Entertainment/Corbis CD

Page 5, p. 150, p. 205: © Active Lifestyles/Corbis CD; **p. 41:** © Business on the Go/PhotoDisc; **p. 249:** © Sports & Recreation/PhotoDisc; **p. 311:** © Sports & Fitness/Corbis CD

Library of Congress Cataloging-in-Publication Data

Magill, Richard A.
    Motor learning : concepts and applications / Richard A. Magill. — 6th ed.
        p.   cm.
    Includes bibliographical references and index.
    ISBN 0–07–232936–X
    1. Motor learning. I. Title.

BF295 .M36   2001
152.3'34—dc21   00–060929
                                                        CIP

www.mhhe.com

BRIEF
CONTENTS

CONTENTS

PREFACE

The learning and performance of motor skills is an important part of the everyday lives of people of all ages. Therefore the study of motor learning continues to be an integral part of the preparation of professionals who will assist people as they learn and perform motor skills. It is largely because of this role that this book is now in its sixth edition. It is a privilege to be able to contribute to the preparation of key professionals in this way. The experience of the previous five editions has reinforced my original goal for the book as an introductory text for undergraduates as they prepare for a variety of professional positions, including physical education teachers, coaches, physical therapists, occupational therapists, instructors in the military and industry, dance teachers, and community education personnel. It is within this context that the sixth edition has been developed.

Although the general scope and orientation of this edition remain consistent with those of previous editions, it contains a few changes intended to enhance the quality and use of the book. These improvements have resulted from suggestions of people who use this book in their classes and from recommendations of reviewers of the previous edition.

HIGHLIGHTS OF THE SIXTH EDITION

New Organization
The most notable change is an organizational one. Rather than being organized by chapter, with several concepts within one chapter, this edition presents each concept as a separate chapter. What were previously chapters are now units. It is important to note that this structural change does not eliminate the "concepts approach" that has been so well received in previous editions. The concepts approach continues. Each chapter begins with a concept statement that identifies the primary topic or principle discussed in the chapter. An application section follows that identifies the relevance of the concept to professional practice. Then the discussion focuses on establishing the basis for the concept statement and its application.

A New Chapter on Memory
Second, an updated and expanded chapter on memory (Chapter 10) is an outstanding addition to this text. Based on well-received material presented in earlier editions, this chapter represents a key element of the unit on attention and memory. In addition to featuring the classic memory issues, the chapter highlights the most recent memory-related research.

Key Restructuring
Third, three concepts have been relocated. Two were previously placed at the end of the book in a chapter focusing on abilities; the third was in the chapter on motor control preparation and attention. The concept of the identification of motor abilities, which is now chapter 2, is a part of the initial unit that introduces certain concepts fundamental to the

study of motor learning. The second abilities concept, which addresses the prediction of future performance, is now chapter 13 and is located in the unit that introduces issues specifically related to the concept of learning. Finally, the concept related to the preparation of action is now chapter 7, which has been relocated to unit II, Introduction to Motor Control.

New Research

Other revisions include an extensive updating of research references cited. In many chapters older references have been replaced by more recent research investigations. This updating is reflected in both the reference lists and the chapter discussions. However, care has been taken to ensure that classic research studies and significant older studies are included. Such research references are important in the study of motor learning because they establish a sense of the history of the investigation of an issue and the development of knowledge about it. These discussions are not intended to be exhaustive reviews of the research literature. Instead, they are designed to present students with relevant examples of research that form the basis of the concept being discussed.

More "A Closer Look" boxes have also been included. As before, these pedagogical aids serve as enhancements to the text rather than being essential parts of it. The information presented in these boxes enhances the text by (1) providing more detail about a research study cited in the text, (2) highlighting or summarizing key points made in a discussion of complex issues, or (3) describing specific professional practice applications that relate to the discussion of a concept.

In addition, the number and variety of professional practice applications have been increased. This change was made to further enhance the students' awareness of the relationship between a specific concept and the range of professional practice environments in which they work to help people learn motor skills.

Finally, this edition continues to present the study of motor learning from a behavioral point of view. This perspective does not negate the impor-

tance or relevance of a physiological approach. However, it does reflect my view that to attempt to present both orientations adequately in the same text would require a volume that would be considerably larger and more complex than would be appropriate for a one-semester undergraduate introductory course in motor learning.

NEW OR EXPANDED TOPICS

Chapter 1: The Classification of Motor Skills
- Revised discussion of skills, actions, and movements
- Skills or actions in relation to goals and required movements
- New presentation of Gentile's taxonomy of motor skills

Chapter 2: Motor Abilities
- Incorporation of motor abilities as introductory material
- Updated discussions about scientific background

Chapter 3: The Measurement of Motor Performance
- Enhanced demonstration of simple, choice, and discrimination reaction time
- Reaction time and movement time in assessing performance problems in decision-making situations (e.g., sport and car driving)

Chapter 4: Motor Control Theories
- Relevance of motor control theory to the practitioner
- Dynamic pattern theory of Kelso
- Comparison of motor program and dynamic pattern theories in relation to relative timing invariance
- Motor program and dynamic pattern theories in relation to spontaneous walk-to-run gait change phenomenon
- Implications of the dynamic pattern view for physical rehabilitation
- Updated discussion of control theory controversy

Chapter 5: Performance Characteristics of Complex Skills

- Three prominent hypotheses concerning explanations of Fitts' law
- Updated discussion of prehension
- Use of functional objects to enhance reaching performance in physical rehabilitation
- Updated section on bimanual coordination

Chapter 6: Proprioception and Vision

- Updated discussion of role of proprioception in motor control, including section on tendon vibration technique
- Anatomy and function of key proprioceptors involved in providing information to central nervous system
- Functions of *tau* in motor control
- New section on coordination of vision and hand movement in manual aiming
- New section on amount of time needed to make visual feedback-based movement corrections
- Monocular and binocular vision in reaching and grasping, and roles of central and peripheral vision in prehension
- Updated information on visual cues as walking aids in patients with Parkinson's disease
- Revised section on vision and catching

Chapter 7: Action Preparation

- Task and performer characteristics in relation to time required to perform an action
- Demonstration of use of fractionated visual reaction time to understand developmental coordination disorder (DCD)
- Demonstration of how functional demand affects action preparation
- Updated discussion of rhythmicity preparation
- New research throughout chapter

Chapter 8: Attention as a Limited Capacity Resource

- Summary of continuous and probe secondary-task techniques
- Attention and automaticity

Chapter 9: Visual Selective Attention

- How we select visual cues
- Updated research on visual search and action preparation
- Training visual search strategies
- Research study describing a visual search training program to teach anticipation skills in squash

Chapter 10: Memory Components, Forgetting, and Strategies

- Revised and updated chapter
- Most recent memory-related research
- Several new boxes

Chapter 11: Defining and Assessing Learning

- Key distinctions between terms *performance* and *learning*
- Examples of performance situations for closed and open skills that require "adaptability" by the performer
- Assessing learning from coordination dynamics
- New research demonstrating how practice performance can misrepresent learning

Chapter 12: The Stages of Learning

- Study of performer and performance characteristics during initial stage of learning
- Revised discussion of Gentile's stages of learning model
- Concept of "freezing the degrees of freedom"
- Experiment demonstrating changes in conscious attention as a function of practice
- Research findings comparing experts and novices in use of vision in motor skill performance situations involving time stress
- Updated research throughout chapter

Chapter 13: Predicting Performance for Later Learning Stages

- Accounting for poor prediction from early to later stage performance
- Recent work by Ackerman relating his model of abilities and stages of learning model of Fitts and Posner

Chapter 14: Transfer of Learning
- Experiment demonstrating use of virtual reality training before experiencing the real environment
- Transfer-appropriate processing view of why transfer occurs
- Specificity of practice principle related to examples of skill practice situations
- Revised discussion of negative transfer
- Study demonstrating bilateral transfer for mirror writing

Chapter 15: Demonstration and Verbal Instructions
- Updated discussion of demonstration
- Verbal instructions and cues
- Experiment showing influence on learning of where a beginner focuses attention during each practice swing in golf

Chapter 16: The Effect of Augmented Feedback on Skill Learning
- Feedback family to better define terms and to provide examples
- Examples of knowledge of results (KR) and knowledge of performance (KP) for situations related to sport, everyday activities, and physical rehabilitation
- Study concerning relationship between teacher feedback in physical education classes and several different practice and performance characteristics
- Updated research cited in discussion section

Chapter 17: The Content of Augmented Feedback
- Augmented feedback content issues
- Erroneous augmented feedback
- Recent study on basing knowledge of performance on a skill analysis
- Recent research on videotape, movement kinematics, and biofeedback as augmented feedback
- Case study involving use of biofeedback for balance training for a stroke patient

Chapter 18: The Timing of Augmented Feedback
- Research investigations into skill learning and rehabilitation
- Updated research throughout chapter
- Frequency of presenting augmented feedback

Chapter 19: Practice Variability
- Gentile taxonomy characteristics of intertrial variability
- New figure illustrating continuum of amount of contextual interference and its relationship to various practice schedule organization options
- New research on limits of contextual interference effect
- Practical implications of contextual interference effect
- Experiment showing effectiveness of moderate contextual interference practice schedule for basketball

Chapter 20: Practice Distribution
- Updated research on intertrial interval and practice distribution
- Implications of massed and distributed practice for scheduling practice or rehabilitation session
- Relation of practice distribution and contextual interference to different skill learning contexts

Chapter 21: The Amount of Practice
- Overlearning strategy and procedural skills
- Overlearning strategy and poor test performance
- Updated research throughout chapter

Chapter 22: Whole and Part Practice
- Fractionization as a part practice strategy for bimanual coordination skills
- Various whole and part practice conditions that facilitate learning of bimanual coordination skills

- New idea for simplification of practice strategy
- Research study on music accompaniment to help patients with Parkinson's disease improve their walking pace

Chapter 23: Mental Practice
- Updated research throughout chapter
- Mental practice aids performance preparation
- Examples of use of imagery in a variety of sports

SUCCESSFUL FEATURES

Motor Learning: Concepts and Applications offers the following helpful features to enhance student learning.

Definition Boxes
Key terms are displayed in the text in boldface type and are defined in corresponding boxes for easy reference. Other important terms in the text appear in italics for emphasis.

Applications
Each chapter begins with an Applications section that explains the chapter concept in practical terms. It helps students understand the relevance of the concept to professional practice.

Discussion
This section explains how the chapter concept will be presented. It gives students the rationale for this presentation, making the concept easier to understand at the outset.

Summary
Each chapter concludes with a summary that presents the main ideas and their significance. The student can then return to a topic in the chapter for clarification or study.

Related Readings
Because some students want to know more about a particular topic, the readings list at the end of each chapter offers carefully selected journal articles and books for exploration.

Study Questions
A set of questions appears at the end of each chapter to allow students to review and analyze the chapter content.

ANCILLARIES

Instructor's Manual and Test Bank
This printed manual contains suggested teaching outlines that correspond with the text. The Test Bank section includes 550 questions: essay, multiple-choice, and fill-in-the-blank.

Laboratory Manual
This online manual is available to students and instructors with a passcard. It includes new laboratory activities on topics such as encoding specificity, preselection effect, and verbal labels and recall.

Computerized Test Bank
Test questions from the printed Test Bank are available on our computerized testing and grading program, MicroTest III, for Windows or Macintosh.

Online Learning Center
The Online Learning Center provides instructors with downloads of helpful ancillaries, such as a PowerPoint presentation (see below) that corresponds with each chapter of *Motor Learning Concepts and Applications*. For students, the Online Learning Center offers self-scoring quizzes, career opportunities, FAQs, and access to web links and updated material.

McGRAW-HILL PAGEOUT: THE COURSE WEBSITE DEVELOPMENT CENTER

PageOut is a program that allows instructors to develop websites for their courses easily. The site includes:

- A course home page
- An instructor home page
- A syllabus (the syllabus is interactive and customizable, allows quizzing and

addition of instructor notes, and can be linked to the Online Learning Center)

- Web links
- Online discussion areas (multiple discussion areas per class)
- Online grade book
- An area to list links to students' web pages
- More than 16 design templates from which to choose

This program is available to registered adopters of *Motor Learning: Concepts and Applications.* To become a registered user, contact your local sales representative. If you would like assistance in using the PageOut program, McGraw-Hill technology experts will create a website for qualified adopters in 30 minutes or less. This program is exciting for those who use *Motor Learning: Concepts and Applications* because the Online Learning Center content can be imported into your web page.

Health and Human Performance Supersite

McGraw-Hill's Health and Human Performance Supersite offers a wide variety of information for both instructors and students—from the latest health topics in the media to career opportunities in the field. Visit this website at: www.mhhe.com/catalogs/sem/hhp.

A sample of what you will find at this supersite includes:

This Just In. Look here for the latest information on "hot" health topics in the news. Read the monthly featured article to find out more about topics that everyone is talking about. Search the archive for a wide selection of resources on health-related topics.

Faculty Support. Find the best resources and services available to teach your course. Click here to find online supplements such as Online Learning Centers and PowerPoint presentations. Other offerings include assessment activities and PowerWeb.

Student Success Center. This is the place for students to find everything from study tips and online study materials to text updates on health information, which often changes daily. They can also look here for scholarship information and career opportunities.

Author Arena. Find out more about our authors—some of the most highly respected educators and pioneers in the field of health and human performance. Check on upcoming professional conventions so you can mark your calendar. Explore the possibility of using your ideas and writing skills to develop new courses and ancillaries.

ACKNOWLEDGMENTS

I want to acknowledge the contributions of several colleagues and friends who were kind enough to give of their time to provide me with valuable suggestions and needed information. Their comments assisted me in a variety of ways as I prepared this sixth edition. Among these, Kellie Hall, Mark Fischman, and Tim Lee deserve special recognition and thanks. In addition, I appreciate the efforts of the reviewers selected by the editors at McGraw-Hill to critique the previous edition and provide suggestions about what to keep, delete, and change in this new edition. The editorial and production staff at McGraw-Hill also deserve many thanks for their able assistance, direction, and support. At Louisiana State University, Amelia Lee, my department chair, has been a wonderful source of support and encouragement throughout the process of developing this revised edition. Finally, I would be remiss if I did not thank the many undergraduate and graduate students who have been in my motor learning classes throughout the years. Although they take the class to learn something about motor learning, I find that each group of students teaches me something about motor learning that influences my own

understanding of the role it should play in professional preparation.

The publisher's reviewers made excellent
comments and suggestions that were very useful in
writing and revising this book. The contributions of
the following reviewers are greatly appreciated:

Elizabeth Bate
University of Northern Colorado

Greg Dale
Winthrop University

Patty Hacker
South Dakota State University

Charlotte Humphries
University of Southern Mississippi

Leon E. Johnson
University of Missouri, Columbia [retired]

Brenda Lichtman
Sam Houston State University

Glenn Roswal
Jacksonville State University

Richard A. Magill
Baton Rouge, Louisiana

To My Mother, Audrey, and Sister, Judy

INTRODUCTION TO MOTOR SKILLS AND ABILITIES

CHAPTER

The Classification
of Motor Skills

*Concept: Motor skills can be classified into
general categories*

APPLICATION

When people run, walk with an artificial limb, throw a baseball, hit a tennis ball, play the piano, dance, or operate a wood lathe, they are engaged in the performance of a type of human skill called *motor skills.* In this book, we focus on helping you understand how people learn, and how you can help people learn, motor skills such as these.

As you engage in this study, you will find it useful to draw general conclusions, applying what you learn to a broad range of motor skills, rather than making many specific statements about many skills. In the Discussion section of this chapter, we provide a starting point for making these kinds of general statements. That starting point is the classification of motor skills into broad categories that emphasize the similarities rather than the differences among skills.

For example, the skill of maneuvering a wheelchair through a crowded hallway and that of hitting a pitched baseball seem quite distinct. However, both skills have one characteristic in common. People must perform both skills in what we will call an "open" environment. This means that to perform the skill successfully, a person must adapt certain aspects of his or her movements to changing characteristics in the performance environment. For the wheelchair skill, this means that the person must be able to maneuver success-

fully through a crowded hallway in which people are standing or walking around. For the baseball-hitting skill, the changing environment includes the ball itself as it moves toward the person. For both of these skills, performance success requires the performer to adapt quickly and accurately to changing conditions. When we view them in terms of this common characteristic, we can see that these two seemingly diverse skills are related.

DISCUSSION

To begin your study of motor learning, you should understand some things about the skills that are at the heart of this study. To enhance this understanding, we will discuss two important points about motor skills. First, we will define motor skills, considering what distinguishes them from other skills; as we do so, we will define some other commonly used terms related to the term *motor skill.* Second, we will discuss four different approaches to classifying motor skills into categories that identify common characteristics of various skills. The benefit of classifying skills is that it can provide us with an appropriate basis for establishing generalizations, or principles, about how we perform and learn motor skills. These generalizations enable us in turn to develop theories about skill performance and learning. Additionally, they help us to establish guidelines for instructors, coaches, and therapists who must develop effective strategies that will enhance motor skill learning and rehabilitation.

Skills, Actions, and Movements

Several terms in the motor learning literature are related to the term *motor skills.* These are *skills, actions,* and *movements.* Each term is used in a specific way; we should understand and use each one correctly.

Skills and actions. The term **skill** is a commonly used word that we will use in this text to denote *a task that has a specific goal to achieve.* For example, we say that "multiplication is a fundamental skill of mathematics," or "playing the piano is a skill that takes practice." Of these two examples, the skill of piano playing includes a **motor skill** because it is *a skill that requires voluntary body and/or limb movement to achieve its goal,* which is to play the piano. Looked at this way, the skill of piano playing involves the goal of striking the correct keys in the proper sequence and at the appropriate time, and it requires finger and hand movement to achieve that goal.

In the motor learning and control literature a term that has become increasingly more common to designate a specific motor skill is the term *actions.* For our purposes, we will use this term as synonymous with *skills.* That is, **actions** are *goal-directed activities that consist of body and/or limb movements.* Another way of defining an action is to say that it is *a family of movements.* Some have referred to an action as *an equivalence class of movements* (see Schmidt & Turvey, 1992).

Note several characteristics that are common to motor skills. First, there is *a goal to achieve.* This means that motor skills have a purpose. Sometimes you will see the term *action goal* to refer to the goal of a motor skill. Second, motor skills of interest in this text are *performed voluntarily;* in other words, we are not considering reflexes as skills. Although an eye blink may have a purpose and involve

movement, it occurs involuntarily and is therefore not a skill in the sense in which we are using the term. Third, a motor skill *requires body and/or limb movement* to accomplish the goal of the task. This characteristic is especially important because it is the basis for distinguishing motor skills from other types of human skills. For example, although calculating math problems is a skill, it does not *require* body and/or limb movement to achieve its goal. We commonly refer to the type of skill used for math problems as a cognitive skill.

One additional characteristic further identifies the types of motor skills of interest in this text: they *need to be learned* in order for a person to achieve the goal of the skill. The piano-playing example clearly has this characteristic. But consider a skill like walking. Although walking may seem to be something that humans do "naturally," it must be learned by the infant who is attempting to move in his or her environment by this new and exciting means of locomotion. And walking is a skill some people may need to relearn. Examples are people who have had strokes, or hip or knee joint replacements, as well as people who must learn to walk with artificial legs.

Movements. In the motor learning and control literature, the term **movements** indicates *behavioral characteristics of a specific limb or a combination of limbs.* In this sense, movements are component parts

---

skill (a) an action or task that has a specific goal to achieve; (b) an indicator of quality of performance.

motor skill a skill that requires voluntary body and/or limb movement to achieve its goal.

action a goal-directed activity that consists of body and/or limb movements.

movements behavioral characteristics of specific limbs or a combination of limbs that are component parts of an action or motor skill.

A CLOSER LOOK

Examples of Skills, Actions, Goals, and Movements

The following examples illustrate how a skill or action can have various goals, which would require movements that differ to achieve the action goal. For each of the goals within a skill/action, consider how the movements would differ to allow the person to achieve the goal while carrying out the same skill/action.

Skills/Actions	Goal
1. Walking	a. To walk from the front of an empty room to the back of the room.
	b. To walk from one store to another store in a crowded mall.
	c. To walk several blocks on a sidewalk.
2. Throwing	a. To accurately throw a small round ball at a target on the wall.
	b. To throw a small round ball as far as possible.
	c. To throw a beach ball to a friend to catch.
3. Reaching and grasping an object	a. To pick up a full coffee mug from a table and drink from it.
	b. To pick up a bowl of soup to move it from one location on a table to another location on the table.
	c. To pick up a can of juice and shake it.

of skills and actions. A variety of different limb behavior characteristics can occur that still enable a person to walk successfully. For example, our limbs move differently in distinct ways when we walk on a concrete sidewalk and when we walk on an icy sidewalk—or on a sandy beach. However, although the actual movements may differ, the skill we perform in each of these different situations is walking.

The important point here is that a variety of movements can produce the same action and thereby accomplish the same goal. For example, walking up a set of stairs is an action. The goal is to get to the top of the stairs. However, to achieve this goal a person can use a variety of different movements. A person can take one step at a time very slowly, or take each step very quickly, or take two steps at a time, and so on. In each situation, the action is the same but the movements the person produces to achieve the goal of the action are different.

Why distinguish movements from skills and actions? There are three reasons why it is impor-

tant, and useful, to consider movements as distinct from skills and actions. First, people learn skills and actions. Although people must produce movements to perform a skill or action, different people may produce different movement characteristics to achieve the same action goal. For example, how many golfers swing a golf club exactly alike? All golfers must learn the action of hitting a golf ball with a golf club, but each person will likely have some unique movement characteristics.

Second, people adapt movement characteristics to achieve a common action goal. Why do golfers have different swing characteristics but yet achieve the same action goal? People differ in physical features that limit the movement characteristics they can produce to perform a skill. This physical feature limitation is an especially critical concern to take into account when working with people in physical rehabilitation settings. Although there may be a "preferred" way for people to walk, certain sensory or motor impairments may not allow a person to walk in that way. But people can make movement

One-Dimension Classification Systems

We can classify motor skills by determining which skill characteristics are similar to those of other skills. The most prevalent approach has been to categorize skills according to one common characteristic. Three skill classification systems use this approach.

For each system, the common characteristic is divided into two categories, which represent extreme ends of a continuum rather than dichotomous categories. This continuum approach allows a skill to be classified in terms of which category the skill characteristic is more like, rather than requiring that the characteristic fit one category exclusively. Consider an analogy. The concepts "hot" and "cold" represent two categories of temperatures. Although we typically consider them as distinct categories, we also can view hot and cold as words describing opposite ends of a temperature continuum, because there are degrees of hot or cold that do not fit exclusively into one or the other category. By considering hot and cold as anchor points on a continuum, we can maintain the category distinctions while at the same time we can more accurately classify various temperature levels that do not fit into only one or the other category.

Size of primary musculature required. One characteristic that distinguishes categories of motor skills is the size of muscle groups required to perform the skill. Skills like walking and hopping do not require as the prime movers muscle groups of the same size as those used for skills like piano playing and eating with chopsticks. By distinguishing skills based on the size of the muscle groups required to accomplish the actions, researchers have established a motor skill classification system in which there are two categories, known as gross and fine motor skills.

To achieve the goals of **gross motor skills,** people need to use *large musculature* to produce the actions. These skills need less movement precision than fine motor skills do. We classify skills such as

The action of hitting a golf ball typically involves different movement characteristics from one shot to the next.

characteristic adjustments and still be able to successfully walk. Even though their gait pattern may look different from the nondisabled pattern, they can successfully achieve the action goal.

Third, as you will see in chapter 3, people evaluate actions and movements with different types of measures. We typically evaluate actions in terms of measures that relate to the outcome of the action, such as the distance a person walked, the length of time it took a person to run a certain distance, or the number of points a basketball shot was worth. Movements, on the other hand, are evaluated by measures that relate to specific characteristics of body, limb, and/or muscle activity, such as kinematic, kinetic, and electromyographic (EMG) measures.

---

gross motor skill   a motor skill that requires the use of large musculature to achieve the goal of the skill.

the so-called *fundamental motor skills*—walking, jumping, throwing, leaping, etc.—as gross motor skills.

Fine motor skills fall at the other end of this classification continuum. Fine motor skills require greater control of the *small muscles,* especially those involved in hand-eye coordination, and require a high degree of precision in hand and finger movement. Handwriting, typing, drawing, sewing, and fastening a button are examples of motor skills that are on the fine motor skill end of the continuum in the muscle size classification system. Note that whereas large muscles may be involved in the action of a fine motor skill, the small muscles are the primary muscles involved to achieve the goal of the skill.

The use of the gross/fine distinction for motor skills is popular in a number of settings. In education settings, special education and adapted physical education curricula and tests commonly distinguish skills on this basis. We also find this classification system in rehabilitation environments. Physical therapists typically work with patients who need to rehabilitate gross motor skills such as walking, whereas occupational therapists more commonly deal with patients who need to learn fine motor skills. People who are involved in early childhood development also find the gross/fine categorization useful and have developed tests of motor development along the gross/fine dimension. Also, industrial and military aptitude tests commonly use the gross and fine motor skill distinction.

The specificity of where actions begin and end. Researchers also classify motor skills on the basis of how specific the beginning and end locations are for an action. If a skill requires a specified beginning and end location, we categorize the skill as a **discrete motor skill.** Discrete skills include flipping a light switch, depressing the clutch of an automobile, and hitting a piano key. Each of these skills involves a specified place to begin and end the action. Also, note from the examples that discrete skills typically are simple, one-movement skills.

Sometimes a skill requires a series or sequence of discrete movements, such as shifting gears in a standard shift car, or playing a song on a piano. We refer to these types of skills as **serial motor skills.** The gear shifting example is a good illustration. To shift gears in a car, the driver must perform a sequence of discrete movements. To shift from second to third gear, the driver performs a sequence of seven discrete movements. First he or she lifts a foot off the accelerator, then depresses the clutch with the other foot, then moves the gear shift forward to neutral, then to the right, then forward again to third gear, then releases the clutch, and finally depresses the accelerator.

At the opposite end of this classification system continuum fall **continuous motor skills,** which are skills with arbitrary beginning and end locations. In addition, continuous skills usually contain repetitive movements. We can classify skills such as steering an automobile, tracking a moving cursor on a computer monitor with a joystick, swimming, and walking as continuous skills. Although some continuous skills, such as walking and swimming have distinct beginning locations, the end location is arbitrary, and the movements are repetitive.

This classification system has been especially prevalent in motor skills research literature when authors are focusing on the control of movement. Researchers have found, for example, that certain phenomena about how we control movement are applicable to discrete skills but not to continuous skills, and vice versa. The distinction between discrete and continuous skills is especially popular in the research literature of those who view the motor skill performance from the perspectives of human engineering and human factors.

The stability of the environment. One classification system has its roots in industrial as well as educational and rehabilitation settings. Researchers base this system on the stability of the environment in which the skill is performed (Gentile, 1972; Poulton, 1957). For this classification system, the term *environment* refers specifically to the object the person is acting on or to the characteristics of the context in which the person performs the skill. For example, if a person is hitting a ball, the critical component of the environment is the ball itself. For the skill of walking, however, the critical environment features are the surface on which the person must walk and the characteristics of the environmental context in which the person must walk.

According to this classification scheme, if the environment is stable, that is, if it does not change while the person is performing the skill, then we classify the skill as a **closed motor skill.** For these skills, *the object to be acted on does not change during the performance of a skill.* In effect, the object waits to be acted on by the performer. For example, picking up a cup from a table is a closed motor skill, because the cup does not move between the time you decide to pick it up until you pick it up. Walking in an uncluttered room is also a closed motor skill, because the environmental context does not change while you are walking. Other examples of closed motor skills are shooting an arrow at a stationary target, buttoning a shirt, stair climbing, and hitting a ball off a tee. For each of these skills, the performer can initiate action when he or she is ready to do so and perform the skill according to his or her own wishes.

Conversely, an **open motor skill** is *a skill that a person performs in a nonstable environment, where the object or context is in motion during the performance of the skill.* To perform such a skill successfully, the performer must act according to the action of the object or the changing characteristics of the environment. For example, skills such as driving a car, stepping onto a moving escalator, walking on a sidewalk crowded with people walking, striking a moving tennis ball, and catching a ball are all open motor skills. People perform each of these skills in a temporally and/or spatially changing environment. For example, during a rally a tennis player cannot stand in one spot and decide when and how he or she will respond to the ball. To be successful, the player must move and act in accordance with the ball's spatial location and speed characteristics. Similarly, walking on a crowded sidewalk is an open motor skill, because

the person's walking characteristics vary depending on the movement of the other people.

Notice that in the last two paragraphs, we have classified the skill of walking as *both an open and a closed skill.* The distinguishing feature is the environmental context in which the walker performs the skill. When walking occurs in an uncluttered environment, it is a closed skill. But when a person must walk in a cluttered environment, walking is an open skill. We can make the same distinction for several skills. For example, hitting a ball from a tee is a closed skill, whereas hitting a pitched ball is an open skill.

Consider how closed and open skills differ in terms of the performance demands placed on the person. A person can initiate his or her movements at will when performing a closed skill. In addition,

---

fine motor skill   a motor skill that requires control of small muscles to achieve the goal of the skill; typically involves eye-hand coordination and requires a high degree of precision of hand and finger movement.

discrete motor skill   a motor skill with clearly defined beginning and end points, usually requiring a simple movement.

serial motor skill   a motor skill involving a series of discrete skills.

continuous motor skill   a motor skill with arbitrary beginning and end points. These skills usually involve repetitive movements.

closed motor skill   a motor skill performed in a stable or predictable environment where the performer determines when to begin the action.

open motor skill   a motor skill that involves a nonstable unpredictable environment where an object or environmental context is in motion and determines when to begin the action.

the person does not need to adjust the movements to changing conditions while the performance is in progress. For example, to climb a set of stairs, a person can initiate his or her first step at will. However, quite the opposite is the case when someone performs open skills. To perform an open skill successfully, a person must time the initiation of movement to conform to the movement of the object involved in the action. If, for example, the person must step onto a moving escalator, the timing or when the first step can be initiated must conform to the speed and position of the escalator. And for many open skills, changes can occur while an action is in progress that will require the person to make movement adjustments to conform to these environmental changes. For example, the spin of a tennis ball will influence the direction and height of its bounce, which may require the tennis player to adjust his or her planned movements to return a serve after the ball hits the ground.

The open/closed classification system has achieved a large degree of popularity in instructional methodology contexts and increasing popularity in rehabilitation contexts. A likely reason for this is that the closed and open skill categories relate so easily to the types of motor skills involved in these settings. Skills in each of these categories follow common principles of instruction that instructors and therapists can readily apply to specific situations. The closed and open distinction between motor skills also has become increasingly common in the motor learning research literature, undoubtedly because of its simplicity and its ability to accommodate both complex "real-world" skills and laboratory skills.

Gentile's Two-Dimensions Taxonomy

A problem with the one-dimension basis for the classification of motor skills is that it does not always capture the complexity of many skills that a professional must take into account when making decisions about instruction or practice routines. To overcome this limitation, Gentile (2000) broadened the one-dimension approach by considering two general characteristics of all skills: (1) the *environ-*

mental context in which the person performs the skill and (2) the *function of the action* characterizing the skill. She then subdivided these two characteristics to create an expansive taxonomy that yields sixteen skill categories, depicted in table 1.1.

Gentile proposed this taxonomy as a functional guide for physical therapists to assist them in carrying out their clinical activities. The various skill categories in the taxonomy place distinct demands on the performer that vary in terms of the complexity of skill characteristics. Gentile saw this taxonomy as having two practical purposes for the therapist. First, it provides a *systematic and comprehensive evaluation guide* to direct the therapist in the clinical process of determining the movement problems characterizing patients. Second, the taxonomy provides the *basis on which the therapist can systematically select functionally appropriate activities* for the patient after having made the evaluation.

Although Gentile developed the taxonomy with physical therapy in mind, it is not limited to that context. The taxonomy provides an excellent basis for understanding the performer demands for a wide variety of motor skills. Everyone who is involved in teaching motor skills should appreciate this taxonomy. It is an excellent means of becoming aware of the skill characteristics that make skills distinct from, as well as related to, other skills, and is an excellent guide for establishing practice or training routines.

Environmental context. The first dimension of Gentile's taxonomy can be seen in the first column of table 1.1. This dimension is the *environmental context* in which a person performs a skill. Two characteristics are involved in this dimension. We see these in the category labels in the first column in table 1.1.

The first environmental characteristic concerns **regulatory conditions,** which are those characteristics of the environmental context that determine (i.e., regulate) the movement characteristics of an action. This means that a person's movements must conform to these specific environmental features to be successful. For example, the surface on which a person walks influences the movements a person uses to walk on that surface. Also, for the action of hitting a ball, the size, shape, and weight of the ball as well as its speed and spatial location in flight influence when a person can initiate hitting the ball and what the movement characteristics of the swing must be like.

An important distinction for differentiating motor skills is whether the regulatory conditions during performance are *stationary* or *in motion.* Sometimes the regulatory conditions are stationary; this is the case when you walk on a sidewalk or hit a ball off a tee. Sometimes the regulatory conditions are in motion; this occurs when you must step onto an escalator or hit a pitched ball. In this part of Gentile's taxonomy, we can see the application of the closed and open motor skills categories. Skills for which the regulatory conditions are stationary are closed skills, whereas those for which they are in motion are open skills. However, this closed/open distinction is too limiting to capture the wide range of skills that people perform every day. Because of this limitation, Gentile added another environmental context characteristic.

The second environmental characteristic in the taxonomy is **intertrial variability,** which refers to *whether the regulatory conditions during performance are the same or different from one attempt to perform the skill to another.* We can distinguish motor skills according to whether intertrial variability is *absent* or *present.* For example, when a person walks across an uncluttered room, intertrial variability is absent because the regulatory conditions do not change from one step to another or each time the person walks across the room. On the other hand, intertrial variability is present when someone walks across a floor crowded with people, because each step may need to have different characteristics for the walker to avoid colliding with other people.

The function of the action. The *function of the action* is the second dimension on which the taxonomy is based. This dimension is presented in the top row of table 1.1. Gentile specified that we can determine the function of an action by deciding

whether or not performing a given skill involves moving the body, and whether or not performance involves manipulating an object. She viewed these characteristics as parts of two broad action functions: body orientation and manipulation.

Body orientation refers to the changing or maintaining of body position. Two types of body orientation are important for classifying skills. Some skills, such as standing, sitting, or shooting an arrow in archery, require *body stability.* Other skills require *body transport,* which means moving from one place to another. Skills such as walking, running, and swimming involve body transport. One point of clarification here is for the skill of riding in a moving vehicle. Although the vehicle transports the person from one place to another, the body orientation action function is to maintain postural body stability.

The second type of action function concerns *object manipulation.* Some motor skills require us to *change or maintain the position of an object,* such as a ball, a tool, or another person. We perform other skills with *no object manipulation.* It is important to note that when a person must manipulate an object, the skill increases in complexity and difficulty, because the person must do two things at once. First, the person must manipulate the object correctly, and second, he or she must adjust body posture to accommodate for the imbalance created by the object.

---

regulatory conditions　characteristics of the environmental context that determine (i.e., "regulate") the required movement characteristics needed to perform an action.

intertrial variability　an environmental characteristic in Gentile's taxonomy of motor skills. The term refers to whether the regulatory conditions that exist for the performance of a skill in one situation or for one trial are present or absent in the next situation or trial.

TABLE 1.1   Gentile's Taxonomy of Motor Skills

Action Function ⇒ Environmental Context ⇓	Body Orientation: **Stability** **and** **No Object** **Manipulation**	Body Orientation: **Stability** **and** **Object** **Manipulation**	Body Orientation: **Transport** **and** **No Object** **Manipulation**	Body Orientation: **Transport** **and** **Object** **Manipulation**
Stationary Regulatory Conditions and No Intertrial Variability	**1** Body stability No object manipulated Stationary regulatory conditions No intertrial variability	**2** Body stability Object manipulated Stationary regulatory conditions No intertrial variability	**3** Body transport No object manipulated Stationary regulatory conditions No intertrial variability	**4** Body transport Object manipulated Stationary regulatory conditions No intertrial variability
Stationary Regulatory Conditions and Intertrial Variability	**5** Body stability No object manipulated Stationary regulatory conditions Intertrial variability	**6** Body stability Object manipulated Stationary regulatory conditions Intertrial variability	**7** Body transport No object manipulated Stationary regulatory conditions Intertrial variability	**8** Body transport Object manipulated Stationary regulatory conditions Intertrial variability
In Motion Regulatory Conditions and No Intertrial Variability	**9** Body stability No object manipulated Regulatory conditions in motion No intertrial variability	**10** Body stability Object manipulated Regulatory conditions in motion No intertrial variability	**11** Body transport No object manipulated Regulatory conditions in motion No intertrial variability	**12** Body transport Object manipulated Regulatory conditions in motion No intertrial variability
In Motion Regulatory Conditions and Intertrial Variability	**13** Body stability No object manipulated Regulatory conditions in motion Intertrial variability	**14** Body stability Object manipulated Regulatory conditions in motion Intertrial variability	**15** Body transport No object manipulated Regulatory conditions in motion Intertrial variability	**16** Body transport Object manipulated Regulatory conditions in motion Intertrial variability

A CLOSER LOOK

Examples of Stationary and In-Motion Regulatory Conditions

Stationary Environmental Context	**In-Motion Environmental Context**
spatial features of the environment control spatial movement characteristics of an action; the *timing* of the initiation of an action is controlled by the performer	*spatial and timing features* of the environment control spatial movement characteristics and timing of the initiation of an action

e.g.	picking up a cup	e.g.	stepping onto an escalator
	walking up a flight of stairs		standing in a moving bus
	hitting a ball from a tee		hitting a pitched ball
	throwing a dart at a target		catching a batted ball

The sixteen skill categories. The interaction of the four environmental context characteristics and the four action function characteristics creates sixteen skill categories. Table 1.1 shows the critical characteristics of these sixteen categories. Gentile specified that each skill category poses different demands on the performer, with *complexity of the skill increasing* from the top leftmost category to the bottom rightmost category. Note that in table 1.1, numbers are included in the taxonomy to label each category (Gentile did not number the categories).

The category containing the simplest skills, shown in box 1 of the table, includes skills in which the environmental context is stationary, there is no intertrial variability, and there is no body transport or object manipulation required. Some examples here are standing and sitting. Skills in this category are comparable to those at the extreme closed-skills end of the closed/open skills continuum we discussed earlier. The next step in complexity is for skills in box 2 of the table, where everything is the same as for skills in box 1, except that the performer must manipulate an object. For example, a person must stand and hold a box.

Complexity of skills increases systematically through box 16 of table 1.1 which is the category of the most complex skills. For these skills, the regulatory conditions are in motion and change from one performance to another, the person is manipulating an object, and the person is moving. Many sport skills fall into this category; one example is running to catch a hit ball in baseball. Skills in this category are comparable to those at the extreme open skills end of the closed/open skills continuum.

Practical application of the taxonomy. Gentile proposed that the taxonomy has practical value for therapists and teachers because they can use it in two ways. First, it can be a useful guide for *evaluation of movement capabilities and limitations.* The therapist or teacher can evaluate deficits by systematically altering environmental contexts and/or action functions to identify skill performance characteristics that pose difficulty for an individual. Contextual versus action-function difficulties suggest different types of problems. By identifying the specific characteristics limiting performance, the therapist or teacher can determine what he or she needs to do to help the person improve his or her performance capabilities.

After the professional assesses performance problems, the taxonomy then becomes a valuable tool for systematically *selecting a progression of functionally appropriate activities* to help the person overcome his or her deficits and increase his or her skill performance capabilities. This is an

A CLOSER LOOK

A Practical Application of the Environmental Context Dimension of Gentile's Taxonomy to Organizing Instruction for Teaching Open Skills

Those who teach motor skills can apply Gentile's taxonomy to the teaching of open skills by placing the four components of the environmental context dimension of the taxonomy on a closed/open skills continuum. As shown in the figure below, we can develop a logical progression from totally closed to totally open skills from these components.

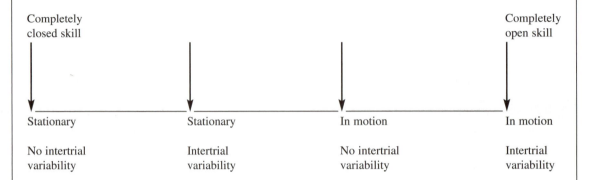

Completely closed skill			Completely open skill
Stationary	Stationary	In motion	In motion
No intertrial variability	Intertrial variability	No intertrial variability	Intertrial variability

Example Teaching goal = to teach a person to hit a baseball thrown by a pitcher under game conditions.

The following sequence of practice events would occur according to the progression in the figure above:

1. Practice begins with a closed version of the open skill; the instructor or coach keeps the regulatory conditions "stationary" and has intertrial variability "absent."

   ⇒ the learner bats the ball from a batting tee at the same height on each practice attempt

2. In the next version of the skill, the instructor or coach keeps the regulatory conditions "stationary" but has intertrial variability "present."

   ⇒ the learner bats the ball from a batting tee, but from different heights on each practice attempt

3. Next, practice proceeds to an open version of the skill; the instructor or coach has the regulatory conditions "in motion" but, intertrial variability "absent."

   ⇒ a pitching machine that can keep the speed and location of each pitch constant puts the ball in motion

4. Finally, the instructor or coach has the learner practice the completely open skill itself; the regulatory conditions are "in motion" and intertrial variability is "present."

   ⇒ a live pitcher pitches the ball using different speeds and locations on each practice attempt.

Note: For research evidence supporting the effectiveness of this progression for helping people learn an open skill, see Hautala and Conn (1993).

important feature of the taxonomy, because it emphasizes the complementary part of the rehabilitation or skill training process. To assess skill deficits is important, but the effectiveness of any rehabilitation or training protocol depends on the implementation of appropriate activities to achieve functional goals for the patient or student. In the activity selection process, the therapist or teacher begins selecting activities related to the taxonomy category in which the person is not capable at first of handling the demands of the skill. Then, the professional can develop a program of rehabilitation or instruction by systematically increasing the complexity of the skills included in the program. Each taxonomy category provides a guide for selecting appropriate activities to help the person overcome his or her deficits and achieve the functional goal of the therapy or training experience.

SUMMARY

We have defined motor skills as skills that require voluntary body and/or limb movement to achieve their goal. There is a wide variety of motor skills, including grasping a cup, walking, dancing, throwing a ball, and playing the piano. We sometimes refer to skills such as these as *actions*. Movements are components of skills and actions. Because there are so many different motor skills, researchers and practitioners have developed motor skill classification systems. These systems identify common characteristics of skills and place skills within distinct categories based on those characteristics. An important purpose of classification systems is to help teachers and therapists apply concepts and principles of motor skill learning to instruction and rehabilitation situations.

We discussed four classification schemes. The first three grouped motor skills into categories based on one common characteristic. One system is based on the size of the primary musculature required to perform the skill, and classifies skills as either gross or fine. The second is based on the distinctiveness of the beginning and end points of a skill, and classifies skills as either discrete or continuous. The third classification system is based on the stability of the environment in which the skill is performed and the object that may be involved. If the environment is stable and the object is not moving, the system categorizes the skills as closed motor skills. If the environment is changeable or the object is in motion it categorizes the skills as open motor skills.

The fourth classification system is based on two common characteristics of skills. Gentile developed a taxonomy that presents sixteen categories of motor skills, created from the environmental context and the action function characteristics of skills. The taxonomy is useful in helping us gain an understanding of the factors that influence skill complexity and unique requirements that are placed on a person when he or she performs skills of different complexity. The practical benefit of this taxonomy is that it provides an effective guide by which therapists and teachers can evaluate the nature of motor skill performance deficits and then systematically select functionally appropriate activities to help people overcome those deficits and increase their motor skill performance capabilities.

RELATED READINGS

Maraj, B., Allard, F., & Elliott, D. (1998). The effect of non-regulatory stimuli on the triple-jump approach run. *Research Quarterly for Exercise and Sport, 69,* 129–135.

Mulder, T., & Geurts, S. (1991). The assessment of motor dysfunctions: Preliminaries to a disability-oriented approach. *Human Movement Science, 10,* 565–574.

STUDY QUESTIONS

1. Discuss how the terms *actions* and *movements* are related to motor skills. Give an example that illustrates this relationship.

2. What are three reasons for distinguishing between actions and movements?

3. Describe the one dimension that distinguishes the two categories in each of the following skill classification schemes, and give three examples of motor skills for each category: (a) gross vs. fine motor skills; (b) discrete vs. continuous motor skills; (c) closed vs. open motor skills.

4. (a) What are the two dimensions used to classify skills in the Gentile taxonomy? (b) Describe the four classification characteristics included under each of these two dimensions.

5. (a) What does the term *regulatory conditions* refer to in Gentile's skill classification system? (b) Why are regulatory conditions important to consider when categorizing skills?

6. Discuss how you would implement the two practical uses Gentile described for her taxonomy of motor skills.

Motor Abilities

*Concept: A variety of abilities underlie motor
skill learning and performance success*

APPLICATION

Some people perform many different physical activities very well. Why is this the case? Are they born with some special "motor ability" that enables them to be successful at all they do? Have they had an abundance of good training and practice in a wide variety of activities? Are they really good at everything, or only at certain activities?

Also, people differ in how quickly and successfully they learn motor skills. If you observe a physical activity class for beginners, you will see various degrees of success and failure during the first few days. For example, in a beginning golf class, when the students first start to hit the ball, some will spend an inordinate amount of time simply trying to make contact with the ball. But some will be at the other extreme, able to hit the ball rather well. The remainder of the class usually will be distributed somewhere along the continuum of success between these two extremes.

We can observe parallel differences in other physical activity situations, such as dance classes, driving instruction classes, and physical therapy sessions. People enter these situations with a wide variety of what some refer to as "entry behaviors." These entry behaviors reflect the very real behavioral phenomenon that individuals differ in their capability to perform motor skills.

DISCUSSION

In chapter 1, you were introduced to motor skills. Now, you will be introduced to a type of personal characteristic known as *ability,* which influences the way people perform and learn motor skills. One of the difficulties in studying the concept of ability as it relates to motor skill performance is that the term ability is used in so many different ways. For example, physical and occupational therapists refer to "functional ability," a baseball coach might refer to a player's "running ability," educators often refer to students' "cognitive ability" or "intellectual ability." The list of examples could go on, but these few examples illustrate the problem. As a result, it is important to specify the precise manner in which the term will be used.

For this discussion, the term *ability* will be used according to its meaning in the area of psychology that involves the study of *individual differences.* People who study individual differences are concerned with the identification and measurement of abilities that characterize and differentiate individuals. Individual difference psychologists also investigate the relationship between abilities and the performance and learning of skills. In this context, the term **ability** means *a general trait or capacity of the individual that is* *a determinant of a person's achievement potential for the performance of specific skills.* When the term **motor ability** is used in this context, it refers to *an ability that is specifically related to the performance of a motor skill.* It is important to note that some researchers and practitioners use terms such as "psychomotor ability" and "perceptual motor ability" to refer to what we will call motor ability.

The identification of specific motor abilities is not an easy task. As a result, few researchers have ventured into this area of study. However, those who have undertaken this challenge have provided us with useful information that helps us have a better understanding of an important factor related to determining why people differ in achievement levels of motor skill performance.

Abilities as Individual Difference Variables

The individual differences we observe in the levels of success that people achieve in the performance of a motor skill depends in large part on the degree to which the person has the motor abilities that are important for the performance of that skill. For example, people with differing levels of the motor abilities important for playing tennis will have differing *achievement potentials* in tennis. This example indicates that various motor abilities underlie the performance of a complex motor skill such as tennis, and that people have different levels of these abilities. It also indicates that if two people have the same training experiences and amount of practice, but differ in their levels of the motor abilities important for playing tennis, the one with the higher levels of the appropriate abilities has the potential to perform at a higher level. Although researchers generally agree with this view, they debated for many years, especially in the 1950s and 1960s, how motor abilities relate to one another within the same person.

The controversy over general versus specific motor abilities. In the debate about the relationship of motor abilities, one viewpoint holds that motor abilities are *highly related* to each other. The opposite view is that they are *relatively independent* of one another. This debate is seldom seen in the current research literature. However, an understanding of the different points of view will facilitate your application of the concept of motor abilities to motor skill performance achievement.

The **general motor ability hypothesis** maintains that although many different motor abilities can be identified within an individual, they are highly related and can be characterized in terms of a singular, global motor ability. It holds that the level of that ability in an individual influences the ultimate success that person can expect in performing any motor skill. This notion has been in existence for quite some time. This hypothesis predicts that if a person is good at one motor skill, then he or she has the potential to be good at all motor skills. The reasoning behind this prediction is that there is *one* general motor ability.

But contrary to the expectations of proponents of the general motor ability hypothesis, very little research evidence supports this viewpoint. One suspects that the basis for the continued existence of this hypothesis is its intuitive appeal. Tests of general motor ability are convenient, appealing to those who seek an easy explanation for why certain people are successful or unsuccessful at performing motor skills. The fact that these tests are poor predictors of specific motor skill performance has not diminished the appeal of the general motor ability hypothesis.

The alternative perspective, for which there has been substantial support, is the **specificity of motor abilities hypothesis.** This view also suggests that individuals have many motor abilities, but these abilities are relatively independent. This means, for example, that if a person exhibited a high degree of balancing ability, we could not predict how well that person would do on a test of reaction time.

Support for the specificity hypothesis has come from experiments that were reported primarily in the 1960s. These experiments were based on the common assumption that if motor abilities are specific and independent, then the relationship between any two abilities will be very low. Thus, in the simplest of cases, the relationship would be very low between any two abilities such as balance and reaction time, or between reaction time and speed of movement, or between static and dynamic balance.

In fact, an influential experiment that was reported many years ago examined balance as an ability, and found that there is no one balancing ability (Drowatzky and Zuccato, 1967). Rather, there are several specific types of balance. In this experiment, participants performed six different balancing tasks that generally have been regarded as measures of either static or dynamic balancing ability. The results of the correlations among all the tests (table 2.1) showed that the highest correlation (.31) was between the sideward stand and the bass stand. Most of the correlations ranged between 0.12 and 0.19. On the basis of these results, it would be difficult to conclude that only one test could be considered a valid measure of balancing ability. We need to subdivide the ability we generally call "balance" into various types of balance.

The "all-around athlete." If motor abilities are numerous and independent, then how can we explain the so-called "all-around athlete," the person who is very proficient at a variety of physical activities? According to the specificity view, abilities fall somewhere along a range containing low, average, and high amounts within individuals. Because people differ, it seems reasonable to expect that some people have a large number of abilities at an average level, and other people have a majority of abilities at either the high or the low end of the scale.

According to the specificity hypothesis, the person who excels in a large number of physical activities has high levels of a large number of abilities. We would expect that a person would do very well in those activities for which the underlying abilities required for successful performance matched the abilities for which the person was at the high end of the scale.

In actual fact, the true all-around athlete is a rare individual. Typically, when a person shows high

performance levels in a variety of physical activities, a close inspection of those activities reveals many foundational motor abilities in common. We would expect a person exhibiting high levels for a variety of abilities to do well in activities for which those abilities were foundational to performance. However, we would expect average performance if this person engaged in activities for which those abilities were less important, activities based on other abilities, of which the person possessed only average levels.

Identifying Motor Abilities

As a capacity, an ability is a relatively enduring attribute of an individual. Researchers who study individual differences assume that we can describe the skills involved in complex motor activities in terms of the abilities that underlie their performance. For example, the ability called spatial visualization is related to the performance of such diverse tasks as aerial navigation, blueprint reading, and dentistry (Fleishman, 1972). An important step in understanding how abilities and skill performance are related is identifying abilities and matching them with the skills involved.

---

ability a general trait or capacity of an individual that is a determinant of a person's achievement potential for the performance of specific skills.

motor ability an ability that is specifically related to the performance of a motor skill.

general motor ability hypothesis a hypothesis that maintains that the many different motor abilities that exist in an individual are highly related and can be characterized in terms of a singular, global motor ability.

specificity of motor abilities hypothesis a hypothesis that maintains that the many motor abilities in an individual are relatively independent.

TABLE 2.1   Results from the Experiment by Drowatzky and Zuccato (1967) Showing the Correlations among Six Different Tests of Static and Dynamic Balance

Test	1 Stork Stand	2 Diver's Stand	3 Stick Stand	4 Sideward Stand	5 Bass Stand	6 Balance Stand
1	—	0.14	−0.12	0.26	0.20	0.03
2		—	−0.12	−0.03	−0.07	−0.14
3			—	−0.04	0.22	−0.19
4				—	0.31	0.19
5					—	0.18
6						—

Source: From Drowatzky, J. N. & Zuccato, F. C. (1967). Interrelationships between selected measures of static and dynamic balance. *Research Quarterly for Exercise and Sport, 38,* 509–510. Copyright © 1967 American Alliance for Health, Physical Education, Recreation, and Dance. Reprinted by permission.

When researchers and practitioners identify specific motor abilities, they usually refer to the work of Edwin Fleishman (see Fleishman & Quaintance, 1984, for a description of this work). His research, which was carried out for four decades beginning in the 1950s, continues to influence our understanding and study of motor abilities and how they relate to motor skill performance. Perhaps the most significant achievement of Fleishman's work was the development of a taxonomy of motor abilities, which he designed to identify the fewest possible ability categories that could be applied to the greatest variety of motor skills.

A taxonomy of motor abilities. From the results of extensive batteries of perceptual motor tests given to many people, Fleishman developed a "taxonomy of human perceptual motor abilities" (Fleishman, 1972; Fleishman & Quaintance, 1984). He proposed that there seem to be eleven identifiable and measurable *perceptual motor abilities.* He identified these abilities as follows: (1) *multilimb coordination,* the ability to coordinate the movement of a number of limbs simultaneously; (2) *control precision,* the ability to make highly controlled and precise muscular adjustments where larger muscle groups are involved; (3) *response orientation,* the

ability to select rapidly where a response should be made; (4) *reaction time,* the ability to respond rapidly to a stimulus when it appears; (5) *speed of arm movement,* the ability to make a gross rapid-arm movement; (6) *rate control,* the ability to change speed and direction of responses with precise timing; (7) *manual dexterity,* the ability to make the skillful, well-directed arm-hand movements that are involved in manipulating objects under speed conditions; (8) *finger dexterity,* the ability to perform skillful, controlled manipulations of tiny objects involving primarily the fingers; (9) *arm-hand steadiness,* the ability to make precise arm-hand positioning movements where strength and speed are minimally involved; (10) *wrist, finger speed,* the ability to move the wrist and fingers rapidly; and (11) *aiming,* the ability to aim precisely at a small object in space.

In addition to perceptual motor abilities, Fleishman also identified nine abilities that he designated as *physical proficiency abilities.* These abilities differ from the perceptual motor abilities in that they are more generally related to gross motor skill performance. Most people would consider these abilities physical fitness abilities. The physical proficiency abilities identified by Fleishman are as follows: (1) *static strength,* the maximum force that a person

A CLOSER LOOK

A Value of Identifying Motor Abilities

Identifying and assessing motor abilities can allow a teacher, coach, or therapist to

- Identify the source of problems or difficulties in performing a skill. Often a person has difficulty learning a new skill because he or she lacks adequate experience involving the motor ability essential to performing that particular skill.

   Example: A child may be having difficulty catching a thrown ball because of a poorly developed ability to visually track a moving object.

- Develop appropriate physical activities to improve performance in a variety of skills involving the same motor ability.

   Example: Balance is a foundational ability to many different skills. As a result, movement experiences that provide people the opportunity to develop their balance ability in a variety of movement situations should benefit learning skills requiring balance.

can exert against external objects; (2) *dynamic strength,* the muscular endurance used in exerting force repeatedly; (3) *explosive strength,* the ability to mobilize energy effectively for bursts of muscular effort; (4) *trunk strength,* the strength of the trunk muscles; (5) *extent flexibility,* the ability to flex or stretch the trunk and back muscles; (6) *dynamic flexibility,* the ability to make repeated, rapid trunk-flexing movements; (7) *gross body coordination,* the ability to coordinate the action of several parts of the body while the body is in motion; (8) *gross body equilibrium,* the ability to maintain balance without visual cues; and (9) *stamina,* the capacity to sustain maximum effort requiring cardiovascular effort.

We should not consider Fleishman's lists to be exhaustive inventories of all the abilities related to motor skill performance, because Fleishman wanted to identify the smallest number of abilities that would describe the tasks performed in the test battery. Although he used hundreds of tasks to identify those abilities, the inclusion of additional types of tasks besides those Fleishman used could lead to the identification of other motor abilities. For example, Fleishman did not include the following abilities in his two lists: *static balance,* the ability to balance on a stable surface when no loco-motor movement is required; *dynamic balance,* the ability to balance on a moving surface or to balance

while involved in locomotion; *visual acuity,* the ability to see clearly and precisely; *visual tracking,* the ability to follow a moving object visually; and *eye-hand* or *eye-foot coordination,* the ability to perform skills requiring vision and the precise use of the hands or feet.

An important assumption of this view of human abilities is that all individuals possess these motor abilities. Another is that because it is possible to measure these motor abilities, it is also possible to determine a quantified measure of the level of each ability in a person. People differ in the amount of each ability they possess. Their motor abilities indicate limits that influence a person's potential for achievement in motor skill performance.

Relating Motor Abilities to Motor Skill Performance

An approach presented by Ackerman (1988) helps us see where motor abilities fit into the broader issue of motor skill performance. He described motor abilities as one of three categories of human abilities that affect motor skill performance. One category is general intelligence, or general ability. Included are cognitively oriented abilities and memory-related processes, such as acquiring, storing, retrieving, combining, and comparing memory-based information, as well as using it in new contexts. The second

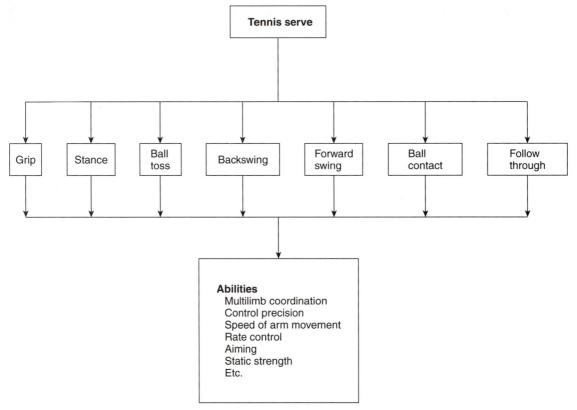

FIGURE 2.1   A task analysis for the tennis serve indicating the component parts of the serve and some examples of perceptual-motor abilities underlying performance of the serve.

category is perceptual speed ability. This category includes abilities associated with a person's facility for solving problems of increasing complexity, and with the person's speed at processing information he or she must use to solve problems. Tests of such tasks as finding the *X*s in an array of letters and transcribing symbols on a list assess these abilities. Finally, *psychomotor ability* (i.e., motor ability) is the third category. Abilities in this category, which is the focus of our discussion, are related to speed and accuracy of movements that place little or no cognitive demand on the person. To fully understand individual differences, we must see performance of all types of skills in terms of these three foundational categories of abilities. However, for the purposes of

the present discussion, we will limit our attention to motor abilities.

Figure 2.1 illustrates the view that motor abilities are underlying, foundational components of motor skill performance. This figure shows how we can analyze complex motor skills by a process known as *task analysis* in order to identify the abilities that underlie any motor skill. For example, to serve a tennis ball successfully, a player must perform certain components of that skill properly. Figure 2.1 identifies these components, which are the first level of analysis of the tennis serve, in the middle tier of the diagram. Identification of these components helps us identify more readily the underlying motor abilities that are involved in the successful performance of this task. The bottom tier of the diagram presents these abilities. Based on Fleishman's lists, they include such abilities as multilimb coordination, control precision, speed of arm movement, rate control, aiming, and static strength. You undoubtedly could add others. However, these few examples should serve to illustrate the foundational role perceptual motor and physical proficiency abilities play in the performance of motor skills.

SUMMARY

The term *ability* refers to a general trait or capacity of the individual that is related to the performance of a variety of skills or tasks. A variety of motor abilities underlie the performance of a motor skill. Different people have different levels of these abilities. An important question that researchers debated for many years concerns how these abilities relate to one another in the same individual. The general motor ability hypothesis proposes that abilities are highly related, whereas the specificity hypothesis argues that abilities are relatively independent of one another. Research evidence consistently has supported the specificity hypothesis.

One approach to identifying motor abilities is Fleishman's taxonomy of perceptual motor and physical proficiency abilities. These abilities play a foundational role in the performance of motor skills. Because it is possible to measure these abilities, we can assess a person's level of each ability. Research evidence shows that people differ in the amounts of each ability they possess. Levels of motor abilities indicate limits that influence a person's potential for skill achievement.

RELATED READINGS

Fleishman, E. A. (1982). Systems for describing human tasks. *American Psychologist, 37,* 821–834.

Proctor, R. W., & Dutta, A. (1995). *Skill acquisition and human performance.* Thousand Oaks, CA: Sage. [Read ch. 10: Individual Differences]

Stelmach, G. E., & Nahom, A. (1992). Cognitive-motor abilities of the elderly driver. *Human Factors, 34,* 53–65.

STUDY QUESTIONS

1. (a) How do people who study individual differences define the term *abilities?* (b) Distinguish the meaning of *abilities* from the term *skill.*

2. (a) What is the difference between the general motor ability hypothesis and the specificity of motor abilities hypothesis? (b) Give an example of research evidence indicating which of these hypotheses is more valid.

3. How can a specificity view of motor abilities explain how a person can be very successful at performing a lot of different motor skills?

4. (a) Name and describe five perceptual motor abilities identified by Fleishman. (b) What other motor abilities can you identify?

5. Describe how Ackerman presented motor abilities as one category of abilities involved in motor skill performance.

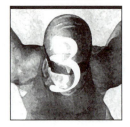

The Measurement
of Motor Performance

Concept: The measurement of motor performance
is critical to understanding motor learning

APPLICATION

Suppose that you are a physical educator teaching your students a tennis serve. What characteristic of performance will you measure to assess students' progress? Consider a few possibilities. You could count the number of serves that land in and out of the proper service court. Or you could mark the service court in some way so that the "better" serves, in terms of where they land, are scored higher than others. Or you could establish a measure that is concerned with the students' serving form.

Now, imagine that you are a physical therapist helping a stroke patient learning to walk again. How will you measure your patient's progress to determine if what you are doing is beneficial to his or her rehabilitation? You have several possible walking characteristics to choose from. For example, you could count the number of steps made or the distance walked on each walking attempt; these measures could give you some general indicators of progress. If you wanted to know more about some specific walking-related characteristics, you could measure the balance and postural stability of the person as he or she walked. Or you could assess the biomechanical progress the person was making by analyzing the kinematic characteristics of the movements of the legs, trunk, and arms. Each of these measurements can be valuable, and will tell

you something different about the person's walking performance.

In both of these performance assessment situations, your important concern as an educator or therapist is using a performance measure, or measures, to make an assessment. As a first step in addressing this problem, you must determine which aspects of performance you should measure to make a valid performance assessment. Then, you must determine how to measure those aspects of performance. The following discussion will help you to know how to accomplish this two-step measurement process by describing several different motor skill performance measures. We will discuss each measure in terms of which feature of performance the measure assesses and how to obtain and interpret the measure.

In addition to helping you better understand the measurement of motor skill performance, this discussion of measuring skill performance should help you better understand the various concepts presented in this book. Throughout this text, we will refer to the various measures introduced in this section, especially as researchers use these measures to investigate various concepts.

DISCUSSION

There are a variety of ways to measure motor skill performance. A useful way to organize the many types of motor performance measures is by creating two categories related to different levels of performance observation. We will call the first category **performance outcome measures.** Included in this category are measures that indicate the outcome or result of performing a motor skill. For example, measures of how far a person walked, how fast a person ran a certain distance, and how many degrees a person flexed his or her knee all are based on the outcome of the person's performance.

Notice that performance outcome measures do not tell us anything about the behavior of the limbs or body that led to the observed outcome. Nor do these measures provide any information about the activity of the various muscles involved in each action. To know something about these types of characteristics, we must use measures in the category called **performance production measures.** These measures can tell us such things as how the nervous system is functioning, how the muscular system is operating, and how the limbs or joints are acting before, during, or after a person performs a skill.

Although additional categories of performance measures could exist, these two represent the motor skill performance measures found in this text. Table 3.1 presents examples of these two categories of measures. For the remainder of this discussion, we will discuss several of the more common performance measures found in the motor learning research literature.

Reaction Time

The common measure indicating how long it takes a person to prepare and initiate a movement is **reaction time (RT).** Figure 3.1 shows that RT is the interval of time between the onset of a signal (stimulus) that indicates the required action and the *initiation* of the action. Note that RT does not include any movement related to the action, but only the time before movement begins.

The stimulus (or "go") signal is the indication to act. In laboratory or clinical settings, the signal can take one of a variety of forms, such as a light, a buzzer, a shock, a word on a screen, or a spoken word or sound. As such, the signal can relate to any

sensory system, i.e., vision, hearing, or touch. The person can be required to perform any type of movement. For example, the person might be required to lift a finger off a telegraph key, depress a keyboard key, speak a word, kick a board or walk a step. Finally, to assess optimal RT, some type of warning signal should be given prior to the stimulus signal.

Types of RT situations. Figure 3.2 depicts three of the most common types of RT situations. For illustration purposes, this figure shows a light as the stimulus signal and lifting a finger from a telegraph key as the required movement. However the three types of RT situations discussed here do not need to be limited to these characteristics.

When a situation involves only one signal and requires only one action in response, the RT situation is known as *simple* RT. In the example presented in figure 3.2 the person must lift a finger from the telegraph key when a light comes on. Another type of RT situation is *choice* RT, where there is more than one signal to which the person must respond, and each signal has a specified response. The example in figure 3.2 indicates that the person must respond to the red light by lifting

---

performance outcome measures   a category of motor skill performance measures that indicates the outcome or result of performing a motor skill (e.g., how far a person walked, how fast a person ran a certain distance, or how many degrees a person flexed a knee).

performance production measures   a category of motor skill performance measures that indicates the performance of specific aspects of the motor control system during the performance of an action (e.g., limb kinematics, force, EEG, EMG, etc.).

reaction time (RT)   the interval of time between the onset of a signal (stimulus) and the initiation of a response.

TABLE 3.1 Two Categories of Motor Skill Performance Measures

Category	Examples of Measures	Performance Examples
1. Performance outcome measures	Time to complete a response, e.g., sec, min, hr	Amount of time to run a mile: type a word
	Reaction time (RT)	Time between starter's gun and beginning of movement
	Amount of error in performing criterion movement, e.g., AE, CE, VE	Number of cm away from the target in reproducing a criterion limb position
	Number or percentage of errors	Number of free throws missed
	Number of successful attempts	Number of times the beanbag hit the target
	Time on/off target	Number of seconds stylus in contact with target on pursuit rotor
	Time on/off balance	Number of seconds stood in stork stance
	Distance	Height of vertical jump
	Trials to completion	Number of trials it took until all responses correct
2. Performance production measures	Displacement	Distance limb traveled to produce response
	Velocity	Speed limb moved while performing response
	Acceleration	Acceleration/deceleration pattern while moving
	Joint angle	Angle of each joint of arm at impact in hitting ball
	Joint torque	Net joint torque of the knee joint at takeoff on a vertical jump
	Electromyography (EMG)	Time at which the biceps initially fired during a rapid flexion movement
	Electroencephalogram (EEG)	Characteristic of the P300 for a choice RT response

the index finger from a telegraph key, to the blue light by lifting the middle finger, and to the green light by lifting the ring finger. The third type of RT situation is *discrimination* RT, where there is also more than one signal, but only one response. In the figure 3.2 example, the person is required to lift his or her finger from the telegraph key only when the red light comes on. If the blue or green light is illuminated, the person should make no response.

Although the examples of simple, choice, and discrimination RT situations just described refer to laboratory conditions, these different types of RT situations also exist in everyday life and in sport environments. For example, a sprinter in track is involved in a *simple RT situation* when he or she starts a race. He or she hears a verbal warning signal from the starter, then hears the gun sound, which is the signal to begin to run. *Choice RT situations* are more common in everyday activities, such as when driving a car you come to an intersection with a traffic signal, which has three possible signals, each of which requires a different action. If the light is red, you must depress the brake pedal and come to a complete stop. If the light is yellow,

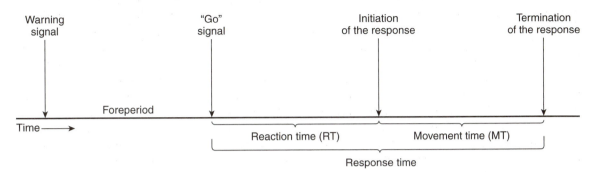

FIGURE 3.1   The events and time intervals related to the typical measurement of reaction time (RT) and movement time (MT).

you need to prepare to stop. And, if the signal is green, you can continue to keep the accelerator pedal depressed to move through the intersection. Joggers experience *discrimination RT situations* when they find something in their path that indicates they need to step over it, such as a log or a curb. There are many different stimuli in the jogger's environment, but only those with specific, distinct features will specify to the jogger to engage in the action of stepping up and over an object. Thus the jogger engages in this specific action only when the environmental stimuli have these features.

RT interval components. Through the use of electromyography (EMG) to measure the beginning of muscle activity in an RT situation, a researcher can *fractionate* RT into two component parts. The EMG recording will indicate the time at which the muscle shows increased activity after the stimulus signal has occurred. However, there is a period of time between the onset of the stimulus signal and the beginning of the muscle activity. This "quiet" interval of time is the first component part of RT and is called the *premotor time.* The second component is the period of time from the increase in muscle activity until the actual beginning of observable limb movement. This RT component is called the *motor time.*

By fractionating the RT interval into two parts, researchers interested in understanding the movement preparation process are able to obtain more specific insights into what occurs as a person prepares to move.

Most researchers agree that the premotor time is a measure of the receipt and transmission of information from the environment, through the nervous system, to the muscle itself. This time interval seems to be an indicator of *perceptual and cognitive decision-making activity* in which the person is engaging while preparing a movement. The motor time interval indicates that there is muscle activity before observable limb movement occurs. Researchers commonly agree that this activity indicates a time lag in the muscle that it needs in order to overcome the inertia of the limb after the muscle receives the command to contract.

The use of RT in research. Reaction time has a long history as a popular measure of human motor skill performance. Although RT can be used as a performance measure to assess how quickly a person can initiate a required action, researchers also use it as a basis for inferring other characteristics. The most common is to identify the information a person may use while preparing to produce a required action, which will be the topic of discussion in chapter 7. For example, if one performance situation yields a longer RT than another situation, the researcher can determine what may have led to the different RT lengths, which then can tell us something about influences on the amount of time it takes us to prepare an action. Another use of RT is to assess the capabilities of a person to anticipate a required action and when to initiate it. In a sport situation, a coach may want to know how long it takes a point guard to recognize that the defender's actions indicate the guard should

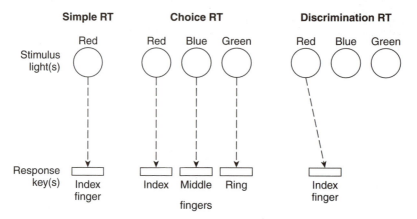

FIGURE 3.2   Three different types of reaction time (RT) test situations: simple RT, choice RT, and discrimination RT.

pass the ball rather than shoot it. When used in this way, RT provides information about decision making. Thus, in addition to indicating how fast a person responds to a signal, RT also provides a window for examining how a person interacts with the performance environment while preparing to produce a required action.

Relating RT to movement time and response time. In any situation in which a person must perform an action in response to a signal, two additional performance measures can be assessed. These are shown in figure 3.1 as movement time (MT) and response time. **Movement time (MT)** begins when RT ends. It is the interval of time between the initiation and the completion of an action. **Response time** is the total time interval, involving both RT and MT.

An important characteristic of RT and MT is that they are relatively *independent* measures. This means that the correlation between them is typically low, indicating that RT does not predict MT, or vice versa. Franklin Henry, considered by many to be the "father" of modern-day motor learning, first provided evidence supporting RT-MT independence many years ago. In a classic, comprehensive experiment (Henry, 1961) compared RT to MT for men and women of different ages and on tasks of various complexities. The experiment

involved 402 subjects between eight and thirty years old. Henry used simple, discrimination, and two-choice RT situations, along with four different conditions of movement complexity. For all situations the *RT-MT correlations were consistently close to zero.* The significance of this result is that it establishes that RT and MT measure different aspects of human performance and that training to improve one will not help improve the other.

Error Measures

The amount of error a person makes as a result of performing a skill has had a prominent place in human performance research and in everyday living activities and sport. Error measures allow us to evaluate performance for skills for which *accuracy* is the action goal. Skills such as reaching to grasp a cup, throwing a dart at a target, walking along a prescribed path, and driving a car on a street require people to perform actions that demand spatial and/or temporal accuracy. In assessing performance outcome for this type of skill, the amount of error a person makes in relation to the goal is a meaningful performance measure.

Error measures not only provide indicators of performance accuracy; certain types of error measures also tell us about possible causes of performance problems. This is especially true if perfor-

A CLOSER LOOK

Examples of the Use of RT and MT to Assess Skill Performance Problems in Decision-Making Situations

Sport-Skill Example

An offensive lineman in football must perform his assignment as quickly as possible after the center snaps the ball. If the lineman is consistently slow in carrying out his assignment, the problem could be: he is not giving enough attention to the ball snap, he is not sure about his assignment, or he moves too slowly when carrying out his assignment. The first two problems relate to RT (the time between the ball snap and the beginning of foot movement); the third relates to MT (the time between the beginning of foot movement and the completion of the assignment). By assessing both RT and MT in an actual situation, the coach could become more aware of the reason for the lineman's problem, and begin working on helping the lineman improve that specific part of the problem.

Driving a Car Example

Suppose you are helping a student in a driving simulator improve the amount of time he or she requires to stop the car when an object suddenly appears in the street. Separating RT and MT would let you know if the slow stopping time is related to a decision-making or a movement speed problem. If RT (the time between the appearance of the object and the person's foot release from the accelerator) increases across various situations, but MT (the time between the foot release from the accelerator and foot contact with the brake pedal) is constant, you know that the problem is primarily related to attention or decision making. But, if RT remains relatively constant but MT changes across various situations, you know the problem is movement related. In either case, you can more specifically help the person to improve his or her performance in these situations.

---

mance is assessed for more than one trial. For a series of trials (typical in a sport skill training or a rehabilitation setting), the instructor or therapist can determine whether the observed movement inaccuracy is due to problems associated with *consistency* or to those associated with *bias*. These important measures provide the professional with a basis for selecting the appropriate intervention to help the person overcome the inaccuracy. *Consistency problems* indicate a lack in acquiring the basic movement pattern needed to perform the skill, whereas *bias problems* indicate that the person has acquired the movement pattern but is having difficulties adapting to the specific demands of the performance situation.

Assessing error for one-dimension action goals.
When a person must move a limb a certain amount in one dimension, as when a patient attempts to achieve a certain knee extension, the resulting error will be a certain distance short of or past the goal. Similarly, if a pitcher in baseball

is attempting to throw the ball at a certain rate of speed, the resulting error will be either too slow or too fast in relation to the goal. Measuring the amount of error in these situations simply involves subtracting the achieved performance value (e.g., 15 cm, 5°, 20 sec) from the target or goal amount.

We can calculate at least three error measures to assess the general accuracy characteristics of performance over repeated performances and to assess what

---

movement time (MT)   the interval of time between the initiation of a movement and the completion of the movement.

response time   the time interval involving both reaction time and movement time; that is, the time from the onset of a signal (stimulus) to the completion of a response.

A CLOSER LOOK

Using Performance Bias and Consistency Assessments

An example demonstrating the value of performance measures assessing bias and consistency occurs when a person is learning archery. In archery, overall performance on a trial is assessed by the total score of a series of six arrows shot at the target. This total score is based on the target rings in which the arrows are located. How the arrows are grouped on the target is not a part of this total score. However, if you are working to help a person improve his or her performance, the total score, which is a general performance score, is not as valuable as the indicators of bias and consistency. If the person's shots are grouped in one portion of the target away from the center, the problem is one of bias. Correcting this problem is relatively simple, as it requires an aiming or release adjustment in a specific direction toward the target center. But a more complex correction problem occurs if the arrows are scattered all over the target. Here the problem is consistency. This characteristic suggests that the person has not acquired the fundamental movement pattern appropriate for performing this skill and needs continued work on this aspect of the skill.

---

may be causing the accuracy problems. To determine a general idea of how successfully the goal was achieved, we calculate **absolute error (AE).** AE is *the absolute difference between the actual performance on each trial and the goal.* For multiple trial situations, summing these differences and dividing by the number of trials will give you the average absolute error for the trials. AE provides useful information about the *magnitude of error* a person has made on a trial or over a series of trials. This score gives you *a general index of accuracy* for the session for this person. But evaluating performance solely on the basis of AE hides important information about the source of the inaccurate performance. To obtain this information, we need two additional error measures.

One reason a person's performance may be inaccurate is that the person has a tendency to overshoot or to undershoot the goal, which is referred to as *performance bias.* To obtain this information, we must calculate **constant error (CE),** which is the signed (+/–) deviation from the goal. When calculated over a series of trials, CE provides a meaningful *index of the person's tendency to be directionally biased* when performing the skill. Calculating CE involves making the same calculations used to determine AE, except that the algebraic signs are used for each trial's performance.

Another reason for performance inaccuracy for a series of trials is *performance consistency* (or, conversely, variability), which is measured by calculating **variable error (VE).** To determine this consistency index, calculate the *standard deviation of the person's CE scores for the series of trials.*

Assessing error for two-dimension action goals. When the outcome of performing a skill requires accuracy in the vertical and horizontal directions, the person assessing error must make modifications to the one-dimension assessment method. The general accuracy measure for the two-dimension situation is called *radial error (RE),* which is similar to AE in the one-dimension case. To calculate RE for one trial, measure the length of the error in both the horizontal (X-axis) and the vertical (Y-axis) directions. Square each of these values, add them together, and then take the square root of this total. For example, if the length of the X-direction error is 10 mm, and the length of the Y-direction error is 5 mm, the RE is 11.2 mm (i.e., $\sqrt{100 + 25}$). Another way to assess RE is to set the target as the 0 X- and 0 Y-coordinates. Then, determine the X and Y locations of the actual response, square each of these values, add them together, and then take the square root of this total. To determine the average RE for a series of trials, simply calculate the mean of the total RE for the series.

Performance bias and consistency are more difficult to assess for the two-dimension case than in one dimension, because the algebraic signs + and – have little meaning for the two-dimension case. Hancock, Butler, and Fischman (1995) have presented a detailed description of calculating measures of bias and consistency in the two-dimension situation. Rather than go into the details of this calculation, we will consider a general approach to the problem here. For a series of two-dimensional movements, a researcher can obtain a qualitative assessment of bias and consistency by looking at the actual grouping of the movement locations. If the grouping tends to be in one quadrant of the target, then a performance bias is evident, whereas responses scattered in all quadrants would indicate no apparent performance bias. In these two examples, consistency would be much better in the former than in the latter case. Again, as for the one-dimension situation, the practical utility of assessing these characteristics is that the strategies used to improve performance would differ for the bias and the consistency cases.

Assessing error for continuous skills. The error measures described in the preceding two sections are based on skills that have discrete accuracy goals. However, continuous motor skills also require accuracy. For example, when a person must walk along a specified pathway, performance assessment can include measuring how well the person stayed on the pathway. Or, if a person is in a car simulator and must steer the car along the road as projected on a screen, a measure of performance can be based on how well the person kept the car on the road. Error measures for these types of skills must be different from those used to assess discrete skill performance.

A common error score for continuous skills is the **root-mean-squared error (RMSE),** which you can think of as AE for a continuous task. To illustrate how this error measure is determined and used, we will consider the following example

taken from performing a continuous skill known as *pursuit tracking*. To perform this skill, subjects move a joystick, steering wheel, or lever to make an object, such as a cursor, follow a specified pathway. The criterion pathway can be described kinematically as a displacement curve. Figure 3.3 provides an example. A displacement curve can represent the subject's tracking performance. To determine how accurately the subject tracked the criterion pathway, we would calculate an RMSE score.

We calculate RMSE by determining the amount of error between the displacement curve produced by the subject's tracking performance and the displacement curve of the criterion pathway (see figure 3.3). The actual calculation of RMSE is complex and requires a computer program that can sample and record the subject's position in relation to the criterion pathway at specified points of time, such as 100 times each second (100 Hz; note that 1 Hz = 1 time/sec). At each sampling point, the difference between the criterion pathway location and

---

absolute error (AE) the unsigned deviation from the target or criterion, representing amount of error. A measure of the magnitude of an error without regard to the direction of the deviation.

constant error (CE) the signed (+/–) deviation from the target or criterion; it represents amount and direction of error and serves as a measure of performance bias.

variable error (VE) an error score representing the variability (or conversely, the consistency) of performance.

root-mean-squared error (RMSE) an error measure used for continuous skills to indicate the amount of error between the performance curve produced and the criterion performance curve for a specific amount of time during which performance is sampled.

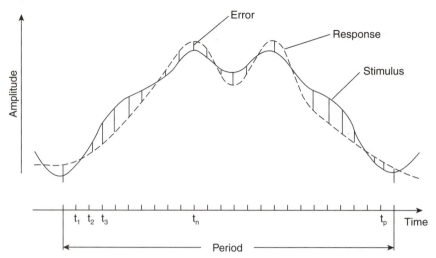

FIGURE 3.3   The difference between the subject's response and the stimulus at each specified time interval is used to calculate one root-mean-squared error (RMSE) score.   [From Franks, I. M. et al. (1982). The generation of movement patterns during the acquisition of a pursuit tracking task. *Human Movement Science*, 1:251–272. Copyright © 1982 Elsevier/North-Holland, Amsterdam, The Netherlands. Reprinted by permission.]

the subject's location is calculated. For the 100-Hz example, this yields 100 error scores each second. If the criterion pattern were 5 sec, there would be 500 error scores for the trial. The computer then derives one score, RMSE, from these by calculating an average error score for the total pathway.

Kinematic Measures

Kinematic measures, traditionally associated with biomechanics, have become important descriptors of performance in research on motor learning and control. The term **kinematics** refers to the description of motion without regard to force or mass. Three of the most common of such descriptors refer to an object's changes in position, its speed, and its changes in speed. The terms used to refer to these kinematic characteristics are *displacement, velocity,* and *acceleration.*

Kinematic measures are performance production measures that are based on recording the movement of specific body segments while a person is performing a skill. A typical procedure is first to mark the body segments of interest in a distinctive way with

tape, a marking pen, special light-reflecting balls, or light-emitting diodes (LEDs). The researcher then records the person's performance of the skill on videotape, or using special LED-reading cameras. Computer software developed to calculate kinematic measures then analyzes the recordings. This approach is used in commercially available movement analysis systems.

Another way to obtain kinematic measures is to use the pursuit tracking task described earlier and depicted in figure 3.3. Here, a computer samples and records the movements of the tracking device. In this example, a horizontal lever on a tabletop was the movement device. A potentiometer attached to the axle of the lever provided movement-related information that the computer could sample. We can take similar samplings of movement from the movement of a joystick, a mouse, or a rollerball.

Displacement. The first kinematic measure of interest is **displacement,** which is *the spatial position of a limb or joint during the time period of the movement.* Displacement describes changes in spatial locations as a person carries out a movement. We calculate displacement by using a movement analysis system to identify where the movement device, marked limb, or joint is in space (in terms of its X-Y coordinate in two-dimensional analysis or its X-Y-Z coordinate in three-dimensional analysis) at a given time. The system then determines the location of that entity for the next sampled time. The analysis system samples (observes) these spatial positions at specific rates, which vary according to the analysis system used. For example, a common videotape sampling rate is 60 Hz. Faster sampling rates are possible, depending on the analysis system used. Thus, the spatial location of a movement device or limb can be plotted for each sampled time as a displacement curve. Examples of displacement curves are in figures 3.3 and 3.4.

Velocity. The second kinematic measure of interest is **velocity,** which is a time-based derivative of displacement. *Velocity,* which we typically call speed in everyday terms, refers to *the rate of change in an object position with respect to time.* That is, how rapidly did this change in position occur and in what direction was this change (faster or slower than its previous rate)? Movement analysis systems derive velocity from displacement by dividing it by time. That is, divide a change in position (between time 1 and time 2) by the change in time (from time 1 to time 2). Velocity is always presented on a graph as a position-by-time curve. Note that in figure 3.4 the velocity curve is based on the same movement as the displacement curve. We refer to velocity in terms of an amount of distance per an amount of time. The tracking example in figure 3.4 shows velocity as the number of degrees per second. As the slope of this curve steepens, it represents increasing velocity, whereas negative velocity is represented by a slope that goes downward. Zero velocity is indicated by no change in positive or negative position of the curve.

Acceleration. The third kinematic measure is **acceleration,** which describes *change in velocity during movement.* We derive acceleration from velocity by dividing change in velocity by change in time. We also depict acceleration curves as a function of time, as you can see in the acceleration graph in figure 3.4, which is based on the displacement and velocity graphs also in that figure. The acceleration curve depicts the speeding up and slowing down of the movements as the subject moves. Rapid acceleration means that a velocity change occurred quickly.

Linear and angular motion. In kinematic descriptions of movement, the measures of displacement, velocity, and acceleration can refer to either linear or angular motion. The distinction between these types of motion is important to understand, and is a critical distinction in the analysis of movement. *Linear motion* describes the movement of all parts of the moving object, whereas *angular motion* refers to movement that occurred for some parts of the object but not for other parts. For example, if you want to describe the kinematics of walking, linear motion descriptions are appropriate for movement from one location to another because the whole body is moving linearly. However, if you want to describe the

---

kinematics   the description of motion without regard to force or mass; it includes displacement, velocity, and acceleration.

displacement   a kinematic measure describing changes in the spatial positions of a limb or joint during the time course of the movement.

velocity   a kinematic measure describing the rate of change of an object's position with respect to time. It is derived by dividing displacement by time (e.g., m/sec, km/hr).

acceleration   a kinematic measure that describes change in velocity during movement; we derive it from velocity by dividing change in velocity by change in time.

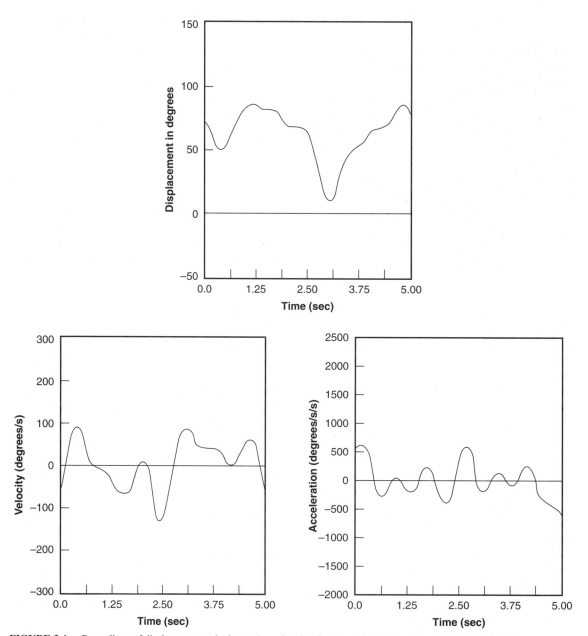

FIGURE 3.4   Recordings of displacement, velocity, and acceleration for a tracking task.   [From Marteniuk, R. G. & Romanow, S. K. E. (1983). Human movement organization and learning as revealed by variability of movement, use of kinematic information, and Fourier analysis. In R. A. Magill (Ed.), *Memory and control of action.* Copyright © 1983 Elsevier/North-Hollond, Amsterdam, The Netherlands. Reprinted by permission.]

foot movement characteristics during walking, angular motion descriptions are more appropriate, because the foot rotates about the ankle joint during walking.

The most common way researchers describe angular motion is by comparing the motion of one joint to the limb segment it rotates about while a movement is occurring. Two examples are shown in figure 3.5. The top part of this figure shows an angle-angle diagram for a skilled runner, where the displacement of the knee joint is compared to that of the thigh during the four phases of a running stride: takeoff, opposite footstrike, opposite foot takeoff, and opposite footstrike. Note that this angle-angle diagram produces a heart-shaped pattern, which is the classic knee-thigh relationship pattern during gait. The bottom part of the figure shows similar diagrams for three persons who have had amputation below the knee. What is noticeable here is that the amputees do not flex the knee joint at the beginning of the stance as the skilled runner does. These examples demonstrate that an important benefit of kinematic measures is that they allow us to describe the characteristics of critical components of a skill during movement.

Kinetics

The term **kinetics** refers to the consideration of force in the study of motion. Whereas *kinematics* refers to descriptors of motion without concern for the cause of that motion, *kinetics refers to force as a cause of motion*. Force has both magnitude and direction, which we need to take into account when we study kinetics. Newton's laws of motion all refer to the role of force in motion. Force is needed for motion to be started, changed, or stopped; it influences the rate of change in the momentum of an object; and it is involved in the action and reaction that occur in the interaction between two objects.

Researchers can investigate various types of forces in the study of human motor skill performance. These include ground reaction force, joint reaction force, muscle force, fluid resistance, elastic force, and inertial force. In addition, an important force-related characteristic of human movement is that human motion involves rotation of

body segments around their joint axes. The effect of a force on this rotation is called *joint torque,* or rotary force (see figure 3.6 for an example of how to graphically present joint torque). Because of the range of influence of different types of force on human movement, researchers studying motor skill learning and control are increasingly including the measurement of forces as part of their research.

Researchers can measure certain forces directly using devices such as force plates, force transducers, and strain gauges. They use force plates to measure ground reaction forces, which are involved in the interaction between an object, such as a person, and the ground. Force plates are popular force measurement devices in laboratories and clinics in which locomotion research and rehabilitation take place. Researchers use force transducers and strain gauges to measure force that is muscle produced; these are popular in laboratory and clinical settings to determine the magnitude of force generated while a subject is performing limb movement tasks.

Newton's second law of motion allows us to measure force indirectly by taking into account the relationship of force to velocity or acceleration and to the mass of the object: force = mass × acceleration. Because of this, we can calculate force without needing to use mechanical and electronic force measurement instruments, if acceleration can be assessed from a kinematic analysis of the movement.

EMG Measures

Movement involves electrical activity in the muscles, which can be measured by **electromyography (EMG).** Researchers commonly accomplish

---

kinetics   the study of the role of force as a cause of motion.

electromyography (EMG)   a measurement technique that records the electrical activity of a muscle or group of muscles. It indicates the muscle activity.

Skilled runner

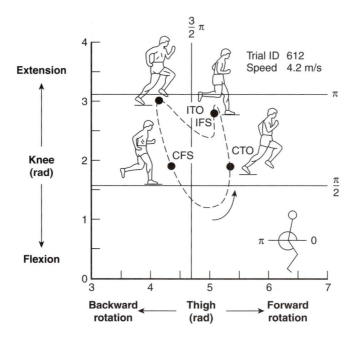

Three below-knee amputees

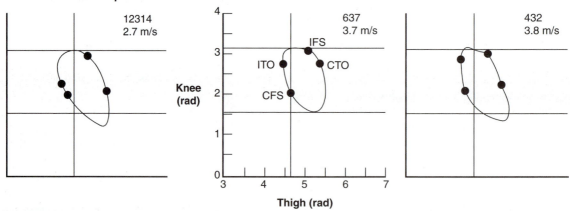

FIGURE 3.5   Angle-angle diagrams showing knee-thigh relationships during running by a skilled runner (top) and three below-knee amputees (bottom). The abbreviations indicate ipsilateral (left) footstrike (IFS), ipsilateral takeoff (ITO), contralateral (right) footstrike (CFS), and contralateral takeoff (CTO), which are the four components of a running stride.   [From Enoka, R. M. et al. (1978). Below knee amputee running gait. *American Journal of Physical Medicine and Rehabilitation, 61*, 70–78. Copyright © 1978 Williams & Wilkins Company, Baltimore, Maryland. Reprinted by permission.]

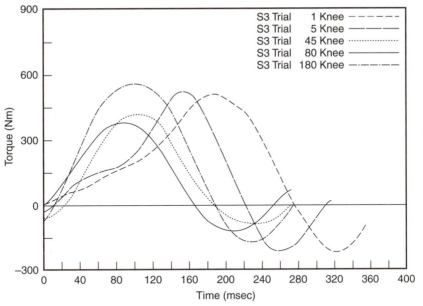

FIGURE 3.6 Results of an experiment by Sanders and Allen showing knee torques for one subject during contact with a surface after the subject drop-jumped from a platform and immediately initiated a vertical jump for maximum height. Each line on the graph represents performance for the trial noted in the key on the graph. [Reprinted from Sanders, R. H., & Allen, J. B. (1993). *Human Movement Science, 12*, pp. 299–326, with kind permission of Elsevier Science-NL, Sara Burgerharstraat 25, 1055 KV Amsterdam, The Netherlands.]

this by attaching surface electrodes to the skin over muscles. These electrodes detect muscle electrical activity, which then can be recorded by a computer or polygraph recorder. Figure 3.7 shows some EMG recordings of electrical activity in the ipsilateral biceps femoris (BFi) and contralateral biceps femoris (BFc) of the legs and the anterior deltoid (AD) of the shoulder girdle for a task that required the person to move his or her arm, on a signal, from the reaction-time key to a position directly in front of the shoulder. The EMG signals presented for these muscles show when electrical activity began in the muscles; we can identify this activity by the increase in the frequency and height of the traces for each muscle. The actual beginning of movement off the RT key is designated in the diagram by the vertical line at the end of the RT recording (line 5 of this figure).

Measuring Coordination

One of the more interesting phenomena of recent motor learning and control research is the investigation of complex skills. One reason for this is methodologically based. Prior to the advent of computer-based technology for movement analysis, kinematic measurement of movement was an expensive, labor-intensive, and time-consuming process involving frame-by-frame analysis of slow-motion film. With the development of the computer-based movement analysis systems, there has been a dramatic increase in research involving complex skills.

A measurement issue that has developed in the study of complex skills concerns how best to assess coordination. As you will study in chapter 4, coordination involves the movement of limb segments in specific time- and space-based

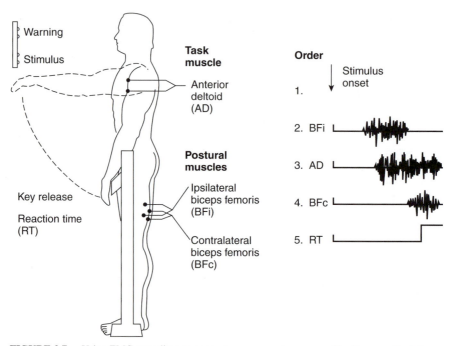

FIGURE 3.7   Using EMG recordings to measure a movement response. The figure on the left shows the reaction-time apparatus and where each electrode was placed to record the EMG for each muscle group of interest. The figures on the right show the EMG recordings for each of the three muscle groups and the reaction-time interval for the response.   [From Lee, Wynne. (1980). *Journal of Motor Behavior, 12*, 187. Reprinted by permission of the author.]

patterns. We can easily observe these patterns in angle-angle plots of the movements of limb segments, such as the ones depicted in figure 3.5. However, a measurement issue has arisen concerning angle-angle diagrams. Many researchers report only these qualitative kinematic descriptions and do not provide quantitative assessments of them. Some researchers question whether the qualitative pattern representation of limb segment relationships is sufficient for inferring coordination and suggest that quantitative assessment of these descriptions is needed as well.

A problem in resolving this issue is that there is little agreement among researchers about how to quantify coordination patterns such as the one in figure 3.5. Although several researchers have suggested techniques (see, e.g., Sparrow et al., 1987; Newell & van Emmerik, 1989; Vereijken et al., 1992), each has inherent problems, contributing to

the current lack of general acceptance of any one technique. Attempts to establish appropriate quantitative techniques continue (e.g., Sidaway, Heise, & Schoenfelder-Zohdi, 1995). Until researchers can resolve this issue, qualitative presentations of limb segment relationships will remain the norm for assessing coordination.

SUMMARY

An essential element in understanding motor learning is the measurement of motor performance. All concepts presented in this text are based on research in which researchers observed and measured motor performance. Measuring motor performance is essential for the assessment of motor deficiencies, as well as for the evaluation of performance by students or patients as they progress through practice

A CLOSER LOOK

Quantifying Coordination Patterns

Motor control researchers have suggested several techniques for quantifying the angle-angle plots that are popular for describing coordination patterns, such as the classic heart-shaped pattern of the knee-hip joints relationship during gait. While the regularity of the pattern is easy to observe, this qualitative approach does not allow for statistical between-pattern comparisons to determine reliable differences or similarities. Following are two quantitative approaches to this problem.

- The most common method is to cross-correlate time-related position changes in the angle of one joint with changes in another joint, (e.g., Newell & van Emmerik, 1989; Vereijken et al., 1992). The resulting correlation coefficient is interpreted as a ratio expressing the extent to which the two joints follow similar patterns of movement. A high correlation indicates strong coordination between the joints, whereas a low correlation shows little between-joint coordination.

- Sidaway, Heise, and Schoenfelder-Zohdi (1995) argue that a correlation approach is flawed because it assumes a linear relationship between the joints. In contrast, angle-angle plots of movement patterns are typically nonlinear. To accommodate both linear and nonlinear situations, they propose a normalized root-mean-squared error technique, which they call NoRMS. This method involves comparing a number of cycles of a continuous task, or a series of trials for a discrete task. From this series, the mean of the angle-angle plots is calculated. Then the root-mean-squared error (RMSE) is determined for each cycle or trial of the series, totaled, and then normalized with respect to the number of cycles or trials.

and therapy regimes. In this chapter, we focused on different ways to measure motor performance, along with the ways we can use these measurements in motor learning research and applied settings. We considered two categories of motor performance measures. The performance outcome measures category includes measures of time, error, and magnitude of a response. We discussed reaction time, movement time, and various error measures more extensively because of their traditional inclusion in motor learning research. The second category, performance production measures, includes kinematic, kinetic, EMG, and EEG measures, which describe characteristics of limbs, joints, muscles, and brain activity during movement. Finally, we discussed the ongoing controversy concerning the assessment of coordination characteristics of complex movement.

RELATED READINGS

Clarys, J. P., Cabri, J., De Witte, B., Toussaint, H., de Groot, G., Huying, P., & Hollander, P. (1988). Electromyography applied to sport ergonomics. *Ergonomics, 31,* 1605–1620.

Enoka, R. M. (1994). *Neuromechanical basis of kinesiology,* 2d ed. Champaign, IL: Human Kinetics. (Read chapters 1 and 2.)

Mah, C.D., Hulliger, M., Lee, R. G., & Marchand, A. R. (1994). Quantitative analysis of human movement synergies: Constructive pattern analysis for gait. *Journal of Motor Behavior, 26,* 83–102.

Reeve, T.G., Fischman, M. G., Christina, R.W., & Cauraugh, J. H. (1994). Using one-dimensional task error measures to assess performance on two-dimensional tasks: Comment on "Attentional control, distractors, and motor performance." *Human Performance, 7,* 315–319.

Sparrow, W. A. (1992). Measuring changes in coordination and control. In J. J. Summers (Ed.), *Approaches to the study of motor control and learning* (pp. 147–162). Amsterdam: Elsevier.

STUDY QUESTIONS

1. (a) Describe the differences between performance outcome measures and performance production measures. (b) Give three examples for each of these measures of motor performance.

2. (a) Describe how simple RT, choice RT, and discrimination RT situations differ. (b) What

does it mean to fractionate RT? (c) How does MT differ from RT?

3. What different information can be obtained about a person's performance by calculating AE, CE, and VE when performance accuracy is the movement goal?

4. How can performance error be determined for a continuous skill such as pursuit tracking?

5. Describe three kinematic measures of movement and explain what each measure tells us about the movement.

6. What is meant by the term *kinetics* as it is related to measuring human movement?

7. What information about a movement can be obtained by using EMG?

8. How can angle-angle diagrams be used to tell us something about the coordination characteristics of two limbs or two limb segments?

INTRODUCTION TO MOTOR CONTROL

CHAPTER

Motor Control Theories

*Concept: Theories about how we control
coordinated movement differ in terms
of the roles of central and environmental
features of a control system*

APPLICATION

To successfully perform the wide variety of motor skills we use in everyday life, we must coordinate various muscles and joints to function together. These muscle and joint combinations differ for many skills. Some skills, such as hitting a serve in tennis or getting out of a chair and into a wheelchair, require us to coordinate muscles and joints of the trunk and limbs. Other skills involve coordination of the arms, hands, and fingers; examples are reaching to pick up a pencil, playing the guitar, and typing on a keyboard. For still other skills, where only one arm and hand are involved, we must coordinate only a few muscles and joints. We do this when we manipulate a computer joystick or a car's gearshift.

Motor skill performance has other important general characteristics in addition to body and limb coordination. For example, we perform some skills with relatively slow movements; think of how we position a bow before releasing an arrow, or pick up a cup to take a drink from it. Other skills, such as throwing a ball or jumping from a bench to the floor, require fast, ballistic movements. Some motor skills, such as writing a numeral or buttoning a shirt, have few component parts; other skills, such as performing a dance routine or playing the piano, are very complex.

Also, we can produce remarkably accurate and consistent movement patterns from one performance attempt to another. We are capable of performing well-learned skills with a remarkable degree of success in a variety of situations, even though we have never before been in similar situations. For example, a skilled tennis player will have to use a forehand stroke in many different situations in matches. The many different characteristics in any situation, such as the ball's flight pattern, speed, spin, bounce, and location on the court, as well as the opponent's position, the wind and sun conditions, and so on, provide little chance that any two situations can be exactly alike. Yet a skilled player can hit the ball successfully.

All of these performance characteristics intrigue scholars who study how the nervous system controls coordinated skill performance. The theories of motor control discussed next represent some of the prominent current views addressing this complex question.

DISCUSSION

Before we discuss some theories of how the nervous system controls coordinated movement, we will consider the importance of having an understanding of the basic components of motor control

Walking down a crowded flight of stairs requires a person to adapt his or her pattern of limb and body movements to the characteristics of the stairs and the other people on the stairs.

theory. Then, we will clarify a few terms, to provide a foundation for understanding those theories.

Theory and Professional Practice

Students who are preparing for professions in which their primary responsibilities involve motor skill instruction often question the need to study motor control theory. This type of questioning often comes from those who see their preparation needs as involving only "practical" information that will help them carry out their day-to-day responsibilities in the workplace. Unfortunately, this view is often the result of a lack of awareness of the relevance of theory to professional practice. In this section, we will discuss what a theory is and

the relevance of motor control theory for teachers, coaches, and therapists.

What is a theory? If we base our understanding of the term theory on how it is commonly used in everyday language, we come away with the view that a theory has little relevance to reality. But, this view is short-sighted and misleading. In science, a theory helps us understand phenomena and explains the reasons why these phenomena exist or behave as they do. Stephen Hawking (1996), the world-renowned theoretical physicist at Cambridge University in England, states that a good theory should satisfy "two requirements. It must accurately describe a large class of observations . . . and it must make definite predictions about the results of future observations" (p. 15). In Hawking's domain of physics, theories are developed to help us understand various aspects of the physical universe in which we live. They do this by providing us with explanations of observable physical events, such as identifying the variables that make a rolling ball eventually stop rolling. By identifying these variables, we can then predict how far a ball will roll given specific characteristics of these variables.

In the behavioral sciences, which include the study of human motor learning and control, theories focus on explaining human behavior. When the human behavior of interest is the performance and learning of motor skills, we look to theories to provide us with explanations about why people perform skills as they do, which means identifying the variables that account for the performance characteristics we observe. For example, we know from our observations of people performing skills that a person can perform the same skill in a variety of different situations. A skilled basketball player can shoot a one-hand jump shot from a variety of locations on the floor and in a variety of game-related situations. A good theory of motor control will explain why this capability is possible.

The relevance of motor control theory for the practitioner. A benefit of a basic understanding of motor control theory is that it provides the practitioner with

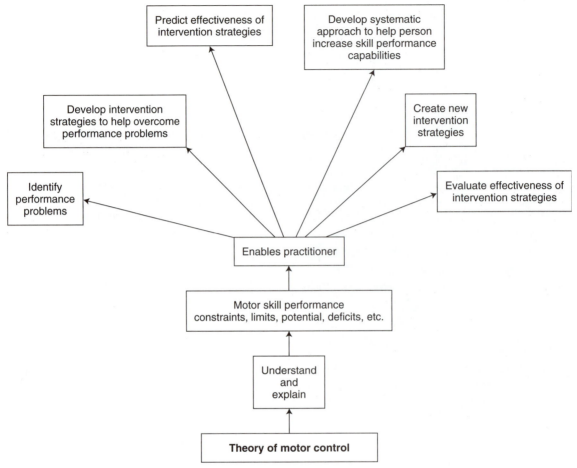

FIGURE 4.1   Motor control theory provides a foundation on which practitioners can base many tasks and responsibilities.

a base of support on which he or she can develop effective skill instruction and practice environments. Figure 4.1 illustrates the connection between theory and practice by indicating some of the many applications that will be enhanced when a practitioner has knowledge about the variables that influence motor skill performance. To use the example given at the end of the preceding section, if we know *why* people can adapt to a variety of situations when they perform a motor skill, we can use this knowledge to develop practice conditions that we can confidently predict will facilitate this adaptation capability.

Consider a different example. Suppose you need to help a person reacquire the capability to walk. Knowledge about the motor control mechanisms that underlie human locomotion and the environmental variables that affect it will allow you to develop more appropriate assessment and intervention strategies, because they will be based on variables that influence locomotion.

Coordination

Skilled motor performance involves a person's organization of the muscles of the body so that the

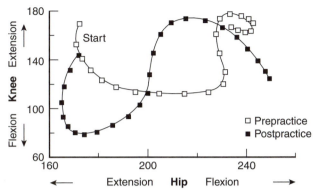

FIGURE 4.2 Angle-angle diagram from an experiment by Anderson and Sidaway showing coordination changes resulting from practice for the hip and knee relationship while performing a soccer kick. [Reprinted with permission from *Research Quarterly for Exercise and Sport,* Vol. 65, pp. 93–99, Copyright © 1994 American Association for Health, Physical Education, Recreation, and Dance, 1900 Association Drive, Reston, VA 20191.]

goal of the skill being performed can be accomplished. It is this organizational feature that is at the heart of the definition of the term *coordination.* For the purposes of this textbook, we will use a definition based on one provided by Turvey (1990): **coordination** is the patterning of body and limb motions relative to the patterning of environmental objects and events.

This definition contains two parts. Each is important to consider further. First, note that the definition specifies that coordination involves *patterns of body and/or limb movements.* Certain patterns of limb movement enable a person to achieve an action goal better than other patterns do. When learning a skill, the person must develop an appropriate limb movement coordination pattern. People typically begin practicing a skill by using a pattern of limb movements that they prefer. However, as they practice the skill and become more successful at performing it, a new and distinct pattern of limb movement emerges.

A common way to portray limb movement patterns is to represent graphically the relationship between the displacement patterns of each limb as it moves while performing the skill. An example of this type of representation can be seen in figure 4.2, where the coordination of the knee-hip joint angles during a soccer kick is shown.

The second part of the definition states that the pattern of limb and body motion is *relative to the pattern of environmental objects and events.* This is important because it establishes the need to consider motor skill coordination in relation to the context in which the skill is performed. The characteristics of the environmental context constrain the body and limbs to act in certain ways so that the goal of the action can be achieved.

For example, to walk along a pathway, people must adapt their body and limb movement patterns to the characteristics of the pathway. If, for example, a person is walking on a sidewalk and encounters a

coordination the patterning of body and limb motions relative to the patterning of environmental objects and events.

A CLOSER LOOK

Looking at the Degrees of Freedom Problem at the Level of Muscles and Joints

We know that there are 792 muscles in the human body that can act to make the one hundred joints behave in different ways. And each joint has mechanical characteristics that define its degrees of freedom for movement. On the basis of these fea-

tures, Turvey (1990) put the coordination control problem into perspective this way. If all the joints were only hinge joints like the elbow, there would be one hundred mechanical degrees of freedom to be controlled at the joint level. But if two specific characteristics, such as position and velocity, needed to be defined for these joints to carry out a specific act, the degrees of freedom would increase to two hundred.

---

tree branch lying across it, he or she must use a new pattern of movement in order to step over the branch. The characteristics of the tree branch will dictate the characteristics of the movement pattern. If it is small, the person may need to take only a large step, whereas if it is a large branch, he or she may have to climb over it.

The Degrees of Freedom Problem

Because coordination involves body and limb movement patterns, an important question in the study of motor control is this: How does the nervous system control the many muscles and joints involved in producing a given pattern? To answer this question, we must consider an important problem that was first posed by Nicolai Bernstein, a Russian physiologist whose work, produced from the 1930s to the 1950s, did not become known to the Western world until 1967. His work continues to influence research and theory related to motor control. Bernstein proposed that to perform a coordinated movement, the nervous system had to solve what he termed the "degrees of freedom problem."

The **degrees of freedom** of any system reflect the number of independent elements or components of the system. The **degrees of freedom problem** arises when a complex system needs to be organized to produce a specific result. The control problem is as follows: How can an effective yet efficient control system be designed so that a complex system, having many degrees of freedom, is constrained to act in a particular way?

Consider the following example of the degrees of freedom control problem in a mechanical system. A helicopter is designed so that it can fly up or down, to the left or the right, forward or backward, and so on, and at a variety of speeds. The helicopter designer must enable the pilot to control many different features so that the helicopter can do all these things. And the designer must help the pilot do so as simply as possible. If the pilot had to control one switch or lever for each component needed to make the helicopter fly a certain way, the pilot's job would be overwhelming. Therefore, the designer reduces the complexity of the task by providing control sticks and pedals that the pilot can control simultaneously with his or her hands and feet. Each stick or pedal controls several functions at once.

When the nervous system must control the human body so that it performs a complex motor skill, such as hitting a baseball, it faces a degrees of freedom control problem similar to that involving the helicopter. The determination of the actual number of degrees of freedom that must be controlled in coordinated human movement depends on which level of control we are considering. At a very basic level, we might consider motor units as the elements that must be controlled. At another level, we could consider muscles as the element of interest. Regardless of the control level considered, it becomes evident that for any motor skill, the control problem involved in enabling a person to perform that skill is an enormous one. It is important that any theory of motor control account for how the nervous system solves this control problem.

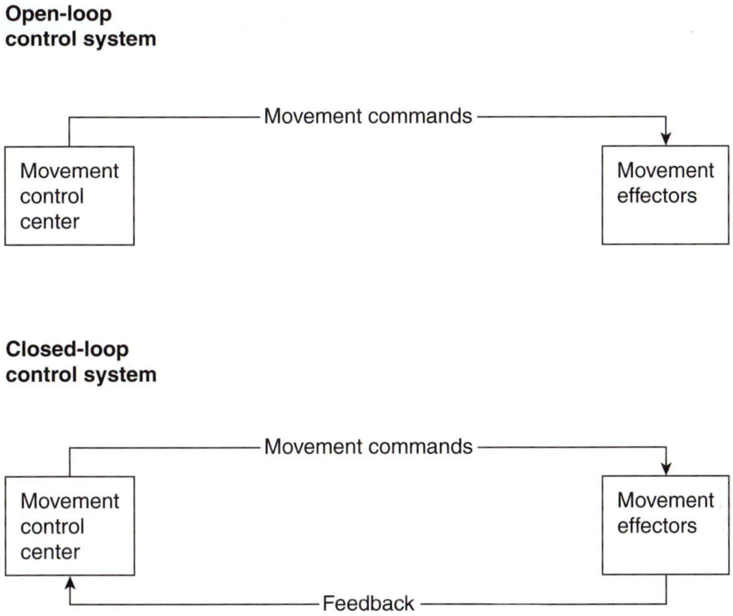

**Open-loop
control system**

**Closed-loop
control system**

FIGURE 4.3   Diagrams illustrating the open-loop and closed-loop control systems for movement control.

Open-Loop and Closed-Loop Control Systems

Most theories of how the nervous system controls coordinated movement incorporate two basic systems of control. These two systems, called **open-loop** and **closed-loop control systems,** are based on mechanical engineering models of control. Rather than provide exact descriptions of the control processes in complex human movement, these two models are basic descriptions of different ways the central and peripheral nervous systems initiate and control action. These models serve as useful guides that illustrate some of the basic components involved in that process.

Figure 4.3 presents diagrams illustrating simple open-loop and closed-loop control systems. These are the typical diagrams you would see in any general presentation of these types of control systems. Notice that each of these systems has a *control center.* The control center is sometimes referred to as an *executive.* An important part of its role is to generate and issue movement commands to the *effectors,* which, in the human, are the muscles and

degrees of freedom   the number of independent elements or components in a control system and the number of ways each component can act.

degrees of freedom problem   a control problem that occurs in the designing of a complex system that must produce a specific result; the design problem involves determining how to constrain the system's many degrees of freedom so that it can produce the specific result.

open-loop control system   a control system in which all the information needed to initiate and carry out an action as planned is contained in the initial commands to the effectors.

closed-loop control system   a system of control in which during the course of an action feedback is compared against a standard or reference to enable an action to be carried out as planned.

A CLOSER LOOK

Mechanical and Human Motor Skill Examples of Open-Loop and Closed-Loop Control Systems

Open-Loop Control
Mechanical Example

- **Videocassette recorder.** It can operate as an open-loop control system by being programmed to tape television programs on specified dates and times. The VCR will turn on and off at the specified times. (Note that it will turn off at the specified time even if the program being taped continues past that time.)

Human Motor Skill Example

- **Throwing a dart at a dartboard.** When the person initiates the throw, the arm movement and dart release occur as specified by movement commands developed before the initiation of the arm movement.

Closed-Loop Control
Mechanical Example

- **Thermostat in a house.** It controls the air-conditioning and heating systems in a house. The desired room temperature is set on the thermostat. This setting becomes a reference against which actual room temperatures are compared. The room temperature serves as the feedback to the thermostat to indicate when to turn the air-conditioning or heating system on or off.

Human Motor Skill Example

- **Driving a car.** When a person drives a car on a street or highway, he or she must keep the car within a specified lane. To do this the driver uses visual and proprioceptive feedback to control the steering wheel to make the needed adjustments to keep the car from going outside the lane boundaries.

---

joints involved in producing the desired movement. Both control systems also contain *movement commands* that come from the control center and go to the effectors.

Differences between the systems. These systems differ in two ways. First, a closed-loop control system involves *feedback,* whereas an open-loop system does not. In human movement, the feedback is *afferent* information sent by the various sensory receptors to the control center. The purpose of this feedback is to update the control center about the correctness of the movement while it is in progress.

In terms of the involvement of feedback in human movement control, figure 4-3 is somewhat misleading. The diagram suggests that the "effectors" that enable the body and limbs to move are the only source of feedback. But in complex human movement, feedback can come from visual and auditory receptors, as well as tactile and proprioceptive receptors.

The second important difference between open- and closed-loop control systems relates to the *movement commands* issued by the control center. In the open-loop system, because feedback is not used in the control of the ongoing movement, the commands contain all the information necessary for the effectors to carry out the planned movement. Although feedback is produced and available, it is not used to control the ongoing movement. This may be so because feedback is not needed, or because there is no time to use feedback to effectively control the movement after it is initiated. In the closed-loop system, the movement commands are quite different. First, the control center issues an initial command to the effectors that is sufficient only to initiate the movement. The actual execution and completion of the movement are dependent on feedback information that reaches the control center. In this case, then, feedback is used to help control the ongoing movement.

Theories of Motor Control

We can classify theories of how the nervous system controls coordinated movement in terms of the relative importance given to movement commands specified by central components of the control system and by the environment. Theories that give prominence to commands specified by the central nervous system in the control process have in common some form of memory representation, such as a motor program, that provides the basis for organizing, initiating, and carrying out intended actions. In contrast, other theories give more influence to movement commands specified by the environment and to the dynamic interaction of this information with the body, limbs, and nervous system.

It is important to note that the theories described here address motor control from a predominantly *behavioral level of analysis.* This means that they focus on explaining observed behavior without attempting to specify neural-level features of the control process (for an example of a neural model of motor control, see Bullock & Grossberg, 1991). An important goal of behaviorally based motor control theories is to propose laws and principles that govern coordinated human motor behavior. A neural-level theory would be expected to describe neural mechanisms or neural mechanism interactions that explain how the nervous system is involved in these behavioral principles.

Motor Program–Based Theory

At the heart of central control–oriented theories is the **motor program,** a memory-based construct that controls coordinated movement. Various theoretical viewpoints attribute different degrees of control to the motor program. Undoubtedly, the view that best characterizes present-day thinking about the motor program comes from the work of Richard Schmidt (1988; Schmidt & Lee, 1999). He proposed that a serious problem with previous views was that they limited the motor program to specific movements or sequences of movements. To overcome this limitation, Schmidt hypothesized the **generalized motor program** as a mechanism that could account for the adaptive and flexible qualities of human coordinated-movement behavior.

Schmidt's generalized motor program. Schmidt proposed that a generalized motor program controls a *class of actions,* rather than a specific movement or sequence. He defined a class of actions as a set of different actions having a common but unique set of features. For Schmidt, these features, which he called **invariant features,** are the "signature" of a generalized motor program, and form the basis of what is stored in memory. In order for a person to produce a specific action to meet the demands of a performance situation, the person must retrieve the appropriate program from memory and then add movement-specific **parameters.**

Rather than use a computer analogy, Schmidt proposed a phonograph record analogy to describe the characteristics of the generalized motor program. The invariant features of a record specify the rhythm and the dynamics (force) of the music. The parameters include the adjustable speed and volume controls. Even if a record is played faster than

---

motor program   a memory representation that stores information needed to perform an action.

generalized motor program   the general memory representation of a class of actions that share common invariant characteristics; it provides the basis for controlling a specific action within the class of actions.

invariant features   a unique set of characteristics that defines a generalized motor program and does not vary from one performance of the action to another.

parameters   features of the generalized motor program that can be varied from one performance of a skill to another; the features of a skill that must be added to the invariant features of a generalized motor program before a person can perform a skill to meet the specific demands of a situation.

A CLOSER LOOK

The Evolution of the Motor Program Concept

- Early Greek philosophers such as *Plato* talked about a person's creation of an "image" of an act preceding the action itself.
- *William James* (1890) alluded to Plato when he stated that to perform an action, a person must first form a clear "image" of that action.
- *Karl Lashley* (1917) is regarded as the first person to use the actual term *motor program*. He initially viewed motor programs as "intention[s] to act," but later described them as "generalized schemata of action which determine the sequence of specific acts" (Lashley, 1951, p. 122). He proposed that these schemata were organized to provide central control of movement patterns.
- *Sir Frederick Bartlett* (1932) implied that a motor program exists when he used the term *schema* to describe internal representations and organizations of movements.
- *Miller, Galanter, and Pribram* (1960) proposed the notion of a "Plan," which was "essentially the same as a program for a computer" (p. 16), and

was responsible for controlling the sequence of events of an action.
- *Franklin Henry* (Henry & Rogers, 1960) gave the motor program concept a needed conceptual and empirical boost. He hypothesized that the "neural pattern for a specific and well-coordinated motor act is controlled by a stored program that is used to direct the neuromotor details of its performance" (p. 449). Henry's concept of the motor program was also that of a computer program. He proposed that when initiated, the program controls the exact movement details, with essentially no modifications possible during the execution of the movement.
- *Stephen Keele* (1968) offered a view similar to Henry's by defining the motor program as "a set of muscle commands that are structured before a movement sequence begins, and that allow . . . the entire sequence to be carried out uninfluenced by peripheral feedback" (p. 387).
- *Richard Schmidt* (1975) proposed that the motor program is not specific muscle commands, but is an abstract memory-based representation of a class of actions, with each class defined by invariant features.

---

normal or louder than normal, the rhythmic and dynamic structure of the music remains intact.

Invariant features and parameters. Although many possible characteristics could be invariant features of the generalized motor program, three are most commonly proposed. These include the **relative time** (which is analogous to rhythm) of the components of the skill; the relative force used in performing the skill; and the order, or sequence, of the components. The term *relative* in *relative time* and *relative force* indicates that what is invariant are the percentages, or proportions, of overall force and timing of the components of a skill.

Figure 4.4 presents an illustration of how to interpret the concept of relative time. Suppose you move your arm as quickly as possible to hit four switches in sequence. Now, suppose that the

four components of this task yield the following movement time proportions: component 1 takes up 30 percent of the total performance time; component 2, 20 percent; component 3, 40 percent; and component 4, 10 percent. If the performance of this skill under typical conditions has an overall duration of 10 sec [represented in part (a) of the figure], then regardless of how much you speed up or slow down this overall duration, the actual amount of time characteristic of each component changes proportionately. In figure 4.4, parts (b) and (c) represent this proportional component change for speeding up the skill [part (b)] and slowing it down [part (c)]. Thus, if you typically perform this skill in 10 sec, then the amount of time you spend performing each component is 3, 2, 4, and 1 sec respectively. If you performed the skill twice as fast, in 5 sec, then each compo-

a. Normal speed (10 sec)

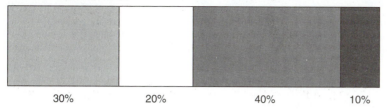

| 30% | 20% | 40% | 10% |

b. Faster (5 sec)

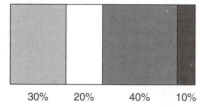

30%   20%   40%   10%

c. Slower (15 sec)

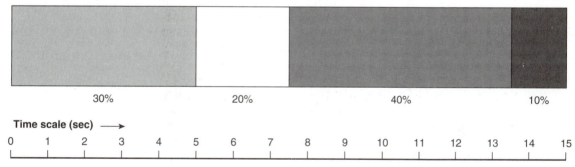

30%   20%   40%   10%

Time scale (sec) ⟶

0   1   2   3   4   5   6   7   8   9   10   11   12   13   14   15

FIGURE 4.4   An illustration of invariant relative time for a hypothetical four-component motor skill when it is performed normally at a 10-sec duration (a), speeded up to a 5-sec duration (b), and slowed down to a 15-sec duration (c).

nent would change proportionately to be 1.5, 1, 2, and 0.5 sec respectively. If you slowed down your overall performance time to 15 sec, then each component would change to 4.5, 3, 6, and 1.5 sec respectively.

Although motor program theory proposes that the invariant features of a generalized motor program are rather fixed from one performance of a skill to another, it also holds that there are other features, called *parameters,* that can be varied. Examples include the *overall force,* the *overall duration,* and the *muscles* that must be used to perform the skill. Performers can easily change these

from one performance situation to another, readily adapting them to the specific requirements of each situation. For example, an individual can speed up a sequence of movements and increase the overall force without altering the invariant characteristics of the motor program.

---

relative time   the proportion of the total amount of time required by each of the various components of a skill during the performance of that skill.

A CLOSER LOOK

Defining the Motor Program: A Memory Representation versus a Plan of Action Prepared Just Prior to Moving

A problem that has arisen over the years has led to difficulties in understanding what the motor program is and how it functions. This problem is that the term *motor program* has been used to describe different functional constructs. In some discussions, the motor program refers to the memory representation of a movement or action. The generalized motor program construct in Schmidt's schema theory is a good exam-

ple. The theoretical arguments about the memory-representation type of motor program focus on which characteristics of a movement or action are stored in memory as a part of the motor program. We use the term this way in the present chapter.

The other use of the term *motor program* refers to what is constructed or prepared just prior to movement initiation, but following an intention to act. This use of the term, sometimes referred to as *motor programming,* is the focus of chapter 7, although we do make some reference to this preparation aspect of motor program–based control in the present chapter.

Schmidt's schema theory. A formalized theory of how the generalized motor program operates to control coordinated movement is Schmidt's schema theory (Schmidt, 1975, 1988). A **schema** is a rule or set of rules that serves to provide the basis for a decision. It is developed by abstracting important pieces of information from related experiences and combining them into a type of rule. For example, your concept of *dog* is the result of seeing many different types of dogs and developing a set of rules that will allow you to identify correctly as a "dog" an animal you have never seen before.

Schmidt used the schema concept to describe two control components involved in the learning and control of skills. Both are characterized as based on abstract rules. The first is the *generalized motor program,* which, as just described, is the control mechanism responsible for controlling the general characteristics of classes of actions, such as throwing, kicking, walking, and running. The second component is the *motor response schema,* which is responsible for providing the specific rules governing an action in a given situation. Thus, the motor response schema provides parameters to the generalized motor program.

The schema theory provides an explanation for a person's ability to successfully perform a skill requiring movements that have not been made in that same way before. This is possible because the person can use the rules from the motor response

schema to generate appropriate parameter characteristics; the person adds these to the generalized motor program to perform the action.

Schmidt's schema theory claims to solve the degrees of freedom problem in movement coordination through an executive control operation that organizes motor programs and schemas. An important emphasis in this approach is the abstract, or general, nature of what is stored in the control center. The generalized motor program and recall schema work together to provide the specific movement characteristics needed to initiate an action in a given situation. The action initiation is an open-loop control process. However, once the action is initiated, feedback can influence its course if there is sufficient time to process the feedback and alter the action.

Testing the invariant relative-time feature. Researchers also have attempted to provide empirical support for motor program–based control by investigating Schmidt's claim that a generalized motor program controls a class of actions defined by specific invariant features. Of the proposed invariant features, relative time has generated the most research interest. Support for the invariance of this feature has come from many experiments investigating several different skills, such as typing, gait, handwriting, prehension, and sequences of key presses, among others. (For reviews of this evidence, see Heuer, 1991; Schmidt, 1985, 1988.)

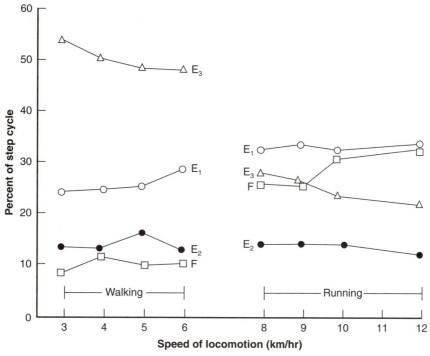

FIGURE 4.5   Results of the experiment by Shapiro et al. showing the relative time for each of the four step-cycle phases (mean values), determined by comparing percentages at the different locomotion speeds.   [From Shapiro, D. C., et al. (1966). Evidence for generalized motor programs using gait-pattern analysis. *Journal of Motor Behavior, 13,* 33–47. Copyright © 1966 Heldref Publication, Inc. Washington, DC. Reprinted by permission.]

Researchers typically have investigated relative time invariance by observing changes in relative time across a range of values of an associated parameter, such as overall duration. A research example that is commonly cited in this regard is a study by Shapiro, Zernicke, Gregor, and Diestal (1981) in which people walked and ran at different speeds on a treadmill. The researchers were interested in the percentages of the total step cycle time (i.e., relative time) that would characterize the four components, or phases, of the step cycle at each treadmill speed (i.e., the overall duration parameter). Their hypothesis was that if relative time is invariant for the generalized motor program involved in controlling walking and/or running gait patterns, then the percentages for a specific gait component should remain constant across the different speeds.

The results were consistent with the hypothesis of relative time invariance (see figure 4.5). As gait sped up or slowed down (at least up to 6 km/hr and beyond 8 km/hr), the percentage of time accounted for by each step cycle component remained essentially the same for different speeds. It is important to notice that for treadmill speeds greater than 8 km/hr a *different* motor program appears to operate. This conclusion must be made because there is an obvious difference in the percentages of step cycle time at this set of speeds compared to slower speeds.

> **schema**   a rule or set of rules that serves to provide the basis for a decision; in Schmidt's schema theory, an abstract representation of rules governing movement.

Interestingly, at this speed, participants were no longer walking, but running. The investigators concluded that different generalized motor programs control walking and running. Within each gait pattern, the overall duration parameter could be sped up or slowed down while the relative timing among the components of the step cycle was maintained.

Dynamic Pattern Theory

In sharp contrast to the motor program–based theory of motor control is an approach commonly referred to as **dynamic pattern theory.** Other terms used to describe this theoretical view include dynamical systems theory, coordination dynamics theory, and action theory. The basis for this theoretical view-

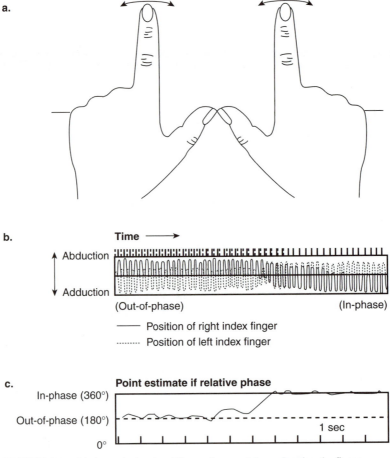

FIGURE 4.6   (a) shows the hand and finger placement for performing the finger movement task used in the experiments by Kelso. (b) and (c) show fingertip movement position as a function of time, during which movement frequency increased. (b) shows fingertip positions for both index fingers as they moved from being out of phase to in phase. (c) shows the relationship of the left index finger's peak extension to the right finger's peak extension as a different way to portray the phase transition shown in (b). [Reprinted from Kelso J.A.S., & Schöner, G. (1988). Self-organization of coordinative movement patterns. *Human Movement Science, 7*, 27–46, with kind permission of Elsevier Science-NL, Sara Burgerharstraat 25, 1055 KV Amsterdam, The Netherlands.)

point is a multidisciplinary perspective involving physics, biology, chemistry, and mathematics. Proponents of this theory see human movement control as a complex system that behaves in ways similar to those of any complex biological or physical system. As a complex system, human motor control is seen from the perspective of *nonlinear dynamics;* this means that behavioral changes over time do not follow a continuous, linear progression. For example, in the physical world, when the velocity of water through a tube is increased gradually, rather than the water flow simply increasing steadily in speed, there is a velocity point at which the water behavior changes from smooth flow to turbulence. This abrupt change represents a **nonlinear behavior.**

Those who study dynamic pattern theory are particularly interested in how a system changes over time from one stable state to another because of the influence of a particular variable. Although this approach has been used to model many complex systems in the physical world (see Gleick, 1987), only since the 1980s has it captured the attention of scientists interested in understanding and explaining human movement control.

Nonlinear changes in movement behavior. A series of experiments by Kelso and his colleagues established for movement scientists that the systematic change in the level of a variable can cause a nonlinear behavioral change in human coordinated movement (e.g., Kelso, 1984; Kelso & Scholz, 1985). The top panel in figure 4.6 illustrates the type of task used in these experiments. Participants began moving their right and left index fingers at a specified rate of speed so that they were *out of phase* (sometimes referred to as antiphase). This means that the muscle groups controlling the right and left fingers were operating simultaneously but in opposite ways: when the right finger was flexed, the left finger was extended. Quantitatively, the fingers were 180° out of phase with each other throughout the movement cycle. The participants systematically increased the speed of their finger movements by keeping their finger speed consistent with that of a metronome con-

trolled by the experimenters. The result was that at a specific speed the finger movements spontaneously shifted to an *in-phase* relationship, where both were flexed or extended at the same time (i.e., 0 or 360° in phase with each other).

The *transition* between the stable out-of-phase and in-phase states was a mixture of both out-of-phase and in-phase finger movements. But, at slower speeds, only out-of-phase movements occurred, whereas at faster speeds, only in-phase movements occurred. Thus, a linear increase in movement speed led to a nonlinear change in the fundamental pattern of movement.

When viewed from the perspective of coordination patterns, these experiments established that distinct coordination patterns can spontaneously develop as a function of a change in a specific variable. In the case of the finger movement task used in the Kelso experiments, the out-of-phase and in-phase finger movement relationships are specific coordination patterns. The importance of these experiments is that they provided an initial step in the investigation of coordination changes that can occur without resorting to a mechanism such as a motor program to account for the change.

Another example of spontaneous coordination change that results from the systematic increase or decrease of a variable is the change from walking

---

dynamic pattern theory an approach to describing and explaining the control of coordinated movement that emphasizes the role of information in the environment and the dynamic properties of the body and limbs; it is also known as the dynamic systems theory.

nonlinear behavior a behavior that changes in abrupt, nonlinear ways in response to systematic linear increases in the value of a specific variable (e.g., the change from smooth to turbulent water flow in a tube at a specific increase in water velocity; the change from a walking to a running gait at a specific increase in gait velocity).

A CLOSER LOOK

Two Views about the Source of Relative Time Invariance

Relative time invariance is a common component of both the generalized motor program and dynamic pattern views of motor control. However, one of the important differences between these views is the source of the invariance.

- The *generalized motor program view* emphasizes that relative time, as an invariant feature of the generalized motor program, is included in the movement commands sent to the musculature. Because of this, the resulting action is obliged to perform according to this time constraint. Relative time invariance across variations of a parameter is an indicator of a class of movements that are controlled by the same generalized motor program.

- The *dynamic pattern view* prefers to use the term "temporal pattern" rather than relative time invariance. Although different with respect to some specific characteristics, a temporal pattern is analogous to the concept of relative time invariance. More important, the invariance seen in relative time for many actions is the result of the person interacting with characteristics of the task and/or environment, or the mechanical dynamics involved in the body and limb movements. Relative time invariance across variations of a control parameter is an indicator of coordination pattern stability.

---

to running coordination patterns that occur at specific speeds. The experiment by Shapiro et al. (1981), which was discussed in this chapter, was an early demonstration of this spontaneous gait pattern change. Since that experiment, the walk-to-run and, conversely, the run-to-walk gait changes that occur as a function of speed have been demonstrated numerous times, and have become the basis for an increasing amount of research (e.g., Diedrich & Warren, 1995, 1998; Wagenaar & van Emmerik, 1994).

Stability and attractors. At the heart of the dynamic pattern view is the concept of **stability.** In dynamic terms, stability refers to the behavioral steady state of a system. This is different from the concept of invariance; stability incorporates the notion of variability by noting that when a system is slightly perturbed, it will return spontaneously to a stable state.

By observing characteristics of a stable state, scientists can gain understanding of the variables that influence a system to behave as it does. For example, in the reciprocal rhythmic finger movements in the Kelso experiment just described, the researchers observed behavioral stability when the fingers were in out-of-phase and in-phase relationships with each other. These two stable states indicate two coordinated movement patterns. Between these states, as finger speed increased, a *phase transition* occurred during which instability characterized the behavioral patterns. The instability continued until finger speed reached a point at which a new stable state spontaneously occurred.

The stable behavioral steady states of systems are known as **attractors** (or *attractor states*). In terms of human coordinated movement, attractors are *preferred behavioral states,* such as the in-phase and out-of-phase states for rhythmic finger movements described in the Kelso experiment. Attractors represent stable regions of operation around which behavior typically occurs when a system is allowed to operate in its preferred manner.

For example, when people locomote at a speed of 3 mi/hr (i.e., 4.8 km/hr), the arms and legs are "attracted to" a coordination relationship that produces a walking gait. This gait pattern represents the preferred behavioral state for engaging in a locomotion action. But, when people locomote at a speed of 10 mi/hr (~ 16 km/hr), the walking gait is not the preferred locomotion state. At this speed, most people run, which involves a coordination pattern that is different from a walking gait pattern.

Finally, attractor states are not only stable states characterized by minimal behavioral variability, but also optimally *energy-efficient* states. This means that when a person is moving at a preferred rate or using a preferred coordination pattern, that person uses less energy than he or she would if moving at a nonpreferred rate.

Order and control parameters. Proponents of the dynamic pattern view place a priority on developing formal nonlinear equations of motion that specify the stability and loss of stability of performance in addition to changes that result from learning and development. To develop these equations, scientists must identify the variables responsible for and associated with coordination. Primary among these variables are **order parameters** (sometimes the term *collective variables* is used). These are functionally specific and abstract variables that define the overall behavior of a system. The order parameters enable a coordinated pattern of movement that can be reproduced and distinguished from other patterns.

Because order parameters define a movement pattern, it is essential to identify specific types. The most prominent of the order parameters identified by researchers is *relative phase* (illustrated in figure 4-4) for rhythmic movements. Relative phase refers to a quantified value that represents the movement relationship between two movement segments. For example, the bottom panel (c) of figure 4.6 illustrates that for the rhythmic finger movement task in the Kelso (1984) experiment, the relative phase for the in-phase movement relationship was 360° (which is the same as 0°); the relative phase for the out-of-phase movement relationship was 180°. These two relative phases were determined by establishing that the maximum adduction of a finger had a phase value of 360°

(i.e., 0°), and the maximum abduction had a phase value of 180°. On the basis of a common starting point, the relative phase was then calculated as the difference between the phase values of the two fingers at any point during the movement. For the in-phase movement, both fingers had a common starting point of maximum adduction (i.e., 360°). The fingers then moved together to a maximum abduction position (180°), and then returned to the initial maximum adduction position. At any time during the fingers' movement, they had a relative phase of 360°, indicating that both fingers are at the same abduction position. The opposite holds for the out-of-phase pattern. At any point, the one finger is abducting the same amount as the other is adducting, which means the two fingers have a relative phase of 180°. Another way to consider this relationship is from the perspective of the amount of simultaneous adduction and/or abduction movement. When moving in-phase with each other, both fingers abduct or adduct the same amount at the same time; when moving out-of-phase with each other, both fingers move the same amount simultaneously, but one is adducting while the other is abducting.

---

stability a behavioral steady state of a system that represents a preferred behavioral state and incorporates the notion of invariance by noting that a stable system will spontaneously return to a stable state after it is slightly perturbed.

attractors the stable behavioral steady states of systems. In terms of human coordinated movement, attractors characterize preferred behavioral states, such as the in-phase and out-of-phase states for rhythmic bimanual finger movements.

order parameters functionally specific variables that define the overall behavior of a system; they enable a coordinated pattern of movement to be reproduced and distinguished from other patterns (e.g., relative phase); known also as collective variables.

The **control parameter** represents the variable that when increased or decreased will influence the stability and character of the order parameter. For example, in the Kelso experiment, movement frequency (i.e., speed) was the control parameter. As the movement frequency was systematically increased by the metronome, the phase relationship between the two fingers underwent distinct changes. As figure 4-6 indicates in both panels (b) and (c), the in-phase relationship was maintained through several frequencies, but then began to destabilize as frequency continued to increase. For several more frequencies, neither an in-phase nor an out-of-phase relationship was detectable during a period of *phase transition.* However, as the frequency continued to increase, there was a certain frequency at which the new out-of-phase relationship emerged and became stable. From an experimental point of view, the control parameter is important to identify because it becomes the variable to manipulate in order to assess the stability of the order parameter, which in turn provides the basis for determining attractor states for patterns of limb movement.

From an applied perspective, the control parameter can be the basis for assessing the stability of a coordination pattern, and may provide insights into a person's coordination characteristics that might not otherwise be observed. This application can be especially useful in rehabilitation settings. For example, van Emmerik and Wagenaar (1996) demonstrated that Parkinson's disease patients had more difficulty than healthy age-matched control participants in adapting a specific coordination pattern while walking to gradually increasing speeds (i.e., the control parameter) on a treadmill. In this study, the relative phase (i.e., the order parameter) of interest was based on the relationship between the arm and leg swings while walking. The researchers concluded from their results that the assessment of the stability of the phase relationship for the arm and leg swings at various walking speeds provides a sensitive technique to diagnose and detect early stages of Parkinson's disease.

Self-organization. An important element of the dynamic pattern perspective is the concept of **self-organization.** This means that when certain conditions characterize a situation, a specific stable pattern of behavior emerges. Many examples of self-organization exist within the physical world that illustrate applications of this concept to the human movement domain. For example, there is no hurricane program in the universe, but hurricanes commonly occur. However, they occur only when certain wind and water temperature conditions exist. When these variables achieve certain characteristics, a hurricane will self-organize in a distinct, identifiable fashion.

When applied to human movement coordination, the concept of self-organization means that when certain conditions characterize a situation, a specific pattern of limb movement emerges. Thus, rather than being specified by a motor program, the coordinated pattern of movement self-organizes within the framework of the characteristics of environmental conditions and limb dynamics. For example, in the bimanual finger-movement task performed in the Kelso experiments, the in-phase coordination pattern self-organized as a function of the movement speed (i.e., the control parameter). This same type of self-organization is seen for the walk-to-run, or run-to-walk, gait transitions that occur as gait speed increases or decreases.

Coordinative structures. Another important aspect of the dynamic pattern view relates to the unit of behavior that is controlled. Proponents of the view assert that skilled action results when a person's nervous system constrains functionally specific *synergies of muscles and joints* to act cooperatively, so that the person can carry out an action according to the dictates of the situation. An individual may develop these functional synergies, called **coordinative structures,** through practice or experience, or they may exist naturally.

An example of a coordinative structure is the muscles and joints (the degrees of freedom to be controlled) involved in the action of reaching and grasping an object. The individual groups of muscles and joints that must act together to enable a person to successfully reach and grasp an object are "converted" through practice into a task-specific ensemble. The action occurs when a person has the intention to reach and grasp a cup and the environmental conditions specify that this action should occur. Then, in accordance to the characteristics of the limb and of the environmental constraints, the coordinative structure self-organizes to carry out the action.

Some coordinative structures appear to be innate, such as those involved in walking, running, and bimanual coordination. For example, research evidence shows that when the two arms must perform simultaneously to achieve an action goal, they tend to move together spatially and temporally. If a person must perform a skill that requires the two arms to simultaneously perform different movements, as is required to perform a tennis serve, the person needs to practice to dissociate the arm movements so that each will perform its own movement. Other coordinative structures are learned, such as the new coordinative structure that would develop as a result of extensive practice of a tennis serve.

In some cases, the innate coordinative structures can be problematic for learning a skill, as in the case of the tennis serve. However, innate and the learned coordinative structures are generally beneficial for performing skills because they allow a person to achieve an action goal even though some slight perturbation occurs during the action. For example, if a tennis player is serving, and during the serve a gust of wind makes the ball deviate from its intended path, the player can adjust the movements involved in his or her serving action and achieve a successful serve. Similarly, if a person is jogging on a sidewalk and must step over a curb, the jogger can adjust movement characteristics of his or her gait pattern to avoid tripping while maintaining the jogging coordination pattern.

Perception and action coupling. Proponents of the dynamic pattern view emphasize the interaction of perceptual and movement variables, which is commonly referred to as **perception-action coupling.** Critical perceptual information includes environment invariances that specify possible behaviors. The dynamic state of the motor control system interacts with the perceptual and motor variables to produce patterns of movement appropriate for achieving the action goal of the situation.

An example of perceptual variables involved in this type of coupling process is the optical variable *tau,* which is a mathematical variable related to the time-to-contact between an object and a person's eye. (We will discuss *tau* further in chapter 6.) Researchers have demonstrated that *tau* guides actions such as steering a car, catching a ball, hitting

---

control parameters   coordinated movement control variables (e.g., tempo, or speed, and force) that when systematically varied (e.g., speed is increased from slow to fast), may remain stable or change its stable state characteristic.

self-organization   the emergence of a specific stable pattern of behavior due to certain conditions characterizing a situation rather than to a specific control mechanism organizing the behavior; e.g., in the physical world hurricanes self-organize when certain wind and water temperature conditions exist.

coordinative structures   functionally specific collectives of muscles and joints that are constrained by the nervous system to act cooperatively to produce an action.

perception-action coupling   the interaction between perceptual and movement variables that results in specific movement dynamics of an action in accordance with a specific characteristic of the perceptual variable (e.g., the specific kinematic characteristics of a reach-and-grasp action associated with specific object characteristics).

Evidence for Relative Time in Brain Activity and Coordinated Movement

In an excellent discussion comparing and contrasting the motor programming and dynamic pattern views of motor control, Kelso (1997) addressed various issues related to relative time, which is a key variable common to both views. One of the issues that motor control researchers have struggled with over the years is determining the relationship between brain activity and observable performance characteristics associated with movement. A possible breakthrough in this struggle appears possible through the use of functional brain imaging technology, which enables researchers to observe brain activity while a person engages in movement.

Below are two key brain activity findings from research by Kelso and his colleagues in which they used this technology to investigate the issue of relative time. In these experiments, participants performed

bimanual coordination skills to produce either in-phase or out-of-phase (antiphase) movement coordination patterns to a signal that specified movement speed, which was systematically increased (see figure 4.6).

- At low speeds, relative time remained stable (i.e., invariant) across a range of speeds for both in- and out-of-phase coordination patterns.
- Spontaneous transitions from out-of-phase to in-phase coordination patterns occurred (i.e., a new coordination pattern self-organized) at a critical movement speed.

These results indicate that for relative time, the brain produces essentially the same pattern of activity as is observed at the movement level during the performance of a motor skill. An important implication of these results for the motor control theory controversy is that the dynamic pattern view predicts these results, whereas the motor programming view does not.

---

a ball, jumping from a platform, and performing the long jump. As a person gains experience, the perceptual variable couples with the dynamics of movement so that a distinct coordination pattern can be reproduced as needed.

Some additional examples of perception-action coupling include the coordination pattern people use to get on or over an obstacle, climb stairs, and go through a doorway. Researchers have found that obstacles in a person's pathway, stairs, and door openings specify size-related information that a person perceives in terms of an invariant relationship between an object's size and her or his own leg length (in the case of obstacles and stairs) or body size (in the case of door openings). Thus the person will step or climb over the obstacle on the basis of this perceived relationship, choose one of various stair-climbing options, and walk through a doorway sideways or face-forward depending on this perceived relationship between the environmental feature and his or her own body size–related feature.

These and other examples will be considered more specifically in chapter 6.

The Present State of the Control Theory Issue

The motor program–based theory and the dynamic pattern theory are the predominant behavioral theories currently addressing how the nervous system produces coordinated movement. Debate and research continue as scientists attempt to answer this important theory question. A benefit of the debate between proponents of these theories is that critical issues have become clarified and future directions more evident. We now know, for example, that a theory of control cannot focus exclusively on the movement information that is specified by the central nervous system. Theorists also must take task and environmental characteristics into account. As Newell (1986) rightly stated, the optimal pattern of coordination is determined by the interaction among constraints specified by the person, the environment, and the task.

A CLOSER LOOK

Walk-to-Run Gait Changes: Interpretations According to Motor Program Theory and Dynamic Pattern Theory

People spontaneously change from a walk to a run gait pattern at a certain speed of locomotion. Although individuals vary in terms of the actual speed at which this change occurs, the shift appears to be common to all people. The motor program and dynamic pattern theories differ in their explanations of why this coordination change occurs.

- **Motor Program Theory** The relative time structure of a coordination pattern distinguishes one generalized motor program from another. Because walking and running gaits are characterized by different relative time structures, they are controlled by different generalized motor programs. The walk-to-run gait pattern change occurs at a certain speed because the person chooses to change from the program that controls walking to the program that controls running.
- **Dynamic Pattern Theory** Interlimb and body coordination patterns self-organize as a function of specific control parameter values and environmental conditions. For walking and running gait patterns, speed is a critical control parameter. The walk-to-run gait transition

involves a competition between two attractors. At slow speeds, the primary attractor state is a walking coordination pattern. But, as walking speed increases, there is a certain range of speeds at which this attractor state loses stability, which means that for this range of speeds, the walking pattern undergoes some change as a running coordination pattern self-organizes and eventually becomes the stable attractor state for gait at a certain speed.

Interpreting the Shapiro et al. (1981) Experiment Results (Figure 4.5)

Motor program theory. Gait is controlled by one generalized motor program when walking gait is observed (3–6 km/hr) and by a different generalized motor program when the running gait is observed (8–12 km/hr).

Dynamic pattern theory. The walking and running gaits represent two attractor states that remain stable within the speed ranges of 3–6 km/hr and 10–12 km/hr. But, for gait speeds of 7–9 km/hr, the order parameter becomes unstable during a transition period in which a new gait pattern (running) self-organizes and becomes stable for a certain range of speeds.

Opinions vary in terms of the resolve of the motor control theory debate. For example, some researchers would prefer to see a compromise between the two theories which would lead to the development of a hybrid theory that incorporates the strengths of each theory (e.g., see Abernethy & Sparrow, 1992; Walter, 1998). However, Abernethy and Sparrow saw this compromise option as unlikely because the two theories represent two vastly different approaches to explaining the control of coordinated movement. They speculate that because of this difference, the history of science would predict that one will even-

tually become the predominant theory. Kelso (1997) expressed a similar view, but was more specific in his projections. He argued that because many aspects of the motor program view can be subsumed within the dynamic pattern theory, especially those related to invariant features and control parameters, and because the dynamic pattern theory can explain and predict more of the behavioral features of coordinated movement, that the dynamic pattern theory will eventually become the predominant theory. However, at this point in time, that predominance has yet to be established.

A CLOSER LOOK

Implications of the Dynamic Pattern View for Physical Rehabilitation

In 1996, the journal *Human Movement Science* published a special issue in which the articles addressed the relevance of the dynamic pattern view of motor control to the field of physical rehabilitation. In the concluding article, van Wieringen highlighted the key implications from the articles. The following summarizes some of those implications.

- Movement problems observed in children with movement disorders may be related to perceptual difficulties. Because of perception-action coupling, deficiencies in detecting visual information can limit movement capabilities.
- Therapy treatments for movement problems should engage patients in the performance of actions that are as realistic as possible. Because many actions occur as a function of environmental context characteristics that afford (i.e., allow) such actions, realistic task environments facilitate the improvement of movement capabilities.

- Assess movement problems and capabilities for functional tasks across a range of personal, environmental, or task characteristics that may, at a critical value, elicit change in a person's movement form. (See Scholz, 1990, for a detailed discussion about using this approach to assess coordination problems for a child with cerebral palsy who locomotes using a "bunny-hop" or hopping pattern.)
- Coordination patterns observed in people with movement disorders may be optimal because of the constraints imposed on the motor control system by the pathological condition. For example, the typical gait pattern of a person with spastic cerebral palsy may be the result of weak muscles that do not allow a "normal" gait pattern, which would suggest that the observed cocontraction of muscles involved in the gait pattern is due to a compensation for the weak muscles rather than to the disease itself. In this case, rehabilitation should be directed toward muscle strengthening rather than decreasing the level of the muscle cocontraction.

SUMMARY

Coordination involves a pattern of body and limb movements characterizing performance of a skill. To acquire this pattern, the nervous system must solve the degrees of freedom problem, which concerns organizing the muscles, joints, etc., which individually are free to behave in various ways, into a unit of action that will allow the achievement of an action goal.

Present-day theories of the control of coordinated movement incorporate features of open-loop and closed-loop control systems. Both involve a command center, commands, and effectors. However, the closed-loop system requires feedback as part of the control process.

Theories about how the nervous system produces and controls coordinated movement attribute different roles to central and environmental factors. The motor program–based theories hold that a central, memory-based mechanism is the primary control mechanism. This theory proposes that this mechanism is a generalized motor program, which is an abstract representation of a class of movements that is stored in memory and retrieved when an action must be produced. Stored in the program are invariant features of the action, such as the order of events, relative time, and relative force. When a specific action must be produced, the program must be parameterized with features such as the overall duration, the overall force of the movement, and the muscles that will be used to perform the movement.

An alternative view of motor control is the dynamic pattern theory. This view takes issue with the idea that there is a central representation of action by proposing that factors such as environmental invariants and limb dynamics can account for much of the control ascribed to the motor program. The dynamic pattern view sees coordinated movement as following the rules and specifications found in nonlinear dynamics. The concept of stability is an essential component of this view. Attractor states are preferred, stable patterns that define specific coordination patterns. Order parameters, such as relative phase, functionally define attractor states. Control parameters, such as speed or frequency, influence the stability and instability of attractor states. Coordinated action self-organizes as coordinative structures according to the characteristics of limb behavior and environmental constraints.

RELATED READINGS

Barton, S. (1994). Chaos, self-organization, and psychology. *American Psychologist, 49,* 5–14.

Clark, J. E. (1995). On becoming skillful: Patterns and constraints. *Research Quarterly for Exercise and Sport, 66,* 173–183.

Feigenberg, I. M., & Meijer, O. G. (1999). The active search for information: From reflexes to the model of the future (1966). *Motor Control, 3,* 225–236.

Lee, T. D. (1998). On the dynamics of motor learning research. *Research Quarterly for Exercise and Sport, 69,* 334–337.

Swinnen, S. (1994). Motor control. *Encyclopedia of human behavior.* (Vol. 3, 229–243). New York: Academic Press.

Wallace, S. A. (1996). Dynamic pattern perspective of rhythmic movement: An introduction. In H. N. Zelaznik (Ed.), *Advances in motor learning and control* (pp. 155–194). Champaign, IL: Human Kinetics.

Whiting, H. T. A., Vogt, S., & Vereijken, B. (1992). Human skill and motor control: Some aspects of the motor control–motor learning relation. In J. J. Summers (Ed.), *Approaches to the study of motor control and learning* (pp. 81–111). Amsterdam: Elsevier.

Worringham, C. J., Smiley-Owen, A. L., & Cross, C. L. (1997). Neural basis of motor learning in humans. In H. N. Zelaznik (Ed.), *Advances in motor learning and control* (pp. 67–86). Champaign, IL: Human Kinetics.

Zanone, P. G., & Kelso, J. A. S. (1991). Relative timing from the perspective of dynamic pattern theory: Stability and instability. In J. Fagard & P. Wolff (Eds.), *The development of timing control and temporal organization in coordinated action* (pp. 69–92). Amsterdam: Elsevier.

STUDY QUESTIONS

1. Define the term *coordination* and describe how a limb movement displacement graph can portray a coordinated movement pattern.

2. What is the *degrees of freedom problem* as it relates to the study of human motor control?

3. Describe the similarities and the differences between a closed-loop control system and an open-loop control system. For each system, describe a motor skill that could be characterized as having that type of control system.

4. Define a generalized motor program and describe two invariant features and two parameters proposed to characterize this program.

5. Describe an example of nonlinear changes in human coordinated movement.

6. Define and give an example of the following key terms used in the dynamic pattern theory of motor control; (a) stability; (b) attractors; (c) order parameters; (d) control parameters; (e) coordinative structures; (f) self-organization.

7. Discuss how relative-time characteristics of human walking and running gaits are explained by (a) motor program–based theory and (b) dynamic pattern theory.

Performance Characteristics
of Complex Skills

Concept: Specific characteristics of the
performance of various motor skills provide the
basis for much of our understanding of the
processes involved in motor control

APPLICATION

Appropriate training and rehabilitation procedures are important to develop to help people acquire skills effectively and efficiently. As you saw in chapter 4, a basic understanding of motor control theory and the processes involved in motor control form important parts of a foundation on which to base the development of these procedures. For example, if a person were having difficulty reaching, grasping, and drinking from a cup, how would the therapist determine the reason for this problem and then develop an appropriate intervention strategy to help the person perform this type of skill? An important part of the answer to these questions comes from research concerned with the motor control involved in prehension. Or, suppose a beginning student in a tennis class is having problems learning to serve because he or she cannot coordinate the ball toss and racquet movement that must simultaneously occur to perform a successful serve. Motor control researchers have identified some distinct characteristics of bimanual coordination that provide teachers and coaches some insight into how to overcome the tennis serve problem. In the discussion that follows, we will look at these and other types of motor skills to consider some of the performance characteristics that

researchers have identified as important for us to understand if we are to understand the motor control processes underlying the performance of skills.

DISCUSSION

The motor control theories discussed in chapter 4 were derived from researchers' observations of people performing a variety of everyday and sport skills in many different situations. These observations have established that each type of skill involves distinct performance characteristics that are essential to consider in a theory of motor control, and to provide guidance for practitioners as they help people learn or rehabilitate skills. In the following sections, we will consider some of the more prominent types of motor skills researchers have investigated with these goals in mind.

Speed-Accuracy Skills

Many motor skills require a person to perform with both speed and accuracy. For example, kicking a penalty kick in soccer, pitching a fastball for a strike in baseball and softball, playing a song on a piano at a fast tempo, and speed typing all require fast and accurate movement to achieve successful performance. When both speed and accuracy are essential to the performance of a motor skill, we commonly observe a phenomenon known as the **speed-accuracy trade-off.** This means that when the person emphasizes speed, accuracy is reduced. And conversely, when he or she emphasizes accuracy, speed is reduced.

Fitts' law.   The speed-accuracy trade-off is such a common characteristic in motor skill performance that a mathematical law describes it. Fitts' law, based on the work of Paul Fitts (1954), has become one of the most significant "laws" associated with human performance. In science, a *law* refers to a situation in which a result, or outcome, can be predicted when certain variables are involved. **Fitts' law** predicts the movement time for a situation requiring both speed and accuracy in which a person must move to a target as quickly and accurately as possible. The variables that predict the performance outcome are the *distance* to move and the *target size*. According to Fitts' law, if we know the spatial dimensions of these two variables, we can predict the movement time required to hit the target. In mathematical terms, Fitts' law describes this relationship as

$$MT = a + b \log_2(2D/W)$$

where

>MT is movement time
>a and b are constants
>D is the distance moved
>W is the target width, or size

That is, movement time will be equal to the $\log_2$ of two times the distance to move divided by the width of the target. As the target size becomes smaller or as the distance becomes longer, the movement speed will decrease in order to allow for an accurate movement. In other words, there is a speed-accuracy trade-off.

Fitts indicated that because of the lawful relationship between target size and movement distance, the equation $\log_2(2D/W)$ provides an **index of difficulty (ID)** for speed-accuracy skills. The index specifies that the higher the ID is, the more difficult the task will be. This is because more difficult tasks will

require more movement time. Figure 5.1 contains several examples of IDs that would characterize different reciprocal tapping task dimensions.

Fitts based his original calculation on a reciprocal tapping task in which participants made repetitive back-and-forth movements as fast as possible between two targets for a specified period of time. For this task, they were told to place an emphasis on accuracy. Since Fitts' initial work, other researchers have found that the lawful speed-accuracy relationship generalizes to a wide range of motor skill performance situations. For example, research evidence shows that when people perform manual aiming tasks, such as moving pegs from one location to insert them into a hole, throwing darts at a target, reaching or grasping containers of different sizes, and moving a cursor on a screen to a target, their actions demonstrate movement time characteristics predicted by Fitts' law.

If we apply Fitts' law to the sport skills described earlier in this section, the implications of this law for instruction and practice become more evident. For example, suppose a soccer player is

---

speed-accuracy trade-off   a characteristic of motor skill performance in which the speed at which a skill is performed is influenced by movement accuracy demands; the trade-off is that increasing speed yields decreasing accuracy, and vice versa.

Fitts' law   a human performance law specifying the movement time for an aiming action when the distance to move and the target size are known; it is quantified as $MT = a + b \log_2(2 \, D/W)$, where a and b are constants and W = target width, and D = distance from the starting point to the target.

index of difficulty (ID)   according to Fitts' law, a quantitative measure of the difficulty of performing a skill involving both speed and accuracy requirements; it is calculated as the $\log_2(2 \, D/W)$, where W = target width, and D = distance from the starting point to the target.

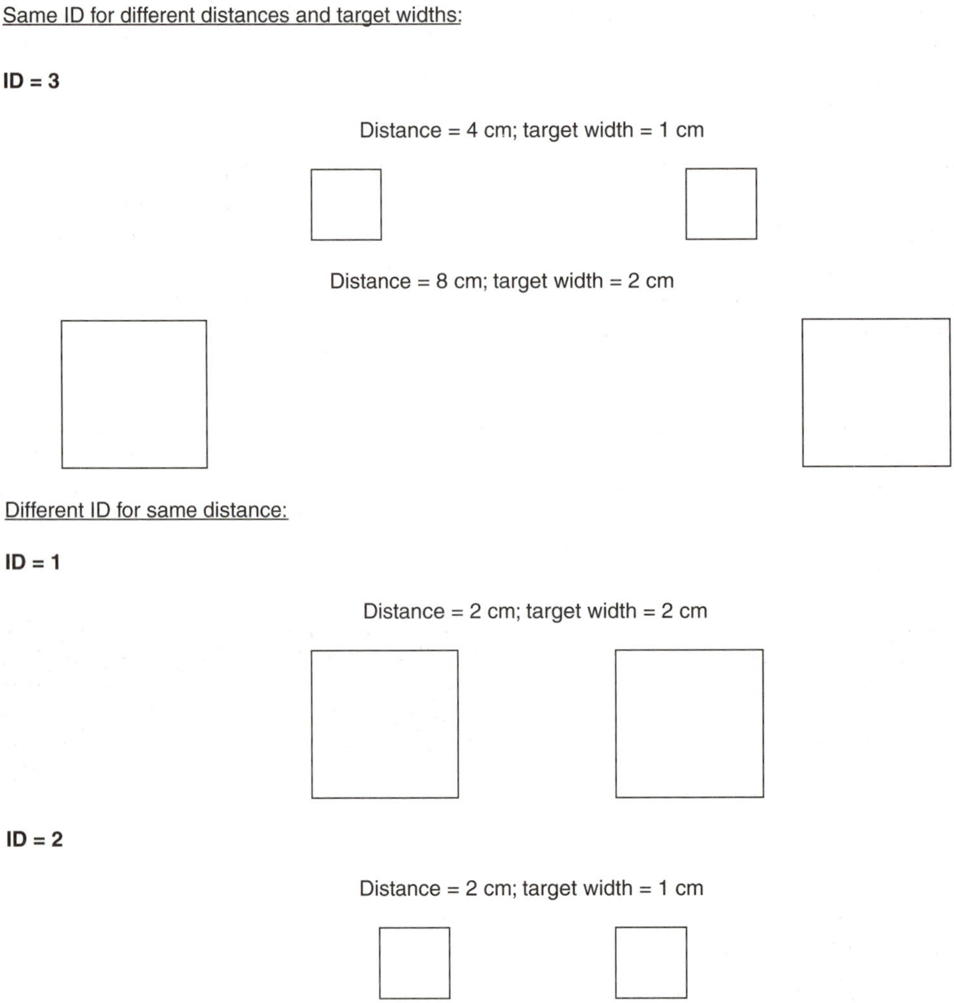

Same ID for different distances and target widths:

ID = 3

Distance = 4 cm; target width = 1 cm

Distance = 8 cm; target width = 2 cm

Different ID for same distance:

ID = 1

Distance = 2 cm; target width = 2 cm

ID = 2

Distance = 2 cm; target width = 1 cm

FIGURE 5.1   Examples of indexes of difficulty (ID) for reciprocal tapping tasks with different target size and/ or distance characteristics. Task difficulty is indexed according to the ID such that the higher the ID is, the more difficult is the task. The ID is calculated according to the Fitts' law equation: $ID = \log_2 (2 \cdot Distance/ Width)$ [Note that W is measured from the near edge of each target.]

asked to practice scoring a goal on a penalty kick by kicking the ball so that it travels as fast as possible to each of three different size areas in the goal. Fitts' law predicts that the highest speed will occur for the ball kicked to the largest area. Conversely, the slowest speed will characterize the ball kicked to the smallest area. Later in this book (Unit VI), we will discuss the practice conditions

that will help a person achieve both speed and accuracy in these types of situations.

Prehension

Prehension is the general term used to describe actions involving the reaching for and grasping of objects. Research evidence has shown that at the movement level, prehension consists of three distinct components:

A CLOSER LOOK

The Controversy Related to Explaining Fitts' Law

Although researchers consistently provide evidence that demonstrates the wide range of skill performance situations to which Fitts' law applies, they have not agreed on a motor control explanation for the speed-accuracy trade-off. Below is a sampling of some of the prominent hypotheses that continue to have proponents. It is important to understand that these hypotheses relate to explanations for the speed-accuracy trade-off associated with rapid manual-aiming tasks, which were the types of tasks involved in the initial demonstration of the trade-off.

- **Intermittent feedback hypothesis.** Crossman and Goodeve (1983) proposed that open-loop control is involved in the initiation of a rapid manual aiming task. But, as the arm moves toward the target, the person intermittently uses feedback to generate submovements, which are small corrections in the trajectory, until the target is contacted. Movement time (MT) increases for longer distances or narrower targets because the number of corrections increases. For a reciprocal aiming task, some of the MT increase occurs because the person spends more time in contact with each target to evaluate visual feedback and plan the movement to the next target.
- **Impulse-timing hypothesis.** Schmidt and colleagues (1979) proposed that many speed-accuracy tasks involve movements that are too fast to allow for the use of visual feedback to make corrections during the movement. In these situations, they hypothesize that a person programs commands in advance of movement initiation. These commands are forwarded to the muscles as "impulses," which are the forces produced during a specific amount of time. The result is the arm is forcefully driven toward the target and achieves accuracy based on the specified amount of force and time. Because amounts of force and time relate to movement variability, increases in movement velocity result in more variable movement. To correct an inaccurate outcome, the person would need to slow arm speed on the next attempt.
- **Multiple submovements hypothesis.** Meyer and colleagues (1988, 1990) adopted elements of both the intermittent-feedback and impulse-timing hypotheses. They proposed that before initiating movement, the person programs an initial impulse, which is then executed. If the movement is accurate, nothing further is required. But, if feedback during the movement indicates the movement will be inaccurate, the person prepares and executes submovements that adjust the initial velocity. This process continues until the person produces an accurate movement. The number of submovements made relates to movement time and the target distance and width (see also Yao & Fischman, 1999).

---

transport, grasp, and *object manipulation.* The object manipulation component refers to the functional goal for the prehension action. In other words, an important part of understanding the control of prehension relates to what the person intends to do with the object after grasping it. The importance of this component is that it influences the kinematic and kinetic characteristics of the transport and grasp components. For example, if a person intends to pick up a cup to drink from it, the transport and grasp characteristics will differ from those associated with the person picking up the cup and moving it to a different location on a table (see Newell & Cesari, 1999, for a discussion of the motor control implications of this issue). In fact, it is because of the relationship of the object manipulation component to the other two components that prehension must be considered an action that is different from the action of reaching and pointing to an object.

---

prehension   the action of reaching for and grasping an object that may be stationary or moving.

The Use of Functional Objects Enhances Prehension Performance in Rehabilitation Settings

An experiment related to the rehabilitation of reaching performance for cerebrovascular accident (CVA) patients demonstrates the benefit of the use of functional objects during therapy. Wu, Trombly, Lin, and Tickle-Degnen (1998) engaged fourteen men and women CVA patients in the performance of two types of tasks, which required them to reach a dis-tance of 20 cm to a food chopper and then grasp and push down its handle. The "enriched" task involved chopping a mushroom, which the participants could see. The "impoverished" task involved chopping, but there was nothing in the chopper, and the chopper itself was covered so that its shape and content could not be seen. All participants performed ten trials of each task. Analysis of the hand movements indicated that the enriched task resulted in patients reaching for the chopper faster, more directly, and more smoothly than the impoverished task.

From a motor control perspective, prehension involves the arm transporting the hand to an object as the hand forms the grip characteristics that are needed to grasp the object. A motor control question of interest here concerns the relationship between the transport and grasp components. Although initial attempts to answer this question proposed that these components were relatively independent (e.g., Jeannerod, 1981, 1984) more recent evidence has established that these two components interact synergistically (i.e., cooperatively) according to task demands. This means that the reach and the grasp are not two separate movement components, but function in an interdependent manner.

The most compelling evidence demonstrating this relationship has come from movement analyses of the fingers and thumb as the hand moves toward the object. For example, Jakobson and Goodale (1991) showed that the object's size and distance influenced the timing of when the distance between the fingers-thumb reached its maximum during the reach as well as the velocity profile of the transport component. Interestingly, they, along with others (e.g., Chieffi & Gentilucci, 1993) found that regardless of object size and distance, hand closure occurred at approximately two-thirds of the total movement time involved in the action. In addition, research evidence has shown that the kinematics of both the transport and grasp components are modified when the object is suddenly and unexpectedly moved during the transport phase (e.g., Gentilucci, Chieffi, Scarpa, & Castiello, 1992), and when an obstacle needs to be avoided to get to the object (e.g., Saling, Alberts, Stelmach, & Bloedel, 1998). These kinematic changes have led to the conclusion that there is a strong "coupling" between the reach and grasp components of a prehension action. Thus, prehension serves as an excellent example of how muscles and joints involved in a complex action operate as a *coordinative structure* to enable people to achieve an action goal in a variety of situations.

It is also important to note that the person's intended manipulation of the object and the visual information the person obtains about the distance to the object, its size, shape, weight, etc., preset the motor control system to initiate the reach and grasp movements. This presetting involves specifying "ballpark" estimates of the spatial and temporal characteristics that the transport and grasp components will need to reach and grasp the object. However, as the arm moves toward the object, visual feedback influences needed modifications to these component specifications (if there is sufficient time). In addition, the grasp itself may undergo further modifications, especially to size and force, after contact with the object and as the intended manipulation is carried out.

One final point that is important to note with regard to the motor control aspects of prehension is

A CLOSER LOOK

Prehension Situations Illustrate Motor Control Adaptability

An experiment by Steenbergen, Marteniuk, and Kalbfleisch (1995) provides a good illustration of how adaptable the motor control system is. We see this adaptability when people alter movements of a specific action to accommodate characteristics of the task situation. The authors asked the participants to reach and grasp with the right or left hand a Styrofoam cup that was either full or empty. Participants had to grasp the cup, located 30 cm in front of them, then place it on a round target 20 cm to the right or left. Movement analyses of the hand transport and grasp phases revealed interesting differences at the movement level

depending on which hand a person used and whether the cup was full or empty. For example, during the transport phase, hand velocity was distinctly faster and peak velocity was earlier when the cup was empty. The grasp aperture time also varied according to the cup characteristic. Maximum grasp aperture occurred earlier in the transport phase for the full cup, a situation demanding more movement precision. In terms of coordination of the joints involved in the action, participants froze the degrees of freedom of the shoulder, elbow, and wrist joints during the prehension movements for both full and empty cups. However, when the cup was full, participants increased stabilization during the movement by making a trunk postural adjustment that moved the shoulder forward.

that it demonstrates speed-accuracy trade-off characteristics. In fact, researchers have established that Fitts' law consistently applies to prehension for both laboratory tasks and activities of daily living. For example, in an experiment by Bootsma, Marteniuk, MacKenzie, and Zaal (1994), movement distance and object width influenced movement time during prehension in accordance with the predictions of Fitts' law. In addition, these object characteristics influenced the movement kinematics of the action. The relevance of the kinematic evidence is that it provides a way to explain why movement time increases as object width decreases. The kinematics showed that as objects decrease in size, the amount of time involved in the deceleration phase of the movement increases, suggesting that the increase in movement time associated with the smaller objects is due to the person reducing the speed of the limb as it approaches the object. This means that when a person reaches for a cup that has a small handle, not only will the transport and grasp kinematics differ from reaching for a cup with no handle, the movement time will also be slower because of the increased accuracy demands of grasping the small handle.

From an applied perspective, the motor control research evidence about prehension has important implications for the development of practice conditions to help people improve their prehension capabilities. Because of the cooperative relationship between the reach, grasp, and object manipulation components, it is essential that prehension practice or therapy strategies involve functional activities (e.g., Wu, Trombly, Lin, & Tickle-Degnen, 1998). In addition, because movement characteristics of reach and grasp components interact in various ways according to object characteristics, it is important that practice involve reaching, grasping, and manipulating a variety of object characteristics and manipulation goals. Finally, because of the interdependent relationship of the components of prehension, it would not be beneficial to separate the reach, grasp, and object manipulation goal so that a person could practice each component separately.

Handwriting

Investigation of the control mechanisms responsible for handwriting is a prominent theme in the study of motor control. Scholars generally agree that different control mechanisms are involved in

A CLOSER LOOK

A Handwriting Demonstration of Motor Equivalence

Write Your Signature

1. with a pen in your preferred hand.
2. with a pen in your nonpreferred hand.
3. with a pen held in your mouth by your teeth.
4. with your preferred hand on the chalkboard.

Compare the Spatial Characteristics of the Four Handwriting Samples

1. Describe the similarities you see.
2. Describe the differences you see.

Undoubtedly, specific elements of your signature remained constant regardless of which muscle groups were involved in the writing action. Your ability to engage various muscle groups to write your signature demonstrates how the act of handwriting illustrates the concept of motor equivalence.

---

controlling what people write (letters, words, numbers, etc.) and how they write it (the writing strokes producing the letters, words, etc., on the writing surface).

When we consider the act of handwriting from an anatomical perspective, we see that there is a great deal of individual variation in terms of limb segment involvement. But when researchers obtain handwriting samples from one person, they offer strong evidence for what Bernstein (1967) referred to as **motor equivalence.** That is, a person can adapt to the specific demands of the writing context and adjust size, force, direction, and even muscle involvement to accommodate those demands. The notable outcome is that there is a great degree of similarity in characteristics such as letter forms, writing slant, relative force for stroke production, and relative timing between strokes. People have little trouble varying characteristics such as movement time and writing size, among others.

The complexity of handwriting control makes it difficult to develop a simple control model describing the components of this process. A person can write his or her signature or a familiar phrase with the preferred hand, with the nonpreferred hand, with a foot, or by holding a pen in the mouth. This suggests that at least the spatial features of writing are represented in the memory system in an abstract form. Also, this motor equivalence capa-

bility suggests the involvement of coordinative structures in handwriting control.

Another interesting feature of the act of handwriting is that several control processes occur at the same time. To write a sentence, a person must use lexical and semantic as well as motor control processes. Writing requires the person to retrieve words from memory. These words must have meanings that fit what the writer intends to convey. The written sentence requires specific grammatical construction. The words require a certain spelling, which involves the person's movement of the limb to produce specific letters that are of an appropriate size and shape for what he or she is writing on. Further, the individual must hold the writing instrument with an appropriate amount of force to allow these letters to be formed. The capability of human beings to carry out these various cognitive and motor elements in relatively short amounts of time demonstrates both the complexity and the elegance of the control processes underlying the act of handwriting.

Bimanual Coordination Skills

In addition to unimanual coordination skills, people perform many motor skills that require the simultaneous performance of the two arms, i.e., **bimanual coordination.** Sometimes the two limbs do essentially the same thing (symmetric bimanual coordination); this occurs when someone rows a boat or when a person in a wheelchair rolls the wheels of the chair in order to go straight forward or backward. But more interesting from a motor control perspective are asymmetric bimanual coordination situations in which each limb must do something different. For example, a guitar player holds strings with one hand to determine chords, while plucking or striking strings with the other hand to produce sound. A skilled drummer can produce one rhythm with one hand while producing another with the other hand. The serve in tennis requires the player to toss the ball into the air with one arm while moving the racquet with a very different movement pattern with the other.

Bimanual coordination preferences. An important characteristic of the performance of skills that require either symmetric or asymmetric bimanual coordination is that the two limbs *prefer* to do the same thing at the same time. This preference helps the performance of symmetric bimanual skills, but can lead to problems for asymmetric skills. For example, why is it difficult to rub your stomach with one hand while at the same time tapping the top of your head with the other hand? The reason is that your two arms want to simultaneously do one of the actions, but not both.

The earliest research to demonstrate the motor control system's preference to coordinate the two arms to move together involved the simultaneous performance of discrete movements. In what is now seen as a classic series of experiments, Kelso, Southard, and Goodman (1979) had people perform rapid aiming movements to targets that had the same or different Fitts' index of difficulty (ID) values (see figure 5.2). Results showed a *temporal basis* for the coordination of the two arms as they moved with similar movement times not only to targets with the same ID values, but also to targets that had different ID values (note that the movement times are not identical, but similar). In addition the results of this experiment demonstrated that the bimanual movements to targets with different ID values did not adhere to Fitts' law. The apparent strength of the preference for the two

arms to temporally move together overcame the influence of the speed-accuracy trade-off characteristic for the same movement when it was performed by only one arm.

In the Kelso et al. bimanual coordination situation, the *more difficult task* influenced the performance of the arm doing the less difficult task. That is, the arm that was required to move a shorter distance (i.e., less difficult) slowed down in comparison to when it moved the same distance alone. Similar results have been shown when *task complexity* differences characterized the bimanual coordination task. For example, the task used in an experiment by Swinnen, Schmidt, Nicholson, Shapiro (1990) required participants to rapidly move their arms in different spatial-temporal patterns. The task involved moving one arm in a simple one-direction arm-flexion movement while at the same time moving the other in a two-part flexion and extension movement. Both arms were to complete their movements in a movement time of 800 ms. At the beginning of practice, participants generally produced the similar movement patterns with each arm, which typically resembled the more complex two-part movement required by one arm.

Researchers are not certain how the motor control system is involved in the control of bimanual coordination. At present, we know that there is a coupling of the arms, which forms a natural coordinative structure that prefers to operate in spatial-temporal symmetry. And, an in-phase relationship between the arms (i.e., both arms flexing and extending at the same time) appears to be the most

---

motor equivalence   the capability of the motor control system to enable a person to achieve an action goal in a variety of situations and conditions (e.g., writing your signature with either hand).

bimanual coordination   a motor skill that requires the simultaneous use of the two arms; the skill may require the two arms to move with the same or different spatial and/or temporal characteristics.

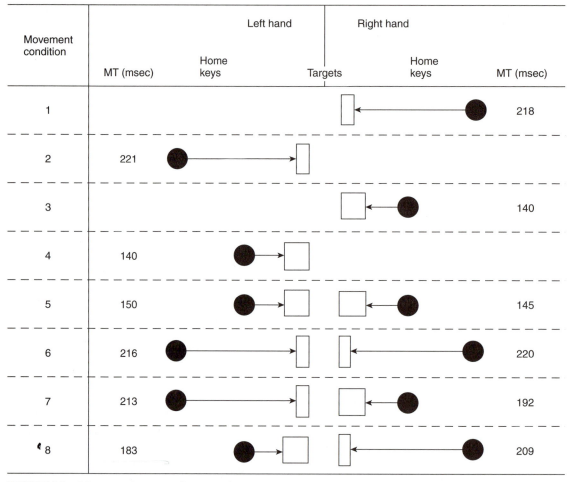

Movement condition	Left hand			Right hand		
	MT (msec)	Home keys	Targets	Home keys		MT (msec)
1						218
2	221					
3						140
4	140					
5	150					145
6	216					220
7	213					192
8	183					209

FIGURE 5.2   Movement time scores for one- and two-hand movements to targets of different distances and sizes reported in Kelso, Southard, and Goodman's second experiment.   [Source: Kelso, J. A., Southard, D.L., & Goodman, D. (1979). On the coordination of two-handed movements. *Journal of Experimental Psychology: Human Perception and Performance, 5*, 229–238. Copyright © 1979 the Amreican Psychological Association. Adapted with permission.]

predominant symmetrical relationship. In addition, we know that with practice, a person can learn to uncouple (sometimes referred to as "dissociate") the two limbs and simultaneously move his or her arms asymmetrically. But, we do not yet understand the control mechanisms involved in this dissociation process, although evidence is accumulating that indicates the importance of proprioceptive feedback in the successful performance of asymmetric bimanual coordination (e.g., Verschueren et al., 1999a).

In terms of motor control theory perspectives on learning to uncouple the limbs, researchers have proposed distinctive views. Those who support the motor program theory argue for generalized motor program involvement, but there is disagreement about whether two new generalized motor programs develop so that each arm becomes controlled by a separate program, or one generalized motor program develops in which each arm can perform somewhat independently. From a dynamic pattern theory perspective, the

A CLOSER LOOK

Applying the Dynamic Pattern View of Gait Control to Physical Therapy Interventions

We can see the involvement in locomotor control of dynamic interactions between the person and the environment in the effectiveness of a therapy strategy that helps reestablish normal rhythmic gait. Based on the dynamic systems control perspective, Wagenaar and van Emmerik (1994) recommended that therapists use various methods to help patients attain spon-

taneous production of the appropriate rhythmic structures for specific gait patterns by systematically altering gait speeds.

Wagenaar and Beek (1992) showed an example of the effectiveness of this procedure. They used a metronome to present rhythms to hemiplegic patients. When the authors systematically increased the rhythmic beat from 60 to 96 steps a minute, these patients improved the phase relationships of their arms and legs; this in turn positively influenced trunk rotation.

---

control issue is rather straightforward. The initial tendency for the arms to be spatially and temporally coupled represents an attractor state in which a specific relative phase relationship is the order parameter. But, with practice, the stable relationship becomes unstable as the new relationship becomes more stable and a new attractor state emerges.

Teachers, coaches, and therapists who are aware of bimanual coordination tendencies will recognize the need to give special attention to people who are learning skills that require the arms to perform different spatial-temporal movement patterns. The required unlinking of bimanual movements can be a difficult process for people. But, as both experience and research evidence (e.g., Lee, Swinnen, & Verschueren, 1995; Swinnen et al., 1990; Walter & Swinnen, 1994) tell us, people can achieve success in performing these types of skills when they receive appropriate instruction, feedback, and practice. We will consider some of the strategies practitioners can use to facilitate the learning of asymmetric bimanual coordination skills in Units V and VI.

Gait

There is little argument that at the nervous system level, we can attribute the basic control of human gait to *central pattern generators* in the spinal cord. These mechanisms provide the basis for stereotypic locomotive patterns. We can trace evidence for this

spinal level of control to the work of the British Nobel laureate Charles Sherrington and his colleagues at the end of the nineteenth and beginning of the twentieth centuries (e.g., Sherrington, 1906).

Using a procedure known as decerebration, which involves severing the spinal cord from the brain, Sherrington observed that decerebrated cats produced locomotor rhythmic muscular activity similar to that produced by intact animals. Later, Brown (1911) went a step further by additionally severing a cat's sensory pathways to the spinal cord; still, the cat showed rhythmic leg contractions appropriate for walking. More recent research (e.g., Grillner & Zangger, 1979) has confirmed and extended these earlier observations.

However, to understand how humans control the wide range of gait they are capable of, we must consider higher-level nervous system involvement, along with musculoskeletal dynamics and environmental interactions. Two aspects of gait control will serve to illustrate the roles of these various factors.

An important characteristic of locomotor actions is their rhythmic structure. You saw some of the research evidence for this in the discussion in chapter 4 of the study by Shapiro et al. (1981). On the basis of an analysis of the four components of the Phillipson step cycle, they found that walking and running each had a distinct rhythmic structure. In fact, this rhythmic characteristic is so common for walking and running gaits, that mathematical models

A CLOSER LOOK

Avoiding Obstacles While Walking or Running

Research by James Cutting and his colleagues at Cornell University (e.g., Cutting, 1986; Vishton & Cutting, 1995) has shown that if a person is walking or running and wishes to maintain footspeed while avoiding an obstacle, three time periods are critical:

The Time Needed to

1. recognize that an object needs to be avoided;
2. adjust the footfall;
3. turn the foot to avoid the obstacle.

Of these three periods, the first is the most critical and takes up about 75 percent of the distance covered while the subject is approaching an object.

Implication for Clinical Rehabilitation and Sport

- Because of the importance of early visual recognition of an object to be avoided, it is important to train people to actively visually search the environment in which they locomote. To avoid collision, a person must recognize objects sufficiently early to allow appropriate movement adjustments. Therefore, the therapist or coach who focuses training on only the movement-adjustment aspect of this task ignores the most critical component of object recognition.

have been developed to describe their structures. Those who have developed these models view walking and running gaits as operating similar to a pendulum (see Wagenaar & van Emmerik, 1994, for discussion about these models).

The rhythmic structure of gait patterns is not limited to leg movements. For example, when a person walks distinct rhythmic relationships exist between the movement of the arms and legs, and the specific character of this relationship relates to walking speed. Craik, Herman, and Finley (1976) first demonstrated this relationship by providing evidence that there are two arm-leg coordination patterns for walking: a 2:1 ratio (i.e., two arm swings to each leg stride) for very slow walking, and a 1:1 ratio for walking at speeds greater than 0.75 m/s (1.7 mi/hr, or 2.72 km/hr). van Emmerik and Wagenaar (1996) reported that additional research has established that the transition from the 2:1 to the 1:1 arm-leg relationship occurs within the walking speed range of 0.2 to 1.2 m/s (0.5 to 2.7 mi/hr, or 0.3 to 4.32 km/hr). In addition to the arm-leg relationship, the pelvis and thorax also demonstrate a rhythmic relationship during walk-

ing. At lower speeds, they move in phase with each other, but out of phase at higher walking speeds.

What is the practical benefit of knowing about these various coordination characteristics of gait patterns? van Emmerik and Wagenaar (1996) presented an excellent argument, along with research evidence, to support their view that knowing about these characteristics and using them as assessment techniques allow us to identify coordination problems in the trunk and extremities, especially for people with Parkinson's disease. For example, when walking at preferred speeds, Parkinson's patients show pelvis and thorax phase relationships that are exactly opposite those described in the previous paragraph for healthy people.

Finally, as you saw in chapter 4, an important gait characteristic is the spontaneous change from a walking to a running gait (and vice versa) at certain speeds. The speed at which the transition occurs varies between individuals. Some people walk at higher speeds than others, whereas some people run at lower speeds than others. In addition, the walk-to-run transition typically occurs at higher speeds than the run-to-walk transition. The issue of interest to researchers who study human locomotion is *why* this transition occurs. There is general agreement that the reason is not due to physical limitations. As a result, researchers have developed and tested several hypotheses. The most prevalent of these has been that the transition occurs to minimize metabolic energy consumption (i.e., VO_2). Although researchers have provided evidence that supports this hypothesis, others have reported results that fail to support it (see Hreljac, 1993). At present, no single cause for gait transitions has been determined. Interestingly, Turvey et al. (1999), after reporting results that did not support their hypothesis based on the role of kinetic energy, expressed doubts that a single cause can be identified because of the nature of complex, biological systems. Thus, the identification of the reason(s) why people change from a walking gait to a running gait at a certain speed remains a puzzle for researchers to solve.

Finally, vision provides an additional component of gait control, as you will see in chapter 6. Vision provides information that directs a person's walking speed, body alignment, and navigation through the environment.

SUMMARY

Much of our understanding of the control processes underlying the performance of motor skills comes from research evidence that has identified specific performance characteristics associated with a variety of types of skills. This discussion highlighted several of these characteristics.

The first type of motor skill discussed requires the performer to produce movement that is both fast and accurate. Performance of the *speed-accuracy skills* typically demonstrates a speed-accuracy trade-off, which means that to be as accurate as possible, speed will be slower than if accuracy is not important. The task characteristics associated with this trade-off are mathematically described by Fitts' law.

Performance of *prehension skills* demonstrates the characteristic of the synergistic coupling of skill components that allow a person to achieve an action goal in a variety of task-related situations. The transport and grasp components of a prehension action function interdependently by adjusting certain kinematic aspects of the movements to adapt to the specific characteristics of the object to be grasped and the manipulation goal of the action. Different from manual aiming, prehension movement kinematics vary during both the transport and grasp phases as a function of what the performer intends to do with the object after it is grasped.

The skill of *handwriting* demonstrates an important characteristic of motor skill performance known as motor equivalence, which means that a person can achieve the action goal in a variety of context conditions that require adjustments to such features as size, force, direction, and muscles involved. These various movement adaptations result in remarkable similarities in handwriting characteristics such as letter forms and relative timing between strokes, among others.

Bimanual coordination skills require the simultaneous performance of the two arms. Some tasks require that both arms perform in the same way at the same time (i.e., symmetric bimanual coordination); others require each arm to perform in a specific manner (i.e., asymmetric bimanual coordination). An important performance characteristic of these skills is the natural coupling between the arms that leads to a preference of simultaneously moving the arms in the same temporal and spatial pattern. We know from personal experience as well as research evidence that people can learn to uncouple the arms to perform asymmetric bimanual coordination tasks. But we do not know the motor control mechanisms that underlie the control of the arms in this uncoupled state.

The performance of *locomotion skills,* such as walking and running, is characterized by the rhythmic relationship between step cycle components as well as arm and leg swings, and the phase relationship between the movement of the pelvis and thorax. An important locomotion characteristic that has yet to be explained in terms of why it occurs is the spontaneous gait transition that occurs from walking to running (and vice versa) at certain gait speeds.

Finally, it is important to point out that vision plays an important role in the control of each of the skills considered in this discussion. Although this involvement has been briefly noted for these skills, the specific contribution of vision to their performance will be considered in chapter 6.

RELATED READINGS

Andres, R. O., & Hartung, K. J. (1989). Prediction of head movement time using Fitt's law. *Human Factors, 31,* 703–713.

Bennett, K. M. B., Adler, C. H., Stelmach, G. E., & Castiello, U. (1993). A kinematic study of the reach to grasp movement in a subject with hemi-Parkinson's disease. *Neuropsychologia, 31,* 709–716.

Bonnard, M., & Pailhous, J. (1993). Intentionality in human gait control: Modifying the frequency-to-amplitude relationship. *Journal of Experimental Psychology: Human Perception and Performance, 19,* 429–443.

Cutting, J. E., Vishton, P. M., & Braren, P. (1995). How to avoid collisions with stationary and with moving objects. *Psychological Review, 102,* 627–651.

Semjen, A., Summers, J. J, & Cattaert, D. (1995). Hand coordination in bimanual circle drawing. *Journal of Experimental Psychology: Human Perception and Performance, 21,* 1139–1157.

Summers, J. J. (1990). Temporal constraints on concurrent task performance. In G. E. Hammond (Ed.), *Cerebral control of speech and limb movements* (pp. 661–680). Amsterdam: North-Holland.

STUDY QUESTIONS

1. How is Fitts' law related to the speed-accuracy trade-off phenomenon observed in many motor skills? What are two explanations of Fitts' law?

2. (a) Describe a prehension situation.
   (b) Indicate the components of this situation.
   (c) Describe the movement characteristics involved in each component.

3. Discuss how the skill of handwriting can provide a good example of the meaning of the term motor equivalence.

4. Discuss how performance of a task requiring bimanual coordination is a good example of a coordinative structure.

5. (a) What are two examples of the rhythmic structures involved in walking and running?
   (b) Describe how gait lends itself to the use of an identified order parameter and control parameter to be the basis for assessment of coordination problems.

CHAPTER

Proprioception and Vision

Concept: Proprioception and vision are
important components of motor control

APPLICATION

When you reach for a glass of water to drink from it, both the proprioceptive and the visual sensory systems come into play as you carry out the action. Vision helps you locate the glass and grasp it with your hand and fingers. Proprioception helps you lift the glass, move it toward your mouth, and not have the glass slip out of your hand. Without the sensory information provided by these two key sensory systems, you would have considerably more difficulty carrying out relatively simple tasks like drinking from a glass. You accomplish other everyday skills, such as putting your door key into the keyhole, maneuvering around people as you walk in a hallway, and driving your car with ease because of the information that proprioception and vision provides your motor control system. Similarly, sport activities also require and benefit from the roles played by the proprioceptive and visual sensory systems. For example, to catch a ball, you must see where the ball is, time its arrival to your hand, position your hand in space, and then close your fingers around the ball when it is in your hand.

Examples such as these help illustrate why proprioception and vision enable the motor control system to carry out action effectively. Without the availability of information from these sensory systems, our successful performance of a wide range of motor skills would be dramatically impaired.

DISCUSSION

A key feature of any theory of motor control is the role played by sensory information in controlling action. Sensory receptors located in various parts of the human body provide this information. Two of the most important types of sensory information sources influencing the control of coordinated movement are proprioception and vision.

Proprioception and Motor Control
Proprioception, which is sometimes called *kinesthesis,* refers to our sensation and perception of limb, trunk, and head movement. Although it is often overlooked as one of our basic senses, proprioception provides sensory information to the central nervous system about such movement characteristics as direction, location in space, velocity, and muscle activation. In closed-loop models of movement control, proprioceptive feedback plays a significant role, whereas in open-loop models, central commands control movement without involving proprioceptive feedback. Questions about whether we can control movements without proprioceptive feedback, and what role proprioceptive feedback plays in the control of coordinated movement have intrigued movement scientists for many years.

Scientists have taken a variety of experimental approaches to determine the role of proprioception

A CLOSER LOOK

Proprioceptors

The sensory receptors responsible for detecting body and limb movements, called proprioceptors, are located in the vestibular apparatus of the inner ear, muscles, tendons, ligaments, and joints. In general, they function to provide the central nervous system (CNS) with information about body and limb position and changes in position. The various types of proprioceptors provide information concerning specific characteristics of body and limb movement. The following is a brief description of the proprioceptors and their function.

- **Vestibular apparatus.** Located inside the temporal lobe in the inner ear; consists of three semicircular canals and two saclike swellings, the utricle and saccule. Functions to provide information about the position of the head in space (i.e., upright, upside down, etc.), and linear and angular acceleration of head movement; assists in visual fixation during head and body movement.
- **Muscle spindles.** Located in all skeletal muscles, lying in parallel with extrafusal muscle fibers and

attached directly to the muscle sheath; consists of two types of sensory neurons: groups Ia (annulospiral endings) and II (flower-spray endings). Functions to detect change in muscle fiber length, limb movement velocity and acceleration, and limb spatial position.
- **Golgi Tendon Organs (GTO).** Located at junction of tendon and skeletal muscle; consists of Ib sensory neuron fibers (approximately one GTO for every ten muscle fibers). Functions to detect force through the tendon due to lengthening of skeletal muscle (works in synergy with muscle spindles); also involved in detecting spatial position.
- **Joint Receptors.** Located in joint capsules and ligaments of all synovial joints; consists of four types of sensory neuron endings: Golgi-type endings (in ligaments), spray-type endings (in joint capsule), Pacinian corpuscle (near ligament attachments), and free nerve endings. Functions to help detect joint spatial position, joint velocity, and joint direction; rather than provide information about the full range of joint position, they appear to act to detect the limits of a flexion or extension.

---

in controlling coordinated action. We discuss a few of these next to introduce you to the current thinking about this issue.

Investigating the role of proprioception. Proprioception is an important source of feedback. When action is under closed-loop control, proprioceptive information allows us to make movement corrections as we move. When an action is under open-loop control, as in a rapid, ballistic movement, proprioceptive feedback is available but we cannot make movement corrections as we move because of time limitations.

Researchers have used several techniques to investigate the role of proprioception in the control of movement. We will consider four techniques in this discussion. Three of the techniques involve the observation of movement after **deafferentation** in some way. This means that the pro-

prioceptive afferent pathways to the central nervous system are not available. The fourth involves the observation of movement while a tendon of a muscle involved in the control of a movement is vibrated, which distorts the proprioceptive feedback that is normally received from the muscle and tendon proprioceptors.

Surgical deafferentation. One method used to investigate the role of proprioception in the control of movement involves the observation of movement of animals or humans following surgical deafferentation, which means that the afferent neural pathways associated with the movements of interest have been surgically severed or removed. Several studies have been reported in which a surgical deafferentation procedure was used with monkeys. Two sets of classic research studies in which this method of investigation was used will serve as examples of how researchers have used this technique to study proprioception.

Taub and Berman (1963, 1968) involved the observation of monkeys before and after surgical deafferentation as they performed well-developed motor skills, such as climbing, reaching, and grasping. Taub and Berman consistently found that the deafferented monkeys were still capable of performing the skills, although the degree of precision was notably less than it had been.

Taub and Berman looked at skills that were well developed. What would happen if experimenters used the same surgical deafferentation procedure with *newly learned skills?* Bizzi and his colleagues at Massachusetts Institute of Technology (e.g., Bizzi & Polit, 1979; Polit & Bizzi, 1978) took this approach in several experiments. They trained monkeys to point an arm at one of a series of lights when it came on. The monkeys could see the lights, but not their arms making the pointing movement. After they learned to point accurately to each light when required, the monkeys were surgically deafferented so that no proprioceptive feedback information from the pointing arm was available during the movement. When the monkeys were again directed to point at each light as it came on, they were able to position their limbs accurately in the deafferented state. In fact, they could make accurate pointing movements from starting positions that were different from the starting positions used during training.

Surgically deafferenting human subjects for experimental purposes is not possible, for obvious reasons. However, some people are surgically deafferented because of certain trauma- or disease-related problems. For example, rheumatoid arthritis patients who have had finger *joint replacement* surgery have no joint receptors available, A good example of using this approach to the study of proprioception is an experiment done many years ago by Kelso, Holt, and Flatt (1980). Patients who had had their metacarpophalangeal joints removed and replaced with flexible silicone rubber implants performed finger-positioning movements. On each trial, participants moved their fingers to a criterion finger position or a criterion distance, returned their fingers to a new starting point, and then attempted to reproduce the criterion position or distance. Results indicated that the patients had little difficulty in accurately reproducing the criterion finger *position* from a starting point that was different from the original starting point. However, they did have problems reproducing the movement *distance* from these new starting points.

Deafferentation due to sensory polyneuropathy. The observation of movement characteristics of people who have a *sensory polyneuropathy* involving a limb provides a non-surgical technique for investigating deafferented humans. For these people, the large myelinated fibers of the limb are lost, leading to a loss of all sensory information except pain and temperature. The efferent motor pathways are typically intact. A good example of this research strategy is an experiment by Blouin et al. (1993). They compared a sensory polyneuropathy patient with normal participants on a pointing task involving an arm moving a pointer. On some trials, participants could see the apparatus environment, whereas on other trials, they performed without this visual information available. Results, shown in figure 6.1, were that with vision, the patient performed as accurately as the normal participants. However, without vision of either the environment or the arm while moving, the deafferented patient

---

proprioception   the perception of limb, body, and head movement characteristics; afferent neural pathways send to the central nervous system proprioceptive information about characteristics such as limb movement direction, location in space, and velocity.

deafferentation   a procedure that researchers use to make proprioceptive feedback unavailable (through surgically severing or removing afferent neural pathways involved in the movement); it also can result from injury or surgery to afferent neural pathways involved in proprioception.

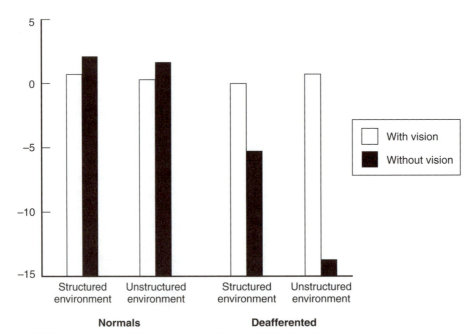

FIGURE 6.1   Results of the experiment by Blouin et al. showing the amount of error during the reproduction of an arm position for normal and deafferented subjects with vision of the environment available (structured) or not available (unstructured), and vision of the moving arm available or not.
[Source: Data from Blouin, J., et al. (1993). Reference systems for coding spatial information in normal subjects and a deafferented patient. *Experimental Brain Research, 93,* 324–331, Springer-Verlag, New York, NY.]

consistently undershot the target. Thus, without visual feedback, the deafferented patient was not able to reproduce movement accurately to a specific location in space.

Temporary deafferentation. The third proprioceptive feedback removal technique, which is used with humans, is known as the *nerve block technique.* To investigate an arm movement, the researcher places a blood pressure cuff just above the participant's elbow and then inflates until the person no longer can feel anything with the fingers. In a phenomenon similar to what you experience when your arm is "asleep," the ischemic condition keeps afferent pathways from functioning. However, the efferent pathways remain unaffected. In several studies (e.g., Kelso, 1977; Kelso & Holt, 1980; Laszlo, 1966, 1967), people could perform finger and arm spatial positioning in the absence of afferent sensory information from the muscles and joints of the fingers, hand, and forearm.

Tendon vibration technique. A procedure in which movement is observed while proprioceptive feedback is distorted rather than removed involves the high-speed vibration of a tendon connected to a muscle that is an agonist in the movement of interest. This vibration distorts muscle spindle firing patterns, which leads to a distortion of proprioceptive feedback. Examples of the use of this technique can be found in several experiments reported by Verschueren. For example, one experiment (Verschueren, Swinnen, Cordo, & Dounskaia, 1999a) applied vibration to the tendon of the biceps and/or anterior deltoids of the preferred arm of blindfolded participants as they simultaneously drew circles with each arm. The results (see figure 6.2) showed that the vibration influenced the spatial characteristics of the circles drawn

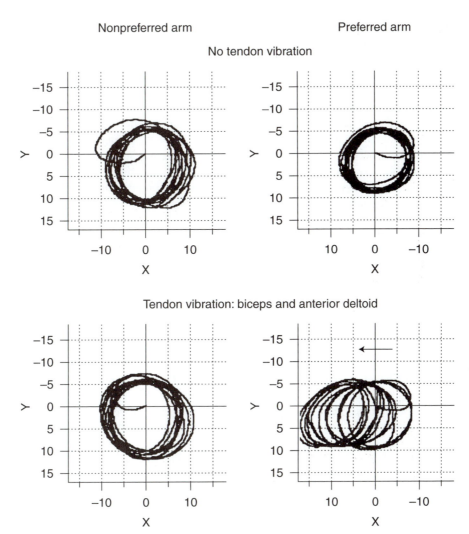

FIGURE 6.2 Results from the experiment by Verschueren et al. showing the effects of vibrating the tendons attached to the biceps and anterior deltoid of the preferred arm during bimanual circle drawing with no vision of the arms. The top row shows of one participant's drawings during one trial when no tendon vibration was applied. The bottom row shows the drawings by the same participant during one trial with tendon vibration.   [Adapted from Figure 1A-D, p. 185, of Verschueren, Swinnen, Cordo, & Dounskaia (1999). *Experimental Brain Research,* 127, 182–192. Copyright © 1999 Springer-Verlag, New York, NY.]

by the vibrated arm, but not for the nonvibrated, non-preferred arm. In addition, the vibration of the preferred arm influenced the relative phase relationship between the two arms during the circle drawing.

The role of proprioceptive feedback. Research evidence shows that people *can* carry out certain limb

movements in the absence of proprioceptive feedback. However, there appears to be distinct limitations to this capability. Primary among these is the *degree of accuracy* possible. Several results from the experiments just discussed support this conclusion. In the Taub and Berman studies, the monkeys were clumsier while climbing, grasping, and reaching than they had been before deafferentation. In fact, they had difficulty grasping food with their hands in this condition. The Bizzi experiments used a relatively wide target area to indicate a correct pointing response for the monkeys. It is difficult, then, to compare the precision of the accuracy responses under normal and deafferented conditions. Researchers did note that when animal's posture was altered, pointing accuracy diminished in the deafferented condition. And in the Kelso, Holt, and Flatt experiment, the human participants maintained only positioning accuracy following joint capsule replacement. Distance movements were severely disrupted when joint capsule proprioceptive feedback was not available.

The influence of proprioception on the degree of movement accuracy appears to be due to the specific kinematic and kinetic feedback provided by the proprioceptors to the central nervous system (CNS). Feedback about limb displacement provides the basis for spatial position corrections, which enable the limb to achieve spatial accuracy by a continuous updating of limb position to the CNS, which in turn can send movement commands that will modify the position accordingly, provided that the movement occurs for a sufficient amount of time to allow movement corrections to occur. In addition, proprioceptors provide feedback about limb velocity and force, which influence movement distance accuracy.

Proprioceptive feedback also influences the *timing of the onset of motor commands.* An experiment by Bard et al. (1992) provides a good example of evidence for this role. They compared movements of normal participants with a patient deafferented due to a sensory polyneuropathy. The participants were asked to simultaneously extend an index finger and raise the heel of the ipsilateral foot. When they performed this task in reaction to an auditory signal, both the normal and the deafferented participants performed similarly by initiating the finger extension first. We would expect this if a common central command were sent to each effector. Because of the difference in distance of efferent neural pathways to the finger and heel, finger movement would occur first. Conversely, when asked to do the task at their

own pace, the normal participants raised the heel first; this suggests that they based timing of the finger movement onset on proprioceptive feedback about heel movement. In contrast, the deafferented patients performed as they had in the reactive situation, indicating that they used a central command rather than proprioceptive movements feedback as the basis for the timing of the onset of the heel and finger movements.

Finally, researchers have shown evidence that proprioception plays an important role in the *coordination of body and limb segments.* Two types of research evidence support this role for proprioception. First researchers have demonstrated the importance of proprioception for postural control. Although postural control is a function of many interacting variables, such as vision, the musculoskeletal system, activity of the cerebellum and basal ganglia, cognitive processes, the tactile sensory system, and proprioception, problems with any of these will lead to postural dysfunction. Jeka and colleagues have demonstrated (e.g., Jeka, Ribiero, Oie, & Lackner, 1998) the importance of proprioception in postural control by showing that proprioception, together with tactile information, functions to provide essential information to the CNS to enable a person to control upright stance posture in body sway situations.

The second type of research evidence was described earlier in the discussion of the experiment by Verschueren et al. (1999a), which showed the effects of tendon vibration on bimanual circle drawing when no vision of the arms is available. That experiment was one of several reported by these researchers that demonstrate the influence of proprioception on intersegmental phase relationships, which refers to the spatial-temporal coupling between body and/or limb segments. Their research has shown that proprioception influences the coupling between two limb segments, such as the upper arm and forearm (Verschueren et al., 1999b), and the coupling between arms in the performance of bimanual coordination tasks (Verschueren et al., 1999a). Also, a study reported by Jackson et al. (2000), which involved a woman whose left arm was temporarily deafferented because of a stroke, provides support for the conclusions about proprioception based on the tendon vibration technique. Similar to the proprioception disruption effects on interlimb phase relationships for bimanual circle drawing, the stroke patient in the Jackson et al. study showed limb-coupling problems during the performance of a task involving prehension.

Vision and Motor Control

There are two components of visual function. Each component receives information in a different segment of the field of vision, which is said to extend to 200 degrees horizontally and 160 degrees vertically. One component is *central vision,* sometimes referred to as foveal or focal vision. Central vision can process information only in small areas, having a range of about 2 to 5 degrees. The detection information in the visual field outside these limits occurs by means of *peripheral vision.*

Vision Predominates Our Sensory-Perceptual Systems

Of all our sensory systems, we tend to use and trust vision the most. For example, when you first learned to type or play the piano, you undoubtedly felt that if you could not see your fingers hit each key, you could not perform accurately. Beginning dancers and stroke patients learning to walk have a similar problem. They often act as if they cannot perform the activity if they cannot watch their feet.

These anecdotal experiences illustrate our tendency to give vision a predominant role when we perform motor skills. Empirical research evidence also supports this phenomenon. The best example is a classic experiment by Lee and Aronson (1974) that is often referred to as the "moving room" experiment. Participants stood in a room in which the walls could move up or down, as well as forward or backward. However, the floor was stationary and did not move. The researchers observed the participants to record their postural responses to the movement of the walls. When the walls moved, children and adults made posture correction adjustments that were in keeping with maintaining their posture in a whole room moving in a certain direction. Because the floor did not move, their proprioceptors were not signaling that their bodies were losing stability. Only their visual systems detected any loss of balance.

The moving room experiment demonstrates the special priority we assign to vision in our daily activities. In that experiment, when the proprioceptive and visual systems provided conflicting information to the central nervous system, people gave attention to vision while ignoring proprioception. The result was that they initiated unnecessary postural adjustments.

In the sections that follow, we will look at several types of motor skills to see the role that vision plays when people perform them. Some of these skills were included in chapter 5, where we considered performance characteristics that provided insight into how the motor control system operates to enable performance. Although vision was described as being involved in the control of these skills, the specific roles played by vision were not discussed. It will be helpful to make the connection between the discussion of these skills in the following sections with what you learned from chapter 5 about the control of these skills.

Vision and Manual Aiming

A manual aiming task requires a person to move one or both arms over a prescribed distance to a target. In real-world settings, this action is required when a person puts a key in a keyhole, places a pen in a penholder, types on a keyboard, or plays the piano. Laboratory approximations of this type of action typically involve a person's holding a stylus on a starting point and then moving it to hit a target as accurately as possible. In some experiments the participants must hit the target while moving as quickly as possible, whereas in others they must move at specific speeds.

Vision's role depends on the phases of the aiming movement. Vision is involved in different ways at different times during an aiming movement. Research evidence has shown that there are three distinct phases of performing a manual aiming movement (see figure 6.3). The role vision plays in the control of the movement is different in each phase.

Preparation phase
Prepare movement based on keyhole size, location, orientation, and distance

Initial flight phase
Ballistic initial portion of arm movement to get key to the keyhole

Termination phase
Error-correction portion of arm movement to get key in the keyhole

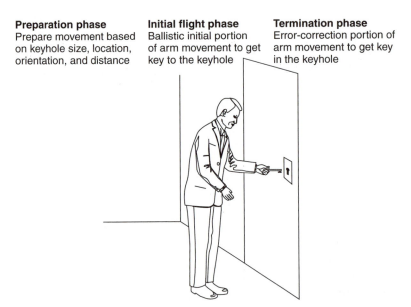

FIGURE 6.3　The three phases of manual aiming task in which vision plays important roles can be illustrated by the task of putting a key into a keyhole in a lock on a door.

The first phase is the *movement preparation phase,* which begins as soon as a person has made the decision to perform a manual aiming action. Here, the person uses vision to determine the specific movement characteristics required by the situation, such as the direction and distance the limb must travel and the target spatial orientation and size. The second phase, the *initial flight phase,* includes the beginning of the actual limb movement in the general direction of the target. This phase is typically ballistic. Vision plays a minor role here, although it acquires early limb displacement and velocity information that is used later for error correction purposes. The third phase is the *termination phase,* which begins just before and ends when the target is hit. If the individual has sufficient time to use visual feedback and make movement modifications, vision plays a critical role in providing the information he or she needs to make these alterations so that the limb will hit the target.

The coordination of vision and hand movement in manual aiming. When a person makes an aim-ing movement with a hand, how do the eyes and hand work together to carry out this action? Researchers have addressed this question by analyzing a person's eye and hand movements when he or she performs a manual aiming task. For eye movement analysis, the characteristic of interest is the point of gaze, which is the specific location in the environment on which central vision is focused at any particular moment. To assess the coordination of vision and hand movement, researchers calculate the relationship between the timing and/or location of the termination of the point of gaze with the timing and/or location of the hand movement. If the point of gaze and hand movement are temporally or spatially coupled during an aiming movement, the point of gaze should be at a specific location at a consistent proportion of the total movement time and/or distance of the hand movement.

A good example of research evidence that demonstrates the coupling between vision and hand movement is an experiment by Helsen, Elliott, Starkes, and Ricker (1998). Participants were seated at a table and were asked to move their index fingers 40 cm to the right from a starting location in front of them to a 1-cm by 2-cm target as fast as possible. The results showed that both point of gaze and hand movements tended to undershoot the target and then made one or more corrections to hit the target. The analysis of their point of gaze and finger movements showed that the participants typically initiated eye movements approximately 70 ms before they began to move their hands from the start location. The initial eye movement moved the point of gaze very close to the target, after which they made a second eye movement to correct the undershooting of the first. The initial hand movement traveled about 95 percent of the total distance, after which one or two additional accelerations were made to home-in on the target. The point of gaze typically arrived at the target 450 msec *before* the finger, which would allow for in-flight hand movement corrections based on visual feedback. In terms of the coupling between the eyes and hand movements, the researchers found evidence for a time-based coupling as the completion of the initial eye movement coincided with the timing of the peak acceleration and velocity of the arm movement. Evidence for spatial coupling was shown by the point of gaze consistently terminating on the target when the hand movement was at 50 percent of the total movement distance.

The results of this experiment, and others like it (e.g., Helsen, Starkes, & Buekers, 1997), support the importance of vision in the three phases of performing an aiming task described earlier. The actual movement part of the aiming task involves only the second and third of these phases, and is often referred to as a two-phase model of limb control for visually directed movements. As the Helsen et al. (1998) results demonstrated, the initial flight phase is a ballistic movement prepared from visually detected information before the initiation of movement. This phase continues for at least the first half of the distance to the target. Then, the termination phase begins in which visual feedback is used to correct the trajectory and speed of the arm movement so that the target will be hit.

The amount of time needed to make visual feedback based movement corrections. An important factor that influences the role of vision in an aiming movement is the amount of time available to use visual feedback to make movement corrections while the movement is in progress. Corrections can occur only when the person has sufficient time to detect and modify the movement. This means there is a minimum total movement time requirement in order for the performer to be able to use visual feedback to correct movement errors prior to the completion of the movement.

The important question here is, *what is the minimum amount of time required* for movement corrections to be carried out on the basis of visual feedback? Researchers have been attempting to answer this question since the end of the nineteenth century (e.g., Woodworth, 1899). The most vigorous effort to investigate this question occurred in the latter part of the twentieth century, beginning with an influential experiment by Keele and Posner in 1968. Unfortunately, all this research effort has not provided us with a precise answer to the question (see Carlton, 1992, for an excellent review of this research). Part of the problem is that different experimental procedures have resulted in a variety of time estimates for the processing of visual feedback.

The most common experimental procedure has been to have people perform manual aiming movements with different goal movement times. On some trials, the lights would go out just as the person began to move, whereas on other trials the lights remained on. The logic to this procedure was that if visual feedback was necessary, aiming accuracy would decrease with the lights out because the person could not see the target and therefore would not be able to use visual feedback. When participants did not know when the lights would be on or off, the amount of time to process visual feedback was estimated to be between 190 and 260 ms. However, later experiments used the same lights-on-or-off technique, but participants knew when they would perform under each condition (e.g., Zelaznik, Hawkins, & Kisselburgh, 1983; Elliott & Allard,

1985). This advance knowledge indicated that visual feedback could be used in less than 100 ms.

Other experimental procedures have led researchers to conclude that visual feedback can be processed in amounts of time that are faster or slower than those estimated by the lights-on-or-off procedure. These have included such procedures as distorting the visual information by having people wear prism glasses (e.g., Smith & Bowen, 1980, estimated the time to be about 150 msec); moving the target location after the person initiated a movement to a target (e.g., Brenner & Smeets, 1997, estimated the time to be about 110 msec); and preventing visual feedback for portions of the distance to the target (e.g., Spijkers & Lochner, 1994, estimated the time to be about 135 msec).

Although it is not possible to establish an exact minimum amount of time required to use visual feedback to enable movement corrections, it appears that an estimate of *100 to 160 msec* is reasonable for simple manual aiming tasks. How well this generalizes to other skills is not known at this time, although several researchers have investigated this question using tasks that require people to intercept a moving object, such as ball catching or hitting (e.g., Bootsma & van Wieringen, 1990). Although the time estimates are again related to the procedures used in the experiments, the 100 to 160 msec estimate would capture the time estimates reported in these experiments.

In terms of the three-phase model of a manual aiming movement described earlier, the minimum amount of time required to make visual feedback–based corrections establishes a time limit for situations to which this model can apply. If the limb movement is faster than the minimum amount of time, only the first two phases of the model describe the movement. In this situation the "initial flight phase" becomes the only flight phase; the movement must terminate at the end of this phase without the possibility of modifying movement errors. Thus, the entire movement would be under open-loop control, which means that the accuracy of the movement would depend on the quality of the preparation before the initiation of movement.

Is this issue about the minimum time required to use visual feedback of any consequence to the performance of skills other than the manual aiming tasks performed in laboratories? If we generalize the notion of manual aiming to skills involving the "aiming" of the arm to catch a ball, or to hit a ball, or the "aiming" of the foot to step on a stair step, then the minimum time issue becomes relevant to sports skills and activities of daily living. For example, whether or not a person will have time to adjust his or her initial hand movement to catch a ball will depend on the speed of the ball. If the ball speed is too fast to allow any movement modification, success at catching the ball will depend on the initial hand position. Similarly, if a person is stair climbing at a pace that is too fast to allow foot-position adjustments while the foot is in flight, the risk of falling increases.

Vision and Prehension

In chapter 5, we considered evidence showing that prehension and manual aiming are different actions. An important difference between them is the object manipulation goal of the prehension action. Although target characteristics influence the control of both manual aiming and prehension, contact with the target does not terminate a prehension action. What the person intends to do with the object after it is contacted is an essential component of prehension. But, because of the similarities between the two actions, vision is involved in the control of prehension in some ways that are similar to its role in the control of manual aiming.

As in manual aiming, vision provides information prior to the initiation of movement, such as the distance to the object and about important regulatory characteristics of the object, such as its shape, texture, and the environmental context in which the object is located. The motor control system uses this information to initiate the transport phase of prehension, during which the hand and fingers begin to form the grasp characteristics required when the object is contacted and manipulated. Then, similar to manual aiming, vision can play an important role in providing information to the CNS

A CLOSER LOOK

Time to Contact: The Optical Variable Tau

In situations in which a person moves toward an object to make contact with it, or the object moves toward the person, such as when a person is catching or hitting a thrown ball, vision plays an important role in specifying *when* to initiate the action and make contact with the object. The important visual information in these situations is the *time to contact,* which is the amount of time remaining until the object contacts the person (or vice versa) from a specific distance (see Bootsma & Peper, 1992). Time to contact is specified according to the relative rate of change of the size of the image of the object on the retina of the eye. As the person approaches the object, or vice versa, the object produces an increasingly larger retinal image. When this image attains a certain critical size, it triggers the action required by the situation.

In the early 1970s, David Lee (1974) provided evidence that time to contact is specified by an optical variable, which he termed *tau* (τ). He also showed that *tau* can be quantified mathematically by relating object size, the distance of the object from the person, and the angle subtended at the person by the object size and distance. In mathematical terms, *tau* is the inverse of the relative rate of change of the visual angle subtended by the moving object, given the speed of approach of the object is constant.

The motor control benefit of the *tau* variable is its predictive function, which allows action initiation and object contact to occur "automatically" at a specific time to contact regardless of the speed of the object or person. When driving a car, for example, the driver's initiation and amount of braking action to avoid collision with another car is not dependent on the driver's cognitive knowledge of the distance to and velocity of the other car. Rather, by specifying the time to contact at any distance and velocity, the rate of change of the size of the retinal image of the other car provides the information needed by the driver to determine the type of braking, or deceleration, required by the situation.

---

while the limb is in flight to make needed movement modifications as the hand approaches and grasps the object. As was the case for manual aiming, a person can make these in-flight arm and hand movement modifications only if there is sufficient time to do so.

One of the questions researchers have investigated concerning vision and prehension relates to *the use of monocular (i.e., one eye) versus binocular (i.e., two eyes) vision* to reach and grasp an object. Research evidence (e.g., Goodale & Servos, 1996; Marotta, Kruyer, & Goodale, 1998; Servos, 2000) has shown that the motor control system operates more effectively and efficiently when it receives visual information from *both* eyes. Although people can reach and pick up objects when the use of only one eye is available, the prehension action is carried out less efficiently than when they use both eyes. This inefficiency appears to be due to a preparation-phase problem that

results from monocular vision leading to an underestimation of the distance to objects and their size prior to the initiation of movement. The evidence for this problem is the lower peak velocities and smaller grip apertures (i.e., the distance between thumb and fingers in the grasp position) during the transport phase. Interestingly, when people are not permitted to use binocular vision, and must reach for and grasp an object using monocular vision, they will move their heads in a manner that enables them to obtain more accurate information about the size of an object and the distance to it (see Marotta, Kruyer, & Goodale, 1998).

Another question of interest concerning the motor control of prehension relates to the *roles of central and peripheral vision.* The current understanding of these roles is that each makes specific contributions to the prehension action. For example, research by Sivak and MacKenzie (1990) showed that peripheral vision provides the CNS

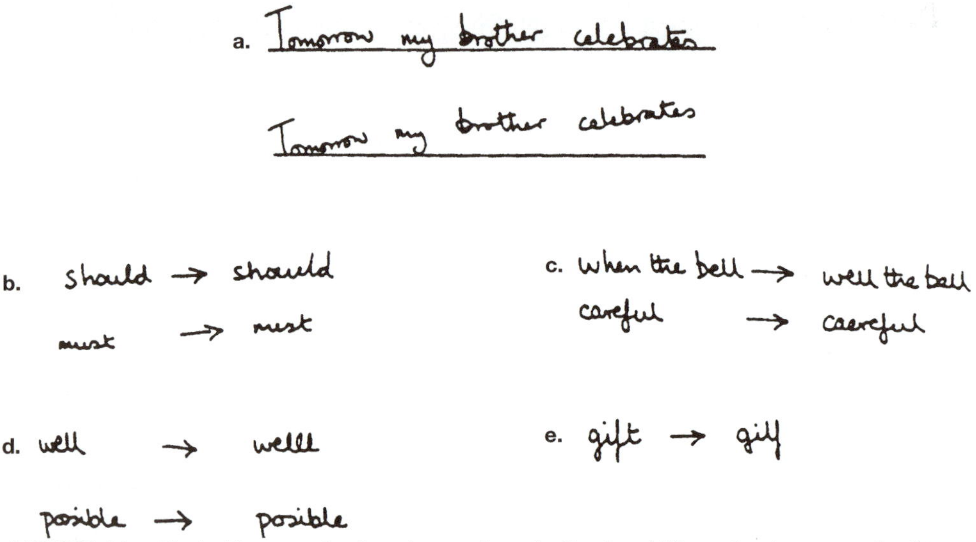

FIGURE 6.4   Handwriting examples from the experiment by Smyth and Silvers showing errors related to writing without vision available (bottom line in (a); right side of arrows in others) as compared to writing with vision available. (a) shows errors as deviating from the horizontal; (b) shows errors as adding and deleting strokes; (c) shows adding and deleting of letters; (d) shows adding or deleting of repetitions of double letters; (e) shows reversing of letters.   [Reprinted from Smyth, M.M., & Silvers, G. (1987). Functions of vision in the control of handwriting. *Acta Phychologica, 65,* 47–64. With kind permission of Elsevier Science-NL, Sara Burgerhartstraat 25, 1055 KV Amsterdam, The Netherlands.]

with information about the environmental context and the moving limb. When they blocked the participants' use of peripheral vision, which meant they could use only central vision for reaching and grasping an object, the organization and control of the transport phase was affected but not the grasp phase. Central vision provides information specific to the object itself, such as the size and shape of the object. When the researchers blocked the participants' use of central vision, which meant they could use only peripheral vision for reaching and grasping an object, problems occurred with both the transport and grasp phases.

Vision and Handwriting

A substantial amount of research evidence indicates that vision plays an important role in the control of handwriting actions. A good example of this role was provided by Smyth and Silvers (1987), who presented evidence showing that a person who

is asked to write with his or her eyes closed adds extra strokes to some letters, omits strokes from some letters, and duplicates some letters. And if visual feedback is delayed while a person is writing, that person makes many errors, including repeating and adding letters.

On the basis of their own research and that of others, Smythe and Silvers proposed that vision performs two distinct functions in the control of handwriting. One function is to help the writer *control the overall spatial arrangement of words on a horizontal line.* We see an example of this function in figure 6.4, where handwriting samples taken from people writing without vision available show distinct deviations from a horizontal line. The second function for vision is to help the writer *produce accurate handwriting patterns,* such as the appropriate strokes and letters required for the written material. Again, evidence of this is seen in figure 6.4. People who wrote without vision avail-

A CLOSER LOOK

Visual Cues Can Aid Walking for People with Parkinson's Disease

One of the primary movement disorders common to people who have Parkinson's disease is slowness of gait (i.e., gait hypokinesia). Two questions have interested researchers and physical therapists concerning this gait problem. One, what movement characteristic accounts for the slowness? Two possibilities are cadence, which would mean that the difficulty relates to the rhythm, or beat, of the walking pace, and stride length, which would mean that the slowness is due to strides that are shorter than normal. The answer to this question is important for the second question: Is there a rehabilitation strategy that would help patients improve their control of walking gait speed?

To address these questions, Morris, Iansek, Matyas, and Summers (1994) compared walking gaits of Parkinson's patients with age-matched controls (60–85 years old) for instructions to walk along a 12-m walkway at "a comfortable pace" and at a "fast speed." *The results showed:*
- *The Parkinson's patients walked slower than the control participants at both speeds, and had shorter stride lengths, but similar cadences.*

Then, the researchers provided visual cues to the Parkinson's patients by placing 50-cm by 5-cm laminated strips of cardboard on the walkway at intervals matching the mean stride lengths of the control participants for each speed. The patients were instructed to walk over each floor marker as they walked along the walkway. *The results showed:*
- *The patients' velocity and stride lengths were similar to the controls for both speeds.*

The researchers concluded from their results that the regulation of stride length was the "key deficit" in gait slowness for patients with Parkinson's disease. And, visual cues can be an effective rehabilitation strategy for helping these patients regulate gait speed.

In light of these results, it is interesting to note that several researchers (e.g., McIntosh, Brown, Rice, & Thaut 1997) have provided evidence to show the effectiveness of rhythmic auditory stimulation, which involves embedding a tone at specific intervals in music to provide a stepping pace for Parkinson's patients. Walking speeds can be varied by using music of different tempos.

---

able added or omitted strokes, added extra letters, deleted letters, and reversed letters.

Vision and Locomotion

Although scientists in a variety of fields have studied locomotion, the study of the role of vision in the control of locomotion does not have a long history. Vision plays an especially important role in locomotion when the person moving has the goal of intercepting or avoiding contact with an object. Scholars now generally agree that the visual information related to the control of this action is the *time to contact,* which is specified by the optical variable *tau.*

In what has become a classic experiment demonstrating this time-to-contact influence for a locomotor skill requiring object contact, Lee, Lishman, and

Thomson (1982) filmed three highly skilled female long jumpers during their approaches to the take-off board. By analyzing stride-length changes as each athlete approached and contacted the take-off board for a series of six long jumps, the researchers observed several important gait pattern characteristics. We will examine these using the results from one of these athletes (an Olympic-level performer), presented in figure 6.5.

Initially, the athlete's stride length increased at a relatively constant rate for the first five to six strides; it then began to become similar for the next six strides. These strides were relatively consistent across the six jumps. Then, on the final six strides, something different began to occur. The athlete made stride-length adjustments so that she could hit the board accurately. In fact, she made almost

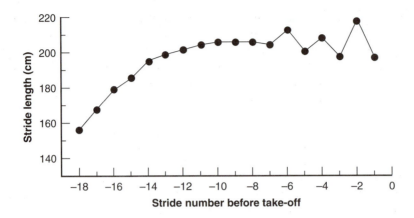

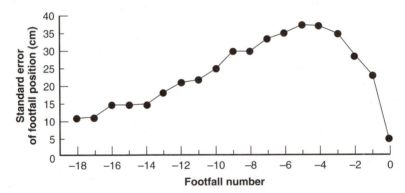

FIGURE 6.5   Redrawn from results of the experiment by Lee, Lishman, and Thomson showing the stride-length characteristics (top) and the standard errors for 6 long jumps by an Olympic-class female long jumper.   [From Lee, D.N., Lishman, J.R., & Thomson, J.A. (1982). Regulation of gait in long jumping. *Journal of Experimental Psychology: Human Perception and Performance, 8,* 448–459. Copyright © 1982 The American Psychological Association. Adapted with permission.]

50 percent of these adjustments on the last stride. The lower half of the figure shows why she had to make these adjustments. As the athlete ran down the track, small inconsistencies in each stride had a cumulative effect, so that when she was five strides from the board the standard error had risen to 37 cm. If she had not adjusted her stride lengths on the remaining strides, she would have missed hitting the take-off board by a long distance.

These stride-length characteristics led the authors to describe the long jump run-up as con-

sisting of two phases: an initial accelerative phase, where an athlete produces stereotypic stride patterns, followed by a zeroing-in phase, where the athlete modifies stride patterns to eliminate accumulated error. They concluded that a long jumper bases the correction process during the second phase on visual information obtained *in advance of* these strides. This means that the visual system picks up time-to-contact information from the board and directs the locomotor control system to make appropriate stride-length modifications for the strides remaining until contact with the take-off board.

It is worth noting that the use of visual time-to-contact information to regulate gait does not depend on the expertise of the person. Although the participants in the Lee and authors long jump study were highly skilled, novice long jumpers also have demonstrated similar stride-length adjustments consistent with the influence of *tau* (Berg, Wade, & Greer, 1994).

Researchers have found that other types of gait also involve adjustments during locomotion on the basis of visual time-to-contact information. Some examples are locomotor activities such as these: walking a given distance and stepping on the target with a specified foot (Laurent & Thomson, 1988); running and stepping on targets, as people do when crossing a creek on rocks (Warren, Young, & Lee, 1986); doing run-ups to the springboard and horse while performing the vault in women's gymnastics (Meeuwsen & Magill, 1987). In all of these activities, the persons adjust stride length on the basis of time-to-contact information as they near the targets.

Vision also specifies critical information that influences how people perform other types of daily locomotor actions. For example, when we need to walk through a doorway or climb stairs, rather than specifying time to contact, vision influences performance through the use of *body-scaled information* about the size of a specific body part in relation to the size of the doorway or stairs. A person decides how to orient his or her body to walk through an open doorway on the basis of visually perceived information related to the proportion of his or her shoulder width to the width of the door opening. Warren and Whang (1987) reported evidence indicating that a doorway needs to be 1.3 times wider than the person's shoulder width for the person to determine that he or she can walk through it without having to turn his or her shoulders. For stair climbing, the relationship between the stair-step height and the person's leg length provides the body-scaled information needed to determine that a stair step can be climbed by a normal, forward-stepping movement. Researchers have shown that a stair step is judged to be climbable in this manner if the riser height is equal to or less than 88 percent of the person's leg length (Warren, 1994; Mark & Vogele, 1987). If the proportion exceeds that amount, the person will use a different movement pattern to climb the stair steps.

Finally, a locomotion control situation that people commonly confront is the need to go safely over an obstacle in their pathway. People can employ a variety of avoidance strategies while walking or running to accomplish this goal. Patla and his colleagues have reported several studies in which they investigated the role vision plays in the strategy people select to go over an obstacle (e.g., Patla, Rietdyk, Martin, & Prentice, 1996). As in the long-jumping situation described earlier, vision provides predictive information that specifies to the motor control system the type of step-pattern alteration that will be needed to step over or on the object. The primary information is specified by the height, width, and shape of the object. In addition, predictions about how solid or fragile the object is are also important. For example, people will increase the height of their leading leg, which increases the amount of toe clearance, more for an obstacle perceived to be fragile than for an object perceived to be solid.

Vision and Jumping from Heights

Jumping from a platform to the floor is another skill for which experimental results have supported the view that the optical variable *tau* triggers specific preparatory actions so that a person can achieve an action goal. In an experiment by Sidaway, McNitt-Gray, and Davis (1989), people jumped from three different heights: 0.72 m, 1.04 m, and 1.59 m. The authors instructed the participants to land with both feet on a force plate on the floor, and to direct their visual attention toward this force plate throughout the jump.

A unique characteristic of this experiment is that the researchers measured the EMG activity of the rectus femoris so that they could assess the onset of activity in this agonist muscle in relation to the distance the person was from landing on the

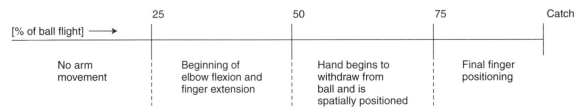

FIGURE 6.6   The arm, hand, and fingers movement characteristics involved in catching a ball in relation to the percentage of ball flight time.   [Data from Williams & McCririe (1988). *Journal of Human Movement Studies, 14,* 241–247.]

floor. The logic here was that according to the role of the optical variable *tau* as a triggering mechanism for initiating a certain action, there should be a specific relationship between *tau* and the onset of rectus femoris activity, regardless of the height of the jump. The results of this experiment support this prediction. Thus, the optical variable *tau* mediated the control of the onset of the muscle activity required for jumping from different heights, indicating that vision plays a critical role in the control of performing this skill.

Vision and Catching

In many ways, catching an object is like the prehension action discussed earlier. However, there are two important differences. First, catching involves a moving object; prehension typically involves a stationary object. Second, the grasp of the object in the catching action ends the action; prehension typically involves doing something with the grasped object. Although in some sport situations, such as baseball and softball, there are occasions in which a player must remove the ball from the glove after the catch and throw the ball, this situation is uniquely sport and situation specific and will not be included in this discussion of catching.

Three phases characterize catching an object. First, the person must move the arm and hand toward the oncoming object. Then, he or she must shape the hand to catch the object. Finally, the fingers must grasp the object.

Williams and McCririe (1988) provided research evidence demonstrating the phases of catching with their study of 11-year-old boys try-

ing to catch a ball with one hand (figure 6.6). A movement analysis of the catching action showed no arm motion for the first 160 to 240 msec of the ball flight. Then, elbow flexion gradually began and continued slowly and uniformly for about 80 percent of the ball flight. At about the same time, the fingers began to extend. The hand began to withdraw from the oncoming ball until about one-half of the ball flight time had elapsed. Then the upper arm accelerated about the shoulder, which resulted in the hand's being transported to the spatial position required for intercepting the ball. Boys who caught the ball began final positioning action 80 msec earlier than boys who failed to catch it. By the time 75 percent of the ball flight was complete (113 msec prior to contact), each successful boy had his hand and fingers in a ready state for catching the ball.

These results indicate that vision provides advance information enabling the motor control system to *spatially and temporally set the arms, hands, and fingers before the ball arrives* so that the individual can catch the ball. It is especially noteworthy here that the person bases the grasping action on visual information obtained *before* the ball actually makes contact with the hand, rather than on feedback obtained after the ball has hit the hand. The extent of involvement of proprioception during pre-ball contact stages is not well understood. However, we know that proprioceptive and tactile feedback become involved after contact because the catcher needs to make adjustments to the grasp. Research evidence also shows that both central and peripheral vision operate when a person picks up information critical to catching an object.

Vision of the object and catching. Catching an object, such as a ball, is a complex action that has challenged researchers in their efforts to understand how the visual and motor control systems interact to enable people to successfully catch a moving object. The results of these research efforts have identified several factors that influence successful catching that relate specifically to the visual observation of the object.

One factor is the *amount of time of visual contact with the moving object.* Research evidence indicates that constant visual contact is needed during two critical periods of time in the object's flight: the initial part of the flight and the period of time just prior to contact with the hand(s). How much time is required during each of these time periods has not been established, and undoubtedly depends on the situation. Some researchers have reported evidence indicating that observation of the initial flight should continue until the ball reaches its zenith (Amazeen, Amazeen, Post, & Beek, 1999), although others have indicated that only the first 300 ms of flight are important (e.g., Whiting, Gill, & Stephenson, 1970). The important point here is that visual contact with the object is needed for an amount of time during its initial flight phase that is sufficient to obtain information to determine estimates of the direction and distance of the flight.

In terms of visual contact with the object during its final portion of flight, research evidence indicates that the time period between 200 and 300 ms before hand contact is critical for successful catching (Savelsbergh, Whiting, Pijpers, & van Santvoord, 1993), although the precise amount of time may depend on the specific characteristics of the situation, especially the length of time the object is in flight and its velocity (see Bennett, Davids, & Craig, 1999). The need to see the ball during the final portion of its flight is to obtain specific time-to-contact information for the final spatial positioning of the hand and fingers, and the timing of the closing of the fingers during the grasp of the object.

What about visual contact with the object in flight between these two time periods? Research evidence, primarily from Elliott and his colleagues (e.g., Elliott, Zuberec, & Milgram, 1994), indicates that continuous visual contact with the ball during this period of time is *not* essential. The Elliott et al. (1994) study showed that people can catch a ball that has a flight time of 1 sec by intermittently seeing brief "snapshots" (approximately 20 msec) of the ball every 80 msec of its flight. Interestingly, these results are remarkably similar to those reported for people walking on a balance beam and across a horizontal ladder (Assaiante, Marchand, & Amblard, 1989). Thus, people can use visual samples of ball flight characteristics to obtain the information they need to catch the ball. This capability to use intermittent visually detected information to catch an object helps us understand how an ice hockey goalie can catch a puck or a soccer goalkeeper can catch a ball even though he or she must visually track it through several pairs of legs on its way to the goal.

Finally, an important motor control theory–related question is, do people use *tau* as the basis for determining time to contact when catching an object? Although there is considerable debate about the answer to this question (see Abernethy & Burgess-Limerick, 1992, for a more complete discussion of this issue), there is a significant amount of research evidence indicating that the optical variable *tau* is involved in solving the time-to-contact problem when catching an object (Abernethy & Burgess-Limerick, 1992; Bootsma & Peper, 1992). When an object moves directly toward a person, the angle created at the person's eyes by the top and bottom edges of the object increases in size in a nonlinear way as the object approaches the person. The nonlinearity refers to the perceived slowness of this angle increase when the ball is farther away from the person and the rapid increase in size as it gets close to the person. It is this rate of expansion of angular size, which is often referred to as *looming,* that the visual system

The Use of Looming in Television and Movies: An Illustration of Our Use of *Tau*

In their review of the issues related to determining the visual information people use to time the approach of an oncoming object, Abernethy and Burgess-Limerick (1992) stated that if a *tau*-based method for picking up time to contact is viable, "observers must first and foremost be sensitive to information provided by optical expansion or 'looming'" (p. 366). They went on to describe several research studies supporting this prediction. Although these studies are important to establish scientific support for *tau,* we can find evidence of our sensitivity to looming from a common everyday experience.

Have you ever watched a television program or movie and experienced the illusion of an object flying out of the screen directly at you? Because television and movies are two-dimensional media, creators of visual effects implement the concept of looming to create the three-dimensional quality of an object moving from far away and then acting as if it were flying out of the screen directly at the viewer. This illusion is created by making the object appear small on the screen and then having it nonlinearly expand in size (i.e., slowly at first and then rapidly). This change in the rate of expansion creates the optical illusion that the object will fly out of the screen and hit you. Undoubtedly you have observed this looming illusion, and have actually responded to it by moving your head to avoid the object hitting you. What is especially interesting about this behavioral reaction is that it occurs even though you know it is not possible for the object to physically fly out of the screen and hit you. The important point here is that the object made no distance and velocity changes, only size changed. It is this size-based change, and its nonlinear rate of expansion, that is the basis for *tau* providing a means for people to time the approach of an oncoming object.

---

uses to determine when collision of the object with the person will occur. For the action of catching, this optical expansion establishes *when* the appropriate movement characteristics for the arm, hand, and finger will be in place to catch the object. For objects that do not move directly toward the person but require the person to run to catch them, *tau* also provides the visual basis for timing the catch, although the mathematics for calculating *tau* are distinctly more complex.

Vision of the hands and catching. An important question related to catching is: *Must a person be able to see his or her hands throughout the flight of a ball to successfully catch the ball?* In one of the first experiments investigating this question, Smyth and Marriott (1982) attached a screen to the participants so they could see the oncoming ball, but not their hands. When the participants were able to see their hands, they averaged 17.5 catches out of 20 balls thrown. However, when they could *not* see their hands, they were able to catch an aver-

age of 9.2 balls out of 20. More important, when they could *not* see their hands, participants typically made a hand-positioning error: they could not get their hands into the correct spatial position to intercept the ball. But when they could see their hands, their typical errors involved grasping: they initiated too early the finger flexion they needed to grasp the ball.

Interesting as the Smyth and Marriott results may be, research since their work has shown that *experience* is an important factor influencing a person's catching success when he or she cannot see his or her hands. We might expect this, as Davids (1988) argued, because the effective use of peripheral vision is a function of age and experience. Because we use peripheral vision to see our hands as we try to catch an oncoming object, it is logical to expect that our need to see our hands to catch a ball will depend on our age and experience.

Fischman and Schneider (1985) reported empirical evidence supporting the influence of experience. Using the same experimental procedures as

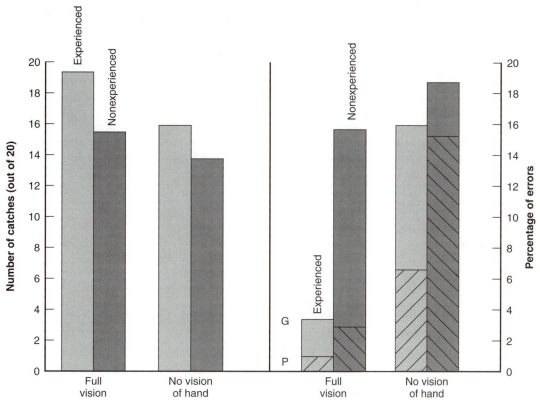

FIGURE 6.7   Results of the experiment by Fischman and Schneider showing the number of right-hand catches made (out of 20 chances) for experienced softball/baseball players and nonexperienced subjects, and the percentage of errors made (based on 360 attempts) by each group that were classified as positioning (P) or grasp (G) errors when subjects either could or could not see their hands.   [Source: Data from Fischman, M.G., & Schneider, T. (1985). Skill level, vision, and proprioception in simple one-hand catching. *Journal of Motor Behavior, 17*, 219–229.]

those of Smyth and Marriott, they included participants who had had at least five years' experience in varsity baseball or softball. The results of this experiment (figure 6.7) showed that while the number of catches decreased when the people could not see their hands, the type of error did not depend on whether or not the participants could see their hands. However, for the inexperienced ball catchers, more positioning errors than grasp errors occurred when they could not see their hands.

Additional research investigating this issue has led researchers to general acceptance of the influence of experience as well as skill level on the need for a person to see his or her hands while catch-

ing a ball (see Bennett, Davids, & Craig, 1999). More-experienced and skilled catchers do not need to see their hands; less-experienced and low-skill catchers require vision of their hands. The reason for this difference appears to relate to a person's capability to use proprioceptive feedback to catch a moving object. The less-experienced, low-skilled person needs visual feedback to assist in the use of proprioceptive feedback to spatially position his or her arms and hands, and to effectively grasp the object. In terms of helping people improve their catching skill, this relationship between experience and the need for vision of the hands suggests that beginners and lesser-skilled people should practice

A CLOSER LOOK

"Watch the Ball All the Way to Your Bat!"

A common instruction coaches give when teaching hitting in baseball is to tell players, "Watch the ball all the way to your bat." In light of this, it is interesting to note that research (e.g., Bahill and LaRitz, 1984) indicates that batters probably never see the bat hit the ball. If they do, it is because they have jumped in their visual focus from some point in the ball flight to the bat contact point. They do not visually track the ball continuously all the way to bat contact because this is virtually a physical impossibility. Batters commonly track the ball to a certain point and then visually jump to a point where they predict the ball will be at bat contact.

It is worth noting that more-skilled batters watch the ball for a longer amount of time than less-skilled players. Beginners tend to have the bat swing initiation movement influence their head position and "pull" their head out of position to see the ball/bat contact area.

From an instruction point of view, these characteristics suggest that *it is worthwhile* to instruct a person, "Watch the ball all the way to your bat." Even though the person can't really do that, this instruction directs the person's visual attention so that the person tracks the ball for as long as physically possible, and keeps his or her head in position to see the ball/bat contact area.

---

catching primarily in situations where they can see their hands throughout the ball flight, from the point where the ball leaves the thrower's hand until the ball is grasped.

Vision and Striking a Moving Object

Two experiments investigating the striking of a moving object illustrate how vision is involved in this action.

Vision and baseball batting. The most commonly cited experiment related to the role of vision in baseball batting was performed many years ago by Hubbard and Seng (1954). Using photographic techniques, they found that professional baseball players tracked the ball only to a point, at which time they made their swing. This point did not coincide with the point where the bat made contact with the ball. Each batter tended to synchronize the start of the step forward with the release of the ball from the pitcher's hand. And, perhaps most important, the durations of the batters' swings were remarkably consistent from swing to swing, indicating that it was the initiation of the swing that batters adjusted according to the speed of the oncoming pitch. Interestingly, these findings agree precisely with expectations from a *tau*-based strategy for hitting. That is, the initiation of the batting action occurred at a critical time to contact.

Some of the findings of Hubbard and Seng have been either verified or extended in research reported since their study. For example, thirty years later, Bahill and LaRitz (1984) used more sophisticated technology to closely monitor eye and head movements of a major league baseball player and several college baseball players. The study was done in a laboratory situation that simulated players' responses to a high-and-outside fastball thrown by a left-handed pitcher to a right-handed batter. The major league player visually tracked the ball longer than the college players did. The college players tracked the ball to a point about 9 ft in front of the plate, at which point their visual tracking began to fall behind the ball. The major league player kept up with the ball until it reached a point about 5.5 ft in front of the plate before falling behind in his tracking. Also, regardless of the pitch speed, the major league player followed the same visual tracking pattern and was very consistent in every stance he took to prepare for the pitch. His head position changed less than one degree across all pitches. Interestingly, he made slight head movements while tracking the ball, but never moved his body.

Vision and table tennis striking. In a study of five top table tennis players in the Netherlands, Bootsma and van Wieringen (1990) showed from movement analysis results that the players could not rely completely on consistent movement production. Players seemed to compensate for differences in the initiation times of their swings in order to hit the ball as fast and as accurately as possible. For example, when time to contact was shorter at swing initiation, players compensated by applying more force during the stroke. And evidence suggests that some of these players were making very fine adjustments to their swings while they were moving. Thus, whereas visual information may trigger the initiation of the swing and provide information about its essential characteristics, vision also provides information that the player can use to make compensatory adjustments to the initiated swing, although these are very slight in terms of time and space quantities.

SUMMARY

Proprioception and vision are two important sources of feedback involved in movement control. To investigate the role played by proprioceptive feedback in movement control, researchers have used several experimental techniques to remove proprioceptive feedback. The most direct method involves surgical deafferentation. When animals have been deafferented after having learned a skill, they continue to perform certain skills, although with distinct performance-capability limitations. Humans who have been deafferented because of joint replacement surgery or neuropathies, or who have simulated deafferentation from a nerve block procedure, show similar characteristics. In addition, researchers have vibrated the tendon of the agonist muscle during movement to distort proprioceptive feedback. Results of these approaches

have shown that proprioceptive feedback is important for controlling the degree of precision in limb movements, for timing the onset of motor commands, and in the coordination of body and limb segments.

Vision tends to dominate as a source of sensory information in the control of coordinated, voluntary movement. This tendency is well illustrated by situations in which vision and proprioceptive feedback provide conflicting information, as in the moving room experiment. Research with manual aiming tasks has shown that the motor control system requires a minimum amount of time to use visual feedback to modify an ongoing movement. We have examined the role vision plays in the control of movement by discussing a variety of motor skills and describing how visual information is important for performing these skills: manual aiming skills, prehension, handwriting, locomotor skills, jumping from heights, catching a ball, and hitting a baseball and a table tennis ball. One of the consistent roles for vision in these skills is to provide context information prior to the initiation of movement to enable the motor control system to preset limb and body movement in accordance with the characteristics of initial limb and body position and the characteristics of the performance environment. For skills requiring accurate limb movement, vision provides error correction information to ensure that an individual makes the movement accurately.

RELATED READINGS

Bootsma, R. J. (1991). Predictive information and the control of action: What you see is what you get. *International Journal of Sport Psychology, 22,* 271–278.

Carnahan, H., Goodale, M. A., & Marteniuk, R. G. (1993). Grasping versus pointing and the differential use of visual feedback. *Human Movement Science, 12,* 219–234.

Higgins, K. E., Wood, J., & Tait, A. (1998). Vision and driving: Selective effect of optical blur on different driving tasks. *Human Factors, 41,* 224–232.

Inhoff, A. W., & Gordon, A. M. (1997). Eye movements and eye-hand coordination during typing. *Current Directions in Psychological Science, 6,* 153–157.

Portier, S. J., & van Galen, G. P. (1992). Immediate vs. post-poned visual feedback in practising a handwriting task. *Human Movement Science, 11,* 563–592.

Whiting, H. T. A., Savelsbergh, G. J. P., & Pijpers, J. R. (1995). Specificity of motor learning does not deny flexibility. *Applied Psychology: An International Review, 44,* 315–332.

STUDY QUESTIONS

1. Describe four methods for investigating the role of proprioception in the control of movement. What do the results of the investigations using these methods tell us about the role of proprioception in controlling movement?

2. What two roles does vision play in controlling manual aiming movements? How is the duration of the movement a variable influencing these roles?

3. Discuss how vision is involved in controlling prehension. Use an example to illustrate.

4. Discuss how time to contact is involved in the control of locomotion when the goal is to contact a target. Include in this discussion the role vision plays in this situation.

5. Discuss how vision is involved when a person must (a) catch a thrown ball; (b) strike an oncoming ball.

CHAPTER

Action Preparation

***Concept: Performing voluntary, coordinated
movement requires preparation of the motor
control system***

APPLICATION

Many sport and daily activities demonstrate our need to prepare the motor control system to carry out an intended action. For example, many sporting events, such as running, swimming, and trap shooting, incorporate the importance of preparation into the rules of the activity, which require an audible signal warning the competitors to get ready.

Certain performance characteristics of activities also provide evidence of the need to prepare for the action. For example, when you decide to pick up a glass of water for a drink, there is a slight delay between your decision and the intended action. In another example, if you are driving a car along a street and another car unexpectedly pulls out in front of you, there is a measurable time delay between the moment you see this and the moment you begin to move your foot off the accelerator and onto the brake pedal. In each of these very different action scenarios, intended action is preceded by an interval of time in which the motor control system is prepared according to the demands and constraints of the situation.

Consider the preparation of action from a different perspective. Undoubtedly, at some time or other you have said, following a poor performance in an activity, "I wasn't ready!" By saying this, you

imply that if you had been "ready," you would have performed much better than you just have. Or, if you work with physical therapy patients, you undoubtedly have heard one tell the therapist, "Don't rush me. If I get out of this chair before I'm ready, I'll fall."

An important motor control question that relates to each of these situations is this: What is so important about getting ready to perform a skill? In other words, what makes preparation such a critical part of successful performance? From this question, others arise. For example, what factors influence how long it takes to prepare an action or how well an action is prepared? And, if a person is prepared to move, are there limits to how long the person can maintain this prepared state? We will attempt to answer these questions in the following discussion.

DISCUSSION

In chapters 4 through 6, we focused on factors influencing the control of an ongoing action. Although there was occasional mention of the initiation of the action, we only touched on what is involved in the actual preparation of an intended action. In the present discussion, our interest is in what occurs between the intention to act and the initiation of the action itself. In the motor control literature, researchers sometimes use the term *movement preparation* to designate this activity. However, in keeping with the distinction we made in chapter 1 between actions and movements, we will use the term **action preparation** when referring to this process.

In this context, *preparation* means not the long-term preparation that occurs during the days prior to an event, but the specific preparation the motor control system makes just prior to initiating an action. We will address two preparation issues here. First, how do different skill, performance-context, and personal factors influence the preparation process? Second, exactly what is the motor control system preparing that makes preparation such a critical part of any performance? Before we discuss these issues, we will establish how we know that the motor control system needs to be prepared for action.

Action Preparation Requires Time

The principle that the motor control system needs preparation before it can initiate an action is an inferred concept. Scholars base this inference on the effects of various factors on observed differences in the amount of time between the production of a signal telling a person to begin performing a skill and the instant experimenters actually observe the beginning of movement. As you studied in chapter 3, we call this interval of time *reaction time (RT)*. When considered in the context of action preparation, *RT is an index of preparation* required to produce an action. By investigating factors that increase or decrease this time interval, we can gain some understanding of the action preparation processes our motor control system engages in to enable us to perform a skill.

One of the things that the RT interval tells us is that preparing to produce voluntary movement takes time. Planned movement does not occur instantaneously. Certain actions and circumstances require more preparation than others. In the following sections, we discuss a variety of factors that influence the amount and type of preparation needed.

Task and Situation Characteristics Influencing Preparation

One set of factors that influence action preparation includes characteristics of both the task itself and the situation in which it must be performed.

The number of response choices. An important characteristic of task and performance situations that influences preparation time is the number of response alternatives the performer has to choose from. *As the number of alternatives increases, the amount of time required to prepare the appropriate movement increases.* The easiest way to demonstrate this relationship is by looking at the choice-RT situation you were introduced to in chapter 3. RT increases according to the number of stimulus or response choices. The fastest RTs occur in simple-RT situations, which have only one stimulus and one response. RT slows down when more than one stimulus and more than one response are possible, as in the choice-RT situation.

The relationship between the amount of RT increase and the number of response choices is so stable that a law, known as Hick's law, was developed that predicts a person's RT when his or her simple RT and the number of choices are known. **Hick's law** (Hick, 1952) states that RT will increase logarithmically as the number of stimulus-response choices increases. The equation that describes this law is $RT = K \log_2 (N + 1)$, where K is a constant (which is simple RT in most cases) and N equals the number of possible choices. This means that RT increases linearly as the number of stimulus-choice alternatives increases. We can predict the magnitude of this increase mathematically by applying Hick's equation (Figure 7.1).

The important component of Hick's law is the $\log_2$ function, because it designates that the RT increase is due to the information transmitted by the possible choices, rather than to the number of choice alternatives. In information theory, *$\log_2$ specifies a bit of information.* A *bit*, short for *bi*nary digi*t*, is a yes/no (i.e., 1/0) choice between two alternatives. In a 1-bit decision, there are two alternatives; there are four alternatives in a 2-bit

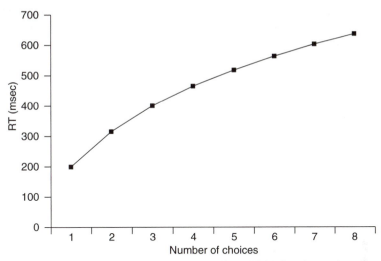

FIGURE 7.1 Predicted reaction times (RT), according to Hick's law, for one through eight choice-RT situations, based on a simple (i.e., one-choice) RT of 200 msec.

decision; a 3-bit decision involves eight choices; and so on. The number of bits indicates the least number of "yes/no" decisions needed to solve the problem created by the number of choices involved. For example, if eight choices were possible in a situation, an individual would have to answer three yes/no questions to determine the correct choice. Thus, an eight-choice situation is a 3-bit decision situation. Accordingly, Hick's law not only correctly predicts that RT increases as the number of choice alternatives increases; it also predicts the specific size of increase to expect.

The predictability of the correct response choice. If a number of response alternatives exist in a performance situation and one alternative is more predictable than the others, response preparation time will be shorter than it would if all the alternatives were equally likely. Research evidence has consistently shown that *as the predictability of one of the possible choices increases, RT decreases.*

An experimental procedure, popularized in the early 1980s by Rosenbaum (1980, 1983), is commonly used to investigate this relationship. In this procedure, known as the *precuing technique,*

researchers provide participants with differing amounts of advance information about which movement must be made in a choice situation. In Rosenbaum's experiments, participants had to move the appropriate finger as quickly as possible to hit the signaled target key. There were three response dimensions, all of which involved a two-choice situation: the *arm* to move (left or right); the *direction* to move (away from or toward the body); and the *extent* of the movement (short or long). Prior to the signal to move, the participants could receive advance information (the precue) specifying the correct upcoming response for none, one, two, or all three of the dimensions. The results

action preparation   the activity that occurs between the intention to perform and the initiation of an action; sometimes, the term *motor programming* is used to refer to this activity.

Hick's law   a law of human performance stating that RT will increase logarithmically as the number of stimulus-response choices increases.

A CLOSER LOOK

Applying Hick's Law to a Sport Performance Situation

A football quarterback running an option play has three response alternatives to choose from. He can hand the ball off to a back, keep the ball and run, or run and pitch out to another back. The problem for the quarterback is that there are so many possible "stimulus" choices. All players on the defensive team, along with certain of his own offensive players, are potential sources of information to help him determine which response alternative to make. However, given the time constraints of the situation, the quarterback must reduce the "stimulus" choices in order to reduce the decision time required. The coach can help by instructing the quarterback to look for only a very few specific characteristics in the defense. These few "keys" reduce the choice alternatives and provide the quarterback a relatively simple basis from which to decide which of the three options to select.

showed that as the number of precued dimensions increased, the RT decreased, with the fastest RT occurring when all three dimensions were precued. The benefit of the advance information was that participants would need to prepare only the remaining non-precued dimensions after the "go" signal.

The influence of the probability of precue correctness.   An interesting twist to the precuing situation occurs when the advance information may or may not be correct. The critical factor influencing preparation time in this situation is the *probability* of the advance information's correctness. For example, in a two-choice situation, if the advance information has only a 50-50 chance of being correct, the performer will ignore it and respond as if no advance information has been given. This occurs because the probability of correctness of the advance information is no greater than the probability of correctness of the information the person already has. However, if the advance information has an 80 percent chance of being correct, the performer will *bias* his or her preparation toward making that response.

What happens when the signal requires the non-prepared movement? In other words, what is the price of preparing the wrong movement before preparing the correct one? We can learn the answer from the results of experiments such as one by Larish and Stelmach (1982), which has become the model approach to study this issue. Participants received advance information about whether the right hand or the left hand should hit the target. But this information was correct only 20 percent, 50 percent, or 80 percent of the time. The results (shown in figure 7.2) illustrate the **cost-benefit trade-off** associated with this situation. When there was a 50-50 chance (50 percent correct condition) of the precue's being correct, participants responded as if the task were a two-choice RT task. However, in the 80-20 condition, participants obviously biased their responses to move in the direction of the precued target. When they were correct, there was a benefit; their RTs were *faster* than if they had not biased their responses. However, when they were wrong (the 20 percent case), there was a cost: their RT was *slower* than it was in the 50-50 condition.

Stimulus-response compatibility.   Another task characteristic that influences the movement preparation time is the physical relationship between the stimulus and response choices. The study of what is termed **stimulus-response compatibility** has a long history that dates back to World War II (Proctor & Reeve, 1990). This extensive study has shown consistently that *RT will be faster as the physical relationship between the stimulus events and their required response becomes more compatible.* Conversely, RT will be slower as this relationship becomes less compatible.

The spatial relationship between the stimulus and response devices is the most common way of considering stimulus-response compatibility. For example, suppose a person has to push one of three

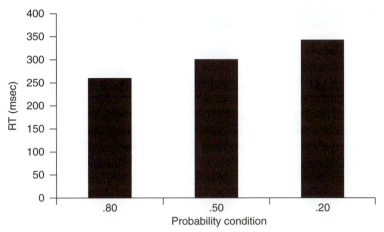

FIGURE 7.2   Results from the experiment by Larish and Stelmach showing the effects on RT of different probabilities of a precue's correctness.   [Adapted from Larish D., & Stelmach, G. E., (1982). Preprogramming, programming, and reprogramming of aimed hand movements as a function of age. *Journal of Motor Behavior, 14,* 322–340. Copyright © 1982 Heldref Publications, Inc., Washington, DC. Reprinted by permission.]

keys in response to the illumination of one of three lights. If the lights and keys are arranged horizontally with the key to be pushed located under the light indicating that response, then the situation is more compatible than if the lights are vertical and the buttons are horizontal. A more compatible relationship would lead to faster RTs than a less compatible situation. Also, as compatibility decreases, the number of choice errors will increase.

To account for the effect of stimulus-response compatibility on RT, Zelaznik and Franz (1990) presented evidence showing that when stimulus-response compatibility is low, RT increases are due to response selection problems. On the other hand, when stimulus-response compatibility is high, response selection processing is minimal, so that any RT changes reflect motoric processes related to preparation of the selected response. Weeks and Proctor (1990) further developed this point by demonstrating that the specific response selection problem is due to translation problems involving the mapping of the stimulus locations to the response locations. Because this translation process requires time, RT increases.

Foreperiod length regularity.   A part of the preparation process begins when a person detects a signal indicating that the signal to respond will occur shortly. The interval between this "warning" signal and the stimulus, or "go" signal, is known as the **foreperiod.** In simple-RT situations the regularity of the length of this interval influences RT.

cost-benefit trade-off   the cost (in terms of slower RT), and benefit (in terms of faster RT) that occur as a result of biasing the preparation of an action in favor of one of several possible actions (as opposed to preparing as if each possible action is equally probable).

stimulus-response compatibility   a characteristic of the spatial arrangement relationship between a stimulus and a response. This relationship will influence the amount of preparation time in a reaction time task involving stimulus and response choices.

foreperiod   in a reaction time paradigm, the time interval between a warning signal and the go signal, or stimulus.

A CLOSER LOOK

Biasing Actions Is Common in Many Sport Contexts

In many sport activities, athletes often bias their action preparation to produce one particular action rather than some other possible one. For example, if a basketball player knows that the player he or she is defending goes to the right to make a shot only on rare occasions, the defensive player undoubtedly will bias his or her movement preparation by "cheating" to defend moves to the left. In racquet sports, players who consistently hit to one side of the court will find their opponents "cheating" to that side. Baseball players commonly bias their hitting decisions and actions according to a pitcher's tendency to throw a certain pitch in a specific situation.

In each of these examples, the players have found that they can gain an advantage by "playing the percentages" and biasing their preparation. The clear advantage is that if they are correct, they can initiate the appropriate action faster than they could otherwise. But they run the risk of being wrong. If they are, the appropriate action will take longer to initiate than it would if no biasing had occurred. And this extra preparation time can lead to an unsuccessful performance.

If the foreperiod is a constant length, i.e., the same amount of time for every trial, RT will be faster than the amount of time that typically characterizes simple RT.

We can attribute the faster RT associated with constant foreperiods to *anticipation* by the performer. Because it is a simple-RT situation, the person knows before the warning signal what response will be required. And, because every trial has the same foreperiod length, he or she knows when the go signal will occur after the warning signal. As a result, the person can prepare the required action in advance of the go signal, such that the actual initiation of it begins before the go signal.

The start of sprint races in track or swimming illustrate the need to implement an understanding of the effect on RT of a constant foreperiod length. If the starter of these races maintains a constant amount of time between his or her signal for the athletes to get ready and the gun or sound to start running or swimming, the athletes can anticipate the go signal and gain an unfair advantage over other athletes who did not anticipate the signal as accurately. We would expect some variation in the actual initiations of movement because people vary in terms of their capability to time the precise amounts of time typically involved in the RT foreperiods of sprint starts.

Movement complexity. Movement complexity is based on the number of parts to a movement. Research evidence demonstrating the effect of movement complexity on RT was reported primarily in the 1960s through the early 1980s, beginning with the now classic experiment by Henry and Rogers (1960). They demonstrated that for a ballistic task, which requires both fast RT and fast movement, RT increases as a function of the number of component parts of the required action. Numerous other experiments have confirmed these findings since that time (e.g., Anson, 1982; Christina & Rose, 1985; Fischman, 1984). From a preparation-of-action perspective, these results indicate that the complexity of the action to be performed influences the amount of time a person requires to prepare the motor control system.

A question that arose from these experiments related to whether, in fact, the key factor is the number of component parts involved in the action. Because the amount of time to perform the action and the number of component parts of the action are confounded when actions of different complexity are compared, it is possible that the amount of time required may be the cause of the RT increase. To investigate which of these possible factors influenced RT in the Henry and Rogers experiment, Christina and colleagues (Christina, Fischman, Vercruyssen, & Anson, 1982; Christina, Fischman, Lambert, &

A CLOSER LOOK

The Classic Experiment of Henry and Rogers (1960)

Henry and Rogers (1960) hypothesized that if people prepare movements in advance, a complex movement should take longer to prepare than a simple one. In addition, the increased preparation time should be reflected in changes in reaction time (RT). To test this hypothesis, they compared three different rapid-movement situations that varied in the complexity of the movement. The least complex movement required participants to release a telegraph key as quickly as possible after a gong (movement A). The movement at the next level of complexity (movement B), required participants to release the key at the gong and move the arm forward 30 cm as rapidly as possible to grasp a tennis ball hanging from a string. The most complex movement (move-

ment C) required participants to release the key at the gong, reach forward and strike the hanging tennis ball with the back of the hand, reverse direction and push a button, and then finally reverse direction again and grasp another tennis ball. Participants were to perform all of these movements as quickly as possible.

The results supported the hypothesis. The average RT for movement A was 165 msec; for movement B the average RT was 199 msec; and for movement C the average RT was 212 msec.

The researchers held that the cause of the increase in RT was the increase in the amount of movement-related information that had to be prepared. They proposed that the mechanism involved in this movement preparation was a motor program, similar to a computer program, that would control the details of the sequence of events required to perform the movement.

Moore, 1985; Fischman 1984) carried out a series of experiments. Their results were consistent in supporting the Henry and Rogers conclusion that the number of component parts of the action is the key variable in the RT increase.

Movement accuracy. *As the accuracy demands for a movement increase, the amount of preparation time required also increases.* Researchers have nicely demonstrated this effect in comparisons of RTs for manual aiming tasks that differed according to the target sizes. For example, Sidaway, Sekiya, and Fairweather (1995) had people perform manual aiming tasks in which they had to hit two targets in sequence as quickly as possible. Two results showed the influence on preparation of the accuracy demands of the task. First, RT increased as target size decreased. Second, when the first target was a constant size, the dispersion of the location of hits on that target was related to the size of the second target. This result indicated that preparation demands increased as movement accuracy demands increased, due to the additional preparation required for a person to constrain his or her limb to move within spatial constraints imposed by the smaller target.

The repetition of a movement. A well-known characteristic of human performance is that when the performance situation requires a person to repeat the same response on the next attempt, that person's RT for the next trial will be faster than it was for the previous attempt. As the number of trials increases, the influence of the repetitions on RT lessens. Again, as in other performance situations, the decrease in preparation time is due to a reduction in the response-selection process (see Campbell & Proctor, 1993).

The time between different responses to different signals. There are some performance situations that require a person to respond to a signal with one action and then very quickly respond to another signal with a different action. For example, when a basketball player is confronted by a defensive player in a one-on-one situation, he or she might fake a move in one direction (the first signal) before moving in the opposite direction (the second signal). Each "signal" by the offensive player requires the defensive player to initiate a movement. In this situation, RT will be slower for the defensive player's second movement than for his or her first.

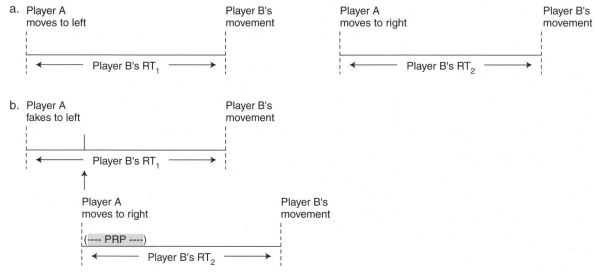

FIGURE 7.3 The psychological refractory period (PRP) illustrated in terms of the time advantage gained by an athlete for moving to the right when it follows a fake for moving to the left. (a) Player B's RT when Player A moves to the left (RT_1) or the right (RT_2), when neither is preceded by a fake in the opposite direction. (b) Player B's RT when Player A first fakes moving to the left but then moves to the right. In this situation, Player A gains extra time to carry out the move to the right because of the increased RT_2 for Player B, which results from the delay caused by the PRP.

The RT delay for the second movement is due to the **psychological refractory period (PRP),** which can be thought of as a delay period (the term *refractory* is synonymous with *delay*) during which a person "puts on hold" the selection of the second movement while he or she selects and initiates the first. As such, the PRP reflects a distinct limitation in the action preparation process.

Figure 7.3 illustrates the PRP using the basketball one-on-one situation described earlier. The player with the ball (Player A) fakes a move to the left but then quickly moves to the right. He or she gains extra time to carry out the move to the right because of the RT delay created by the PRP that results from Player B's initial reaction to the fake. The illustration shows that Player B's RT would be the same amount of time for Player A's move to the right if it had not been preceded by a fake move to the left. But the fake requires Player B to initiate a response to the fake before he or she can initiate a response to the move to the right.

**Performer Characteristics
Influencing Preparation**

In addition to task and situation characteristics, certain characteristics of the performer also influence the process of action preparation. We should think of these characteristics as situational, because they refer to the state of the person at the time a skill must be performed. It is important to note here that these performer characteristics typically influence not only the time needed to prepare a voluntary movement but also the quality of its performance.

Alertness of the performer. An important principle of human performance is that the degree of alertness of the performer influences the time he or she takes to prepare a required action, as well as the quality of the action itself. In two types of performance situations, the role of alertness is especially critical. One type is the RT task, where a person does not have to wait for any length of time beyond a few seconds, but must respond as quickly and as

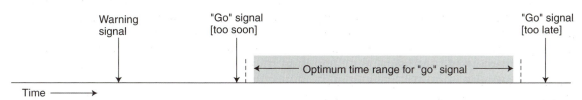

FIGURE 7.4   An illustration of the warning signal to "go" signal time relationship necessary to ensure optimal readiness to respond in a reaction time situation. The actual amounts of time for these events depend on the task and situation in which they are performed.

accurately as possible. The other type, involving the long-term maintenance of alertness, is the task for which fast and accurate responding is important, but the signals to which the person must respond occur infrequently and irregularly.

For RT tasks, a way to increase the likelihood that a person is optimally alert and prepared to respond appropriately is to provide some type of *warning signal* that indicates he or she must respond within the next few seconds. Researchers demonstrated the benefit of this warning signal more than a century ago, in the early days of human performance research. For example, in a review of RT research, Teichner (1954) reported that there was sufficient evidence accumulated in the first half of the 1900s, to conclude that RT is significantly faster when the signal to respond is preceded by a warning signal than when there is no warning signal.

An important point is that after the warning signal, there is an optimal length of time for the person to develop and maintain alertness while waiting for the go signal. If the go signal occurs too soon after the warning signal, or if the person must wait too long, RT will be longer than if the go signal occurs sometime between these two points in time. These performance effects indicate that people require a minimum amount of time to develop optimal alertness and that we can maintain that level of alertness for a limited amount of time.

As you can see in figure 7.4, there is an optimal time range during which the go signal should occur following the warning signal. The exact amounts of time to insert in this figure will depend on the skill and situation. However, for simple-RT situations, a

reasonable rule of thumb is: *the optimal foreperiod length should range between 1 and 4 sec.*

Tasks that involve long-term maintenance of alertness are known as **vigilance** tasks. In vigilance situations, an individual must perform an appropriate action when he or she detects a signal to act. The problem is that *signals occur very infrequently and irregularly.* There are many vigilance situations in skill performance contexts. In sports, a situation involving vigilance occurs when a baseball outfielder must maintain alertness throughout an inning in the field despite having only one ball hit his or her way, out of the many pitches thrown. In industry, a worker who must detect and remove defective products from the assembly line will see many products move past him or her for long periods of time, but only a few will be defective. Similarly, driving a car along an uncrowded freeway is a vigilance task when a person drives for an extended time. Lifeguarding at a pool or beach can be a vigilance problem, because during a long shift on duty situations requiring a response are very infrequent. Medical personnel often are required to work long hours and still be

psychological refractory period (PRP)   a delay period during which a person seems to put planned action "on hold" while executing a previously initiated action.

vigilance   maintaining attention in a performance situation in which stimuli requiring a response occur infrequently.

A CLOSER LOOK

Vigilance Problems Result from Closed-Head Injury

Closed-head injury involves brain damage and often results from an auto accident or a fall. Numerous cognitive and motor problems can accompany this type of injury, depending on the area of the brain that is damaged. Included in the problems associated with closed-head injury is difficulty sustaining attention over a period of time in vigilance tasks.

Loken et al. (1995) provided evidence for this by comparing patients with severe closed-head injuries to non-brain-injured people. All participants observed on a computer screen sets of two, four, or eight small blue circles (1.5 mm diameter). On some trials, one of the circles was solid blue (this occurred on only 60 percent of the 200 trials). When participants detected the solid blue circle, they were to hit a specified keyboard key.

The set of trials lasted 20 min, with only 2 to 5 sec between trials.

The authors pointed out that the following results were most noteworthy because they added to previous knowledge of vigilance problems related to closed-head injury. *In contrast to the non-brain-injured participants,* the patients showed that their

1. **overall vigilance performance** was differentially affected by the complexity of the stimulus array on the computer screen (i.e., detection performance decreased as the set size of circles increased).
2. **detection time latency** (RT) increased as a function of the length of time engaged in performing the task (i.e., the amount of time taken to detect a solid blue circle increased linearly across the 200 trials).

---

able to identify symptoms of health problems correctly and perform surgical techniques requiring precise motor control.

In each of these situations, RT increases as a function of the amount of time the person must maintain alertness to detect certain signals. Detection errors increase as well. Scientists first reported this phenomenon during World War II (see Mackworth, 1956). In experiments investigating the detection of signals simulating those observed on a radar screen, results showed that both the RT to a signal and the accuracy of detecting signals deteriorated markedly with each half hour during a two-hour work interval.

Eason, Beardshall, and Jaffee (1965) nicely demonstrated that alertness deterioration contributes to the performance decrements associated with long-term vigilance. They provided physiological evidence consistent with decreases in vigilance performance over one-hour sessions. Skin conductance in participants decreased, indicating increased calming and drowsiness over the session. In addition, participants' neck tension steadily increased, as their nervous systems attempted to compensate by increasing muscle activity in the neck.

Attention focused on the signal versus the movement. Many motor skills, such as sprints in track and swimming, require a person to move as fast as possible when the signal to move occurs. In these situations, there are two important components, the RT and the movement time (MT). To prepare to initiate his or her movement the person can focus on the signal itself (a *sensory set*) or on the movement required (a *motor set*). Research evidence, first provided by Franklin Henry (1961), indicates that which of the two components the performer consciously focuses attention on influences RT.

However, because Henry's results were based on the participants' opinions of what their sets were, Christina (1973) imposed on each participant either a sensory or a motor set to initiate a fast arm movement. The sensory-set group was told to focus attention on the sound of the go signal, a buzzer, but to move off the response key as fast as possible. The motor-set group was told to focus on moving as quickly as possible. Results showed that the sensory-set group had an RT 20 msec faster than that of the motor-set group. Interestingly, MT was not statistically different for the two groups. Thus,

A CLOSER LOOK

A Summary of Task and Performer Characteristics That Influence the Amount of Time Required to Prepare an Action

Characteristics That *Increase* Action Preparation Time	Characteristics That *Decrease* Action Preparation Time
• An increase in the number of movement alternatives	• A decrease in the number of movement alternatives
• An increase in the unpredictability of the correct movement response alternative	• An increase in the predictability of the correct movement response alternative
• Following an expectation bias toward performing one of several movement alternatives, the required movement is not the one expected	• Following an expectation bias toward performing one of several movement alternatives, the required movement is the one expected
• An increase in the degree of spatial incompatibility between environmental features and the movements required	• An increase in the degree of spatial compatibility between environmental features and the movements required
• An increase in the irregularity of foreperiod lengths in an RT situation	• An increase in the regularity of foreperiod lengths in an RT situation
• No previous experience (i.e., practice) performing the task in the required situation	• An increase in the amount of experience (i.e., practice) performing the task in the required situation
• A decrease in performer alertness	• An increase in performer alertness
• An attention focus on the movement rather than the "go" signal	• An attention focus on the "go" signal rather than the movement

participants' focusing of attention on the signal and allowing the movement to happen naturally shortened the preparation time required and did not penalize movement speed, yielding a faster overall response time.

Jongsma, Elliott, and Lee (1987) replicated these laboratory results in a sport performance situation. They compared sensory and motor sets for a sprint start in track. To measure RT, the authors embedded a pressure-sensitive switch in the rear-foot starting block. They measured MT as the time from the release of this switch until a photoelectric light beam was broken 1.5 meters from the starting line. Results showed that for both novices and experienced sprinters, RT was faster for the sensory-set condition.

What Occurs during Preparation?
On the basis of the discussion so far, you can see that the process of preparing an action is complex.

It includes perceptual, cognitive, and motor components. One way to demonstrate that the preparation process includes these components is to divide an EMG recording of the RT interval into components by using a technique known as *fractionating RT,* which was introduced in chapter 3.

Evidence from fractionating RT. To fractionate RT, we divide into two distinct components the EMG recording taken from the agonist muscle involved in a movement (see figure 7.5). The first is the *premotor* component (sometimes referred to as electromechanical delay). Notice that the EMG signal does not change much from what it was prior to the onset of the signal. However, shortly after the onset of the signal, the EMG signal shows a rapid increase in electrical activity. This indicates that the motor neurons are firing and the muscle is preparing to contract, even though no observable

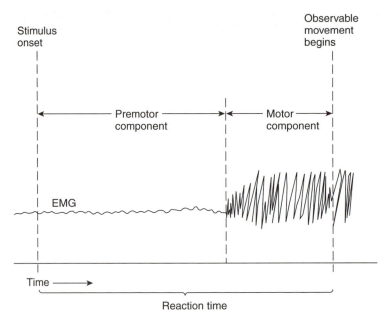

FIGURE 7.5   Schematization of fractionated reaction time indicating the relationship between the EMG signal activity and the premotor and motor components of the RT interval.

movement has yet occurred. In this period of time, the *motor* component, is the increased EMG activity preceding the observable movement.

The premotor and motor components of RT represent two distinct activities that occur prior to observable movement and reflect different types of movement preparation processes. The premotor component includes the perceptual or cognitive processing of the stimulus information and preparing the movement features of the required action. The motor component begins the actual motor output phase of a movement. During this time, the specific muscles involved in the action are firing and preparing to begin to produce observable movement.

By fractionating RT, we can gain insight into what occurs during the action preparation process. Researchers look at which of these RT components is influenced by the various factors we discussed earlier that influence RT. For example, Christina and Rose (1985) reported that the changes in RT due to increases in *response complexity* were reflected in

increases in the premotor component. For a two-part arm movement, the premotor component increased an average of 19 msec over that for a one-part arm movement, whereas the motor component increased only 3 msec. Siegel (1986) found that whereas RT increased linearly as *movement durations* increased from 150, through 300 and 600, to 1200 msec, the length of the premotor component also increased linearly. The motor component, on the other hand, remained the same length until the response duration became 1200 msec; then it showed a slight increase. Sheridan (1984) showed that the premotor component was also responsible for RT increases due to increases in *movement velocity*. However, Carlton, Carlton, and Newell (1987) found changes in both the premotor and motor components by altering *force-related characteristics* of the response.

Postural preparation.   When a person must perform arm movements while in a standing position, a part of the preparation process involves organizing

Fractionated Visual Reaction Time Can Provide Insights into the Locus of Developmental Coordination Disorder

Children with developmental coordination disorder (DCD) have no evident physical or mental condition that would result in motor disabilities, yet they display motor performance levels below those of age-matched peers, and have significant difficulties with activities of daily living. In their attempts to better understand DCD, researchers have presented evidence that children with DCD have slower visual reaction time (RT) for a simple voluntary movement compared to normally coordinated children. Many of those researchers hypothesized that this slower RT is due to problems related to selecting the appropriate action or preparing the movements required for that action. Annette Raynor (1998) investigated this hypothesis by fractionating simple visual RT for six-

and nine-year-old children with and without DCD. With the children in a sitting position, she asked them to kick their right leg forward as fast as possible when a light in front of them illuminated. The results showed:

- Children with DCD had slower RTs than children who were not diagnosed with DCD.
- The fractionated RTs showed slower *premotor and motor* components for the DCD children.

The results of the fractionated RT not only supported the premotor locus hypothesis, but also presented new evidence that the motor component contributes to the coordination difficulties. Thus, the RT fractionation technique enabled the researcher to gain insights into DCD not previously seen. From this new base of understanding, researchers can plan investigations to identify the specific reasons for the movement planning and implementation delays.

supporting postural activity. EMG recordings of postural muscle activity provide evidence for this preparation. For example, Weeks and Wallace (1992) asked people to perform an elbow-flexion aiming movement in the horizontal plane while standing in an erect posture. Participants learned to make this movement in three different velocities defined by criterion movement times. The authors made EMG recordings from various muscles of both legs and the responding arm. The results (figure 7.6) showed that for each movement velocity, a specific sequence of supporting postural events occurred. The arm movement, which is shown in the figure on the potentiometer (POT) recording, begins just after 0.2 sec for each velocity, with the elbow flexion occurring just after 0.4 sec. Note that the muscles of the contralateral and ipsilateral legs (biceps femoris and rectus femoris) activated *prior to* the onset of the arm agonist muscles (biceps brachii). And as the arm velocity increased, the onset of the anticipatory postural muscle activity occurred at an earlier time prior to arm agonist muscle activation. The authors found different onset

orders for the various postural muscles. This finding shows that postural preparation involves organizing features of a *flexibly organized synergy* of postural muscles. This conclusion is important because movement scientists traditionally have assumed that postural muscle preparation is rigidly temporally organized. The advantage of the flexibly organized synergy is that anticipatory postural activity can occur according to the person's equilibrium needs of various premovement postures.

Preparation of limb movement characteristics. An essential part of the action preparation process is selecting and organizing the specific movement characteristics of the limbs to perform according to the dictates of task constraints and characteristics. Because an individual often can perform the same action using several different limbs or different segments of the same limb, he or she must specify and prepare the limb or limb segments to be involved in performing a given task.

One feature of limb movement a person must prepare is the *direction* or directions in which the

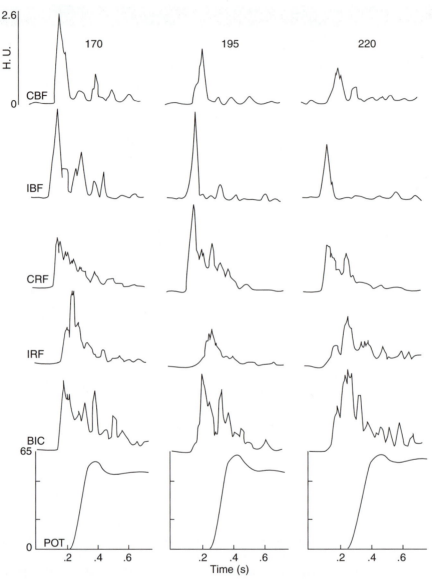

FIGURE 7.6   EMG recordings from the experiment by Weeks and Wallace. One trial of a rectified and smoothed EMG record is shown for one subject performing an elbow-flexion aiming movement in the horizontal plane while standing in an erect posture. Shown are records for three different velocities (170, 195, and 220 ms) for various muscles of both legs and the responding arm (CBF = contralateral biceps femoris, IBF = ipsilateral biceps femoris, CRF = contralateral rectus femoris, IRF = ipsilateral rectus femoris, BIC = biceps brachii, POT = potentiometer). Note that the POT recording shows the arm movement, which is synchronized in time with the EMG recordings. [Reprinted from *Human Movement Science,* Vol. 11, D. L. Weeks and S. A. Wallace, Premovement posture and focal movement velocity effects on postural responses accompanying rapid arm movement, pp. 717–734, 1992, with permission of Elsevier Science.]

A CLOSER LOOK

Achieving a Standing Posture from Various Sitting Postures: An Example of How Functional Demands Affect Action Preparation

Changing from a sitting posture to a standing posture (referred to as a sit-to-stand action) is a common everyday activity that provides a good example of how the motor control system adapts to allow the same action to occur from a variety of initial postural positions. Shepherd and Gentile (1994) presented evidence of this adaptability by having healthy adults sit in different postures on a chair (an erect trunk, a fully flexed trunk, and a partially flexed trunk, i.e., flexed between the fully flexed and erect positions) and then stand. Analyses of the various joint movements involved in this action showed:

- *In the erect and partially flexed sitting postures:* The knee began to extend before the hip joint began to extend.
- *In the fully flexed sitting posture:* the hip joint began to extend before the knee began to extend.

These different initiation patterns of joint movements illustrate how functional demands influence the order of muscle activation in preparing an action. Because different sitting postures will require different support, propulsion, and balance characteristics during the sit-to-stand action, the order of the initiation of movement of the knee or hip joints is a critical factor in enabling a person to carry out the intended action without losing balance.

---

limbs must move. For a very rapid movement, a person may prepare several different directions before initiating the movement. Another feature related to direction preparation is the *trajectory* the arm will follow during movement. For a task requiring a ballistic movement and spatial accuracy, an individual must prepare in advance: constraining the limb movement to meet the *accuracy* constraints of the task. In addition, as we discussed in chapter 6 a person catching a ball must prepare his or her hand and finger movements before an oncoming ball reaches him or her.

Preparation of movements for object control. When the action to be performed involves manipulating an object, a part of the preparation process involves specifying certain movement features needed to control the object. Two examples illustrate what can be involved in this aspect of movement preparation.

One feature of the preparation process for handwriting is the specification of pen pressure on the writing surface and grip force of the fingers on the writing instrument (Wann & Nimmo-Smith, 1991). Experienced writers adjust the amount of pen pres-

sure on the writing surface according to certain characteristics of the surface to allow energy-efficient, continuous, fluent motion. In contrast, children with handwriting problems often use excessive pen pressure and grip the pen barrel with excessive force.

Another object control feature that individuals prepare is what Rosenbaum and Jorgenson (1992) referred to as "end-state comfort." This means that when a person has several options for specifying how an object will be manipulated, as when he or she must pick up an object and place it in a specified location, the person will organize the limb movements so that a comfortable limb position will result at the completion of the action. For example, if a person must pick up an object and place it upside down on a tabletop, the person typically will pick up the object with a hand position that will yield the most comfortable position when the object is placed upside down.

Of the several hypotheses proposed to explain the end-state comfort effect, one that continues to gain support is the precision hypothesis (Rosenbaum et al., 1993; Rosenbaum, van Heutgen, & Caldwell, 1996; Short & Cauraugh, 1999). This hypothesized

A CLOSER LOOK

Correcting Handwriting Problems Due to Grip and Pen Force

The results of the experiment by Wann and Nimmo-Smith (1991) showed that when handwriting, children with handwriting problems often do so because they use excessive pen pressure and grip the pen barrel with excessive force. The have not acquired the necessary association between the "feel" of the pen against the surface and the appropriate pen pressure to apply. The researchers speculated that adults who made the appropriate force adjustments had acquired this capability through experience, which had led to their nonconsciously learning the amount of pressure required based on sensations in the fingers holding the pen.

Teachers and therapists who work with children struggling with this type of problem can encourage an increasing sensitivity in the children to appropriate pen pressure. One way to do this is by providing handwriting experiences with a variety of writing surfaces. A teacher or therapist should monitor each child's grip force, with the goal of keeping it at the minimum amount of force needed to produce a visible trace on the writing surface.

---

explanation proposes that precision in limb positioning will be greater, and the movement will be faster, when a person's limb is in a comfortable position. Thus, to ensure a faster and more accurate final limb and object position, a person prepares movement characteristics according to the comfort of the final rather the starting position of the limb. Although this strategy may require some awkward hand and arm postures when picking up an object, it enables the person to more effectively and efficiently achieve the object manipulation goal.

Preparation of spatial coding. In performance situations requiring specified responses to certain stimuli, such as choice-RT situations, people take into account the spatial relationships of the stimulus and response locations in the movement preparation process. They translate these relationships into meaningful codes that they then use to produce the required responses. Research has shown that this spatial coding accounts for many stimulus-response compatibility effects (see Weeks & Proctor, 1990 for a discussion of these). The simplest spatial coding, which leads to the fastest preparation (i.e., RT), occurs when left and right stimulus locations are compatible with left and right response locations. Beyond that arrangement, it appears that up-to-right and down-to-left stimulus-to-response relationships lead to faster preparation times. The limb involved in performing the required response is not so critical as the spatial relationship of the stimulus location to the response location.

Rhythmicity preparation. Many skills require that the component movements follow specific rhythmic patterns. We can see this characteristic in any of the various types of gait, performance of a dance sequence, shooting of a free throw in basketball, and so on. In some of these activities, the participant can take time before performing it to engage in some preperformance activities that are commonly referred to as rituals. Interestingly, rhythmic patterns also characterize preperformance rituals and appear to influence performance. Although this relationship has not been widely studied, the few research studies investigating it have consistently shown a positive correlation between the rhythm of the preperformance routine and the success of the performance itself (e.g., Southard & Miracle, 1993; Southard & Amos, 1996; Wrisberg & Pein, 1992).

The Southard and Amos (1996) study will serve as a good example of how these researchers have determined that such a relationship exists. They video recorded fifteen basketball free throws, golf putts, and tennis serves for experienced university men who had established rituals for each of these

TABLE 7.1 Types of Behaviors Involved in Preperformance Rituals in Activities Investigated by Southard and Amos (1996)

Activity	Behaviors in Preperformance Rituals
Golf putt	1. Swinging the putter back and forth without contacting the ball 2. Pause; no movement for 1 sec or more 3. Moving the toes or either foot up and down 4. Swaying the body back and forth without swinging the putter 5. Lifting the putter vertically
Tennis serve	1. Bouncing the ball with the racquet or the hand not holding the racquet 2. Pause; no movement for 1 sec or more 3. Moving the racquet forward to a position in front of the body waist high 4. Moving the racquet back from the front of the body and then forward again 5. Moving the racquet to a ready position in order to initiate serving the ball
Basketball free throw	1. Bouncing the ball 2. Pause, no movement for 1 sec or more 3. Bending at the knees or waist 4. Moving the ball upward with the arms 5. Spinning the ball 6. Bringing the ball to an initial shooting position

Table based on text and table 1 (p. 290) in Southard, D., & Amos, B. (1996). Rhythmicity and preperformance ritual: Stabilizing a flexible system. *Research Quarterly for Exercise and Sport, 67,* 288–296.

activities. Each video recording was analyzed to determine the preperformance behaviors each participant used on each trial. The types of behaviors for each activity are listed in table 7.1. It is important to note that although each of the behaviors was observed, individual participants did not exhibit every behavior. The researchers also analyzed the total time to perform the ritual and the relative time for each behavior in the ritual, which was the percentage of time engaged in each behavior in the ritual. Results showed a moderately high .77 correlation between the relative time for the ritual behaviors and successful performance. This relationship suggests that the consistent relative timing of preperformance ritual behaviors may be an important part of the successful performance of closed motor skills that provide an opportunity for the performer to engage in preperformance rituals.

In terms of the preparation of action, the preperformance rituals would appear to stabilize the motor control system and orient it to engaging in a rhythmic activity.

SUMMARY

To perform a motor skill, a person must prepare the motor control system. This preparation requires time, as we can see from research evidence showing that various task, situation, and personal factors influence RT. Task and situation factors include the number of response alternatives the performer has to choose from; the predictability of the correct response choice; stimulus-response compatibility; foreperiod length regularity; movement complexity; movement accuracy; the repetition of a response; and the time between different responses. Personal factors influencing preparation include the degree of the person's alertness and whether attention is focused on the signal or on the movement. We know that people prepare action-related movement characteristics during the RT interval. Movement scientists have gained insight into the extent to which these are perceptual, cognitive, or motor by fractionating the RT intervals from the EMG signals of the primary agonist muscles into their premotor and motor components. Research has shown that some of the various action features people prepare during the RT interval include: postural organization, limb performance characteristics, object control characteristics, spatial coding, and rhythmicity.

RELATED READINGS

Carson, R., Chua, G. R., Goodman, D., & Byblow, W. D., (1995). The preparation of aiming movements. *Brain and Cognition, 28,* 133–154.

Klapp, S. T. (1996). Reaction time analysis of central motor control. In H. N. Zelaznik (Ed.); *Advances in motor learning and control* (pp. 13–35). Champaign, IL: Human Kinetics.

Meulenbroek, R. G. J., Rosenbaum, D. A., Thomassen, A. J. W. M., & Schomaker, L. R. B. (1993). Limb-segment selection in drawing behaviour. *Quarterly Journal of Experimental Psychology, 46A,* 273–299.

Stelmach, G. E., Teasdale, N., & Phillips, J. (1992). Response initiation delays in Parkinson's disease patients. *Human Movement Science, 11,* 37–45.

Weeks, D. J., Proctor, R. W., & Beyak, B. (1995). Stimulus-response compatibility for vertically oriented stimuli and horizontally oriented responses: Evidence for spatial coding. *Quarterly Journal of Experimental Psychology, 48A,* 367–383.

STUDY QUESTIONS

1. Discuss how we can use reaction time (RT) as an index of the preparation required to perform a motor skill.

2. Discuss how Hick's law is relevant to helping us understand the characteristics of factors that influence motor control preparation.

3. What is the cost-benefit trade-off involved in biasing the preparation of an action in the expectation of making one of several possible responses? Give a motor skill performance example illustrating this tradeoff.

4. Describe two performer characteristics that can influence action preparation. Discuss how these characteristics can influence preparation.

5. Select a motor skill and describe two motor control features of that skill that a person prepares prior to the initiation of performance of the skill.

ATTENTION AND MEMORY

CHAPTER

8

Attention as a Limited
Capacity Resource

*Concept: Preparation for and performance of
motor skills are influenced by our limited
capacity to select and attend to information*

APPLICATION

When you are driving your car on an open high-way that has little traffic, it is relatively easy for you to carry on a conversation with a passenger in the car or on a cell phone at the same time. But what happens when the highway you are driving on becomes congested with other traffic? Isn't it difficult to carry on a conversation with your pas-senger or on your phone while driving under these conditions?

This driving example raises an important human performance and learning question: Why is it easy to do more than one thing at the same time in one situation, but difficult to do these same things simultaneously in another situation? As you will discover in this chapter, we can consciously attend to, or think about, only so much at one time. As long as we can handle what we are doing within the capacity limits of our information-processing sys-tem, we can carry out several activities effectively at the same time. But if what we are doing requires more of our attention than we can give to the things we are trying to do, we have to either stop doing some things in order to do others well, or do all of them poorly.

There are many other examples in which this concept of attention limits comes into play. For example, a skilled typist can easily carry on a con-versation with someone while continuing to type—but a beginner cannot. A child learning to dribble a ball has difficulty dribbling and running at the same time, whereas a skilled basketball player does these two activities and more at the same time. Another type of situation in which attention limits come into play involves the instructional environ-ment. For example, have you ever heard a physical therapy patient tell the therapist not to tell him or her to think about so many things at the same time? Or have you experienced the difficulty a beginning tennis player has determining what and how much to look for when trying to return a serve or a groundstroke?

DISCUSSION

Since the earliest days of investigating human behavior, scholars have had a keen interest in the study of attention. For example, as early as 1859, Sir William Hamilton conducted studies in Britain dealing with attention. Around the same time, William Wundt, generally acknowledged as the "father of experimental psychology," investigated the concept of attention at the University of Leipzig in Germany. In America, William James

116

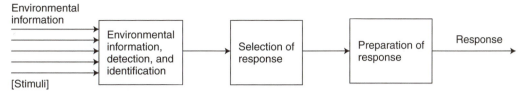

FIGURE 8.1 A generic information-processing model on which filter theories of attention were based. The figure illustrates the several stages of information processing and the serial order in which information is processed. Filter theories varied in terms of the stage at which the filter occurred. Prior to the filter, the system could process several stimuli at the same time. In the model illustrated in this figure, the filter is located in the detection and identification stage.

provided one of the earliest definitions of attention in 1890, describing it as the "focalization, concentration, of consciousness."

Unfortunately, this late-nineteenth- and early-twentieth-century emphasis on attention soon waned, as those under the influence of behaviorism deemed the study of attention no longer relevant to the understanding of human behavior. A renaissance in attention research occurred, however, when the practical requirements of World War II included the need to understand human performance in a variety of military skills. Researchers were interested in several attention-related areas, such as the performance of more than one component of a skill or more than one skill at the same time; the performance of tasks where people had to make rapid decisions when there were several response choices; and the performance of tasks where people had to maintain attention over long periods of time. This renewed interest in the study of attention continues today, as scholars attempt to understand one of the most significant limitations influencing human learning and performance.

Attention as a Human Performance Limitation
When the term is used in the context of human performance, **attention** refers to engagement in the perceptual, cognitive, and motor activities associated with performing skills. These activities may be performed consciously or nonconsciously. For example, detecting information in the environment is an attention-demanding activity. We observe and attend to the environment in which we move to detect features that help us determine what skill to perform and how to perform it. Although this observation and detection activity demands our attention, it does not always require that we are consciously aware of what we observe and detect that directs our actions.

Researchers investigating human performance have shown that attention-related activities are tied to an important human performance limitation. This limitation is well illustrated by the problem we often have doing more than one thing at a time, when we are required to divide our attention among the tasks to be performed.

Scientists have known for many years that we have attention limits that influence performance. In fact, in 1886, a French physiologist named Jacques Loeb showed that the maximum amount of pressure that a person can exert on a hand dynamometer actually decreases when the person is engaged in mental work. Unfortunately, it was not until the 1950s that researchers began to try to provide a theoretical basis for this type of behavioral evidence.

> **attention**   in human performance, the conscious or nonconscious engagement in perceptual cognitive, and/or motor activities before, during, and after performing skills; the human information-processing system includes limitations to the number of these activities that can be performed simultaneously.

Attention Theories

The most prominent among the first theories addressing attention limitations was the *filter theory* of attention, sometimes referred to as the *bottleneck theory*. This theory, which evolved into many variations, proposed that a person has difficulty doing several things at one time. The reason for this limitation is because the human information-processing system performs each of its functions in serial order, and some of these functions can process only one piece of information at a time. This means that somewhere along the stages of information processing, the system has a *bottleneck,* where it filters out information not selected for further processing (see figure 8.1). Variations of this theory were based on the processing stage in which the bottleneck occurred. Some contended it existed very early, at the stage of detection of environmental information (e.g., Welford, 1952, 1967; Broadbent, 1958), whereas others argued that it occurred later, after information was perceived or after it had been processed cognitively (e.g., Norman, 1968).

This type of theoretical viewpoint remained popular for many years, until it became evident that the filter theories of attention did not adequately explain all performance situations. The most acceptable alternative proposed that attention limits were the result of the *limited availability of resources* needed to carry out the information-processing functions. Just as you have limited economic resources to pay for your activities, we have limited attention resources to do all the activities that we may attempt at one time.

Theories emphasizing attentional resource limits propose that we can perform several tasks simultaneously, as long as the resource capacity limits of the system are not exceeded. However, if these limits are exceeded, we experience difficulty performing one or more of these tasks. Theorists following this viewpoint differ in their views of *where* the resource limit exists. Some propose that there is one central resource pool from which all attention resources are allocated, whereas others propose multiple sources for resources.

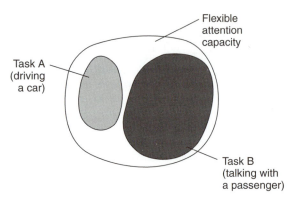

FIGURE 8.2   Diagram showing that two tasks (A and B) can be performed simultaneously (e.g., driving a car while talking with a passenger) if the attention demanded by the tasks does not exceed the available attention capacity. Note that the amount of available capacity and the amount of attention demanded by each task to be performed may increase or decrease, a change that would be represented in this diagram by changing the sizes of the appropriate circles.

Central-resource capacity theories.   According to some attention theories, there is a central reserve of resources for which all activities compete. Following the analogy of your economic resources, these **central-resource theories** compare human attention capacity to a single source from which all activities must be funded. To further understand this view, consider the available attention resources as existing within one large circle, like the one depicted in figure 8.2. Next, consider as smaller circles the specific tasks that require these resources, such as driving a car (task A) and talking with a friend (task B). Each circle by itself fits inside the larger circle. But for a person to successfully perform both tasks simultaneously, both small circles must fit into the large circle. Problems arise when we try to fit into the large circle more small circles than will fit.

A good example of a central resource theory is one proposed by Kahneman (1973). Although this theory was originally presented many years ago, it continues to influence our present views about attention. In his model (see figure 8.3), the *capacity limits of the central pool of resources are flexible.* This means that the amount of available attention can vary depending on certain conditions related to

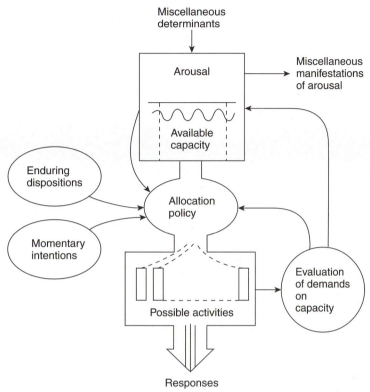

FIGURE 8.3   Kahneman's model of attention.   [From Kahneman, D. (1973).
Attention and effort, © 1973, p. 10. Reprinted by permission of Prentice Hall, Inc., Englewood
Cliffs, NJ]

the individual, the tasks being performed, and the
situation. According to the illustration in figure 8.2,
this flexible central-capacity theory states that the
size of the large circle can change according to certain personal, task, and situation characteristics.

Kahneman views the *available* attention that a
person can give to an activity or activities as a general *pool of effort,* which involves the mental
resources necessary to carry out activities. The person can subdivide this one pool so that he or she
can allocate attention to several activities at the
same time. Allocation of resources is determined
by characteristics of the activities and the allocation policy of the individual, which in turn is influenced by situations internal and external to the
individual. Figure 8.3 depicts the various condi-

tions that influence how a person will allocate the
available resources.

First, notice that the central pool of available
resources (available capacity) is represented as a
box at the top of the model. The wavy line indicates that the amount of attention available, the
capacity limit, is flexible. Attention capacity will
increase or decrease according to the *arousal level*

---

central-resource theories   attention-capacity
theories that propose one central source of attention
resources for which all activities requiring attention
compete.

A CLOSER LOOK

An Attention-Capacity Explanation of the Arousal-Performance Relationship

A widely held view of the relationship between arousal and performance is that it takes the form of an inverted U. This means that when we graph this relationship, placing on the vertical axis the performance level ranging from poor to high, and placing on the horizontal axis the arousal level ranging from very low to very high, the plot of the relationship resembles an inverted U. This type of relationship indicates that arousal levels that are either too low or too high will result in poor performance. However, between these extremes is a range of arousal levels that should yield high performance levels.

If, as Kahneman's model indicates, arousal levels influence available attention capacity in a similar way, then it would follow that we can attribute the arousal level–performance relationship to available attention capacity. This means that arousal levels that are too low or too high lead to poor performance, because the person does not have the attentional resources needed to perform the activity. When the arousal level is optimal, sufficient attention resources are available and the person can achieve a high level of performance.

---

of the person. **Arousal** is the general state of excitability of a person, reflected in the activation levels of the person's emotional, mental, and physiological systems. If the person's arousal level is too low or too high, he or she has a smaller available attention capacity than he or she would if the arousal level were in an optimal range. This means that for a person to have available the maximum attention resources, the person must be at an optimal arousal level.

Another critical factor determining whether there are sufficient attentional resources is the attention demands, or requirements, of the tasks to be performed. This factor is represented in Kahneman's model in figure 8.3 as the *evaluation of demands on capacity*. Because tasks differ in the amount of attention they demand, the person must evaluate these demands to determine if he or she can do them all simultaneously, or if he or she will not be able to perform some of them.

Finally, certain rules come into play that influence how people allocate attentional resources. One is that we allocate attention to ensure that we can complete one activity. Another is that we allocate attentional resources according to our *enduring dispositions*. These are the basic rules of "involuntary" attention, which concern those things that seem to naturally attract our attention (i.e., distract us). We

typically will "involuntarily" direct our attention to (or be distracted by) at least two types of characteristics of events in our environment, even though we may be attending to something else at the time.

One is that the event is *novel*, or perhaps more interesting. For example, how many times have you directed your attention away from the person teaching your class to one of your classmates when he or she sneezes very loudly or drops a book on the floor? Why does this incident influence where you direct your attention? The primary reason is that it is an unexpected event in the class environment. Consider a different type of example. Why is a professional golfer who is preparing to putt distracted by a spectator talking, but a basketball player who is preparing to shoot a free throw is not distracted by thousands of spectators yelling and screaming? The reason relates to the novelty of the talking or yelling in each situation. The golfer does not expect to hear someone talking while preparing to putt, but for the basketball player, the noise is a common part of the game. As a result, the noise is novel in one situation but not in the other.

The second characteristic of events that will involuntarily direct our attention is the *meaningfulness* of the event to us personally. A classic example of this characteristic is known as the "cocktail party phenomenon," which was first described in the 1950s (Cherry, 1953). Undoubtedly, you have experienced this phenomenon yourself. Suppose you are at a party in a room filled with people. You are attending to your conversation with another person. Suddenly you hear someone near you mention your name in a conversation that person is having with other people. What do you do? You probably redirect your attention away from your own conversation to the person who said your name. Why did you do this? The reason relates to the meaningfulness of your name to you. Even though you were attending to your own conversation, this meaningful event caused you to spontaneously shift your attention. In sports, it is not uncommon to hear athletes say that while they are performing, the only person they hear saying something to them is the coach. Why? In this competitive situation, the person's coach is very meaningful to the athlete.

The final rule in Kahneman's model concerning our allocation of attention relates to a person's *momentary intentions.* That is, a person allocates attention in a situation according to his or her specific intentions. Sometimes, these intentions are self-directed, which means the person has personally decided to direct attention to a certain aspect of the situation. At other times, momentary intentions result from instructions given to the person about how or where to direct his or her attentional resources. For example, if a physical therapist tells a patient to "pay close attention to where you place your foot on the stair step," the patient has the "momentary intention" to allocate his or her attention according to the therapist's instruction.

Multiple-resource theories. **Multiple-resource theories** provide an alternative to theories proposing a central resource pool of attention resources. Multiple-resource theories contend that we have several attention mechanisms, each having limited resources. Each resource pool is specific to a component of performing skills. Using a government analogy, the resources are available in various government agencies and competition for the resources occurs only among those activities

related to the specific agencies. The most prevalent of the multiple-resource theories were proposed by Navon and Gopher (1979), Allport (1980), and Wickens (1980, 1992).

Wickens proposed what has become the most popular of these theories. He stated that resources for processing information are available from three different sources (see figure 8.4). These are the *input and output modalities* (e.g., vision, limbs, and speech system), the *stages of information processing* (e.g., perception, memory encoding, response output), and the *codes of processing information* (e.g., verbal codes, spatial codes). Our success in performing two or more tasks simultaneously depends on whether those tasks demand our attention from a common resource or from different resources. When two tasks must be performed simultaneously and share a common resource, they will be performed less well than when the two tasks compete for different resources.

For example, the multiple-resource view would explain variations in the situation involving driving a car while talking with a passenger in the following way. When there is little traffic, driving does not demand many resources from any of the three different sources. But when traffic gets heavy, resource demand increases from these two sources: input-output modalities and stages of information processing. These are the same two sources involved in providing attention resources for carrying on a conversation with a friend. As a result, to maintain safe driving, the person must reduce the resource demand of the conversation activity.

---

arousal   the general state of excitability of a person, involving physiological, emotional, and mental systems.

multiple-resource theories   theories of attention proposing that there are several attention resource mechanisms, each of which is related to a specific information-processing activity, and is limited in how much information it can process simultaneously.

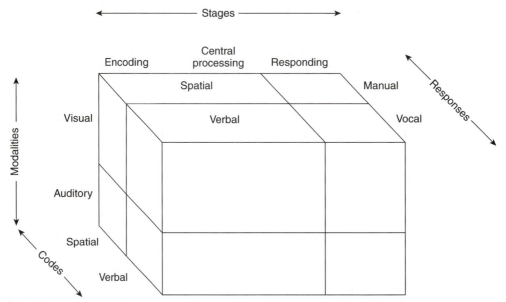

FIGURE 8.4   The component structure of Wickens's multiple-resource model of attention.   [From Wickens, C. D. (1984). Processing resources in attention. In R. Parasuraman and R. Davies (Eds.), *Varieties of attention.* Copyright © 1984 Academic Press, Orlando, FL. Reprinted by permission.]

An advantage of multiple-resource theories is their focus on the types of demands placed on various information-processing and response outcome structures, rather than on a nonspecific resource capacity. The resource-specific attention view provides a practical guide to help us determine when task demands may be too great to be performed simultaneously. For example, if one task requires a hand response and one requires a vocal response, a person should have little difficulty performing them simultaneously, because they do not demand attention from the same resource structure. Conversely, people have difficulty performing two different hand responses simultaneously because they both demand resources from the same structure.

Procedures for Assessing Attention Demands
The most common experimental procedure used to investigate attention-limit issues has been the **dual-task procedure.** The general purpose of experiments using this technique is to determine the attention demands and characteristics of two dif-

ferent tasks that are performed simultaneously. Experimenters' general approach has been to determine the attention demands of one of the two tasks by noting the degree of interference caused on that task while it is performed simultaneously with another task, called the *secondary task.*

The *primary task* in the dual-task procedure is typically the task of interest, whose performance experimenters are observing in order to assess its attention demands. Depending on the purpose of the experiment, the performer may or may not need to maintain consistent primary-task performance, whether performing that task alone or simultaneously with the secondary task.

If instructions in the experiment require the participant to pay attention to the primary task so that it is performed as well alone as with the secondary task, then secondary-task performance is the basis researchers use to make inferences about the attention demands of the primary task. On the other hand, if the experiment does not direct the person to attend primarily to either task, performance on

A CLOSER LOOK

Dual-Task Techniques Used to Assess Attention Demands of Motor Skill Performance

Researchers typically have used one of two dual-task techniques in their investigations of the attention demands associated with the preparation and performance of motor skills. Each technique relates to a specific attention-demand issue.

Continuous Secondary-Task Technique
Purpose. To determine if attention capacity is required *throughout* the performance of a motor skill.

Procedure. A person performs the primary and secondary tasks separately and simultaneously. When the person performs both tasks simultaneously, he or she is instructed to concentrate on the performance of the primary task while continuously performing the secondary task.

Rationale. If the primary task demands full-attention capacity, performance will be poorer on a secondary task while performing it together with the primary task than when performing only the secondary task. If attention capacity can be shared by both tasks, simultaneous performance should be similar to that of each task alone.

Example. As a person walks from one end of a hallway to the other, he or she must listen to words spoken through earphones; when the person hears each word, he or she must repeat the word that was spoken

just prior to that word (i.e., the secondary task is a short-term memory task that involves interference during the retention interval).

Secondary-Task Probe Technique
Purpose. To determine the attention demands required by the *preparation* of a skill, by the performance of *specific components* of a skill, or at *specific times* during the performance of a skill.

Procedure. A person performs the primary and secondary tasks separately and simultaneously. The secondary task (a discrete task) is performed at predetermined times before or during primary-task performance (i.e., the secondary task "probes" the primary task).

Rationale. If a probed site of the primary task demands full-attention capacity, performance will be poorer on a secondary task while performing it together with the primary task than when performing only the secondary task. If attention capacity can be shared by both tasks at the probed site, simultaneous performance should be similar to that of each task alone.

Example. As a person reaches for and grasps a cup of water to drink from it, he or she must listen through earphones for a "beep" sound at any time just before or during the performance of the activity. As soon as the person hears the "beep," he or she says "bop" into a microphone (i.e., the secondary task is a simple auditory-reaction time task that requires a vocal response).

both tasks is compared to performance when each task is performed alone.

Focusing Attention
In addition to having to divide attention among several activities, people also direct attention to specific features of the environment and to action preparation activities. This attention-directing process is known as **attentional focus.** As opposed to attentional demands, which concern the distribution of attentional resources to various tasks that

dual-task procedure   an experimental procedure used in the study of attention to determine the amount of attention required to perform an action, or a part of an action; the procedure involves assessing the degree of interference caused by one task when a person is simultaneously performing another task.

attentional focus   the directing of attention to specific characteristics in a performance environment, or to action-preparation activities.

A CLOSER LOOK

Comparison of Attention Demands of Balance Control for People with and without Lower-Limb Amputations

Geurts and Mulder (1994) studied people in the Netherlands with and without unilateral lower-limb amputations to determine the degree of attention those with amputations needed to control their balance. The participants with amputations had been fit with prostheses for the first time when this study began. All participants performed a static balance task of standing on a force platform on the floor for 30 sec. They were instructed to stand as still and symmetrically as possible with their hands folded behind their backs. After establishing baseline fore-aft and lateral sway characteristics while doing this task, participants simultaneously performed an arithmetic task. They had to listen to a relatively simple addition problem and state verbally if the sum was correct or incorrect. The participants without amputations showed, as expected, no

postural difficulties in the dual-task situation. In contrast, those with amputations showed an increase in both body sway and the number of arithmetic errors. Interestingly, eight weeks later, after weekly rehabilitation therapy, participants with amputations did not show these same dual-task deficits and performed more as the no-amputation participants had.

These results demonstrate that

- people who are initially acquiring the capability to use a lower-limb prosthesis following amputation require attention capacity to perform a simple static postural control task. A sufficient amount of attention to perform a mental task simultaneously is not available.
- the amount of attention participants need to balance using a prosthesis decreases after a period of therapy to a point at which they can allocate attention to a mental task so that they can perform both tasks successfully.

---

need to be performed simultaneously, attentional focus concerns the marshalling of available resources in order to direct them to specific information sources.

We can consider attentional focus in terms of both width and direction of focus. *Width* indicates that our attention can have a *broad or narrow* focus on environmental information and mental activities. *Direction* indicates that our attention focus can be *external or internal:* attention may be focused on cues in the environment or on internal thoughts, plans, or problem-solving activities. Nideffer (1993) has shown that the broad and narrow focus widths and the external and internal focus directions interact to establish four types of attention-focus situations that relate to performance.

Individuals in performance situations require specific types of attention focus to achieve successful performance. For example, a person needs a broad/external focus to walk successfully through a crowded hallway, but a narrow/external focus to catch a ball. Sometimes, situations require us to shift the type of attention focus and the object of

that attention. We do this by engaging in what is referred to as *attention switching.* It is an advantage to switch attention focus rapidly among environment and situational pieces of information when we must use a variety of sources of information for rapid decision making. For example, a football quarterback may look to see if the primary receiver is open; if not, he must find an alternate receiver. In the meantime, the quarterback must be making certain that he is not about to be tackled or kept from delivering a pass. Each of these activities requires attention and must be carried out in the course of a few seconds. To do this, the player must rapidly switch attention between external and internal sources of information.

However, certain kinds of attention switching can be a disadvantage in the performance of some activities. For example, a person performing a skill that requires a rapid, accurate series of movements, such as typing, piano playing, or dancing, will be more successful if he or she focuses attention on a primary source of information for extended periods of time. Problems can arise if the person's attention

A CLOSER LOOK

An Attention-Related Strategy for Preparing to Perform a Closed Skill

Based on a review of research related to attention and performance, Singer and colleagues (Singer et al., 1991) presented a three-component strategy that should be employed by people as they prepare to perform a closed skill. People can use this strategy when performing a variety of sport skills (e.g., shooting a free throw in basketball, serving in tennis or badminton, shooting in archery and gun sports, hitting a golf ball) and everyday skills (e.g., getting out of bed, getting out of a chair, walking along a designated pathway, buttoning a jacket).

Those who use this strategy engage in three activities just prior to performing a skill:

1. **Relaxation** involves using breathing control and muscle relaxation to reduce tensions, to enhance attention focus and develop an optimal arousal level.
2. **Visualization** involves mentally seeing and feeling the desired performance before actually performing it.
3. **Focus** involves concentrating on a positive aspect of task performance that is vital to performing effectively.

is switched too frequently between appropriate and inappropriate sources of information. For example, if a pianist is constantly switching visual attention from the written music to the hands and keys, he or she will have difficulty maintaining the precise timing structure required by the piece being played.

Attention and Automaticity

Automaticity is an important concept in our understanding of attention and motor skill performance. The term **automaticity** is commonly used to indicate that a person performs a skill or engages in an information-processing activity without demands on attention capacity. We briefly considered the attention capacity demands of a skill in the discussion of the evaluation of the task demands component of Kahneman's model of attention. Information-processing activities include the visual search of the environment that occurs as a person assesses the environmental context regulatory characteristics associated with performing a skill; the use of *tau* when moving toward an object to make or avoid contact with it, or an object is moving toward a person who needs to catch or strike it; the storing of information in memory and the retrieval of information from memory; the selection of an action to perform and the movement characteristics that must be applied to carry out the action; and the actual production of an action. From an attention point of

view, the question of interest with regard to these activities concerns the attention capacity demand of each activity.

Logan (1985, 1988, 1998), who has produced some of the most important research and thinking about the concept of automaticity and motor skill performance, views automaticity as an acquired skill that should be viewed as a continuum of varying degrees of automaticity. This means that rather than considering the attention capacity demand of an information-processing activity in terms of "yes, it demands capacity," or "no, it doesn't demand capacity," the continuum view considers automaticity as related to demanding varying amounts of attention capacity. Logan proposes that, similar to a skill, people acquire automaticity with practice. As a result, the degree of automaticity for a skill or information-processing activity may be only partially automatic when the attention demand of the activity is assessed.

An important skill learning question that comes out of this view is: *How automated do complex skills*

---

automaticity   the term used to indicate that a person performs a skill, or engages in certain information-processing activities, without requiring attention resources.

become? Some skills such as performing a dance or gymnastics routine or playing a piano piece, are highly complex. Do these become automated throughout the piece so that little, if any, attention is needed? The more likely response to this question is that the performer develops automated "chunks" of the entire piece. These chunks are parts of the piece that have been put together into groups and performed with little attention required within the chunks. Attention appears to be demanded, however, at the beginning or initiation of each chunk.

Anecdotal evidence for this view comes from discussions with skilled individuals. During performances, individuals indicate that they perform many parts of a routine without thinking about these parts. However, these performers indicate that there are also places in the routine to which they must direct conscious attention. Those places seem to be identified by distinct characteristics. The dancer may attend to the place where the tempo changes or a partner must be contacted or lifted; the pianist may attend to tempo changes. The gymnast may direct attention to parts of the routine that would be dangerous if missed. All of these individuals indicate that they give attention to parts of the routine with which they have had difficulty.

SUMMARY

We have considered attention as our capacity to engage in the perceptual, cognitive, and motor activities associated with performing skills. People have a limited capacity to engage in these activities. As a result, we often have difficulty performing more than one task at a time. The most popular theories of attention limits propose that we have a limited capacity to process information. Some theories consider this limitation to be a central pool of attentional resources. For example, Kahneman's flexible limited-capacity model proposes that attentional resources are allocated from a single pool. The amount of resources available at any given time is determined by the person's arousal level. An optimal arousal level yields the maxi-

mum amount of attentional resources. Allocation of resources is influenced by several factors related to the individual and to the activities to be performed. Multiple-resource theories arise from an alternative view that proposes several resources from which attention can be allocated. The typical experimental procedures used to investigate attentional demands of skill performance are called dual-task procedures.

An important aspect of attention and motor skill performance is *attentional focus:* where and how a person directs his or her attention in a performance situation. Attention can be focused either broadly or narrowly, and either externally, on some aspect of the environmental situation, or internally, on some aspect of the skill preparation or performance. People can switch focus quickly among these widths and directions.

Automaticity is an important attention-related concept. In terms of the performance of motor skills, automaticity relates primarily to skilled performance in which the person can implement knowledge and procedures with little or no demand on attention capacity.

RELATED READINGS

Abernethy, B. (1988). Dual-task methodology and motor skills research: Some applications and methodological constraints. *Journal of Human Movement Studies, 14,* 101–132.

Bourdin, C., Teasdale, N., & Nougier, V. (1998). Attentional demands and the organization of reaching movements in rock climbing. *Research Quarterly for Exercise and Sport, 69,* 406–410.

Briem, V., & Hedman, L. R. (1995). Behavioural effects of mobile telephone use during simulated driving. *Ergonomics, 38,* 2536–2562.

Peters, M. (1994). When can attention not be divided? *Journal of Motor Behavior, 26,* 196–199.

van Gemmert, A. W. A., Teulings, H. L., & Stelmach, G. E. (1998). The influence of mental and motor load on handwriting movements in Parkinsonian patients. *Acta Psychologica, 100,* 161–175.

Spikman, J. M., Timmerman, M. E., van Zomeren, A. H., & Deelman, B. G. (1999). Recovery versus retest effects in attention after closed head injury. *Journal of Clinical Experimental Neuropsychology, 21,* 585–605.

Whitall, J. (1996). On the interaction of concurrent verbal and manual tasks: Which initial task conditions produce interference? *Research Quarterly for Exercise and Sport, 67,* 349–354.

STUDY QUESTIONS

1. Discuss the similarities and differences between fixed and flexible central-resource theories of attention capacity.

2. Describe a motor skill situation in which two or more actions must be performed simultaneously, and then discuss how Kahneman's model of attention could be applied to the situation to explain conditions in which all the actions could be performed simultaneously and when they could not be.

3. Discuss two different dual-task techniques that researchers use to assess the attention demands of performing a motor skill. Give an example of each.

4. (a) Describe the different types of attention focus a person can employ when performing a motor skill. (b) For each type, describe a motor skill situation in which that type of focus would be preferred.

5. What is the meaning of the term *automaticity* as it relates to attention and the performance of motor skills? Give an example.

CHAPTER

Visual Selective Attention

Concept: Visual selective attention plays an important role in preparing and performing many motor skills

APPLICATION

To carry out many of the motor skills you use in your daily activities, you need to visually attend to specific features of the environmental context before actually carrying out the actions. For example, when you reach for a cup to drink the coffee in it, you visually note where the cup is and how full it is before you reach to pick it up. When you put your door key into the keyhole, you first look to see exactly where it is. When you need to maneuver around people and objects as you walk along a corridor, you look to see where they are, what direction they are moving in, and how fast they are going. To drive your car, you also must visually select information from the environment so that you can get safely to your destination.

In sport activities, visual attention to environmental context information is also essential. For many skills, unless athletes attend to critical cues first, their performance success is seriously impaired. For example, visually attending to ball- and server-based cues allows the player to prepare to hit a return shot in tennis or racquetball. Skills such as determining where to direct a pass in soccer or hockey, or deciding which type of move to put on a defender in basketball or football, are all dependent on a player's success-

ful attention to the visual cues prior to initiating action.

In each of these daily living and sport activities, vision plays a critical role in preparing a person to perform a skill. Visually searching the environment helps the individual obtain information he or she needs to make decisions about which actions to produce, how to carry out the actions, and when to initiate the actions.

DISCUSSION

The consideration of visual selective attention extends the discussion of chapter 6, in which you saw that vision plays an important role in the control of motor skills. Visual selective attention concerns the role vision plays in motor skill performance in directing visual attention to environmental information (sometimes referred to as "cues") that influences the preparation and/or the performance of an action. Researchers have disputed since the end of the nineteenth century about whether visual selective attention is active or passive (sometimes phrased as "top-down or bottom-up," or "goal directed or stimulus driven"). That is, do we visually select relevant environmental cues according to our action intentions and

goals, or do we visually attend to environmental cues because of their distinctiveness or meaningfulness in the situation? In their review of the visual attention research literature, Egeth and Yantis (1997) concluded that these two types of visual attention control "almost invariably interact" (p. 270). This means that in most performance situations, our intentions and goals as well as certain characteristics in the environment influence visual attention. In other words, although we may actively seek environmental cues based on our action intentions and goals, we may also attend to certain cues because of their distinct characteristics. You will see evidence of this active-passive visual attention throughout this discussion.

The term **visual search** is used to describe the process of directing visual attention to locate relevant environmental cues. During the preparation process for performing many skills, people carry out visual search to select from the environment those cues that are relevant for the performance of a skill in a specific situation. In the following sections, we discuss the actual process of selecting appropriate information from the environment, and give examples from various sport and everyday skills to illustrate how visual search is an important component of the performance of both open and closed motor skills.

Procedures for Investigating Visual Search in Motor Skills

Before considering the visual search process itself, we will examine how researchers have investigated visual selective attention as it relates to performing motor skills. Three experimental procedures have become popular for determining the visual search strategies used in skill performance situations. Two involve video simulation of a skill performance situation. The third involves monitoring of the person's eye movements as he or she performs a skill. A fourth technique, *which will not be discussed* has yet to be used for visual search research purposes, but holds much promise. It is the use of virtual reality devices.

Video simulation techniques. In one popular technique for investigating visual search, researchers videotape real skill performance situations and then use the video to simulate the real situation. In the testing situation, the participant observes the video (or sometimes a film or a series of slides), and then is asked to perform specific actions as if he or she were actually in that situation. For example, a tennis player may be asked to act as if he or she is actually receiving the serve of the tennis player in the video. For the action component, the participant may be required to designate as quickly as possible the ball's landing position on the court of the serve.

Researchers have used two different procedures in the video simulation technique. Each determines one of two characteristics of the visual search process. One procedure assesses the amount of time the person takes to select the information he or she needs in order to respond. The other determines which characteristics of the observed performance the person uses to make a correct response.

The procedure for addressing the time issue is the *temporal occlusion procedure.* The film or video stops at various time points during the action and the observer is required to make a response. An excellent example of the use of this procedure is in an experiment by Abernethy and Russell (1987), in which badminton players watched film sequences of a player making different shots. When the film stopped, participants marked their predictions of the landing positions of the shuttle. To determine when in the course of the observed action the participants made their decisions, the film stopped at different times prior to, during, and after ball contact. By noting the relationship between the accuracy of a participant's predicted shuttle landing location and the moment he or she made the decision, the researchers could determine when in the time course of the observed action the participant

---

visual search the process of directing visual attention to locate relevant information in the environment that will enable a person to determine how to prepare and perform a skill in a specific situation.

FIGURE 9.1   Examples of what subjects saw in the Abernethy and Russell experiment when they watched a film of a badminton serve where various parts of the serving action were masked and could not be seen.   [*Source:* Abernethy, B., & Russell, D.G. (1987). Expert-novice differences in an applied selective attention task. *Journal of Sport Psychology, 9,* 326–345.]

had picked up by visual search the information needed to make a decision.

To identify the specific information a person uses to make the required response, researchers use the *event occlusion procedure.* Parts of each frame of film or video are masked so that the observer cannot see selected parts of the action. Figure 9.1 presents an example of this procedure, taken from the second part of the Abernethy and Russell (1987) study. In their experiment, participants predicted the landing location of the shuttle when they could not see the arm and racquet, racquet, head, or

legs of the person hitting the shuttle. The logic of this approach is that if the person performs worse without being able to see a specific feature of the opponent's action, then that feature includes the visual information the person uses to determine the location of the shot.

Eye movement recording technique.   Another experimental procedure researchers use to investigate visual attention in motor skills is *eye movement recording.* This procedure requires the use of specialized equipment that tracks the movement of the eyes and records where the eyes are "looking" at a particular time. A researcher can record the displacement of *central vision* for a specific time interval, as well as the place and the length of time the person fixates his or her gaze while tracking. One way researchers use this technique is to have the participant observe a film simulation of a performance situation and then make a response. The movement of the eye is then plotted on the film scene to determine the spatial location of the participant's eye movements (displacement), along with his or her gaze fixation characteristics related to observing the serving action. A more difficult way to use this procedure is to record eye movements while a person is actually performing a skill in the performance setting. Later in this discussion, we will discuss several examples of experiments that have used the eye movement recording technique.

Eye movements and visual attention. Although eye movement recordings track the displacement characteristics of central vision while people observe a scene, an important question arises concerning how well this procedure assesses visual attention. The logic underlying the use of the procedure is that what a person is looking at should give researchers insight into what information in the environment the person is attending to. But there is an important research question here: Is this a valid assumption? Can we validly relate eye movements to visual attention?

Two characteristics of the use of eye movement recordings provide an answer. First, research evidence (see Henderson, 1996, and Zelinsky et al., 1997, for reviews of this evidence) has shown consistently that it is possible to give attention to a feature in the environment without moving the eyes to focus on that feature. However, it is *not* possible to make an eye movement without a corresponding shift in attention. Second, because eye movement recordings are limited to the assessment of central vision, they do not assess peripheral vision. Research evidence has shown that peripheral vision is involved in visual attention in motor skill performance (see Bard, Fleury, & Goulet, 1994 for

a brief review of this research). As a result of these two factors, eye movement recordings cannot provide a complete picture of the environmental features to which the person is directing visual attention, which leads to an *underestimation* of what a person is visually attending to. However, even with these limitations, the recording of eye movements is a useful technique to provide good estimates of those features in the environment that a person directs visual attention to as he or she prepares and performs a motor skill.

How We Select Visual Cues

Theories concerning how we select certain cues in the environment address the selection of cues for nonmoving as well as moving objects. Both situations are important for the performance of motor skills. For example, visual search for regulatory characteristics of stationary objects is critical for successful prehension actions. Without detection of these characteristics a person would not have the information needed to prepare and initiate movement to reach for and grasp a cup, or any stationary object.

One of the more popular theories that is specifically concerned with this type of visual search is the *feature integration theory* proposed by Treisman in the 1980s (e.g., Treisman & Gelade 1980; Treisman 1988). This view indicates that during visual search, we initially group stimuli together according to their unique features, such as color or shape. This grouping occurs automatically. These groups of features form "maps" related to the various values of various features. For example, a color map would identify the various colors in the observed scene, whereas a shape map would indicate which shapes are observed. These maps become the basis for further search processes when the task demands that the person identify specific cues. For further processing, we must use attention, and must direct it to selecting specific features of interest.

The selection of features of interest occurs when a person focuses the *attentional spotlight* on the master map of all features. People can direct

A CLOSER LOOK

Visual Search and Attention Allocation Rules

If the key to successful selection of environmental information when performing motor skills is the distinctiveness of the relevant features, an important question is this:

What Makes Certain Features More Distinctive than Others?

Insight into answering this question comes from the attention allocation rules in Kahneman's theory of attention (1973), which were discussed in chapter 8:

- **Unexpected features attract our attention.** You can see this in your own daily experience. While concentrating on your professor during a lecture, haven't you been distracted when a classmate has dropped some books on the floor? Undoubtedly,

you switched your visual attention from the professor to search for the source of the noise. When the environment includes features that typically are not there, the distinctiveness of those features increases. The result is that people have a tendency to direct visual attention to them.

- **We allocate attention to the most meaningful features.** In the performance environment, the most meaningful cues "pop out" and become very evident to the performer. Meaningfulness is a product of experience and instruction. As a person experiences performing in certain environments, critical cues for successful performance are invariant and increase in their meaningfulness, often without the person's conscious awareness. Instruction also plays a part in the way certain features of cues become more meaningful than others.

---

attention over a wide or a narrow area, and it appears that the spotlight can be split to cover different map areas. If the person's task is to search for a target having a certain distinct feature, then the target will "pop out" as a result of this search process, because the feature is distinct among the groupings of features. Thus, the more distinctive the feature is that identifies the target of the visual search, the more quickly the person can identify and locate the target. If the distinctive feature is a part of several cues, the search slows as the person assesses each cue in terms of how its characteristics match those of the target.

For movement situations McLeod, Driver, Dienes, and Crisp (1991) proposed a *movement filter* in the visual system that would allow visual attention to be directed at just the moving items in the person's environment. They suggested that this movement filter mechanism can be related to Treisman's feature integration theory's emphasis on the importance of grouping in visual search by operating as a subsystem to a group's common movement characteristics. In light of this view it is interesting to note that Abernethy (1993) described research evidence to

demonstrate that in sports involving fast ball action, such as racquet sports, skilled players visually search the playing environment for the "minimal essential information" necessary to determine an action to perform. This information has been shown to be the invariant perceptual features of a situation. We described one of these invariant features in chapter 6 when we discussed the importance of the use of time-to-contact information to catch a ball, contact or avoid an object while walking or running, and strike a moving ball.

Abernethy adds to this example of minimal essential information the detection of the coordination kinematics of an opponent's action, which involves the grouping of displacement characteristics of the joints involved in a coordinated movement pattern. As a person becomes more skillful, his or her visual attention becomes increasingly more attuned to detecting the important kinematic features, which provides the skilled player an advantage over the less-skilled player in anticipating the opponent's action in a situation. In effect then, this minimal essential information "pops out" for the skilled player, and directs the player's visual

A CLOSER LOOK

Two Examples of Severe Time Constraints on Visual Search

There are some situations in sport in which researchers can determine the actual amount of time a person has to engage in visual search and to prepare an action. Two of these are returning a serve in tennis and hitting a baseball. In each of these situations, it is clearly to the player's advantage to detect the information needed as early as possible in order to prepare and initiate the appropriate action.

Preparing to Return a Tennis Serve

A serve traveling at 90 to 100 mi/hr (145 to 161 km/hr) allows the receiver only 0.5 to 0.6 sec to hit the ball. This means that the person must search as soon as pos-

sible for the cues that will provide information about the direction, speed, landing point, and bounce characteristics of the ball so that he or she can select, organize, and execute an appropriate return stroke.

Preparing to Hit a Baseball

When a pitcher throws a ball at a speed of 90 mph, it will arrive at home plate in approximately 0.45 sec. Suppose that it takes 0.1 sec for the batter to get his or her bat to the desired point of ball contact. This means that the batter has less than 0.35 sec after the ball leaves the pitcher's hand to make a decision and to initiate the swing. If the pitcher releases the ball 10 to 15 ft in front of the rubber, the batter has less than 0.3 sec of decision and swing initiation time.

---

attention as he or she prepares an appropriate action to respond to his or her opponent's action.

Visual Search and Action Preparation

Visual search picks up critical cues that influence three parts of the action control process: *action selection, constraining of the selected action,* and *timing of action initiation.* By influencing these processes, the visual system enables a person to prepare and initiate an action that conforms to the specific requirements of the performance situation.

Research investigating visual search in performance situations has produced evidence about what is involved in these important preparation processes. The following research examples illustrate how researchers have investigated a variety of sports and everyday skills, and provide a sense of what we currently know about the characteristics of visual search processes related to the performance of open and closed motor skills.

Visual search in badminton. The experiments by Abernethy and Russell (1987) described earlier in this chapter provide the best example of research investigations of visual search by expert badminton

players. They found that the time between the initiation of the badminton server's backswing and the shuttle's hitting the floor in the receiver's court is approximately 400 msec (0.4 sec). Within that time period, there appears to be a critical time window for visually picking up critical cues predicting where the shuttle will land. This window, which lasts from about 83 msec before until 83 msec after racquet-shuttle contact, provides information about racquet movement and shuttle flight that seems to resolve uncertainty about where the served shuttle will land. Experts use the 83-msec period prior to racquet-shuttle contact more effectively than novices. As a result, experts have more time to prepare their returns. The racquet and the arm are the primary sources to visually search for the anticipatory cues needed to prepare the return.

Visual search in baseball batting. An example of research describing characteristics of the visual search processes involved in baseball batting is a study by Shank and Haywood (1987). They recorded eye movements for college and novice players as they watched a videotape of a right-handed pitcher as if they were right-handed batters.

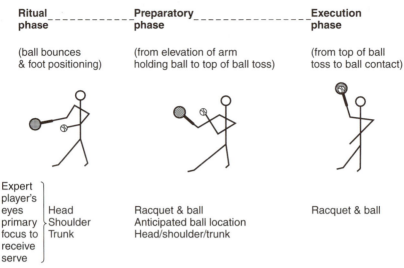

Ritual phase (ball bounces & foot positioning) — Preparatory phase (from elevation of arm holding ball to top of ball toss) — Execution phase (from top of ball toss to ball contact)

Expert player's eyes primary focus to receive serve } Head Shoulder Trunk

Racquet & ball
Anticipated ball location
Head/shoulder/trunk

Racquet & ball

FIGURE 9.2   Illustration showing where expert tennis players in the Goulet, Bard, and Fleury experiment were looking during the three phases of a tennis serve.   [*Source:* Based on discussion in Goulet, C., et al. (1989). Expertise differences in preparing to return a tennis serve: A visual information processing approach. *Journal of Sport and Exercise Psychology, 11,* 382–398.]

Twenty randomly presented fastballs and curves from both the windup and stretch positions were observed. For each pitch, the players' task was to indicate verbally if the pitch was a fastball or a curve. The expert players correctly identified almost every pitch, whereas the novices were correct only about 60 percent of the time. Participants in both groups did not begin to track the ball until about 150 msec after the ball had left the pitcher's hand. During the windup, experts fixated on the release point, whereas novices tended to shift fixations from the release point to the pitcher's head. These results show that the expert batter, knowing where the most relevant cues are prior to the release of a pitch, visually attends to the release point and ignores other possible sources of information prior to the release.

Visual search in returning a tennis serve.
Results from two experiments by Goulet, Bard, and Fleury (1989) demonstrate how critical visual search strategies are to preparing to return tennis serves. Expert and novice tennis players watched a

film showing a person serving and were asked to identify the type of serve as quickly as possible. The authors recorded the participants' eye movements as they watched the film. Three phases of the serve were of particular interest: the "ritual phase" (the 3.5 sec preceding the initiation of the serve); the "preparatory phase" (the time between the elevation of the arm for the ball toss and the ball's reaching the top of the toss); and the "execution phase" (from the ball toss to racquet-ball contact).

As illustrated in figure 9.2, during the ritual phase, the expert players focused mainly on the head and the shoulder/trunk complex, where general body position cues could be found. During the preparatory phase, they directed visual search primarily around the racquet and ball, where it remained until ball contact. An interesting note was that the experts also looked at the server's feet and knees during the preparatory phase. The important difference between experts and novices was that the visual search patterns of the expert players allowed them to correctly identify the serve sooner than novices could.

In an effort to investigate the visual search characteristics of expert players in a more realistic setting, Singer et al. (1998) assessed the eye movement behaviors of five nationally ranked university male and female tennis players as they returned ten serves on a tennis court. Interestingly, all five players did not use the same visual search strategies. During the phases of the serve that Goulet et al. (1989) called the ritual and preparatory phases, the two highest-ranked players fixated primarily on the arm-racquet-shoulder region of the server, whereas two fixated on the racquet and expected ball toss area. All the players included head fixations during these phases. The players demonstrated more individual variation during the ball toss phase of the serve. Two players visually tracked the ball from the server's hand to the highest point of the toss, one player made a visual jump from the server's hand to the highest point of the toss, one player fixated only on the predicted highest point of the toss, and one player did not fixate on the ball toss but only on the racquet. Differences again were found for the visual search strategies used by the players after the server hit the ball. The two highest-ranked players visually tracked the ball to its landing location, two players did not track the ball after contact but visually jumped to the predicted landing location, and one player used a combination of these two strategies to return serves.

When compared to the Goulet et al. (1989) results, the Singer et al. (1998) study shows that expert players exhibit more individual variation in their visual search strategies than Goulet and his colleagues reported. With this qualification in mind, it is important to note that the description of visual search characteristics of expert tennis players presented in figure 9.2 can be viewed as a general description of these characteristics; individual players may not match them completely. However, both studies, in keeping with others reported in the research literature, illustrate the importance of a person focusing visual search on specific features in the environment as early as possible to obtain essential information for the preparation of an appropriate action.

Visual search in soccer actions. To determine whether to shoot, pass, or dribble in soccer, the player must use visual search that is different from that involved in the situations described above. The soccer situation involves many players in the visual scene that must be searched for relevant cues. An experiment by Helsen and Pauwels (1990) provides a good demonstration of visual search patterns used by experienced and inexperienced male players to determine these actions. Participants acted as ball handlers as they viewed slides of typical attacking situations. For each, the person indicated as quickly as possible whether he would shoot at the goal, dribble around the goalkeeper or opponent, or pass to a teammate. As expected, the experts took less time to make the decision. More important, eye-tracking results showed that the experts gained this time advantage because they knew what to look for in a scene. Although the visual search patterns of the experts and the novices were similar, the experts fixated on fewer features of the scene and spent less time at each fixation.

Another visual search situation in soccer involves anticipating where a pass will go. Williams, Davids, Burwitz, and Williams (1994) showed that experienced players and inexperienced players look at different environmental features to make this determination. Results based on subjects' eye-tracking characteristics while watching action from an actual soccer game showed that the experienced players fixated more on the positions and movements of other players, in addition to the ball and the ball handler. In contrast, inexperienced players typically fixated only on the ball and the ball handler.

Visual search when shooting a basketball free throw. Each of the sports skills just discussed is an open skill. Visual search was clearly an important part of the preparation for performing these skills. But visual search is important for closed skills as well. The free throw in basketball provides a good example of a closed skill in which the quality of the visual search prior to shooting the ball plays a critical role in the success of the shot. Vickers (1996) reported an experiment that nicely demonstrates this

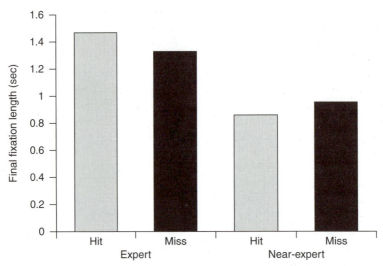

FIGURE 9.3   Results from Vickers (1996) showing expert and near-expert basketball players' mean duration of their final eye movement fixations just prior to releasing the ball during basketball free throws during shots they hit and missed. These final fixations were on the backboard or hoop.   [Modified figure 6 (p. 348) in Vickers, J. (1996). Visual control when aiming at a far target. *Journal of Experimental Psychology: Human Perception and Performance, 22,* 342–354. Copyright © 1996 the American Psychological Association. Adapted with permission.]

effect. She recorded the eye movements of elite Canadian women basketball players as they prepared to shoot, and then shot, free throws. Two results are especially noteworthy. First, the "experts" (they made an average of 75 percent of their free throws during the just-completed season) looked directly at the backboard or hoop for a longer period of time just prior to shooting the ball than did the "near experts" (they made an average of 42 percent of their free throws during the just-completed season). This was especially the case for the final eye movement fixation just prior to the release of the ball. Second, as can be seen in figure 9.3, the amount of time devoted to the final fixation prior to releasing the ball was related to the shooting success of the players Vickers classified as experts. They fixated on the backboard or hoop for just over 1.4 sec for shots they made, but almost 0.2 sec less for shots they missed. It is interesting to note that the final fixation duration for the near experts was just the opposite, with a longer fixation time on shots they missed

than made. Vickers interpreted this finding as evidence that the near experts did not fixate long enough just prior to the release of the ball for either the shots they made or missed to allow them to attain the shooting percentage of the expert.

Visual search when putting a golf ball.   Another closed skill that involves visual search as a part of the preparation for performing the skill is putting a golf ball. In another experiment by Vickers (1992), she reported eye movement data for lower-handicap golfers (0 to 8 handicaps) and higher-handicap golfers (10 to 16 handicaps). In golf, the lower-handicap golfers are more skilled than those with higher handicaps. Vickers reported that during a series of putts, several differences were found between these two groups during the preparation phase of each putt, which she defined as the interval of time just after the golfer completed positioning the ball and just before the initiation of the backswing of the putter. First, the low-handicap golfers had a shorter preparation phase (approximately 3.7 sec) than the high-handicap golfers (approximately 4.8 sec). Second, the low-handicap golfers directed more eye movement fixations to the ball during this phase than the high-handicap golfers, who directed more fixations to the putter. Third, there was a relationship between the eye movement fixation during the preparation phase and the success of a putt. Fixations on the club led to more missed putts, whereas fixations on the ball led to more successful putts.

Vickers also described an interesting point that is relevant to our discussion on visual attention. She noted that golfers generally are not consciously aware of eye movements during putting. Golfers tend to associate visual attention with head position, which means they consider a change in visual attention to be related to a change in head movement. However, their head movement to shift visual attention from one location to another is generally initiated by eye movement.

Visual search while driving a car.   Driving a car is a nonsport performance situation in which vision provides information to select and constrain action. In a study that is commonly cited as a demonstration of this role for vision, Mourant and Rockwell (1972) had novice and experienced drivers drive a 2.1-mi neighborhood route and a 4.3-mi freeway route. The novices were students in a driver education class. The results of the eye movement recordings showed that novice drivers concentrated their eye fixations in a small area more immediately in front of the car. More experienced drivers visually search a wider area that was further from the front of the car. This broader scanning range increases the probability for the detection of important cues in the environment. On the freeway, the novices made pursuit eye movements, whereas the experienced drivers made specific eye fixations that jumped from location to location. That is, the experienced drivers knew which cues were important and specifically searched for those cues. The experienced drivers looked into the rear- and side-view mirrors more frequently than the novices, whereas the novices looked at the speedometer more than the experienced drivers did.

More recently, Chapman and Underwood (1998) extended these findings. They monitored eye movements of novice and experienced drivers as they watched various driving-related scenes that included at least one dangerous situation. In these situations, both types of drivers narrowed their visual search and increased the durations of their eye movement fixations. But the more experienced drivers tended to fixate for shorter amounts of time on specific parts of the scene than the novice drivers. This result indicates that the more experienced drivers required less time to detect and process the information obtained from a fixation, which gives them an advantage in determining the appropriate driving action to take in the situation. In addition, the experienced drivers tended to be less variable in where they fixated their eye movements while watching the driving scenes, which, in agreement with the findings of Mourant and Rockwell (1972), indicates their greater knowledge of which environmental cues to look at to obtain the most relevant information.

Visual search during prehension while walking. When a person must walk to a table to pick up an object, such as a pen or book, visual search plays an important role in setting into motion the appropriate action coordination. An experiment by Cockrell, Carnahan, and McFayden (1995) demonstrated this role for visual search. Participants were required to walk 3.75 m to a table and pick up an aluminum can or a pencil as they walked by. Results showed that before they began any prehensive action, their eyes moved to fixate on the target. Head movement also preceded the initiation of reaching movements. Thus, the eyes' searching of the environment to determine the location and characteristics of the object started a chain of events to allow the participants to grasp the object successfully.

Visual search while locomoting through a cluttered environment. Walking and running through a cluttered environment can occur in everyday situations—we walk around furniture in

A CLOSER LOOK

A Visual Search Training Program to Teach Anticipation Skills in Squash

Abernethy, Wood, and Parks (1999) engaged university male and female students in a four-week training program designed to teach them to improve their anticipation skills in squash by improving their visual search strategies. None of the students had competitive experience in any racquet sport. The training program consisted of the following:

- A 20-min session of supervised perceptual training exercises related to squash on four days of each week. These exercises involved
  — formal instruction on the biomechanics of the forehand and backhand drives, which emphasized the proximal-to-distal development of stroke kinematics
  — formal instruction on locating the most important anticipatory cues for racquet sports and a brief summary of expert-novice differences in the use of these cues
  — practice in focusing on appropriate information sources in video sequences
  — practice in verbally predicting stroke direction and force from spatially occluded video

displays, with feedback given about prediction accuracy
  — practice on making anticipatory predictions from temporally occluded video displays, with feedback given about prediction accuracy
  — practice in which a simulated movement rather than verbal response was required to the video

- A 20-min session of supervised practice of squash on one day of each week. This practice session involved
  — hitting forehand drives while moving or stationary (balls were projected from a ball machine)

A posttest given after the completion of this training program showed that the participants improved their prediction accuracy for ball direction and location, and they were able to consistently make their predictions before ball contact in a temporal occlusion test. In addition, these participants performed these tasks better than other participants who had experienced a more general training program or who had experienced only physical practice of squash.

the house or walk through a crowded mall—and in sport situations: a player runs with a football or dribbles a basketball during a game. People's ability to maneuver through environments like these indicates that they have detected relevant cues and used them in advance to avoid collisions. Visual search is an important part of this process.

According to research by Cutting, Vishton, and Braren (1995), the most important cues involved in avoiding collision in these situations come from the relative location or motion of objects around the object the person needs to avoid. When visually fixating on the object he or she needs to avoid, the person uses relative-displacement and/or velocity information about both the object to be avoided and other objects in front of or behind the object. It is important to note that this decision making is

done automatically by the visual system and provides the basis for appropriate action by the motor control system. The key practical point here is that the person needs to visually fixate on the object or objects that he or she wishes to avoid.

Training Visual Search Strategies

Each of the motor skill performance examples discussed in the preceding section had in common the characteristic that people with more experience in an activity visually searched their environment and located essential information more effectively and efficiently than people with little experience. Therefore, we know that as people become more experienced and skilled in an activity, they acquire better visual search skills. How do people acquire this capability? In many cases, experience alone is the key factor in the acquisition of effective visual search strategies. These strategies are often acquired without specific training and without the person's conscious awareness of the strategies they use. But is it possible to facilitate the acquisition of effective search strategies by teaching novices to use strategies that experts use? A positive answer to this question would provide teachers, coaches, and physical rehabilitation therapists with guidance about how to more effectively design practice and intervention strategies.

Researchers have demonstrated the benefits of providing novices with instructions concerning what to look for and attend to, along with giving them a sufficient amount of practice implementing these instructions. A result of this type of intervention strategy is an increase in the probability that important environmental cues will "pop out" when the person is in the performance situation (see Czerwinski, Lightfoot, & Shiffrin, 1992). However, Abernethy, Wood, and Parks (1999) emphasized that it is essential for this type of training to be specific to an activity. They pointed out that research evidence has demonstrated the lack of benefit derived from generalized visual training programs, such as those often promoted by sports optometrists (e.g., Wood & Abernethy, 1997). The problem with a generalized training approach to the improvement of visual attention is that it ignores the general finding that experts recognize specific patterns in their activity more readily than do novices (a point that will be discussed in chapter 12).

Several examples of effective visual search training programs have been reported in the research literature (e.g., Abernethy, Wood, & Parks, 1999; Farrow, et al., 1998; Haskins, 1965; Singer et al., 1994). Each of these programs has been sport specific, and has shown that video-based simulations can serve as the basis for effective self-paced training of athletes outside of their organized practice time. However, as Abernethy, Wood, and Parks (1999) point out, the studies that have reported the effectiveness of these programs have not tested their efficacy in actual performance situations or in competition environments. Although these programs

show promise to benefit athletes' performance, it remains for researchers to establish that this type of visual search training will transfer to the sports performance environment. In addition, whether similar training programs could be effective in physical rehabilitation contexts to facilitate the performance of skills requiring visual search also remains to be determined.

SUMMARY

Visual attention to critical cues in the environment is an important part of preparing to perform a skill. An individual selects these cues by visually searching the environment for advance information that will enable the person to anticipate the action required in a situation. Effective visual search influences action selection, constraining of the selected action, and timing of action initiation. We have discussed examples of visual search in sports skill situations in badminton, baseball batting, tennis, soccer, basketball, and golf. We also discussed visual search in everyday skills such as driving a car, prehension, and walking or running through cluttered environments. Research evidence shows that activity-specific training can facilitate novices' use of effective visual search strategies.

RELATED READINGS

Abernethy, B. (1990). Anticipation in squash: Differences in advance cue utilization between expert and novice players. *Journal of Sports Science, 8,* 17–34.

Abernethy, B., & Burgess-Limerick, R. (1992). Visual information for the timing of skilled movements: A review. In J. J. Summers (Ed.), *Approaches to the study of motor control and learning* (pp. 343–384). Amsterdam: Elsevier.

Osborne, K., Rudrud, E., & Zezoney, F. (1990). Improved curveball hitting through the enhancement of visual cues. *Journal of Applied Behavior Analysis, 23,* 371–377.

Rayner, K. (1998). Eye movements in reading and information processing: 20 years of research. *Psychological Bulletin, 124,* 372–422.

Tenenbaum, G., Levy-Kolker, N., Sade, S., Liebermann, D. G., & Lidor, R. (1996). Anticipation and confidence of decisions related to skilled performance. *International Journal of Sport Psychology, 27,* 293–307.

Williams, A. M., & David, K. (1998). Visual search strategy, selective attention, and expertise in soccer. *Research Quarterly for Exercise and Sport, 69,* 111–128.

STUDY QUESTIONS

1. What is the meaning of the term *visual search* when it applies to the performance of a motor skill? Give an example.

2. (a) Describe two different types of video simulation techniques and the eye-movement recording technique that can be used to help us understand visual search in a motor skill performance situation. (b) What are the benefits and limitations of each of these three techniques?

3. Discuss how skilled performers engage in visual search in the performance of four different types of motor skills.

CHAPTER

Memory Components, Forgetting, and Strategies

*Concept: Memory storage and retrieval
influence motor skill learning and performance*

APPLICATION

Have you ever had the experience of calling an information operator to ask for a telephone number and then found out that you didn't have a pen? Hurriedly, you dialed the number as quickly as possible after the operator gave it to you. Why did you do this? "Obviously," you say, "because I would have forgotten it if I hadn't dialed right away." Do you need to do this with your home telephone number? You can quite readily recall your home number at almost any time, without any assistance.

Consider a few other memory situations. When you are at a party and you are introduced to someone, you often find it very difficult to recall that person's name, even a very short time later. Compare that to remembering a teacher's name from your elementary school. You can probably name most of your teachers with little difficulty. Consider also a situation when you were shown how to serve a tennis ball for the first time. When you tried it, you found that you had some difficulty remembering all the things that you were supposed to do to perform a successful serve. That situation differs quite drastically from how well you can hop onto a bicycle, even after you have not been on one for many years, and ride it down the street.

The situations described here point out an important characteristic of human memory; its

structure involves a distinction in how permanently information is stored. Information may be only temporarily stored or it may be more permanently stored. The telephone number you received from the information operator and the tennis serve instructions you received before you tried to serve were stored in a temporary memory storage system, whereas your home number is kept more permanently in a long-term memory storage system.

In each of the examples just described, information in memory was forgotten to some degree. Information in one memory storage system was forgotten more easily than in another, and different types of information were forgotten in various amounts in the long-term storage system. The question of interest here is, what are the causes of forgetting? A related question is, what can I do to decrease the amount of forgetting and increase how much I remember? Fortunately, researchers have discovered answers to these questions, which have direct applications to motor skill instruction situations.

In the discussion that follows, we will consider these various issues and questions concerning human memory as it applies to the learning and performance of motor skills. First, we will discuss the different storage systems included in memory. We will then build on this foundation by considering the issue of the causes of forgetting, and finally

141

address how these causes can be overcome by the use of strategies that can help develop a more durable and accessible memory for the skills being learned.

DISCUSSION

Memory plays an important role in virtually all our daily activities Whether in conversation with a friend, working mathematical problems, or playing tennis, we are confronted by situations that require the use of memory to produce action.

What is memory? We often think of memory as being synonymous with the words *retention* or *remembering.* As such, most people consider that the word *memory* indicates a capacity to remember. Endel Tulving (1985), a leading contemporary memory researcher and theorist, stated that **memory** is the "capacity that permits organisms to benefit from their past experiences" (p. 385). Given this view, it is not surprising that the study of human memory involves a variety of topics. In this discussion, we will look at several of these topics by looking into memory issues that are relevant to the study of motor learning.

Some Introductory Issues

Before considering the various topics to be discussed in our study of memory, it will be helpful to first clarify two issues concerning terminology that could cause confusion as you progress through this discussion.

Motor memory and verbal memory. The first issue concerns the use of two terms used frequently in the research literature related to human memory: *motor memory* and *verbal memory.* These expressions seem to imply that motor and verbal memory are separate entities. We will consider the memory for motor skills and for verbal skills as being part of the same memory system. Research evidence shows that people can have memory problems in performing certain activities that are related to verbal skills while still being able to perform certain motor activities. For example, some head injury

patients have been shown to have difficulty recalling words they had just seen but had no difficulty putting together pieces of a puzzle. On the other hand, there are situations where memory functions related to performing both verbal and motor skills are impaired by an injury. This suggests then, that human memory consists of components, or modules, that are designed to deal with certain types of information. However, these modules interact in ways that allow us to engage in our daily activities. This means that memory modules are both information specific and interactive. This arrangement allows the memory system to be adaptable to the demands of a variety of situations in which memory functions are important.

Retention and forgetting. The second issue concerns the meanings of two terms common to any discussion about memory. These terms, *retention* and *forgetting,* are closely related. In fact, it could be said that they are opposites. Retention refers to what we remember while forgetting refers to what we do not remember. However, a potential problem exists when we use the term forgetting. The problem is that this term can mean two different things. When we say that something has been "forgotten," we indicate that we cannot remember something. But, in terms of relating this statement to human memory functions, it can mean that the information either is not in memory or is in memory but unretrievable at the moment.

Consider an example that illustrates this problem. Suppose you were asked a question on a test, such as "In what city is the world's tallest building located?" You remember having studied this but right now you are unable to answer the question. You say, "I forget." But does your inability to answer mean that the information is not in memory, or that you just can't retrieve it? This distinction is important if we are to understand human memory. We must know which is the case in this forgetting situation if we are to understand memory functions. To get at the meaning of "I forget" in this case, the same question could be presented in a multiple-choice format. Suppose that you are now able to select the correct answer. This would indicate that the information needed to answer the question was in fact in memory. However, you needed something to help you locate that information. Seeing the correct answer among several alternatives enabled you to remember the answer to the question. Keep this problem about the definition of forgetting in mind because it will be a recurring theme in various discussions in this chapter and in other parts of this book.

Memory Structure

Views about the structure of memory have gone through many different phases throughout the history of the study of memory, which can be traced back to the early Greek philosophers. However, one characteristic of memory structure that is now commonly accepted is that a part of memory is oriented toward events that have just occurred while a part is related to information about events in the past. This is not a new idea. In fact, in 1890, William James wrote of an "elementary" or "primary" memory that makes us aware of the "just past." He distinguished this from a "secondary memory" that is for "properly recollected objects." To primary memory, James allocated items that are lost and never brought back into consciousness; whereas to secondary memory, he allocated ideas or data that are never lost. Although they may be "absent from consciousness," they are capable of being recalled.

The debate about the structure of memory has centered around how this distinction between memory for immediate things and for things in a more distant past fits into a structural arrangement in memory. Is the memory for the immediate or "just past" a special function of one unitary memory system, or is it a separate component of memory that is distinct from the component responsible for remembering information from the more distant past? You might think of this issue as attempting to describe the functional anatomy of human memory.

At present, the bulk of the evidence points to the latter of these viewpoints. That is, there are two components of memory.* The evidence for this comes

from two different but complementary research approaches to the study of human memory. One of these is taken from the study of cognitive psychology where inferences about the structure and function of memory are based on observing the behavior of individuals in memory situations. The other approach is that of the neuropsychologist or neurophysiologist, who is interested in explaining the structure of memory in terms of what is occurring in the nervous system during behavioral changes related to memory. Research evidence from both of these approaches provides convincing evidence that the memory system comprises at least two components that are definable by their distinct functions. Also, it is important to note that after reviewing and evaluating the relevant research literature, Healy and McNamara (1996) concluded that although some elaboration of various aspects of the component model of memory is needed, the model remains a useful means of understanding human memory.

A two-component memory model.   Several different models of human memory have been developed to represent its component structure. One of the most enduring and influential was presented by Atkinson and Shiffrin in 1968. Using a computer analogy, they conjectured that memory structure should be thought of as similar to computer hardware. They considered that the software that allows the computer to function are "control processes," which involve memory processes such as storage and retrieval of information, and are under the control of the person. The structural

---

*Although some models and discussions of memory include "sensory memory" as a third component, its role in motor skill learning and performance has not been well established. As a result, it is not included in this discussion.

---

memory   (a) our capacity to remember or be influenced by past experiences; (b) a component of the information-processing system in which information is stored and processed.

components, they concluded, comprise a sensory register, short-term store, and long-term store.

Since the time of Atkinson and Shiffrin's presentation of theory of memory structures, the primary theoretical problem has been to determine the exact nature of these structures. While debate continues about memory structure, there is general agreement that this structure of memory should include different memory storage components in addition to serving a functional role for what the person does with the information in each component. Such a view bases remembering and forgetting on the characteristics of the memory component in which the information resides and on the characteristics of the processes operating in each component.

One approach that accommodates these characteristics was proposed by Baddeley (1986, 1995). According to this view, memory is seen as comprising two functional components, *working memory* and *long-term memory*. Each memory component is defined in terms of its functions. Although a number of different functions have been proposed, we will focus primarily on three types of processes: those that relate to putting information in memory (referred to as storage processes), getting information out of memory (referred to as retrieval processes), and functions involved in processing information residing in each component.

Working Memory

The **working memory** should be thought of as a system that incorporates characteristics and functions traditionally associated with sensory, perceptual, attentional, and short-term memory processes that are involved in processing information. Working memory acts in all situations requiring the temporary use and storage of information and the execution of memory and response production processes (see Baddeley, 1995).

Working memory functions. Working memory must be thought of both as a place where information is stored for a short time and as a functionally active structure where critical information-processing activity occurs. This functional characteristic of

working memory enables people to respond according to the demands of a "right now" situation. As such, working memory plays a critical role in decision making, problem solving, movement production and evaluation, and long-term memory function. With regard to influencing long-term memory function, working memory provides essential processing activity needed for the adequate transfer of information into long-term memory. Finally, it is important to note that an important working memory function is to serve as an *interactive workspace* where various memory processing activities can occur, such as integrating the information in working memory with information that has been retrieved from the more permanent, long-term memory.

Because working memory involves both storing and processing information, it is important to consider each function separately. In terms of storing information, two characteristics of working memory are essential to understand: the length of time information will remain in working memory, which is called *duration,* and the amount of information that will reside in working memory at any one time, which is called *capacity.* Each of these characteristics will be discussed in the following sections.

Duration. Our understanding of the duration of information in working memory is relatively recent in terms of the history of science. Peterson and Peterson (1959) were the earliest to report research related to the remembering of word presented one time each. They showed that we tend to lose information (i.e., forget) from working memory after about only 20 to 30 sec. The first experiment published relating working memory to motor skills was by Adams and Dijkstra in 1966. Results of their experiment indicated that arm positions in space that are experienced one time each are lost from working memory at a rate comparable to that of words.

The results of many other studies that followed the Adams and Dijkstra investigation generally supported the conclusion that the duration of movement information in working memory is about 20 to 30 sec. Information that is not processed further or rehearsed is lost.

A CLOSER LOOK

Pitching in Baseball: A Demonstration of the Interactive Work Space Function of Working Memory

The situation.   You are a baseball catcher or coach who needs to decide which pitch the pitcher should throw next. To make this decision, you must consider information about both the present situation and past experiences. In terms of the present situation you need to consider: *who the batter is, the score, who and where the runners on base are, the number of outs, the locations of defensive players in the infield and outfield, the ball and strike count,* and so on. In terms of past experiences you need to consider: *the batter's batting history in similar situations, the opposing team's tendencies in this situation—especially if they have runners on base, the pitcher's history of pitching in similar situations,* and so on.

Working memory involvement.   The working memory serves as a temporary work space to enable you to integrate the information about the present situation and past experiences so that you can select the best pitch for right now. After receiving your pitch choice, the pitcher will involve the working memory to retrieve from long-term memory the invariant characteristics of the type of pitch required, and then use the temporary work space to apply specific movement-related features to the pitch, such as speed and location. After the pitch is delivered, the information in working memory is deleted to provide space for new information to allow the pitcher to respond to what the batter does, or to throw the next pitch you select.

Capacity.   We are not only concerned with *how long* information will remain in short-term storage but also *how much* information we can accommodate. The issue of capacity in working memory was originally presented by George Miller in 1956, in an article that has become a classic in the memory literature. Miller provided evidence to indicate that we have the capacity to hold about *seven items (plus or minus two items)* such as words or digits, in short-term storage. To increase the "size" of an item in memory involves a control process termed *organization,* which we will consider later in this discussion. The newly created larger item, or "chunk" as Miller called it, enables people to recall far more than five to nine individual items at a time. However, with no practice or rehearsal of newly presented information, the capacity limit of working memory is five to nine individual items.

Although few researchers have investigated the capacity limits of working memory for motor skills, the available evidence agrees with the 7 ± 2 range proposed by Miller. For example, in one of the first investigations of this issue, Wilberg and Salmela (1973) reported that an eight-movement sequence of arm-positioning movements was the upper limit of working memory capacity for movements. More recently, Ille and Cadopi (1999) asked twelve- and thirteen-year-old female gymnasts to reproduce a sequence of discrete gymnastics movements after watching the sequence one time on a videotape. The gymnasts' recall performance demonstrated a six-movement capacity limit for the more-skilled gymnasts and a five-movement limit for the less-skilled gymnasts. The results for these young gymnasts are in line with those reported by Starkes, Deakin, Lindley, and Crisp (1987) for young skilled ballet dancers, who showed evidence that an eight-movement sequence was their capacity limit.

> **working memory**   a functional component of the structure of memory that operates to temporarily store and use recently presented information; it also serves as a temporary work space to integrate recently presented information with information retrieved from long-term memory so that problem-solving, decision-making, and action-preparation activities can be carried out as needed in a situation. It also serves as a processing center to transfer information to long-term memory.

A CLOSER LOOK

**Experimental Procedures to Assess
the Duration of Movement
Information in Working Memory**

The Adams and Dijkstra (1966) experiment set the
standard for the procedural protocol researchers have
used to investigate the question concerning the duration of movement information in working memory.
Because the researchers were interested in movement
information, their procedures were designed to
require participants to use only proprioceptive information to perform the task.

- **Apparatus.** An arm-positioning apparatus
  consisted of an almost friction-free handle that
  could be moved left or right along a metal
  trackway. This apparatus sat on a table facing the
  participant in the experiment.
- **Task.** To begin a trial, a blindfolded participant
  moved the handle of the apparatus along the
  trackway to a location specified by a physical
  block (the criterion arm position to be
  remembered). After returning the handle to the
  starting point and waiting for a certain amount of
  time (the retention interval) the participant
  performed a recall test by moving the handle to
  his or her estimate of the arm position just
  experienced (the physical block had been
  removed). The experimenter recorded the location
  and the participant returned the handle to begin a
  new trial, which involved moving to a new
  position along the trackway.
- **Determining duration.** To determine the length
  of time movement location information stayed in
  working memory, the researchers compared

various durations of the retention interval. They
determined the accuracy of the participants' recall
movements for each retention interval length.
Duration of the memory for the arm position was
assumed to be related to the degree of accuracy of
the recall movement. As you can see in figure 10.1
below, arm-positioning recall accuracy decreased
(i.e., error increased) very sharply for retention
intervals up to 20 sec, and continued to decrease
for longer interval lengths.

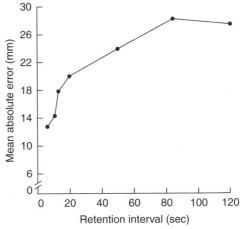

FIGURE 10.1   Results from the experiment by
Adams and Dijkstra showing the mean absolute error
for the recall of an arm-positioning task following
different lengths of retention intervals.   [From Adams,
J.A., & Dijkstra, S. (1966). Short-term memory for motor
responses. *Journal of Experimental Psychology, 71,* 314–318.
Copyright © 1966 by the American Psychological Association.
Reprinted with permission.]

To account for research evidence that has shown
that highly skilled individuals (i.e., experts) seem
to have a working memory capacity that is greater
than that of the general population, Ericsson and
Kintsch (1995) proposed a memory mechanism
they called *long-term working memory.* In addition
to having a larger working memory storage capacity, experts also show evidence that performing
certain secondary tasks does not interfere with their

performance of the activity at which they are
skilled. Experts in an activity use long-term working memory when they must have access to a large
amount of relevant knowledge at their disposal to
use while performing the activity. In addition, the
experts use long-term working memory to integrate
new information with previously acquired knowledge. It is important to note that as is commonly
characteristic of expertise (which we will discuss

more fully in chapter 12), long-term working memory is skill specific, which means that it develops as expertise in a skill rather than being a common component of working memory.

Processing activities. Information from the immediate past is processed in working memory so that it can be used to accomplish the goal of the problem at hand. The goal may be to remember what you have just been told or shown to do so that you can do the task. Or, you may need to use this information to solve a specific movement problem. And in both cases, you would like to remember what you did in each performance situation so that you can use your experience as a reference to help you in some future performance situation. In each case, you will involve working memory processing activities to enable you to achieve different goals.

Consider some examples of motor skill performance situations in which these different information uses could occur. Suppose your golf instructor has just given you a specific instruction to concentrate on your hand position as you swing a golf club. You must not only remember this instruction as you swing, but you must also retrieve from long-term memory the correct hand position and evaluate your present hand swing compared with the ideal. Of course, how successfully you make this comparison on your own depends on your stage of learning. But carrying out this verbal instruction invokes the working memory.

Suppose you have just watched a dancer perform a sequence of dance movements and you must now perform that sequence, which is a common occurrence in instruction and dance audition situations. Working memory processing activity would be involved because you must keep in memory the visually presented sequence of movements and translate that visual information into motor performance. Involved in this translation process would be retrieving from long-term memory the movement information required to carry out the sequence.

Consider also the following example. You are a patient in an occupational therapy session and are given a complex puzzle to put together. You study

the pieces and try to determine how the specific pieces fit together. You continually try to match pieces as in the completed puzzle. And you try to determine an appropriate movement strategy that would allow you to put the pieces together quickly and with little error. Working memory would be actively involved in this problem-solving situation because you carried out several activities requiring several different perception, remembering, and performance characteristics that must be done virtually simultaneously.

Other information-processing activities are also the function of working memory, such as preparing the information for storage in the more permanent long-term memory. In each of the examples just described, it would be to the performer's advantage to store in some permanent way information critical to performing the task at hand. Thus, it is important to be aware that working memory is more than a storage depository for newly presented information. It also serves a critical function as a work space so that the information in working memory can be processed to solve a problem, make a decision, or transfer the information to long-term memory.

Long-Term Memory

We are calling the second component of the structure of memory *long-term memory*. As indicated earlier, **long-term memory** is a more permanent storage repository of information. It is what we typically think of when the term *memory* is mentioned. William James (1890) considered long-term memory as "memory proper." This is the component of memory that contains information about specific past events as well as our general knowledge about the world.

In terms of the *duration* of information in long-term memory, it is generally accepted that the

---

long-term memory a component of the structure of memory that serves as a relatively permanent storage repository for information.

An Alternate View of Long-Term Memory Capacity: "When the Brain's Mailbox Is Full"

An article titled "When the Brain's Mailbox Is Full" appeared in *The New York Times On The Web** on July 27, 1999. The article described an experiment by Dr. H. Lee Swanson, from the University of California at Riverside, that takes issue with the commonly held view that long-term memory has a limitless capacity. Swanson's study, which was reported in the July 1999 issue of the research journal *Developmental Psychology,* found evidence he interpreted as indicating that "As we get older, we run out of places to store information. We have a limited amount of space in our memory system." The decrease in memory capacity, he said, begins around age forty-five for most people, although "not all 'mailboxes' are the same size and people organize them differently. We have different abilities in what we store and some of us are more efficient in what we can store." From an aging perspective, Swanson's view would indicate that when older people have memory lapses, it may not he due to a failure on the brain's part to adequately process information, but "may signal that a mailbox of memory is full."

Because Swanson's study is unique in finding evidence for such a memory capacity limitation, other scholars were quoted in the article as being skeptical about the reliability of the evidence. Dr. Timothy Salthouse, a highly regarded cognitive psychologist at Georgia Tech who investigates age-related memory and human performance, commented that one problem researchers face in the investigation of this issue is, "We don't know how to measure storage capacity." Dr. Robert L. Kahn, a retired psychology professor who coauthored the book *Successful Aging,* which was based on the study of aging by the MacArthur Foundation, rejected Swanson's ". . . mechanistic notion that treats the brain as a bunch of shelves and pigeonholes which run out of space." Instead, he preferred the concept of "the life-long elasticity of the human brain" and that training and mnemonic devices can sharpen memory skills.

*http://www.nytimes.com.

information resides in a relatively permanent state in long-term memory. (Note however a discussion of this by Loftus, 1980; Loftus & Loftus, 1980.) Usually, "forgotten" information that is stored in long-term memory is there, but the person is having difficulty locating it. Thus, measuring forgetting and remembering in long-term memory situations can be a tricky problem and one that often cannot be satisfactorily addressed by traditional recall and recognition tests. We will come back to this important point later in this chapter.

With regard to the *capacity* of long-term memory, it is generally agreed that there is a relatively unlimited capacity for information in long-term memory (e.g., Chase & Ericsson, 1982). In fact, we neither know how much information a person can store in memory nor know how to measure the capacity of long-term memory. An unlimited capacity leads to unique problems, however. For example, organization of information in memory becomes much more critical in an unlimited capacity system than in one of a limited capacity. Thus, there is a need to understand how people organize the information stored in long-term memory. This and other related issues unique to long-term memory will be discussed throughout this chapter.

In terms of information duration and capacity characteristics, it becomes obvious that long-term memory is distinct from working memory. Another distinct characteristic of long-term memory is the type of information that is stored there. In the following sections, three types of information stored in long-term memory will be discussed.

Procedural, episodic, and semantic memory.   In a commonly referred-to model of long-term memory, Tulving (1985) proposed that there are at least three "systems" in long-term memory: *procedural, episodic,* and *semantic* memories. Each of these systems differs in terms of how information is acquired, what information is included, how information is represented, how knowledge is expressed, and the kind of conscious awareness that characterizes the operations of the system. We will briefly consider each of these systems and how they function and differ.

Procedural memory may have the most direct relevance to our discussion of long-term memory because it relates specifically to storing information about motor skills. **Procedural memory** is best described as the memory system that enables us to know "how to do" something, as opposed to enabling us to know "what to do." This distinction is readily seen in situations where you can perform a skill very well (i.e., "how to do it"), but you are not able to verbally describe very well what you did (i.e., "what to do").

The procedural memory system enables us to respond adaptively to our environment by carrying out learned procedures so that we can achieve specific action goals. For the performance of motor skills, procedural memory is critical because motor skill is evaluated on the basis of producing an appropriate action, rather than simply verbalizing what to do. According to Tulving, an important characteristic of procedural memory is that procedural knowledge can only be acquired through "overt behavioral responses" which, for motor skills, means physical practice. Information stored in procedural memory serves as a "blueprint for future action."

Semantic memory is, according to Tulving, characterized by "representing states of the world that are not perceptually present" (p. 387). This means that we store in this memory system our general knowledge about the world that has developed from our many experiences. This includes specific factual knowledge, such as when Columbus discovered America or the name of the tallest building in America, as well as conceptual knowledge, such as our concepts of "dog" and "love." How information is represented in seman-

tic memory is currently the source of much debate. The debate ranges from suggestions that all experiences are represented in some fashion in memory to suggestions that individual experiences are not represented in semantic memory, but rather, only abstractions, such as prototypes or schemas, are represented. However, to discuss this debate in any detail is beyond the scope of this text. The knowledge stored in semantic memory can be expressed in various ways. You may verbally express this knowledge, or you may use typewriting or handwriting. There is no one way that semantic knowledge must be expressed.

Episodic memory consists of knowledge about personally experienced events, along with their temporal associations, in subjective time. It is this memory system that Tulving believes enables us to "mentally 'travel back' in time" (p. 387). An example here would be your memory of an important life event. You are very likely to recall this event in terms of both time and space. For example, if you were asked, "Do you remember the first time you drove a car by yourself?" you would retrieve that information from episodic memory. Episodic memory is usually expressed in terms of remembering some experience, or episode. For performing motor skills, episodic memory can be the

---

procedural memory   a subsystem of long-term memory that stores and provides knowledge about "how to do" a skill or activity.

semantic memory   a subsystem of long-term memory in which we store our general knowledge about the world that has developed from many experiences; this knowledge includes factual and conceptual knowledge.

episodic memory   a subsystem of long-term memory in which we store our knowledge about personally experienced events, along with information about the time that they were experienced.

source for information that prepares you for an upcoming performance or helps you determine what you are now doing wrong that at one time you did correctly.

Distinguishing between knowing "what to do" and doing it. An important part of relating the three memory systems of long-term memory with processes underlying motor control is the distinction between knowing "what to do" and being able to successfully perform the action to accomplish that goal. Some learning theorists have argued that the information in the episodic and semantic memory systems should be considered **declarative knowledge** (e.g., Anderson, 1987). This knowledge is specified as what we are able to describe (i.e., declare) if we are asked to do so. Thus, declarative knowledge is specific to knowing "what to do" in a situation. This type of knowledge is distinct from *procedural knowledge,* which typically cannot be verbalized. As described earlier, **procedural knowledge** enables the person to know "how to do" a skill. This distinction is a useful one and will be referred to in various parts of this chapter.

One of the only experiments that has directly distinguished these two types of knowledge in a motor skill context was reported by McPherson and Thomas (1989). They classified nine- to twelve-year-old boys as "expert" or "novice" tennis players based on length of playing experience and tournament play. Novices had never played in tournaments and had only three to six months playing experience. The "experts," on the other hand, had at least two years of experience and had played in junior tournaments. These boys were clearly in an elite group for their age. The players were interviewed after each point (something that the researchers had previously established did not disrupt the quality of performance). Players were asked to state what they had attempted to do on the previous point. When this information was later compared with what they had actually done (which was analyzed from a videotape recording), some interesting results were obtained. First, in terms of having an effective strategy or action goal, the experts knew what to do nearly all

Hitting a backhand groundstroke during a rally in tennis requires the player to know what to do in the situation and how to execute the stroke.

the time, whereas the novices generally never knew what to do. Second, although the experts were quite capable of demonstrating that they knew what action goal to establish in a specific situation, they were not always able to accomplish it in their performance of the action. This suggests that the appropriate goal was established but there were problems in attaching the appropriate parameter values to the selected motor program. This evidence, then, supports the importance of distinguishing "what to do" from "how to do it" when discussing learning and control processes underlying complex motor skills.

Remembering and Forgetting

In our discussion of the structure of memory you saw that information stays in working memory for a very limited amount of time. On the other hand, information in long-term memory seems to remain there indefinitely. Thus, it would appear that time alone can cause forgetting of information in working memory; but an inability to retrieve, or gain access to the stored information, accounts for forgetting in long-term memory. Although these two conclusions seem to have research support, they only partially explain forgetting. In this section of our discussion, we will consider some evidence to indicate that a variety of reasons exist to explain forgetting.

Some terms used in the following parts of this section need to be identified and defined. **Encoding** is the transformation of information to be remembered into a form that can be stored in memory. **Storage** of information is the process of placing information in long-term memory. **Rehearsal** is a process that enables the individual to transfer information from the working memory to long-term memory. **Retrieval** involves the search through long-term memory for information that must be accessed in order to perform the task at hand.

Assessing Remembering and Forgetting

Before considering the various reasons why we forget and how we can facilitate remembering, it will be helpful to consider how we generally determine what or how much has been remembered or forgotten. Two categories of memory tests will be discussed to introduce you to different types of tests that are commonly used in memory research to assess remembering and forgetting.

Explicit memory tests.   When we ask people to remember something, we are asking them to consciously call something to mind. There are tests of memory that do this same type of thing. These tests are known as *explicit* memory tests. That is, they assess what a person can consciously remember. Two types of explicit memory tests that have been popular in memory research are known as recall tests and recognition tests. On the basis of the results of these tests, we are able to determine how much or what a person has consciously remembered, or, conversely, forgotten.

A **recall test** requires a person to produce a required response with few, if any, available cues or aids. This test asks the person to "recall" information that has been presented. In the verbal domain, these tests typically take the form of essay or fill-in-the-blank tests. For example, a recall test could ask, "Name the bones of the hand." In motor skills, a recall test requires the subject to produce a certain movement on command, such as "Perform the skill I just demonstrated to you" or "Show me how you tie your shoe."

A **recognition test,** on the other hand, provides some cues or information on which to base a response. In this type of test, a person's task is to

recognize the correct response by distinguishing it from several alternatives. In the verbal domain, multiple-choice or matching tests are examples of recognition tests. For example, you could be asked, "Which of these is a bone of the hand?" You are then given four alternative answers from which to choose where only one is correct. To answer the question, you need only to recognize which is the correct alternative, or which are the incorrect alternatives, to answer the question. For motor skills, recognition tests can involve having a person produce several different movements and then asking

---

declarative knowledge   knowledge about "what to do" in a situation; this knowledge typically is verbalizable.

procedural knowledge   knowledge that enables a person to know "how to do" a skill; this knowledge typically is difficult to verbalize, or is not verbalizable.

encoding   a memory process involving the transformation of information to be remembered into a form that can be stored in memory.

storage   a memory process involving the placing (i.e., storing) of information in long-term memory.

rehearsal   a memory storage process that enables a person to transfer information from the working memory to long-term memory, and to enhance the memorability of information in long-term memory.

retrieval   a memory process involving the search through long-term memory for information needed to perform the task at hand.

recall test   an explicit memory test that requires a person to produce a required response with few, if any, available cues or aids.

recognition test   an explicit memory test that requires a person to select a correct response from several alternative responses.

which of these is the one just demonstrated or most appropriate for a specific situation.

In terms of learning and performing motor skills, we are often confronted with both recall and recognition "tests," sometimes in the same situation. For example, if a person must climb a ladder, he or she must recall what to do and how it should be done in order to safely and effectively climb the rungs to the desired height. And a recognition test situation exists in a sport context when a football quarterback must visually inspect the defensive players to determine if their alignment is as it should be if he is to use the offensive play that has been called. Both recall and recognition tests are relevant to a baseball batter when deciding whether or not to swing at a pitch. He or she engages in a recognition test when determining if the ball is in the strike zone or not. Then, to produce the appropriate swing, the batter must recall what to do to carry out this action and then be able to recognize if the swing that has been initiated is appropriate for hitting the pitch where it is thrown. It is important to point out that recall and recognition do not necessarily demand conscious attention by the person. Accordingly, in these examples, recall and recognition activities can be occurring without the person being aware of being engaged in them.

An important benefit of recall and recognition tests is that each provides different information about what has been remembered or forgotten. It may not be possible for a person to produce a correct response on a recall test but be able to produce that response when it is one among several alternatives in a recognition test. A value of the recognition test, then, is that it enables the researcher to determine if information is actually stored in memory, but retrieval cues or aids are needed by the person in order to gain access to that information.

Implicit memory tests.   Many times people have information stored in memory but it is stored in such a way that they have difficulty accessing that information so that they can respond correctly on explicit memory tests. For example, a person may be asked to describe the grammatical components

of a sentence he or she is shown and be unable to do so. However, if the person were asked a question that required a sentence using the same grammatical structure, the person may be quite capable of producing that sentence. This would show that although knowledge about grammar rules that was needed to answer the explicit test was not available or accessible, knowledge about the grammar rules was in memory, but in a form that could not be brought to conscious level to be able to verbalize. Only when a person is required to use the rules in a way that did not require verbalizing the actual rules is it evident that the person had knowledge about the rules.

In the domain of motor skills, we can assess implicit memory by asking a person to perform a skill. The importance of this type of assessment is that it is often the case, especially with highly skilled people, that a person can successfully perform a skill but cannot verbally describe what he or she did. For example, if you were asked to verbally describe how you tie your shoes, you may not be able to do it, or you may experience some difficulty doing it. Does this mean you don't know how to tie your shoes, or that you have forgotten how to tie your shoes? No, in terms of our earlier distinction between procedural and declarative knowledge, it means that you do not have access to, or immediate access to, your declarative knowledge about tying shoes. How would you provide evidence that you know how to tie your shoes? You would physically demonstrate tying your shoes, which would indicate that you have the procedural knowledge necessary to perform this skill.

On the other hand, it is possible to know what to do (i.e., declarative knowledge), but not be able to actually do what you know you should do (i.e., poor procedural knowledge). This phenomenon was demonstrated very nicely in the experiment by McPherson and Thomas (1989) that was discussed earlier. They gave young male basketball players an explicit paper-and-pencil test and asked them to indicate what they would do in a given basketball game situation. This information indicated declarative knowledge about what to do. An implicit test

A CLOSER LOOK

Typical Explicit Memory Test Paradigms Used in Experiments to Assess Remembering and Forgetting

Researchers who investigate the causes of forgetting and remembering typically use procedures that follow three basic paradigms, depending on whether they are interested in the effects of time or activity.

These paradigms are illustrated below from the participant's point of view in terms of the events that take place at specific times during the experiment.

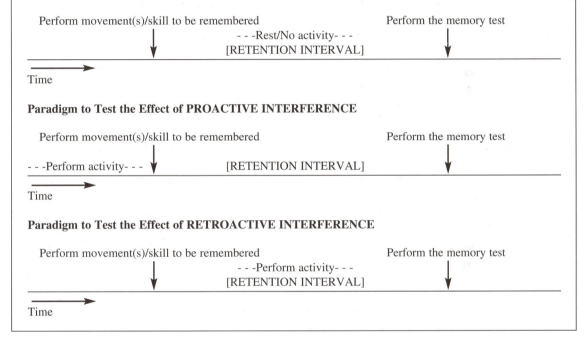

Paradigm to Test the Effect of TIME

Perform movement(s)/skill to be remembered   Perform the memory test

- - -Rest/No activity- - -
[RETENTION INTERVAL]

Time

Paradigm to Test the Effect of PROACTIVE INTERFERENCE

Perform movement(s)/skill to be remembered   Perform the memory test

- - -Perform activity- - -   [RETENTION INTERVAL]

Time

Paradigm to Test the Effect of RETROACTIVE INTERFERENCE

Perform movement(s)/skill to be remembered   Perform the memory test

- - -Perform activity- - -
[RETENTION INTERVAL]

Time

was also administered by observing what the players actually did in a situation to determine if they had the procedural knowledge necessary to do what they indicated should be done. The results showed that many of the players knew what to do in each situation, but couldn't actually do it in a game.

The Causes of Forgetting

Trace Decay.   When forgetting occurs with the passing of time, the cause is generally termed *trace decay* in the memory literature. It should be noted that the term "trace" is not commonly used in contemporary memory research literature. However, it

can be thought of as synonymous with what is referred to in this discussion as the representation of the movement in memory.

An important point about trace decay is that it can be effectively tested as a cause of forgetting only in working memory. A major problem with testing it for the long-term memory situation is the practical impossibility of maintaining a no-interference situation. For example, if you try to recall how to hit a slice serve in tennis after several years of not having performed it, you will have some initial difficulty remembering how to do it. Although time is a factor, you undoubtedly experienced the potentially interfering influences of the verbal and motor tasks you have performed since you last performed this type of serve. Hence, we observe the interaction of interference and time in the long-term memory situation. As a result, we know very little about the influence of time on forgetting information stored in long-term memory.

Although time undoubtedly influences forgetting of information stored in long-term memory, it is more likely that the term forgetting refers to the misplacing of information rather than to decay or deterioration. The reason for this is based on the relative permanence characteristic for information stored in long-term memory. Thus, forgetting becomes a retrieval problem rather than an indication of information lost from memory.

Proactive interference.   Activity that occurs prior to the presentation of information that is to be remembered and negatively affects the remembering of that information is known as **proactive interference.** Relatively convincing research evidence suggests that proactive interference is a reason for forgetting movement information held in *working memory.* One of the best examples of this was provided in an experiment by Stelmach (1969). Participants moved to either zero, two, or four locations on an arm-positioning task *before* moving to the location to be recalled. Following a retention interval of 5, 15, or 50 sec, they moved in reverse order to their estimates of each of the locations they had moved to. Thus, the first location recalled was the criterion location. Results showed proactive interference effects as four prior movements and a retention interval of at least 15 sec yielded the largest amount of recall performance error compared to the other time and activity conditions.

Several attempts have been made to explain why proactive interference affects remembering movement information. One plausible suggestion is that when the proactive interference takes the form of other movements, especially those that are similar to the criterion activity, *confusion* occurs. The individual is unable to make the criterion movement precisely because of the influence of the prior activities on the distinctiveness of the criterion movement.

Proactive interference seems to occur only when there is similarity between what is to be remembered and the interfering activity. This similarity seems to relate to "attribute" similarity. That is, if the information to be remembered and the interfering activity relate to the same movement attribute or characteristic, then proactive interference will build up as the number of similar movements preceding the movements to be remembered increases.

For movement information that has been transferred into *long-term memory,* the role of proactive interfering activities is virtually unknown. It appears that we can quite readily overcome proactive interference effects by actively rehearsing the information. This means that by active practice of a movement, we strengthen the representation of the movement in memory and thus notice few, if any, effects of proactive interference.

Retroactive interference.   If an interfering activity occurs *during* the retention interval and results in poorer retention performance than if no activity had occurred, the forgetting is said to be due to **retroactive interference.** In *working memory,* it seems that rather than just any activity causing interference to the extent that retention performance is negatively affected, the degree of similarity between the interfering activity and the movement that must be remembered is an important factor. For example, participants in experiments by Smyth and Pendleton (1990) were shown a sequence of four movements, such as a forward bend of the head, both arms raised to shoulder level in front of the body, a bend of the knees, and left leg raised to the side. Following a retention interval, they had to perform these movements, either in sequence (serial recall) or in any order (free recall).

The influence of five different retention interval time and activity conditions on recall performance can be seen in figure 10.2. As you can see, these results showed that only when the retention interval involved subjects in recalling movements that were similar to those they had to remember did recall performance significantly suffer from activity in the retention interval.

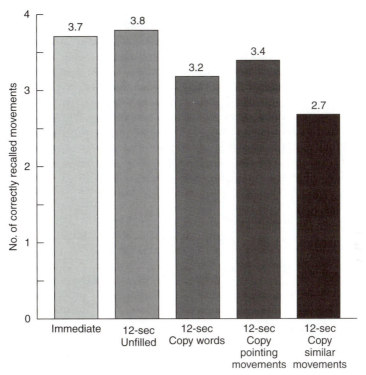

FIGURE 10.2 Free recall results of the experiment by Smyth and Pendleton showing the retroactive interference effects of performing similar movements to those that had to be remembered. [From Smyth, M. M., & Pendleton, L. R. (1990). Space and movement in working memory. *Quarterly Journal of Experimental Psychology, 42A,* 291–304. Reprinted by permission of the Experimental Psychology Society.]

Another characteristic of retroactive interference effects in working memory is one that we discussed for proactive interference. That is, activity during the retention interval causes interference that increases recall performance error only when there is a certain amount of activity. As long as the amount of information stays within this limit, remembering is not affected. However, when that limit is exceeded, forgetting occurs, which results in recall performance error increase (see, e.g., Roy & Davenport, 1972).

Thus, the available research evidence indicates that retroactive interference for remembering just-presented movements occurs in specific circumstances. These appear to be when the activity during the retention interval is similar to the movements that must be remembered, and when this activity and the movements to be remembered exceed working memory or attention-capacity limits.

Retroactive interference and long-term memory. It appears that retention interval length and/or activity

> **proactive interference** a cause of forgetting because of activity that occurs prior to the presentation of information to be remembered.
>
> **retroactive interference** a cause of forgetting because of activity occurring during the retention interval.

A CLOSER LOOK

Implications for Motor Skill Instruction of the Effects on Working Memory of Proactive and Retroactive Interference

- After you give instructions that describe or demonstrate what to do in a skill or how to do a skill, keep the amount of time before people physically practice the skill as short and activity (verbal and motor) free as possible.
- Do not describe or demonstrate examples of "what *not* to do" before you give instructions that describe or demonstrate what to do in a skill or

how to do a skill, and before people have an initial opportunity to physically practice the skill.

- If you describe or demonstrate examples of "what *not* to do" either before or after you give instruction about what to do in a skill or how to do a skill, do it after people have practiced the skill several times and limit the examples to one or two.
- If people ask questions after you give instructions about what to do in a skill or how to do a skill, repeat the instructions (i.e., verbally or demonstrate) after answering the question just before the people physically practice the skill.

does not have the same forgetting effects for all types of motor skills stored in *long-term memory*. Research evidence indicates that certain types of motor skills are remembered better over long periods than are other types. Your own experiences may provide some support for this. You probably had very little trouble remembering how to ride a bicycle, even after not having been on one for several years. However, you did experience some difficulty in putting together the pieces of a puzzle that you had assembled quickly around the same time you learned to ride a bicycle.

The characteristic of skills that distinguishes these two situations relates to one of the classification systems discussed in chapter 1. That is, continuous motor skills are typically more resistant to long-term forgetting than are discrete skills, especially when the skill involves producing a series of discrete movements. This latter type of skill is sometimes referred to as a serial discrete skill or as a procedural skill.

Several reasons have been suggested to explain why this discrete, procedural skill versus continuous skill retention difference occurs. Adams (1987), for example, suggested that the difference is related to procedural skills having a large verbal component, which seems to deteriorate over time more readily than a motor component of a skill. Another reason less forgetting occurs for continuous skills is that they typically are practiced more

than are discrete skills. This is evident if you consider what a "trial" is for these two types of skills. One trial for a discrete skill is usually one performance of the skill whereas one trial for a continuous skill is several repetitions of the skill over a much longer period of time. Thus, fifty trials of a continuous skill yields many more practice repetitions of the skill than it does of a discrete skill.

Movement Characteristics Related to Memory Performance

Location and distance characteristics. Actions have many characteristics that we can store in memory. For example, we could store the spatial position of various points of a movement, such as the beginning and the end point of a golf swing. We could also store the distance of a movement, its velocity, its force, and/or the direction of a movement. These characteristics represent specific spatial and temporal features of movement. Two of these, *location* and *distance,* have been extensively examined with regard to how easily they can be stored in and retrieved from memory.

Investigation of the issue was very popular in the 1970s and focused primarily on working memory, and the remembering of spatial positioning movements of the arm. It is from the results of this research that we currently know something about the short-term remembering of location and distance characteristics of movements. The initial research studies investigating this issue found that movement end-point location is remembered better than movement distance (e.g., Diewert, 1975; Hagman, 1978; Laabs, 1973). However, an important finding by Diewert and Roy (1978) showed that when movement end-point location information is a relatively reliable recall cue, people will use a location-type strategy to recall the movement. However, when location information is totally unreliable and only distance information will aid recall, people will use some nonkinesthetic strategy, such as counting, to help remember the distance of the criterion movement. Interestingly, spontaneous use of this dual strategy to aid the remembering of location and distance information has been demonstrated only in children older than nine years of age (Thomas et al., 1983).

Another aspect of remembering location information is that an arm-movement end location is more easily remembered when it is within the person's own body space (see, e.g., Chieffi, Allport, & Woodfin, 1999; Larish & Stelmach 1982). For limb-positioning movements, people typically associate the end location of the criterion movement with a body part and use that as a cue to aid their recall performance. Other research that will be considered later suggests that people will also spontaneously associate the end location of limb positions with well-known objects, such as a clock face, to aid recall.

What does all this mean for teaching motor skills? One implication is that if limb positions are important for successful performance of the skill, instructional emphasis can be placed on these positions. For example, if you are teaching a beginner a golf swing, the important phases of the swing that he or she should concentrate on are critical location points in the swing. The keys could be the beginning point of the backswing or the location point of the top of the backswing. Or if a therapist is working with a patient who needs to work on flexing or extending his or her knee, emphasizing the position of the lower leg can help the patient remember where the last movement was or to establish a goal

for future flexion attempts. If a dancer is having difficulty remembering where her arm should be during a particular sequence, a body-part cue about the location of the arm can help her remember the position more effectively.

The meaningfulness of the movement.   Another characteristic that influences remembering movements is the *meaningfulness* of the movement. A movement or sequence of movements can be considered meaningful to an individual if that person can readily relate the movement to something he or she knows. For example, a movement that forms the shape of a triangle is considered more meaningful than one that makes an unfamiliar, abstract pattern. Or, if a movement is similar to one the person can do, then the new movement being learned takes on increased meaningfulness to the person.

The results of an experiment by Laugier and Cadopi (1996) illustrate the influence movement meaningfulness has on remembering movements. Adult novice dancers watched a video of a skilled dancer perform a four-element sequence of dance movements, each of which involved two to four body, head, and/or limb movements. One sequence, which the researchers labeled as a "concrete" sequence, was a sequence commonly performed in dance. Another sequence, labeled as an "abstract" sequence, involved elements that did not belong to any particular style of dance. After fifteen viewings of the dancer performing the sequences, the participants performed the sequence one time. Analysis of the participants' performance indicated that the observation of the concrete sequence led to better form and quality than the observation of the abstract sequence (see figure 10.3). Interviews of the participants indicated that the concrete sequence had a higher degree of meaningfulness to them, which helped them remember the sequence when they performed it.

Strategies That Enhance Memory Performance

In addition to certain movement characteristics, the strategy a person uses to help him or her remember influences memory performance. The strategy may be one generated by the person who must remember

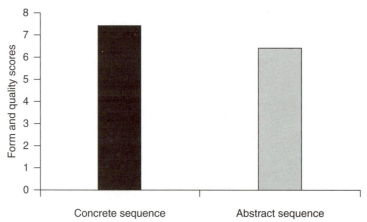

FIGURE 10.3   Results from the experiment by Laugier and Cadopi (1996) showing the influence of movement meaningfulness on remembering a four-element dance sequence. Scores reflect form and quality measures of novice dancers' one-time performance of the sequence after fifteen viewings of a skilled dancer performing the sequence. Participant interviews indicated that the "concrete" sequence was more meaningful to the participants than the "abstract" sequence.   [Modified figure 2, p. 98, in Laugier, C., & Cadopi, M. (1996). Representational guidance of dance performance in adult novices: Effect of concrete vs. abstract movement. *International Journal of Sport Psychology, 27,* 91–108. Adapted with permision of the International Society of Sport Psychology.]

the movement, or it may be one imposed by the teacher, coach, or therapist. In either case, different memory strategies may have different influences on how well a movement is remembered or how much is forgotten. In this section, we will consider four strategies that may influence how well a movement is remembered.

It is important to note that any consideration of memory strategies takes into account what are known as *control processes* in memory. In theoretical accounts of the functioning of human memory, control processes represent the means by which we use our memories. Primarily, control processes are employed to enable us to remember information. Some of these processes are under our direct control, and therefore demand attentional resources, whereas other control processes are automatic, and not under our direct control. Automatic processes are assumed not to require attentional resources. Control processes involve functions such as selecting particular aspects of presented information to place

in working memory, the retrieval of appropriate information from long-term memory to interact with the information in working memory, and rehearsal processes used to transfer and organize information from the working memory to long-term memory.

Knowledge about effective memory strategies is important for people who learn skills and for those who teach skills. For those involved in instructional or rehabilitation settings, the benefit of knowing about the effectiveness of certain strategies is that it can lead to enhancing their own learning performance. Teachers, coaches, and therapists can benefit from an awareness of the effectiveness of memory strategies by being better prepared to incorporate the most effective strategies into their instructional or rehabilitative situations. Thus, this discussion of strategies will not only help you gain a better understanding of memory processes, it will also provide you with useful information to aid your own learning and teaching of motor skills.

Increasing a movement's meaningfulness. In the preceding section, you saw that people remember movements that are higher in their meaningfulness to the person than those that are less meaningful. When people first practice a new skill, it is very likely that the skill will require that they coordinate their body and limbs in a new way. This characteristic makes it also likely that the new coordination pattern of movements will be more abstract than it is concrete. That is, the skill typically has little inherent "meaningfulness" to you in terms of the required organizational structure of the spatial and temporal characteristics of the limb coordination needed to perform the skill.

In this section, we will consider some ways in which you can increase the meaningfulness of the movements you are trying to remember as you learn a skill. By doing so, you will find that it becomes easier to learn the skill as you practice it. By considering this type of strategy, we are able to relate our knowledge about a characteristic of movement known to influence the memorability of a movement with a memory strategy that applies this knowledge.

One of the most commonly used strategies to increase the meaningfulness of a movement involves the use of *imagery.* Imagery as a memory strategy involves developing in your mind a picture of what a movement is like. It is best to use an image of something that is very familiar. We know that this strategy is effective because there is research evidence supporting the benefit of the use of imagery to increase the memorability of a movement.

The use of mental imagery appears to be a powerful rehearsal strategy for learning motor skills. As such, it can also be an effective instructional strategy. For example, rather than provide the complex instructions for how to coordinate the arm movements to perform a sidestroke in swimming, the instructor can provide the students with a useful image to use while practicing the stroke. The image given the students is of themselves picking an apple from a tree with one hand, bringing the apple down, and putting the apple in a basket. The remembering of the sidestroke is enhanced by changing the abstract, complex components involved in the skill into a concrete, meaningful movement.

Another effective strategy that increases the meaningfulness of a movement so that it is more accurately remembered is to attach a useful or meaningful *verbal label* to the movement, then using that label-movement association to aid the recall of the movement. One of the earliest demonstrations of the beneficial influence of attaching verbal labels to simple movements was by John Shea (1977), who had participants move to a stop on a semicircular arm-positioning apparatus. When the participants arrived at the criterion location, one group was provided with a number that corresponded to the clockface location of the criterion location; another group received an irrelevant verbal label such as a nonsensical three-letter syllable; another group received no verbal label about the criterion location. Results, as seen in figure 10.4, indicated that the group given a clock face label showed no increase in error over a 60-sec unfilled retention interval, whereas the other two groups showed a large increase in recall error. In a related experiment Winther and Thomas (1981) showed that when useful verbal labels are attached to positioning movements, young children's (age seven) retention performance can become equivalent to that of adults.

Why do strategies involving the use of imagery and verbal labels benefit memory for performing motor skills? Based on available research evidence, the answer appears to be that motor imagery activates brain areas involved in movement planning (Johnson, 1998). This indicates that the use of imagery facilitates the selection of appropriate movements to be performed. From a memory perspective, this means that images and verbal labels speed up the memory retrieval process involved in the selection of movements associated with an action. Thus, these strategies serve as *mnemonics,* which are simply techniques that aid remembering. Undoubtedly, you have used mnemonics many times to help you remember lists of words, such as a grocery list or the bones of the hand. Chase and Ericsson (1982) argued that mnemonics derive their

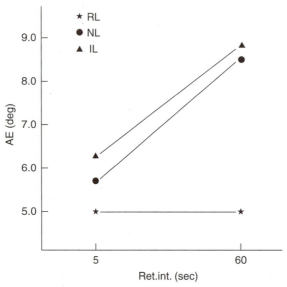

FIGURE 10.4   Mean absolute error computed across positions for the 5-sec and 60-sec retention intervals (ret. int.) for Experiment 1 by Shea. (RL = relevant label, NL = no label, IL = irrelevant label.)   [From Shea, J.B. (1997). Effects of labelling on motor short-term memory. *Journal of Experimental Psychology: Human Learning and Memory, 3,* 92–99. Copyright © 1977 by the American Psychological Association. Reprinted with permission.]

power from their ability to narrow the search in long-term memory to just the information needed.

The intention to remember.   In all the memory experiments considered so far, participants have always known in advance that the movements they were presented or had to practice would be later subject to a recall test. But, suppose they were not told in advance? Suppose they were told that the goal of the experiment was to see how well they could move their arms to a specified location. If an unexpected recall test was given later, how well would they recall the movements made earlier? The two situations just described are known in the memory research literature as *intentional* and *incidental* memory situations, respectively. In addition to investigating the influence of intention to remember as an effective remembering strategy, the comparison of these two situations provides insight into the encoding of movement information processes. That is, do we only store information to

which we give conscious attention, as in the case of the intentional memory situation, or do we store more information, as would be shown by good memory performance, in the incidental memory situation?

This question has received little research interest in the study of memory for movements. However, the research that has been done indicates that, in general, intention to remember leads to better remembering than no intention to remember. (See Crocker & Dickinson, 1984 for a review of this research.) Yet retention test performance in the incidental situation is typically better than if no previous experience with the test movements had occurred. In fact, some reports show incidental memory test performance to be as good as it was for the intentional situation.

The investigation of intentional and incidental memory strategies is an important one to increase our understanding of memory processes related to encoding and storing information. Research indicates that we encode and store much more information than we are consciously aware of.

One implication that the intentional and incidental memory research provides for instructional situations is that memory performance and skill learning can be enhanced by telling students when they begin to practice a skill that they will be tested on the skill later. The effect of this advance knowledge about a test is that students will undoubtedly increase the amount of effort given in practice, a characteristic that you will repeatedly see in this text as beneficial for memory and learning. Also, when there are specific characteristics of a skill performance situation that must be remembered for a later test, a better test performance will result from telling people what these characteristics are.

Subjective organization. A strategy frequently used by learners of large amounts of information is grouping or organizing the information into units. This strategy, which is known as **subjective organization,** involves the organizing of information that must be remembered in a way that is meaningful to the individual. Other terms that researchers have used to describe this strategy are chunking, clustering, and grouping, among others. An example of implementing this strategy is commonly seen when people need to learn a long monologue for a play, or a list of terms for a test. They often will organize the monologue or list by dividing it into shorter, more manageable chunks to begin memorizing the information. You would likely use a similar strategy if you had to play from memory a long piece of music on an instrument, or had to learn a dance or gymnastics routine. In each of these situations, continued practice typically leads to increasing the size of the chunks.

Although the role of subjective organization in motor skill learning has not been the subject of a large amount of research, there is evidence indicating that when given the opportunity to subjectively organize a sequence of movements, some people will spontaneously create an organized structure. And this subjectively determined organizational structure imposed on the sequence benefits recall performance (e.g., Magill & Lee,

1987). In addition, it is interesting to note that memory performance deficits often seen following a stroke (i.e., cerebrovascular accident) have been found to be due in part to a lack of ability to implement effective organizational strategies (e.g., Lange, Waked, Kirshblum, & DeLuca, 2000). Similarly, people with Parkinson's disease have been shown to have problems with implementing a subjective organization strategy without external guidance (Berger et al., 1999).

One way to apply the benefit of subjective organization to motor skill learning situations is to consider the way a novice approaches the learning of a complex skill. He or she tends to consider complex motor skills as comprising many parts. As the beginner develops his or her ability to execute the skill, the number of components of the skill seems to decrease. This does not mean the structure of the skill itself has changed. Rather, the learner's view of the skill has changed. A good example is a dance or gymnastic floor exercise routine, where each of the routines is made up of many individual parts. To the beginner, a dance routine is thought of step-by-step and movement-by-movement. Beginning gymnasts think of a floor exercise as so many individual stunts. As they practice, their approach to the skills changes. They begin to organize the routines into units or groups of movements. Three or four component parts are now considered as one. The result will be performing the entire routine with the requisite timing, rhythm, and coordination. With that result, moreover, will be the added effect of developing a more efficient means of storing the complex routine in memory.

It is important to note that skilled individuals organize information to such an extent that it appears they have an increased working memory

---

subjective organization a memory strategy that involves the organizing of a complex array or list of information in a way that is meaningful to the person performing the task (also referred to as chunking, clustering, grouping, etc.).

capacity, which led Ericsson and Kintsch (1995) to propose the long-term working memory described earlier in this discussion. A good example of this type of evidence can be seen in the experiment with "novice" and "expert" eleven-year-old dancers by Starkes et al. (1987) that was mentioned earlier in the discussion of working memory capacity. When these dancers were presented sequences of eight elements that were organized as in a ballet routine, the expert dancers recalled the routine almost perfectly, whereas the novices recalled about half of the sequence correctly. However, when the same number of elements was presented in an unstructured sequence, there was no difference between the skilled and novice dancers in terms of the number of elements they correctly recalled. This result indicates that the organizational structure of the sequence of dance movements was an important factor in the experts' recall performance.

As a result of much practice, the dancers organized sequences of movements into longer and longer units, or chunks. As a result a long dance routine sequence became easier to incorporate into working memory when a sequence had to be repeated from memory. An interesting anecdote was provided by Starkes et al. They reported observing an adult principal national-level ballet dancer being able to perform a sequence of ninety-six steps after having seen the sequence demonstrated one time. Thus, organization was apparently a strategy used to reduce the working memory load of this sequence and to increase the memorability of the sequence.

Because most complex motor skills have a specific organizational structure, there are a variety of ways to break up that structure for teaching or practicing the skills. Skills should not be arbitrarily broken into parts for practice. Better and more efficient learning will result from keeping together those components of a movement sequence that are interrelated and dependent on each other. For example, the motion for pitching a softball is often initially practiced by using only the underhand backswing and forward motion of the pitch. A better organizational approach would be to incorporate the forward swing of the initial part of the windup to allow the student the opportunity to understand the full structure of the movement.

Practice-Test Context Effects

An important influence on the retention of motor skills is the relationship between the context of practice and the context at the time of the test. The context of a movement relates to both the environmental conditions in which the movement is performed as well as to characteristics related to the person performing the movement. For example, if a memory experiment is performed in a laboratory, the environmental context includes such things as the room in which the experiment is done, the experimenter, the time of day, the noise the participant can hear, the lighting, and so on. Personal context involves such things as the mood of the individual, the limb used to make the movement, the sitting or standing position of the subject, and the sensory feedback sources that are available to the subject. As you will see in this section, differences in these conditions during the time the movement to be remembered or learned is presented or practiced and during the time the movement must be recalled can influence the success of the recall performance.

The encoding specificity principle.   An important point to consider regarding the influence of movement context on remembering or learning a motor skill is the relationship between the practice and test contexts. In some situations, especially for closed skills, the test goal is essentially the same as the practice goal. That is, to shoot a free throw, you must stand in essentially the same place and shoot the ball through a hoop that is the same distance from you as it was when you practiced it. In such closed-skill situations, what is known as the **encoding specificity principle** applies.

The encoding specificity principle was introduced by Tulving and Thomson (1973). According to this principle, the more the test context resembles the practice context, the better the retention performance will be. Evidence that this principle applies to motor skills has come primarily from laboratory-based experiments (e.g., Lee & Hirota, 1980; Magill & Lee, 1987). However, as you will see in the discussion in chapter 14 concerning the transfer of learning, ample evidence exists to have confidence in generalizing this principle to the learning and performance of motor skills.

The encoding specificity principle is important for increasing our understanding of memory processes. An essential finding is that the memory representation for a movement has stored with it important sensory feedback information that is specific to the context conditions in which the movement was practiced. Evidence also supports a memorial representation for movements that have specific movement context information associated with them. Thus, the more the test, or recall, conditions match the practice, or encoding, conditions, the more accurate the test performance will be expected to be.

The practical implications of the encoding specificity principle seem especially relevant to remembering and learning closed skills. In a closed skill, the test context is typically stable and predictable. Because of this, practice conditions can be established that will closely mimic the test conditions. In these cases, then, the more similar the practice setting is to the test setting, the higher the probability or successful performance during the test. Consider, for example, practice for shooting free throws in a basketball game. Free throws are always one, two, or one-and-one situations. According to the encoding specificity principle, it is essential that players have practice experiences in which these gamelike conditions prevail. This does not say that this is the only way that free throws can be practiced. However, if game performance is the test of interest, it is essential that gamelike practice be provided.

Consider also a physical therapy example where a knee joint replacement patient is working on knee joint flexion and extension. Based on the encoding specificity principle, because test condi-

tions involve active limb movement, practice conditions should emphasize active rather than passive limb movement. Similar practice-test relationships can be established for a variety of skill practice situations.

SUMMARY

Memory is best viewed as consisting of two functional components: working memory and long-term memory. Working memory is a short-term storage system for just-presented information and for information retrieved from long-term memory. It has a limited capacity for information storage and the information remains for only a brief amount of time. Working memory also serves as a temporary work space for the integration of information just received and retrieved from long-term memory so that a specific problem can be solved, a decision can be made, or an appropriate action can be developed or evaluated. Long-term memory stores different types of information on a more permanent basis. It appears to have no limits in terms of how much information can be stored, or the length of time the information will remain there.

Forgetting concerns the loss of, or the inability to retrieve, information from memory. It is usually measured by determining the amount of information that a person can recall or recognize following a retention interval. Both time and activity influence forgetting in both working memory and long-term memory. The causes of forgetting related to these factors are known as trace decay, which

---

encoding specificity principle a memory principle that indicates the close relationship between encoding and retrieval memory processes; it states that memory test performance is directly related to the amount of similarity between the practice and the test contexts, i.e., the more similarity, the better the test performance will be.

A CLOSER LOOK

Active and Passive Limb Movements: Evidence for the Application of the Encoding Specificity Principle to Motor Skills

An excellent example of research evidence supporting the application of the encoding specificity principle to the remembering of movements is an experiment done many years ago by Lee and Hirota (1980).

- **Apparatus.** An arm-positioning apparatus on a table facing the participant.
- **Task and experimental conditions.** On some trials, blindfolded participants *actively* moved the handle of the apparatus along the trackway to a criterion arm position that was specified by a physical block. On other trials, they were *passively* moved by the experimenter to a criterion arm position. For the recall test on each trial, participants were told to actively move to the arm position just experienced or were passively moved by the experimenter until the participant told the experimenter to stop. This procedure continued until all participants had actively and passively experienced the presentation of each criterion arm position and had performed recall tests in either the same or

opposite way they had experienced the presentation of the criterion position.

- **Encoding specificity principle predictions.**
  — Active movements to the criterion arm movements should be recalled better when the movements are actively recalled than passively recalled.
  — Passive movements to the criterion arm movements should be recalled better when the movements are passively recalled than when they are actively recalled.

- **Results.** As you can see in figure 10.5 below, the results supported the encoding specificity principle. When the movement during the recall test was performed in the same way as it was during the presentation of the criterion arm position (i.e., active-active, passive-passive), recall performance was more accurate than when the recall test was performed differently from the way it was during the presentation of the criterion arm position (i.e., active-passive, passive-active).
  — Note that there was no advantage to active over passive movements. The difference in recall accuracy related to the relationship between the presentation and recall conditions.

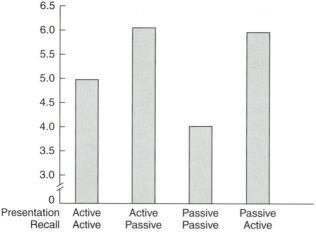

FIGURE 10.5 Results of the experiment by Lee and Hirota showing absolute error for recalling arm-position movements presented as either active or passive and recalled in either the same or opposite conditions. [From data in Lee, T.D., & Hirota, T.T. (1980). Encoding specificity principle in motor short-term memory. *Journal of Motor Behavior, 12,* 63–67.]

means that the memory representation deteriorates over time, and interference, which results from the influence of activity. Interfering activity can occur before the presentation of the information to be remembered (i.e., proactive interference) or during the retention interval (i.e., retroactive interference). Certain types of motor skills, especially continuous skills, show little forgetting over long periods of time.

Three categories of factors influence the remembering of motor skill related information. One category includes certain movement characteristics, such as distance and spatial location characteristics and the meaningfulness of the movement. The second category relates to strategies a person uses to improve how well a movement is remembered. These include the use of verbal labeling and imagery to increase a movement's meaningfulness, the subjective organization of a complex sequence of movements into meaningful units, or chunks, that can reduce the memory load for remembering a long sequence of movements and enhance remembering, and the intention to remember. Finally, the relationship between the practice and test context characteristics influences the remembering of movements. The encoding specificity principle, which applies to this situation, states that increasing the similarity between these context characteristics increases recall performance.

RELATED READINGS

Awh, E., Jonides, J., Smith, E. E., Buxton, R. B., Frank, L. R., Love, T., Wong, E. C., & Gmeindl, L. (1999). Rehearsal in spatial working memory: Evidence from neuroimaging. *Psychological Science, 10,* 433–437.

Christina, R. W., & Bjork, R. A. (1991). Optimizing long-term retention and transfer. In D. Druckman & R. A. Bjork (Eds),

In the mind's eye: Enhancing human performance (pp. 23–56). Washington, DC: National Academy Press.

Forssberg, H., Jucaite, A., & Hadders-Algra, M. (1999). Shared memory representations for programming of lifting movements and whole body postural adjustments in humans. *Neuroscience Letters, 273,* 9–12.

Imanaka, K., & Abernethy, B. (1992). Interference between location and distance information in motor short-term memory: The respective roles of direct kinesthetic signals and abstract codes. *Journal of Motor Behvavior, 24,* 274–280.

Kimberg, D. Y., D'Esposito, M., & Farah, M. J. (1998). Cognitive functions in the prefrontal cortex: Working memory and executive control. *Current Directions in Psychological Science, 6,* 185–192.

Roediger, H. L. (1990). Implicit memory: Retention without remembering. *American Psychologist, 45,* 1043–1056.

STUDY QUESTIONS

1. Discuss how working memory and long-term memory differ in terms of the duration and capacity of information in each.

2. Describe the meaning of the terms *declarative* and *procedural* knowledge. Give a motor skill example of each.

3. Discuss the primary causes of forgetting in working memory and in long-term memory.

4. Discuss two effective strategies a person can use to help him or her remember a movement or sequence of movements that he or she must perform. Give an example of the use of each strategy in a motor skill performance situation.

5. What is the *encoding specificity principle,* and how does it relate to the performance of motor skills?

UNIT

IV

INTRODUCTION TO MOTOR SKILL LEARNING

CHAPTER

Defining and Assessing Learning

Concept: People who assess learning must make inferences from observing performance during practice and tests

APPLICATION

Any professional involved in motor skills instruction typically has to provide some type of assessment to determine whether or not the student or patient has learned what the professional has taught. The following two situations, common in physical education and rehabilitation settings, provide examples of the importance of assessing learning.

Suppose you are a physical educator teaching a tennis unit. If you are teaching your students to serve, how do you determine if they are actually learning what you are teaching them? What will you look for to assess their progress in learning to serve? How can you be certain that what you are observing is the result of learning and not just luck?

Or suppose you are a physical therapist helping a stroke patient to learn to walk without support. What evidence will tell you that this patient is learning to do what you have taught him or her to do? What characteristics of the patient's performance will make you confident that the patient is learning this skill and will be able to walk without assistance at home as well as in the clinic?

The answers to these questions are important for effective professional practice in any setting in which people need to learn motor skills. As you

think about possible answers to these questions, consider two important characteristics of learning that you need to take into account whenever you assess skill learning. First, we do not directly observe learning; we directly observe behavior. Second, because of this, we must make inferences about learning from the behavior we observe. Any learning assessment procedure must incorporate these two critical characteristics of learning. In the discussion that follows, we will address these points by first, establishing a definition of learning, and then discussing several learning assessment procedures.

DISCUSSION

In any discussion about the assessment of learning, we need to keep two important terms distinct: *performance* and *learning*. This distinction helps us establish an appropriate definition for the term *learning;* it also helps us consider appropriate conditions under which we should observe performance so that we can make valid inferences about learning.

Performance Distinguished from Learning

Simply put, **performance** is *observable behavior.* If you observe a person walking down a corridor, you

A CLOSER LOOK

The Terms "Performance" and "Learning"

Performance	Learning
• Observable behavior	• Inferred from performance
• Temporary	• Relatively permanent
• May not be due to practice	• Due to practice
• May be influenced by performance variables	• *Not* influenced by performance variables

are observing him or her perform the skill of walking. Similarly, if you observe a person hitting a baseball, you are observing a performance of the skill of hitting a ball. When used in this way, the term *performance* refers to the execution of a skill at a specific time and in a specific situation. *Learning,* on the other hand, cannot be observed directly, but can only be inferred from characteristics of a person's performance.

Before considering a more formal definition for learning, think about how often we make inferences about people's internal states based on what we observe them doing. For example, when someone smiles (an observable behavior), we infer that he or she is happy. When someone cries, we infer that he or she is sad, or perhaps very happy. When a person yawns, we assume that the person is tired. In each of these situations, certain characteristics about the individual's behavior are the basis for our making a particular inference about some internal state we cannot observe directly. However, because we must base our inference on observed behavior, it is possible for us to make an incorrect inference. For example, if a student sitting beside you in class yawns during the lecture, you might infer from that behavior that the person is tired because of lack of sleep the night before. However, it may be that he or she is bored.

Learning defined. We will use the following general definition for the term **learning:** *a change in the capability of a person to perform a skill that must be inferred from a relatively permanent improvement in performance as a result of practice*

or experience. It is important to note from this definition that the person has increased his or her *capability, or potential,* to perform that skill. Whether or not the person actually performs the skill in a way that is consistent with this potential will depend on the presence of what are known as *performance variables.* These include factors that can affect a person's performance but not the degree of learning the person has achieved. Some examples include the alertness of the person, the anxiety created by the situation, the uniqueness of the setting, fatigue, and so on. As a result, it is critical that methods used to assess learning take factors such as these into account to allow accurate inferences about learning.

General Performance Characteristics of Skill Learning

We generally observe four performance characteristics as skill learning takes place.

Improvement. First, *performance of the skill shows improvement over a period of time.* This means that

---

performance the behavioral act of performing a skill at a specific time and in a specific situation.

learning a change in the capability of a person to perform a skill; it must be inferred from a relatively permanent improvement in performance as a result of practice or experience.

the person performs at a higher level of skill at some later time than at some previous time. It is important to note here that learning is not necessarily limited to improvement in performance. There are cases in which practice results in bad habits, which in turn result in the observed performance's failure to show improvement. In fact, performance actually may become worse as practice continues. But because this text is concerned with skill acquisition, we will focus on learning as it involves improvement in performance.

Consistency. Second, as learning progresses, *performance becomes increasingly more consistent.* This means that from one performance attempt to another, a person's performance characteristics should become more similar. Early in learning, performance is typically quite variable from one attempt to another. Eventually, however, it becomes more consistent.

A related term here is *stability,* which was introduced in chapter 4. As performance consistency of a skill increases, certain behavioral characteristics of performance become more stable. This means that the acquired new behavior is not easily disrupted by minor changes in personal or environmental characteristics.

Persistence. The third general performance characteristic we observe during learning is this: *the improved performance capability is marked by an increasing amount of persistence.* This means that as the person progresses in learning the skill, the improved performance capability lasts over increasing periods of time. A person who has learned a skill should be able to demonstrate the improved level of performance today, tomorrow, next week, and so on. However, because of some forgetting or other factors, the person may not achieve the same performance level on each of these occasions as he or she did at the end of the practice time devoted to the skill. The persistence characteristic relates to the emphasis in our definition of learning on a *relatively permanent improvement* in performance.

Adaptability. Finally, an important general characteristic of performance associated with skill learning is that *the improved performance is adaptable to a variety of performance context characteristics.* We never really perform a skill for which everything in the performance context is exactly the same each time. Something is different every time we perform a skill. The difference may be our own emotional state, the characteristics of the skill itself, an environmental difference such as a change in weather conditions, the place where we perform the skill, and so on. Thus, successful skill performance requires adaptability to changes in personal, task, and/or environmental characteristics. The degree of adaptability required depends on the skill and the performance situation. As a person progresses in learning a skill, his or her capability to perform the skill successfully in these changed circumstances also increases. Later in this book, we will explore some instruction and practice condition characteristics that can influence how well a person adapts to these various situations.

Assessing Learning by Observing Practice Performance

One way we can assess learning is to record levels of a performance measure during the period of time a person practices a skill. A common way to do this is to illustrate performance graphically in the form of a **performance curve.** This is a plot of the level achieved on the performance measure for each time period, which may be time in seconds or minutes, a trial, a series of trials, a day, etc. For any performance curve, the levels of the performance measure are always on the Y-axis (vertical axis), and the time over which the performance is measured is on the X-axis (horizontal axis).

Performance curves for outcome measures. We can graphically describe performance by developing a performance curve for an outcome measure of performance. An example is shown in figure 11.1, which depicts one person's practice of a complex pursuit tracking task. The task required the person to track, or follow the movement of, a cursor on a

A CLOSER LOOK

Examples of Motor Skill Performance Adaptability Demands

Closed Skills

- *Hitting a sand wedge in golf*
  - from wet sand, dry sand, etc.
  - from various locations in the sand trap
  - to various pin locations on the green
  - when shot has various implications for score

- *Shooting free throws in basketball*
  - one- and two-shot free throws at various times of the game
  - one-and-one shot situations at various times of the game
  - with various crowd conditions (e.g., quiet, loud, visible behind the basket)
  - various types of backboards

- *Walking*
  - on various types of surfaces
  - in various settings (e.g., home, mall, sidewalk)
  - while carrying various types of objects
  - alone or while carrying on a conversation with a friend

Open Skills

- *Hitting a baseball/softball*
  - various types, speeds, and locations of pitches
  - various ball-and-strike counts
  - various people-on-base situations with various numbers of outs
  - left-handed and right-handed pitchers

- *Catching a ball*
  - balls that are different shapes, weights, sizes, etc.
  - various speeds and directions
  - in the air, on the ground
  - with one or two hands

- *Driving a car*
  - various sizes of cars
  - various street and highway conditions
  - with or without passengers
  - various weather conditions

---

computer monitor by moving the mouse on a tabletop. The goal was to track the cursor as closely as possible in both time and space. Each trial lasted about 15 sec. The outcome measure of performance was the root-mean-squared error (RMSE).

Notice that in this graph we can readily observe two of the four behavioral characteristics associated with learning. First, *improvement* is evident by the general direction of the curve. From the first to the last trial, the curve follows a general downward trend (indicating decreasing error). Second, we can also see *increased performance consistency* in this graph. The indicator of this performance character-

istic is performance on adjacent trials. According to figure 11.1, this person showed a high degree of inconsistency early in practice but became slightly

performance curve   a line graph describing performance in which the level of achievement of a performance measure is plotted for a specific sequence of time (e.g., sec, min, days) or trials; the units of the performance measure are on the Y-axis (vertical axis) and the time units or trials are on the X-axis (horizontal axis).

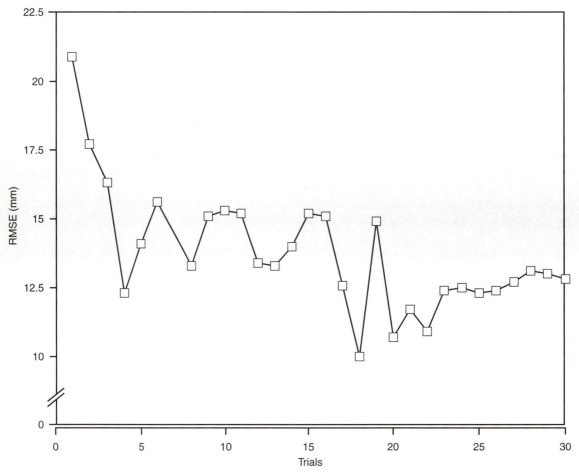

FIGURE 11.1   Performance curve for one person learning a pursuit tracking task. The performance measure is the root-mean-squared error (RMSE) for each trial.

more consistent from one trial to the next toward the end of practice. The expectation would be that the person would increase this consistency with additional practice trials.

When a person is acquiring a new skill, the performance curve for an outcome measure typically will follow one of *four general trends* from the beginning to the end of the practice period for a skill. This period of time may be represented as a certain number of trials, hours, days, etc. The trends are represented by the four different shapes of curves in figure 11.2. Curve (a) is a *linear curve,*

or a straight line. This indicates proportional performance increases over time; that is, each unit of increase on the horizontal axis (e.g., one trial) results in a proportional increase on the vertical axis (e.g., one second). Curve (b) is a *negatively accelerated curve,* which indicates that a large amount of improvement occurred early in practice, with smaller amounts of improvement later. This curve represents the classic power function curve of skill learning, which we will discuss in some detail in chapter 12 as a characteristic of the power law of practice. Curve (c) is the inverse of curve

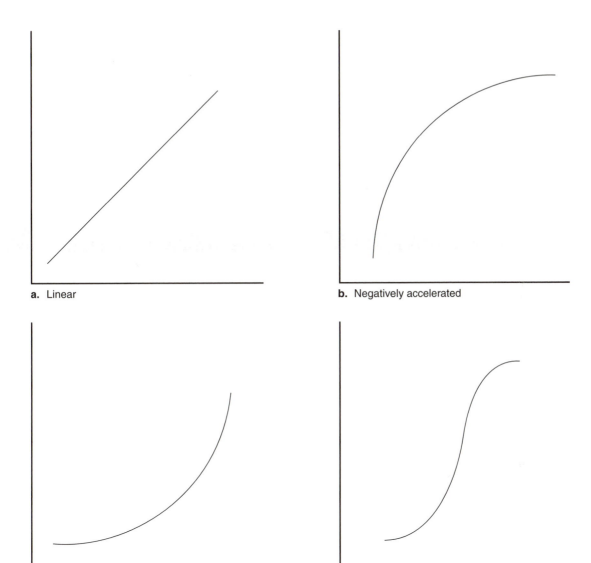

a. Linear

b. Negatively accelerated

c. Positively accelerated

d. Ogive or S-shaped

FIGURE 11.2 Four general types of performance curves.

(b) and is called a *positively accelerated curve.* This curve indicates slight performance gain early in practice, but a substantial increase later in practice. Curve (d) is a combination of all three curves, and is called an *ogive* or *S-shaped curve.*

It is important to note that each curve in figure 11.2 shows better performance as the curve

slopes upward. There are, however, instances in which the slope of the curve in a downward direction indicates performance improvement. This occurs when the performance measure is one for which a decrease in the performance level means better performance. Measures involving error or time (such as absolute error and reaction time) follow this characteristic as performance is improving when the amount of error or time decreases. In such cases, the directions of the performance curves would be opposite to those just described, although the shapes of the curves would be the same.

The four curves presented in figure 11.2 are hypothetically smoothed to illustrate general patterns of performance curves. Typically, performance curves developed for individuals are not smooth but erratic, like the one in figure 11.1. However, there are various statistical procedures that can be used for curve smoothing when the reporting of research results warrants it. Finally, various individual, instructional, and motor skill characteristics can influence the type of curve that will characterize a person's performance as he or she learns a skill. You will learn about several of these characteristics in various chapters of this textbook.

Performance curves for kinematic measures.
When we use performance production measures, such as kinematics, we cannot always develop performance curves like the one in figure 11.1. This is because a kinematic measure typically does not lend itself to being represented by one number value for each trial. Kinematic measures involve performance over time *within* a trial. It is important to include this time component in the graphic representation of a kinematic measure.

To assess improvement and consistency in performance for a series of practice trials, researchers commonly show one performance curve graph for each trial. To show improvement and consistency changes, they depict a representative sample of trials from different stages of practice.

We can see an example of this approach to kinematic measures in figure 11.3. The task that generated these measures is commonly used in motor learning research. It required participants in an experiment to move a lever on a tabletop to produce the criterion movement pattern shown at the top of this figure. Each participant observed the criterion movement on a computer monitor. The four

graphs located below the criterion movement pattern represent the performance of one person for 800 trials. To provide a more representative picture of performance, the researchers analyzed practice trials in blocks of ten trials each. To represent performance changes during practice, figure 11.3 shows four blocks of trials, each representing a different segment of the 800-trial session. Each graph shows two performance characteristics. One is the person's average pattern drawn for the block of trials; this is indicated by the solid line (mean). The second is the variability of the patterns drawn for that same block of trials; this is indicated by the dashed lines (SD, or standard deviation).

To determine *improvement in performance,* compare the early to the later practice trials by examining how the shape of the person's produced pattern corresponds to the shape of the criterion pattern. As the person practiced more, the produced pattern became more like the criterion pattern. In fact, in trials 751 through 760, the participant was making a pattern almost identical to the criterion pattern.

To assess *changes in consistency,* compare how far the standard deviation lines are from the mean pattern for each block of trials. For trials 1 through 10, notice how far the standard deviation lines are from the mean. This shows a large amount of trial-to-trial variability. However, for trials 751 through 760, these lines are much closer to the mean, indicating that the person more consistently produced the same pattern on each trial of that block of trials.

Assessing Learning by Retention Tests
Another means of inferring learning from performance examines *the persistence characteristic of improved performance* due to practicing a skill. A common means of assessing this characteristic is to administer a retention test. You have been experiencing this approach to assessing learning since you began school. Teachers regularly give tests that cover units of instruction. They use these **retention tests** to determine how much you know, or have retained from your study. The teacher makes an inference concerning how much you

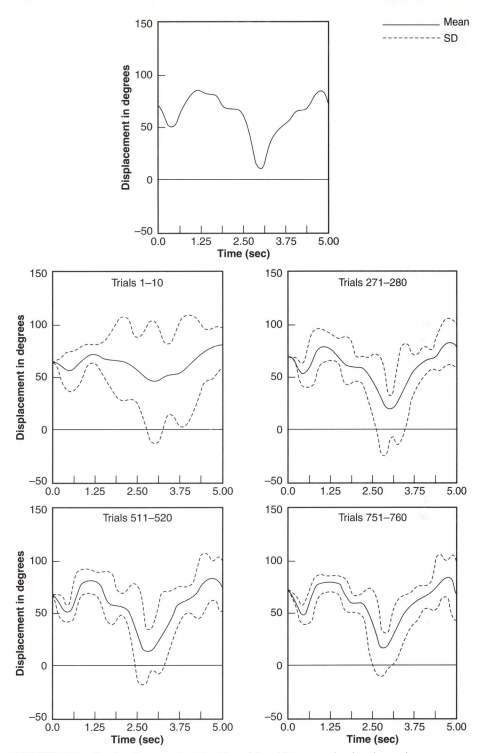

FIGURE 11.3 Results of an experiment by Marteniuk and Romanow showing changes in performance accuracy (displacement) on a tracking task at different practice trial blocks for one participant. The graph at the top shows the criterion pathway for the tracking task. [From Marteniuk, R. G., & Romanow, S. K. E. (1983). Human movement organization and learning as revealed by variability of movement, use of kinematic information, and fourier analysis. In R. A. Magill (Ed.), *Memory and control of action.* Copyright © 1983 Elsevier/North-Holland, Amsterdam, The Netherlands. Reprinted by permission.]

have learned about a particular unit of study on the basis of your test performance.

The typical way to administer a retention test in a motor skill situation is to have people perform the skill they have been practicing after a period of time during which they have not actually practiced the skill. The purpose is to determine the degree of permanence or persistence of the performance level achieved during practice; having a period of time with no practice allows this type of assessment. The actual length of time between the end of practice and the test is arbitrary. But the amount of time should be sufficiently long to allow the influence of any performance variables to dissipate to determine what was learned during practice. The critical assessment is the difference between the person's performance level on the first practice day and that on the test. If there is a significant improvement between these two periods of time, then you can be confident that learning has occurred.

Assessing Learning by Transfer Tests

The third means of inferring learning examines the *adaptability aspect of performance changes* related to learning. This assessment method involves using **transfer tests,** which are tests involving some novel situation, so that people must adapt the skill they have been practicing to the characteristics of this new situation. Two types of novel situations are especially interesting. One is a new context in which the people must perform the skill; the other is a novel variation of the skill itself.

Novel context characteristics. Test administrators can use various kinds of context changes in transfer tests. One characteristic they can change is the *availability of augmented feedback,* which is the performance information a person receives from some external source. For example, in many practice situations, the person receives augmented feedback in the form of verbal information about what he or she is doing correctly or incorrectly. If you were assessing learning to discover how well the person can rely on his or her own resources to perform the skill, then your requirement that the

person perform without augmented feedback availability would be a useful context change for the transfer test. It is important to note that some researchers refer to a test that involves this type of context change as a retention rather than a transfer test, because the practiced skill is performed during the test.

Another context characteristic a test administrator can change is the *physical environment* in which a person performs. This is especially effective for a learning situation in which the goal is to enable a person to perform in locations other than those in which he or she has practiced. For example, if you are working in a clinic with a patient with a gait problem, you want that patient to be able to adapt to the environmental demands of his or her everyday world. Although performing well in the clinic is important, it is less important than performing well in the world in which the patient must function on a daily basis. Because of this need, the transfer test in which the physical environment resembles one in the everyday world is a valuable assessment instrument.

The third aspect of context that can be changed for a transfer test is the *personal characteristics* of the test taker as they relate to skill performance. Here, the focus is on how well a person can perform the skill while adapting to characteristics of himself or herself that were not present during practice. For example, suppose you know that the person will have to perform the skill in a stressful situation. A test requiring the person to perform the skill while emotionally stressed would provide a useful assessment of his or her capability to adapt to this situation.

Novel skill variations. Another aspect of adaptability related to skill learning is a person's capability to successfully perform a novel variation of a skill he or she has learned. This capability is common in our everyday experience. For example, no one has walked at all speeds at which it is possible to walk. Yet, we can speed up or slow down our walking gait with little difficulty. Similarly, we have not grasped and drunk from every type of cup or glass that exists in the world. Yet when we are confronted with some new cup, we adapt our movements quite well to the cup characteristics and successfully drink from it. These examples illustrate the importance to people of producing novel variations of skills. One of the ways to assess how well a person can do this is to use a transfer test that incorporates this movement adaptation characteristic.

Note that one of the ways we get people to produce a novel skill variation is to alter the performance context in some way so that they must adapt their movements to it. In this way, the transfer test designed to assess capability to produce novel skill variations resembles a transfer test designed to assess capability to adapt to novel performance context features. The difference is the learning assessment focus.

Assessing Learning from Coordination Dynamics

Another method of assessing learning involves the observation of the stabilities and transitions of the dynamics of movement coordination related to performing a skill. Proponents of this approach, which is gaining in popularity in learning research, assume that when a person begins to learn a new skill, he or she is not really learning something new, but is evolving a new spatial and temporal coordination pattern from an old one. When viewed from this perspective learning involves the transition between the initial pattern, represented by a preferred coordination mode the person uses when first attempting the new skill, to the establishment of the new coordination mode. *Stability and consistency* of the coordination pattern are important criteria for determining which coordination state (initial, transition, or new) characterizes the person's performance.

For example, a person who is learning handwriting experiences an initial state represented by the coordination characteristics of the upper arm, forearm and hand while engaged in handwriting at the beginning of practice. These characteristics make up the preferred spatial and temporal structure the person and the task itself impose on the

limb, so the limb can produce movement approximating what is required. This initial stable state must be changed to a new stable state in which the person can produce fluent handwriting. Learning is the transition between these two states.

An example of this approach to assessing skill learning is an experiment by Lee, Swinnen, and Verschueren (1995). The task (see figure 11.4) required participants to learn a new bimanual coordination pattern. To perform the task, they simultaneously moved two levers toward and away from the body at the same rate (15 times in 15 sec). Their goal was to produce ellipses on the computer monitor. But to accomplish this, they had to coordinate the movement of their arms so that the right arm on each cycle was always 90 degrees out of phase with the left arm. The initial coordination pattern for the two arms for one participant is shown in figure 11.4 as the arm-to-arm displacement relationship demonstrated on the pretest on the first day of practice. The series of diagonal lines resulted when the person moved the arms in phase, in a motion resembling that of windshield wipers. The stability of this coordination pattern is indicated by the consistency of the fifteen diagonal lines produced during the pretest trial, and by the person's tendency to produce that same pattern on the pretest trial on day 2, after having performed sixty practice trials of the ellipse pattern on day 1.

By the end of day 3, this person had learned to produce the ellipse pattern. Evidence for this is the consistent production of fifteen ellipses in both the pretest and the posttest trials on day 3. However,

---

retention test   a test of a practiced skill that a learner performs following an interval of time after practice has ceased.

transfer test   a test in which a person performs a skill that is different from the skill he or she practiced, or performs the practiced skill in a context or situation different from the practice context or situation.

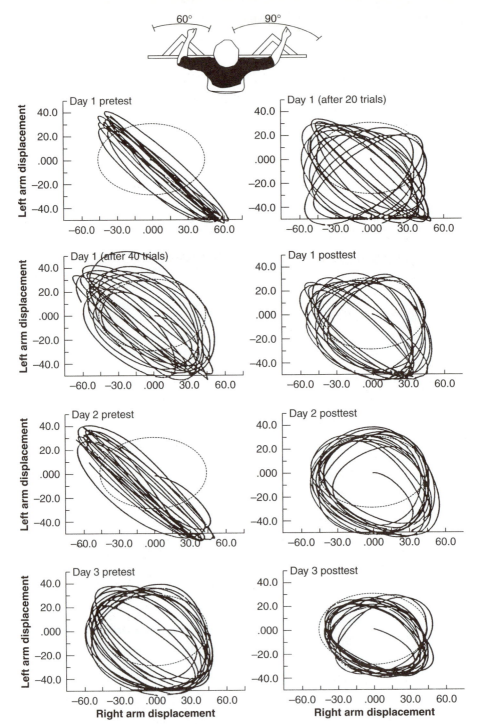

FIGURE 11.4   The task and results from the experiment by Lee, Swinnen, and Verschueren. The top panel shows the task, in which participants moved two levers to draw ellipses on the computer monitor (the dotted lines on each graph represent the goal ellipse pattern). The series of graphs shows the results as the left-arm × right-arm displacements of one person for the pretest and posttest (and some intermediate) trials for each of three practice days.   [From Lee, T. D. et al. (1995). Relative phase alterations during bimanual skill acquisition. *Journal of Motor Behavior, 27,* 263–274. Reprinted with permission of the Helen Dwight Reid Educational Foundation. Published by Heldref Publications, 1319 Eighteenth Street NW, Washington, DC 20036–1802. Copyright © 1995].

notice the instability of the performance in the many trials between the old and the new stable patterns (exhibited on the day 1 pretest and the day 3 posttest). This instability occurs during the transition between two stable states and characterizes the process of learning a new skill.

Practice Performance May Misrepresent Learning

It may be misleading to base an inference about learning solely on observed performance during practice. There are at least two reasons for this. One is that the practice situation may involve a performance variable, which was described earlier in this discussion as having the potential to artificially inflate or depress performance. The second reason is that practice performance may be misleading if it involves performance plateaus.

Practice performance may overestimate or underestimate learning. In this textbook, you will see examples of variables whose presence during practice influences performance in such a way that performance overestimates or underestimates learning. One way to overcome these problems is to use retention or transfer tests to assess learning. If a person's practice performance does represent learning, then that person's performance on a retention test should demonstrate the persistence characteristic and not deviate too much from his or her performance at the end of practice. Similarly, transfer test performance should demonstrate the person's increased capability to adapt to novel conditions.

Performance plateaus. Over the course of learning a skill, it is not uncommon for a person to experience a period of time during which improvement seems to have stopped. But for some reason, at some later time, improvement starts to occur again. This period of time during which there appears to be no further performance improvement is known as a **performance plateau.**

Examples of performance plateaus are difficult to find in the motor learning research literature because most of this research presents performance

curves that represent the average for a group of participants. To find evidence of a performance plateau, individual participant's results are needed. An experiment reported by Franks and Wilberg (1982) is an example of this latter case, and it provides a good illustration of a performance plateau (figure 11.5). This graph shows one individual's performance on a complex tracking task for ten days, with 105 trials each day. Notice that this person showed consistent improvement for the first four days. Then, on days 5 through 7, performance improvement stopped. However, this was a temporary characteristic; performance began to improve again on day 8 and the improvement continued for the next two days. The steady-state performance on days 5 through 7 is a good example of a performance plateau.

The concept of a performance plateau has had a historical place in motor learning research. The first evidence of a plateau during skill learning is attributed to the work of Bryan and Harter (1897), who published their observations of new telegraphers learning Morse code. The authors noted steady improvement in the telegraphers' letters-per-minute speed for the first twenty weeks. But then a performance plateau occurred that lasted six weeks; this was followed by further performance improvement for the final twelve weeks. Since this early demonstration, researchers have been debating about whether a plateau is a real learning phenomenon or merely a temporary performance artifact (see Adams 1987 for the most recent review of plateau research). At present, most agree that plateaus are *performance rather than learning characteristics.* This means that plateaus may appear during the course of practice, but it appears that learning continues during these times.

---

performance plateau   while learning a skill, a period of time in which the learner experiences no improvement after having experienced consistent improvement; typically, the learner then experiences further improvement with continued practice.

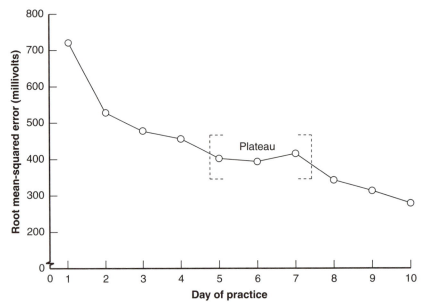

FIGURE 11.5   Results from the experiment by Franks and Wilberg showing the results from one participant performing the complex tracking task for ten days, with 105 trials per day. Notice the performance plateau for three days (days 5, 6, and 7) where performance leveled off before the subject showed improvement again.   [From Franks, I. M., & Wilberg, R. B. (1982). The generation of movement patterns during the acquisition of a pursuit tracking task. *Human Movement Science, 1,* 251–272. Copyright © 1982 Elsevier/North-Holland, Amsterdam, The Netherlands. Reprinted by permission.]

There are several *reasons performance plateaus occur.* One is that the plateau represents a period of transition between two phases of acquiring certain aspects of a skill. During this transition, the person is developing a new strategy that the task requires to increase the level of performance already achieved. Consequently, no performance improvement occurs until the new strategy is successfully implemented. Other possible explanations for a performance plateau may be that it represents a period of poor motivation, a time of fatigue, or a lack of attention directed to an important aspect of a skill. Finally, it is possible the plateau may be due not to these performance characteristics but to limitations imposed by the performance measure. This is the case when the performance measure involves what are known as *ceiling* or *floor effects.* These effects occur when the performance mea-

sure will not permit the score to go above or below a certain point.

SUMMARY

To effectively study concepts and issues related to the learning of motor skills, it is important to distinguish the terms performance, which is an observable behavior, and learning, which is inferred from the observation of performance. When people learn motor skills, they typically demonstrate four performance characteristics: performance improvement over a period of time, an increase in performance consistency, a persistence of an improved performance capability for long periods of time, and the capability to adapt to a variety of performance context characteristics. The

A CLOSER LOOK

An Example of Practice Performance that Misrepresents Learning

An experiment by Winstein et al. (1996) is a good example of how practice performance may not represent the influence of a variable on the learning of a motor skill.

- **Purpose of the experiment:** Which of three different augmented feedback conditions would be best as an aid to help people learn a partial-weight bearing task? This task is a skill often taught by physical therapists. (Augmented feedback refers to performance-based information a person receives from a source external to himself or herself.)
- **The task:** The participants' goal was to learn to support 30 percent of their body weight while stepping on a floor scale with a preferred leg while on crutches. The target amount of weight was marked on the scale for each person. Participants in one group could see the scale needle move as they were stepping on the scale (concurrent augmented feedback). These participants were able to correctly adjust their weight on each trial. Two other groups received augmented feedback after performing the task (terminal augmented feedback). Participants in these groups could not see the scale needle during each trial, but saw a red line on the scale after completing one trial or a five-trial set (the five-trial group saw five red lines, each marked with the corresponding trial number of the set).
- **Practice trials and retention test:** All three groups performed eighty practice trials on one

day. Two days later, they performed a retention test that consisted of twenty trials without any feedback about the amount of weight they applied to the scale.
- **Results:** *During the practice trials* the concurrent feedback group performed with very little error. The two terminal feedback groups performed with significantly more error than the concurrent group. However, *on the retention test* the concurrent group performed significantly worse than at the end of the practice trials, and worse than both of the terminal groups. The terminal feedback groups performed with about the same amount of error as they produced at the end of the practice trials.
- **Conclusion:** It is important to notice that if the retention test had not been given, the conclusion about the best augmented feedback condition for learning this task would have favored the concurrent condition. However, this conclusion would be based on performance when the various types of augmented feedback were available to the participants. The more valid way to determine which feedback condition is best for learning is when no augmented feedback is available, because it reflects the therapy goal of enabling people to perform the partial-weight bearing task in daily living conditions, which is with no augmented feedback. When the participants were tested under this condition on the retention test, the conclusion was that the *concurrent feedback was the worst learning condition.* Thus, performance during practice misrepresented the influence of the augmented feedback conditions on learning.

---

assessment of one or more of these characteristics forms the basis for four methods commonly used to assess skill learning. One method is to look for the improvement and consistency characteristics of performance as the person practices. We can see these when we plot performance curves of outcome and kinematic performance measures during practice. The second method is to use a retention test

which assesses the persistence characteristic by requiring a person to perform a practiced skill after a period of time during which he or she has not practiced. Third, transfer tests assess a person's acquired capability to adapt to new performance conditions. A transfer test requires a learner to perform either the practiced skill in a new situation or a new variation of the practiced skill. The fourth learning assessment method involves the observation of the consistency and stability characteristics of coordination patterns during practice and on tests. This method provides an opportunity to observe previously learned and newly acquired coordination patterns as well as the transition between them.

To assess learning only on the basis of practice performance can sometimes lead to invalid inferences. Certain performance variables can artificially inflate or depress performance so that the test over- or underestimates the amount a person has learned. Additionally, a performance artifact known as a performance plateau can occur, giving the appearance that learning has stopped when it has not. Retention and transfer tests provide ways to avoid the potential problem of the influence of performance variables during practice. And, the observation of additional practice provides a means of determining if a performance plateau occurred during the learning of a skill.

RELATED READINGS

Christina, R. W. (1997). Concerns and issues in studying and assessing motor learning. *Measurement in Physical Education and Exercise Science, 1,* 19–38.

Langley, D. J. (1997). Exploring student skill learning. A case for investigating subjective experience. *Quest, 49,* 142–160.

Lee, T. D., & Swinnen, S. P. (1993). Three legacies of Bryan and Harter: Automaticity, variability, and change in skilled performance. In J. L. Starkes & F. Allard (Eds.), *Cognitive issues in motor expertise* (pp. 295–315). Amsterdam: Elsevier.

Slifkin, A. B., & Newell, K. M. (1998). Is variability in human performance a reflection of system noise? *Current Directions in Psychological Science, 7,* 170–177.

Zanone, P., & Kelso, J. A. S. (1994). The coordination dynamics of learning: Theoretical structure and experimental agenda. In S. P. Swinnen, H. Heuer, J. Masson, & P. Caesar (Eds.), *Interlimb coordination: Neural, dynamical, and cognitive constraints* (pp. 461–490). San Diego: Academic Press.

STUDY QUESTIONS

1. Explain how the terms *performance* and *learning* differ, and why we must *infer* learning from performance situations.

2. What four performance characteristics are generally present if learning of a skill has occurred?

3. What is an advantage of using transfer tests in making a valid assessment of learning? Give an example of a real-world situation that illustrates this advantage.

4. What is a performance plateau? What seems to be the most likely reason a performance plateau occurs in motor skill learning?

5. Describe a motor skill learning situation in which it may be possible to under- or overestimate the amount of learning during practice. Indicate how you would demonstrate this misrepresentation.

The Stages of Learning

Concept: Distinct performance and performer
characteristics change during skill learning

APPLICATION

Have you ever noticed that people who are skilled at performing an activity often have difficulty teaching that activity to a beginner? This difficulty is due in part to the expert's failure to understand how the beginner approaches performing the skill each time he or she tries it. To facilitate successful skill acquisition, the teacher, coach, or therapist must consider the point of view of the student or patient and ensure that instructions, feedback, and practice conditions are in harmony with the person's needs.

Think for a moment about a skill you are proficient in. Remember how you approached performing that skill when you first tried it as a beginner. For example, suppose you were learning the tennis serve. Undoubtedly you thought about a lot of things, such as how you held the racquet, how high you were tossing the ball, whether you were transferring your weight properly at contact, and so on. During each attempt and between attempts, your thoughts focused on fundamental elements of the serve. Now, recall what you thought about after you had had lots of practice and had become reasonably proficient at serving. You probably did not continue to think about all the specific elements each time you served. If you continued practicing for many years so that you became skilled, your thoughts while serving undoubtedly changed even

further. Rather than thinking about the specific elements involved in serving, you could concentrate on other aspects of the skill. Although you still concentrated on looking at the ball while tossing it and during contact, you also thought about things like where you were going to place this serve in your opponent's service court, or what you were going to do after you served.

Although this performance example involves a sport skill, the underlying concept helps explain the difficulty experienced by skilled people teaching beginners in all skill instruction contexts. In the rehabilitation clinic, for example, the same problem exists. Imagine that you are a physical therapist working with a stroke patient and helping him or her regain locomotion function. Like the tennis pro, you are a skilled performer (here, of locomotion skills); the patient is like a beginner. Although there may be some differences between the sport and the rehab situations because the patient was skilled prior to the stroke, in both cases you must approach skill acquisition from the perspective of the beginner.

In the examples just described, we have seen that different characteristics distinguish beginners from skilled people. At the instruction level, this indicates that the skilled person teaching the beginner must approach performing the skill the way he or she did as a beginner. The extent to which the skilled person can do this will influence the degree of success he or she has teaching beginners. In addition, those who teach or coach skilled people likewise must understand characteristic of the skilled performer. In both cases, those who provide motor skill instruction benefit from being aware of those characteristics people demonstrate at these different skill levels.

DISCUSSION

An important characteristic of learning motor skills is that all people seem to go through distinct stages as they acquire skills. Several models have been proposed to identify and describe these stages. We discuss two of the more influential of these next.

The Fitts and Posner Three-Stage Model

Paul Fitts and Michael Posner presented the acknowledged classic learning stages model in 1967. Their model continues to be referred to by researchers today. They proposed that learning a motor skill involves three stages. During the *first stage,* called the **cognitive stage** of learning, the beginner focuses on cognitively oriented problems. For example, beginners typically try to answer questions such as these: What is my objective? How far should I move this arm? What is the best way to hold this implement? Where should this arm be when my right leg is here? Additionally, the learner must engage in cognitive activity as he or she listens to instructions and receives feedback from the instructor.

Performance during this first stage is marked by a large number of errors, and the errors tend to be large ones. Performance during this stage also is highly variable, showing a lack of consistency from one attempt to the next. And although beginners may be aware that they are doing something wrong, they generally do not know what they need to do to improve.

The *second stage* of learning in the Fitts and Posner model is called the **associative stage** of learning. The cognitive activity that characterized the cognitive stage changes at this stage, because the person has learned to associate certain environmental cues with the movements required to achieve the goal of the skill. The person makes fewer and less gross errors since he or she has acquired the basic fundamentals or mechanics of the skill, although they need to be improved. Because this type of improvement still is required, Fitts and Posner referred to this stage as a *refining* stage, in which the person focuses on performing the skill successfully and being more consistent from one attempt to the next. During this refining process, performance variability begins to decrease. Also during this associative stage, people acquire the capability to detect and identify some of their own performance errors.

After much practice and experience, which can take many years, some people move into the **autonomous stage** of learning, which is the *final stage* of learning. Here the skill has become almost *automatic,* or habitual. People in this stage do not consciously think about what they are doing while performing the skill, because they can perform it without conscious thought. They often can do another task at the same time; for example, they can carry on a conversation while typing. Performance variability during this stage is very small: skilled people perform the skill consistently well from one attempt to the next. Additionally, these skilled performers can detect their own errors, and make the proper adjustments to correct them. Fitts and Posner pointed out the likelihood that not every person learning a skill will reach this autonomous stage. The quality of instruction and practice as well as the amount of practice are important factors determining achievement of this final stage.

It is important to think of the three stages of the Fitts and Posner model as parts of a continuum of practice time, as figure 12.1 depicts. Learners do not make abrupt shifts from one stage to the next. There is a gradual transition or change of the learner's characteristics from stage to stage. Because of this, it is often difficult to detect which stage an individual is in at a particular moment. However, as we will consider in more detail later in

| Cognitive stage | Associative stage | Autonomous stage |

Practice time →

FIGURE 12.1   The stages of learning from the Fitts and Posner model placed on a time continuum.

this discussion, the beginner and the skilled performer have distinct characteristics that we can observe and need to understand.

Gentile's Two-Stage Model

Another model that motor learning researchers commonly refer to was proposed by Gentile (1972, 1987, 2000). In contrast to Fitts and Posner, she viewed motor skill learning as progressing through two stages, and presented these stages from the perspective of the goal of the learner in each stage.

In the *first stage* the goal of the learner is **"getting the idea of the movement."** We can understand the "idea of the movement" in general terms as what the person must do to achieve the goal of the skill. In movement terms, the "idea" involves the *appropriate movement coordination pattern* required for achieving the action goal of the skill. For example, if a person is rehabilitating his or her capability to reach for and grasp a cup, the person's focus in the first stage of learning is on acquiring the appropriate arm and hand coordination that will lead to his or her successfully reaching for and grasping a cup.

In addition to establishing the basic movement pattern, the person also must learn to *discriminate between environmental features* that specify how the movements must be produced from those that do not influence movement production. Gentile referred to these features as regulatory and nonregulatory environmental conditions. You may recall from the discussion in chapter 1 of Gentile's taxonomy of motor skills that *regulatory conditions* are characteristics of the performance environment that influence, i.e., regulate, the characteristics of the movements used to perform the skill. In the example of learning to reach for and grasp a cup,

the regulatory conditions include information such as the size of the cup, the shape of the cup, the distance the cup is from the person, and so on. On the other hand, there are characteristics of the performance environment that do not influence the movement characteristics of the skill. These are called *nonregulatory conditions.* For example, the color of the cup or the shape of the table the cup is on are nonrelevant pieces of information for reaching for and grasping the cup, and therefore do not influence the movements used to perform the skill.

To achieve these two important goals, the learner explores a variety of movement possibilities. Through trial and error, he or she experiences movement characteristics that are successful as well as unsuccessful, and begins to focus practice on those that are successful. In addition, because the learner has numerous problems to solve to

---

cognitive stage   the first stage of learning in the Fitts and Posner model; the beginning or initial stage on the learning stages continuum.

associative stage   the second stage of learning in the Fitts and Posner model; an intermediate stage on the learning stages continuum.

autonomous stage   the third stage of learning in the Fitts and Posner model; the final stage on the learning stages continuum, also called the *automatic stage.*

"getting the idea of the movement"   the learner's goal in the first stage of learning in Gentile's model; it refers to the need for the learner to establish an appropriate movement coordination pattern to accomplish the goal of the skill.

A CLOSER LOOK

Implications of Gentile's Learning Stages Model for Instruction and Rehabilitation Environments

During the First Stage

- Have the learner focus on developing the basic movement coordination pattern of the skill for both open and closed skills.
- Establish practice situations that provide opportunities to discriminate regulatory from nonregulatory characteristics.

During the Second Stage

Closed skills. In practice situations, include characteristics as similar as possible to those the learner will experience in his or her everyday world, or in the environment in which he or she will perform the skill.

   Examples:

- walking on similar surfaces in similar environments
- writing with the same type of implement on the same type of surface
- shooting basketball free throws as they would occur in a game
- shooting arrows under match conditions

Open skills. In practice, systematically vary the controllable regulatory conditions of actual performance situations, while allowing naturally varying characteristics to occur as they normally would.

   Examples:

- walking from one end of a hallway to the other while various numbers of people are walking in different directions and at various speeds (systematically vary the hallway size and numbers of people; allow the people to walk at any speed or in any direction they wish)
- returning volleyball serves under gamelike conditions (systematically vary the location of the serve, the offensive alignment of players, etc.; the speed and action of the ball will vary at the server's discretion)

determine how to achieve the action goal, he or she engages in a large amount of cognitive problem-solving activity. When the learner reaches the end of this stage, he or she has developed a movement coordination pattern that allows action goal achievement, but this achievement is neither consistent nor efficient. However, as Gentile (1987) described it, the learner "does have a framework for organizing an effective movement" (p. 119).

In the *second stage* the learner's goal is described as *fixation/diversification.* During this stage the learner must acquire several characteristics to continue skill improvement. First, the person must develop the capability of *adapting* the movement pattern he or she has acquired in the first stage to the specific demands of any performance situation requiring that skill. Second, the person

must increase his or her *consistency* in achieving the goal of the skill. Third, the person must learn to perform the skill with an *economy of effort.*

A unique feature of the second stage in Gentile's model is that the learner's goals depend on the type of skill. More specifically, the open skill and closed skill classifications specify these goals. *Closed skills require* **fixation** of the basic movement coordination pattern acquired during the first stage of learning. This means that the learner must refine this pattern so that he or she can consistently achieve the action goal. The learner works toward developing the capability to perform the movement pattern with little, if any, conscious effort (i.e., automatically) and a minimum of physical energy. Thus, practice of a closed skill during this stage must give the learner the opportunity to "fixate" the required movement coordination pattern in such a way that he or she is capable of performing it consistently. On the other hand, *open skills require* **diversification** of the basic movement pattern acquired during the first stage of learning. An important characteristic of open skills, which differs from closed skills, is the requirement for the performer to quickly adapt to the continuously changing spatial and temporal regulatory conditions of the skill. These conditions change within a performance trial as well as between trials. This means that the learner must become attuned to the critical features of the regulatory conditions and acquire the capability to modify the movement patterns to meet their constantly changing demands on the performer. As a result, rather than learning to automatically produce a specific movement pattern, the learner must acquire the capability to monitor the environmental conditions and modify the movement pattern accordingly. Thus practice of an open skill during this stage must provide the learner with experiences that will require these types of movement pattern modifications.

One aspect of the second stage of learning in Gentile's model that requires further consideration concerns the features of the acquired movement pattern that the performer must change to meet performance situation demands. Although Gentile's model indicates that fixation of the pattern is the goal of the second stage for closed skills, the performer may need to make movement pattern modifications. But, closed skill pattern modifications differ from those required for open skills. You saw some examples of these differences in the discussion of the adaptability component of our definition of learning in chapter 11. These differences relate to the distinction between invariant features and parameters of a coordination pattern, which were discussed in chapter 4. For closed skills, pattern modifications typically involve movement parameter changes rather than changes of the invariant features of the pattern itself. For example, in bowling, on the second ball of a frame the bowler is confronted with a different pattern of pins than he or she experienced with the first ball.

But, rather than change the movement coordination pattern in order to bowl the ball, the bowler modifies characteristics such as location of ball release or ball speed. In golf, a ball in different types of grass or sand may require the golfer to modify his or her stance or the trajectory of the downswing, but not the invariant features of the swing itself. Similarly, situations requiring prehension may require various widths of grasp apertures or amounts of grasp force, but the basic invariant features of the reach-and-grasp action will remain consistent. However, for open skills, the performer may be required to change either the invariant features or parameters of the movement pattern. For example, if the action goal for a tennis player is to return a serve, he or she may prepare to hit a forehand groundstroke but have to change to a backhand when the serve is hit. Or, if the action goal of a pedestrian is to cross a street at an intersection, he or she may begin to walk but have to change to a run partway across because the traffic signal has changed.

Finally, it is important to note that the types of movement pattern changes required by closed and open skills involve different action planning and preparation demands for the performer. Closed skills allow the learner to plan and prepare either without any or a minimum of time constraints. However, time constraints severely limit the amount of time the performer has to plan and prepare the performance of an open skill. This difference indicates that

---

fixation   the learner's goal in the second stage of learning in Gentile's model for learning closed skills in which learners refine movement patterns so that they can produce them correctly, consistently, and efficiently from trial to trial.

diversification   the learner's goal in the second stage of learning in Gentile's model for learning open skills in which learners acquire the capability to modify the movement pattern according to environmental context characteristics.

The Initial Stage of Learning to Bowl

A study by Langley (1995) provides a good illustration of the performer and performance characteristics described for the initial stage of learning in both the Fitts and Posner and the Gentile learning stages models. Langley assessed student thought processes during a beginning bowling class that met for ten weeks. He had each student complete a questionnaire at the end of each class, he took extensive observational and interpretive notes, and he interviewed the students at the beginning, middle, and end of the ten-week session.

The results of this study indicated that student thoughts focused primarily on errors in task perfor-

mance. In the first week, the primary errors of concern related to lack of control of the ball, which related to inconsistency of throws and aiming problems. In the middle week, students began to describe the movement characteristics and outcomes of their throws as keys to what they needed to focus on to improve. By the end of the course, students indicated problems with consistency and accuracy of the hook ball. Consistent with expectations of learning stages models, these beginning bowlers showed evidence of an initial lack of an appropriate movement pattern to achieve the action goal, inconsistent performance, a lack of knowledge about specific components of the skill (e.g., aiming), and the development of error detection capabilities.

---

during practice of open skills, the performer must acquire the capability to quickly attend to the environmental regulatory characteristics that direct action as well as to anticipate changes before they actually occur.

Performer and Performance Changes across the Stages of Learning

Stages-of-learning models indicate that in each learning stage, both the person and the skill performance show distinct characteristics. In this section, we will look at a few of these characteristics. This overview has two benefits: first, it provides a closer look at the skill learning process, and second, it helps explain why instruction or training strategies need to be developed for people in different learning stages.

Changes in rate of improvement. As a person progresses along the skill learning continuum from the beginner stage to the highly skilled stage, the *rate* changes at which the person improves. Although, as figure 11.2 showed, there are four different types of performance curves representing different rates of improvement during skill learning, the *negatively accelerated pattern is more typical of skill learning* than the others. This means that early in practice, a

learner usually experiences a large amount of improvement relatively quickly. But as practice continues, the amount of improvement decreases.

This change in the rate of improvement during skill learning has a long and consistent history in motor learning. In fact, in 1926 Snoddy mathematically formalized a law known as the **power law of practice.** According to this law, early practice is characterized by large amounts of improvement. However, after this seemingly rapid improvement, further practice yields improvement rates that are much smaller. Exactly how long the change in rates takes to occur depends on the skill.

Crossman (1959) reported what is today considered a classic experiment demonstrating the power law of practice. He examined how long it took cigar makers to produce a cigar as a function of how many cigars each worker had made in a career. Some workers had made 10,000 cigars, whereas others had made over 10 million. The skill itself was a relatively simple one that could be done very quickly. The first notable finding was the relationship between performance improvement and the amount of experience. Workers still showed performance improvement after seven years of experience, during which time they had made over 10 million cigars (see figure 12.2). In addition to

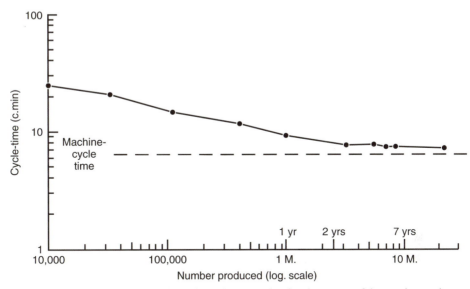

FIGURE 12.2   The results from the study by Crossman showing the amount of time workers took to make a cigar as a function of the number of cigars made across seven years of experience. Note that both axes are log scales.   [From Crossman, E. R. F. W. (1959). A theory of the acquisition of speed skill. *Ergonomics, 2,* 153–166. Copyright © 1959 Taylor and Francis, London.]

this remarkable result, he found evidence of the power law of practice for these workers. As you can see in figure 12.2, the majority of all the improvement occurred during the first two years. After that, performance improvement increments were notably smaller.

The difference in rate of improvement between early and later practice is due partly to the amount of improvement possible at a given time. Initially, there is room for a large amount of improvement. The errors people make during early practice trials are large and lead to many unsuccessful attempts at performing the skill. Because many of these errors are easy to correct, the learner can experience a large amount of improvement quickly. However, as practice continues, the amount of improvement possible decreases. The errors people make later in practice are much smaller. As a result, their correction of these errors yields less improvement than they experienced earlier in practice. And certainly from the leaner's perspective, attaining notable improvement seems to take longer than it did before.

Changes in limb-segment coordination. When the skill being learned requires the person to coordinate various segments of a limb, the typical learner will use the common initial strategy of trying to control the many degrees of freedom of the limb segments by holding some joints rigid. Nikolai Bernstein, the late Russian scientist whose writings continue to influence the development of motor learning theory, described a strategy beginners use to gain control of the degrees of freedom associated with performing a complex motor skill (Bernstein, 1967; Whiting, 1984). Today, motor learning researchers refer to this

power law of practice   a mathematical law describing the change in rate of performance improvement during skill learning; large amounts of improvement occur during early practice, but smaller improvement rates characterize further practice.

strategy as **freezing the degrees of freedom.** For example, suppose a beginner must perform a skill such as a racquetball forehand shot, which involves the coordination of the wrist, elbow, and shoulder joints of one arm. This means that for the arm movement component of this skill, the person needs to control three degrees of freedom. The common strategy the beginner uses to achieve this control, so that he or she can hit the ball, is to keep the wrist and elbow joints "locked" (i.e., "frozen"). This strategy makes the arm and hand move as if they were a stick, with the arm and hand segments acting as one segment. But as the person practices the skill, a freeing of the degrees of freedom emerges as the "frozen" joints begin to become "unfrozen" and operate in a way that allows the arm and hand segments to function as a multisegment unit. This new unit eventually demonstrates characteristics of a *functional synergy,* which means the individual arm and hand segments work together in a cooperative way to enable optimal performance of the skill. It is interesting to note that Southard and Higgins (1987) reported evidence demonstrating this kind of coordination development for the arm movement component of the racquetball forehand shot. They showed that a primary benefit of the development of the functional synergy of the arm segments was an increase in racquet velocity at ball impact.

Researchers have demonstrated similar coordination development characteristics for several other skills. For example, Anderson and Sidaway (1994) showed that when beginning soccer players initially tried to kick a ball properly, they limited the movements of their hip and knee joints. The problem with this strategy is that it limits the velocity that can be generated by the hip joint, because the player cannot use the knee joint effectively. With practice, however, players' kicking velocity increased, as their hip and knee joints acquired greater freedom of movement and increased functional synergy.

In a final example, note that these coordination changes are not limited to sports skills or to people acquiring new skills. Stroke patients going through physical therapy to help them move from sitting to standing and then to sitting again show coordination development characteristics similar to those of people acquiring a new skill (Ada, O'Dwyer, & Neilson, 1993). In this experiment, recovering stroke patients progressed from being able to sit-stand-sit without assistance one time to being able to perform this sequence three times in a row in 10 sec. It is noteworthy that the coordination between the hip and the knee joints showed marked improvement changes as the patients progressed, demonstrating the development of the functional synergy required for these joints to allow unaided standing.

Changes in altering a preferred coordination pattern. Because we have learned to perform a variety of motor skills throughout our lives, we have developed preferred ways of moving. In fact, each of us has developed a rather large repertoire of movement patterns that we prefer to use. When confronted with learning a new skill, we often determine that it resembles a skill we already know how to perform. As a result, we typically begin practicing the new skill using movement characteristics similar to those of the skill we already know. For example, it is common for an experienced baseball player to use a swing resembling baseball batting when he or she first practices hitting a golf ball.

When a person is learning a new skill that requires altering an established coordination pattern, an interesting transition from old to new pattern occurs. The experiment by Lee, Swinnen, and Verschueren (1995) that we discussed in chapter 11 provides a good example of this change. Recall that participants had to lean to bimanually move two levers simultaneously in a 90-degree out-of-phase arm movement relationship in order to draw ellipses on the computer monitor. Figure 11.4 showed that when they first were confronted with this task, the participants' preferred way of coordinating their arms was to move both arms at the same time, producing diagonal patterns. The influence of this preferred movement pattern remained

A CLOSER LOOK

Controlling Degrees of Freedom as a Training Strategy in Occupational Therapy

A case study of a thirty-four-year-old hemiplegic woman who had suffered a stroke demonstrates how a therapist can use an understanding of the degree-of-freedom problem to develop an occupational therapy strategy (Flinn, 1995). To increase impaired left-arm strength and function during the first two months of outpatient therapy, the therapist engaged the patient in using the impaired arm to perform several functional tasks for which the degrees of freedom were restricted. To achieve this, the therapist decreased the number of joints involved in the task by stabilizing or eliminating some joints and decreasing the amount of movement of the limb against gravity. For example, the patient used the impaired arm to lock her wheelchair brakes, dust tables, and provide stability while she stood and brushed her teeth using her sound arm. During the next two months, as the patient's left-arm use improved, the therapist increased the degrees of freedom by requiring the control of more joints. For example, initially the patient simply had pushed silverware from the counter into the drawer; now the patient grasped the objects from the counter, lifted them, and placed them in the drawer. Finally, the therapist again increased the degrees-of-freedom demands a couple of months later. Now the treatment focused specifically on the everyday multiple degrees-of-freedom tasks the patient would have to perform at her regular workplace.

for more than sixty practice trials. Participants did not produce the new coordination pattern consistently until they had performed 180 practice trials. Instability characterized the coordination patterns they produced on trials between these two demonstrations of stable patterns.

The Lee et al. experiment demonstrates several things. First, it shows that people approach skill learning situations with distinct movement pattern biases that they may need to overcome to achieve the goal of the skill to be learned. Second, it is possible for people to overcome these biases, but often this takes a lot of practice (the actual amount varies among people). Finally, an observable pattern of stability-instability-stability characterizes the transition between production of the preferred movement pattern and production of the goal pattern. The initially preferred and the newly acquired goal movement patterns are distinguished by unique but stable kinematic characteristics over repeated performances. However, during the transition period between these stable patterns, the limb kinematics are very irregular or unstable.

People who provide skill instruction should note that this transition period can be a difficult and frustrating time for the learner. The instructor or therapist who is aware of this can be influential in helping the person work through this transition stage. One helpful strategy is providing extra motivational encouragements to keep the person effectively engaged in practice.

Changes in muscles used to perform the skill. If practicing a skill results in coordination changes, we should expect a related change in the muscles a person uses while performing the skill. EMG patterns produced while people practiced skills have shown that early in practice a person uses his or her muscles inappropriately. Two characteristics are particularly noteworthy. First, more muscles than are needed commonly are involved. Second, the timing of the activation of the involved muscle

freezing the degrees of freedom a common initial strategy of beginning learners to control the many degrees of freedom associated with the coordination demands of a motor skill; the person holds some joints rigid (i.e., "freezes" them) while performing the skill.

A CLOSER LOOK

Muscle Activation Changes during Dart-Throwing Practice

An experiment by Jaegers et al. (1989) illustrates how the sequence and timing of muscle activation reorganizes as a person practices a skill. Individuals who were inexperienced in dart throwing made forty-five throws at a target on each of three successive days. Several arm and shoulder muscles were monitored by EMG.

The three muscles primarily involved in stabilizing the arm and upper body were the anterior deltoid, latissimus dorsi, and clavicular pectoralis. On the first day, these muscles erratically activated both before and after the dart release. But at the end of the last day, these mucles followed a specific sequence of activation initiation. The clavicular pectoralis and anterior deltoid muscles became active approximately 40 to 80 msec prior to the dart release and turned off at release. The latissimus dorsi became active just before the release and remained active for 40 msec after release. Then, the anterior deltoid became active again.

The primary muscle involved in producing the forearm-extension–based throwing action was the lateral triceps. During the initial practice trials, this muscle initiated activation erratically, before and after dart release. But by the end of the third day, it consistently initiated activation approximately 60 msec prior to dart release and remained active until just after release.

---

groups is incorrect. As a person continues to practice, the number of muscles involved decreases so that eventually a minimal number of muscles needed to produce the action are activated, and the timing of when the involved muscles are activated becomes appropriate.

Researchers have provided evidence showing these types of change during practice for a variety of physical activities. For example, muscle activation changes have been demonstrated for sport skills such as the single-knee circle mount on the horizontal bar in gymnastics (Kamon & Gormley, 1968), ball throwing to a target (Vorro, Wilson, & Dainis, 1978), and dart throwing (Jaegers et al., 1989). Also, researchers have shown muscle activation differences resulting from practice in laboratory tasks, such as complex, rapid arm movement and manual aiming tasks (Schneider et al., 1989), as well as simple, rapid elbow flexion tasks (Gabriel & Boucher, 1998), and arm-extension tasks (Moore & Marteniuk, 1986).

The change in muscle use that occurs while a person learns a skill reflects a *reorganization of the motor control system* as that skill is acquired. As Bernstein (1967) first proposed, this reorganization results from the need for the motor control system to solve the degrees-of-freedom problem it confronts when the person first attempts the skill. By structuring muscle activation appropriately, the motor control system can take advantage of physical properties of the environment, such as gravity or other basic physical laws. By doing this, the motor control system reduces the amount of work it has to do and establishes a base for successful skill performance.

Changes in energy use. Because the performer and performance changes we have described in the preceding sections occur as a result of practicing a skill, we can reasonably expect that the amount of energy a person uses while performing the skill should change with practice as well. Although there has been little empirical study of this effect, evidence supports this expectation. Economy of movement refers to minimizing the energy cost of performing a skill. Beginners expend a large amount of energy (have a high energy cost), whereas skilled performers perform more efficiently, with minimum expenditure of energy.*

Several energy sources have been associated with performing skills. One is the *physiological*

---

*Note that many prefer the term *economy* to *efficiency;* see Sparrow and Newell (1998).

energy involved in skilled performance; researchers identify this by measuring the amount of oxygen a person uses while performing a skill. They also determine physiological energy use by measuring the caloric cost of performing the skill. People also expended *mechanical energy* while performing; scientists determine this by dividing the work rate by the metabolic rate of the individual. As we learn a skill, changes in the amount of energy we use occur for each of these sources. The result is that we perform with greater efficiency; in other words, our energy cost decreases as our movements become more economical.

Scientists have been accumulating research evidence only recently to support the widely held assumption that energy use decreases as a result of practicing a skill. For example, *oxygen use* decreased for people learning to perform on a complex slalom ski simulator in twenty-min practice sessions over a period of five days (Durand et al., 1994). Sparrow (Sparrow & Irizarry-Lopez, 1987; Sparrow & Newell, 1994) demonstrated that oxygen use, heart rate, and *caloric costs* decrease with practice of a motor skill for persons learning to walk on their hands and feet (creeping) on a treadmill moving at a constant speed. And Heise (1995; Heise & Cornwell, 1997) showed *mechanical efficiency* to increase as a function of practice for people learning to perform a ball-throwing task.

Changes in achieving the kinematic goals of the skill. Kinematic characteristics define the spatial and temporal features of performing a skill. Skilled performance has certain displacement, velocity, and acceleration limb-movement-pattern goals. As a person practices a skill, he or she not only becomes more successful in achieving these goals, but also acquires these kinematic goals at different times during practice, although in the same sequence. Displacement is the first kinematic goals persons achieve, indicating that spatial characteristics of a skill are the first ones people successfully acquire. The next goal people achieve is velocity; this is followed by acceleration. The instructional significance of this progression of kinematics is

that it suggests the importance of focusing on spatial features of a skill first, and then progressing to the more temporal features.

Marteniuk and Romanow (1983) provided the best demonstation of this systematic progression of kinematic goal acquisition in an experiment that was briefly introduced in chapter 11. Participants practiced moving a horizontal lever back and forth to produce a complex displacement pattern (shown in figure 11-3). During 800 trials of practice, they became increasingly more accurate and consistent at producing the criterion pattern. An evaluation of the kinematic performance measures showed that the participants first achieved accuracy and consistency with the displacement characteristics. Then they acquired the velocity and finally the acceleration characteristics as practice progressed.

Changes in visual attention. Because vision plays a key role in the learning and control of skills, it is interesting to note how the use of vision changes as a function of practicing a skill. Because we discussed most of these changes at length in chapter 6, we will mention them only briefly here. Beginners typically look at too many things; this tendency leads them frequently to direct their visual attention to inappropriate environmental cues. As a person practices a skill, he or she directs visual attention toward sources of information that are more appropriate for guiding his or her performance. In other words, the person gains an increased capability to direct his or her vision to the regulatory features in the environment that will provide the most useful information for performing the skill. Also, people get better at appropriately directing their visual attention earlier during the time course of performing a skill. This timing aspect of directing visual attention is important because it increases the time available in which the person can select and produce an action required by the situation.

Changes in conscious attention when performing a skill. According to the Fitts and Posner learning stages model, early in practice the learner consciously thinks about almost every part of performing the skill.

A CLOSER LOOK

Driving Experience and Attention Demands of Driving a Standard-Shift Car

Shinar, Meir, and Ben-Shoham (1998) used a dual-task procedure to determine the influence of years of driving experience on the attention demands for driving a standard shift car. They asked forty licensed drivers (ages eighteen to sixty-six years) to drive their own manual or automatic transmission cars through a 5-km route through downtown Tel Aviv. The route involved streets with multiple lanes, many intersections, many traffic signs, heavy traffic, and many pedestrians and pedestrian crossings. The secondary task involved the drivers observing traffic signs and

verbally reporting each sign that indicated "Slow—Children on the Road" and "No Stopping."

The results showed that the experienced drivers (median = eight years of experience) of either the manual or automatic transmission cars detected similar percentages of the two signs. However, the novice drivers (median = one and one-quarter years of experience) of manual transmission cars detected lower percentages of the signs than those who drove automatic transmission cars. Thus, driving experience led to a reduction in the attention demanded by the action of gear shifting to such an extent that driving a manual transmission car in heavy traffic became similar to the attention demanded when driving an automatic transmission car.

But as the person practices the skill and becomes more proficient, the amount of conscious attention he or she directs to performing the skill itself diminishes to the point at which he or she performs it almost automatically.

We see an everyday example of this change in the process of learning to shift gears in a standard shift car. If you have learned to drive a standard shift car, you undoubtedly remember how you approached shifting gears when you first learned to do so. Each part of the maneuver required your conscious attention. You thought about each part of the entire sequence of movements: when to lift off the accelerator, when to push in the clutch, how to coordinate your leg movements to carry out these clutch and accelerator actions, when and where to move the gear shift, when to let out the clutch, and finally, when to depress the accelerator again. But what happened as you became a more experienced driver? Eventually, you performed all these movements without conscious attention. In fact, you undoubtedly found that you were able to do something else at the same time, such as carry on a conversation or sing along with the radio. You would have had great difficulty doing any of these things while shifting when you were first learning to drive.

Changes in error detection and correction capability. Another performance characteristic that improves during practice is the capability to identify and correct one's own movement errors. An individual can use this capability either during or after the performance of the skill, depending on the time constraints involved. If the movements are slow enough, a person can correct or modify an ongoing movement while the action is occurring. For example, if a person grasps a cup and brings it to the mouth to drink from it, he or she can make some adjustments along the way that will allow him or her to accomplish each phase of this action successfully. However, for rapid movements, such as initiating and carrying out a swing at a baseball, a person often cannot make the correction in time during the execution of the swing, because the ball has moved past a hittable location by the time the person makes the correction. For both types of skills, performers can use errors they detect during their performance to guide future attempts.

Expertise

If a person practices a skill long enough and has the right kind of instruction, he or she eventually may become skilled enough to be an *expert*. On the

A CLOSER LOOK

A Summary of Performer and Performance Changes across the Stages of Learning

- *Rate of improvement* — The amount of improvement decreases (*power law of practice*)
- *Limb-segment coordination* — Coordination patterns change from a "freezing" of limb segments to the segments working together as a functional synergy
- *Altering an old or preferred coordination pattern* — Coordination patterns change from the old pattern to a transitional state of no evident pattern to a new pattern
- *Muscles involved* — The number of muscles involved decreases and the timing pattern of muscle group activation becomes appropriate for the action situation
- *Energy use/movement efficiency* — The amount of energy used decreases; movement efficiency increases
- *Achievement of kinematic goals* — Spatial-to-temporal goals sequence
- *Visual attention* — Increasingly becomes directed to more appropriate sources of information
- *Conscious attention* — Amount of conscious attention to movement characteristics reduces
- *Error detection and correction* — Capability increases to detect and correct performance errors

learning stages continuum we presented earlier in this discussion (figure 12.1), the expert is a person who is located at the extreme right end. This person is in an elite group of people who are exceptional and outstanding performers. Although motor skill expertise is a relatively new area of study in motor learning research, we know that experts have distinct characteristics. Most of our knowledge about experts in the motor skills domain relates to athletes, dancers, and musicians. Although they are in seemingly diverse fields, experts in these skill performance areas have some similar characteristics. Some of these will be examined next.

Amount and type of practice leading to expertise. In an extensive study of experts from a diverse number of fields, Ericsson, Krampe, and Tesch-Romer (1993) reported that expertise in all fields is the result of *intense practice for a minimum of ten years.* Critical to achieving expertise is not only the length of time in which the person practices intensely, but also the type of practice. According to Ericsson and his colleagues, the specific type of intense practice a person needs to achieve expertise

in any field is *deliberate practice.* During this type of practice, the person receives optimal instruction, as well as engages in intense, worklike practice for hours each day. As the person develops toward expertise, he or she begins to need personalized training, or supervision of the practice regime.

A characteristic of expertise that emerges from the length and intensity of practice required to achieve expertise in a field is this: *expertise is domain specific* (see Ericsson & Smith, 1991). This means that characteristics of experts are specific to the field in which they have attained this level of success. There is little transfer of the capabilities in the field of expertise to another field in which the person has no experience.

Experts' knowledge structure. A notable characteristic common to expert skill performers is that they know more about an activity than nonexperts do. More important, this expert knowledge is structured quite differently as well. Research investigating experts in a number of diverse skills, such as chess, computer programming, bridge, and basketball, has shown that the expert has developed his or her

A CLOSER LOOK

Experts Compared to Novices: Vision

Bruce Abernethy, one of the world's leading researchers on the issue of expertise as it relates to the use of vision in the performance of motor skills, summarized some primary research findings in an article published in 1999 in the *Journal of Applied Sport Psychology.* The following are some of his key points about the comparison between experts and novices in their use of vision in performance situations in which there is a very brief window of time to detect and use visual information, such as hitting a pitched baseball or returning a racquetball serve.

No Differences

- General vision measures (e.g., visual acuity) and nerve function measures (e.g., nerve conduction velocity) *Experts' superior performance relates more to the superior use of visual information.*
- Visual search patterns may or may not differ *Experts exhibit superior use of visual information even when search patterns are similar.*

Differences

- Experts are faster and more accurate in recognizing patterns in their own skill domain *"Patterns" refer to coordination patterns related to an action and to patterns involving several people.*
- Experts detect and use important action-directing cues faster *The result is better anticipation and faster implementation of a required action.*

knowledge about the activity into more organized concepts and is better able to interrelate the concepts. The expert's knowledge structure also is characterized by more decision rules, which he or she uses in deciding how to perform in specific situations. Additionally, because of the way the knowledge is structured, the expert can remember more information from one observation or presentation.

The benefit of these knowledge structure characteristics is that they enable the expert to solve problems and make decisions faster and more accurately than a nonexpert can, and to adapt to novel environments more easily. For example, an expert basketball player bringing the ball down the floor can look at one or two players on the other team and know which type of defense the team is using; he or she then can make decisions about whether to pass, dribble, or shoot. The beginner would need to take more time to make these same decisions because he or she would need to look at more players to obtain the same information.

Experts' use of vision. When experts perform an activity, they use vision in more advantageous ways than nonexperts do. We discussed many of these

characteristics in chapters 6 and 9. For example, experts search their environment faster, give more attention to this search, and select more meaningful information in less time. Also, experts do not need as much environmental information for decision making, primarily because they "see" more when they look somewhere. Undoubtedly due in part to their superior visual search and decision-making capabilities, experts can use visual information better than nonexperts to anticipate the actions of others. And experts recognize patterns in the environment sooner than nonexperts do. Experts achieve these vision characteristics after many years of experience performing a skill; studies have shown the characteristics to be a function more of experience than of better visual acuity or eyesight.

SUMMARY

Learning is a process that involves time and practice. As an individual moves from being a beginner in an activity to being a highly skilled performer, he or she progresses through distinct, although continuous, stages. Two different models were discussed to describe these stages. Fitts and Posner proposed that the learner progresses through three stages: the cognitive, the associative, and the autonomous stages. Gentile proposed two stages, which she identified in terms of the goal of the learner. The learner's goal in the first stage is "getting the idea of the movement." In the second stage, the learner's goal is fixation or diversification for closed and open skills, respectively.

As people progress through the learning stages, distinct performer and performance changes are notable. We have discussed several here: changes in the rate of improvement, coordination pattern characteristics, the muscles involved in performing the skill, energy use and movement efficiency, the achievement of the kinematic goals of the skill, visual attention, conscious attention, and the learner's capability of detecting and correcting errors.

Finally, we discussed the expert end of the learning continuum. Experts are characterized by exceptional performance. They take a minimum of ten years of intense practice to achieve expertise. These highly skilled people have common performance characteristics in their use of vision and in their knowledge structures, which provide the basis for their exceptional performance capability.

RELATED READINGS

Abernethy, B., Thomas, K. T., & Thomas, J. T. (1993). Strategies for improving understanding of motor expertise [or mistakes we have made and things we have learned!!]. In J. L. Starkes & F. Allard (Eds.), *Cognitive issues in motor expertise* (pp. 317–356). Amsterdam: Elsevier.

Benguigui, N., & Ripoll, H. (1998). Effects of tennis practice on the coincidence timing accuracy of adults and children. *Research Quarterly for Exercise and Sport, 69,* 217–223.

Broderick, M. P., & Newell, K. M. (1999). Coordination patterns in ball bouncing as a function of skill. *Journal of Motor Behavior, 31,* 165–188.

Etnier, J. L., Whitwer, S. S., Landers, D. M., Petruzzello, S. J., & Salazar, W. (1996). Changes in electroencephalographic activity associated with learning a novel motor task. *Research Quarterly for Exercise and Sport, 67,* 272–279.

Robertson, S., & Elliott, D. (1996). The influence of skill in gymnastics and vision on dynamic balance. *International Journal of Sport Psychology, 27,* 361–368.

Sparrow, W. A., & Newell, K. A. (1998). Metabolic energy expenditure and the regulation of movement economy. *Psychonomic Bulletin & Review, 5,* 173–196.

Steenbergen, B., Marteniuk, R. G., & Kalbfleisch, L. E. (1995). Achieving coordination in prehension: Joint freezing and postural contributions. *Journal of Motor Behavior, 27,* 333–348.

STUDY QUESTIONS

1. Describe some characteristics of learners as they progress through the three stages of learning proposed by Fitts and Posner.

2. How does Gentile's learning stages model differ from the Fitts and Posner model? How does her model relate specifically to learning open and closed skills?

3. Describe four performer or performance changes that research has shown to occur as a person progresses through the stages of learning a motor skill.

4. Describe what an expert is and how a person can become an expert motor skill performer. What are some characteristics that distinguish an expert from a nonexpert?

Predicting Performance
for Later Learning Stages

*Concept: Performance during the initial stage
of learning is not a good predictor of
performance during later stages*

APPLICATION

How often do you observe someone who has just begun to learn a motor skill and think about how well that person will perform the skill after he or she has had a lot of practice and experience? Predicting a person's future achievement is something we commonly talk about with friends and colleagues as we watch beginners perform a skill. A part of the reason for this may be a rather natural inclination for people to want to predict the future, which is something we see and hear regularly in the news. However, there are valid professional reasons for making these kinds of predictions. For example, a teacher who wants to subdivide a large physical education class into smaller, more homogeneous groups may make the decision about how to select the groups on the basis of how each student performs a skill on a pretest or during the first class in which the skill is taught. The teacher may place students who exhibit high initial performance levels into one group, those who exhibit poor initial performance levels into another group, and so on. Predictions about future performance achievement also occur in other contexts. In sports, young athletes will be invited to participate in "development" leagues or camps if they show potential to become national- or international-level players. In industry and the military, people are placed into specific types of jobs on the basis of their performance on a variety of types of tests or experiences. And in physical rehabilitation, therapists often determine the therapy intervention strategies to use with a patient on the basis of the patient's initial performance on a skill for which therapy is required. The question that arises from these various situations is, What is the relationship between a person's performance during the initial stage of learning a skill and later stages of learning the skill? The discussion that follows addresses this question.

DISCUSSION

The focus of this discussion is on predicting a person's *potential* for future achievement rather than a person's actual future achievement. Whether or not an individual actually achieves his or her potential will depend on many factors, such as motivation, training, opportunities, etc. Thus, those who make predictions must limit their judgment to the assessment of a person's potential for success, given the appropriate opportunities to develop that potential.

Relating Initial and Later Achievement

Researchers have used three different approaches to address the question of how well early learning stage achievement predicts later stage achievement. Two of these involve determining the degree of relationship between early and later stage performance by employing correlational statistics. The third considers the role played by motor abilities at each learning stage.

Correlating initial and later performance. One way to determine the relationship between initial and later performance achievement is to correlate performance scores of a person as he or she progresses across the stages of learning. The simplest method is to correlate early performance scores with later performance scores. In most cases, this correlation will be low, indicating a low relationship between initial and later achievement.

Although it was published many years ago, an experiment by Ella Trussell (1965) continues to be a classic example of research evidence with this typical result. College women practiced juggling three tennis balls for twenty-seven practice sessions (three sessions per week for nine weeks). Each session included seventy-five tosses. The author defined juggling performance as the number of errors or dropped balls. As expected, the women's performance improved with practice. As the top panel of figure 13.1 shows, error scores dropped from fifty errors per seventy-five tosses in the first practice period to twenty errors per seventy-five tosses in the final session. More important, however, is the bottom graph of this figure, which shows the extent to which scores for each practice period predicted final scores (practice periods 24 through 27). Note that the statistic denoting the prediction value is R^2, which is on the vertical axis of the graph. This statistic was derived by squaring the correlation between the participants' scores for a practice period and the average of the final four practice periods. Interpret the R^2 as indicating the degree of commonality, that is, similarity, between the initial

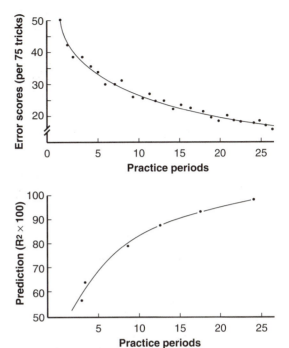

FIGURE 13.1   The top graph shows the performance curve from the experiment by Trussell for a juggling task. The errors are indicated for the practice periods. The bottom graph indicates the accuracy of prediction of final performance in the juggling task as a function of the amount of practice used for prediction.   [From Trussell, E. (1965). Prediction of Success in a Motor skill on the basis of early learning achievement. *Research Quarterly, 36,* 342–347. 1965 American Alliance for Health, Physical Education, Rrecreation, and Dance. Reprinted by permission.]

and final sets of performance scores. In this experiment, the first five practice period scores correctly predicted the scores of the final periods only 50 to 60 percent of the time. These odds are about the same as those involved in flipping a coin. But this prediction capability increased with more practice periods. Note, for example, that performance during practice period 15 predicted final performance with about 85 percent accuracy.

Intertrial correlations. A more complex correlation procedure involves correlating all the practice trials with each other. This approach provides

TABLE 13.1 The Intertrial Correlation Matrix from Performance on a Rhythmic Arm Movement Task Reported by Thomas and Halliwell (The correlations are based on the spatial error scores from the task.)

Trial	1	2	3	4	5	6	7	8	9	10	11	12	13	14	15
1	—	27	−.05	.33	.23	.08	.27	.15	.00	−.04	−.09	.11	−.05	.13	−.12
2		—	.63	.71	.57	.57	.64	.54	.57	.38	.54	.29	.15	.67	.25
3			—	.60	.46	.18	.56	.50	.45	.53	.48	.12	.09	.37	.24
4				—	.73	.45	.61	.62	.45	.29	.51	.15	.17	.49	.12
5					—	.37	.67	.57	.59	.32	.52	.22	.28	.52	.21
6						—	.53	.54	.50	.39	.68	.52	.41	.61	.35
7							—	.71	.67	.70	.65	.51	.57	.80	.50
8								—	.67	.67	.65	.52	.43	.59	.48
9									—	.47	.73	.54	.61	.78	.41
10										—	.56	.59	.63	.62	.64
11											—	.49	.57	.72	.62
12												—	.63	.58	.47
13													—	.71	.63
14														—	.53
15															—

Source: Thomas, J. R., & Halliwell, W. (1976). Individual differences in motor skill acquisition. *Journal of Motor Behavior, 8,* 89–100. Copyright © 1976 Heldref Publications, Inc., Washington, DC. Reprinted by permission.

information about the relationship between the performance scores of any two trials. The common finding from this analysis has been that *trials that are close to each other in time are more highly correlated than trials that are farther from each other.* This between-trials relationship follows what has been called a **superdiagonal form.** This term describes the way the trial-to-trial correlations appear on a correlation matrix that compares all trials against each other, with the same trials located on both the vertical and the horizontal axes of the matrix. The correlation of a trial with the trial that succeeds it, such as that of trial 2 with trial 3, is found just above the diagonal of the matrix, where a trial would be correlated with itself. On the basis of the use of the prefix super to mean above, a superdiagonal form occurs when the highest correlations in the matrix are along the diagonal that is just above the main diagonal of the matrix.

An excellent example of this approach is in one of the few motor skill studies to apply this approach. In an experiment by Thomas and Halliwell (1976), participants learned three motor skills: the rotary pursuit task, the stabilometer task, and a rhythmic arm movement task. The correlation matrix in table 13.1 presents the results of participants' initial fifteen trials of practice on the rhythmic arm movement task. This task involved learning to move a lever held at the side of the body to a visual target in time with a metronome. Both spatial and temporal error constituted the performance score. As you can see in the table, the highest between-trial correlations are typically along the diagonal located just *above* the main diagonal of the correlation matrix. As you can see by looking to your right to compare a particular trial to other trials, the correlation between trials farther away is generally lower. For example, the correlation between trials 4 and 5 is 0.73, whereas the correlation between trials 4 and 12 drops to 0.15. Thus, these results provide additional evidence that performance early in practice is a poor predictor of performance later in practice.

A CLOSER LOOK

Individual Differences in Skill Learning from a Dynamic Pattern Perspective

According to a dynamic pattern view of skill learning (e.g., Zanone and Kelso, 1994), a person initiates practice to learn a new skill by using a coordination pattern that is familiar to him or her yet is similar in some way to the pattern that the person must learn. The pattern the person uses on the initial practice trial spontaneously results from his or her attempt to achieve the action goal of the new skill.

Because of previous skill performance experiences and certain physiological and biomechanical constraints, the person has developed distinct coordination-pattern preferences (*attractor states*). These preferences represent stable patterns that the

person can repeat with little variation and that involve optimal efficiency of energy use. Examples include preferred walking and running gaits and speeds, as well as rhythmic bimanual limb movements that are both in-phase (with simultaneous activation of homologous muscles) and antiphase (with alternate activation of homologous muscles).

Learning a new skill involves a transition between the preferred, stable coordination dynamics of the new skill are similar to those characterizing the preferred pattern, competition between attractor states will lead to slower learning of the new skill than if the patterns were dissimilar. Thus, the practitioner must consider the individual's coordination-pattern tendencies at the time he or she begins practice for learning a new skill. These tendencies constitute an individual difference factor that influences the rate of skill learning.

The relationship between motor abilities and the stages of learning. The third approach to investigating the relationship between performance achievement early and later in learning is to compare the motor abilities that account for performance achievement at each stage. Although controversy exists concerning whether the abilities associated with performance remain constant or change during skill learning, the prevailing view is that abilities required to perform a skill can change as the person becomes more proficient at performing the skill. This means that the abilities related to performing the skill in the early stage of learning may not be the same as those related to performance in later stages. When considered in terms of how poorly we can predict performance between early and later stages of learning, this view provides a basis for accounting for this poor prediction.

Ackerman (1988, 1992) provided insight into these changes when he proposed a model broadly describing the relationship between the types of abilities that are primarily responsible for performance in each of the three stages of learning of the Fitts and Posner model (discussed in chapter 12). Figure 13.2 presents a graphic representation of

this relationship. In the cognitive stage of learning, in which the learner must acquire knowledge about task goal, rules, and strategies, general cognitive and broad-content abilities predominate to account for performance. General cognitive abilities include reasoning, problem solving, and verbal abilities, among others; broad-content abilities include spatial orientation, attention control, etc. As the person progresses to the associative stage, perceptual speed ability becomes more predominant in accounting for performance. This includes the facility to solve problems quickly, especially problems related to visual search and memory use. Finally, in the autonomous phase, the demand on perceptual and motor abilities increases so that

---

superdiagonal form   a term describing the way the trial-to-trial correlations appear in a correlation matrix where all trials are correlated with each other; trials that are closer to each other have scores more highly correlated; the correlation decreases as trials become farther apart.

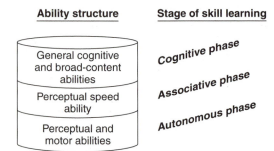

Ability structure   **Stage of skill learning**

General cognitive and broad-content abilities

Perceptual speed ability

Perceptual and motor abilities

Cognitive phase

Associative phase

Autonomous phase

FIGURE 13.2   Ackerman's hierarchical model of the relationship between types of abilities and the Fitts and Posner stages of learning.   [Adapted from Ackerman, P.L. (1992). Predicting individual differences in complex skill acquisition: Dynamics of ability determinants. *Journal of Applied Psychology, 77,* 598–614. Copyright © 1992 the American Psychological Association. Adapted with permission.]

they become the abilities that are most highly correlated with performance.

Ackerman (1992) cites several examples of experiments that provide support for his model. In addition, he associates the relationship between the types of abilities that account for performance and the three learning stages. He indicates that the simple relationship between abilities and learning stages shown in figure 13.2 may relate *only* to skills in which motor performance requirements of the task are critical for task performance and the information-processing requirements do not change in various contexts in which the skill is performed. Although Ackerman does not use motor skill classification terminology, his description of these types of tasks would be most closely related to those classified in chapter 1 as closed motor skills in which regulatory conditions do not change from trial to trial. In contrast, for skills where information-processing demands change from one situation to another, the three types of abilities do not change in their relationship to performance at each stage of learning. Ackerman presented evidence based on the learning of an air traffic controller task as an example of this type of skill.

The Ackerman model must be viewed as a general description of three broad categories of human abilities and their relationship to skill performance at various stages of learning. Unfortunately, we do not know enough about the task-specificity aspect of the model to relate it to specific sport skills or skills of daily living. We must wait for additional research to provide this information. However, because the progression presented in the model depicted in figure 13.2 is in general agreement with other views (e.g., Fleishman & Mumford, 1989) about the change of the abilities-performance relationship during skill acquisition, we can view this model as a key component of the explanation for poor early to later learning stage performance for most complex motor skills.

The key point is that it is very difficult to predict future achievement in learning a motor skill when we base the prediction on early performance only. Abilities that account for a person's level of performance change in importance as the person moves from the early stage of learning to later stages. Those abilities that are important in accounting for a person's performance score early in practice are typically not as important later in practice. However, prediction of future performance improves if the teacher, coach, or therapist is aware of both the specific abilities that are essential to performance in the different stages of learning, and also the corresponding abilities within the learner.

SUMMARY

Research evidence consistently demonstrates that we cannot predict with any degree of accuracy a person's potential for future achievement based on initial practice trials when first learning a skill. This evidence comes from three different approaches researchers have used to investigate this prediction issue. The first involves correlating initial practice trials with later practice trials when the person has achieved what would appear to be his or her highest performance level. The resulting correlations show that the prediction is no better than flipping a coin. The second approach also involves correlating practice trials, but in this case all trials are correlated with each other with the

A CLOSER LOOK

Teaching and Rehabilitation Implications of the Influence of Changes in Motor Abilities from Early to Later Practice

- A person eventually may perform better than his or her initial performance indicates. This means that you should not "give up" on a person because of such undependable evidence as early performance alone.
- Awareness of the coordination characteristics of a person's initial practice attempts can help a teacher or therapist determine the ease or difficulty the person will have learning the new

skill. A change in the coordination pattern itself is more difficult to achieve than are changes in parameter components of the pattern.
- Skill analyses are important in helping the teacher or therapist distinguish between individual ability factors that will contribute to more or less successful skill performance during early and later practice trials.
- Screening tests to assess potential for future performance success should emphasize assessing in novices the specific abilities that are related to successful performance by people who are skillful performers.

results presented on an intercorrelation matrix. The matrix typically follows a superdiagonal form where the highest correlated pairs of trials lie just above the main diagonal of the matrix. This means that the highest correlations for performance trials are found for adjacent trials, and become progressively lower as the number of trials between the correlated pairs of trials increases. The third approach involves investigating the relationship between motor abilities and performance at each stage of learning. Results of this type of research typically show that the motor abilities that account for successful performance are different for the initial and final stages of learning. Ackerman's model further indicates that the types of abilities accounting for performance at each stage are similar to expectations from the descriptions of the three stages of learning in the Fitts and Posner model.

RELATED READINGS

Cox, R. H. (1988). Utilization of psychomotor screening for USAF pilot candidates: Enhancing prediction validity. *Aviation, Space, and Environmental Medicine, 59,* 640–645.

Day, E. A., Arthur, Jr., W., & Shebilske, W. L. (1997). Ability determinants of complex skill acquisition: Effects of training protocol. *Acta Psychologica, 97,* 145–165.

Fleishman, E. A. (1982). Systems for describing human tasks. *American Psychologist, 37,* 821–824.

Henry, R. A., & Hulin, C. L. (1987). Stability of skilled performance across time: Some generalizations and limitations on utilities. *Journal of Applied Psychology, 72,* 457–462.

Levine, E. L., Spector, P. E., Menon, S., Narayanan, L., & Cannon-Bowers, J. (1996). Validity generalization for cognitive, psychomotor, and perceptual tests for craft jobs in the utility industry. *Human Performance, 9,* 1–22.

STUDY QUESTIONS

1. How accurately can you predict a person's future performance achievement on the basis of his or her performance in the practice sessions in which he or she begins to learn the skill? Discuss two types of research evidence that support your answer.

2. Discuss how Ackerman's model relates human abilities to stages of learning a motor skill?

CHAPTER

Transfer of Learning

*Concept: Transfer of learning from one
performance situation to another is an integral
part of skill learning and performance*

APPLICATION

Why do we practice a skill? One reason is to increase our capability of performing the skill in a situation requiring it. We want to be able to accomplish specific action goals when we need to whether we perform everyday skills, work skills, or sport skills. For example, if your goal is to walk through a mall to get to a store, you will want to perform the required actions without problems. Similarly, if your goal is to pitch well for your baseball team, you will need to perform well the skills involved in pitching a baseball. To achieve goals like these, we practice the skills we need to perform the appropriate actions involved in accomplishing these goals.

These skill performance examples involve an important motor learning concept known as *transfer of learning*. This concept lies at the very heart of understanding motor skill learning. An important focus of this concept is the capability we acquire through experience to perform a skill in some novel situation. We want to be able to do what we have done before in any situation we may experience. This suggests, then, that one of the goals of practicing a skill is developing the capability to transfer performance of the skill from the practice environment to some other environment in which the individual must perform the skill so that he or she can achieve the same action goal.

Consider this point in light of the examples we have just described. If you were working with a stroke patient, you would want the hours of rehabilitation to help that person be able to walk in a mall. In terms of transfer of learning, this example illustrates that an important goal of the rehabilitation experience is to help the patient develop the capability to transfer the skill acquired in the clinic to his or her everyday world. Similarly, if you were working with a baseball pitcher, you would want that person to be able to pitch effectively in a game, and not just in a practice environment.

DISCUSSION

Transfer of learning is one of the most universally applied principles of learning in education and rehabilitation. In educational systems, this principle is an important part of curriculum and instruction development, because it provides the basis for arranging the sequence in which the students will learn skills. In the rehabilitation clinic, this principle forms the basis for the systematic development of protocols that therapists implement with patients. Because of the widespread importance of

Performance during a swimming competition provides an opportunity for a coach to assess the swimmers' learning during practices prior to the competition.

transfer of learning, you need to have an understanding of this learning phenomenon as part of your conceptual foundation for studying motor learning.

In chapter 11, we used the concept of transfer of learning when we discussed transfer tests as a method of assessing learning. Those tests are based on the transfer of learning principle. That discussion provided you with a good basis for the present discussion, which will provide you with an understanding of the transfer of learning principle itself.

What Is Transfer of Learning?

Learning researchers generally define **transfer of learning** as the infuence of previous experiences on performing a skill in a new context or on learning a new skill. This influence may be positive, negative, or neutral (zero). **Positive transfer** occurs when previous experience facilitates performance of a skill in a new context or the learning of a new skill. Each of the examples presented at the beginning of this chapter involved positive transfer. **Negative transfer** occurs when previous experience hinders or interferes with performance of a skill in a new context or the learning of a new skill. For example, a person who has learned the forehand in tennis before learning the forehand in badminton often experiences some initial negative transfer for learning the mechanics of the stroke. The badminton

forehand is a wrist snap, whereas the tennis forehand requires a relatively firm wrist. The third type of transfer of learning effect is *zero transfer,* which occurs when previous experience has no influence on performance of a skill in a new context or learning of a new skill. Obviously, there is no transfer from learning to swim to learning to drive a car. Nor can we assume that experience with some motor skills will always have an influence on learning new motor skills.

Why Is Transfer of Learning Important?

We pointed out earlier that the principle of transfer of learning is an important part of educational curriculum development and instructional methodology, as well as the development and implementation of systematic approaches to rehabilitation protocols. Thus, from a practical point of view, the transfer principle is very significant. But the transfer principle also has theoretical significance, because it helps us understand processes underlying the learning and control of motor skills.

Sequencing skills to be learned. The sequencing of mathematics skills provides a very useful practical example of the transfer principle as it relates to curriculum development in schools. The curriculum from grades K through 12 is based on a simple-to-complex sequence. Teachers present

---

transfer of learning   the influence of having previously practiced or performed a skill or skills on the learning of a new skill.

positive transfer   the beneficial effect of previous experience on the learning or performance of a new skill, or on the performance of a skill in a new context.

negative transfer   the negative effect of prior experience on the performance of a skill so that a person performs the skill less well than he or she would have without prior experience.

numeral identification, numeral writing, numeral value identification, addition, subtraction, multiplication, and division in this specific sequence, because each concept is based on the concepts that preceded it. A person presented with a division problem needs to know how to add, subtract, and multiply in order to solve the problem. We do not teach algebra before basic arithmetic. We do not teach trigonometry before geometry.

We can make the same point about skills taught in a physical education program, a sports program, or a rehabilitation clinic. Those who develop a curriculum or a protocol should incorporate the transfer of learning principle when they sequence skills. Learners should acquire basic or foundational skills *before* more complex skills that require mastery of these basic skills. In other words, there should be a logical progression of skill experiences. An instructor should decide when to introduce a skill by determining how the learning of that skill will benefit the learning of other skills. If the instructor does not use this approach, time is wasted while people "go back" to learn prerequisite basic skills.

Gentile's taxonomy of motor skills (discussed in chapter 1) provides a good example of how the transfer principle can be implemented in any skill training situation. That taxonomy presents sixteen categories of skills, systematically sequenced from less to more complex according to specific skill characteristics (see table 1.1). One use for this taxonomy is as a guide to help the therapist select functionally appropriate activities for a rehabilitation patient after making a clinical evaluation of the patient's motor function problems. Gentile based this taxonomy on the principle of positive transfer. She organized the sequence of activities by listing first the activities that a person must perform before performing more complex or difficult ones. The therapist can select appropriate functional activities for a rehabilitation regime by starting with activities related to the taxonomy category in which the therapist identified the skill performance deficit. Then the therapist can increase activity complexity by moving up the taxonomy from that point.

Instructional methods. The second important practical application of the transfer of learning principle to motor skill instruction is in the area of instructional methods. For example, an instructor might use dry land drills when teaching students the basic swimming strokes, before letting them try the strokes in the water. The instructor assumes that there will be positive transfer from the dry land drills to the performance of the strokes in water.

There are numerous other examples of incorporating the transfer principle in instructional settings. It is common, for example, to practice a part of a skill before practicing the entire skill (we will discuss this practice method in chapter 22). Sometimes an instructor simplifies an activity for a person before requiring the person to perform the skill in its actual context; for example, the coach has a person hit a baseball from a batting tee before hitting a moving ball. If the skill being acquired involves an element of danger, the instructor often allows the person to perform the skill with some type of aid so that the danger is removed. For example, a therapist provides physical guidance for a patient who is learning to get out of bed and into a wheelchair, so that the patient will not fall when first practicing this skill.

Assessing the effectiveness of practice conditions. When an instructor or therapist designs a practice regime, he or she also must assess its effectiveness. A transfer test can provide such an assessment. In fact, when an instructor or therapist is comparing the effectiveness of several practice conditions, he or she should identify the one that leads to the best transfer test performance as the preferred practice condition, and implement that one in a training or rehabilitation protocol. Thus, the principle of transfer of learning comes into play once again, as it provides the basis for assessing the effectiveness of the practice conditions an instructor selects to facilitate skill learning.

In fact, one of the predominant theoretical viewpoints of why transfer of learning occurs, emphasizes the importance of the transfer basis for assessing the effectiveness of any practice

A CLOSER LOOK

Assessing Positive Transfer of Learning

Researchers commonly use a simple experimental design to determine if positive transfer has occurred from either (1) experience with one skill to learning another skill or (2) performing a skill in one situation to performing it in another context. The design is:

Experimental group	(1) Practice skill A	Perform skill B
	(2) Perform a skill in context A	Perform the same skill in context B
Control group	No practice	Perform skill B
		Perform the same skill in context B

The performance score of interest to the researcher is for skill B (1), or context B (2). If positive transfer is evident, then the performance of the experimental group should be better than that of the control group. Thus, prior experience is better than no prior experience for the skill or practice situation of interest.

To quantify the amount of positive transfer, researchers commonly calculate the *percentage of transfer,* which is the percentage of difference between the experimental and control groups' performance scores on skill B or in context B:

$$Percentage\ of\ transfer = \frac{Experimental\ group - Control\ group}{Experimental\ group + Control\ group} \times 100$$

condition. The transfer-appropriate processing theory of transfer, which will be presented later in this discussion, asserts that *the effectiveness of any practice condition should be determined only on the basis of how the practiced skill is performed in a "test" context.* This means that if we are deciding whether one procedure is superior to another to facilitate skill learning, we should not reach a conclusion until we have observed the skill in a test performance situation.

Think of the "test" referred to here in several ways. It may be a specific skills test, where a person performs the practiced skill in a test constructed for that skill. In another type of test, the person performs the practiced skill in an everyday functional environment. Or, the test may require the person to use the skill in an organized competition or game. The point is that regardless of the exact nature of the test, the person's performance in the test context itself should be the primary measure of the effectiveness of a practice condition.

Why Does Positive Transfer of Learning Occur?

The theoretical significance of the concept of transfer of learning becomes evident as we attempt to determine why transfer occurs. For example, if we know why transfer occurs, we have a better understanding of what a person learns about a skill that enables the person to adapt to the performance requirements of a new situation.

Although researchers have proposed several reasons over the years to explain why transfer of learning occurs, we will discuss only two of the more prominent hypotheses here. Both consider the *similarities* between the two situations to be critical for explaining transfer. However, they differ in their explanations of which similarities account for transfer. One hypothesis proposes that transfer of learning occurs because the components of the skills and/or the context in which skills are performed are similar. The other proposes that transfer occurs primarily because of similarities

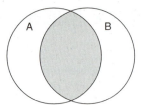 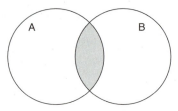

FIGURE 14.1   The two circles (A and B) in this figure can represent two skills or two performance contexts. For either the identical elements theory or transfer-appropriate processing theory proposed to explain why transfer of learning occurs, consider the amount of overlap between the two circles (the shaded area) as representing the degree of similarity between the two skills or performance contexts. For the identical elements theory, the similarity relates to components or characteristics of the two skills or contexts; for the transfer-appropriate processing theory, the similarity relates to the learning- or performance-related cognitive processes involved in the two skills or contexts. More transfer should occur between the two skills or contexts in the set of circles on the left than on the right.

between the amounts and types of learning processes required (see figure 14.1).

Similarity of skill and context components. The more traditional view of why positive transfer occurs contends that transfer is due to the similarity between the components of two skills or of two performance situations. In this view, the more similar the component parts of two skills or two performance contexts are, the greater will be the amount of positive transfer between them.

This view has its roots in some of the earliest motor learning research, which Thorndike did at Columbia University in the early part of the 1900s. To account for transfer effects, Thorndike (1914) proposed the **identical elements theory.** In this theory, "elements" are general characteristics of a skill or performance context—such as the purpose of the skill or the attitude of the person performing the skill—or specific characteristics of the skill, such as components of the skill being performed. Additionally, Thorndike considered identical elements to include mental processes that shared the same brain cell activity as the physical action.

According to this view, we would expect the amount of transfer between the tennis serve and the volleyball serve to be greater than that between the tennis serve and the racquetball serve. We likewise

would expect a high degree of transfer to occur when practice conditions emphasize performance characteristics similar to those required in a "test" situation. In a clinical situation, for example, physical therapy protocols to increase a stroke patient's capability to walk in the patient's everyday environment including experiences in that environment will yield more positive transfer than those that involve experiences only in the clinic.

Similarity of processing requirements. The second hypothesis explaining why positive transfer occurs proposes that it results from the *similarity of the cognitive processes* required by the two skills or two performance situations. This hypothesis finds its clearest expression in the view that explains transfer effects in terms of transfer-appropriate processing (see Lee, 1988). This view maintains that although similarity in skill and context components explains some transfer effects, it cannot explain all transfer effects. A key point of the **transfer-appropriate processing theory** is the similarity between the learning or performance cognitive processes required by the two performance situations. In this view, two components of positive transfer are critical: the cognitive processing activity a person must do to be successful in performing the transfer task, and the similarity

A CLOSER LOOK

Transfer from Virtual Reality Experience to a Real Environment

Virtual reality refers to three-dimensional computer-generated environments that can be explored and experienced in real time. Although there appear to be many potential applications of the use of virtual reality as a training strategy for motor skills, this potential remains to be determined. However, an interesting experiment by Wilson, Foreman, and Tlauka (1997) in England offers a look into one use of virtual reality in motor skills training contexts.

The focus of this study was on the training of people to be familiar with the spatial layout of a building, especially in terms of locating specific objects on three floors. Participants were in three groups: the real group, which experienced training in the real environment by being guided through the building floors; the computer group, which experienced being guided through a three-dimensional virtual reality version of the floors; and the control group, which did

not experience training. Following training, participants performed several tests to assess their spatial knowledge of the location of the objects pointed out during training. The results showed that the real and computer training groups performed better on the tests than the control group, and were not different from each other for two of the three floors. Interestingly, further investigation showed that the simulation of the floor for which the real group performed better was not as detailed as for the other two floors.

In addition to providing support for the identical elements theory of transfer, this study also suggests potential applications for motor skills training. For example, in rehabilitation contexts virtual reality training could provide a preparatory experience for patients who need to experience locomoting in a variety of environmental contexts. Similar applications can be made for sports skills training where participation in new contexts will have an impact on the athletes' performance.

---

between that activity and the activity required during the training experience.

Some examples of transfer-appropriate processing include when the transfer task requires a person to engage in problem-solving activity, rapid decision making, application of rules, attention control, and the simultaneous performance of two or more tasks. For positive transfer to occur between the training and transfer tasks, the training task also must involve these same types of activities. What is especially important to note here is that the training and transfer tasks do not need to have similar movement components. The critical characteristic is the similarity between the cognitive processing demands of the training task and those of the transfer task.

Merit in both hypotheses. Although much remains unknown about the cause of transfer of learning, evidence points to the value of both hypotheses in accounting for transfer effect. As

indicated by figure 14.1, we can expect the amount of positive transfer to be related to the amount of similarity between skills and performance contexts. It appears that the similarity-of-processing view is actually an extension of the components view that comes into play when skill components and context similarities are minimal,

---

identical elements theory   an explanation of positive transfer proposing that transfer is due to the degree of similarity between the component parts or characteristics of two skills or two performance contexts.

transfer-appropriate processing theory   an explanation of positive transfer proposing that transfer is due to the similarity in the cognitive processing characteristics required by the two skills or two performance situations.

A CLOSER LOOK

Relating Transfer of Learning to Practice Conditions: The Specificity of Practice Principle

One of the oldest principles of motor learning is the "specificity of practice principle." Simply stated, this principle tells us that *to achieve optimal performance in a test, a person should experience practice conditions that match test conditions as closely as possible.* The specificity principle is a natural outgrowth of the various explanations about why positive transfer occurs. In fact, according to figure 14.1, the greatest amount of positive transfer would occur when practice and test conditions are the same. Although it is not always possible to create practice situations that will exactly match test situations, consider the following examples of some general practice and test features that can be matched as closely as possible.

Sensory/Perceptual Characteristics

Visual conditions. If the test requires performance without visual feedback about either the outcome of the performance or the limb or limbs performing the skill, practice should include performance situations without the visual feedback, e.g.

- *practicing typing skills or piano playing*—Include practice opportunities without vision of the hands and keyboard
- *practicing basketball dribbling*—Include practice opportunities without vision of hands and ball

- *practicing "form/technique" with a mirror (e.g., gymnastics, dancing, weightlifting)*—Include practice opportunities without a mirror

Performance Context Characteristics

Environmental context. Include practice opportunities in the same environmental context as will exist for the test, e.g.,

- *rehabilitating locomotion*—Include practice opportunities in the person's home, workplace, shopping mall, etc.
- *rehabilitating occupational skills*—Include practice opportunities in the same or simulated setting as the person experiences in daily living
- *preparing for a night football game*—Include practice opportunities at night under the lights

Personal characteristics. Include practice opportunities that simulate the types of physical, mental, and emotional conditions the person may experience in the test, e.g.,

- *fatigue*—Practice shooting basketball free throws at the end of practice when fatigued
- *decision making*—Develop drills for soccer practice that will require a player with the ball to decide if he or she should pass to a teammate, shoot at the goal, or continue to keep control of the ball
- *anxiety*—Simulate conditions in practice that will require the person to control his or her anxiety levels while performing the skill

---

but cognitive processing activities are similar. However, as Schmidt and Young (1987) concluded in their extensive review of transfer in motor skills, we do not know very much about what accounts for the transfer phenomenon. Unfortunately, research investigating this question has been minimal during recent years, despite the fact that much more research is needed if we are to answer the question of *why* transfer occurs.

Negative Transfer

Although negative transfer effects appear to be rare and temporary in motor skill learning, people

involved in motor skill instruction and rehabilitation need to be aware of conditions that may contribute to negative transfer. Because negative transfer effects can occur, it is important to know how to avoid such effects and to deal with them when they occur.

Negative transfer situations. Simply stated, negative transfer effects occur when an old stimulus requires a new but similar response. This means that the *environmental context characteristics of two performance situations are similar, but the movement characteristics are different.* Two situations that are especially susceptible to negative transfer effects involve a *change in the spatial locations of a movement* and a *change in the timing structure of the movement.*

An example of the *spatial location change* occurs when you must drive a car different from your own. If both cars are five-speed stick shifts, what happens when reverse is in a different location from the one you are accustomed to in your own car? Typically, you find yourself trying to shift to the location of reverse for your own car. This happens especially when you are not paying close attention to shifting. This example demonstrates that when we learn a specific spatially oriented movement to accomplish an action goal, we require attention and time to learn a similar movement that is in a new direction or end-location, because of the negative transfer effect of the previous learning experience.

The second situation that leads to negative transfer effects involves a *change in the timing structure* of a sequence of movements from a previously learned sequence. Two different types of timing structure conditions are involved here. One is the rhythmic pattern, or relative time structure, learned for a sequence of movements. When people learn a specific relative time structure for a sequence of movements, such as when they learn a piece of music, a dance sequence, etc., and then they are asked to perform the sequence and ignore the rhythmic structure they learned, they typically produce the learned rhythmic structure for a number of trials (e.g., Summers, 1975). The second timing structure condition involves what appear to be innate bimanual coordination timing relationships. An example of this situation can be seen in the results of the experiment by Lee, Swinnen, and Verschueren (1995) that was described in chapter 11. In this experiment, participants were asked to produce a bimanual coordination pattern that is difficult to perform and varied markedly from their natural coordination pattern tendency, which was to move the arms in temporal synchrony. Recall that after achieving a small amount of progress in performing the new pattern by the end of the first day of practice (refer to figure 11.4), the participants reverted back to producing their natural bimanual synchrony pattern. Thus the innate coordination tendency to move the arms in temporal and spatial synchrony interfered with the participants' learning a new nonsynchronous movement pattern for the arms.

Either of the conditions that induce negative transfer effects are often seen when a person tries to "unlearn" a way of performing a skill and learn a new way to perform it. This type of situation occurs in many skill learning contexts. For example, athletes who go from high school to college commonly have to learn to perform a skill in a way that is different from how they performed it in high school. Even though the way they performed it in high school was successful, the college coach knows that to achieve success at the college level, the athlete needs to learn to perform the skill differently. In the rehab clinic, physical and occupational therapists often interact with patients who have learned to perform a skill in a certain way because of a disability. However, the therapist knows that continued performance in this manner will lead to additional physical problems, which means the patient must acquire a different manner of performing the skill. In these types of situations, people typically show a decrement in performance when they begin practicing the skill in a new way. But with continued practice, performance begins to improve and eventually exceeds the level achieved previously.

Negative transfer effects are temporary. In each of the negative transfer situations described in this discussion a common characteristic has been that the negative effects do not continue through all stages of learning. This is because negative transfer effects are temporary in nature and typically influence skill learning only in the early learning stage. However, it is important for the practitioner to be aware of this characteristic because the negative transfer effects a person experiences early in practice may discourage a person's interest in pursuing the learning of the new skill or a new way to perform a well-learned skill. In addition, it is important that the practitioner be aware of the aspects of a skill that will be most affected by negative transfer effects, and give particular instructional attention to these aspects to help the person overcome these effects.

A CLOSER LOOK

An Example of Bilateral Transfer for Mirror Writing

Mark Latash (1999) reported a study in which students in his undergraduate class at Penn State University were required to learn a new skill as part of their class experience. The new skill was mirror writing, which involved handwriting a sentence on a piece of paper while looking in a mirror so that it would read correctly in the mirror, not on the paper. During a pretest the students wrote the sentence, "I can write while looking in the mirror," five times with one hand and then the other hand. For each trial, they timed how long it took to write the sentence and

counted the errors they made. The students then practiced writing the sentence fifteen times a day, five days a week, for three weeks using the dominant hand only. At the end of the practice period, they did a posttest that required them to perform the task as in the pretest. By comparing the writing performance of the nondominant hand during the pre- and posttests, the students could determine if bilateral transfer resulted from the 225 practice trials with the dominant hand. The results showed that on the posttest for the nondominant hand, they wrote the sentence 40 percent faster than on the pretest, and their errors decreased by 43 percent.

Why do negative transfer effects occur? There are at least two likely reasons why negative transfer occurs. The first relates to the memory representation developed as a result of learning a skill. As a result of much practice performing a skill in one specific way, a specific perception-action connection (sometimes referred to as coupling) has developed between the perceptual characteristics of the task and the motor system. This connection becomes a part of the memory representation for the action. When a person sees a familiar perceptual layout, the motor system has a preferred way of organizing itself to respond to those characteristics. Although this perception-action connection allows for fast and accurate performing, it is problematic when the familiar perceptual situation requires a movement that is different from what was learned. As you have seen in several discussions in this book, to change from the preferred state (i.e., the learned movement for the perceptual event) to a new state is difficult and takes practice.

Another possibility is a cognitive processing explanation. Negative transfer results from *cognitive confusion.* In the car shift example, the requirements for shifting into reverse in the new car undoubtedly lead to some confusion in the driver about what to do. Undoubtedly you have had a similar experience when

you have had to type on typewriters or keyboards that differ in the locations of certain keys, such as the backspace or delete key. When you first begin typing on the new keyboard, you have difficulty striking the keys that are in different locations. What is notable here is that the problem is not with your limb control; you know how to strike keys in a sequence. Rather, the problem is related to the confusion created by the unfamiliar locations of the keys.

Fortunately, negative transfer effects can be overcome with practice. You probably have experienced this for either gear shifting or typing, or for both. Just how much practice is required depends on the person and the task itself.

Bilateral Transfer

When transfer of learning relates to learning of the same task but with different limbs, it is known as **bilateral transfer.** This well-documented phenomenon demonstrates our ability to learn a particular skill more easily with one hand or foot after we already have learned the skill with the opposite hand or foot.

Experimental evidence of bilateral transfer. Experiments designed to determine whether bilateral transfer does indeed occur have followed similar experimental designs. The most typical design has been the following:

	Pretest	Practice Trials	Posttest
Preferred limb	X	X	X
Nonpreferred limb	X		X

This design allows the experimenter to determine if bilateral transfer to the nonpracticed limb occurred because of practice with the other limb. In the sample experimental design, note that the practice limb is the preferred limb. However, this does not need to be the case; the preferred limb/nonpreferred limb arrangement could be reversed. In either case, the researcher compares pretest-to-posttest improvements for each limb. Although the practiced limb should show the greatest improvement, a significant amount of improvement should occur for the nonpracticed limb, indicating that bilateral transfer has occurred.

Investigation of the bilateral transfer phenomenon was popular from the 1930s through the 1950s. In fact, the bulk of the evidence demonstrating bilateral transfer in motor skills can be found in the psychology journals of that period. One of the more prominent investigators of the bilateral transfer phenomenon during the early part of that era was T. W. Cook. Between 1933 and 1936, Cook published a series of five articles relating to various concerns of bilateral transfer, or cross-education, as they called it. Cook terminated this work by asserting that the evidence was sufficiently conclusive to support the notion that bilateral transfer does indeed occur for motor skills.

Given such a foundation of evidence, few experiments published since those by Cook have investigated only the question of the occurrence of the bilateral transfer phenomenon (although, see Latash, 1999). The research literature since the 1930s has addressed several issues related to bilateral transfer. Among these are the direction of the greater amount of transfer, and the reason bilateral transfer occurs which will be discussed next.

Symmetry versus asymmetry of bilateral transfer. One of the more intriguing questions about the bilateral transfer effect concerns the direction of the transfer. The questions is this: Does a greater amount of bilateral transfer occur when a person learns a skill using one limb before learning it using the other limb (**asymmetric transfer**), or is the amount of transfer similar no matter which limb the person practices with first (**symmetric transfer**)?

Reasons for investigating this question are theoretical as well as practical. From a theoretical perspective, knowing whether bilateral transfer is symmetric or asymmetric would provide insight, for example, into the role of the two cerebral hemispheres in controlling movement. That is, do the two hemispheres play similar or different roles in movement control?

A more practical reason for investigating this question is that its answer can help professionals design practice to facilitate optimal skill performance with either limb. If asymmetric transfer predominated, the therapist, instructor, or coach would decide to have a person always train with one limb before training with the other; however, if symmetric transfer predominated, it would not make any difference which limb the person trained with first.

The generally accepted conclusion about the direction of bilateral transfer is that it is *asymmetric.* But there is some controversy about whether this asymmetry favors transfer from preferred to nonpreferred limb, or vice versa. The traditional view has been that there is a greater amount of

---

bilateral transfer   transfer of learning that occurs between two limbs.

asymmetric transfer   bilateral transfer in which there is a greater amount of transfer from one limb than from the other limb.

symmetric transfer   bilateral transfer in which the amount of transfer is similar from one limb to another, no matter which limb is used first.

transfer when a person practices initially with the preferred limb.

Although some controversy continues about this question, there is sufficient evidence to recommend that for most skill training and rehabilitation situations, the greater amount of transfer occurs *from the preferred to the nonpreferred limb*. This approach not only is consistent with the bulk of the research literature concerned with bilateral transfer, but also is supported by other factors that need to be taken into account, such as motivation. Initial preferred-limb practice has a greater likelihood of yielding the types of success that will encourage the person to continue pursuing the goal of becoming proficient at performing the skill with either limb.

Why does bilateral transfer occur? As we saw for explanations proposed to account for positive and negative transfer effects, cognitive and motor control explanations have been offered to answer the question of why bilateral transfer occurs. The *cognitive explanation* states that the basis for the positive transfer from a practiced to a nonpracticed limb is the important cognitive information related to what to do to achieve the goal of the skill. This information is relevant to performing the skill regardless of the limb involved, and is critical information acquired during the initial stage of skill learning. As a result of practice with one limb, the relevant cognitive information is acquired, which makes it available when the skill is performed with the other limb.

The cognitive explanation of bilateral transfer can be related to the "identical elements" theory Thorndike proposed, which we discussed earlier. This explanation gives strong consideration to those elements of a skill related to the performer's knowing "what to do." For example, we can consider the performance of a skill with one limb and then the other to be essentially two distinct skills. Throwing a ball at a target using the right arm is a different task from throwing a ball with the left arm. However, elements of these skills are common to both, regardless of the hand the thrower is

using. Examples would be the arm-leg opposition principle, the need to keep the eyes focused on the target, and the need to follow through. Each of these elements represents what to do to successfully throw the ball at a target and does not specifically relate to either arm.

Proponents of this view predict that if a person achieves proficiency at a skill using the right arm, the person does not need to relearn the common cognitive "what to do" elements when he or she begins practicing with the left arm. The person should begin with the left arm at a higher level of proficiency than he or she would have had if he or she had never practiced with the right arm.

The *motor control explanation* for bilateral transfer incorporates the generalized motor program and the transfer of motor output characteristics through the nervous system. There are two ways to establish this explanation. In the first, theorists look at the generalized motor program, which was described in chapter 4. Recall that the muscles required to produce an action are *not* an invariant characteristic of the generalized motor program. Rather, muscles are a *parameter* that a person must add to achieve the goal of the action.

Because the generalized motor program develops from practice, we would expect that following sufficient practice with one limb, a person would develop an appropriate memory representation of the action so that he or she could perform at a better-than-beginning level with a nonpracticed limb. However, because of other factors, such as problems with perception, biomechanics, and specificity of training, we would not expect initial performance with the nonpracticed limb to be as good as performance with the practiced limb. But we would expect this initial performance to be better than it would if there were no practice at all with the other limb.

The second argument proponents of a motor control explanation offer is based on evidence showing that at least some bilateral transfer of skill is mediated in the brain by interhemispheric transfer of the motor components of the task (Hicks, Gualtieri, & Schroeder, 1983). Researchers have

A CLOSER LOOK

Implementing Bilateral Transfer Training

For the person involved in motor skill instruction or rehabilitation, an important question concerns how to take advantage of the bilateral transfer phenomenon and implement it into the instructional or rehabilitation setting.

Recommended Guidelines

- Initiate practice with the preferred limb.

- In early practice sessions, concentrate on developing a reasonable degree of proficiency with one limb *before* begining practice with the other limb.
- After initiating practice with the second limb, alternate practice for both limbs on the basis of set blocks of trials or amounts of time for practice with each limb.
- Use verbal encouragement to motivate the person to continue to practice with the nonpreferred limb.

---

demonstrated this mediation by measuring the EMG activity in all four limbs when one limb performs a movement. When EMG activity occurs, it tells researchers that the central nervous system has forwarded commands to those muscles. In fact, research conducted as long ago as 1942 showed that the greatest amount of EMG activity occurs for the contralateral limbs (i.e., the two arms), a lesser amount occurs for the ipsilateral limbs (i.e., arm and leg on the same side), and the least amount occurs for the diagonal limbs (Davis, 1942).

Which of the two explanations of bilateral transfer is correct? Research evidence indicates that both cognitive and motor factors are involved in bilateral transfer. There is no doubt that cognitive components related to "what to do" account for much of the transfer that results from practicing a skill with one limb. This is quite consistent with what we have discussed thus far in this book. For example, both the Fitts and Posner and the Gentile models of the stages of skill learning described in chapter 12 propose that determining "what to do" is a critical part of what a learner acquires in the first stage of learning. There is likewise no doubt that bilateral transfer involves a motor control basis as well. This is consistent with our discussion in chapter 4 of the control of coordinated action. It is also consistent with research evidence that there is some motor outflow to other limbs when one limb performs a skill.

SUMMARY

Transfer of learning concerns the influence of previous experiences on the performance of a skill in a new context or on learning a new skill. The influence of the previous experience may facilitate, hinder, or have no effect on the learning of the new skill. The transfer of learning concept is integral to curriculum development in educational environments, as well as to training protocol development in rehabilitation programs. The concept also forms the basis for many methods instructors, coaches, and rehabilitation therapists use to enhance skill acquisition. In addition, the transfer of learning concept is an essential part of understanding motor learning, because it is basic to the process of making inferences about the influence of practice conditions on learning skills.

We have discussed two hypotheses that attempt to account for positive transfer. The first states that positive transfer increases as a function of the similarities of the components of motor skills and of the contexts in which the skills are performed. The second hypothesis states that the amount of positive transfer is related to the similarity of the cognitive processing activity involved in the two situations.

Negative transfer effects occur primarily when a new movement is required for a familiar environmental context. Researchers attribute negative transfer to the difficulty inherent in altering the preferred perception-action connection that a person has developed for moving in a specific context. Negative transfer also may result from initial cognitive confusion that results when a person does not know what to do in a new performance situation. Negative transfer effects are temporary, and people usually overcome them with practice.

Bilateral transfer is a phenomenon in which a person experiences improvement in the performance of a nonpracticed limb as a result of practice with the opposite limb. Typically, bilateral transfer is asymmetric, because the preferred-to-nonpreferred direction typically yields greater transfer than vice versa. A cognitive basis for explaining bilateral transfer is that people acquire knowledge about what to do with practice of one limb, and do not need to acquire this knowledge when beginning practice with the opposite limb. A motor control explanation is also relevant because of generalized motor program invariant and parameter characteristics and the motor outflow of motor commands to the opposite limb.

RELATED READINGS

Christina, R. W., & Bjork, R. A. (1991). Optimizing long-term retention and transfer. In D. Druckman & R. A. Bjork (Eds.), *In the mind's eye: Enhancing human performance* (pp. 23–56). Washington, DC: National Academy Press.

Ferrari, M. (1999). Influence of expertise on the intentional transfer of motor skill. *Journal of Motor Behavior, 31,* 79–85.

Hesketh, B. (1997). Dilemmas in training for transfer and retention. *Applied Psychology: An International Review, 46,* 317–386.

Ma, H. I., Trombly, C. A., & Robinson-Podolski, C. (1999). The effect of context on skill acquisition and transfer. *American Journal of Occupational Therapy, 53,* 138–144.

Schmidt, R. A., & Young, D. E. (1987). Transfer of movement control in motor skill learning. In S. M. Cormier & J. D. Hagman (Eds.), *Transfer of learning* (pp. 47–79). Orlando, FL: Academic Press.

Shields, R. K., Leo, K. C., Messaros, A. J., & Somers, V. K. (1999). Effects of repetitive handgrip training on endurance, specificity, and cross-education. *Physical Therapy, 79,* 467–475.

Tremblay, L., & Proteau, L. (1998). Specificity of practice: The case of powerlifting. *Research Quarterly for Exercise and Sport, 69,* 284–289.

Winstein, C. J. (1991). Designing practice for motor learning: Clinical implications. In M. J. Lister (Ed.), *Contemporary management of motor control problems* (pp. 65–76). Fredericksburg, VA: Bookcrafters.

STUDY QUESTIONS

1. What are two reasons proposed to explain why transfer occurs? For each of these, give a motor skill example.

2. What situation characteristics predict negative transfer? Give two motor skill performance examples of these characteristics and indicate why negative transfer would occur.

3. What is bilateral transfer? What is the issue underlying the question of whether bilateral transfer is symmetric or asymmetric?

4. Discuss two hypotheses that attempt to explain why bilateral transfer occurs.

5. Describe how you would organize practice for a skill in which the use of *either* arm or *either* leg to perform the skill would be beneficial.

INSTRUCTION AND AUGMENTED FEEDBACK

CHAPTER

Demonstration and Verbal Instructions

Concept: The most effective method of providing
instructions for helping a person to learn a
motor skill depends on the skill and the
instructional goal

APPLICATION

If you want to instruct someone in doing a skill, how would you do it? Probably, you would verbally describe what to do, demonstrate the skill, or use some combination of both approaches. But do you know enough about the effectiveness of these different means of communication to know which one to prefer or when to use each one or both?

Demonstrating skills is undoubtedly the most common means of communicating how to perform them. We find demonstrations in a wide range of skill acquisition situations. For example, a physical education teacher may demonstrate to a large class how to putt in golf. An aerobics teacher may demonstrate to a class how to perform a particular sequence of skills. A baseball coach may show a player the correct form for bunting a ball. In a rehabilitation context, an occupational therapist may demonstrate to a patient how to button a shirt, or a physical therapist may demonstrate to a wheelchair patient how to get from the floor into the chair.

The instructor demonstrates a skill because he or she believes that in this way the learner receives the most amount of information in the least amount of time. Whether you are teaching a large class, working with a small group, or providing individ-

ual instruction, and whether you are teaching a complex skill or a simple skill, you probably hold this generally accepted view that demonstration is the preferred instruction strategy. But we should not assume the wisdom of this view of demonstration without addressing several issues. We must establish when demonstration is effective, and when it may be less effective than some other means of communicating how to perform a skill. And *if demonstration is used,* we must know how to use it to provide the best possible information about how to perform a skill.

Similarly, the instructor should know when verbal instructions are an effective means of communicating how to perform a skill. And if verbal instructions are given, what characterizes the most effective instructions?

DISCUSSION

As we mentioned, the two most popular ways to communicate how to perform a skill are to demonstrate the skill and to give verbal instructions about how to do the skill. One of the problems encountered by any person providing skill instruction is determining which of these communication

218

forms is better for a particular skill or skill instruction situation.

Demonstration

It is ironic that although demonstration is a very common method of providing information about how to perform a skill, there is very little research related to it. In fact, most of what we know about the use of demonstration comes from research and theory related to modeling and social learning (e.g., Bandura, 1984). However, in recent years movement scientists have shown an increased interest in the role of demonstration in motor skill learning. (Note that the terms **modeling** and **observational learning** often are used interchangeably with the term *demonstration*. Because *demonstration* is more specific to the context of instruction about how to perform a skill, we will use this term in this text.)

There seem to be at least two reasons for the increased interest in demonstration and skill learning. One reason is the phenomenal growth of interest in the role of vision in skill learning. Because demonstrating how to do a skill involves visual observation on the part of the learner, researchers have been able to use the study of demonstration and skill learning to assess how the visual system is involved in skill acquisition and performance. Another reason for the current interest is that we know so little about how to effectively implement this very common instructional strategy. As a result, researchers have been making an increased effort to improve our understanding of the role of demonstration in skill instruction and learning.

In the most recent comprehensive review of research investigating the role of demonstration in motor skill acquisition, McCullagh (1993) concluded that demonstration is more effective under certain circumstances than under others. This conclusion suggests that an instructor should use demonstration only after determining that the instructional situation indeed warrants the use of demonstration, rather than some other form of providing information about skill performance. In the following sections, we consider some of the concerns that professionals need to take into account before making this instructional decision.

What the observer perceives from a demonstration. The decision about the situations in which demonstration would be preferred should be based on our knowledge of what a person actually "sees" when a skill is demonstrated. Note the use of the word "sees" rather than "looks at." As we pointed out in chapter 6, what we see and what we look at can be very different. What we "see" is what we *perceive* from what we look at. This distinction is particularly relevant to the discussion of demonstration, because what a person perceives from a skill demonstration is not necessarily something that he or she specifically looks at or looks for. It is also important to keep in mind that what we perceive may be at a conscious or nonconscious level of awareness. For example, when people are asked later to describe verbally what they saw in a demonstration that helped them perform a skill, they do not always give a very accurate accounting.

Research evidence has shown consistently that the observer perceives from the demonstration information about the coordination pattern of the skill (e.g., Scully & Newell, 1985; Schoenfelder-Zohdi, 1992; Whiting, 1988). More specifically, the observer perceives and uses *invariant features of the coordinated movement pattern* to develop his or her own movement pattern to perform the skill.

Two types of research evidence support this view. One involves the investigation of the visual perception of motion; the other is the investigation of the influence of demonstration on learning a complex skill.

---

modeling   the use of demonstration as a means of conveying information about how to perform a skill.

observational learning   learning a skill by observing a person perform the skill; also known as *modeling*.

A CLOSER LOOK

Perceiving a Throwing Action from Observing a Point-Light Display

An experiment by Williams (1988) provides an example of use of the point-light technique. Eighty adults (ages eighteen to twenty-five years) and eighty children (ages fourteen to fifteen years) observed a video point-light display of a side view of the arm of a seated person throwing a small plastic ball at a target (see figure 15.1). The video showed only dots of light at the shoulder, elbow, and wrist joints of the person throwing the ball. The author showed participants the video three times and then asked them what they had seen. Results showed that 66 percent of the children and 65 percent of the adults responded that they had seen a throwing motion. An additional 25 percent of the adults and 23 percent of the children made this response after seeing the video one additional time.

a.

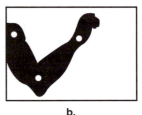

b.

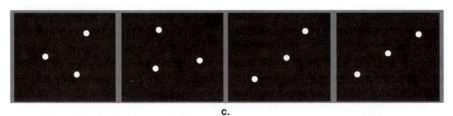

c.

FIGURE 15.1　　An example of use of the point-light technique in motor learning research. (a) shows the model demonstrating the throwing of a small ball at a target. (b) shows a static image of the point-light display of the model's arm with lights at the shoulder, elbow, and wrist joints. (c) shows four still frames of the video shown to subjects. From left to right, these depict the arm at the start of the throw, at maximal flexion, at release of the small ball, and at completion of the throw.　　[Reproduced with permission of author and publisher from Williams, J. G. (1989). Visual demonstration and movement production: Effects of timing variations in a model's action. *Perceptual and Motor Skills, 68,* 891–896. © Perceptual and Motor Skills 1989.]

First, research investigating the perception of human motion attempts to answer questions about how people recognize movement patterns they see in their world. An important principle developed from this research is that people rarely use specific characteristics of the individual components of a pattern to make judgments about the pattern. Rather, they use relative information about the relationships among the various components.

Using a procedure known as the **point-light technique,** researchers have identified the relative information involved in the perception of human movement. This procedure involves placing lights or bright spots on the joints of a person who is then filmed or videotaped performing an action or skill. Then the researcher plays the film or video so that the person who watches the film or video sees only bright dots in motion. The first reported use of this procedure (Johansson, 1973) showed that people could accurately label different gait patterns, such as walking and running, by observing the moving dot patterns. Later, Cutting and Kozlowski (1977) showed that from observing moving dot patterns, people actually could identify their friends. Using a computer simulation, Hoenkamp (1978) showed that the movement characteristic people use to identify different gait patterns is not any one kinematic variable, but the ratio of the time duration between the forward and return swings of the lower leg.

This groundbreaking research on the perception of human movement has shown two things that help our understanding of observational learning. First, people can recognize different gait patterns accurately and quickly without seeing the entire body or all the limbs move. Second, the most critical information people perceive in order to distinguish one type of gait pattern from another is not any one characteristic of the gait, such as velocity of the limbs. Instead, people use the invariant relative time relationship between two components of gait. From these conclusions we can hypothesize that these invariant relationships in coordinated movement constitute the critical information involved in observational learning.

The second type of research providing evidence about what an observer uses from a skill demonstration provides more direct evidence that people perceive invariant relationships. An example is an experiment by Schoenfelder-Zohdi (1992) in which subjects practiced the slalom ski simulator task shown in figure 15.2. This simulator consisted of two rigid, convex, parallel tracks on which a movable platform stood. A participant stood on the platform with both feet and was required to move the platform to the right and then to the left as far as possible (55 cm to either side) with rhythmic slalom skilike movements. The platform was connected on either side to each end of the apparatus by strong, springlike, rubber bands, which ensured that the platform always returned to the center (normal) position. Thus, the participant had to learn to control the platform movement by using smooth skilike movements, just as he or she would if actually skiing. Participants practiced this skill for several days after they had either observed a skilled model perform the task or received verbal information about the goal of the task. A movement analysis of limb movements showed that participants who had observed the skilled demonstration developed coordinated movement patterns earlier in practice than did those who had not observed the demonstration. figure 15.3 shows one example of these results.

Taken together, these two types of research indicate that the visual system automatically detects in a movement pattern invariant information for determining how to produce the observed action. In some manner, which scientists do not

---

point-light technique   a research procedure used to determine the relative information people use to perceive and identify coordinated human actions; it involves placing LEDs or light-reflecting material on certain joints of a person, then filming or videotaping the person performing an action; when an observer views the film or video, he or she sees only joints in action.

FIGURE 15.2   A person performing on the slalom ski simulator. Note that the person has attached LED markers for movement analysis purposes.

fully understand and continue to debate, the person translates the perceived information into movement commands to produce the action.

The influence of skill characteristics. Research investigating the influence on learning of demonstration has produced equivocal findings about the effectiveness of skill demonstration. Some researchers have found that demonstration leads to better skill learning than other forms of instruction; others have found that it does not. But as Magill and Schoenfelder-Zohdi (1996) pointed out, a closer inspection of that research leads to the conclusion that the influence of demonstration on skill acquisition depends on characteristics of the skill being learned. The most important characteristic leading to the beneficial effect of demonstration is that the skill being learned requires the *acquisition of a new pattern of coordination.*

We see this clearly when we organize into two categories the results of research investigating the effect of demonstration on skill learning. In one category are those experiments in which participants learned more quickly after demonstration than after other forms of instruction. In experiments in this category, participants typically learned skills requiring them to acquire new patterns of limb coordination. In the other category are experiments in which participants usually learned skills no better after observing demonstrations than after receiving other forms of instruction. In these experiments, the participants practiced skills that required them to acquire new parameter characteristics for well-learned patterns of limb coordination.

Observing correctly performed demonstrations. A common guiding principle for demonstrating a skill is that the demonstrator should perform the

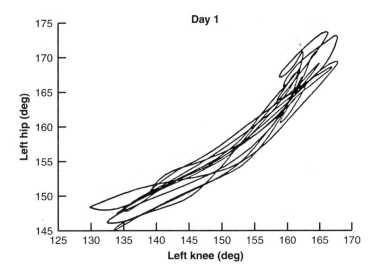

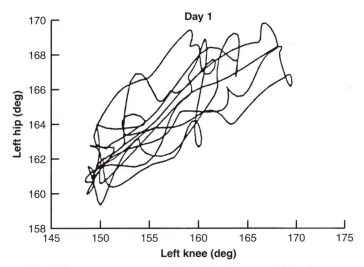

FIGURE 15.3   Angle-angle diagrams of the left knee and left hip for two people practicing on the slalom ski simulator. Both graphs show the relationship of these joints after one day of practice. The top graph is from the person who watched a skilled model demonstrate; the lower graph is from the person who did not watch a demonstration.   [From Schoenfelder-Zohdi, B. G. (1992). *Investigating the informational nature of a modeled visual demonstration,* Ph. D. dissertation, Louisiana State University. Reprinted by permission.]

A CLOSER LOOK

Beginners Learn by Observing Other Beginners: Learning the Tennis Volley

An experiment by Hebert and Landin (1994) nicely illustrates how instructors can facilitate skill acquisition for beginners by having them observe other beginners. Female university students who had no previous formal training or regular participation in tennis practiced the tennis forehand volley with the nondominant hand. All of these students first saw a brief instructional videotape emphasizing the basic elements of the volley. Then one group practiced the volley for fifty trials while receiving verbal feedback from the instructor after each trail. Each of these students had a fellow participant observe and listen to a videotape of their practice trials. Then these observers were divided into two groups and began their own fifty trials of practice. One of these latter groups received verbal feedback from the instructor during practice, whereas the other group did not. A fourth control group practiced without either observing other participants of receiving verbal feedback. The results showed that those who had observed other beginners practice before beginning practice performed better on a posttest than those who had not, regardless of the feedback condition during practice.

---

skill correctly. Why would more accurate demonstration lead to better learning? Two reasons are evident from the research literature (see McCullagh, 1993). The first reason follows our discussion of perception of information in the preceding section. If the observer perceives and uses information related to invariant movement patterns, it is logical to expect the quality of performance resulting from observing a demonstration to be related to the quality of the demonstration. Another reason is that in addition to picking up coordination information, an observer also perceives information about the strategy used by the model to solve the movement problem. Typically, the observer then tries to imitate that strategy on his or her initial attempts at performing the skill.

Observing unskilled demonstrators. Although the theoretical predictions and the empirical evidence point to the preferability of observing skilled demonstrators, evidence indicates that beginners can derive learning benefits even from observing unskilled demonstrators, especially if both the observers and the models are beginners. What this means is that the models are "demonstrators" only in that the observers are watching them practice.

One proposed benefit of this use of demonstration is that it discourages imitation of a skilled model's performance of the skill, and encourages the observer to engage in more active problem solving. We can trace evidence for the benefit of this approach to the 1930s (e.g., Twitmeyer, 1931), although widespread interest in this approach did not develop until Adams (1986) published some experiments. Since then, others have pursued the investigation of the use and benefit of observing an unskilled model (e.g., McCullagh & Meyer, 1997; Pollock & Lee, 1992; Weir & Leavitt, 1990). Results of this research have consistently shown that observers of other beginners practicing a skill will perform at a higher level when they begin to perform than the beginners they observed.

One way to effectively implement this use of demonstration is by pairing students, athletes, or patients in situations where one of the pair performs the skill while the other observes. After a certain number of trials or amount of time, the pair switches roles. On the basis of what we know from the research literature, learning of the skill can be facilitated for both the performer and the observer by having the teacher, coach, therapist, or some other knowledgeable person provide verbal feedback to the performer. Another effective strategy is to provide the observer of the pair with a checklist of key aspects of the skill. The observer should look for each aspect, check it on the list, and then provide some feedback to the performer. Under these conditions, the observer actively engages in problem-solving activity that is beneficial for learning. The learner observes what the unskilled model does, what the "expert" tells him or her is wrong with the attempt, what the model does to correct errors, and how successful he or she is on the succeeding attempts.

The frequency of demonstrating a skill. One of the reasons for demonstrating a skill is to communicate how to perform the skill. For the beginner, demonstration provides an effective means of communicating the "idea" of the action or skill, which includes the general movement pattern. As we discussed in chapter 12, Gentile considered this to be the goal of the first stage of learning. When applied to the use of demonstration, Gentile's view suggests two things. The first is that it is beneficial to demonstrate a skill before the person begins practicing it. The second, and perhaps more important, is that the instructor should continue demonstrating during practice as frequently as necessary. Earlier, we pointed out that a skilled demonstration communicates the invariant characteristics of a movement pattern. If this is the case, then we would expect that the more frequently a beginner observes a skilled demonstration, the more opportunity the beginner will have to acquire the movement pattern. At least two research studies support this latter point. One, by Carroll and Bandura (1990), involves the learning of complex movement patterns of a computer joystick; the other, by Hand and Sidaway (1993), involves the learning of a golf skill. Both experiments provided evidence that more frequent observations of the model yielded better skill learning.

Auditory modeling. Our discussion so far has focused on visual demonstration. However, there are skills for which visual demonstration is less effective for learning than other forms of demonstration. An example is a skill for which the goal is to move in a certain criterion movement time. For this type of skill an auditory form of demonstration seems to work best.

A good research example illustrating the use and effectiveness of auditory modeling is an experiment by Doody, Bird, and Ross (1985). The task required people to perform a complex sequential movement with one hand in a criterion movement time of 2.1 sec. Visual and auditory demonstration groups observed a videotape of a skilled model before each practice trial. The visual demonstration group saw only the video portion of the tape and heard no sound. The auditory demonstration group heard only the audio portion of the modeled performance and did not see the task performed by the model. Results indicated that the group that heard the audio portion of the performance did better than both the visual demonstration–only group.

Additionally, there are skills for which auditory modeling can be as effective for learning as visual modeling. A good example of this is learning the rhythmic sequence of a series of dance steps. For example, in an experiment by Wuyts and Buekers (1995), people who had no prior dance or music experience learned a sequence of thirty-two choreographed steps. For acquiring the rhythmic timing of this sequence, participants who only heard the timing structure learned it as well as those who both saw and heard the sequence performed by a model.

How the observing of demonstrations influences learning. At the learning theory level, an important question is this: Why does observing demonstrations influence motor skill learning in a beneficial way? Two different views address this question.

The predominant current view is based on the work of Bandura (1984) concerning modeling and social learning. This view, called the **cognitive mediation theory,** proposes that when a person observes a model, he or she translates the observed

---

cognitive mediation theory   a theory for explaining the benefit of a demonstration proposing that when a person observes a skilled model, the person translates the observed movement information into a cognitive code that the person stores in memory and uses when the observer performs the skill.

movement information into a symbolic memory code that forms the basis of a stored representation in memory. The reason the person transforms movement information into a cognitive memory representation is so that the brain can then rehearse and organize the information. The memory representation then serves as a guide for performing the skill and as a standard for error detection and correction. To perform the skill, the person first must access the memory representation and then must translate it back into the appropriate motor control code to produce the body and limb movements. Thus, cognitive processing serves as a mediator between the perception of the movement information and the performance of the skill by establishing a cognitive memory representation between the perception and the action.

According to Bandura, four subprocesses govern observational learning. The first is the *attention process,* which involves what the person observes and the information he or she extracts from the model's actions. The second is the *retention process,* in which the person transforms and restructures what he or she observes into symbolic codes that the person stores in memory. Certain cognitive activities, such as rehearsal, labeling, and organization are involved in the retention process and benefit the development of this representation. The *behavior reproduction process* is the third subprocess; during it, the person translates the memory representation of the modeled action and turns it into physical action. Successful accomplishment of this process requires that the individual possess the physical capability to perform the modeled action. Finally, the *motivation process* involves the incentive or motivation to perform the modeled action. This process, then, focuses on all those factors that influence a person's motivation to perform. Unless this process is completed, the person will not perform the action.

The second view of how observing a demonstration benefits skill learning is based on the direct perception view of vision proposed many years ago by J. J. Gibson (1966, 1979). Scully and Newell (1985) adapted Gibson's view to the visual observation of a skilled demonstration and proposed the **dynamic view of modeling** as an alternative to Bandura's theory. The dynamic view questions the need for a symbolic coding step (the memory representation step) between the observation of the modeled action and the physical performance of that action. Instead, it maintains, the visual system is capable of automatically processing visual information in such a way that it constrains the motor control system to act according to what the vision detects. The visual system "picks up" from the model salient information that effectively constrains the body and limbs to act in specific ways. The person does not need to transform the information received via the visual system into a cognitive code and store it in memory. This is the case because the visual information directly provides the basis for coordination and control of the various body parts required to produce the action. Thus, the critical need for the observer in the early stage of learning is to observe demonstrations that enable him or her to perceive the important invariant coordination relationships between body parts. Additional observations of the model will benefit the learner by helping the person learn to parameterize the action.

Unfortunately, there is no conclusive evidence in the research literature that shows one of these two views of the modeling effect to be the more valid one. At present, both appear to be viable theoretical explanations of why modeling benefits skill acquisition. The cognitive mediation theory has been the more prominent of the two, receiving more attention in motor skills research. However, the dynamic view is growing in popularity; this should lead to research that will test its viability as an alternative explanation of the modeling effect.

Verbal Instructions and Cues

Verbal instructions rank with demonstration as undoubtedly the most commonly used means of communicating to people how to perform motor skills. Evidence supports the value of verbal instructions for facilitating skill acquisition. Several factors are particularly important for developing effective verbal instruction.

Implementing Demonstration in Skill Instruction Settings

- Keep in mind that demonstrating a skill will have its greatest benefit when the skill being learned requires the acquisition of a new pattern of coordination. Examples include learning to serve in tennis, learning a new dance step, and learning to get into a wheelchair from the floor.
- Be aware that if the skill being learned involves learning a new control parameter characteristic for a previously learned pattern of coordination, demonstration will be no more beneficial than verbal instructions. Examples include learning to throw a ball at different speeds, learning to kick a ball from different distances, and learning to grasp and lift different sizes of cups.
- Demonstrate frequently and provide no verbal commentary while demonstrating, to reduce a potential attention-capacity problem.

- Be certain the observer can see the critical features of the skill you are demonstrating. It may be helpful to verbally direct the observer's attention to these features just before the demonstration.
- If you cannot demonstrate a skill very well, use some other way to provide a skilled demonstration, such as a film or videotape, or another person who can demonstrate the skill.
- In some situations, allow beginners to observe other beginners practice a skill. This can be an effective use of demonstration, and works well when there is limited space and/or equipment for every person in a group to perform the skill at the same time.
- Use auditory demonstrations of timing and rhythm goals. This is an effective way to communicate how to achieve these types of action goals.

Verbal instructions and attention capacity. An important performer characteristic that an instructor needs to keep in mind when presenting verbal instructions is that the person has a limited capacity to attend to incoming information. This means that the instructor must take into account the quantity of instructions. It is easy to overwhelm the person with instructions about what to do to perform a skill. On the basis of our knowledge of attention-capacity limits, we can reasonably expect that a beginner will have difficulty paying attention to more than one or two instructions about what to do. Because the beginner will need to divide attention between remembering the instructions and actually performing the skill, a minimal amount of verbal information can exceed the person's attention-capacity limits (e.g., Wiese-Bjornstal & Weiss, 1992).

Verbal instructions to focus attention on movement components of a skill. An important function of instructions is to direct learners' attention to focus on the features of the skill or environmental

context that will enhance their performance of the skill. A key point with regard to the content of these instructions relates to our discussion of attention and consciousness in chapter 8. We indicated that attention can be either conscious or nonconscious, with the person's awareness, or lack of awareness, of what was being attended to as the basis for the distinction between consciousness and nonconsciousness. When we relate this point about awareness to attention focus during the performance of a motor skill, an important question is, Is the extent to

dynamic view of modeling a theoretical view explaining the benefit of observing a skilled model demonstrate a skill; it proposes that the visual system is capable of automatically processing the observed movement in a way that constrains the motor control system to act accordingly, so that the person does not need to engage in cognitive mediation.

which the performer needs to be consciously aware of the features of a skill or environmental context critical to successful performance? The answer to this question has important implications for verbal instructions because it will serve as a guideline for determining the content of instructions.

Research evidence indicates that a key part of skill learning is *where* a person directs his or her conscious attention when performing a skill. One approach researchers have taken to address this question is by providing instructions that direct the performer's attention to specific movement components of the skill or to specific features of the environmental context. A study reported by Wulf and Weigelt (1997) provides an excellent example of this type of research. Participants practiced the slalom ski simulator task (described earlier in this chapter and pictured in figure 15.2). Everyone was told that the goal of the task was to continuously move the platform for 90 sec as far as possible from the middle to the left and right and back to the middle at a rate of one complete cycle every 2 sec. Participants in one group were given an additional attention-directing instruction, which was based on a movement characteristic of people who demonstrated high performance levels on the ski simulator. The instruction was to try to exert force on the platform only after it passed the center of the ski simulator. Another group was not given this instruction, which previous research had shown could result in a high performance level on this task. However, the expectation was that receipt of instructions that provided information about a movement characteristic of skilled performers would facilitate learning the skill compared to not receiving these instructions. However, as figure 15.4, shows, just the opposite occurred. The additional attention-directing instructions led to poorer performance during practice trials and on a transfer test in which participants performed under stress (they were told they were being observed and evaluated by a skiing expert). Interestingly, in a follow-up experiment, which was based on the assumption that more experience with the task would allow participants to direct more attention to the specific information in the instruc-

tions, the attention-directing instructions were given after three days of practice. But, once again, rather than aid learning, the instructions had a negative effect.

Why would instructions to direct attention to a specific movement component of a skill hinder learning the skill? The most likely reason is one presented by Wulf, Hoess, and Prinz (1998), which they called the *action effect hypothesis* (see Prinz, 1997). This hypothesis proposes that actions are best planned and controlled by their intended effects. The theory basis for this hypothesis relates to how we code in memory sensory and motor information. Prinz contends that we represent both in memory in a common code, which argues against the separation of perception and action as unique and distinct events. Without going further into the theory issues involved, the common coding view predicts that actions will be more effective when they are planned in terms of their intended outcomes rather than in terms of the movement patterns required by the skill. Interestingly, although Prinz proposed this hypothesis in the 1990s, William James described a similar view a century earlier (James, 1890). However, different from James, Prinz based his hypothesis on the results of controlled, laboratory research.

Verbal instructions to focus attention on environmental context features for open skills. Another issue associated with the content of instructions as they compare to conscious awareness relates to the common instructional technique of telling people what in the environment to look for that will help them perform a skill. Sometimes we ask people to tell us what they were looking for or looking at when they performed a skill, so that we can help them correct their visual attention focus. However, research investigating the need for conscious awareness of environmental cues when learning skills reveals that these types of techniques do not have to be included in the student-teacher or patient-therapist interaction. This research shows that we learn to select relevant cues from the environment without being consciously aware of what those cues are.

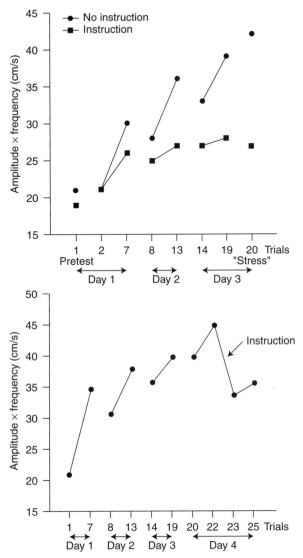

FIGURE 15.4 The top graph shows the results of the first experiment by Wulf and Weigelt which compared a group that received instructions about a movement component of the slalom ski simulator task and a group that did not receive the instructions. The bottom graph shows the results of their second experiment in which one group received the movement component instructions on the fourth day of practice. [Reprinted with permission from *Research Quarterly for Exercise and Sport,* Vol. 1, No. 4, 262–367. Copyright © 1997 by the American Alliance for Health, Physical Education, Recreation and Dance, 1900 Association Drive, Reston, VA 20191.]

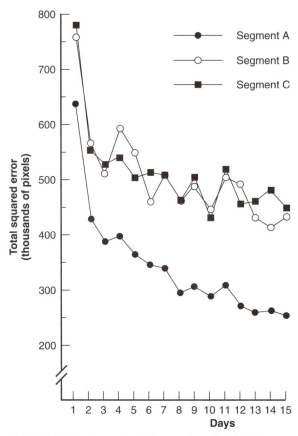

FIGURE 15.5   The results of the experiment by Magill, Schoenfelder-Zohdi, and Hall (1990) showing the superior performance on the repeated segment A compared to the random segments B and C for a complex tracking task.   [Source: R. A. Magill, et al., "Further Evidence for Implicit Learning in a Complex Tracking Task" paper presented at the annual meeting of hte Psychonomics Society, Novermber, 1990, New Orleans, LA.]

A good example of research demonstrating that people attend to and use important environmental context features without conscious awareness of them is an experiment reported by Magill (1998). Participants watched a target cursor move in a complex waveform pattern across a computer monitor screen for 60 sec. The participants' task involved pursuit tracking of the target cursor: they were to manipulate a horizontal lever on a table top to make their own cursor stay as close as pos-

sible to the target cursor. The unique feature of the target cursor movement was that it moved randomly for the second and third 20-sec segments on every trial, but it made the same movements on every trial during the first 20-sec segment. The participants practiced this pursuit-tracking task for approximately twenty-four trials on each of fifteen days. The results shown in figure 15.5, indicated that as they practiced, they performed better on the first segment than on the other two segments. But what is more important is that when interviewed, none of the participants indicated that they knew that the target cursor made the same pattern during the first segment on every trial. Thus the participants attended to and used the regularity of the cursor movement during the first segment, even though they were unaware of that characteristic.

Although the research just described indicates that people can learn to use relevant environmental context features without being instructed to look for them, there is a common assumption that we can facilitate skill learning by giving instructions that make people aware of these features. For example, a tennis teacher may tell a student that a certain racquet-head angle at ball contact during a serve indicates a specific type of serve, which the student should try to look for to predict that type of serve. However, what is not so commonly known is that this type of instruction could actually hinder rather than facilitate learning, especially when the specific feature looked for occurs infrequently in a series of trials.

Green and Flowers (1991) reported an experiment that serves as a good example of the research evidence demonstrating this negative effect. Participants played a computer game in which they manipulated a joystick to move a paddle horizontally across the bottom of the monitor to try to catch a "ball," which was a dot of light, that moved for 2.5 sec from the top to the bottom of the screen. The ball moved according to one of eight pathways, four of which involved a single curve and four of which involved an S-curve. On some trials (75 percent), the ball made one of two types of deviations from the normal pathway. When these occurred, they related to a specific final position of the ball. Thus participants' detection of these characteristics could help them increase their catching accuracy. One group of participants received instructions about this characteristic and its probability of occurring; the other group did not. Participants practiced for five days for a total of 800 trials. The results showed that both groups improved. However, the instructed group made more errors than the group that had had no instruc-

tion. The authors concluded that the instructed participants directed so much of their attentional resources to trying to remember the rule and looking for its occurrence that their performance was disrupted, because they did not have sufficient attention to devote to the catching task itself.

Verbal instructions influence goal achievement strategies. Another factor that we need to consider is that verbal instructions direct the person's attention to certain performance aspects of the skill. A good example of this is the way verbal instructions can bias a person in terms of the strategy he or she uses to learn skills that must be performed both quickly and accurately. An experiment by Blais (1991) illustrates the way verbal instructions can invoke strategy bias for learning these skills. The task was a serial pursuit tracking task in which participants controlled a device like a steering wheel to align a pointer in one of four positions on a screen in front of them. When a target position was illuminated, a participant had to move the pointer to that small area as quickly and as accurately as possible. When the person had achieved that goal, another target area was illuminated. This process was repeated many times. Three groups of participants received verbal instructions that emphasized being accurate, being fast, or being both accurate and fast.

The instruction emphasis was especially evident during the first of the five days of practice. On this day, the "speed instruction" group recorded the fastest movement times, whereas the "accuracy group" produced the most accurate performance. An interesting result was that the group told to emphasize both speed and accuracy adopted a strategy that led to fast movement times—but at the expense of performance accuracy. And although the "accuracy instruction" group performed the most accurately, its members did so in a manner that eventually gave them the fastest average overall response time, which included reaction time, movement time, and movement-correction time for errors. Thus, for this task, where both speed and accuracy were equally important for overall

A CLOSER LOOK

Attention Focus Instructions for Learning a Golf Swing

An experiment reported by Wulf, Lauterbach, and Toole (1999) presents interesting evidence showing that *where* a beginner directs his or her attention focus during each practice golf swing can influence the learning of the swing. University students who had no prior experience playing golf practiced hitting pitch shots into a circular target from a distance of 15 m. Everyone was given the same demonstration and instructions about gripping the club and stance. But, instructions concerning the swing differed between two groups. The *internal-focus* group was told to focus on the swinging motion of the arms dur-

ing each swing. This group received specific instructions about the various movements involved in the swing and practiced several swings without holding a club. The *external-focus* group was instructed to focus on the club movement during the swing. Specific instructions to this group emphasized the need to allow the club to perform a pendulumlike motion, and to let the club swing freely and focus attention on the weight of the clubhead, its pathway on the back- and downswing, and acceleration during the downswing. During eighty practice trials with augmented feedback and thirty retention trials one day later with no augmented feedback, the external-focus group consistently produced higher scores than the internal-focus group.

---

performance, instructions emphasizing accuracy led to the best achievement of the two-component goal.

Verbal cues. One of the potential problems associated with verbal instructions is that they can contain too little or too much information and not provide the learner with what he or she needs to know to achieve the goal of the skill. To overcome this problem, instructors can use verbal cues to direct people to know what to do to perform skills (Landin, 1994). **Verbal cues** are short, concise phrases that serve to (1) direct people's attention to regulatory information relevant for performing skills, or (2) prompt key movement-pattern elements of performing skills. For example, the cue "Look at the ball" directs visual attention, whereas the cue "Bend your knee" prompts an essential movement component. Research has shown these short, simple statements to be very effective as verbal instructions to facilitate learning new skills, as well as performing well-learned skills.

Teachers, coaches, or therapists can implement verbal cues in several different ways in skill learning settings. One way is to *give verbal cues along with a demonstration* to supplement the visual informa-

tion (e.g., Carroll & Bandura, 1990; McCullagh, Stiehl, & Weiss, 1990). When used this way, verbal cues aid in directing attention, and can guide rehearsal of the skill a person is learning. One caution about this use of verbal cues is that they may interrupt attention to the relative time patterns of skills and actually hinder skill learning (see Wiese-Bjornstal & Weiss, 1992).

Another way to use verbal cues is to *give cues to help learners focus on critical parts of skills.* For example, in an experiment by Masser (1993), first-grade classes were taught to do headstands. In one class, before students made each attempt to swing their legs up into the headstands, the instructor said, "Shoulders over your knuckles," to emphasize the body position critical to performing this skill. The cued students maintained their acquired skill three months after practice, whereas the students who had not received this verbal cue performed the headstand poorly three months later. A similar result occurred in an experiment using verbal cues to emphasize critical parts of the forward roll.

Performers also can *use verbal cues while performing* to cue themselves to attend to or perform key aspects of skills. Cutton and Landin (1994) provided a research example demonstrating the

A CLOSER LOOK

Guidelines for Using Verbal Cues for Skill Instruction and Rehabilitation

- Cues should be short statements of one, two, or three words.
- Cues should relate logically to the aspects of the skill to be prompted by the cues.
- Cues can prompt a sequence of several movements.

- Cues should be limited in number. Cue only the most critical elements of performing the skill.
- Cues can be especially helpful for directing shifts of attention.
- Cues are effective for prompting a distinct rhythmic structure for a sequence of movements.
- Cues must be carefully timed so that they serve as prompts and do not interfere with performance.
- Cues should initially be spoken by the performer.

effectiveness of this technique for nonskilled individuals. Instructors taught university students in a beginning tennis class five verbal cues to say out loud each time they were required to hit a ball. These were as follows: "ready," to prompt preparation for the oncoming ball; "ball," to focus attention on the ball itself; "turn," to prompt proper body position to hit the ball, which included turning the hips and shoulders to be perpendicular with the net and pointing the racquet toward the back fence; "hit," to focus attention on contacting the ball; and "head down," to prompt the stationary position of the head after ball contact. The students who used verbal cues learned tennis groundstrokes better than those who did not, including a group that received verbal feedback during practice.

Verbal cues have also been used to improve the performance of skilled tennis players. For example, Landin and Hebert (1999) had university female varsity tennis players use self-cueing to help them improve their volleying skills. Players learned to say the word "split," to cue them to hop to a balanced two-foot stop that would allow them to move in any direction. Then, they said, "turn," to cue them to turn their shoulders and hips to the ball. Finally, they said, "hit," to direct their attention to tracking the ball to the point of contact on the racquet and to cue themselves to keep the head still and hit the ball solidly. After practicing this cueing strategy for five weeks, the players showed marked improvements in both performance and technique.

Verbal cues can be used for two different purposes. Sometimes the cue *directs attention* to a specific environmental event or to specific sources of regulatory information (in our example, "ready," "ball," and "hit" are such cues). In other cases, the cue *prompts action,* for either a specific movement ("head down") or a sequence of movements ("turn"). The key to the effectiveness of verbal cues is that as the person practices and continues to use the cues an association develops between the cue and the act it prompts. The benefit is that the person does not need to give attention to a large number of verbal instructions and can focus attention on the important perceptual and movement components of the skill.

SUMMARY

A demonstration conveys information about how to perform a skill. The benefit of observing a skilled demonstration is that it presents to the

verbal cues short, concise phrases that direct a performer's attention to important environmental regulatory characteristics, or that prompt the person to perform key movement pattern elements while performing a skill.

observer the invariant characteristics of the movement pattern necessary for performing the skill. Because of this, more learning benefits will result from observing skills requiring new patterns of coordination than from observing skills for which people must learn new parameters for already established patterns of movement. Observing another beginner learning a skill also can lead to skill learning benefits. Increased frequency of demonstration appears to influence skill learning positively. When people must learn timing characteristics of skills, auditory modeling is an effective technique for communicating these characteristics.

Two prominent theoretical viewpoints attempt to explain how modeling influences skill learning. One view, called the cognitive mediation theory, argues that a person develops a memory representation from observing a model, and that the person must access this representation prior to performing the skill. The alternative view, called the dynamic view, holds that people do not need cognitive mediation, because the visual system can automatically constrain the motor system to act in accordance with what has been observed.

When an instructor uses verbal instructions to provide information about how to perform a motor skill, several factors must be taken into account. The amount of information provided in instructions should not exceed the learner's attention capacity. Because instructions direct the learner's focus of attention, they should emphasize an attention focus that is not on the movement itself or on nonregularly occurring environmental context features. In addition, instructions should influence the learner to use an effective strategy while practicing a skill, such as emphasizing accuracy before speed when learning a skill that requires both speed and accuracy. Verbal cues provide an effective technique that beginners and skilled performers can use to direct attention to specific environmental context features and components of the skill, and to prompt action for a specific movement or sequence of movements.

RELATED READINGS

Carroll, W. R., & Bandura, A. (1990). Representational guidance of action production in observational learning: A causal analysis. *Journal of Motor Behavior, 22,* 85–97.

Laugier, C., & Cadopi, M. (1996). Representational guidance of dance performance in adult novices: Effect of concrete vs. abstract movements. *International Journal of Sport Psychology, 27,* 91–108.

McCullagh, P. (2001). Modeling: Learning, development, and social psychological considerations. In R. N. Singer, H. A. Hausenblaus, & C. Janelle (Eds.), *Handbook of research in sport psychology* (2nd ed.). New York, NY: Wiley.

Starek, J., & McCullagh, P. (1999). The effect of self-modeling on the performance of beginning swimmers. *The Sport Psychologist, 13,* 269–287.

Sweeting, T., & Rink, J. E. (1999). Effects of direct instruction and environmentally designed instruction on the process and product characteristics of a fundamental skill. *Journal of Teaching Physical Education, 18,* 216–233.

STUDY QUESTIONS

1. What are two types of research evidence that show that observing a skilled demonstration of a motor skill influences the acquisition of the coordination characteristics of the skill?

2. Describe how observing an unskilled person learning a skill could help a beginner learn that skill?

3. What are the main features of the two predominant theories about how observing a demonstration helps a person to learn that skill? How do these theories differ?

4. Give an example of how instructions influence *where* a person directs his or her attention when performing a motor skill. Why is this a point of concern in a motor skill learning situation?

5. How can verbal cues be used to help overcome some of the problems often associated with giving verbal instructions?

The Effect of Augmented Feedback on Skill Learning

Concept: Augmented feedback can improve,
hinder, or have no effect on skill learning

APPLICATION

Think about a time when you were beginning to learn a new physical activity. How much success did you experience on your first few attempts? Most likely, you were not very successful. As you tried to improve, you probably had many questions that you needed someone to answer to help you better understand what you were doing wrong and what you needed to do to improve. How were these questions answered for you? If you were in a class or taking lessons from a private instructor, you probably sought the answers from the instructor. Although you may have been able to answer many of your questions on your own as you continued to try different things while you practiced, you found that getting an answer from the instructor saved you time and energy.

This situation is an example of what commonly occurs in the early stage of learning a skill. It is equally typical for a person learning a new sport skill and a person relearning a skill following an injury or illness. The significance of this example is that it points out an important role played by the teacher, coach, therapist, or trainer, which is to give information to the learner to facilitate the skill acquisition process. This information, known as augmented feedback, is the topic of the following discussion as well as the next two chapters.

DISCUSSION

Although motor learning researchers generally agree that augmented feedback can be an important part of skill instruction, they do not agree on how instructors should implement it to influence skill learning most effectively. As a first step in the process of addressing this issue, we will discuss what augmented feedback is. This step is important because of the long history of terminology problems that have characterized discussions about this important instructional variable. Our goal here is to establish a common ground of terms and definitions so that we can see more clearly that augmented feedback can have various effects on skill learning, depending on the type of information given and the skill being learned.

The Feedback Family

When people perform a motor skill, they can have available to them two general types of performance-related information (i.e., feedback) that will "tell" them something about the outcome of the performance or about what caused that outcome. One is **task-intrinsic feedback,** which is the sensory-perceptual information that is a natural part of performing a skill. Each of the sensory systems can provide this type of feedback. For example, if a person throws a dart at a target on the wall, he or she receives *visual* task-intrinsic feedback from seeing the flight of the dart and where it lands on the target. In addition, the person receives *proprioceptive* task-intrinsic feedback movement of his or her body posture along with arm and hand movement as the person prepares to throw the dart and as the dart is thrown. Other sensory systems can also provide task-intrinsic feedback, such as the *auditory* system, when the person hears the dart hit, or not hit, the target.

The second general type of performance-related information a person can receive is *in addition to* task-intrinsic feedback. Although various terms have been used to identify this type of feedback, the term that will be used in this book is **augmented feedback.** This adjective "augmented" refers to adding to, or enhancing something, which in this case involves adding to or enhancing task-intrinsic feedback. Consider the dart-throwing task just described. The task-intrinsic feedback could be augmented in various ways. For example, a person who is standing by the dartboard could tell the performer the dart's location on the target, which would augment the visual task-intrinsic feedback. Or, a teacher or coach may tell the person something about his or her arm movement that led to the dart location on the dartboard, which would augment the proprioceptive task-intrinsic feedback.

It is important to note that the term *feedback* is common to both categories of performance-related information described in the preceding paragraphs. As a result, consider the term feedback as a generic term that describes information people receive about their performance of a motor skill during or after the performance. To help conceptualize the relationship of the two general types of performance-related feedback to each other and to feedback itself, consider these two types of feedback as related members of the same family. Figure 16.1 graphically describes the feedback family relationships for task-intrinsic feedback and augmented feedback, as well as for the related specific types of each. The focus of the discussion of the remainder of the chapters in this unit is on augmented feedback.

Types of Augmented Feedback

Augmented feedback augments task-intrinsic feedback in two distinct ways. In some situations, it *enhances* the task-intrinsic feedback the person's sensory system can readily detect on its own. For example, a teacher or coach might tell a golfer where his or her hands were positioned at the top of the swing, even though the person could feel for himself or herself where they were. In a clinical environment, a therapist might show an amputee patient EMG traces on a computer monitor to enhance the patient's own proprioceptive feedback to help the patient know when the appropriate muscles are functioning.

In other situations, augmented feedback *adds* information that the person cannot detect using his or her sensory system. For example, the golf teacher or coach might tell the golfer where the ball went because the golfer was concentrating so much on keeping his or her head down during the swing that he or she did not see it after it was hit. Likewise, a therapist might tell a clinical patient how much his or her body swayed because vestibular problems prevent the patient from being able to detect this information. In each of these situations, augmented feedback provides performance information that otherwise would not be available to the person.

In Figure 16.1, it is important to note that there are *two categories of types of augmented feedback:* knowledge of results and knowledge of performance. Each category can involve a variety of ways of presenting augmented feedback; this will be the topic of discussion in chapter 17.

Also, it is important to point out here that augmented feedback can be provided at different times. Researchers use specific terms to designate the time periods when it is given. If augmented feedback is given *while the movement is in progress,* we call it **concurrent augmented feedback.** If it is given *after the skill has been performed,* we call it **terminal augmented feedback.**

Knowledge of results (KR). The category of augmented feedback known as **knowledge of results**

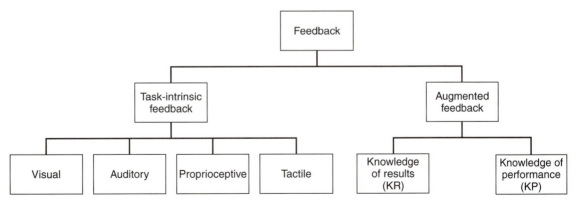

FIGURE 16.1   Illustration of the different types of feedback in the feedback family that are related to learning and performing motor skills.

(commonly referred to as **KR**) consists of *externally presented information about the outcome of performing a skill or about achieving the goal of the performance.* In some situations, KR describes something about the performance outcome. For example, if a teacher tells a student in an archery class, "The shot was in the blue at 9 o'clock," the teacher is providing performance outcome information. Similarly, if a therapist shows a patient a computer-generated graph indicating that this leg extension was 3 degrees more than the last one, the therapist is giving KR to the patient about the outcome of his or her leg extension movement.

Sometimes, KR does not describe the performance outcome, but simply tells the performer whether he or she has achieved the goal of the performance. This is the case when some external device gives a "yes" or "no" signal indicating whether or not the performance goal was achieved. For example, to augment proprioceptive and visual feedback for a patient working on achieving a goal leg extension, the therapist could set a buzzer to be activated when the patient achieved the goal number of degrees of movement. Although the buzzer would provide no information about how close to the goal or how far from it the movement was if it had not been achieved, the patient would know that

he or she had not achieved the goal unless the buzzer sounded. See table 16.1 for some additional examples.

task-intrinsic feedback   the sensory feedback that is naturally available while performing a skill.

augmented feedback   a generic term used to describe information about performing a skill that is added to sensory feedback and comes from a source external to the person performing the skill; it is sometimes referred to as extrinsic or external feedback.

concurrent augmented feedback   augmented feedback that is provided while a person is performing a skill or making a movement.

terminal augmented feedback   augmented feedback that is provided after a person has completed the performance of a skill or a movement.

knowledge of results (KR)   a category of augmented feedback that gives information about the outcome of performing a skill or about achieving the goal of the performance.

TABLE 16.1   Examples of Augmented Feedback

• **A golf instructor tells a student:**	KR ⇒ "Your shot went into the right rough." KP ⇒ "You did not take your backswing back far enough before you began your downswing."
• **A physical therapist tells a patient:**	KR ⇒ "You walked 10 feet more today than you did yesterday." KP ⇒ "You should bend your knees more as you walk."
• **A student driver in a simulator:**	KR ⇒ sees the number of errors he or she made after completing a session. KP ⇒ sees a light flash each time he or she makes an error while driving in a session.
• **A sprinter in track:**	KR ⇒ sees a posting on the scoreboard of the amount of time to run the race. KP ⇒ sees a videotape replay of his or her race.
• **A gymnast:**	KR ⇒ sees the judges' scores after completing a routine. KP ⇒ looks at a computer monitor to see a stick figure representation of his or her body, limb, and head displacement when he or she performed the routine.
• **A knee rehabilitation patient:**	KR ⇒ reads a display on an exercise machine that indicates the number of degrees of leg extension he or she had on that leg extension exercise repetition. KP ⇒ hears a buzzer when a target muscle is active during a leg extension exercise.

Knowledge of performance (KP). The second category of augmented feedback is **knowledge of performance** (known as **KP**). This is information about the *movement characteristics that led to the performance outcome.* The important point here is that KP differs from KR in terms of which aspect of performance the information refers to. For example, in the archery situation described above, the teacher would provide KP by telling the student that he or she pulled the bow to the left at the release of the arrow. Here, the teacher would be verbally augmenting the task-intrinsic feedback by telling the student what he or she did that caused the arrow to hit the target where it did.

In addition to giving KP verbally, there are various nonverbal means of providing KP. For example, videotape replay is a popular method of showing a person what he or she did while performing a skill. Videotape replay allows the person to see what he or she actually did that led to the outcome of that performance. Another means of providing

KP that is increasing in popularity as computer software becomes more accessible is showing the person computer-generated kinematic characteristics of the just-completed performance. In clinical environments, therapists also use biofeedback devices to give KP. For example, a therapist can attach a buzzer to an EMG recording device so that the person hears the buzzer sound when he or she activates the appropriate muscle while performing a movement. In each of these situations, sensory feedback is augmented in a way that informs the person about what he or she did while performing the skill that yielded the outcome of that performance.

The Roles of Augmented Feedback in Skill Acquisition

Augmented feedback plays two roles in the skill learning process. One is to *facilitate achievement of the goal of the skill.* Because augmented feedback provides information about the success of the skill in progress or just completed, the learner can

A CLOSER LOOK

Augmented Feedback as Motivation

An instructor can use augmented feedback to influence a person's perception of his or her own ability in a skill. This is an effective way to influence the person's motivation to continue pursuing a task goal or performing a skill. The verbal statement "You're doing a lot better" can indicate to a person that he or she is being successful at an activity. Evidence supporting the motivational effectiveness of this type of verbal feedback comes from research relating to self-efficacy and performance of skills.

For example, Solmon and Boone (1993) showed that in a physical education class environment, stu-

dents with high ability perceptions demonstrated longer persistence at performing a skill and had higher performance expectations than those with low ability perceptions.

In her review of the self-efficacy literature as it relates to skill performance, Feltz (1992) concluded that the success or failure of past performance is a key mediator of a person's self-perceptions regarding ability. The logical implication of these findings is that an instructor, coach, or therapist can present augmented feedback in a way that influences a person's feelings of success or failure which, in turn, influence a person to continue or to stop his or her involvement in participating in a physical activity.

---

determine whether what he or she is doing is appropriate for performing the skill correctly. Thus, the augmented feedback can help the person achieve the skill goal more quickly or more easily than he or she could without this external information.

The second role played by augmented feedback is to *motivate the learner to continue striving toward a goal.* In this role, the person uses augmented feedback to compare his or her own performance to a performance goal. The person then must decide to continue trying to achieve that goal, to change goals, or to stop performing the activity. This motivational role of augmented feedback is not the focus of our discussion here. Others, however, have discussed it in the motor learning literature (e.g., Little & McCullagh, 1989). Scholars interested in the pedagogical aspects of physical education teaching (e.g., Solmon & Lee, 1996; Silverman, Woods, & Subramaniam, 1998) increasingly are studying the effects of augmented feedback on people's motivation to engage in, or continue to engage in, physical activities. And exercise psychologists have shown that augmented feedback is influential in motivating people to adhere to exercise and rehabilitation programs (e.g., Annesi, 1998; Dishman, 1993).

How Essential Is Augmented Feedback for Skill Acquisition?

When a researcher or practitioner considers the use of augmented feedback to facilitate skill acquisition, an important theoretical and practical question arises: Is augmented feedback *necessary* for a person to learn motor skills? The answer to this question has theoretical implications for the understanding of the nature of skill learning itself. The need, or lack of need, for augmented feedback to acquire motor skills tells us much about what characterizes the human learning system and how it functions to acquire new skills. From a practical perspective, determining the necessity for augmented feedback for skill learning can serve to guide the development and implementation of effective instructional strategies. As you will see, the answer to this question is not a simple yes or

---

knowledge of performance (KP) a category of augmented feedback that gives information about the movement characteristics that led to a performance outcome.

no. Instead, there are *four different answers.* Which one is appropriate depends on certain characteristics of the skill being learned and of the person learning the skill.

Augmented feedback can be essential for skill acquisition. In some skill performance situations, performers cannot use the task-intrinsic feedback to determine what they need to do to improve performance. For performers to learn skills in such situations, augmented feedback is essential. There are at least three types of situations in which a person may *not* be able to use important task-intrinsic feedback effectively.

First, some skill situations do not make critical sensory feedback available to the person. For example, when a performer cannot see a target that he or she must hit, the performer does not have important visual feedback available. In this case, augmented feedback adds critical information that is not available from the task performance environment itself.

Second, in some situations the person, because of injury, disease, etc., does not have available the sensory pathways needed to detect critical task-intrinsic feedback for the skill he or she is learning. For these people, augmented feedback serves as a substitute for this missing information.

Third, in some situations the appropriate task-intrinsic feedback provides the necessary information and the person's sensory system is capable of detecting it, but the person cannot use the feedback. For example, a person learning to move a limb a certain distance or to throw a ball at a certain rate of speed may not be able to determine the distance moved or the rate of speed of the throw because of lack of experience. In these situations, augmented feedback helps to make the available task-intrinsic feedback more meaningful to the performer.

Research evidence supports the need for augmented feedback in these learning situations. For example, many of the earliest experiments on this topic showed the need for augmented feedback in situations in which the performance environment did not provide the learner with critical sensory

feedback. In many of these experiments, participants were blindfolded and thus could not see their movements or the performance environments. These experiments consistently showed augmented feedback, typically in the form of KR, to be essential for learning when, for example, the blindfolded persons had to learn to draw a line of a certain length (Trowbridge & Cason, 1932) or move a lever to a criterion position (e.g., Bilodeau, Bilodeau, & Schumsky, 1959). When the authors did not give KR in these situations, participants did not learn the skills.

Augmented feedback may not be needed for skill acquisition. Some motor skills inherently provide sufficient task-intrinsic feedback, so augmented feedback is redundant. For these types of skills, learners can use their own sensory feedback systems to determine the appropriateness of their movements and to make adjustments on future attempts. An experiment by Magill, Chamberlin, and Hall (1991) provides a laboratory example of this type of situation. Participants learned a coincidence-anticipation skill in which they simulated striking a moving object, which was a series of LEDs sequentially lighting along a 281-cm-long trackway. As they faced the trackway, they had to use a handheld bat to knock down a small wooden barrier directly under a target LED coincident with the lighting of the target. KR was the number of msec that they contacted the barrier before or after the target lighted. Four experiments showed that participants learned this task regardless of the number of trials on which they received KR during practice. In fact, receiving KR during practice did not lead to better learning than practice without KR.

A motor skill that does not require a person to have augmented feedback to learn it has an important characteristic: a detectable external referent in the environment that the person can use to determine the appropriateness of an action. For the anticipation timing task in the Magill et al. experiment, the target and other LEDs were the external referents. The learner could see when the bat made contact with the barrier in comparison to when the target lighted; this enabled him or her to see the

A CLOSER LOOK

Teacher Feedback Relationships in Physical Education Classes

Silverman, Woods, and Subramaniam (1999) examined the relationship between teacher feedback and several different practice and performance characteristics for eight classes of middle school physical education. Although each teacher taught one activity, the eight classes involved a variety of activities: volleyball, soccer, badminton, basketball, and ultimate. The teachers were videotaped for two classes in a row in which motor skill was the focus of instruction. The researchers observed the videotapes and recorded characteristics of several different teacher behavior categories, including teacher feedback. Among the various results of the analysis of the data from this study was the finding that *the amount of teacher feedback given to students was significantly correlated with the amount of appropriate practice in which students engaged,* regardless of skill level. These results indicate that even though research has shown that teacher feedback and skill achievement are not highly correlated, teacher feedback has a positive impact on the students' participation in class by influencing them to engage in activity that is appropriate for helping them learn the skills that are the focus of the class instruction.

---

relationship between his or her own movements and the goal of those movements. It is important to note here that the learner may *not* be consciously aware of this relationship. The sensory system and the motor control system operate in these situations in a way that does not demand the person's awareness of the environmental characteristics (see Magill, 1998). Thus, the enhancement of these characteristics by providing augmented feedback does not increase or speed up learning of the skill.

In addition to skill characteristics, practice condition characteristics also influence the need for augmented feedback. One of these characteristics is the existence of an observational learning situation. Experimental results have shown that two different types of observational learning conditions can be influential. In one, the learner observes a skilled model perform the skill. For example, in an experiment by Magill and Schoenfelder-Zohdi (1996), people who observed a skilled demonstration learned a rhythmic gymnastics rope skill as well as did those who received verbal KP after each trial. In addition, Hebert and Landin (1994) showed that beginning tennis players who watched other beginners practice learned the tennis forehand volley as well as or better than beginning players who received verbal KP. In both of these situations, the observational learning situation provided beginners an opportunity to acquire knowledge about how to do the skill correctly; they then were able to practice and improve on their own without needing augmented feedback.

There is an interesting parallel between skill learning situations in which learners do not need augmented feedback and results of studies investigating the use of teacher feedback in physical education class settings. These studies consistently have shown low correlations for the relationship between teacher feedback and student achievement (e.g., Lee, Keh, & Magill, 1993; Silverman, Tyson, & Krampitz, 1991). This finding suggests that the amount and quality of teacher feedback is influential for improving the skills of beginners in sport skills class settings, but we should not see it as the *most* important variable. Other variables, such as observational learning, appear to be capable of precluding the need for augmented feedback. Our understanding of the extent of this influence awaits further research.

Augmented feedback can enhance skill acquisition. There are some types of motor skills that people can learn without augmented feedback, but they will learn them more quickly or perform them at a higher level if they receive augmented feedback during practice. For these skills, augmented feedback is neither essential nor redundant. Instead, it *enhances* the learning of these skills.

Skills in this category include those for which improvement does occur through task-intrinsic feedback alone, but because of certain skill or learner characteristics, performance improvement reaches only a certain level. The research literature has shown two types of skill characteristics to fit this description.

The first type involves relatively simple skills for which achievement of the performance goal is initially easy to assess. An example is a movement goal of moving as quickly as possible. Initially, a person can assess if a particular attempt was faster than a previous one. However, usually because of the learner's lack of experience, which results in his or her decreased capability to discriminate small movement-speed differences, improvement seems to stop at a certain level of performance. To improve beyond this level of performance, the person requires augmented feedback. Research evidence shows that there is a point during practice at which people who receive KR about movement time for this type of skill continue to improve performance, whereas those who do not receive it level off in their performance.

The second type of skill for which augmented feedback enhances learning is any complex skill that requires a person to acquire an appropriate multilimb pattern of coordination. For such skills, learners can attain a certain degree of success simply by making repeated attempts to achieve the performance goal. But this goal achievement process can be speeded up with the addition of KP. More specifically, the KP that works best is information about critical components of the coordination pattern.

The best research example that illustrates this type of augmented feedback effect is an experiment by Wallace and Hagler (1979). The complex skill participants learned was a one-hand basketball set shot with the nondominant hand. The shot they practiced was 3.03 m from the basket and 45 degrees to the left side of the basket. After each shot, one group received verbal KP about errors in their stance and limb movements during the shot. Another group received only verbal encourage-

ment after each shot. Both groups could see the outcome of each shot. Figure 16.2 depicts the results. Note that KP provided an initial boost in performance for the first fifteen trials. Then, the verbal encouragement group caught up. However, similarity in performance between the two groups lasted only about ten trials; after this point, the verbal encouragement group showed no further improvement, whereas the group receiving KP continued to improve.

Augmented feedback can hinder skill learning. An effect of augmented feedback on skill learning that many might not expect is that it can hinder the learning process and, in some cases, actually make learning worse than it would have been otherwise. This effect is especially evident when a beginning learner becomes dependent on augmented feedback that will not be available in a test situation. Typically, the performance improvement the learner experienced during practice deteriorates in the test situation. In fact, in some situations, not only does performance deteriorate when augmented feedback is withdrawn, but the test performance is no better than if augmented feedback had not been given at all.

There are *three different skill learning situations* in which research has shown that this hindering effect can occur. One is when the instructor or therapist presents augmented feedback *concurrently* with the person's performance of the skill. This effect has a long history in the research literature (e.g., Annett, 1959).

The characteristic of tasks that are the most likely to lead to a dependency on augmented feedback are those in which the task-intrinsic feedback is minimal or difficult to interpret. When initially performing these types of tasks, people typically substitute concurrently provided augmented feedback for task-intrinsic feedback, because it gives them an easy-to-use guide for performing correctly. The problem with this approach is that rather than learning to use important task-intrinsic feedback characteristics associated with performing the skill, people become dependent on the augmented feed-

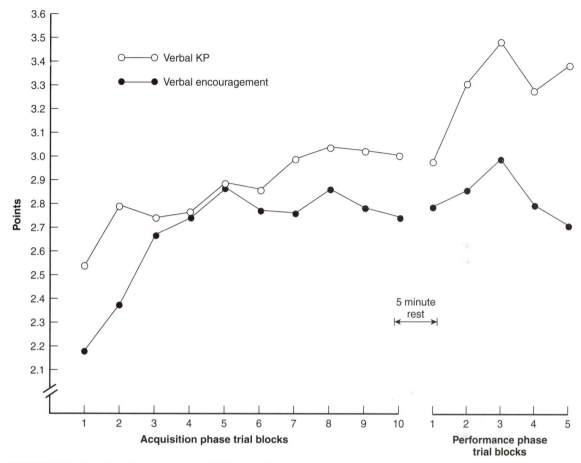

FIGURE 16.2   Results of the experiment by Wallace and Hagler showing the benefit of verbal KP for learning a basketball shooting skill.   [Reprinted with permission from *Research Quarterly for Exercise and Sport, Vol. 50, No. 2,* 265–271. Copyright © 1979 by the American Alliance for Health, Physical Education, Recreation and Dance, 1900 Association Drive, Reston, VA 20191.]

back to perform the skill (see Lintern, Roscoe, & Sivier, 1990).

It is important to note that concurrent augmented feedback does not always hinder learning. We will discuss conditions favoring the effective use of concurrent augmented feedback in chapters 17 and 18.

A second situation in which augmented feedback during practice can lead to performance deterioration during transfer occurs when the instructor or therapist presents terminal augmented feedback *after every practice trial.* There are many research examples that show this effect. Because this point is discussed more specifically in chapter 18, we will not present any research examples here.

Proteau and his colleagues (Proteau et al., 1987; Proteau & Cournoyer, 1990) proposed an interesting hypothesis about why dependency on augmented feedback occurs in this type of situation. They suggested that the augmented feedback becomes a part of the memory representation that develops during practice, and thus becomes a part of what the person has learned. Thus, when the person must perform the skill in a situation without augmented feedback, task-intrinsic feedback alone is not sufficient for them to perform the skill successfully.

A third situation in which augmented feedback can hinder skill learning occurs when the instructor or therapist presents augmented feedback *erroneously* for a skill that the person could learn without augmented feedback. In this situation, task-intrinsic and augmented feedback are in conflict with each other. Especially in the early stage of skill learning, people resolve this conflict by performing according to the augmented feedback. When this information is erroneous, they learn the skill incorrectly. Some examples of research that has shown this effect will be described in the next chapter. The primary reason people resolved the conflict between sensory and augmented feedback in favor of the erroneous information is that they were not certain how to use or interpret the task-intrinsic feedback. As a result, they chose the augmented feedback as their information source for making movement adjustments on future trials.

SUMMARY

Augmented feedback is a type of performance-related feedback that is provided by an external source and either adds to or enhances task-instrinsic feedback, which is directly available when performing a skill. We distinguish two types of augmented feedback on the basis of the part of a skill performance to which the information refers. Knowledge of results (KR) refers to the outcome of the skill performance, whereas knowledge of performance (KP) refers to performance characteristics that led to the outcome. An instructor can provide augmented feedback concurrently, while the learner is performing the skill, or terminally, after the performance is completed. Augmented feedback can serve to inform the learner about the success of the skill perfor-

mance or the performance errors made; it also can serve to motivate the learner to continue striving toward a goal.

Augmented feedback can have four different effects on skill learning. Research evidence has shown that augmented feedback can be essential, not essential, an enhancement, or even detrimental for learning skills. The effect varies according to certain skill and learner characteristics. What remains to be determined from future research are the specific skill and learner characteristics and/or skill learning conditions that underlie each of these four effects. Some hypotheses do exist concerning these characteristics and conditions. It appears that when the performance of a skill provides the performer with task-intrinsic feedback that the performer can interpret effectively so that he or she can evaluate the performance, augmented feedback is not necessary. When the person cannot interpret task-intrinsic feedback from the environment or from the movements involved in the skill itself, he or she needs some form of augmented feedback. The exact type the person needs and how or when it should be provided appear to depend on the skill the person is performing. Three situations exist in which the learner can become dependent on augmented feedback and therefore learning will be hindered by the availability of augmented feedback during practice.

RELATED READINGS

Adams, J. A. (1987). Historical review and appraisal of research on the learning, retention, and transfer of human motor skills. *Psychological Bulletin, 101,* 41–74. (Read the sections on KR: pp. 43–44, 48–49, 61–62.)

Magill, R. A. (2001). Augmented feedback and skill acquisition. In R. N. Singer, H. A. Hausenblaus, & C. Janelle (Eds.), *Handbook on research in sport psychology* (2nd ed.) New York: Wiley.

Swinnen, S. P. (1996). Information feedback for motor skill learning. A review. In H. N. Zelaznik (Ed.), *Advances in motor learning and control* (pp. 37–66). Champaign, IL: Human Kinetics.

1. Describe the two general types of performance-related feedback a person can receive during or after performing a motor skill. In your description, indicate the characteristic that differentiates the two.

2. What are the two types of information referred to by the terms KR and KP? Give two examples of each.

3. What are the two roles played by augmented feedback in the skill learning process? Give an example of each.

4. Describe skill learning conditions where augmented feedback would (a) be necessary for learning, (b) not be necessary for learning, and (c) not be necessary for learning but would enhance learning.

5. Describe three situations in which augmented feedback could be given in such a way that it hinders skill learning.

The Content
of Augmented Feedback

*Concept: Augmented feedback can be given
in a variety of ways*

APPLICATION

When you help a person learn or relearn a skill, do you ever think about the augmented feedback you provide? For example, when you give a person verbal feedback, how do you decide what to tell the person? If the person is making a lot of mistakes while performing the skill, how many mistakes do you tell him or her about and which do you choose? Do you ever consider that there may be more effective ways to provide augmented feedback? Can you state the advantages, disadvantages, or limitations of these various means?

Consider the following situations. Suppose that you are teaching a golf swing to a class, or working in a clinic with a patient learning to walk with an artificial limb. In each situation, the people practicing these skills can make lots of mistakes and will benefit from receiving augmented feedback. When they make mistakes, which they do in abundance when they are beginners, how do you know which mistakes to tell them to correct on subsequent attempts? If you had a video camera available, would you videotape them and then let them watch their own performances? Or would it be even more beneficial to take the videotapes and have them analyzed so that you could show them what their movements looked like kinematically? There are many alternative methods you can use to

provide augmented feedback. But before you as the instructor, coach, or therapist use any one of these, you should know how to implement that method most effectively and when to use it to facilitate learning.

All of these points relate to a fundamental issue confronting every person involved in motor skill instruction, regardless of setting or type of skill. The issue is how to provide adequate information for the learner's optimal benefit. In the following discussion the goal is to increase your understanding of the variety of ways it is possible to give augmented feedback.

DISCUSSION

In this discussion, we will focus on important issues concerning the content of augmented feedback, and then examine several types of augmented feedback that professionals can use in instructional settings. Before we look at these, we will consider a characteristic of augmented feedback that has direct bearing on the choice of type and content of augmented feedback an instructor makes in any situation.

Augmented Feedback Directs Attention
When deciding the type and content of augmented feedback to give, an instructor must consider this:

A CLOSER LOOK

KP about Certain Features of a Skill Helps Correct Other Features

Participants in an experiment by den Brinker, Stabler, Whiting, and van Wieringen (1986) learned to perform on the slalom ski simulator. Their three-part goal was to move the platform from left to right as far as possible at a specific high frequency, and with a motion that was as fluid as possible. On the basis of these performance goals, each of three groups received a different type of information as KP after each trial. Researchers told participants in one group the *distance* they had moved the platform; they told another group's participants how close they were to

performing at the criterion platform movement *frequency;* and they told participants in the third group how fluid their movements were (i.e., fluency). All three groups practiced for four days, performing six 1.5-min trials each day, with a test trial before and after each day's practice trials. Early in practice, the type of KP an individual received influenced only the performance measure specifically related to that feature of performing the skill. However, on the last two days of practice, KP about *distance* caused people to improve all three performance features. Thus, giving KP about one performance feature led to improvement not only of that one, but also of the two other performance features.

---

the feedback will influence how the learner directs his or her attention while performing a skill. Recall from our discussion of Kahneman's model of attention (chapter 8) that an influential factor in determining how attention capacity is allocated is what Kahneman called "momentary intentions." Augmented feedback can serve as a type of momentary intention, because it can direct the individual's attention to a particular feature of performing the skill.

Because of the attention-directing influence of augmented feedback, it is important to make sure that the feedback you give directs the person's attention to the particular aspect of the skill that, if improved, will improve the performance of the entire skill or the part of the skill the person is trying to improve. For example, suppose you are teaching a child to throw a ball at a target. Also suppose this child is making many errors, as is typical of beginners. The child may be looking at his or her hand, stepping with the wrong foot, releasing the ball awkwardly, or not rotating the trunk. Probably the most fundamental error is not looking at the target. This, then, is the error about which you should provide feedback, because it is the part of the skill to which you want the child to direct his or her attention. It is the part of the skill

that, if corrected, will have an immediate, significant, positive influence on performance. By correcting this error, the child undoubtedly will also correct many of the other errors that characterize his or her performance.

Augmented Feedback Content Issues

We will consider here four issues related to the content of augmented feedback. Each of these concerns some of the kinds of information augmented feedback may contain.

Information about errors versus correct aspects of performance. A continuing controversy about augmented feedback content is whether the information the instructor conveys to the learner should concern the mistakes he or she has made or those aspects of the performance that are correct. The answer to this question is difficult to determine, primarily because of the different roles augmented feedback can play in the skill acquisition process. When the instructor is giving error information, augmented feedback is functioning in its informational role related to facilitating skill improvement. On the other hand, when the instructor is telling a person what he or she did correctly, augmented feedback has a more motivational role.

Research evidence consistently has shown that *error information* is more effective for encouraging skill improvement. This evidence supports an important hypothesis by Lintern and Roscoe (1980), which was an expanded version of one originally proposed many years earlier by Annett (1959). The hypothesis is that focusing on what is done correctly while learning a skill, especially in the early stage of learning, is not sufficient by itself to produce optimal learning. Rather, the experience the person has in correcting errors by operating on error-based augmented feedback is especially important for skill acquisition.

Another way of looking at this issue is to consider the different roles augmented feedback plays. Error information directs a person to change certain performance characteristics; this in turn facilitates skill acquisition. On the other hand, information indicating that the person performed certain characteristics correctly tells the person that he or she is on track in learning the skill and encourages the person to keep trying. When we consider augmented feedback from this perspective, we see that whether this feedback should be about errors or about correct aspects of performance depends on the goal of the information. Error-related information works better to facilitate skill acquisition, whereas information about correct performance serves better to motivate the person to continue.

It makes good sense to provide both error-based and correct performance information during practice. The real question of importance, then, concerns the optimal proportion of each type. Although some sport pedagogists (e.g., Docheff, 1990) have suggested that some combination of both types of information is beneficial, no research results exist on which we can base an answer to this question. A conclusion on whether there is an optimal combination to facilitate skill learning awaits experimental study. However, until such evidence is available it seems that the use of some combination is an excellent way to involve both roles of augmented feedback in a skill learning setting.

KR versus KP. Two relevant questions concerning the comparison of the use of KR and KP in skill learning situations are: Do practitioners use one of these forms of augmented feedback more than the other? Do they influence skill learning in similar or different ways?

Most of the evidence addressing the first question comes from the study of physical education teachers in actual class situations. The best example is a study by Fishman and Tobey (1978). Although their study was conducted many years ago, it is representative of more recent studies, and it involves the most extensive sampling of teachers and classes of any study that has investigated this question. Fishman and Tobey observed teachers in eighty-one classes teaching a variety of physical activities. The results showed that the teachers overwhelmingly gave KP (94 percent of the time) more than KR. The majority of the KP statements (53 percent) were appraisals of students' performance, and 41 percent of the statements involved instructions on how to improve performance on the next trial. It is also worth noting that teachers gave praise or criticism 5 percent of the time.

These results from physical education teachers seem to be in line with what occurs in other motor skill instructions contexts. Discussions with coaches and physical and occupational therapists would undoubtedly yield similar KP and KR percentages.

An answer to the second question, concerning the relative effectiveness of KR and KP, is more difficult to provide because of the lack of sufficient and conclusive evidence from research investigating this question. The following four examples of experiments illustrate the problem and provide some insight into a reasonable answer.

Two of the experiments indicate that KP is better than KR to facilitate motor skill learning. Kernodle and Carlton (1992) compared videotape replays and verbally presented technique statements as KP with KR in an experiment in which participants practiced throwing a soft, spongy ball as far as possible with the nondominant arm. KR was presented as the distance of the throw for each practice trial. The results showed that KP led to better throwing technique and distance than KR. Zubiaur, Oña, and Delgado (1999) reported a similar conclusion in a study in which university students with no previous volleyball experience practiced the overhead serve in volleyball. KP was specific information about the most important error to correct as it related either to action before hitting or in hitting the ball. KR referred to the outcome of the hit in terms of the ball's spatial precision, rotation, and flight. The results indicated that KP was more influential for learning the serve.

The other two experiments presented evidence that demonstrates the benefit of both KR and KP for learning a skill. Brisson and Alain (1997) reported an experiment in which the task required participants to learn a complex spatial-temporal arm movement pattern. The goal was to produce the most efficient arm movement pattern to connect four targets on the computer monitor within a criterion amount of time. One group received KP after each trial as the displacement profile for that trial. Another group received the same KP but also saw a superimposed image of the most efficient spatial pattern. A third group received KP (without the superimposed pattern) and KR, which was the total absolute timing and amplitude error for the trial. Finally, a fourth group saw the KP with the superimposed pattern and KR. Results showed that KR was an influential variable for learning the criterion pattern because both groups that received KR in addition to KP learned the pattern better than those that did not receive KP. The authors concluded that participants used KR as a reference for interpreting KP.

Finally, a study by Silverman, Woods, and Subramaniam (1999) provided additional evidence for the benefit of both KR and KP for skill learning, but in a slightly different way. Rather than evaluate the effectiveness of each form of augmented feedback on the basis of how well participants learned the skill, they compared how each related to how often students in physical education classes would engage in successful and unsuccessful practice trials during a class. The researchers observed eight middle school teachers teach two classes each, which involved skill instruction in various sport-related activities. The results indi-

When giving verbal KP, it is important to provide information that is meaningful to the person to whom it is given.

cated that teacher feedback as KR, which was teacher feedback about performance outcome, and as KP about a particular part of a skill performance, showed relatively high correlations with the frequency of students engaging in successful practice trials (0.64 and 0.67, respectively). Interestingly, KP about multiple components of a skill performance correlated notably lower at 0.49.

Although these four studies do not provide a clear-cut answer to the question about the relative effectiveness of KR and KP, they indicate that *both forms of augmented feedback can be valuable* in skill learning sessions. But, as was discussed in the previous chapter, the importance of augmented feedback for learning skills depends on specific characteristics of the skill and the learner. The same conclusion can be made with respect to the relative importance of KR and KP. With this in mind, consider the following hypotheses about conditions in which each of these forms of augmented feedback would be beneficial. At present, these hypotheses, and undoubtedly others, await empirical investigations to determine their validity.

KR will be beneficial for skill learning for at least four reasons: (1) Learners often use KR to confirm their own assessments of the task-intrinsic feedback, even though it may be redundant with task-intrinsic feedback. (2) Learners may need KR because they cannot determine the outcome of performing a skill on the basis of the available task-intrinsic feedback. (3) Learners often use KR to motivate them to continue practicing the skill. (4) Practitioners may want to provide only KR in order to establish a discovery learning practice environment in which learners are encouraged to engage in trial and error as the primary means of learning to perform a skill.

On the other hand, KP can be especially beneficial when: (1) Skills must be performed according to specified movement characteristics, such as gymnastics stunts or springboard dives. (2) Specific movement components of skills that require complex coordination must be improved or corrected. (3) The goal of the action is a kinematic, kinetic, or specific muscle activity. (4) KR is redundant with the task-intrinsic feedback.

Qualitative versus quantitative information. Augmented feedback can be qualitative, quantitative, or both. If the augmented feedback involves a numerical value related to the magnitude of some performance characteristic, it is called **quantitative augmented feedback.** In contrast, **qualitative augmented feedback** is information referring to the quality of the performance characteristic without regard for the numerical values associated with it.

For verbal augmented feedback, it is easy to distinguish these types of information in performance situations. For example, a therapist helping a patient to increase gait speed could give that patient qualitative information about the latest attempt in statements such as these: "That was faster than the last time"; "That was much better"; or "You need to bend your knee more." A physical education teacher or coach teaching a student a tennis serve could tell the student that a particular serve was "good," or "long," or could say something like this: "You made contact with the ball too far in front of you." On the other hand, the therapist could give the patient quantitative verbal augmented feedback using these words: "That time you walked 3 sec faster than the last time," or "You need to bend your knee 5 more degrees." The coach could give quan-

titative feedback to the tennis student like this: "The serve was 6 cm too long," or "You made contact with the ball 10 cm too far in front of you."

Therapists and instructors also can give quantitative and qualitative information in nonverbal forms of augmented feedback. For example, the therapist could give qualitative information to the patient we have described by letting him or her hear a tone when the walking speed exceeded that of the previous attempt, or when the knee flexion achieved a target amount. The teacher or coach could give the tennis student qualitative information in the form of a computer display that used a moving stick figure to show the kinematic characteristics of his or her serving motion. Those teaching motor skills often give nonverbally presented quantitative information in combination with qualitative forms. For example, the therapist could show a patient a computer-based graphic representation of his or her leg movement while walking along, displaying numerical values of the walking speeds associated with each attempt, or the degree of knee flexion observed on each attempt. We could describe similar examples for the tennis student.

How do these two types of augmented feedback information influence skill learning? Motor learning researchers traditionally have investigated this question in experiments designed to address the *precision* of verbally presented KR. In doing so, they have assumed that quantitative KR is more precise than qualitative KR. The traditional view is that quantitative is superior to qualitative information for skill learning. However, researchers have been questioning this conclusion following a reassessment by Salmoni, Schmidt, and Walter (1984) of the research on which the conclusion is based. They showed that most of the experiments investigating the precision issue did not include retention or transfer tests.

Consider the following experiment as an example of a more appropriate conclusion about the precision effect. Each participant in an experiment by Magill and Wood (1986) learned to move his or her arm through a series of wooden barriers to produce a specific six-segment movement pattern. Each seg-

A CLOSER LOOK

Quantitative versus Qualitative Augmented Feedback and the Performance Bandwidth Technique

Cauraugh, Chen, and Radlo (1993) had subjects practice a timing task in which they had to press a sequence of three keys in 500 msec. Participants in one group received quantitative KR about their movement times (MT) when MT was *outside* a 10 percent performance bandwidth. A second group, in the reverse of that condition, received quantitative KR only when MT was *inside* the 10 percent performance bandwidth. Two additional groups had participants "yoked" to individual participants in the outside and inside bandwidth conditions. Members of these two groups received KR on the same trials their "yoked" counterparts did. This procedure provided a way to have two conditions with the same frequency

of augmented feedback, while allowing a comparison between bandwidth and no-bandwidth conditions.

In terms of KR frequency, those in the outside bandwidth condition received quantitative KR on 25 percent of the sixty practice trials; those in the inside condition received KR on 65 percent of the trials. The interesting feature of this difference is that the remaining trials for both groups were implicitly qualitative KR trials, because when they received no KR, the participants knew that their performance was "good" or "not good." The retention test performance results showed that the two bandwidth conditions did not differ, but both yielded better learning than the no-bandwidth conditions. These results show that establishing performance bandwidths as the basis for providing quantitative KR yields an interplay between quantitative and qualitative KR that facilitates skill learning.

---

ment had its own criterion movement time, which participants had to learn. Following each of 120 practice trials, participants received either qualitative KR for each segment (i.e., "too fast," "too slow," or "correct") or quantitative KR for each segment (i.e., the number of msec too fast or too slow). Performance for the first sixty trials showed no difference between the two types of information. However, during the final sixty trials and on the twenty no-KR retention trials, quantitative-KR resulted in better performance than qualitative.

From these results we can conclude that people in the early stage of learning give attention primarily to the qualitative information, even if they have quantitative information available. The advantage of this attention focus is that the qualitative information provides an easier way to make a first approximation of the required movement. Put another way, this information allows learners to control more easily the many degrees of freedom and produce an action that is "in the ballpark" of what they need to do. After they achieve this "ballpark" action, quantitative information becomes more valuable to them, because it enables them to

refine the action to make it more effective for achieving the action goal. In terms of Gentile's learning stages model, qualitative information can allow a person to "get the idea of the movement," but the learner needs quantitative information in the next stage to achieve its fixation or diversification goals.

Augmented feedback based on performance bandwidths. A question that has distinct practical appeal is, How large an error should a performer make before the instructor or therapist gives augmented

---

quantitative augmented feedback augmented feedback that includes a numerical value related to the magnitude of a performance characteristic (e.g., the speed of a pitched baseball).

qualitative augmented feedback augmented feedback that is descriptive in nature (e.g., using such terms as *good, long*), and indicates the quality of performance.

feedback? To many teachers and therapists, it seems reasonable to provide feedback only when errors are large enough to warrant attention. This practice suggests that in many skill learning situations, teachers or therapists develop **performance bandwidths** that establish tolerance limits specifying when they will or will not give augmented feedback. When a person performs within the tolerance limits of the bandwidth, the teacher or therapist does *not* give augmented feedback. But if the person makes an error that is out side that limit, the person instructing does give feedback.

Research supports the effectiveness of the performance bandwidth approach. For example, in the first reported experiment investigating this procedure, Sherwood (1988) had subjects practice a rapid elbow-flexion task with a movement-time goal of 200 msec. Participants in one group received KR about their movement-time error after every trial, regardless of the amount of error (i.e., 0 percent bandwidth). Participants in two other groups received KR only when their error exceeded bandwidths of 5 percent and 10 percent of the goal movement time. The results of a no-KR retention test showed that the 10 percent bandwidth condition resulted in the least amount of movement time variability (i.e., variable error), whereas the 0 percent condition resulted in the most variable error. Other researchers have replicated these results (see, e.g., Lee, White, & Carnahan, 1990; Cauraugh, Chen, & Radlo, 1993).

An important question related to implementing the performance-bandwidth technique in skill learning situations concerns its relationship with the learner's stage of learning. It might seem reasonable, for example, to reduce the size of the error bandwidth as the learner advances from an early to a later stage of learning. However, at least two experiments have demonstrated that this type of reduction is not necessary. Goodwin and Meeuwsen (1995) compared a 0 percent and a 10 percent bandwidth for all practice trials with expanding (0-5-10-15-20 percent) and contracting (20-15-10-5-0 percent) bandwidths for learning a golf putting task. Their results, which can be seen in figure 17.1, indicated that changing the bandwidth size during practice did not provide any additional learning benefit. In fact, both the expanding and constant 10 percent bandwidth conditions produced similar performance on a 48-hour retention test, and were superior to the contracting and 0 percent bandwidth conditions. Others have reported similar evidence that the changing of bandwidth sizes during practice does not improve learning beyond the level achieved with a constant bandwidth during practice (e.g., Lai & Shea, 1999a).

Another practical issue concerning the use of the bandwidth technique relates to the instructions learners receive about the bandwidth procedure. This issue is relevant because when the learners receive no augmented feedback about their performance, the implicit message is that it was "correct." The instruction-related question here is: Is it important that the learner explicitly be told this information, or will the learner implicitly learn this information during practice? Butler, Reeve, and Fischman (1996) investigated this question by telling one group of participants that when they received no KR after a trial, their performance was "essentially correct." A second group was not told this information. The task required a two-segment arm movement to a target in a criterion movement time. The results showed that the bandwidth technique led to better learning when the participants knew in advance that not receiving KR meant they were essentially correct.

Erroneous augmented feedback. In the Discussion section in chapter 16, one of the ways that was described that could result in augmented feedback hindering learning was to provide people with erroneous information. While this statement may seem unnecessary because it seems to make such common sense, the statement gains importance when it is considered in the context of practicing a skill that can be learned *without* augmented feedback. In this skill learning situation, augmented feedback is redundant with the information available from task-intrinsic feedback. As a result, most people would expect that to provide augmented feedback would be a waste of time because it would not influence the learner. But, research evidence shows that this is not the case because even when augmented feedback is redundant information, learners, especially beginners, will use it rather than ignore it.

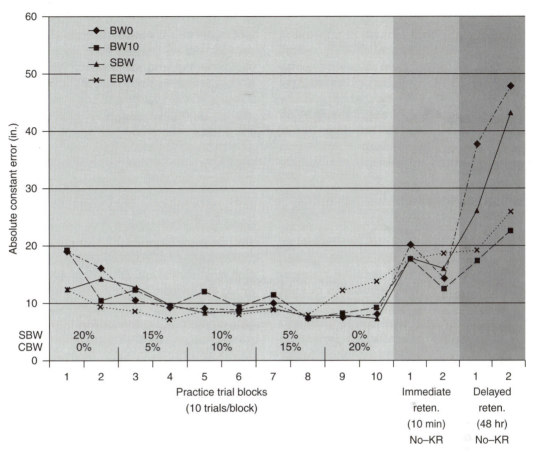

FIGURE 17.1   The results of the experiment by Goodwin and Meeuwsen, which compared four different performance-based bandwidth (BW) conditions for KR during the practice of a golf putting task. The BW0 is a 0 percent bandwidth, BW10 is a 10 percent bandwidth, SBW is a shrinking bandwidth, and EBW is an expanding bandwidth. Practice trial blocks show the mean of ten trials for each. The actual bandwidth for the SBW and EBW conditions are shown for each set of twenty trials.   [Adapted from data in Goodwin, J. E., & Meeuwsen, H. J. (1995). Using bandwidth knowledge for results to alter relative frequencies during motor skill acquisition. *Research Quarterly for Exercise and Sport, 66*, 99–104.

One way to demonstrate this effect is to consider the influence of erroneous (i.e., incorrect) augmented feedback. The hypothesis is that if the learner ignores augmented feedback when it is redundant with task-intrinsic feedback, then the erroneous information should have no effect on learning the skill. But, if the learner uses the augmented feedback, then the erroneous information should influence learning in such a way that will bias the learner to perform according to the erroneous information.

The first test of this hypothesis was reported by Buekers, Magill, and Hall (1992). Participants practiced an anticipation timing task similar to the one

performance bandwidth   in the context of providing augmented feedback, a range of acceptable performance error; augmented feedback is given only when the amount of error is greater than this tolerance limit.

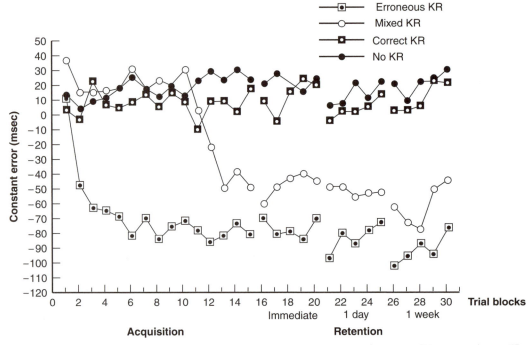

FIGURE 17.2 Results of the experiment by Buekers et al., showing the effects of erroneous KR compared to no KR and correct KR for learning an anticipation timing skill. Note that members of the mixed-KR group received correct KR for their first fifty trials and then received erroneous KR for their last twenty-five practice trials.   [From Buekers, M. J., Magill, R. A., & Hall, K. G. (1992). The effect of erroneous knowledge of results on skill acquisition when augmented information is redundant. *Quarterly Journal of Experimental Psychology. 44* (A), 105–117. Reprinted by permission of The Experimental Psychology Society.]

used by Magill, Chamberlin, and Hall (1991), which was described in chapter 16 as a task for which KR about movement time error is not needed to learn the task. In the Buekers et al. (1992) experiment, three of four groups received KR after every trial. The KR was displayed on a computer monitor and indicated to the participants the direction and amount of their timing error. For one of these groups, KR was always correct. But for another group, KR was always erroneous by indicating that performance on a trial was 100 msec later than it actually was. The third KR group received correct KR for the first fifty trails, but then received the erroneous KR for the last twenty-five trials. A fourth group did not receive KR during practice. All four groups performed twenty-five trials without KR one day later, and then twenty-five more no-KR

trials one week later. The results (Figure 17.2) showed two important findings. First, the correct- and the no-KR groups did not differ during the practice or the retention trials, which confirmed the KR redundancy results of the Magill et al. (1991) experiments. Second, the erroneous KR information led participants to perform according to the KR rather than according to the task-intrinsic feedback. This latter result suggested that the participants used KR, even though it was erroneous information. Even more impressive was that the erroneous KR influenced the group that had received correct KR for fifty trials and then was switched to the erroneous KR. After the switch, this group began to perform similarly to the group that had received the incorrect KR for all the practice trials. And the erroneous information not only influenced performance when it was available, it also influenced retention performance one day and one week later when no KR was provided. A subsequent experiment (McNevin, Magill, & Buekers, 1994) demonstrated that the erroneous KR also influenced performance on a no-KR transfer test in which participants were required to respond to a faster or slower speed than they practiced.

More recent investigations have focused on why erroneous KR affects learning a skill for which KR is redundant information. The most likely reason appears to be that beginners rely on augmented feedback to help them deal with their *uncertainty* about what the task-intrinsic feedback is telling them. For the anticipation timing task the uncertainty may exist because the visual task-intrinsic feedback is difficult to consciously observe, interpret, and use. Evidence for an uncertainty-based explanation has been demonstrated in experiments by Buekers, Magill, and Sneyers (1994), and Buekers and Magill (1995).

While practicing the anticipation timing task, beginners use the erroneous KR to adjust the timing of the initiation of their movement, rather than the movement component of the task (Van Loon, Buekers, Helsen, & Magill, 1998). This evidence further supports the view that even when augmented feedback is redundant with task-intrinsic feedback, beginners use augmented feedback. And it also tells us something about how beginners actually use the erroneous information. For the anticipation timing task, they use it to interpret, or calibrate, the visual task-intrinsic feedback, which means they use the augmented feedback to confirm their visual task-intrinsic feedback. When there is a conflict between these two sources of feedback, beginners resolve the conflict in favor of augmented feedback.

The important message for practitioners here is that people who are in the early stage of skill learning will use augmented feedback when it is available, whether it is correct or not. This is especially the case for skills for which the task-intrinsic feedback is difficult for beginners to interpret and use to improve performance. Because of their

uncertainty about how to use or interpret task-intrinsic feedback, beginners rely on augmented feedback as a critical source of information on which to base movement corrections on future trials. As a result, instructors need to be certain that they provide correct augmented feedback, and establish a means for beginners to learn to use task-intrinsic feedback in a way that will enable them to eventually perform without augmented feedback. Beginning learners are of particular concern here because they will ignore their own sensory feedback sources, and adjust future performance attempts on the basis of the information the instructor provides to them, even though it may be incorrect.

From a learning theory perspective, this reliance on augmented feedback by learners in the early stage of learning suggests that cognitive information can override the perception-action link, which suggests that the perceptual motor control system does not "automatically" use task-intrinsic feedback appropriately. The perceptual component of this system appears to require some calibration. If augmented feedback is available, the learner uses this information to carry out this calibration process. However, if augmented feedback is not available, and if the task is one where augmented information is not necessary for learning the skill, then this calibration process appears to occur by means of trial-and-error experience occurring during practice.

Different Types of Knowledge of Performance

Most of the research on which we base our knowledge of augmented feedback and skill learning comes from laboratory experiments in which researchers gave KR to participants. Although most of the conclusions from that research also apply to KP, it is useful to look at some of the research that has investigated different types of KP. As discussed earlier teacher performance research indicates that most people engaging in motor skill instruction give KP more than they give KR. But, as movement analysis technology becomes more available, nonverbal forms of KP are becoming more prominent in skill acquisition settings. As a

An Example of Basing Verbal KP on a Skill Analysis

In an experiment by Weeks and Kordus (1998), twelve-year-old boys who had no previous experience in soccer practiced a soccer throw-in. The participants' goal was to perform throw-ins as accurately as possible to a target on the floor. The distance to the target was 75 percent of each participant's maximum throwing distance. They received verbal KP on one of eight aspects of technique, which the researchers referred to as "form." Which aspect of form each participant received was based on the primary form problem identified for a throw-in. The researchers constructed a list of eight "form cues" on the basis of a skill analysis of the throw-in, and used this list to give verbal KP. The eight form cues were:

1. The feet, hips, knees, and shoulders should be aimed at the target, feet shoulder width apart.

2. The back should be arched at the beginning of the throw.

3. The grip should look like a "W" with the thumbs together on the back of the ball.

4. The ball should start behind the head at the beginning of the throw.

5. The arms should go over the head during the throw and finish by being aimed at the target.

6. There should be no spin on the ball during its flight.

7. The ball should be released in front of the head.

8. Feet should remain on the ground.

result, it is important to understand the influences on skill learning of various types of KP.

Verbal KP. One of the reasons practitioners give verbal KP more than verbal KR is that KP gives people more information to help them improve the movement aspects of skill performance. One of the problems that arises with the use of verbal KP is determining the appropriate content of what to tell the person practicing the skill. This problem occurs because skills are typically complex and KP usually relates to a specific feature of skill performance. The challenge for the instructor or therapist, then, is selecting the appropriate features of the performance on which to base KP.

To solve this problem, the first thing a teacher, coach, or therapist must do is perform a *skill analysis* of the skill being practiced. This means identifying the various component parts of the skill. Then, he or she should prioritize each part in terms of how critical it is for performing the skill correctly. Prioritize by listing the most critical part first, then the second most critical, and so on. To determine which part is most critical, decide which

part of the skill absolutely must be done properly for the entire skill to be performed correctly. For example, in the relatively simple task of throwing a dart at a target, the most critical component is looking at the target. This part of the skill is the most critical because even if the beginning learner did all other parts of the skill correctly (which would be unlikely), there is a very low chance that he or she would perform the skill correctly without looking at the target. In this case, then, looking at the target would be first on the skill analysis priority list, and would be the first part of the skill assessed in determining what to give KP about.

After determining which aspect of the skill to give KP, the practitioner needs to decide the content of the statement to make to the learner. There are *two types of verbal KP statements.* A **descriptive KP** statement simply describes the error the performer has made. The other type, **prescriptive KP,** not only identifies the error, but also tells the person what to do to correct it. For example, if you tell a person, "You moved your right foot too soon," you describe only the problem. However, if you say, "You need to move your right foot at the same time you move your right arm," you also give prescriptive information about what the person needs to do to correct the problem.

Which type of KP better facilitates learning? Although there is no empirical evidence, common sense dictates that the answer varies with the stage of learning of the person practicing the skill. The statement, "You moved your right foot too soon," would be helpful to a beginner only if he or she knew that the right foot was supposed to move at the same time as the right arm. Thus, descriptive KP statements are useful to help people improve performance only once they have learned what they need to do to make a correction. This suggests that prescriptive KP statements are more helpful for beginners. For the more advanced person, a descriptive KP statement often will suffice.

Videotape as augmented feedback. The increasing use of videotape as augmented feedback argues for the need for instructors and therapists to know more about how to use it effectively.

It is common to find articles in professional journals that offer guidelines and suggestions for the use of videotape replays as feedback (e.g, Franks & Maile, 1991; Jambor & Weekes, 1995; Trinity & Annesi, 1996). However, very little empirical research exists that establishes the effectiveness of videotape replays as an aid for skill acquisition. In fact, the most recent extensive review of the research literature related to the use of videotape replay as a source of augmented feedback in skill learning situations was published many years ago by Rothstein and Arnold (1976). Their review included over fifty studies that involved eighteen different sport activities, including archery, badminton, bowling, gymnastics, skiing, swimming, and volleyball, among others. In most of these studies, the students were beginners, although some included intermediate- and advanced-level performers.

Despite the age of the review, current research and practice related to the use of videotape as augmented feedback tends to follow or is based on its general conclusions. Overall, Rothstein and Arnold reported that the results of the studies

they reviewed were mixed with regard to the effectiveness of videotape as a means of providing augmented feedback. However, an important conclusion from that review was that the critical factor for determining the effectiveness of videotape as an instructional aid was the skill level of the student rather than the type of activity. For beginners to benefit from videotape replay, they required the assistance of an instructor to point out critical information. Advanced performers did not appear to need instructor aid as frequently, although discussions with skilled athletes suggests they receive greater benefit from observing replays when some form of attention-directing instructions are presented, such as verbal cues and checklists.

Kernodle and Carlton (1992) provided evidence that demonstrated the benefit of having an instructor point out what the observer of the videotape replay should look for. Participants practiced throwing a soft, spongy ball as far as possible with the nondominant arm. One group of participants received specific technique–related cues about what to look for on the videotape replays of each trial. Participants in a second group received this same information plus a verbal prescriptive KP statement that told them how to correct the technique problem. A third group watched only the video and received no cues or verbal KP. And a fourth group received verbal KR about the distance of each throw. The results showed that the participants in the two groups who received the specific technique

---

descriptive KP   a verbal knowledge of performance (KP) statement that describes only the error a person has made during the performance of a skill.

prescriptive KP   a verbal statement of knowledge of performance (KP) that describes errors made during the performance of a skill and states (i.e., prescribes) what needs to be done to correct them.

cues to look for while watching the videotape replays learned to throw the ball farther and with better technique than the other two groups.

Another conclusion about the use of videotape replay comes from research since the time of the Rothstein and Arnold review. Videotape replays *transmit certain types of performance-related information to the learner more effectively than other types.* One of the best examples of research evidence that supports this conclusion was an experiment conducted many years ago by Selder and Del Rolan (1979). They compared videotape replays and verbal augmented feedback (in the form of KP) in a study in which twelve-to-thirteen-year-old girls were learning to perform a balance beam routine. All the girls used a checklist to critically analyze their own performance after each trial. The verbal augmented feedback group used verbal KP to complete the checklist; the videotape feedback group completed the checklist after viewing videotape replays of each trial. Two results are especially noteworthy. After four weeks of practice, performance scores for the routine did not differ between the two groups. But at the end of six weeks of practice the videotape group scored significantly higher on the routine than the verbal feedback group. Second, when each factor of the total routine score was evaluated, the videotape group scored significantly higher on only four of the eight factors: precision, execution, amplitude, and orientation and direction. The two groups did not differ on the other four: rhythm, elegance, coordination, and lightness of jumping and tumbling. The importance of these results is that they demonstrate that although videotape replay can be effective, it does not facilitate the learning of all aspects of a complex motor skill.

The results of the Selder and Del Rolan study suggest that videotape replay facilitates the learning of those performance features that the performer can readily observe and determine how to correct on the basis of the videotape replay. However, for performance features that are not as readily discernible, videotape replay is not as effective as verbal KP.

A more recent study by Hebert, Landin, and Menickelli (1998) provided further evidence concerning the effectiveness of videotape replay but, more important, identified steps skilled athletes go through to use this information. Skilled college female tennis players who needed to improve their attacking stroke, either observed or did not observe videotape replays of their practice sessions. The performance results demonstrated that the players who observed the videotape replays improved more than the players who did not. And evidence from recordings of players' comments during videotape observation sessions and the researchers' field notes indicated that the players progressed through four stages in their use of the videotape replay information. During the first stage, players familiarized themselves with observing themselves on videotape and made general observations about how they personally looked on videotape as well as their technique. In the second stage, players began to recognize specific technical errors. The third stage was more analytical as the players made connections between technique and outcome. In the fourth stage, players began to show evidence of the use of their previous observations of replays by correcting their technique errors. As a result of this final stage, the players acknowledged what they considered to be the important key points related to successfully hitting the attack shot.

An alternative use of videotape replays as augmented feedback was demonstrated in an interesting study by Starek and McCullagh (1999). They showed adult beginning swimmers three-minute videotape replays of their swimming performance during the lesson of the previous day. The replay showed four swimming behaviors they had performed correctly, and four they had trouble performing. Then, some of the students saw only their own successfully performed skills from the previous day, whereas other students saw a skilled swimmer successfully perform these skills. The results showed that swimmers who saw their own videotaped performance performed better than those who saw the same skills performed by someone else. This use of videotape replay in which people see themselves performing a skill correctly is referred to as *self-modeling,* which combines modeling as a form of instruction with modeling as also a form of augmented feedback.

Movement kinematics as augmented feedback.
With the widespread availability of computer software capable of providing sophisticated kinematic analysis of movement, it has become increasingly common to find sport skill instruction situations in which students can view graphically presented kinematic representations of their performances as a form of feedback. Unfortunately, as was the case with the use of videotape replays, there is very little empirical evidence that provides definitive answers to questions concerning the effectiveness of this means of providing augmented feedback. However, the few studies that have been reported provide some insight into the use of this form of augmented feedback.

One of the first studies to investigate the use of movement kinematics as augmented feedback did not involve a computer, and was carried out many years ago. However, this study is important because it illustrates the historical interest in this type of feedback, it involved a real-world training situation, and it exemplifies the positive effect that kinematic information can have on skill learning when it is used as augmented feedback. Lindahl (1945) investigated the methods used to train industrial machine operator trainees to precisely and quickly cut thin disks of tungsten with a machine that required fast, accurate, and rhythmic coordination of the hands and feet. The traditional approach to training for this job was a trial-and-error method. To assess an alternative method, Lindahl created a mechanism that would make a paper tracing of the machine operator's foot movement pattern during the cutting of each disk. During training, the trainers showed the trainees charts illustrating the correct foot action (see the top portion of figure 17.3), and periodically showed them tracings of their own foot action. The results (see the bottom portion of figure 17.3) indicated that this training method based on movement

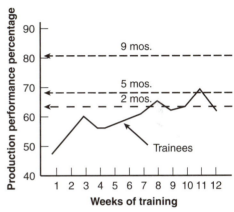

FIGURE 17.3 The upper panel illustrates the foot action required by the machine operator to produce an acceptable disk cut in the experiment by Lindahl. The graph at the bottom indicates the production performance achieved by the trainees using graphic information during twelve weeks of training. The dashed lines indicate the levels of performance achieved by other workers after two, five, and nine months of experience. [From Lindahl, L. G. (1945) Movement analysis as an industrial training method. *Journal of Applied Psychology, 29,* 420–436, American Psychological Association.]

kinematic information as augmented feedback enabled the trainees to achieve production performance levels in eleven weeks compared to the five months required by trainees who used the traditional trial-and-error method. In addition, the trainees reduced their percentage of broken cutting wheels to almost zero in twelve weeks, a level not achieved by those trained with the traditional method in less than nine months.

Most of the research evidence we have about the use of movement kinematics as augmented feedback comes from laboratory-based experiments (e.g., Hatze, 1976; Newell, Quinn, Sparrow, &

Walter, 1983). A comprehensive series of experiments reported by Swinnen and his colleagues serve as good examples of this research (Swinnen et al., 1990; Swinnen, Walter, Lee, & Serrien, 1993). Participants in these experiments practiced a bimanual coordination task that required them to move two levers at the same time, but with each lever requiring a different spatial-temporal movement pattern. Kinematic information was presented as augmented feedback in the form of the angular displacement characteristics for each arm superimposed over the criterion displacements. In several experiments, the kinematic augmented feedback was compared with various other forms of augmented feedback. The results consistently demonstrated the effectiveness of the displacement information as augmented feedback.

These laboratory-based experiments generalize very well to real-world skill learning contexts. For example, Wood, Gallagher, Martino, and Ross (1992) provided a good example of the use of graphically displayed movement kinematics for learning a sport skill. Participants practiced a full-swing golf shot with a five iron from a platform into a backstop net. A commercially marketed golf computer monitored the kinematics of the golf swing as the head of the club passed over light sensors on the platform. The computer assessed the velocity, displacement, and trajectory path of each swing and displayed this information on a monitor for learners in two groups. One group saw a template of an optimum pattern along with the kinematics; the other group did not see this template. A third group received kinematic information verbally in the form of numbers referring to kinematic outcomes of the swing. A fourth group received no augmented feedback. On a retention test given one week later without augmented feedback, the group that had observed the graphic presentation of the swing kinematics along with the optimum pattern template performed best.

Finally, it is important to point out that when teachers, coaches, and therapists use graphic displays of movement kinematics as augmented feedback, they should take the stage of learning into account. Beginners benefit from kinematic infor-

mation only when they can interpret and use it to improve their own performance. Thus, it is useful to show a template of the kinematic goal to beginners. More skilled people can take advantage of more complex kinematic information.

Biofeedback as augmented feedback. The term **biofeedback** refers to an augmented form of task-intrinsic feedback related to the activity of physiological processes, such as heart rate, blood pressure, muscle activity, etc. Several forms of biofeedback have been used in motor skill learning situations. The most common is *electromyographic (EMG) biofeedback,* which provides information about muscle activity. Most of the research concerning the use EMG as biofeedback has been undertaken in physical rehabilitation settings, and has shown positive results as an effective therapy intervention. The following two examples illustrate different types of intervention purposes for the use of this form of augmented feedback.

Brucker and Bulaeva (1996) used EMG biofeedback with long-term cervical spinal cord–injured people to determine if it would help them increase their voluntary EMG responses from the triceps during elbow extension. Some of the 100 participants received only one forty-five-minute treatment session, whereas the others received an average of three additional sessions. Results of a posttreatment test indicated that participants who experienced only one session significantly increased their triceps EMG activity, and those who experienced the additional treatment sessions demonstrated even further increases.

The purpose of a study by Intiso and colleagues (1994) was to determine the effectiveness of EMG biofeedback to help poststroke patients overcome foot drop of the paretic limb during the swing phase of walking. Some patients received EMG biofeedback during their physical therapy, whereas others did not. A unique characteristic of this study was the use of gait analysis to assess foot drop during the gait cycle. Results of this analysis demonstrated that the EMG biofeedback intervention led to better recovery than physical therapy without the biofeedback.

A CLOSER LOOK

A Case Study of the Use of Biofeedback for Balance Training for Stroke Patients

A form of biofeedback that has been used for balance training in physical therapy contexts is the visual presentation on a computer monitor of a person's center of gravity. A case study reported by Simmons and associates (1998) is an interesting example of the effectiveness of this type of biofeedback in a clinical setting. The patient was a seventy-four-year-old post-stroke, hemiparetic male with whom therapists were working to help him regain balance control while standing. Following a pretest, the patient engaged in three balance training therapy sessions a week for four weeks. During each therapy session the patient stood on two force plates while looking at a computer monitor placed at eye level. On the monitor, he could see a small white dot superimposed on a white cross, which indicated an appropriate center of gravity while standing. During each therapy session, a clear plastic template marked with a circular pattern of eight alphabetic letters was placed on the monitor. A verbal command to the patient indicated that he should initiate a weight shift that would cause the white dot to move from the center and hit the target letter and then return the dot back to the center cross. The patient did this for six 1-min intervals with a 45-sec rest between intervals. A posttest followed at the end of the four-week training period, and a retention test was given two weeks later. One of the tests simulated a sudden loss of balance, which involved a quick (400-msec) 5.7-cm forward and backward movement of the force plates on which the patient was standing. The patient's performance on this motor control test during the two-week retention test showed a 60 percent improvement for response strength of the affected leg, and a marked shift in balance onto the affected leg in the patient's attempts to regain balance.

Chollet, Micallef, and Rabischong (1988) used another type of biofeedback with skilled swimmers to help them improve and maintain their high level of performance. The authors developed swimming paddles that would provide information to enable highly skilled swimmers to maintain their optimal velocity and number of arm cycles in a training session. The swimming paddles contained force sensors and sound generators that transmitted an audible signal to transmitters in a swimmer's cap. The sensors were set at a desired water-propulsion-force threshold; when the swimmer reached this threshold, the paddles produced a sound audible to the swimmer. The authors found this device helped swimmers maintain their stroke count and swimming speed when they otherwise would have found it decreasing through the course of a long-distance practice session.

Finally, a rather unique type of biofeedback in motor skill learning contexts has been applied in the training of competitive rifle shooters (Daniels & Landers, 1981). Heartbeat biofeedback was pre-sented auditorally to help these athletes learn to squeeze the rifle trigger between heartbeats, which is a characteristic of elite shooters.

In general, research evidence has supported the effectiveness of biofeedback as a means of facilitating motor skill learning. However, debate continues concerning the specific situations in which the use of biofeedback is an effective and preferred form of augmented feedback (Moreland & Thomson, 1994). In addition, biofeedback is usually presented as concurrent augmented feedback, which leads to concerns related to the development of a dependency on the availability of the augmented feedback to maintain an acquired level of

> **biofeedback**   a type of augmented feedback that provides information about physiological processes through the use of instrumentation (e.g., EMG feedback).

A CLOSER LOOK

Guidelines for Giving Augmented Feedback

- **The person must be capable of using the information.** More specific or sophisticated augmented feedback is not necessarily better. Beginners need information to help them make a "ballpark" approximation of the required movements; they need more specific information as skill learning progresses.
- **A combination of error-based augmented feedback and information based on what was done correctly is most helpful,** to take advantage of the roles of augmented feedback for facilitating skill improvement and for motivating a person to continue practicing the skill.
- **Verbal KP should be based on the most critical error** made during a practice attempt; the

professional should identify this on the basis of a skill analysis and a prioritized list of components of the skill.
- **Prescriptive KP is better for novices,** whereas descriptive KP is more appropriate for more skilled people.
- **Videotape replays can be effective with beginners** if instructors or therapists provide direction to help them detect and correct errors as they watch the tape.
- **Computer-generated displays of the kinematics of a skill performance will be more effective for more advanced performers** than for novices to help facilitate skill improvement.
- **Biofeedback needs to give people information they can use to alter movements.** In addition, it must be presented in such a way that people do not become dependent on it.

---

performance. This dependency issue will be discussed more specifically in chapter 18.

SUMMARY

Because augmented feedback is such an important part of skill learning, it is important to understand what information the therapist or instructor should provide to facilitate learning and how often he or she should give that information. The professional should keep three important points in mind when deciding what augmented feedback information to give. First, he or she should determine the precision of the information. Augmented feedback can be either too precise or too general to aid learning. Second, he or she should determine the content of the augmented feedback. In doing so, the therapist or teacher must understand that augmented feedback serves to direct attention to certain parts of the skill; therefore, augmented feedback should direct attention to the part of the skill that it is most important to improve on the next trial. Third, the professional

should establish the form of presentation of the augmented feedback. Although verbal augmented feedback is the most common type, alternative methods such as videotape replay, graphic representations of movement kinematics, and biofeedback also can be effective.

RELATED READINGS

Lee, A. M., Keh, N. C., & Magill, R. A. (1993). Instructional effects of teacher feedback in physical education. *Journal of Teaching in Physical Education, 12,* 228–243.

Moreland, J. D., Thomson, M. A., & Fuoco, A. R. (1998). Electromyographic biofeedback to improve lower extremity function after stroke: A meta-analysis. *Archives of Physical Medicine and Rehabilitation, 79,* 134–140.

Swinnen, S. P. (1998). Age-related deficits in motor learning and differences in feedback processing during the production of a bimanual coordination pattern. *Cognitive Neuropsychology, 15,* 439–466.

Wrisberg, C. A., Dale, G. A., Liu, Z., & Reed, A. (1995). The effects of augmented information on motor learning: A multidimensional assessment. *Research Quarterly for Exercise and Sport, 66,* 9–16.

STUDY QUESTIONS

STUDY QUESTIONS

1. How do quantitative and qualitative augmented feedback differ, and how do they influence the learning of motor skills?

2. What two important points must a practitioner strongly consider when deciding on augmented feedback content? Give an example of a motor skill situation that illustrates these two points.

3. Describe a situation in which you would use videotape as a form of augmented feedback to (a) help a beginner learn a new skill, (b) help a skilled person correct a performance problem.

4. (a) What do we currently know about the use and benefit of kinematic information as augmented feedback to help someone learn a motor skill? (b) Describe a situation in which you would use this type of information and explain why you would use it.

5. (a) Discuss the different types of learning effects that biofeedback has been shown to have on skill learning. (b) Describe a skill learning situation in which you would use some form of biofeedback. Indicate how you would use it, and why you would expect it to enhance the learning of the skill.

CHAPTER

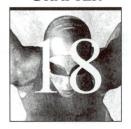

The Timing
of Augmented Feedback

*Concept: Several timing characteristics
of augmented feedback influence skill learning*

APPLICATION

Three important questions arise about the timing of giving augmented feedback. First, should the motor skills instructor present it during or after the performance of a skill? Second, how do the length of and activity during time intervals preceding and following the presentation of augmented feedback affect skill learning? Third, how often should a person give augmented feedback during practice? The following example illustrates how these questions are involved in skill instruction.

Suppose you are teaching a person to play golf. Each of our three questions comes into play in a practice session. The first question is relevant here because you could give augmented feedback while the person swings, after he or she has hit the ball, or both times. If you give feedback after the person hits the ball, the second question comes into play, because two time intervals are now important. The first is the time interval from the person's hitting of the ball until you give augmented feedback. The second is the time that elapses from your giving that information until the person hits another ball. Finally, the third question is involved in this situation because you could give augmented feedback every time the learner hits the ball, or only a few times during practice.

The answers to the three timing questions relate to some important practical concerns. For example, does

it matter whether feedback is given during or after a movement is completed? Does it matter how long a person must wait to get augmented feedback after completing a movement? How important is the amount of time between the completion of one movement and the beginning of the next movement? Does it matter how frequently during practice the learner receives augmented feedback? Does the notion that "more is better than less" apply here? We address these questions in the following discussion section.

DISCUSSION

The first of the three augmented feedback timing issues we will consider here is whether it is better to give augmented feedback while a person is performing a skill, in what is known as *concurrent augmented feedback,* or at the end of a practice attempt, in what we call *terminal augmented feedback.* In addressing the second issue, we consider two specific intervals of time that are created when a learner receives terminal augmented feedback. One interval (the **KR-delay interval**) is between the end of one practice attempt and the augmented feedback. It is important to consider this interval because we examine the question of when, after a skill is performed, a teacher, coach, or therapist should give augmented feedback. The second interval (the

264

post-KR interval) is between the augmented feedback and the beginning of the next practice attempt.[1] The third timing issue concerns how often the practitioner should give augmented feedback during practice to facilitate skill learning. This issue has generated a great deal of research in recent years under the label of the *frequency* of augmented feedback.

Concurrent versus Terminal Augmented Feedback

An important training question is whether concurrent or terminal presentation of augmented feedback is better for facilitating skill acquisition. Unfortunately, a search through the motor learning research literature suggests that there is no unequivocal answer to this question. However, a guideline emerges from that literature that can help us answer the question. Terminal augmented feedback can be effective in almost any skill learning situation, although the teacher or therapist must consider the nature of its effect in light of our discussion in chapter 16 of the four different effects augmented feedback can have on skill learning. Concurrent augmented feedback, on the other hand, seems to be most effective when task-intrinsic feedback is very low and the person cannot determine from the task-intrinsic feedback how to perform the skill or improve performance. It is in these situations that concurrent augmented feedback seems to work best.

Implementing Concurrent Augmented Feedback. When augmented feedback is given concurrently, it involves the enhancement of task-intrinsic feedback while a person is performing the skill. The following four examples illustrate the various forms that this enhancement can take. One, when the task requires movement accuracy, such as throwing a dart at a tar-

get, reaching to grasp an object, moving a stylus through a maze, or steering a driving simulator through a narrow, winding street, concurrent augmented feedback could be given by providing a visible or audible signal that lets the performer know when a movement is on- or off-target. Two, when the task involves the performance of a bimanual coordination task, concurrent augmented feedback could be given by using a computer to calculate and display to the performer the displacement characteristics of the limbs as he or she performs the task. Three, when the task requires that the person learn to produce a specific force-time curve, such as pressing on a knee-extension device with a specified amount of force for a certain amount of time, a curve showing the amount of force produced could be shown to the person on a computer monitor or oscilloscope as the person performs the task. Four, when the task requires learning to use a physiological feature or process in a specific way, such as learning to activate a specific muscle group to help overcome foot-drop during walking, or to learn to time the trigger pull to shoot a rifle between heartbeats, different forms of biofeedback could be used as a means of providing concurrent augmented feedback.

Research evidence has shown two general types of effects for the use of concurrent augmented feedback in skill learning situations. The more common is *a negative learning effect.* Although performance improves very well during practice when the concurrent augmented feedback is available, it declines on retention or transfer trials during which the augmented feedback is removed. In these situations, the concurrent augmented feedback influences learners to direct their attention away from the critical task-intrinsic

---

[1]Note that the terminology used to describe these two intervals follows the traditional labels used in the majority of the research literature, even though we have been using the term KR in a more specific way than these interval labels imply. It is important to see these intervals as relevant to *all* forms of augmented feedback.

> **KR-delay interval**   the interval of time between the completion of a movement and the presentation of augmented feedback.
>
> **post-KR interval**   the interval of time between the presentation of augmented feedback and the beginning of the next trial.

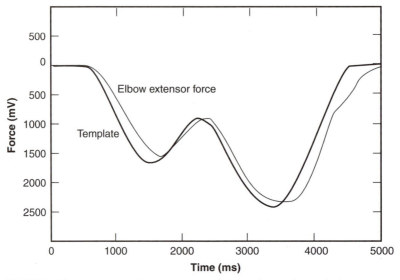

FIGURE 18.1 An example from the Vander Linden et al. experiment of what a participant saw during and/or after a trial on which they attempted to produce a 5-sec elbow-extension force trace that replicated as closely as possible the template trace. [Reprinted from Vander Linden, D. W. et al. (1993). "The effect of frequency of kinetic feedback on learning an isometric force production task in nondisabled subjects," *Physical Therapy, 73,* 79–87 with permission of the American Physical Therapy Association.]

feedback and toward the augmented feedback. The result is that they substitute the information derived from augmented feedback for the important information they should acquire from task-intrinsic feedback. The result is that the augmented feedback becomes an integral part of what is learned, and therefore necessary for future performance.

Two experiments will serve as examples of research that has demonstrated this negative learning effect. Verschueren, Swinnen, Dom, and DeWeerdt (1997) had elderly healthy adults and Parkinson's patients practice the continuous bimanual coordination task described in chapters 11 and 12 (see figure 11.4). The task required that they learn to move two levers simultaneously for 20 sec in such a way that they would draw ellipses on the computer monitor. During the practice trials, participants saw on the monitor the drawings produced as they moved their arms. The results showed that both groups of participants made considerable improvement during practice when the concurrent visual augmented feed-

back was available. But their performance dropped dramatically on retention test trials without the augmented feedback.

The negative learning effect has also been demonstrated for the learning of a discrete task. Vander Linden, Cauraugh, and Greene (1993) compared concurrent and terminal augmented feedback for learning a 5-sec isometric elbow-extension force production task, which is illustrated in figure 18.1. Participants in one group received concurrent kinetic augmented feedback by seeing the force produced during the performance of the task on each trial. Two other groups received terminal augmented feedback by seeing the results of a trial after they completed performing the task. One of these two groups saw this information after every trial, the other saw it after every other trial. During the practice trials, the group that received the concurrent augmented feedback performed the task better than the two terminal groups. However, forty-eight hours later on a retention test with no augmented feedback, the concurrent group's performance declined to a level that was the poorest of the three groups.

The second general effect is that concurrent augmented feedback *enhances skill learning.* A variety of situations have produced this effect. Some of these are the training of flight skills for airplane pilots (e.g., Lintern, 1991), the rehabilitation of motor skills in physical therapy (e.g., Intiso et al., 1994), the activation of specific muscles or muscle groups (e.g., Brucker & Bulaeva, 1996), and the learning of certain types of bimanual coordination laboratory tasks (e.g., Swinnen et al., 1993). In these experiments, concurrent augmented feedback enhanced relevant features of the task-intrinsic feedback that were difficult to discern without the enhancement. Because most of these experiments are described elsewhere in this book, there is no need to describe them here.

Predicting learning effects of concurrent augmented feedback. Two related hypotheses have been proposed to help us better understand how to predict when concurrent augmented feedback will have a positive or negative effect on learning. First, Annett (1959, 1969, 1970) stated that augmented feedback should be considered in terms of its information value, which he related to the "informativeness" of the task-intrinsic feedback and the augmented feedback. When the information value of task-intrinsic feedback is low, but the information value of the augmented feedback is high, concurrent augmented feedback will most likely lead to a dependency on the augmented feedback.

Lintern and his colleagues (Lintern, 1991; Lintern, Roscoe, & Sivier, 1990) added another dimension to Annett's hypothesis by proposing that practicing with augmented feedback will benefit learning to the extent that the feedback sensitizes the learner to properties or relationships in the task that specify how the system being learned can be controlled. This means that for concurrent augmented feedback to be effective, it must facilitate the learning of the critical characteristics or relationships in the task as specified by the task-intrinsic feedback. Negative learning effects will result when the augmented feedback distracts attention away from these features. But positive learn-

ing effects will result when the augmented feedback directs attention to these features.

Consider how these two hypotheses apply to the experiments described earlier as examples of the negative and positive learning effects of concurrent augmented feedback. In the Verschueren et al. and Vander Linden et al. experiments, which yielded negative effects, task-intrinsic feedback was difficult to interpret for both tasks. The limb movement relationship required by the bimanual coordination task and the amount of isometric force required by the elbow-extension task involved the need to discern proprioceptive feedback in ways that are unusual to most people. Thus the information value of the task-intrinsic feedback was low, which made it difficult to use to perform the skill. As a result, the concurrent augmented feedback became a very appealing source of information to help perform the skill. Although this information enabled the learners to improve their performance quite rapidly when it was present, it led to a dependence that distracted them from learning the proprioceptive task-intrinsic feedback critical to successful performance of the tasks. However, in the situations in the experiments in which concurrent augmented feedback facilitated learning, the concurrent augmented feedback directed the learners' attention to important features of the tasks that would be almost impossible to attend to otherwise because there is nothing inherent in the tasks themselves that tells a person how to perform the skill correctly.

The KR-Delay and Post-KR Intervals

The second timing issue related to augmented feedback concerns when the feedback is given terminally. Two intervals of time are created between two trials: the KR-delay interval and the post-KR interval. These intervals are depicted graphically in figure 18.2. To understand the relationship between these intervals and skill learning, we must understand the influence of two variables: *time,* i.e., the length of the interval, and *activity,* i.e., the cognitive and/or motor activity during the interval.

The length of the KR-delay interval. It is not uncommon to see statements in textbooks indicating

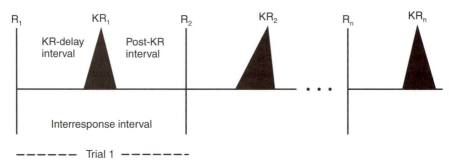

FIGURE 18.2   Intervals of time related to KR during the acquisition of a skill.

that a learner should receive augmented feedback as soon as possible after performing a skill, because delaying it beyond a certain amount of time would lead to poorer learning. A significant problem with this viewpoint is that it has little research evidence to support it. Such a view comes from research based predominantly on animal learning (see Adams, 1987). Research has established that human learners see augmented feedback as more than a reward: augmented feedback has informational value that humans use to solve problems associated with learning a skill. Whereas animal learning studies have shown that delaying reward leads to decreased learning, human skill learning studies have shown that delaying augmented feedback does not have this negative effect.

Although delaying the presentation of augmented feedback does not appear to affect skill learning, there does seem to be a *minimum amount of time* that must pass before it is given. Swinnen, Schmidt, Nicholson, and Shapiro (1990) demonstrated this in two experiments in which participants learned to move a lever through a two-reversal movement to achieve a specific movement-time goal (experiment 1), or to move a lever coincident in time with the appearance of a target light (experiment 2). They received KR at three different times: immediately upon completing the required movement (i.e., "instantaneously"), 8 sec after completing it (experiment 1) or 3.2 sec after completing it (experiment 2). The results of both experiments showed that giving KR instantaneously upon completing a movement had a negative effect on learning.

Why would receiving augmented feedback immediately after completing a movement not be good for learning a skill? One possibility is that when learners receive augmented feedback too soon after the completion of a movement, they are not able to engage in their own analysis of task-intrinsic feedback, which is essential for them to develop error-detection capabilities. When augmented feedback is delayed by just a few seconds, these capabilities can develop more effectively.

Activity during the KR-delay interval. Researchers investigating the effects of activity during the KR-delay interval have found *three types of outcomes.* In some circumstances, activity has no effect on skill learning. In others, activity hinders learning. At still other times, activity benefits learning. These different types of results have provided insight into the learning processes involved in the KR-delay interval, as well as providing distinct implications for developing effective instructional strategies.

The most common effect of activity during the KR-delay interval on skill learning is that it has *no influence on learning.* Experiments have demonstrated this result since the 1960s (e.g., Bilodeau, 1969; Boulter, 1964; Marteniuk, 1986). For example, in the Marteniuk experiment, subjects practiced moving a lever to produce a specific sine wave-like pattern on a computer screen. One group received KR within a few seconds after completing the movement and engaged in no activity during the KR-delay interval; another group had a 40-sec KR-delay interval, but did not engage in any activity during the interval; and a third group also had a 40-sec KR-delay interval, but engaged in a lever movement task in which the subjects attempted to reproduce a movement pattern that the experimenter had just performed. The results showed no differences among the groups on a no-KR retention test.

The second type of effect is much less common. There is some evidence, although it is sparse, that activity during the KR-delay interval *hinders learning*. Two specific types of activities have shown this negative effect, which provides insight into the types of learning processes that occur during this interval. The study by Marteniuk (1986) also included activities that interfered with learning. These activities required the learning of other skills. He hypothesized that if the KR-delay interval activity were to interfere with learning, it would have to interfere with the exact learning processes required by the primary task being learned. In two experiments, Marteniuk added conditions in which subjects had to learn either a motor or a cognitive skill during the KR-delay interval. Results of both experiments indicated that these types of learning activities interfered with learning of the primary skill.

The other type of KR-delay interval activity that research has shown to hinder skill learning involved estimating the movement-time error of another person's movement, which the second person performed during the interval. In an experiment by Swinnen (1990), people learned to move a lever a specified distance, involving two reversals of direction, in a criterion movement time. Participants who engaged in the error estimation activity during the KR-delay interval showed worse performance on a retention test than those who did nothing or who performed a nonlearning task during the interval.

Third, certain activities during the KR-delay interval actually can *benefit learning*. One type of activity that has consistently demonstrated this effect requires the person to evaluate his or her own performance. We will refer to this activity as the subjective performance evaluation strategy. Research has established the effectiveness of two

approaches to the use of this strategy. One requires the estimation of the outcome of the performance, the other requires the evaluation of the movement-related characteristics of the performance of the skill. Hogan and Yanowitz (1978) reported the first demonstration of the learning benefit of this strategy. In an experiment in which participants practiced a discrete movement that had a specified movement-time goal, those who verbally estimated their own movement-time error during the KR-delay interval learned to perform the task more accurately than those who did not use this estimation strategy.

More recently, Swinnen (1990), in the experiment described above, and Liu and Wrisberg (1997) have also presented evidence supporting the learning benefit of the subjective performance estimation strategy. The Swinnen experiment is especially noteworthy because it compared the strategies of the participant estimating his or her own performance outcome error with estimating performance outcome error of another person's movement. Figure 18.3 shows that the subjective performance estimation strategy led to a learning benefit, but the strategy of estimating another person's performance hindered learning. The importance of this comparison is that it indicates that the key part of the estimation strategy is not the estimation of performance itself, but the estimation of the learner's own performance.

The second type of beneficial subjective performance estimation is presented in the Liu and Wrisberg (1997) experiment. In addition to subjectively estimating their performance outcome, participants in this experiment estimated specific characteristics of some of the movement-related components of an action. The task required participants to throw a ball at a target as accurately as possible with the nonpreferred arm and without vision of the target. Participants received KR by seeing where on the target the ball had landed on each trial. During the KR-delay interval, two groups, which differed in terms of the length of the KR-delay interval, rated on 5-point scales the appropriateness of the force, angle of ball release, and ball trajectory

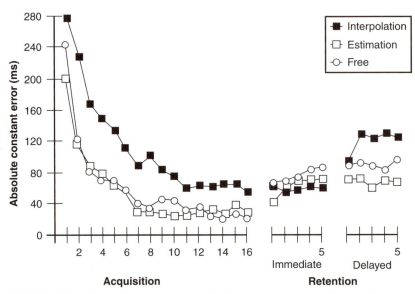

FIGURE 18.3　　Results from the experiment by Swinnen showing the influence of estimating the experimenter's movement error (interpolation group) and the influence of estimating the subject's own error (estimation group) during the KR-delay interval, compared with no activity during the interval (free group).　　[From Swinnen, S. P. (1990). Interpolated activities during the knowledge of results delay and post-knowledge of results interval: Effects on performance and learning. *Journal of Experimental Psychology: Learning, Memory, and Cognition, 16,* 692–705. Copyright © 1990 by the American Psychological Association. Reprinted with permission.]

of the throw, and then estimated the throw's point value on the target. The results indicated that these two groups performed more accurately on a retention test given twenty-four hours after the end of the practice session than the two groups that had not used the estimation strategy.

We find an interesting parallel to the subjective performance estimation strategy in what researchers call the **trials-delay procedure.** Here, experiment participants receive KR for a trial after they complete performance on a later trial. Anderson, Magill, and Sekiya (1994) reported one of the most recent experiments providing evidence for the effectiveness of this effect. Participants practiced making a blindfolded aiming movement. One group received KR about distance error after every trial (delay–0). A second group received KR two trials later (delay–2), which meant that they were told their error for trial 1 after completing trial 3. Results (fig-

ure 18.4) were that while the delay condition hindered performance during practice, it led to better performance on a twenty-four-hour retention test.

What do these different effects of activity reveal about learning processes that occur during the KR-delay interval? Our conclusion is that during this time interval the learner is actively engaged in learning processes involving activities such as developing an understanding of the task-instrinsic feedback and establishing essential error detection capabilities. When activity requiring similar processing occurs at the same time, interference with essential learning processes occurs, because the learner's attention capacity is too limited to allow both to occur simultaneously. On the other hand, when other activity during this interval enhances these processes, learning is facilitated.

For instructional purposes, the most significant implication of the various types of effects of

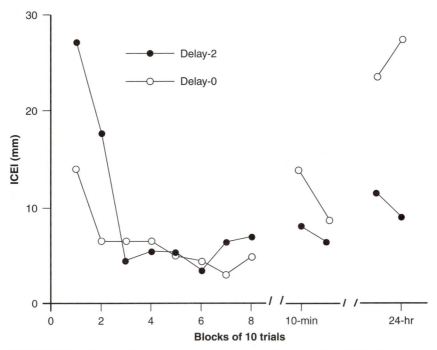

FIGURE 18.4   Results of the Anderson et al. experiment showing the beneficial effects of delaying KR for two trials (delay–2) compared to presenting KR after each trial (delay–0) for learning a manual aiming task.   (Reprinted with permission from *Research Quarterly for Exercise and Sport, Vol. 65, No. 3*, 286–290. Copyright © 1994 by the American Association for Health, Physical Education, Recreation, and Dance, 1900 Association Drive, Reston, VA 20191.)

activity during the KR-delay interval is that people who are practicing a skill can use a beneficial strategy after they complete the performance of a skill and before a teacher, coach, or therapist gives them augmented feedback. Before they receive augmented feedback, they should verbally describe what they think they did wrong that led to a less than desired performance outcome. There are two likely benefits that will result from the use of this strategy. One is that it will have a positive influence on skill learning, because the strategy forces the learner to subjectively evaluate his or her task-intrinsic feedback in relation to his or her own performance. Additionally, on the basis of our knowledge of the motivational role of augmented feedback, asking learners to occasionally describe what they think they did correctly should also ben-

efit skill learning because of the positive influence this type of activity can have on self-esteem.

The length of the post-KR interval. Many motor learning scholars have viewed the post-KR interval as an important interval for skill acquisition. They reason that it is during this period of time that the

---

trials-delay procedure   an experimental procedure used in the study of augmented feedback; it involves giving augmented feedback for a trial not after a person completes that trial, but following completion of a later trial (e.g., for a two-trial delay, an experimenter gives augmented feedback for trials 1, 2, and 3 after trials 3, 4, and 5, respectively).

learner develops a plan of action for the next trial. This planning occurs during this interval because the learner now has available both task-intrinsic feedback and augmented feedback.

If the learner processes critical skill learning information during the post-KR interval, we would expect there to be a *minimum length* for this interval. Although there is not an abundance of research that has investigated this issue, there is empirical evidence that has shown that indeed, this interval can be too short (e.g.,Weinberg, Guy, & Tupper, 1964; Rogers, 1974; Gallagher & Thomas, 1980). However, the amount of minimum time appears to be skill specific. It is worth noting here that the post-KR interval resembles the KR-delay interval; for optimal learning to be achieved, a learner needs a minimum amount of time to engage in the learning processes required. Conversely, there is no evidence indicating an optimal length for the post-KR interval. Research consistently has shown no apparent upper limit for the length of this interval.

Activity during the post-KR interval. The effect of engaging in activity is similar for the post-KR interval to that for the KR-delay interval. Depending on the type of activity, activity can have no effect on learning, interfere with learning, or benefit learning.

The most common finding has been that activity during the post-KR interval *has no effect on skill learning.* The best example is in an experiment by Lee and Magill (1983). People practiced making an arm movement through a series of three small wooden barriers in 1050 msec. During the post-KR interval, one group engaged in a motor activity (learning the same movement in 1350 msec), one group engaged in a cognitive activity involving number guessing, and a third group did not do any activity. At the end of the practice trials the two activity groups showed poorer performance than the no-activity group. However, this was a temporary performance effect rather than a learning effect: on a no-KR retention test, the three groups did not differ.

Several researchers have reported results indicating that activity during the post-KR interval *hin-*

ders learning. Of these, only those by Benedetti and McCullagh (1987) and Swinnen (1990, experiment 3) included appropriate tests for learning. In both of these experiments, the interfering activity was a cognitive activity. Participants in the experiment by Benedetti and McCullagh engaged in a mathematics problem-solving task, whereas those in the experiment by Swinnen guessed the movement-time error of a lever movement the experimenter made during the post-KR interval.

Only one experiment (Magill, 1988) has demonstrated that *beneficial learning effects* can result from activity in the post-KR interval. Participants learned a two-component arm movement in which each component had its own criterion movement time. During the post-KR interval, one group had to learn two additional two-component movements, one group had to learn a mirror-tracing task, and a third group did not engage in activity. Results showed that although there were no group differences on a no-KR retention test, the two groups engaged in activity during the post-KR interval performed better than the no-activity group on a transfer test in which participants learned a new two-component movement.

What do these different effects of activity tell us about learning processes that occur during the post-KR interval? They support the view we discussed earlier that learners engage in important planning activities during this time period. They use this planning time to take into account the discrepancy between the task-intrinsic and the augmented feedback, to determine how to execute the next attempt at performing the skill. Much of this planning seems to require cognitive activity; we see this in the experiments showing that engaging in cognitive problem-solving activity during this interval hinders learning. Why would beneficial transfer effects result when people must learn another motor skill in this interval? One hypothesis follows the transfer-appropriate processing view we discussed in chapter 14. This type of activity is beneficial because it increases the person's motor skill problem-solving experience; this in turn enables the person to transfer more successfully to a situation that requires similar problem-solving activity.

A CLOSER LOOK

Practical Implications of the Effects of KR-Delay and Post-KR Intervals

- A brief time interval should occur between a person's completion of a movement and the teacher's or therapist's giving of augmented feedback.
- Although an instructor's delaying of augmented feedback for a considerable length of time does not negatively affect learning of the skill, it undoubtedly influences the motivation of the person to continue to try to achieve the activity goal.

- A useful technique to facilitate skill learning is to have the person overtly focus attention on what he or she did wrong on a practice attempt by having the person respond, before being told what he or she did wrong, to this question: "What do you think you did wrong that time?"
- There is little need to be concerned about the length of the activity engaged in during the post-KR interval in terms of its influence on the degree of skill learning. However, the teacher or therapist should take motivational considerations into account on an individual basis.

Frequency of Presenting Augmented Feedback

The third question related to the timing of giving augmented feedback concerns how frequently it should be given during practice to optimize skill learning. For many years, the view was that it should be given during or after every practice trial because no learning occurred on trials without augmented feedback. However, beginning with the influential review and evaluation of the KR literature by Salmoni, Schmidt, and Walter (1984) and continuing to the present time, this traditional view has been revised as researchers have provided evidence that is contrary to predictions of that viewpoint.

The reduced frequency benefit. Sufficient research evidence has now accumulated for us to say confidently that the optimal frequency for giving augmented feedback is *not* 100 percent. The best example of the initial evidence to support this conclusion was from an experiment by Winstein and Schmidt (1990). They had participants practice producing the complex movement pattern shown in the top panel of figure 18.5 by moving a lever on a tabletop to manipulate a cursor on a computer monitor. During the two days of practice, participants received KR after either 100 percent or 50 percent of the trials. For the 50 percent condition, the experimenters used a **fading technique** in which they systematically reduced the KR frequency; they pro-

vided KR after each of the first twenty-two trials of each day, then had participants perform eight trials with no KR, then systematically reduced the frequency from eight to two trials for the remaining eight-trial blocks each day. The results of this experiment are presented in the bottom panel of figure 18.5. In a no-KR retention test given one day later, the faded 50 percent frequency condition led to better retention performance than the 100 percent condition produced. In fact, people who had received KR after every practice trial showed retention test performance at a level resembling that of their first day of practice.

The Winstein and Schmidt (1990) study has generated a great deal of research since it was published. The research has focused on two predominant themes: providing additional empirical support for the reduced frequency benefit, and determining whether or not an optimal frequency exists to enhance skill learning (e.g., Lai & Shea, 1998, 1999b; Wulf,

---

fading technique   a method of decreasing the frequency of augmented feedback by systematically reducing the frequency during the course of practice so that the person is effectively "weaned" from depending on its availability.

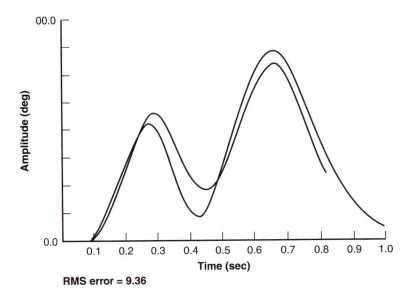

RMS error = 9.36

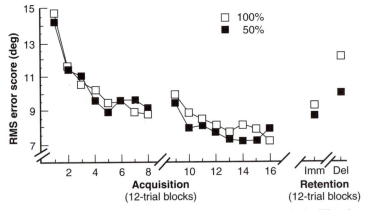

FIGURE 18.5 The top panel shows the goal movement pattern in the Winstein and Schmidt experiment. A sample of one participant's attempt to produce this pattern is superimposed. The RMS error score is shown as the subject saw it. Note that the goal pattern lasted for 0.8 sec while the participant produced a 1.0-sec pattern. The bottom panel shows the results of this experiment for the 100 percent KR frequency and 50 percent KR frequency groups, where the 50 percent group had KR frequency "faded" from 100 percent to 0 percent. [From Winstein, C. J., & Schmidt, R. A. (1990). Reduced frequency of knowledge of results enhances motor skill learning. *Journal of Experimental Psychology: Learning, Memory and Cognition, 16,* 677–691. Copyright © 1990 American Psychological Association. Reprinted by permission.]

Schmidt, & Deubel, 1993; Wulf, Lee, & Schmidt, 1994). Two interesting conclusions resulted from these research efforts. First, although a reduced frequency of augmented feedback can benefit motor skill learning, it may *not* benefit the learning of all motor skills. Second, an optimal relative frequency appears to be specific to the skill being learned.

These two conclusions lead to the question, what are the skill-related characteristics that would predict relative frequency effects? One of the more interesting possibilities is the *complexity* of the skill being learned (Wulf, Shea, & Matschiner, 1998). The reduced augmented feedback frequency appears to be better than, or as effective as, 100 percent frequency, primarily for the learning of tasks that are relatively simple. Many of the laboratory tasks for which a reduced frequency was beneficial required simple ballistic movements, or the moving of a lever to produce a specific spatial-temporal movement pattern. On the other hand, studies that have reported that a reduced augmented feedback frequency does not benefit skill learning typically have involved relatively complex skills, such as a slalom ski simulator.

A possible interpretation to this skill complexity view is to consider complexity not only in terms of the skill itself, but also in terms of the number of components of the skill about which augmented feedback could be given. This interpretation would lead to the hypothesis that when a skill involves only one performance or outcome characteristic on which to base augmented feedback, as is the case in the simple tasks described above, then people do not require this information repeated on every practice trial. But when the task is complex, and involves several possible performance characteristics on which to base augmented feedback, then more frequent presentations of augmented feedback may be required. The expectation for the complex skill would be that the learner would require more frequent feedback presentations, but the performance characteristic about which feedback would be given would vary from trial to trial. In this approach, the augmented feedback frequency for any one component of the task would

be low, but the frequency for the overall skill could be relatively high.

Until further research establishes a different picture of the frequency issue, the best conclusion for now is that optimal learning does not depend on a person's receiving augmented feedback after every practice trial. Research has been consistent in demonstrating that when people receive augmented feedback on fewer than 100 percent of the practice trials, their learning is as good as or better than their learning with augmented feedback provided on every practice trial. In fact, there is sufficient evidence so that we can conclude that receiving augmented feedback after every trial of practice increases the likelihood a person will become dependent on it. This dependence leads to poor test performance when the augmented feedback is not available.

Theoretical implications of the frequency effect. The challenge for those interested in developing motor learning theory is to establish why giving augmented feedback less than 100 percent of the time during practice is better for skill learning. One possible reason is that when people receive augmented feedback after every trial, they eventually experience an attention-capacity "overload." After several trials, the cumulative effect is that there is more information available than the person can handle.

A more likely possibility is that giving augmented feedback on every trial leads to engaging the learner in a fundamentally different type of learning processing than he or she would experience if it were not given on every trial. Schmidt and his colleagues (e.g., Salmoni, Schmidt, & Walter, 1984; Winstein & Schmidt, 1990) proposed this view, which they called the **guidance hypothesis.** According to this

---

guidance hypothesis   a hypothesis indicating that the role of augmented feedback in learning is to guide performance to be correct during practice; however, if it is provided too frequently, it can cause the learner to develop a dependency on its availability and therefore to perform poorly when it is not available.

A CLOSER LOOK

Practical Implications of the Reduced Frequency Effect

The conclusion that augmented feedback does not need to be given after every practice trial

- reduces the demand on the instructor, coach, or therapist to provide augmented feedback all the time. This should be especially comforting for those who work with groups, because research evidence shows that they typically do not provide augmented feedback with 100 percent frequency. In fact, in group practice situations, the teacher, coach, or therapist provides augmented feedback

about one or two times per minute, with the same student rarely receiving more than a few feedback statements throughout a class session or practice period (e.g., see Eghan, 1988; Fishman & Tobey, 1978; Silverman, Tyson, & Krampitz, 1991).

- is based on the use of augmented feedback to provide error correction information. However, it is important not to ignore the role of augmented feedback as a source of motivation when considering the frequency question. Although learners do not need externally presented error correction information after every trial, they may benefit from feedback statements that are motivation oriented on some intervening trials.

hypothesis, if the learner receives augmented feedback on every trial (i.e., at 100 percent frequency), then it will effectively "guide" the learner to perform the movement correctly. However, there is a negative aspect to this guidance process. By using augmented feedback as the guidance source, the learner develops a dependency on the availability of augmented feedback so that when he or she must perform the skill without it, performance will be poorer than if augmented feedback were provided. In effect, augmented feedback becomes a crutch for the learner that is essential for performing the skill.

The hypothesis further proposes that receiving augmented feedback less frequently during practice encourages the learner to engage in more beneficial learning strategies during practice. For example, active problem-solving activities increase during trials with no augmented feedback. The learner does not become dependent on the availability of augmented feedback, and therefore can perform the skill well, even in its absence.

Techniques That Reduce Augmented Feedback Frequency

Now that we have established that it is generally more effective to provide augmented feedback less frequently than on every practice trial, a question

that remains concerns how to implement ways that reduce frequency. The fading technique, described in the previous section, is one useful approach to reducing frequency. But there are several other techniques that are effective as well.

Performance-based bandwidths. When the decision to give augmented feedback is determined by performance-based bandwidth criteria, which we discussed in chapter 17, the frequency of giving augmented feedback will be less than on every trial. Recall from that discussion that this bandwidth technique for giving augmented feedback involves providing it only when performance is *not* within a preestablished tolerance limit (i.e., bandwidth). If we relate the bandwidth technique to the augmented feedback frequency issue, we can see how the bandwidth technique influences the frequency of presenting augmented feedback.

Lee, White, and Carnahan (1990) were the first to investigate this relationship. In their experiment they paired individual participants so that one of each pair received KR only on the trials on which the other of the pair received KR in 5 percent and 10 percent bandwidth conditions. The reason for the pairing of participants (a procedure known as "yoking") was to control for the possibility that the performance-based bandwidth benefit for learning was due to a reduced KR frequency. Thus, KR frequency was the same for each pair of participants, but the KR frequency for the participant of the pair in the bandwidth condition depended on the 5 percent and 10 percent criteria. Results showed that the bandwidth-based KR conditions led to better retention performance than the paired frequency conditions for learning a ballistic two-segment limb movement. The researchers concluded from these results that although the performance-based bandwidth technique reduces augmented feedback frequency, there are additional reasons why the technique enhances learning.

Two additional experiments will serve as examples of research that help us better understand the relationship between the performance-based bandwidth technique and augmented feedback frequency. In an experiment by Goodwin and Meeuwsen (1995), which was described in chapter 17 in the discussion of the performance-based bandwidth technique, 0 percent and 10 percent error bandwidth conditions were compared with those that were systematically expanded (0-5-10-15-20 percent) and contracted (20-15-10-5-0 percent) while practicing putting a golf ball a criterion distance. Results showed that retention performance did not differ between the expanded and 10 percent conditions, although both were better than the 0 percent and contracted bandwidth conditions. Interestingly, the KR frequencies for the 10 percent bandwidth condition reduced from 62 percent during the first twenty trials, to between 47 percent and 50 percent on the remaining four blocks of trials. For the expanding bandwidth condition, KR frequencies began at 99 percent for the first twenty trials when the bandwidth was 0 percent, but then reduced to 69 percent, 48 percent, 29 percent, and 19 percent on the last four blocks of trials, respectively, for the increasing bandwidths. These results indicate that rather than the actual amount of the reduction of KR frequency, it is the reduction of KR frequency during practice that is important to improved learning. More recently, Lai and Shea (1999a) reported similar findings by showing that a 15 percent error bandwidth led to better

learning of a complex spatial-temporal movement pattern than either a 0 percent bandwidth or switching from 15 percent to 0 percent bandwidths midway through the practice trials.

The results of these experiments raise interesting questions concerning why the bandwidth technique facilitates skill learning. We know part of the reason is because the technique reduces augmented feedback presentation frequency. But, the frequency reduction differs from the fading technique because the bandwidth conditions that relate to the best learning do not always involve a systematic frequency reduction toward zero. And, different from the fading technique, the learner's performance establishes the frequency rather than the experimenter, teacher, coach, or therapist establishing it, which is the case for the fading technique.

Lee, White, and Carnahan (1990) proposed that the benefit resulting from the bandwidth technique is due to combining the presentation of augmented feedback with what the motor control system is capable of doing. Early in practice, the system is not capable of correcting errors with the precision required within a narrow bandwidth, such as when errors must be corrected within a 5 percent or 10 percent tolerance limit. However, later in practice the system has acquired this capability.

From an instructional perspective, the bandwidth technique provides a useful means of individualizing the systematic reduction of the frequency of augmented feedback in practice situations. The bandwidth technique gives the practitioner a specific guideline for when to provide augmented feedback that encourages the learner to engage in important learning strategies. And, because the bandwidth is related to individual performance, the learner can engage in these strategies at his or her own rate.

Self-selected frequency. Another technique that bases the frequency of augmented feedback on the individual involves the practitioner giving the learner augmented feedback only when he or she asks for it. The learning benefits derived from this approach result from allowing the learner to participate more actively in determining characteristics of the practice conditions by self-regulating the presentation of augmented feedback. An experiment by Janelle, Kim, and Singer (1995) provided initial evidence that this strategy can enhance the learning of motor skills. College students practiced an underhand golf ball toss to a target on the ground. The students received KP about ball force, ball loft, and arm swing during practice. Compared to groups that received KP according to experimenter-determined frequencies (all of which received it less frequently than on every trial), the participants who controlled KP frequency themselves performed more accurately on the retention test.

Janelle substantiated and extended these results in a later study in which videotape replay was a source of augmented feedback in addition to verbal KP (Janelle, Barba, Frehlich, Tennant, & Cauraugh, 1997). Participants in the self-regulated group controlled the augmented feedback schedule by requesting KP at will during 200 practice trials. An important characteristic of this experiment was that individual participants in another group were paired (i.e., yoked) to participants in the self-regulated condition to receive KP on the same trials, but without requesting it. The importance of this yoked condition was to control for the possibility that the effect of self-regulation of augmented feedback is due only to reduced frequency. Results showed that participants in the self-regulated condition learned the throwing accuracy task with more accuracy and better throwing technique than participants in the other KP and yoked conditions.

In terms of augmented feedback frequency, it is interesting to note that participants in the self-controlled condition requested KP on only 7 percent of the practice trials in the Janelle et al. (1995) experiment, and on only 11 percent in the Janelle et al. (1997) experiment. These low frequencies indicate that there is some relationship between the self-controlled procedure and the reduced relative frequency of augmented feedback. However, because people in the self-controlled conditions in both experiments performed better on retention tests than

those in the frequency-yoked conditions, the benefit of the self-controlled situation is more than a simple frequency effect.

Janelle et al. (1997) described several hypotheses that have been proposed to account for this learning benefit. One is that a self-controlled learning environment allows a person to process important skill-related information at a deeper level. Another is that the self-controlled situation encourages the learner to engage in more effective learning strategies. A third possibility is that being able to control one's own learning environment increases the person's confidence in his or her capability to perform the skill (i.e., self-efficacy) when improvement is experienced. Although there is a lack of agreement about the specific reason why the self-selected technique benefits learning, the evidence concerning the technique indicates that it is one that deserves serious consideration for inclusion in skill learning situations.

Summary augmented feedback. Another way to reduce the frequency of augmented feedback presentations is to give a listing of performance-related information after a certain number of practice trials. This technique, which is known as **summary augmented feedback,** reduces the presentation frequency of augmented feedback while providing the same amount of information as if it were given after every trial.

The summary technique could be advantageous in several types of skill learning situations. For example, suppose that a therapy patient must do a series of ten leg extensions in relatively rapid succession. To give augmented feedback after every extension may not be possible, if time limits restrict access to performance information after each attempt. A summary of all ten attempts could help overcome this limitation. Or, suppose that a person is practicing a shooting skill for which he or she cannot see the target because of the distance involved. Efficiency of practice could be increased if that person did not receive augmented feedback after each shot, but received information about each shot after every ten shots.

Two examples of experiments, one involving a laboratory task and the other a real-world skill, will

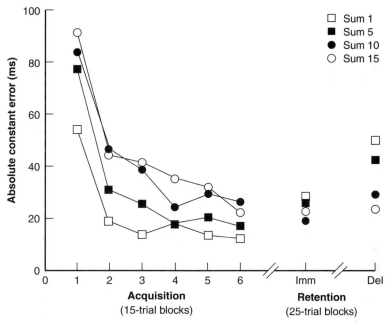

FIGURE 18.6   Results of the experiment by Schmidt et al., showing the effects of learning a timing movement with different summary KR conditions. (Sum 1 = KR after every trial; Sum 5 = KR for five trials presented every five trials, etc.)   [From Schmidt, R. A., et al., (1989). Summary knowledge of results for skill acquisition: support for the guidance hypothesis. *Journal of Experimental Psychology: Learning, Memory and Cognition. 15,* 352–359. Copyright © 1989 American Psychological Association. Reprinted by permission.]

illustrate the summary technique. The first study to generate a great deal of interest in the summary technique was a laboratory-based experiment by Schmidt, Young, Swinnen, and Shapiro (1989). The task involved moving a lever along a trackway to achieve a goal movement time. During the ninety practice trials, participants received KR after every trial or in summary form after five, ten, or fifteen trials. The results of this experiment (see figure 18.6) showed very little difference between the conditions during practice and on a retention test given ten minutes after practice. But, on a retention test two days later, the group that had received KR after every trial performed the worst, whereas the group that had received summary KR after every fifteen trials performed the best.

In an experiment involving the learning of target shooting with rifles, Boyce (1991) provided one group with KP after every shot, and another group with KP about every shot after each fifth shot. The results showed no difference in eventual shooting performance by these groups. Although the summary method did not yield better performance than the method giving KP after every shot, its effectiveness as an instructional technique was established, because it was just as effective for improving performance as the other method.

---

summary augmented feedback   a method of reducing the frequency of augmented feedback by giving a person augmented feedback for a certain number of trials at the completion of those trials (e.g., KR for each of five trials after the completion of every fifth trial).

The decade of the 1990s saw several studies published that provided evidence supporting benefit of the summary technique for motor skill learning, although most used laboratory tasks (e.g., Schmidt, Lange, & Young, 1990; Wright, Snowden, & Willoughby, 1990; Guay, Salmoni, & Lajoie, 1999). However, several questions remain concerning the use of this technique and why it is effective.

A very practical question that remains to be answered is: What is the optimal number of performance attempts, or practice trials, to include in a summary augmented feedback statement? Although there have been several attempts to determine if a specific number of trials is optimal, the results have been equivocal. Two answers appear reasonable at the present time on the basis of results of research that has investigated this question. First, Sidaway, Moore, and Schoenfelder-Zohdi (1991) concluded that the positive effects of the summary technique are not due to the number of trials summarized, and stated that their results argue against the notion of an "optimal summary length." Instead, they argued that the summary effect is related either to the reduced frequency of presenting augmented feedback, or to the time delay involved in presenting augmented feedback using the summary technique (note that the summary technique has characteristics similar to the trials-delay procedure, which we discussed in chapter 17). An alternative answer to the question is one we have seen related to many of the issues discussed in this book. The "optimal" summary length may be specific to the skill being learned. Guadagnoli, Dornier, and Tandy (1996) provided evidence for this possibility by showing that longer summaries are better for the learning of simple skills, whereas shorter summaries lead to better learning of more complex skills.

Another question of interest concerns how the effectiveness of the summary technique relates to a person's stage of learning. The only evidence at the present time that indicates there may be a relationship comes from the experiment by Guadagnoli et al. (1996). They found that that shorter KR summaries were more beneficial than longer ones for

beginners, but just the opposite was the case for more experienced performers.

One of the possible strategies people may use when presented with a listing of augmented feedback is to estimate an average for the series of trials that the summary includes. The research literature provides some evidence that this may occur. In experiments in which the learner receives the average score for all the trials in a series, the results have shown that this procedure leads to better learning than presenting augmented feedback after every trial (Young & Schmidt, 1992), and no better or worse than after every trial or after every third trial (Wulf & Schmidt, 1996). But, when compared to the summary technique, no differences are found in terms of their influence on skill learning (Guay, Salmoni, & Lajoie, 1999; Weeks & Sherwood, 1994; Yao, Fischman, & Wang, 1994).

Finally, why is the summary method effective? Its effectiveness is undoubtedly due to the same factors that lead to the benefit of reducing augmented feedback frequency, as explained by the guidance hypothesis. During practice trials on which they receive no augmented feedback, people engage in beneficial learning activities that are not characteristic of people who receive augmented feedback after every trial.

SUMMARY

Three issues related to the timing aspects of augmented feedback are important to consider if we seek to understand the influence of augmented feedback on skill learning. One of these concerns is whether a learner should receive augmented feedback during or after the performance of a skill. Although there is no conclusive answer to this concern, we know that terminal augmented feedback can be effective in most skill learning situations, and concurrent augmented feedback can be beneficial when it is difficult for a person to determine what to do to achieve a task based on the task-intrinsic feedback. The research literature shows both negative and positive effects on skill learning for concurrent augmented feedback. The second timing issue addresses the time intervals involved for terminal augmented feedback. Both the KR-delay and the post-KR intervals are important time periods for skill learning. Both intervals have minimum lengths, but appear to have no maximum effective lengths. Also, engaging in activity during these intervals typically has no effect on skill learning, although engaging in certain types of activities can either hinder or benefit learning. The third timing issue concerns how frequently the practitioner should give augmented feedback to facilitate skill learning. Research evidence shows that giving augmented feedback after every practice attempt is generally not the optimal conditions, and that some frequency of less than 100 percent is desirable. The guidance hypothesis represents the most commonly held view for explaining the reduced frequency benefit. Methods for reducing frequency include the fading technique, performance-based bandwidth technique, self-selected frequency strategy, and the summary method. One reason to investigate issues related to the timing of providing augmented feedback is that this is a means of addressing questions about the learning processes involved between trials during practice. Evidence shows that attention to processing task-intrinsic feedback is critical for effective skill learning. In fact, when practice conditions create a dependence on augmented feedback by shifting a learner's attention away from task-intrinsic feedback, learning is impeded.

RELATED READINGS

Carnahan, H., Vandervoort, A. A., & Swanson, L. R. (1996). The influence of summary knowledge of results and aging on motor learning. *Research Quarterly for Exercise and Sport, 67,* 280–287.

Schmidt, R. A. (1991). Frequent augmented feedback can degrade learning: Evidence and interpretations. In J. Requin & G. E. Stelmach (Eds.), *Tutorials in motor neuroscience* (pp. 59–75). Dordrecht, The Netherlands: Kluwer.

Schmidt, R. A., & Wulf, G. (1997). Continuous concurrent feedback degrades skill learning: Implications for training and simulation. *Human Factors, 39,* 509–525.

Swinnen, S. P. (1996). Information feedback for motor skill learning: A review. In H. N. Zelaznik (Ed.), *Advances in motor learning and control* (pp. 37–66). Champaign, IL: Human Kinetics.

STUDY QUESTIONS

1. What is the difference between concurrent and terminal augmented feedback? Give two examples of each.

2. Name the two time intervals associated with the giving of terminal augmented feedback during practice. Discuss why researchers are interested in investigating these intervals.

3. (a) What are two types of activity during the KR-delay interval that have been shown to benefit skill learning? (b) Why does this benefit occur?

4. (a) What seems to be the most appropriate conclusion to draw regarding the frequency with which an instructor should give augmented feedback during learning? (b) How does the guidance hypothesis relate to the issue of augmented feedback frequency?

5. Describe a skill learning situation in which (a) giving summary augmented feedback would be a beneficial technique, (b) using the self-selected frequency strategy would be beneficial.

UNIT

VI

PRACTICE CONDITIONS

CHAPTER

Practice Variability

*Concept: Variability of practice experiences is
important for learning motor skills*

APPLICATION

The reason a person practices a skill is to increase
his or her capability of performing it in future situations that will require the skill. For example, some
people will need to perform sport skills successfully in skills tests, games, and matches. Dancers
need to perform in recitals, performances, and
competitions. And rehab patients practice skills so
that they can perform them as needed in the everyday environment. Because of this future performance requirement, teachers, coaches, and therapists must design and establish practice conditions
that will lead to the greatest probability of successful performance in the situations that will require
the skills.

One practice characteristic that increases the
chances for future performance success is the variability of the learner's experiences while he or she
practices. This includes variations of the characteristics of the context in which the learner performs the skill, as well as variations of the skill he
or she is practicing. The teacher, coach, or therapist must address several important questions to
determine how to optimize the types and amount
of variation to include in practice experiences.
First, what aspects of performing the skill should

he or she vary? Second, how much variety of
experiences is optimal? Third, how should the
variety of experiences be organized in the practice
sessions? We consider these questions in the discussion that follows.

DISCUSSION

A consistent characteristic of theories of motor
skill learning is their emphasis on the learning benefits derived from practice variability. In these theories, **practice variability** refers to the variety of
movement and context characteristics the learner
experiences while practicing a skill. For example,
in Schmidt's (1975) schema theory, a key prediction is that successful future performance of a skill
depends on the amount of variability the learner
experiences during practice. Similarly, Gentile's
learning stages model (1972, 2000) emphasized the
learner's need during practice to experience variations of regulatory and nonregulatory context characteristics. And dynamic pattern views of skill
learning stress the learner's need to explore the
perceptual motor workspace and to discover optimal solutions to the degrees-of-freedom problem
posed by the skill (e.g., McDonald, Oliver, &
Newell, 1995; Vereijken & Whiting, 1990).

The Future Performance Benefit of Practice Variability

The primary benefit a learner derives from practice experiences that promote movement and context variability is an increased capability to perform the skill in a future test situation. This means that the person has acquired an increased capability to perform the practiced skill, as well as to adapt to novel conditions that might characterize the test situation. When viewed from the perspective of transfer learning, the inclusion of movement and context variability in practice can be seen as a means of enhancing the probability of positive transfer from the practice to the test contexts.

An interesting irony here is that an increased amount of practice variability usually is associated with an *increased amount of performance* error *during practice.* However, research evidence shows that more performance error can be better than less error for skill learning, when it occurs in the initial learning stage. A good example of this evidence is an experiment by Edwards and Lee (1985). Each participant had to learn to move his or her arm through a specified pattern in 1200 msec. Participants in the prompted group were told that if they moved according to a "ready and 1, 2, 3, 4, 5" count on a tape, they would complete the movement in the criterion time. Each person practiced until he or she could do three trials in a row correctly at 1200 msec. Those in the trial-and-error group were told the goal movement time and received KR about their timing error after each trial. The results (figure 19.1) indicated that the two groups performed similarly on the retention test, but the trial-and-error group performed the 1800-msec novel transfer task more accurately.

What is particularly interesting about these results is how much the two groups differed in the amount of error each produced during practice. The prompted group performed with very little error during practice, whereas the trial-and-error group experienced much error, especially during the first fifteen trials. Yet experiencing less error during practice was no more beneficial for retention test performance, and it was detrimental for transfer to a novel variation of the practiced movement.

Implementing Practice Variability

The first step in determining how to provide an appropriate amount of practice variability is to assess the characteristics of the future situations in which the learner will perform a skill. Of particular relevance here are the *characteristics of the physical context* in which he or she will perform the skill and the *skill characteristics* that the performance situation will require. If you again view this situation as a transfer of learning situation, then you will see the value of using the test conditions to determine what the practice environment should be like. As we discussed in chapter 14 and illustrated in Figure 14.1, effective transfer is a function of the similarities between skill, context, and cognitive processing characteristics of the practice and test situations. A high degree of similarity between these characteristics in the two situations enhances transfer between the practice and the test.

Varying practice contexts. It is important to keep in mind that when people perform skills, they do so in contexts that have identifiable characteristics. As Gentile (2000) pointed out, some features of the performance context are critical for determining the movement characteristics of an action (which she called regulatory conditions), whereas other features (nonregulatory conditions) have no influence.

Consider some examples of *regulatory conditions* that influence a person's walking behavior. Certain movement characteristics will be different when you walk on a concrete sidewalk from when you walk on ice or on sand. Also, you walk differently on a busy

---

practice variability   the variety of movement and context characteristics a person experiences while practicing a skill.

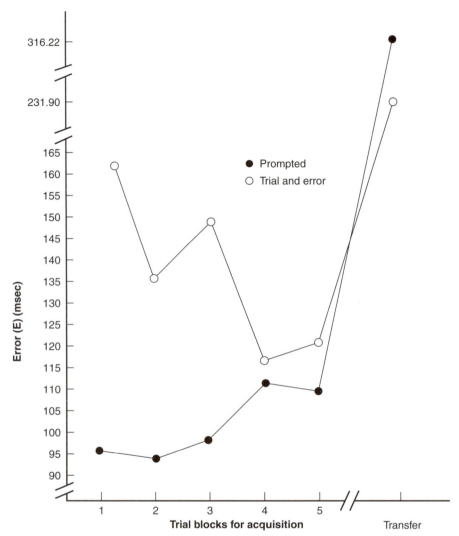

FIGURE 19.1   Results from the experiment by Edwards and Lee showing performance on a 1200-msec movement-time goal task during the acquisition trials and on an 1800-msec goal for the transfer task for two types of practice conditions: prompted by a tone lasting 1200 msec or practicing with KR (trial and error) [Reprinted with permission from *Research Quarterly for Exercise and Sport, Vol. 56, No. 3*, 286–290. Copyright © 1985 by the American Alliance for Health, Physical Education, Recreation, and Dance, 1900 Association Drive, Reston, VA 20191.]

sidewalk that is cluttered with other people than on a sidewalk empty of people. When regulatory conditions like these may vary from one performance context to another, it is important that practice conditions include a variety of similar conditions.

Nonregulatory conditions also play a role in influencing transfer between practice and test. For walking, some nonregulatory conditions would include the physical environment around the walking pathway, such as buildings, trees, and open

---

TABLE 19.1 Examples of Varying Practice Conditions for Two Types of Closed Skills

---

Intertrial Variability of Regulatory Conditions	No Intertrial Variability of Regulatory Conditions
Golf shot using a 7-iron The goal is to successfully make shots with the 7-iron during a golf match.	**Basketball free throw** The goal is to shoot free throws successfully in basketball games.
Regulatory conditions that remain constant in a match • 7-iron characteristics • golf ball characteristics	**Regulatory conditions that remain constant in games** • basket height • basket distance from free-throw line • basketball characteristics
Regulatory conditions that can vary in a match • goal for the shot • distance of required shot • location of ball	**Nonregulatory conditions that can vary in games** • number of free throws to be taken • importance to game of making the free throws • crowd noise • length of the game
Nonregulatory conditions that can vary in a match • number of hole being played • number of strokes ahead or behind • cloudy or sunny skies • importance of a particular shot	*Practice conditions* should include as many *nonregulatory* conditions as possible to be similar to those that could be experienced in a game.
Practice conditions should simulate as many *regulatory* and *nonregulatory* conditions as possible to be similar to those that could be experienced in a match.	

---

space. Although these features do not influence the pattern of movement directly, they nonetheless can influence the degree of success a person may achieve in carrying out the action in a unique context. Again, when nonregulatory conditions will vary from one performance context to another, practice conditions should provide opportunities to experience these characteristics.

Varying practice conditions for closed skills. The first step in making the decision about what to vary during the practice of a closed skill is to determine whether or not the skill involves intertrial variability for the regulatory conditions in the test situation. *For closed skills that do not involve intertrial vari-*

ability for regulatory conditions, nonregulatory conditions may be novel. For the practice of these types of skills, regulatory conditions should remain constant but nonregulatory conditions should vary according to expectations for the test situation. For closed skills that involve intertrial variability, both regulatory and nonregulatory conditions are likely to be novel in the test situation, which means that both should be varied in practice. Examples of practice condition characteristics for each of these types of closed skills are presented in table 19.1.

Varying practice conditions for open skills. Each performance of an open skill is unique, because in each performance of the skill, certain characteris-

		Class day					
		1	2	3	4	5	6
Blocked practice	30 min	All overhand	All overhand	All underhand	All underhand	All sidearm	All sidearm
Random practice	5 min 5 min 5 min 5 min 5 min 5 min	Underhand Overhand Underhand Sidearm Underhand Overhand	Overhand Sidearm Sidearm Underhand Overhand Overhand	Sidearm Overhand Sidearm Underhand Underhand Sidearm	Overhand Sidearm Sidearm Underhand Overhand Overhand	Underhand Overhand Underhand Sidearm Underhand Overhand	Sidearm Overhand Sidearm Underhand Underhand Sidearm
Serial practice	5 min 5 min 5 min 5 min 5 min 5 min	Overhand Underhand Sidearm Overhand Underhand Sidearm	Overhand Underhand Sidearm Overhand Underhand Sidearm	Overhand Underhand Sidearm Overhand Underhand Sidearm	Overhand Underhand Sidearm Overhand Underhand Sidearm	Overhand Underhand Sidearm Overhand Underhand Sidearm	Overhand Underhand Sidearm Overhand Underhand Sidearm

FIGURE 19.2   A six-day unit plan demonstrating three different practice structures (blocked, random, and serial) for teaching three different throwing patterns (overhand, underhand, and sidearm). All classes are 30 min long and all but the blocked practice schedule are divided into 5-min segments. Each practice condition provides an equal amount of practice for each throwing pattern.

tics are novel to the performer. That is, to perform the skill the person must produce certain movements that he or she has not made before in the manner this situation requires. The performer needs to modify previously produced movements in order to achieve the goal of the skill. For example, if you are preparing to return a serve in tennis, it is likely that certain characteristics of the ball action will be unique to this particular serve. Thus, in addition to variations of nonregulatory conditions, practice of open skills also needs to include experiences with regulatory conditions that change from one attempt to another.

Organizing Variable Practice

Having established that practice variability benefits skill learning, we next must consider how the teacher, coach, or therapist should organize the variable experiences within a practice session or unit of instruction. The following example illustrates how this practice organization question is involved as the motor skills professional develops practice conditions.

Suppose you are an elementary school physical education teacher organizing a teaching unit on throw-

ing for your classes. You have determined that you will devote six class periods to this unit. You want the students to experience three variations of the throwing pattern: the overhand, underhand, and sidearm throws. How should you arrange these three different throws for practice during the six class periods? Figure 19.2 shows three possible arrangements. One is to practice each throw in blocks of two days each (blocked practice). Another possibility is to practice each throw in a random arrangement with 5-min blocks devoted to each particular pattern (random practice). Thus, each day students would experience six 5-min blocks, with no specified order of occurrence for the three patterns; the only stipulation would be that they practice all three an equal amount over the course of the unit. The third arrangement, serial practice, also involves a 5-min block for each pattern. However, in this approach students practice each pattern for two sets of five minutes every day in the same order.

This organization problem is not unique to the teaching of physical education activities. It is characteristic of any situation in which learners must practice several variations of a skill. In a therapy situation, a patient may need to practice grasping

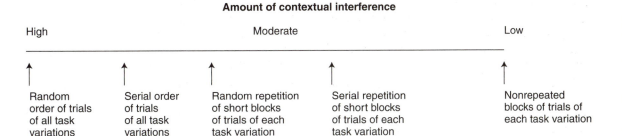

Amount of contextual interference

High	Moderate	Low

Random order of trials of all task variations	Serial order of trials of all task variations	Random repetition of short blocks of trials of each task variation	Serial repetition of short blocks of trials of each task variation	Nonrepeated blocks of trials of each task variation

Practice schedules

FIGURE 19.3   The amount of contextual interference that is possible in a practice situation is portrayed as a continuum ranging from high to low. Also presented are sample variable practice schedules in terms of how each relates to the amount of contextual interference created by the schedule.

objects of different sizes, weights, and shapes. Or a patient who has had a knee joint replacement may need to practice walking on different types of surfaces. In a dance setting, a dancer may need to practice tempo variations in a routine or other variations of particular components of a routine. All of these situations involve the same organization problem: How should the schedule of practice for these variations be organized within the practice time available?

The contextual interference approach to organizing variable practice. One way to solve the variable practice schedule problem is to apply the learning phenomenon known as the *contextual interference effect.* William Battig (1979), who first demonstrated this effect, introduced the term **contextual interference** to refer to the interference that results from practicing various tasks or skills within the context of practice. Different amounts of contextual interference can result from the organization of the practice schedule. The practice schedule organization options described earlier can be viewed as located along a continuum of contextual interference (see figure 19.3). A *high amount of contextual interference* occurs at one extreme when the practice schedule involves a random arrangement of trials so that all the task variations are practiced in each practice session. In this schedule, the task variation practiced on each trial would

be randomly determined. At the opposite extreme, a *low amount of contextual interference* results from a schedule that organizes the practice of each task variation in its own block, or unit, of time. Other schedules, such as the serial schedule described earlier, fall along the continuum between these two extremes.

The **contextual interference effect** occurs when a high amount of contextual interference results in better learning (i.e., retention and transfer performance) of the task variations than a low amount. What is especially noteworthy about this effect is that prior to Battig's initial demonstration of it, researchers traditionally viewed interference as something that hinders learning. According to that view, a low amount of contextual interference during practice should lead to better learning than

---

contextual interference   the interference that results from practicing variations of a skill within the context of practice.

contextual interference effect   the learning benefit resulting from practicing multiple skills in a high contextual interference practice schedule (e.g., random practice), rather than practicing the skills in a low contextual interference schedule (e.g., blocked practice).

a high amount. However, Battig's research showed an important exception to the traditional view of interference. It is important to note in this regard that a negative influence of interference is often found for high contextual interference schedules during practice. But this interference turns out to be a learning benefit because the high contextual interference practice schedules result in better performance on retention and transfer tests than low contextual interference practice schedules.

The first evidence of the contextual interference effect for motor skill learning was reported by Shea and Morgan (1979). Participants practiced three variations of movement patterns in which the goal was to move one arm through a series of small wooden barriers as rapidly as possible. One group followed a blocked practice schedule (i.e., low contextual interference) in which each movement pattern was practiced in its own unit of trials. A second group practiced the three patterns according to a random practice schedule (i.e., high contextual interference) in which the practice of each pattern was randomly distributed throughout the practice trials. Results showed that the random practice schedule led to poorer performance during practice, but better performance on retention and transfer tests. Thus, random practice resulted in better learning of the three pattern variations and allowed for better performance for a new pattern. Since the Shea and Morgan experiment, numerous other studies have been reported (see Brady, 1998; Magill & Hall, 1990). The evidence from this research establishes that the contextual interference effect is generalizable to learning motor skills.

One of the striking negative effects of low contextual interference practice is that it inhibits performance of the practiced skills in novel performance contexts. Contextual interference experiments commonly show this. Although blocked practice sometimes leads to blocked retention test performance that is similar to performance following random practice, a large decrement in retention performance is typical when researchers test the skills under random conditions (e.g., Shea, Kohl, & Indermill, 1990). On the other hand, high contextual interfer-

ence practice does not show the same transfer problem. Thus, low contextual interference practice appears to develop a practice context dependency that decreases a person's capability to adapt to novel test contexts.

The contextual interference effect outside the laboratory. Battig's original demonstration of the contextual interference effect was based on the learning of cognitive skills, such as word lists. Much of the research involving motor skills has been based on the learning of laboratory tasks, such as the barrier-knockdown task used by Shea and Morgan (1979). Because it is important to establish that learning phenomena demonstrated in the laboratory also exist in real-world settings, we will look at some of the research that provides evidence that the contextual interference effect applies to learning situations outside the laboratory.

One of the first experiments that presented this type of evidence was reported by Goode and Magill (1986). College women with no prior badminton experience practiced the short, long, and drive serves from the right service court. They practiced these serves three days a week for three weeks with 36 trials in each practice session, for a total of 324 trials (108 trials per serve) during the practice period. The low contextual interference condition was a modification of the blocked condition used in previous studies; in this study, the blocked practice group practiced one serve each day of each week. The group on a random practice schedule practiced each serve randomly in every practice session. In this condition, the experimenter told each participant which serve she should perform next.

As you can see in figure 19.4, the results demonstrated the contextual interference effect. The group that practiced with the random schedule outperformed the blocked practice group on the retention and transfer tests. What is especially remarkable is that on the transfer test, which involved serving from the left service court, the random group showed no deterioration in performance. On the other hand, students in the group that had practiced in a blocked schedule were not able to adapt well to

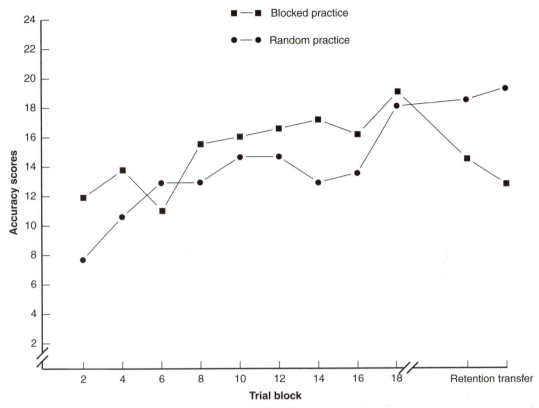

FIGURE 19.4 Results from the experiment by Goode and Magill showing the effects of blocked and random structured practice for three types of badminton serves on acquisition, one-day retention, and transfer. [Reprinted with permission from *Research Quarterly for Exercise and Sport, Vol. 57, No. 4*, 308–314. Copyright © 1986 by the American Alliance for Health, Physical Education, Recreation, and Dance, 1900 Association Drive, Reston, VA, 20191.]

this new performance context. In fact, learners in this group performed in the new context about as well as they had when they had begun practicing the serves from the right court three weeks earlier.

The Goode and Magill study showed the benefit of high contextual interference for beginners learning an actual sport skill (the badminton serve). However, although their experiment used a sport skill, the authors carried it out in controlled experimental conditions. Those who seek even more real-world validity should note that Wrisberg and Liu (1991) attained the same results as Goode and Magill, but in an actual class setting. In that study, students learned the serves in a unit of instruction in an actual physical education class.

Another experiment worth noting demonstrates not only that the contextual interference effect for real-world skills exists for beginners, but also for skilled individuals. Hall, Domingues, and Cavazos (1994) had skilled baseball players practice hitting different types of pitches to improve their batting performance. The players engaged in forty-five extra pitches of batting practice three days a week for five weeks. Batters hit fastballs, curves, or change-ups according to a blocked or random schedule. In the blocked schedule, players practiced hitting one of these pitches on each day, whereas in the random schedule, they hit all three types of pitch, randomly presented, each day. The results showed that on a test involving a random sequence of pitches, like one that

A CLOSER LOOK

A Professional Golfer's Use of Random Practice

Amy Alcott, a professional golfer on the LPGA tour, described in *Golf Magazine* (December, 1991) a drill she uses to help her make a swing of the correct length and strength for the distance. She practices pitch shots that are 20, 40, 60, and 80 yards from

flags marking each distance. Before she hits a ball, her teacher, Walter Keller, calls out the yardage for the shot. She looks at the flag, sets up, and swings. Then, her teacher calls out another yardage for the next shot. She says that "One after another, he'd call out yardages—60, 20, 40, 80, 40, 60." Alcott states that she finds this type of practice "invaluable," and repeats it from time to time throughout the season.

would occur in a game, players who had experienced the random practice schedule performed better than those who had practiced according to the blocked schedule.

In addition to these few examples, several other studies have found evidence that demonstrates the contextual interference effect for the learning of real-world skills. These include basketball shooting skills, tennis ground strokes, volleyball serves, rifle shooting, and computer game skills (see Brady, 1998, for discussions of the various studies involving these skills). When considered together with the research based on laboratory tasks, research involving real-world skills establishes the contextual interference effect as an important motor learning phenomenon.

What are the limits of the contextual interference effect? Although researchers have provided a large amount of evidence supporting the contextual interference effect, they also have shown that it does not apply to all motor skill learning situations. As a result, it is important to determine those characteristics that limit the generalization of the effect. Both task and learner characteristics have been the focus of speculations and investigations of this issue.

Task characteristics were proposed as the primary limiting factor for the contextual interference effect in the first comprehensive review of the research literature (Magill & Hall, 1990). They hypothesized that the contextual interference effect would more likely be found for task variations controlled by different generalized motor programs

(discussed in chapter 4) than by the same program. For example, when a person practices learning several skill variations characterized by different relative time patterns, a high contextual interference practice schedule should lead to better learning than a low contextual interference schedule. However, when the skill variations are characterized by the same relative time patterns, but different overall speeds, there should be no advantage to a high over a low contextual interference practice schedule. Thus, when removed from the context of the generalized motor program, the Magill and Hall hypothesis proposed that for the learning of skill variations, the contextual interference effect should be found when the characteristics of the variations are more dissimilar than similar.

In his assessment of the research that has investigated this hypothesis, Brady (1998) concluded that research involving laboratory tasks tends to support the hypothesis (e.g., Wood & Ging, 1991; Wulf & Lee, 1993). But, when research involves applied settings, higher amounts of contextual interference tend to enhance the learning of skill variations that are more similar than different. For example, compared to a low contextual interference practice schedule, moderate and high contextual interference practice schedules produced better learning of one-hand basketball set shots from different distances and angles (Landin & Hebert, 1997), but not for the learning of three different volleyball skills (French, Rink, & Werner, 1990).

Two reasons may account for this discrepancy between the laboratory and applied settings. First, the learning of sport skills requires more practice than has been included in those studies that have not found the effect. Because sport skills tend to be more complex and difficult than the typical laboratory skills used in contextual interference research, much more practice would be required to learn the sport skills. The second reason is that the learning of sports skills may require a progression of low to high amounts of contextual interference rather than only a high amount. Unfortunately, these two possibilities remain speculative until we have research evidence that supports or does not support them.

Researchers have also proposed that several *learner characteristics* may limit the effect of contextual interference on skill learning. Of the characteristics suggested, age and skill level appear to be the most likely limiting factors. When participants in studies have been children, the highest amounts of contextual interference typically do not enhance learning. In fact, Brady's (1998) review points out that for children, practice schedules that produce lower amounts of contextual interference tend to produce better learning. In terms of skill level, Hebert, Landin, and Solmon (1996) found that low-skilled students in university tennis classes performed forehand and backhand strokes better on a retention test following blocked practice, whereas high-skilled students performed no differently following blocked or alternating-trials practice schedules.

In summary, we know that certain factors limit the extent of the generalization of the contextual interference effect in motor skill learning situations. Unfortunately, we do not have a definitive account of the specific characteristics that establish those limits. Although there is general agreement that both task- and learner-related characteristics influence the degree to which contextual interference influences the learning of motor skill variations, we must wait for much more research evidence to allow us to confidently identify the specific characteristics.

Implications for the practitioner. Given the inconclusive nature of our present knowledge about the specific factors that limit the generalization of the effect of contextual interference on skill learning, what should the practitioner do? First, if you refer to figure 19.3, it is important to keep in mind that our present knowledge is different for the top and bottom portions of the continuum in this figure. In terms of the top half, we know that moderate and high amounts of contextual interference generally produce better learning of skill variations than low amounts. However, the bottom half of the figure remains unresolved in terms of the amount of contextual interference specific practice schedules produce when they are used for the learning of specific skill variations. As a result, view the continuum in figure 19.3 as representing a generic relationship between the various practice schedules and the amount of contextual interference each produces.

For the practitioner, when several variations of a skill must be learned, the best course of action would be to select a practice schedule that should produce a moderate to high amount of contextual interference (according to figure 19.3). But he or she should be prepared to modify the schedule after practice begins in order to accommodate individuals who do not respond well to the practice schedule. For example, some individuals may require a practice schedule that produces a lower amount of contextual interference, such as a blocked schedule, until they acquire the basic movement patterns of the skill variations. However, it is important that the practitioner base any practice schedule modification on performance difficulties evident from retention or transfer tests rather than from practice sessions.

Accounting for the Contextual Interference Effect

An important question that remains unanswered is this: *Why* does the contextual interference effect occur? Two hypotheses predominate the several accounts for this effect. One is the *elaboration hypothesis;* the other is known as the *action plan reconstruction hypothesis.* Although we will not debate these two hypotheses at length, we will consider each briefly.

The elaboration hypothesis. In their experiment that first showed the contextual interference effect for learning motor skills, Shea and Morgan (1979) proposed that the effect is related to the elaboration of the memory representation of the skill variations that a learner is practicing.[1] During random practice, a person engages in more strategies, as well as more different strategies, than an individual who practices according to a blocked schedule. Also, because in a random practice schedule the person retains in working memory all the skill variations he or she is practicing, the person can compare and contrast the variations so that each becomes distinct from the other. The result of engaging in these cognitive activities during practice is that the learner develops a memory representation for the skills that he or she then can access more readily during a test.

The action plan reconstruction hypothesis. An alternative hypothesis, by Lee and Magill (1985), stated that high amounts of contextual interference benefit learning because the interference requires a person to reconstruct an action plan on the next practice trial for a particular skill variation. This is necessary because the person has partially or completely forgotten the action plan he or she developed on the previous practice trial for that skill variation, because of the interference of the intervening practice trials of the other skill variations. In contrast, the person following a blocked practice schedule can use the same action plan he or she used on the previous trial, or a slightly modified one.

Consider the following illustration of how these different practice schedules would require different types of action plan activity. If you must add a long set of numbers and then you are immediately asked to do the same problem again, you probably will not re-add the numbers, but will remember and repeat only the answer. In contrast, if you are required to add several additional lists of numbers and then are given the first list again, you probably

will have forgotten the solution to that problem, and therefore will have to add the same numbers again. The intervening problem-solving activity requires you to re-solve a problem you have solved already.

Lee and Magill hypothesized that the high contextual interference practice condition is like the addition situation in which there are several other problems to solve before you see the first problem again. When a learner practices a motor skill, the interference created by the practice trials between two trials of the same skill variation causes the person to forget much of the action plan he or she developed for the first trial. As a result, the learner must reconstruct and modify that plan to attempt the skill on the next trial. On the other hand, the blocked practice schedule is like the addition problem in which the next trial follows immediately, and it is easy to remember the solution and therefore be successful on the next trial.

In the motor learning context, high contextual interference conditions require subjects to engage more actively in problem-solving activity during practice. Although this activity typically leads learners to perform more poorly during practice than they would with a low contextual interference schedule, this short-term performance deficit becomes a long-term benefit, because it leads to better retention and transfer test performance.

Research supports both hypotheses. Much research is needed to determine which of the two hypotheses best accounts for the contextual interference effect. In his review of the research literature, Brady (1998) discussed several studies that provide support for each hypothesis. This means that it may be that more than one explanation accounts for the contextual interference effect. However, this inconclusive state of affairs about the explanation should not detract from general agreement among researchers that this effect is an established learning phenomenon. Clearly, we need to know more about it. In addition to needing to know why it occurs, we need to know about the conditions that affect when it will occur and when it will

---

[1]Shea and Zimny (1983) developed a more formal version of the elaboration hypotheses.

A CLOSER LOOK

The Effectiveness of a Moderate Contextual Interference Practice Schedule

It may be preferable to learn some motor skill variations by practicing according to a schedule that involves a moderate rather than a high amount of contextual interference. A study by Landin and Hebert (1997) provides a good example of this type of practice situation.

Participants were university undergraduate students who had very little experience playing basketball. They practiced the one-hand set shot from six positions on the basketball court that varied in angle and distance from the basket. The *low contextual interference* group practiced according to a blocked schedule by shooting six consecutive shots from each position on each of three practice days. The *moderate contextual interference* group followed a blocked-serial schedule by shooting three shots from each position in sequence and then repeating the sequence.

The *high contextual interference* group followed a serial schedule by taking one shot from each position in sequence and then repeating the sequence six times.

On the day after the end of practice, each group performed three transfer tests: a twelve-trial blocked schedule for three of the practice positions; a twelve-trial serial schedule for the same three positions; and a ten-trial free-throw test (the free-throw line was one of the six practiced positions). All three groups improved their shooting performance during practice, buy they did not differ from each other at the end of practice. However, the blocked-serial practice schedule group performed better than the other two groups on all three tests. In addition, low amounts of contextual interference during practice led to poor adaptation to change. The blocked practice group maintained their end-of-practice performance level for the blocked and free-throw tests, but their performance on the serial test decreased to the level of their first day of practice.

---

not. And we need to determine why different practice schedules lead to different learning effects.

SUMMARY

Variations of movement and context experiences are important ingredients for practice conditions that increase a person's capability to perform the practiced skill successfully and to adapt to conditions he or she has not experienced previously. To determine an appropriate type and amount of practice variability, the teacher, coach, or therapist first must assess the performance characteristics of future situations in which the learner will perform the skill. The specific characteristics of the performance context that instructors need to vary in practice are regulatory and nonregulatory conditions. In addition, which of these conditions should be varied in practice depends on whether the skill is a closed or open skill. For closed skills that involve

regulatory conditions that do not change from one trial to the next, nonregulatory conditions should be varied in practice. But for closed skills that involve intertrial variability of the regulatory conditions, and for open skills, both regulatory and nonregulatory conditions should be varied.

A related practice condition concern is how to organize the variety of experiences within a practice session, unit of instruction, or treatment protocol. Researchers have gained insight into the best type of organization by implementing the contextual interference effect into practice scheduling. They have found that increasing the amount of interference created by practicing several skill variations within each practice session is preferable. For example, following a blocked practice schedule, such as practicing only one skill variation during a practice session, leads to poorer learning than following a random practice schedule in which the learner practices several skill variations randomly during each session. The contextual interference effect is a robust learning phenomenon; researchers have found it to apply to beginners as well as skilled performers, and to laboratory as well as real-world motor skills. However, the effect is not applicable to all skill learning situations. Although both task and learner characteristics appear to set the limits of the generalization of the effect, researchers have not reached a definitive conclusion concerning the specific factors related to these characteristics. Two hypotheses predominate as explanations for why this effect occurs. The first asserts that higher levels of contextual interference increase the elaborateness and distinctiveness of the memory representation of the skills the learner is practicing. The second holds that the learner must reconstruct the action plan for a preceding trial of a skill more actively when trials of a different skill have intervened.

RELATED READINGS

Hall, K. G. (1998, November/December). Using randomized drills to facilitate motor skill learning. *Strategies*, pp. 27–28, 35.

Horak, M. (1992). The utility of connectionism for motor learning: A reinterpretation of contextual interference in movement schemas. *Journal of Motor Behavior, 24,* 58–66.

Lee, T. D., Swanson, L. R., & Hall, A. L. (1991). What is repeated in a repetition? Effects of practice conditions on motor skill acquisition. *Physical Therapy, 71,* 150–156.

Lee, T. D., Wishart, L. R., Cunningham, S., & Carnahan, H. (1997). Modeled timing information during random practice eliminates the contextual interference effect. *Research Quarterly for Exercise and Sport, 68,* 100–105.

Sherwood, D. E. (1996). The benefits of random variable practice for spatial accuracy and error detection in a rapid aiming task. *Research Quarterly for Exercise and Sport, 67,* 35–43.

Shewokis, P. A., Del Rey, P., & Simpson, K. J. (1998). A test of retroactive inhibition as an explanation of contextual interference. *Research Quarterly for Exercise and Sport, 69,* 70–74.

Wright, D. L., Li, Y., & Coady, W. (1997). Cognitive processes related to contextual interference and observation learning: A replication of Blandin, Proteau, and Alain (1994). *Research Quarterly for Exercise and Sport, 68,* 106–109.

STUDY QUESTIONS

1. What is meant by the term *practice variability* and why is it important for skill learning?

2. Give an example of how you would implement practice variability for (a) a closed skill without intertrial variability; (b) a closed skill with intertrial variability; (c) an open skill.

3. (a) How is contextual interference related to the issue of organizing practice for learning several related motor skills and variations of a motor skill? (b) Describe four practice schedules and locate each on a contextual interference continuum.

4. Describe an example that illustrates how you would implement an appropriate amount of contextual interference into the practice schedule for (a) a novice learning a skill; (b) a skilled person.

5. What are two reasons researchers have proposed why contextual interference benefits motor skill learning?

Practice Distribution

*Concept: The spacing or distribution of practice
can affect both practice performance and
learning of motor skills*

APPLICATION

The professional who schedules instruction or rehabilitation sessions must make several decisions regarding how much time to devote to various activities within and across sessions. He or she must determine the amount of time to devote to each activity in a session, the amount of rest between activities within a session, the length of each session, and the amount of time between sessions.

For example, if you are a physical education teacher organizing a volleyball unit, you need to determine how much time you should devote in each class period to working on the various skills, drills, and other activities that you plan to include. If you have determined the total amount of practice time you want to devote to a given activity in the unit, and you know how many class periods you will have in the unit, you will know how much time you need to spend in each class period on that activity.

Similarly, if you are a physical or occupational therapist, you need to determine how much time a patient will spend on each activity within a session, how much rest time you should allow between activities in a session, when the next session should be, and so on. You also may need to instruct the patient concerning how to arrange his or her time schedule to do prescribed activities at home.

These examples illustrate two important practice scheduling decisions that are necessary next steps to the schedule decisions discussed in chapter 19. These two decisions concern how to distribute the time available for practicing a skill. As we discuss them, we will assume that you have determined the total amount of practice or therapy time needed for or available to this person. The first decision concerns how much time the person should spend performing a specific activity in a given practice or therapy session. In order to address this problem, you first must decide whether it is better to perform the activity for shorter or longer periods each day. Your answer will influence the number of days the person needs to achieve the total amount of practice or therapy time. The second scheduling concern is the optimal amount of rest between practice trials.

DISCUSSION

Practice distribution, or the spacing of practice, as researchers sometimes call it, has been a popular topic for research in motor learning for many years. The most popular era for this study extended from the 1930s through the 1950s when practice distribution was seen as a way to test learning theories popular at that time. However, researchers have continued to investigate practice distribution issues because of its relevance to applied settings in a variety of contexts.

One of the issues that was the focus of much of the early research concerned the amount of rest people need between practice trials to ensure an optimal learning environment. At issue was the question of whether *massed or distributed* practice trials provided for better learning of motor skills. Some researchers argued that distributed practice was better; others maintained that it did not make much difference which spacing strategy an instructor followed.

Although this early controversy focused on between-trial rest intervals, the study of practice distribution also concerns the amount of practice during each session of practice and the amount of rest between sessions. In this second practice distribution issue, the question of concern is whether it is better to have fewer but longer sessions, or more but shorter sessions.

Defining Massed and Distributed Practice

Researchers use the terms **massed practice** and **distributed practice** in a general way to distinguish practice distribution schedules rather than assign specific amounts of time, which would allow for more objective definitions for these terms. The best way to understand these terms is to know that a massed practice schedule involves longer active practice, or work time, and shorter rest periods than a distributed schedule. This rather vague definition is necessary because of the types of situations to which they apply.

When these terms apply to the *length and distribution of practice sessions,* a massed schedule will have fewer practice sessions than a distributed schedule, with each massed practice session requiring more and/or longer practice. A distributed schedule, on the other hand, will distribute the same amount of practice time across more sessions, so that each session is shorter than each session in the massed schedule; the distributed practice sessions must be extended over a longer period to achieve the same total amount of practice. When these terms apply to the *rest intervals between trials,* a massed schedule will have either no rest or a very short rest interval between trials. A distributed schedule will have much longer rest intervals than a massed schedule.

The Length and Distribution of Practice Sessions

For most instruction and rehabilitation situations, the primary practice distribution concern is how to use an allotted amount of time within and between practice sessions. An important consideration here is that many instruction and rehabilitation situations have specified limits for the amount of time available. For most clinical applications, a patient may receive treatment for only a limited number of sessions because of health care management restrictions. Also, in teaching and coaching situations, there is often little flexibility in the number of days available for classes or practice sessions. For example, if a teacher has only ten days for a unit of instruction, then the practice schedule must fit that limit. Similarly, if a dancer must perform in a concert that is one month away, then the rehearsal schedule must adjust accordingly. Thus, outside limitations may determine how many days a person should devote to practice. However, the instructor, coach, or therapist still decides the number of practice sessions and the length of each one.

The benefit of more and shorter sessions. Although there is not an abundance of research addressing the optimal number and length of practice sessions, the available evidence points to *the benefit of distributed practice.* The general result of experiments comparing a few long practice sessions with more frequent and shorter sessions is that practicing skills during shorter sessions leads to better learning.

The classic example of research supporting this general conclusion is a study published by Baddely and Longman (1978). They were attempting to determine the best way to schedule training sessions for postal workers on a mail-sorting machine, which

TABLE 20.1 Results of the Baddeley and Longman Experiment with Practice Distribution Schedules for Training Postal Workers

Practice Schedule	Number of Hours to Learn Keyboard	Number of Hours to Type 80 Keystrokes/Minute
1 hr/session-1 session/day (12 weeks training)	34.9	55
1 hr/session-2 sessions/day (6 weeks training)	43	75
2 hrs/session-1 session/day (6 weeks training)	43	67
2 hrs/session-2 session/day (3 weeks training)	49.7	80+

Source: Data from Baddeley, A. D., & Longman, D. J. A. (1978). The influence of length and frequency training session on the rate of learning to type. *Ergonomics, 21,* 627–635.

required operating a typewriterlike keyboard. All trainees received 60 hours of practice time and practiced 5 days each week. However, the researchers distributed this practice time in four different ways. Two groups practiced for 1 hour in each session. One of these groups practiced for only one session each day, which resulted in a total training time of 12 weeks, whereas the second group had two sessions each day, thereby reducing the number of weeks in training to 6. Two other groups practiced for 2 hours in each session. One of these groups had only one session each day, whereas the other had two sessions per day. These latter two groups therefore had 6 weeks and 3 weeks of training, respectively. As this situation demonstrates, there are a variety of ways to distribute 60 hours of practice. The most distributed schedule required workers to train for 12 weeks, whereas the most massed schedule allowed them to complete their training in only 3 weeks. The difference lay in how long each session was and how many sessions occurred each day.

Table 20.1 describes two performance measures used to determine the effectiveness of the different practice schedules. One was the amount of time the trainees needed to learn the keyboard. The shortest time was 34.9 hours, whereas the longest was 49.7 hours; these figures represent the most distributed and the most massed schedules, respectively. Thus, for learning the keyboard, keeping practice

sessions short and having only one session a day led to faster learning.

The second performance measure, which assessed motor performance, was typing speed. The trainees' goal was to type eighty keystrokes per minute. Only those in the most distributed schedule group attained this goal in the allotted training time of 60 hours (they did it in 55 hours). All of the other groups required additional practice time. It is interesting that those in the most massed schedule group, which practiced two 2-hour sessions each day, never achieved this goal. After 80 hours of practice they were still doing only a little better than seventy keystrokes per minute.

Retention tests were given 1, 3, and 9 months after the workers had finished training. After 9 months, the most massed group performed worse on the typing speed test than the other groups, which performed about equally. Finally, the researchers obtained a very

---

massed practice a practice schedule in which the amount of rest between practice sessions or trials is very short.

distributed practice a practice schedule in which the amount of rest between practice sessions or trials is relatively long.

revealing result from the trainees' own ratings of the training schedules. Although most workers preferred their own schedule, those in the most massed group preferred theirs the most, whereas members of the most distributed liked theirs the least. Interestingly, these preferences were exactly opposite to the performance test results.

The results of this experiment indicate that fitting 60 hours of training into 3 weeks, where there had to be two 2-hour practice sessions each day, was a poor practice schedule. Although those in the most distributed schedule generally attained performance goals in the shortest time, they did not perform any better than two of the other groups on the retention tests. Given all the results, the authors concluded that the 1-hour training sessions were more desirable than the 2-hour sessions, and that one session per day was only slightly more effective than two sessions per day. However, having two 2-hour sessions each day was not a good training regime.

More recent studies have shown similar learning benefits for distributed practice. For example, Annett and Piech (1985) found that two 5-trial training sessions separated by one day led to better learning of a computer target-shooting game than one ten-trial session. One trial involved shooting at ten singly presented moving targets. The authors assessed learning by a performance test given one day after the end of the training session. The distributed group not only had more "hits" on the test but also had less error in the shooting attempts. Bouzid and Crawshaw (1987) reported similar results for the learning of word processing skills. Typists who practiced twelve skills during two sessions of 35 and 25 min each, separated by a 10-min break, required less time to learn the skills and had fewer errors on a test than typists who practiced the skills during one 60-min session.

The Intertrial Interval and Practice Distribution

By far the greatest amount of research on the distribution of practice has investigated the length of the intertrial interval. One of the problems confronted when trying to understand this research relates to the definition problem described earlier in this discussion. For example, some researchers have defined massed practice rather narrowly, to mean practice with no rest between trials, and distributed practice to mean including rest intervals between trials. Other researchers have defined massed practice more broadly, to mean practice in which the time spent during a practice trial is greater than the amount of rest between trials, and distributed practice to mean practice in which the amount of rest between trials equals or exceeds the amount of time during a trial.

To elaborate on the general definitions presented earlier, we shall define *massed practice* as practice in which the amount of rest between trials is either very short or nonexistent so that practice is relatively continuous. *Distributed practice* is practice in which the amount of rest between trials or groups of trials is relatively long. Although the terms "very short" and "relatively long" in these definitions are somewhat ambiguous, we use them here so that we can generalize as much as possible from the research literature on massed versus distributed practice to motor skill learning situations. The precise meanings of these terms will vary with the skill and learning situation to which they apply.

A history of controversy. Although a great deal of research literature exists concerning the distribution of practice as it relates to the length of the intertrial interval, it is filled with controversy about which schedule leads to better learning. The controversy is evident in reviews of this literature as well as motor learning textbooks; both provide a variety of answers to the practice distribution question.

Two problems underlie the controversy surrounding this issue. The first relates to the issue of practice performance versus learning effects. Many of the experiments on massed versus distributed practice did not include retention or transfer trials. The second problem is that researchers generally have failed to consider that the two practice distribution schedules may have different learning effects on different types of skills.

Two reviews of the distributed practice research literature have helped resolve these two problems

**Implications from Research
on Massed versus Distributed
Practice for Scheduling Practice
or Rehabilitation Sessions**

- **Practice sessions can be too long.** When in
doubt about how long a session should be, opt for
a shorter rather than a longer amount of time. If
learners need more time, add more sessions.
- **More frequent practice sessions are preferable**
to fewer sessions.
- **Time saved in terms of the number of days of
practice can be a false savings,** because massing
sessions too close together can lead to poorer
long-term results.
- **The length and number of sessions desired by
students, trainees, or patients may not
represent the best schedule** for learning the
skill. In the Baddeley and Longman study, if the
postal trainees had been given their choice, they
would have chosen the schedule that allowed
them to complete their training in the fewest

days, but that was the poorest schedule for
learning the skill.
- **Make practice trials relatively short for skills
that last a reasonably long time and require
repetitive movements.** For beginners learning
skills such as swimming, bicycling, typing, piano
playing, and dancing: shorter practice trials that
are repeated more frequently lead to better
learning than longer trials that are infrequently
repeated. For more advanced learners, the
common dictum, "Keep trying it until you get it
right," should only be used if the continuous
attempts are relatively short in length and
interspersed with ample amounts of rest (or other
activity).
- **Make rest intervals relatively short for skills
that involve relatively brief amounts of time.**
For beginners learning skills such as hitting a golf
ball, serving a tennis ball, shooting a basketball,
throwing darts, prehensive actions: short rest
intervals between trials lead to better learning
than longer rest intervals between trials.

and the controversy about which practice schedule
is better for learning motor skills (Donovan &
Radosevich, 1999; Lee & Genovese, 1988). Both
reviews involved a statistical analysis, known as
meta-analysis, to evaluate the research literature.
Their conclusion was that the type of task was an
important variable in determining practice distribution effects for schedules related to the length of
intertrial rest intervals. More specifically, Lee and
Genovese (1988, 1989) provided evidence that the
type of practice distribution schedule that results in
better learning depends on whether the skill is continuous or discrete. We will look at each of these
types of skills next.

Continuous skills. Continuous skills have been the
most common type of motor skills used to investigate the effects of massed versus distributed practice between trials. And the most popular task has
been the rotary pursuit task, in which a person must

keep a handheld stylus in contact with a small disk
on a rotating turntable for as long as possible. A
trial is usually a specified length of time, such as 20
or 30 sec. What makes this type of task useful for
investigating the issue of massed versus distributed
practice is that it is quite easy to specify massed
and distributed intertrial interval lengths. Massed
practice schedules typically have few, if any, seconds of rest between trials, whereas the intervals in
distributed schedules are as long as or longer than
the trials themselves. Because of this, researchers
can establish intertrial interval lengths that are
readily identifiable as distinctly massed or distributed. The Lee and Genovese (1988) review found
that the consistent result has been that *distributed
schedules lead to better learning* than massed
schedule for learning continuous motor skills.

Discrete skills. When researchers use discrete skills
to investigate the issue of intertrial massed versus

**Relating Practice Distribution
and Contextual Interference
to Skill Learning Contexts**

The concept of contextual interference can be incorporated into practice distribution by organizing practice sessions to include principles related to both. The following are some examples that relate to three different skill learning contexts.

- **Physical education class.** If several drills or other kinds of activity are planned for the day's lesson, use a station-organization approach by assigning each skill or activity to a location in the gym or on the field so that there are several stations. Divide the class into groups and assign each to a station. Let the groups stay in their stations for about 12–15 minutes and then rotate to the next station. Continue this rotation

approach for the entire period. If the class period is sufficiently long, allow for two or more rotations.
- **Sports-related practice.** Practices for team and individual sports typically include several activities. Rather than spend an extended amount of time on any one activity, divide in half the amount of time planned for each activity, and do each activity as two sets during practice. The two sets can be randomly or serially scheduled during the practice session.
- **Physical rehabilitation session.** Similar to sports-related practice sessions, rehab sessions typically involve several activities. If the planned activities allow, apply the approach described for sports-related practice by dividing in half the total amount of time planned for each activity, and do each activity as two randomly or serially scheduled sets during the session.

distributed practice, a problem arises that is directly related to the definition problem we discussed earlier. If a massed schedule allows no rest between trials, whereas a distributed schedule involves a rest interval that is the same length as the practice trial, then the two contrasted intertrial intervals will be essentially the same length, because a discrete response is typically very short. For example, if people are practicing a rapid-aiming task that has a duration of approximately 150 msec, the distributed practice condition could, by definition, have a 150-msec intertrial interval. But if the massed condition had no rest between trials, only 150 msec would separate the two practice schedules. Thus, the operational definition of the terms massed and distributed becomes especially important in experiments using discrete tasks. Probably one reason this has not troubled researchers is that discrete tasks seldom have been used for comparing massed to distributed practice. In fact, in their comprehensive review, Lee and Genovese (1988) found only one study in the research literature that used a discrete task (Carron, 1969). The results of that study, and one subse-

quently reported by Lee and Genovese (1989), provided evidence that *massed practice schedules* result in better learning for discrete motor skills.

SUMMARY

An important decision teachers, coaches, and therapists must make is how to distribute the time that they have been allotted for practicing specific skills. Researchers investigating this issue have compared massed and distributed schedules of practice. Two types of practice schedule concerns are relevant to this issue. One involves the length and frequency of practice sessions. Research evidence is consistent in showing that practice sessions can be too long and too infrequent to lead to optimal learning. Generally, people learn skills better in larger numbers of shorter sessions of practice than in sessions that are long and fewer in number. The second practice schedule issue is the length of the intertrial interval, which is the rest period between trials. Researchers have found that the optimum intertrial interval length depends on the type of skill being learned. For continuous skills, distributed schedules are generally better than massed ones for learning. However, for discrete skills, researchers have found massed practice schedules are preferable.

RELATED READINGS

Ammons, R. B. (1988). Distribution of practice in motor skill acquisition: A few questions and comments. *Research Quarterly for Exercise and Sport, 59,* 288–290.

Chamberlin, C., & Lee, T. (1993). Arranging practice conditions and designing instruction. In R. N. Singer, M. Murphey, & K. Tennant (Eds.), *Handbook of research on sport psychology* (pp. 213–241). New York: Macmillan. (Read section on "Distribution of Practice," pp. 219–221.)

Rhodenizer, L., Bowers, C. A., & Bergondy, M. (1998). Team practice schedules: What do we know? *Perceptual and Motor Skills, 87,* 31–34.

Schmidt, R. A., & Bjork, R. A. (1992). New conceptualizations of practice: Common principles in three paradigms suggest new concepts for training. *Psychological Science, 3,* 207–217.

STUDY QUESTIONS

1. Describe how the concept of practice distribution is related to the intertrial interval and to the length and distribution of practice sessions. Describe a motor skill learning situation for each.

2. Discuss the Baddeley and Longman study with postal worker trainees in terms of how the study demonstrates the benefit of distributed over massed practice sessions for learning a motor skill.

3. How do massed and distributed intertrial interval schedules differentially influence the learning of discrete and continuous motor skills?

4. Why do you think there is a difference in how massed and distributed intertrial interval schedules influence the learning of discrete and continuous skills?

5. Describe how you would implement your knowledge about massed and distributed practice in *one* of the following situations: a physical education or dance class; a practice session for a sport; a physical or occupational therapy session.

CHAPTER

The Amount of Practice

Concept: The amount of practice influences the amount of learning, although the benefit is not always proportional to the time required

APPLICATION

It seems reasonable to assume that the more practice a person has, the better his or her performance will be in some future situation. In fact, the conventional wisdom about skills seems to be that how well a person will perform a skill is directly related to the amount of practice the person has had. Consider some examples. A dance teacher would encourage a dancer who was a bit tentative in certain parts of a routine to spend as much time as possible going over the routine repeatedly in practice. A golf instructor would try to help a person be more successful when putting in golf by encouraging the person to spend as much time as possible on the practice putting green. And a therapist would encourage a rehabilitation patient to practice the skill he or she was relearning as often as possible. Our experiences in situations like these lead us to accept the "more practice is better" approach. But ironically, although this approach seems logical, research evidence indicates that it is not always the best alternative.

The potential problem is that when a person practices a motor skill, he or she may reach a point of "diminishing returns" in terms of the benefits derived from the practice in proportion to the amount of time the practice takes. More simply

stated, this means that the performance benefit the person gains is less than the cost in time he or she must spend practicing. This "benefits versus time" trade-off is an important consideration that professionals should not overlook when they design practice sessions.

DISCUSSION

The amount of practice a person devotes to a skill is critical for learning motor skills. This is especially the case when the person has the attaining of expertise as a goal. As we discussed in chapter 12, the impressive work by Ericsson has shown that expertise in any field is the result of intense practice for a minimum of ten years (Ericsson et al., 1993). Clearly, for achieving expertise, more practice is better than less. However, the amount of practice required to attain expertise is not our focus here. Instead, we will focus on the amount of practice a person needs to ensure achieving a specific learning goal associated with a specific period of practice.

There are many situations in which it is important to determine the amount of practice people should experience to achieve specific performance goals. For example, a person might need to prepare for a skills test in a physical education activity during the unit of instruction covering that activity. In sports settings, the amount of practice time available is restricted by a season's schedule or by rules establish by professional associations. And, in rehabilitation contexts, the amount of time available for therapy is typically restricted by healthcare provider agencies.

As we address the issue of optimal amounts of practice, we will limit our discussion to these types of situations, and establish some guidelines for the effective and efficient use of available practice time. As suggested by the examples we just considered, this limited focus is particularly relevant to those involved in settings that involve strict practice time limitations on teachers, coaches, and therapists.

Overlearning and Learning Motor Skills

Researchers historically have investigated the relationship between the amount of practice and the achievement of specific performance goals within the topic of *overlearning*. **Overlearning** is the continuation of practice beyond the amount needed to achieve a certain performance criterion. A teacher, coach, or therapist implements overlearning by establishing a performance criterion, determining the amount of practice time the learner needed to attain that criterion, and then requiring some percentage of that practice time as extra practice.

When we view it from a theoretical perspective, the idea of assigning extra practice has merit. Those who hold a motor program–based view of motor learning would say that extra practice helps strengthen the generalized motor program and response schema for the skill a person is learning, so that the person can call it into action more readily when necessary. From a dynamic patterns perspective, extra practice is a means by which a learner increases the stability of the coordination and control characteristics in the performance of the skill.

Driskell, Willis, and Copper (1992) presented a review and analysis of fifteen research studies that investigated several hypotheses related to overlearning. The first notable point about this review is that the issue of overlearning has not generated a

great deal of research over the years. The fifteen studies covered research articles published from 1929 to 1982. However, these studies involved almost 4,000 subjects, which gives us a good basis for discerning the influence of overlearning on skill acquisition and how various factors influence overlearning. The results of this review indicated that for motor skill learning, overlearning has a positive influence on retention performance. And when 50 to 200 percent amounts of extra practice were analyzed, the higher percentages resulted in relatively proportionate higher retention test performance.

Although the Driskell et al. (1992) review provides a comprehensive overview of overlearning as it relates to skill acquisition, it does not evaluate effects related to specific types of motor skills. Because motor learning research has shown that certain types of skills relate to some distinct characteristics with regards to overlearning, we will consider three examples in the following sections.

The overlearning strategy for learning procedural skills. *Procedural skills* constitute one type of motor skill particularly well suited to deriving benefits from an overlearning practice strategy. A procedural skill is an interesting combination of cognitive and motor components. It typically requires a person to perform a series of discrete movements, which individually are relatively easy to execute. However, to accomplish the total task, the performer must know which movements to make, and in what order. These types of skills are especially common in occupational, industrial, and military settings. For example, people are performing procedural skills when their jobs require them to sort mail into appropriate bins, put together the components of a circuit board for a computer, or type from a written text.

---

overlearning   practice that continues beyond the amount needed to achieve a certain performance criterion.

A common problem with procedural skills is that people tend to forget what to do to carry out the entire procedure. This is particularly characteristic of procedural skills that they do not perform routinely every day. For example, several years ago, the U.S. Army was interested in improving the performance of soldiers assembling and disassembling a machine gun. This skill is especially interesting to study because soldiers typically learn it in a short training period, but do not perform it again until some time after training; it is not a routine part of their daily duties. The problem was that when they performed a later test on this skill, the soldiers typically showed a large decrement in performance, compared to how they had performed at the end of training. To overcome this problem, researchers for the U.S. Army Research Institute (Schendel & Hagman, 1982) proposed that an overlearning training strategy (which they referred to as *overtraining*) would be effective for decreasing the amount the soldiers forgot about the procedure.

The researchers compared two forms of overtraining with a no-overtraining situation. An "immediate" overtraining condition required soldiers to perform 100 percent more trials than were necessary to achieve a performance criterion of one correct assembly/disassembly trial. The second overtraining condition also involved an additional 100 percent more practice trials, but these trials were administered as "refresher" training midway through the 8-week retention interval used for all subjects. Results showed that both of these overtraining groups performed better than the no-overtraining control group on the retention test, which required the soldiers to practice until they were again able to assemble and disassemble the gun correctly on a trial. However, the two overtraining groups did not differ from each other in the number of trials it took to retrain to the criterion performance of one correct trial.

Based on the results of this experiment, the authors recommended the immediate overtraining procedure, because it was more cost- and time-effective. Because the trainees were already in the training session, it would take less time and money to have them engage in additional practice there than to bring them back several weeks later for a refresher training session.

The overlearning strategy for learning dynamic balance skills. In an experiment that involved learning a skill that has less of a cognitive component than the gun disassembly/assembly skill, Melnick (1971) investigated the use of overlearning for a dynamic balance skill. In addition to addressing the question of whether practice beyond what the learner needed to achieve a performance criterion was beneficial, Melnick asked whether there was an optimal amount of extra practice. In this experiment, people practiced balancing on a stabilometer until they were able to achieve a performance criterion of 28 out of 50 sec. After achieving this criterion, each group was required to perform further trials in one of the following amounts: 0 percent (none), 50 percent, 100 percent, or 200 percent of the initial number of trials of practice. Then, all participants performed a retention test twice, one week and then one month after practice.

The results showed that extra practice was beneficial. All the groups that engaged in practice beyond what they needed to achieve the performance criterion performed better on the retention tests. More interesting, however, was the result that there appeared to be *a point of diminishing returns* for the amount of retention performance benefit in relation to the amount of extra practice. The group that had 50 percent additional practice did as well on the retention tests as the groups that had 100 percent and 200 percent extra practice. So, although additional practice was beneficial, increasing the amount of additional practice beyond a certain amount was not proportionally more beneficial to retention performance.

The overlearning strategy in a physical education class. Researchers also have demonstrated the presence of this phenomenon of "diminishing returns" from increases in the amount of practice for learning skills in physical education classes. A good example of this is an experiment by

Goldberger and Gerney (1990). In a unit of instruction, fifth-grade boys and girls practiced several football skills. The goal of this unit was to help students improve their performance of these skills. To simplify matters, we will look only at the two-step football punt. One group practiced these skills according to a teacher-rotated format, in which the teacher divided the class into five subgroups and assigned each to one of five stations where they practiced the skills for 5 min. At the end of every 5 min, students rotated to a new station. Another group of students practiced according to a learner-rotated format: they received index cards describing what they needed to do at each station and then were told to use their 25 min efficiently to practice each skill. Everyone practiced like this for two class periods on 2 days. The next week, the students performed the skills in a test.

The results showed that the two groups differed in terms of the number of practice trials for this skill, but not in test performance. The teacher-rotated format group actually practiced the skill an average of 7 more trials than the learner-rotated format group. Students in the learner-rotated format group performed from 0 to 67 trials, whereas students in the teacher-rotated group performed from 0 to 87 trials. But there was no difference between the groups in the amount of improvement in their punting performance scores. The additional practice time induced by the teacher-rotated format did not yield an additional skill improvement benefit. Thus, given the time constraints of the unit of instruction, the learner-rotated format was superior, because it provided more efficient use of that time.

The Overlearning Strategy Can Lead to Poor Test Performance

Although the overlearning strategy typically benefits skill learning, some evidence shows that learning deficits may result from providing *too many* extra practice trials. Shea and Kohl (1990) reported an example of this effect in an experiment in which participants learned to push a handle with a specified amount of force (175N). One group practiced this skill for 85 trials. Another group also practiced this skill for 85 trials, but in addition practiced the same skill at four other force goals (125N, 150N, 200N, and 225N) for 51 trials each, for a total of 289 practice trials. A third group practiced the skill with the 175N goal force for 289 trials. One day later, all participants engaged in a retention test in which they performed the skill with the goal force of 175N for 10 trials.

The results showed that the group that practiced the 175N goal force for 289 trials had the poorest performance on the initial 5 trials of the retention test. In contrast, the group that practiced the variable goals performed best. Results for the group that practiced only 85 trials of the 175N goal fell between those of the two other groups. The differences between these groups were most distinct on the first retention trial. However, on the final 5 trials of the retention test, all three groups performed similarly. These results were replicated in another experiment by the same authors (Shea & Kohl, 1991).

The significance of the results reported in the Shea and Kohl experiments is that they run counter to what most people would expect. First, adding more practice beyond a certain amount did not improve retention performance. Second, practice of variations of the criterion skill in addition to practice of the criterion skill itself resulted in retention performance better than that following practice of only the criterion skill. Third, additional practice beyond a certain amount was detrimental for initial performance trials on a test given some time after practice ended.

Overlearning and Other Practice Variables

It can be useful for a learner to continue to practice a skill even though he or she can perform it correctly; such practice increases the permanence of the person's capability to perform the skill at some future time. However, the research investigating the overlearning strategy has shown rather conclusively that *the amount of practice is not the critical variable influencing motor skill acquisition.* The amount of practice invariably interacts with some other variable to influence learning. You have seen this interaction with such variables as the type of

A CLOSER LOOK

Implementing the Overlearning Strategy

- The overlearning practice strategy works best when the teacher, coach, or therapist knows how much practice (i.e., number of trials or amount of time) a learner needs to achieve a certain performance level.
- Overlearning practice is effective for skills that a learner will practice during a specified period only, but will not perform for some time after that. The task in the Schendel and Hagman (1982) experiment of disassembling and assembling the machine gun is a good example. Although the soldiers did not need to perform this task every day, they needed to know how to do so in case a situation arose in which they were required to follow those procedures. The most effective

practice procedure required the soldiers to engage in 100 percent more practice trials than the number they required *to perform the skill correctly one time.*

- The instructor should *not* base the amount of extra practice on the notion that "more is better." There can be a point of diminishing returns, and it is even possible that the additional practice can lead to negative test performance. Although the instructor needs to determine the actual amount of extra practice that is best for each situation, a good place to start is to require 100 percent additional practice beyond the amount the learner requires to achieve the specified performance criterion.
- Practice requiring the performance of variations of skill characteristics can be an effective means of establishing an overlearning practice situation.

KR and the variability of practice. From this perspective, the typical overlearning research study indicates that a certain amount of practice is beneficial to a point. However, for continued performance improvement that is more proportionate to the time and effort given to the practice, the instructor and/or learner also must take other practice condition characteristics into account. This does not mean that the amount of practice is unimportant. It does mean that the amount of practice cannot be considered in isolation, but in terms of its interaction with other practice condition variables.

SUMMARY

Research investigating the practice strategy of engaging in extra practice demonstrates that the view that "more is better" is not always true for the learning of motor skills, at least in terms of the benefits derived in relation to the amount of practice experienced. There appears to be a point of "dimin-

ishing returns" for amount of practice. Although the amount of practice is an important concern for the instructor, it is more important to consider how the amount of practice interacts with other variables influencing motor skill learning. As the amount of time a person spends in practicing a skill increases, the value of certain conditions of practice decreases. However, the person's need to incorporate other variables into the practice routines does increase.

RELATED READINGS

Chamberlin, C., & Lee, T. (1993). Arranging practice conditions and designing instruction. In R. N. Singer, M. Murphey, & K. Tennant (Eds.), *Handbook of research on sport psychology* (pp. 213–241). New York: Macmillan. (Read section on "Amount of Practice," pp. 236–237.)

Croce, R. V., & Jacobson, W. H. (1986). The application of two-point touch cane technique to theories of motor control and learning: Implications for orientation and mobility training. *Journal of Visual Impairment and Blindness, 80,* 790–793.

STUDY QUESTIONS

1. What is meant by the term *overlearning* as it relates to learning motor skills?

2. Describe a skill learning situation in which an overlearning practice strategy would help a person learn that skill.

3. (a) Define the term "procedural skill" as it is commonly used in the motor learning literature. (b). What was the recommendation from the results of the Schendel and Hagman study for using an overlearning strategy to help people learn a procedural skill. Indicate why they made this recommendation.

4. Describe how the results of the study by Melnick demonstrate that the view "more is better" may not be the best approach to implementing an overlearning strategy to help people learn a motor skill.

5. Considering various types of practice conditions, discuss why it would be possible for two groups of people who are learning a new motor skill to have the same amount of practice, but one group learns the skill better than the other group.

Whole and Part Practice

*Concept: Base decisions about practicing skills
as wholes or in parts on the complexity and
organization characteristics of the skills*

APPLICATION

An important decision you must make when you teach any motor skill concerns whether it is better to have the learner practice the skill in its entirety or by parts. An argument in favor of practicing a skill as a whole is that this experience would help a learner get a better feel for the flow and timing of all the component movements of the skill. The opposing argument is that practicing the skill by parts reduces the complexity of the skill and allows the learner to emphasize performing each part correctly before putting the whole skill together.

One of the reasons this decision is important is that it affects efficiency of instruction. For many skills, both methods of practicing the skill—as a whole and in parts—will be effective in helping the students learn the skill. However, it is not likely that both methods will help the student attain the same level of competency in the same amount of time. One method generally will be more efficient than the other as a means of attaining competent performance.

Consider the following sport skill instruction situation as an example of the significance of the decision to use whole versus part practice. Suppose you are teaching a beginning tennis class. You are preparing to teach the serve. Most tennis instruc-

tion books break down the serve into six or seven parts: the grip, stance, backswing, ball toss, forward swing, ball contact, and follow-through. You must decide whether to have the students practice all of these parts together as a whole or to have them practice each component or group of components separately.

The question of whether to use whole or part practice also confronts professionals in a rehabilitation setting. For example, when a patient needs to learn the task of getting out of bed and getting into a wheelchair, this decision comes into play. Although this task has distinct and identifiable parts, the therapist must determine whether to have the patient practice each part separately or always practice the whole sequence.

DISCUSSION

The issue of whether to use whole or part practice has been a topic of discussion in the motor learning literature since the early 1900s. Unfortunately, that early research often led to more confusion than to understanding. One of the reasons was that researchers tended to investigate the issue in terms of whether one or the other type of practice is better for learning specific skills, without concern for observing skill-related characteristics that could help them make useful generalizations about which practice scheme would be preferable for certain skills. For example, the question of whole versus part practice was investigated by Barton (1921) for learning a maze task; Brown (1928) for learning a piano score; Knapp and Dixon (1952) for learning to juggle; and Wickstrom (1958) for learning gymnastic skills. Although this research provided useful information about teaching these specific skills, it did little to establish a guiding principle for decisions about whether to use whole or part practice.

Skill Complexity and Organization

A breakthrough in understanding the issue of whole versus part practice occurred in the early 1960s when James Naylor and George Briggs (1963) hypothesized that the organization and complexity characteristics of a skill could provide the basis for a decision to use either whole or part practice. This hypothesis made it possible for instructors to predict for any skill which method of practice would be preferable.

Naylor and Briggs defined *complexity* in a way that is consistent with the term's use in this text. They stated that *complexity* refers to the number of parts or components in a skill, as well as the information-processing demands of the task. This means that a highly complex skill would have many components and demand much attention, especially from a beginner. Performing a dance routine, serving a tennis ball, and getting out of bed and into a wheelchair are examples of highly complex skills. Low-complexity skills have few component parts and demand relatively limited attention. For example, the skills of shooting an arrow and picking up a cup are low in complexity. It is important to keep the term *complexity* distinct from *difficulty*. As you saw in the discussion of Fitts' law in chapter 5, a low-complexity skill can be difficult to perform.

The **organization** of a skill refers to the relationship among the component parts of a skill. When the parts are very interdependent—when the way one part is performed depends on the way the

An important part of teaching the skill of rollerblading is the decision to have the students practice it as a whole skill or to use a part practice strategy.

previous part is performed—then the skill has a high degree of organization. Shooting a jump shot in basketball and walking are examples. On the other hand, when the parts of a skill are rather independent of one another, the skill is considered to be low in organization. Examples here include many dance routines and handwriting certain words.

---

organization when applied to a complex motor skill, the relationship among the components of the skill.

Skill characteristics and the decision to use whole or part practice. Based on the Naylor and Briggs hypothesis, assessing the degrees of complexity and organization of a skill and determining how these two characteristics relate helps a teacher, coach, or therapist decide whether to use whole or part practice. If the skill is *low in complexity and high in organization,* practice of the whole skill is the better choice. This means that people learn relatively simple skills in which the few component parts are highly related most efficiently using the whole practice method. For example, the skills of buttoning a button, throwing a ball, and putting a golf ball have this combination of characteristics. On the other hand, people learn skills that are *high in complexity and low in organization* most efficiently by the part method. For example, the skills of serving a tennis ball; reaching for, grasping, and drinking from a cup; and shifting gears on a car have these characteristics.

To determine effectively which of these complexity and organization combinations describe a particular skill, first analyze the skill. This analysis needs to focus on identifying the skill's component parts and the extent to which those parts are interdependent. When performance of one part of a skill depends on what precedes or follows that part, the skill is higher in organization. Next, it is necessary to decide which part of the continuum of skill complexity and organization best represents the skill.

Practicing Parts of a Skill

The decision to use a part practice strategy unfortunately solves only part of the problem, because there are several different ways to implement a part practice approach to the practice of a skill. When selecting a part practice strategy, it is important to apply transfer of learning principles, which we discussed in chapter 14. Part practice strategies should involve positive transfer between and among the practiced parts of a task, and between the practiced parts and the whole task.

In their important review of the research literature related to skill training methods, Wightman and Lintern (1985) classified three commonly used part-task strategies. One called **fractionization,** involves practicing individual limbs first for a bimanual coordination skill. A second method, called **segmentation,** involves separating the skill into parts and then practicing the parts so that after the learner practices one part, he or she then practices that part together with the next part, and so on. Researchers also have called this method the *progressive part method* and the chaining method. A third method of part practice is called **simplification.** This method is actually a variation of a whole practice strategy and involves reducing the difficulty of the whole skill or of different parts of the skill.

Fractionization: Practicing bimanual coordination skills. Many of the motor skills discussed throughout this text have required people to simultaneously move their arms to achieve a specific spatial and/or temporal goal. We have referred to these skills as bimanual coordination skills. Recall from the discussion of coordination in chapter 4 that the coordination tendency is for the arms to move spatially and temporally together. What this means in terms of part versus whole practice is that because of this coordination tendency, the task is high in organization, which indicates that a whole practice approach would be preferable. However, when the task requires the two arms simultaneously to do different spatial and/or temporal movements, the question of the use of a part practice strategy becomes more of an issue.

The playing of many musical instruments, such as the violin and accordion, require the person to produce distinctly different movement patterns. Other instruments, such as the piano and drums, may require this type of bimanual movement characteristic. Sport skills such as the sidestroke in swimming and the tennis serve also involve this type of bimanual coordination. Is a part practice strategy the best approach for learning these types of skills, or would a whole practice approach be preferable? Although some controversy exists among researchers, there is evidence to support either approach (see Walter & Swinnen, 1994). If a

A CLOSER LOOK

An Example of Making the Decision Regarding Use of Whole or Part Practice

Use skill analysis to determine whether to practice juggling three balls as a whole or in parts:

Skill Analysis

Complexity characteristics
1. Hold the three balls in two hands.
2. Toss ball 1 from hand 1.
3. Catch ball 1 in hand 2 while tossing ball 2 with hand 2.
4. Catch ball 2 in hand 1 while tossing ball 3 with hand 2.
5. Catch ball 3 in hand 1 while tossing ball 1 with hand 2.
6. Repeat steps 2 and 5.
7. Between-component timing: critical for performance.

Organization characteristics. Doing any one part without doing the part that precedes or follows it does not allow the learner to experience critical between-component timing aspects.

Conclusion. Three-ball juggling involves several component parts that are highly interdependent. Therefore, juggling three balls is relatively high in complexity and in organization. *Practicing the whole skill* is the predicted appropriate method.

Empirical Evidence Supporting the Whole Practice Prediction

Knapp and Dixon (1952) told university students who had no previous juggling experience to practice until they could make 100 consecutive catches while juggling 3 paddle tennis balls. Results showed that students who followed a whole practice approach achieved this goal in 65 trials, whereas those who followed a part practice regime needed 77 trials.

---

part practice approach is used, the most appropriate strategy is *fractionization.*

The fractionization strategy involves practicing each arm or hand individually before performing the skill bimanually. A relevant question related to the use of this strategy is, Does it matter which arm or hand practices first? A feature of bimanual coordination skills that is important to consider in answering this question is that one arm or hand will sometimes perform a movement, or sequence of movements, that is more difficult or complex than the other. For example, one hand may perform a movement that requires a higher degree of movement accuracy than the other, or one hand may perform a movement that involves more component parts to it. Research that has addressed this question (e.g., Sherwood, 1994) suggests that practice should begin with the hand or arm that must perform the more difficult or complex movement.

Segmentation: The progressive part method. Although practicing individual parts can be helpful

in learning a skill, the learner can experience difficulty later, when he or she has to put the part back together with the whole skill. One way to overcome this problem is to use the *progressive part*

---

fractionization a part-task training method related to bimanual skills that involves practicing each arm separately before performing with the arms together.

segmentation a part-task training method that involves separating the skill into parts and then practicing the parts so that after one part is practiced, it is then practiced together with the next part, and so on; also known as the progressive part method.

simplification a part-task training method that involves reducing the difficulty of specific parts or features of a skill.

A CLOSER LOOK

Whole and Part Practice Conditions That Facilitate the Learning of Bimanual Coordination Skills

Bimanual coordination skills that require each arm to simultaneously perform different movements are difficult to learn because of the tendency for the two arms to spatially and temporally move together. Walter and Swinnen (1994) discussed various training approaches that would facilitate learning to break this "habit" for skills that require different simultaneous arm movements. Their research involved a task that required participants to place each forearm on a lever on a tabletop, and to move them simultaneously so that one arm made a one-direction elbow-flexion movement and the other made a two-direction elbow-flexion-extension movement in a criterion amount of time. Their research demonstrated that the following

three techniques accomplished this learning goal. Note that one involved part-task practice and two involved whole-task practice.

- **Fractionization.** The movement patterns were practiced separately for each arm, and then with the two arms moving simultaneously.
- **Speed-based simplification.** Initial practice of the bimanual task was at a slower speed than the criterion; subsequent sets of trials involved the progressive increase of the speed until the criterion speed was practiced.
- **Augmented feedback.** Practice involved the two arms simultaneously moving and augmented feedback provided after each trial as KP (the acceleration-time traces for each limb) or KR (correlation values indicating the degree of between-arm relationship).

method. Rather than practicing all parts separately before putting them together as a whole skill, the learner practices the first part as an independent unit, then practices the second part—first separately, and then together with the first part. In this way, each independent part progressively joins a larger part. As practice continues, the learner eventually practices the entire skill as a whole.

A common example of the progressive part method is a frequently used practice scheme for learning the breaststroke in swimming. The breaststroke is easily subdivided into two relatively independent parts, the leg kick and the arm action. Because a difficult aspect of learning the breaststroke is the timing of the coordination of these two parts, it is helpful for the learner to reduce the attention demands of the whole skill by practicing each part independently first. This enables the student to devote his or her attention to just the limb action requirements, because he or she can learn each part without attending to how to coordinate the two parts as a unit. After practicing each part independently, the swimmer can put them together to practice them as a whole unit, with his or her

attention now directed toward the temporal and spatial coordination demands of the arm and leg actions.

Skills that involve learning movement sequences lend themselves particularly well to the progressive part method. Researchers have demonstrated this for both laboratory and real-world skills. For example, Watters (1992) reported that the progressive part method was beneficial for learning to type an eight-key sequence on a computer keyboard. And Ash and Holding (1990) found that people learning a musical score on a piano benefited from a progressive part practice approach. In this experiment, participants learned a musical score of twenty-four quarter notes, grouped into three sets of eight notes. The first two segments were easy and the third segment was difficult. Two types of the progressive part method were better than the whole method for learning to perform this musical score, for which performance was based on errors made, rhythmic accuracy, and rhythmic consistency. Of the two progressive part methods, the one that prescribed an easy-to-difficult progression tended to be better than the one stipulating a difficult-to-easy progression.

A key characteristic of the progressive part method is that it takes advantage of the benefits of both part and whole methods of practice. The part method offers the advantage of reducing the attention demands of performing the whole skill, so that the person can focus attention on specific aspects of a part of the skill. The whole method, on the other hand, has the advantage of requiring important spatial and temporal coordination of the parts to be practiced together. The progressive part method combines both of these qualities. Thus, the attention demands of performing the skill are under control, while the parts are put together progressively so that the learner can practice important spatial and temporal coordination requirements of performing the parts as a whole.

Simplification: Reducing task difficulty. For a complex skill, simplification can make either the whole skill or certain parts of the skill less difficult for people to perform. There are several ways to implement a simplification approach to skill practice. We will discuss four of these here. Each is specific to learning a certain type of skill. All of them involve practicing the whole skill, but simplify certain parts of the skill in various ways.

When a person is learning an object manipulation skill, one way to simplify learning the skill involves *reducing the difficulty of the objects.* For example, someone learning to juggle three balls can practice with scarves or bean bags. This reduces the difficulty of the task by involving objects that move more slowly and are therefore easier to catch. Because these objects move more slowly, the person has more time to make the appropriate movements at the right moments. However, the person still must follow the principles of juggling while learning to juggle the easier objects. We would expect early practice using easier objects to enable the person to learn these juggling principles, and then easily transfer them to juggling with more difficult objects. In fact, research evidence supports this approach to learning to juggle three balls (Hautala, 1988).

Another way to reduce task difficulty is to *reduce the attention demands of the skill without changing the*

action goal. This strategy reduces task difficulty by reducing task complexity. One approach to implementing this strategy is to provide physical assistance devices that allow the person to practice the goal of the skill but at the same time reduce the attention demands of the task. For example, Wulf and her colleagues (Wulf, Shea, & Whitacre, 1998; Wulf & Toole, 1999) found that people who used ski poles while they practiced the slalom ski simulator task learned to perform the task without ski poles better than people who practiced without ski poles. The poles allowed the performers to focus more attention on the movement coordination demands of the task. This was possible because of the reduced attention demands for the dynamic balancing component of the task, which resulted from the poles enabling better body stability. It is also notable that in these experiments, transfer from performing with poles to without the poles led to no appreciable reduction in performance level.

Third, for skills having a distinct rhythmic characteristic, *providing auditory accompaniment* that cues the appropriate rhythm works well to reduce task difficulty and facilitate a person's learning of the activity. This approach is especially interesting because it actually simplifies a task by adding an extra component to it. For example, musical accompaniment can assist people with gait disorders while they practice walking. An example of research support for the effectiveness of this simplification procedure was reported by Thaut et al. (1996). The researchers provided patients with Parkinson's disease with an auditory device that consisted of audiotapes with metronome sounds embedded in instrumental music to designate the rhythmic structure and tempo (i.e., speed) of the music. The patients used the device as part of a three-week home-based gait-training program to pace their steps while walking. Compared to patients who did not use the device, the patients who trained with the auditory accompaniment showed greater improvement in their gait velocity, stride length, and step cadence. In addition, they accurately reproduced the speed of the last training tape without the assistance device.

A fourth simplification method is useful for the learning of complex skills requiring both speed and

A CLOSER LOOK

The Simplification Method for Learning Three-Ball Juggling

An experiment reported by Hautala (1988) demonstrated that beginning juggling practice by using easier objects is beneficial for learning to juggle three balls.

The participants were boys and girls ten to twelve years old with no previous juggling experience. All of them practiced 5 min per day for 14 days and then were tested for 1 min with the juggling balls.

The experiment compared four practice conditions:

1. Learners began practice using three "juggling balls" of three different colors.

2. Learners began practice using cube-shaped beanbags.

3. Learners followed a progressive simplification scheme:
   a. scarves of different colors
   b. beanbags
   c. juggling balls

4. Learners began practice using weighted scarves and then switched to the balls.

The results of the three-ball juggling test showed this:

• The beanbags practice condition led to the best test performance.

Note: The ball-juggling score for participants in the beanbag practice group was over 50 percent higher than those for the juggling balls group and the progression group, and over 100 percent higher than that of the group that practiced with weighted scarves and then beanbags before using the balls.

---

accuracy. *Reducing the speed* at which a learner first practices a skill can simplify practice. This approach places emphasis on the relative-time relationships among the skill components and on the spatial characteristics of performing the whole skill. Because a characteristic such as relative time is an invariant feature of a well-established coordination pattern and because people can readily vary overall speed, we would expect that a person could learn a relative-time pattern at a variety of overall speeds. By practicing at a slower speed, the learner would establish the essential relative-time characteristics of a coordination pattern.

It is interesting to note that the training strategy of reducing the speed of a task also benefits the learning of bimanual coordination tasks in which each arm performs different spatial-temporal patterns but with the same overall duration of time. What makes this interesting is that in the earlier discussion about the fractionization part-task training strategy, that strategy also facilitated the learning of this type of bimanual task. Evidence for the beneficial effects of the speed-reduction strategy was provided in an experiment by Walter and Swinnen (1992). Participants practiced a bimanual coordination task that required them to use one arm to move a horizontal lever in a one-direction elbow-flexion movement while at the same time using the other arm to move a lever in a two-direction elbow-flexion-extension movement. One group practiced two sets of twenty trials at reduced speeds before practicing the task at the criterion speed. The other group practiced all trials at the criterion speed. Transfer test results showed that the reduced-speed training group learned to perform the task more accurately than the group that practiced the criterion speed only.

A caution against using miming as a simplification method. A common practice in occupational therapy is to have patients mime task performance, or pretend they are performing a task. For example, rather than have a person reach for and grasp a glass of water and drink from it, the therapist asks the person to mime this complete action without the glass present. The problem with this approach is that different patterns of movement characterize the mimed and the real actions.

Mathiowetz and Wade (1995) clearly demonstrated these movement pattern differences for three different tasks for normal adults and adults with multiple sclerosis (MS). The three tasks were eating applesauce from a spoon, drinking from a glass, and turning pages of a book. The authors compared two different types of miming: with and without the object. For both the normal and the MS participants, the kinematic profiles for the three tasks revealed uniquely different characteristics for the real and the mimed situations.

Although this experiment and situation relate specifically to a therapy environment, the results have implications for all skill-learning situations. When simplifying the practice of a skill, a therapist, teacher, or coach should have the person perform the natural skill. In each of the four simplification methods we recommend here, this is always the case.

An Attention Approach to Involving Part Practice in Whole Practice

Sometimes it is not advisable or practical to separate the parts of a skill physically for practice. This, however, does not mean that a learner cannot practice parts of the whole skill. It is possible to practice the whole skill, but focus attention on specific parts that need work. This approach provides both the advantage of part practice, where emphasis on specific parts of the skill facilitates improvement of these parts, and the advantage of whole practice, in which the emphasis is on how the parts of the skill relate to one another to produce skilled performance.

Both attention theory and research evidence support this attention approach. In Kahneman's model of attention (chapter 8), an important factor in attention allocation policy is called *momentary intentions.* When applied to a performance situation, this factor comes into play when a person focuses his or her attention on a specific aspect of the performance. Because we can manipulate our attention resources in this way, we can direct attention to a specific part of a skill while performing the whole skill.

An example of research evidence supporting the use of this attention-directing strategy for part practice is an experiment by Gopher, Weil, and Siegel (1989). Participants learned a complex computer game, known as the Space Fortress Game,

that requires a person to master perceptual, cognitive, and motor skills as well as to acquire specific knowledge of the rules and game strategy. The player must shoot missiles at and destroy a space fortress. He or she fires the missiles from a movable spaceship, controlling spaceship movement and firing using a joystick and a trigger. To destroy the fortress, the player must overcome several obstacles, such as the fortress's rotating to face the spaceship to defend itself, protection of the fortress by mines that appear on the screen periodically and can destroy the spaceship if it runs into them, and so on (see Mané & Donchin, 1989, for a complete description of this computer game).

In the experiment by Gopher, Weil, and Siegel, three groups received instructions during the first six practice sessions that emphasized a strategy requiring them to direct attention to one specific component of the skill. One group's instructions emphasized focusing attention on controlling the spaceship. The second group's instructions emphasized focusing attention on handling the mines around the fortress. The third group received spaceship control instructions for the first three practice sessions and then mine-handling instructions for the next three sessions. When the researchers compared the performance of these three groups against that of a control group that had not received any strategic instructions, the effectiveness of the attention-directing instructions was evident. As you can see in figure 22.1, the control group improved with practice, but not as much as the three instruction groups did. And the group that received two different strategies outperformed those that received only one.

These results provide empirical evidence that attention-directing instructions can serve to establish a part practice environment while allowing the person to practice the whole skill. And these instructions are more effective than having the person practice the skill without providing such strategies. Neither the motor learning nor the teaching methods literature has addressed this type of part practice with any degree of intensity. It clearly deserves more consideration and investigation.

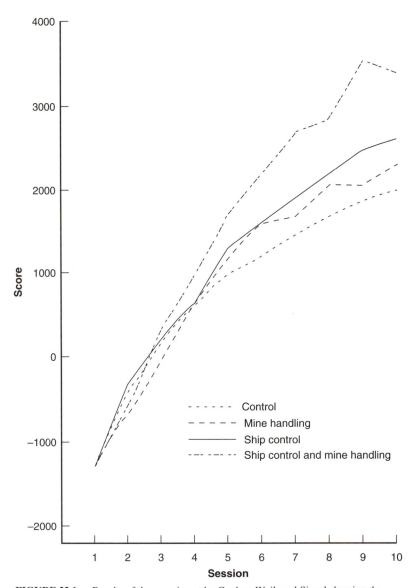

FIGURE 22.1   Results of the experiment by Gopher, Weil, and Siegel showing the change in performance on the computer game Space Fortress for attention-directing instructions related to specific parts of the skill.   [Reprinted from Gopher, D. et al. (1989). Practice under changing priorities: An approach to the training of complex skills. *Acta Psychologica, 71,* 147–177, with kind permission of Elsevier Science-NL, Sara Burgerharstraat 25, 1055 KV Amsterdam, The Netherlands.]

SUMMARY

An important practice conditions decision is whether to have a person practice a skill as a whole or in parts. The instructor should make the initial decision according to the complexity and organization of the skill. Whole practice is advisable when the skill to be learned is low in complexity and high in organization. Part practice is advisable when the skill is more complex and involves less organization. When a teacher, coach, or therapist makes the decision to follow a part practice method, it is important that he or she have the learner practice those components of the skill that are spatially and temporally interdependent together, as a "natural unit." The learner can practice separately those parts of the skill that are relatively independent. At least three different methods can be effective for part practice. The fractionization method involves practicing parts of each hand's movement of a bimanual coordination skill separately and then practicing them together. The segmentation method is a progressive-part method that allows the learner to practice parts, but provides for a building of parts toward performance of the whole skill. The third method involves simplifying the whole skill or parts of the skill for practice. We considered four different simplification strategies. Each is specific to certain types of skills or skill characteristics. These include reducing the difficulty of the objects for object manipulation skills, reducing the attention demands for a task while maintaining the action goal, providing acoustical accompaniment for skills characterized by a specific rhythm, and reducing the speed of complex skills requiring spatial-temporal accuracy. Additionally, learners can use attention focus strategies when practicing the whole skill, to obtain a part practice type of experience.

RELATED READINGS

Chamberlin, C., & Lee, T. (1993). Arranging practice conditions and designing instruction. In R. N. Singer, M. Murphey, & K. Tennant (Eds.), *Handbook of research on sport psychology* (pp. 213–241). New York: Macmillan. (Read section on "Part versus Whole Task Practice," pp. 229–232.)

French, K., Rink, J., Rikard, L., Mays, A., Lynn, S., & Werner, P. (1991). The effects of practice progressions on learning two volleyball skills. *Journal of Teaching in Physical Education, 10,* 261–274.

Klapp, S. T., Nelson, J. M., & Jagacinski, R. J. (1998). Can people tap concurrent bimanual rhythms independently? *Journal of Motor Behavior, 30,* 301–322.

Pellett, T. L., & Lox, C. L. (1997). Tennis racquet length comparisons and the effect on beginning college players' playing success and achievement. *Journal of Teaching in Physical Education, 16,* 490–499.

STUDY QUESTIONS

1. (a) Define the term "organization" as it relates to the relationship among the parts (or components) of a complex motor skill. (b) Give an example of parts of a skill that demonstrate a high degree of organization. Indicate why you consider these parts to be highly organized.

2. (a) How can you decide whether people would learn a skill best if they practiced it as a whole or in parts? (b) Give a motor skill example to show how to apply these rules.

3. Describe examples of how practitioners can apply the part practice methods of fractionization and segmentation to the practice of skills.

4. Describe three ways practitioners can apply the simplification method to the practice of skills.

5. Describe how you could apply an attention allocation policy factor in Kahneman's model of attention to practicing a motor skill as a means of implementing a type of part practice while practicing a whole skill. Give an example.

Mental Practice

Concept: Mental practice can be effective
for learning skills, especially when combined
with physical practice

APPLICATION

Situations abound in which teachers, coaches, and therapists can apply mental practice to the learning and performing of motor skills. These situations range from helping a patient employ mental practice to learn a new skill to aiding a world-class athlete perform in a major competitive event. Consider a few examples of situations in which people can use mental practice to their benefit.

A gymnast is standing beside the floor exercise mat waiting to begin his or her routine. Before actually beginning that routine, the gymnast goes through the entire routine mentally, visualizing the performance of each part of the routine, from beginning to end. Following this, the gymnast steps onto the mat and begins the routine.

A stroke patient is having difficulty walking down a flight of stairs. After several failed attempts, the patient is becoming frustrated. The therapist tells the patient to stop practicing and instead to stand on the top step and mentally visualize and feel himself or herself walking down the stairs perfectly ten times in a row. The patient goes through the entire sequence mentally on each practice attempt. Following this procedure, the therapist has the patient go back to physically practicing this skill.

Think about a situation in which you have just performed a skill very well and you would like to perform it the same way the next time. But because of the nature of the activity, you cannot physically practice what you have just done. Golf is a good example of this type of situation. If you have just hit a beautiful drive right down the middle of the fairway, you would like to be able to hit a few more practice drives just to try to reproduce and reinforce the swing that produced such a beautiful result. Although you can't do that, you *can* practice that swing mentally as you walk down the fairway to your next shot.

Notice that each of these three situations had a different goal for mental practice. The gymnast used mental practice to prepare for an immediate performance of a well-learned routine. The rehabilitation patient used mental practice to acquire a new skill. Finally, the golfer used a mental practice procedure to reinforce an appropriate action and thereby aid an upcoming performance of that action.

DISCUSSION

In the skill learning and performance literature, the term **mental practice** refers to the cognitive rehearsal of a physical skill in the absence of overt physical movements. We should not confuse this type of mental practice with meditation, which generally connotes an individual's engagement of his or her mind in deep thought in a way that blocks out awareness of what is happening to or around him or her. We can think of meditation as a form of mental practice; in fact, it seems to be a potentially effective means for enhancing physical performance. However, in this discussion, we limit the term *mental practice* to mean active cognitive or mental rehearsal of a skill, where a person is *imaging* a skill or part of a skill. During this process, an observer would notice no involvement of the body's musculature. This imaging may occur while the learner is observing another person live, another person on film or videotape, or the learner himself or herself on film or videotape. Or it may occur without any visual observation at all.

The act of imaging can involve internal or external forms of imagery (Mahoney & Avener, 1977). In **internal imagery,** the individual approximates the real-life situation in such a way that the person actually "imagines being inside his/her body and experiencing those sensations which might be expected in the actual situation" (p. 137). During **external imagery,** on the other hand, the person views himself or herself from the perspective of an observer, as in watching a movie. We will not compare the efficacy of these two types of imagery conditions in this discussion.

Two Roles for Mental Practice

The study of mental practice as it relates to the learning and performance of motor skills follows two distinct research directions. One concerns the role of mental practice in the *acquisition* of motor skills. Here the critical question is how effective mental practice is for a person in the initial stages of learning or relearning a skill. The other research direction addresses how mental practice can aid in the *performance* of a well-learned skill.

People use mental practice as a performance aid in two ways. We presented the first in the gymnast example in the Application section. The gymnast used mental practice to prepare for the immediately upcoming performance. When used this way, mental practice is a means of action preparation. We saw the second approach in the example of the golfer mentally imaging a successful swing as he or she walked down the fairway. Here mental practice combines characteristics of both acquisition and performance situations by providing a person with a means of facilitating the storage and retrieval from memory of an appropriate action.

Beginning as early as the 1890s, research literature is replete with mental practice studies. Several excellent reviews of this research literature can be consulted for more specific information than will be discussed here (see Driskell, Copper, & Moran, 1994; Martin, Moritz, & Hall, 1999). These reviews describe the convincing evidence that is available to support the point that mental practice is an effective strategy for aiding both skill acquisition and performance preparation.

Mental Practice Aids Skill Acquisition

Investigations of the effectiveness of mental practice in motor skill acquisition typically compare mental and physical practice conditions with a no-practice control condition. In general, research results show that physical practice is better than the other conditions. However, mental practice is typically better than no practice. This finding alone is

---

mental practice   the cognitive rehearsal of a physical skill in the absence of overt physical movements; it usually involves imaging oneself performing a skill.

internal imagery   a form of mental practice in which a person imagines being inside his or her own body while performing a skill and experiencing the sensations that are expected in the actual situation.

external imagery   a form of mental practice in which a person imagines viewing himself or herself performing a skill from the perspective of an observer.

important, because it demonstrates the effectiveness of mental practice in aiding acquisition. Even more impressive is the effect of using a combination of physical and mental practice.

One of the more extensive comparisons of combinations of mental and physical practice was an experiment by Hird et al. (1991). The authors compared six different physical and mental practice conditions. At one extreme was 100 percent physical practice, while at the other extreme was 100 percent mental practice. In-between were practice routines requiring 75 percent physical and 25 percent mental practice, 50 percent physical and 50 percent mental practice, and 25 percent physical and 75 percent mental practice. The sixth condition required neither physical nor mental practice, but had participants doing a different type of activity during the practice sessions. Participants practiced two tasks. One required them to place as many round and square pegs in appropriately marked places in the pegboard as they could in 60 sec. The other was a rotary pursuit task in which the target moved in a circular pattern at 45 rpm for 15 sec.

Results of this experiment (figure 23.1) showed three noteworthy effects. First, consistent with other research findings was the result that mental practice alone was better than no practice for both tasks. Second, as the proportion of physical practice increased for both tasks, the level of posttest performance rose. Third, although physical practice alone was better than combinations of mental and physical practice, the differences were small.

The relative similarity in learning effects between physical practice only and combinations of physical and mental practice has been a common finding in research. What is especially notable about this similarity is that the use of a combination of physical and mental practice often involves only half as many physical practice trials as physical practice only.

Why would a combination of mental and physical practice trials lead to learning effects that are as good as physical practice only? We can derive one answer to this question by considering some points discussed throughout this text about the need to engage in effective practice strategies. An important characteristic of effective strategies for optimizing skill acquisition is cognitive problem-solving activity. Physical practice appears not to be the only means of establishing these beneficial conditions. Mental practice can invoke them as well, although not to the same extent. However, the combination of physical and mental practice appears to establish a learning condition that can optimize these important characteristics.

Mental practice benefits in rehabilitation settings. In addition to being beneficial for the acquiring of new skills, mental practice can be effective for the relearning of skills, as well as for the improvement of skill performance, in rehabilitation contexts. A research example that demonstrates this is an experiment by Linden et al. (1989). They examined the effects of using mental practice on improving walking balance for women aged 67 to 90 years. The task required the women to perform several actions at designated places along an activity course. They began by standing on two footprints and then walked along a simulated balance beam, which was actually a strip of masking tape 4 in. (10.16 cm) wide placed down the center of a carpeted walkway. Then they walked up a ramp that had a 4-degree slope, stepped off the ramp, and walked to a table, where they picked up juice and cookies.

For eight days women in the mental practice group engaged in 6 min of mentally imaging themselves walking along the simulated balance beam. A control group spent the same amount of time sitting and playing word and memory games. The participants performed pretests and posttests for the equilibrium task on the simulated balance beam and for walking the activity course on the day before beginning the mental practice or control activity, and the days after the fourth and eighth days of the mental practice or control activity. Results showed that the mental practice was beneficial for walking balance, as measured by equilibrium and foot placement measures, only when participants carried an object in each hand. Thus,

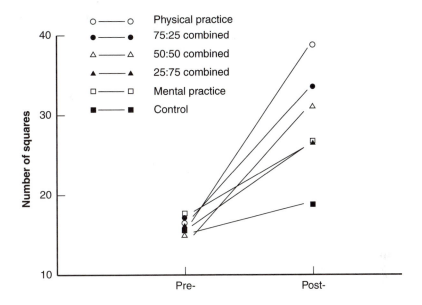

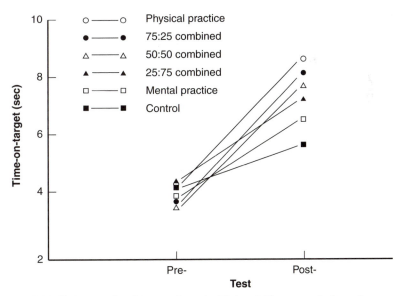

FIGURE 23.1   Results of the experiment by Hird et al. The top graph shows the pre- and posttest results for the different practice conditions for the pegboard task. The bottom graph shows results for the pursuit rotor task.   [Reprinted by permission from Hird, J. S., Landers, D. M., Thomas, J. R., & Horan, J. J. (1991). Physical practice is superior to mental practice in enhancing cognitive and motor task performance. *Journal of Sport & Exercise Psychology, 13* (3), p. 288. Human Kinetics, Champaign, IL.]

A CLOSER LOOK

Imagery Training as a Posture Development Technique

Two experiments by Fairweather and Sidaway (1993) showed that imagery training can help people diagnosed with postural problems related to abnormal curvature of the spinal column. In one of these experiments, participants were seventeen-year-old males who regularly experienced low back pain and were assessed as having varying degrees of lordosis and kyphosis. The authors compared two different treatments. One involved flexibility and abdominal exercises; the other involved deep muscular relaxation exercises prior to kinesthetic awareness exercises and visualization practice. The visualization technique consisted of creating images of four different action situations involving trunk, buttocks, pelvis, and thighs. For example, participants were told to visualize their buttocks as unbaked loaves of dough and watch them slide downward toward their heels. Results showed that following a three-week training period during which participants engaged in their respective techniques, both techniques led to improved postural form, as measured by spinal angles, and a reduction in back pain.

---

although the mental practice routine was not as successful as the researchers had hoped, it was clinically beneficial.

Mental practice benefits for power training. A characteristic of many motor skills is the need to generate speed over relatively short distances. Sprint events in running, bicycling, and crew are examples of skills involving this characteristic. An experiment by Van Gyn, Wenger, and Gaul (1990) demonstrated that mental practice can be beneficial for improving power for people learning a 40-m bicycle sprint. After being pretested on a bicycle ergometer (stationary bicycle) to determine peak power for a 40-m sprint, participants began three training sessions each week for six weeks on the bicycle ergometer to improve power performance. This training involved physical practice in which they had to maintain maximum speed for 10 sec.

Two groups imaged themselves performing the sprint eight times. One of these groups did only the mental practice, whereas the other imagery group did imagery practice while they practiced physically. A third group received only the power training. A fourth group served as a control group by receiving neither the imagery nor the power training. The results showed the benefits of combining mental and physical practice. Only the group that received both the imagery and the power training showed an improvement in sprint times at the end of the six-week training period. An interesting result was that only the imagery training group and the imagery and power training group improved their peak power scores between the pre- and posttests.

Mental practice as a part of a general preparation strategy that aids learning. We see an interesting example of incorporating mental practice into a practice routine in some work from Singer (1986, 1988). He proposed a five-step general learning strategy that involves elements of mental practice in three of the steps. The first step is to get ready physically, mentally, and emotionally. The second step involves mentally imaging performing the action, both visually and kinesthetically. The third step involves concentrating intensely on only one relevant cue related to the action, such as the seams of a tennis ball. The fourth step is to execute the action. Finally, the fifth step is to evaluate the performance outcome.

Several studies have demonstrated the effectiveness of this general strategy for learning a specific skill. For example, Lidor, Tennant, and Singer (1996) compared people who used this strategy with those who didn't to learn a task involving ball-throwing accuracy. Participants sat on a chair 6 m from a target that was standing on the floor

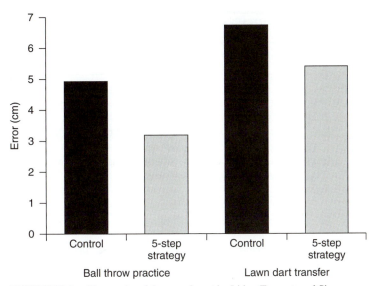

FIGURE 23.2   The results of the experiment by Lidor, Tennant, and Singer (1996) that show the comparison of using Singer's Five-Step Strategy and not using the Strategy (Control) on performance during practice of an overhand ball throw to a target and during a transfer test involving an underhand lawn-dart throw to a target.   [*Source:* Modification of figures 3 and 4 in Lidor, Tennant, & Singer (1996). *International Journal of Sport Psychology 27,* 23–36. Modified with permission.]

behind a badminton net that was 1.32 m high. The task required them to use an overhand motion to throw a ball over the net at the target. Points for each throw were awarded according to where the ball hit the target. However, for the assessment of performance for research purposes, the actual distance from the center of the target was calculated. The results, which are shown in figure 23.2, indicated that participants who engaged in the five-step general preparation strategy learned to perform the skill more accurately than those who did not use the strategy. It is interesting to note that the transfer test of learning in this study involved the same strategy conditions to perform an underhand throw of a lawn dart from a distance of 3 m from a target mounted on a wall 1.3 m from the floor.

Mental Practice Aids Performance Preparation
In their review of the research literature related to imagery use in sport, Martin, Moritz, and Hall (1999) described five types of imagery that athletes

use for various purposes (see table 23.1). The specific situations in which athletes use imagery are in training periods between competitive events, immediately prior to and during a competitive event, and when they are rehabilitating an injury. The situation of interest for our purposes is the use of imagery immediately prior to and during a competitive event. Although Martin et al. specifically addressed the use of imagery by athletes, it is not necessary to limit the use of imagery in these situations to athletes. The use of imagery can be related to anyone engaged in a situation in which he or she must perform a practiced skill for evaluation purposes.

Surveys and anecdotal evidence indicate that athletes use imagery as part of their preparation strategies for a variety of purposes (e.g., Hall, Rodgers, & Barr, 1990; Murphy, 1994). Among these are arousal-level regulation, attention focus, and the maintenance of positive and confident feelings. This means that prior to competition, athletes

TABLE 23.1   Five Types of Imagery Related to Motor Skill Performance*

Imagery Type	Description/Example
Motivational	
(a) Specific	Imagery that represents specific goals and goal-orienting behaviors, e.g., *winning a medal for first place; receiving congratulations for a specific accomplishment*
(b) General mastery	Imagery that represents effective coping and mastery of challenging situations, e.g., *being confident; being focused*
(c) General arousal	Imagery that represents feelings of relaxation, stress, arousal, and anxiety in a situation, e.g., *being relaxed prior to an event*
Cognitive	
(a) Specific	Imagery of performing specific skills, e.g., *performing a golf shot; walking down a flight of stairs*
(b) General	Imagery of strategies related to an event, e.g., *strategy to overcome full-court press in basketball; strategy to organize items for cooking a meal*

*Adapted from text of Martin, Moritz, & Hall (1999), p. 250.

tend to use the motivational types of imagery described in table 23.1. Unfortunately, because of the lack of controlled research investigations on the effectiveness of these imagery strategies, empirically based conclusions are not possible. The primary research problem is that in what would seem to be a simple investigation that compares athletes who use an imagery preparation strategy with those who don't, there are no established valid methods for determining if those in the imagery group actually used an imagery strategy, and if they did, what it involved. However, given this limitation, the Martin et al. (1999) review indicates that researchers have reported sufficient evidence to provide "tentative support" (p. 256) for the benefits of the use of imagery as an effective competition preparation strategy.

Why Is Mental Practice Effective?

At present, there are no comprehensive theories that explain why the various types of imagery are effective (see Martin et al., 1999, for a discussion of proposed explanations). However, there are two generally accepted explanations for why mental practice benefits the learning and performance of specific motor skills: a neuromuscular explanation and a cognitive explanation.

A neuromuscular explanation. We can trace the notion that mental practice of a motor skill has a neuromuscular basis to the work of Jacobson (1931). When he asked people to visualize bending the right arm, Jacobson observed EMG activity in the ocular muscle, but not in the biceps brachii. However, when he asked them to imagine bending the right arm and lifting a 10-lb weight, he noted EMG activity in the biceps brachii on more than 90 percent of the trials. Since Jacobson's early study, many other researchers have provided evidence for this type of electrical activity in the muscles of people asked to imagine movement (e.g., Bakker, Boschker, & Chung, 1996).

The creation of electrical activity in the musculature involved in a movement as a result of the performer's imaging of an action suggests that the appropriate neuromotor pathways involved in the action are activated during mental practice. This activation aids skill learning by helping estab-

A CLOSER LOOK

The Use of Mental Imagery by Skilled Athletes

The Martin, Moritz, and Hall (1999) review of research related to athletes' use of imagery included information about the specific uses of imagery in a variety of sports. Listed below is a sampling of these sports and a brief description of the purposes for using imagery in each sport.

- Basketball — Improve free-throw shooting performance
- Football — Rehearse 2-min. drill; rehearse specific plays
- Baseball — Rehearse batting strategies (e.g., hitting the ball the opposite way, waiting for a specific type of pitch; running past first base and sliding into second base)
- Figure skating — Rehearse routines
- Gymnastics — Rehearse routines
- Wrestling — Rehearse strategies against a specific opponent
- Badminton — Establish confidence and arousal control
- Golf — Develop attention focus and control during putting
- Various sports — Increase or decrease precompetition anxiety
- Sports-related injuries — Use relaxation strategy; motivation to adhere to rehab program; pain management; mentally practiced rehab exercises; enhance self-confidence after return to competition

lish and reinforce the appropriate coordination patterns that are so essential to develop. For someone performing a well-learned skill, this activation tunes, i.e., primes, the neuromotor pathways that will be activated when the person performs the skill. This tuning process increases the likelihood that the person will perform the action appropriately and reduces the demands on the motor control system as it prepares to perform the skill.

A cognitive explanation. Researchers generally agree that the first stage of learning a motor skill involves a high degree of cognitive activity. Much of this activity is related to questions about "what to do" with this new task. It should not be surprising, then, that mental practice would be an effective strategy for people acquiring a new skill or relearning an old one. Mental practice can help the person answer many performance-related questions without the pressure that accompanies physical performance of the skill. In the later stages of learning, mental practice can be benefi-

cial in assisting the person to consolidate strategies as well as to correct errors.

Mental Practice and Imagery Ability

Although researchers have proposed both physiological and psychological reasons for the effectiveness of mental practice for learning and performing motor skills, a related factor also might be operating. There is evidence indicating that the effectiveness of mental practice is related to a person's **imagery ability,** or ability to image an action when requested to do so. Some people have great difficulty imaging

---

imagery ability an individual-difference characteristic that differentiates people who can image an action with a high degree of vividness and control from people who have difficulty imaging an action.

A CLOSER LOOK

Examples of Movement Imagery Questionnaire (MIQ) Items

An Item from the Visual Imagery Subscale

Starting position: Stand with your feet slightly apart and your hands at your sides.

Action: Bend down low and then jump straight up in the air as high as possible with both arms extended above your head. Land with your feet apart and lower your arms to your sides.

Mental task: Assume the starting position. Form as clear and vivid a mental image as possible of the movement just performed. Now rate the ease/difficulty with which you were able to do this mental task.

An Item from the Kinesthetic Imagery Subscale

Starting position: Stand with your feet slightly apart and your arms at your sides.

Action: Jump upwards and rotate your entire body to the left such that you land in the same position in which you started. That is, rotate to the left in a complete (360 degree) circle.

Mental task: Assume the standing position. Attempt to feel yourself making the movement just performed without actually doing it. Now rate the ease/difficulty with which you were able to do this mental task.

Imagery Ability Rating Scales
Visual Imagery Scale

1	2	3	4	5	6	7
Very Easy to Picture	Easy to Picture	Somewhat Easy to Picture	Neutral (Not Easy nor Hard)	Somewhat Hard to Picture	Hard to Picture	Very Hard to Picture

Kinesthetic Imagery Scale

1	2	3	4	5	6	7
Very Easy to Feel	Easy to Feel	Somewhat Easy to Feel	Neutral (Not Easy nor Hard)	Somewhat Hard to Feel	Hard to Feel	Very Hard to Feel

a described action, whereas others can image with a high degree of vividness and control.

Evidence demonstrating that imagery ability is an individual-difference variable came from research using the Movement Imagery Questionnaire (MIQ), a test of imagery ability designed specifically to apply to motor skill performance (Hall & Pongrac, 1983; Hall & Martin, 1997). The MIQ consists of various action situations that a person is asked to physically perform. Then the person is asked to do one of two mental tasks, to either "form as clear and vivid a mental image as possible of the movement just performed" or "attempt to positively feel yourself making the movement just performed without actually doing it." In this test, the first mental task is called "visual imagery," whereas the second mental task is called "kinesthetic imagery." After performing one of these mental tasks, the person rates how easy or difficult it was to do it. A person may be able to do both visual and kinesthetic imagery easily, do one easily and the other with difficulty, or do both with difficulty.

Because imagery ability is an individual difference, Hall proposed that *imagery ability influences the success of mental practice.* People with a high level of imagery ability will benefit more readily from mental practice of motor skills than those with a low level. To test this hypothesis, Goss et al. (1986) selected people who were categorized from their MIQ scores as high visual/high kinesthetic (HH), high visual/low kinesthetic (HL), or low visual/low kinesthetic (LL). Before each practice trial of four complex arm movement patterns, participants kinesthetically imaged the movement about which they received instructions. The results supported the hypotheses, as the HH group performed the patterns to criterion in the fewest trials, with the HL group next, and the LL group taking the greatest number of trials to achieve criterion. Retention performance showed a similar effect.

The importance of this experiment is that it supports the hypothesis that a relationship exists between imagery ability and the effectiveness of mental practice. In addition, it demonstrates that people with low imagery ability can benefit from mental practice.

SUMMARY

Mental practice involves mentally seeing or feeling oneself performing a physical skill while not actually physically performing the skill. Experimental evidence shows that mental practice can be effective as an aid for learning skills as well as for preparing to perform well-learned skills. As a practice technique when people are learning skills, mental practice works best when used in combination with physical practice. Both neuromuscular and cognitively based explanations account for why mental practice is effective. The neuromuscular explanation stems from evidence showing EMG recordings in muscle groups that would be involved in the actual physical performance of the imaged skills. The cognitive explanation points to the benefit of mental practice in helping learners answer many questions about what to do during the first stage of learning. Finally, the ease or difficulty a person may have using mental practice appears to be related to a person's imagery ability. People who have low levels of imagery ability experience more difficulty engaging in mental practice than those who are high in this ability, although both ability levels can benefit from mental practice.

RELATED READINGS

Annett, J. (1995). Motor imagery: Perception or action? *Neuropsychologia, 33,* 1395–1417.

Gould, D., & Udry, E. (1994). Psychological skills for enhancing performance: Arousal regulation strategies. *Medicine and Science in Sports and Exercise, 26,* 478–485.

Johnson, S. H. (1998). Cerebral organization of motor imagery: Contralateral control of grip selection in mentally represented prehension. *Psychological Science, 9,* 219–222.

Jones, L., & Stuth, G. (1992). The uses of mental imagery in athletics: An overview. *Applied and Preventative Psychology, 6,* 101–115.

Kohl, R. M., Ellis, S. D., & Roenker, D. L. (1992). Alternating actual and imagery practice: Preliminary theoretical considerations. *Research Quarterly for Exercise and Sport, 63,* 162–170.

Warner, L., & McNeil, M. E. (1988). Mental imagery and its potential for physical therapy. *Physical Therapy, 68,* 516–521.

STUDY QUESTIONS

1. Define *mental practice.*

2. Describe an example of how you would implement mental practice procedures to aid the learning of a new skill.

3. Describe an example of how you would implement a mental practice strategy to aid your preparation to perform a well-learned skill.

4. What are two reasons researchers have proposed to explain why mental practice aids motor skill learning and performance?

5. (a) Discuss what is meant by the term "imagery ability." (b) How does imagery ability relate to the effectiveness of mental practice?

REFERENCES

Abernethy, B. (1993). Searching for the minimal essential information for skilled perception and action. *Psychological Research, 55,* 131–138.

Abernethy, B. (1999). The Coleman Roberts Griffith Address: Movement expertise: A juncture between psychology theory and practice. *Journal of Applied Sport Psychology, 11,* 126–141.

Abernethy, B., & Burgess-Limerick, R. (1992). Visual information for the timing of skilled movements: A review. In J. J. Summers (Ed.), *Approaches to the study of motor control and learning* (pp. 343–384). Amsterdam: Elsevier.

Abernethy, B., & Russell, D. G. (1987). Expert-novice differences in an applied selective attention task. *Journal of Sport Psychology, 9,* 326–345.

Abernethy, B., & Sparrow, W. A. (1992). The rise and fall of dominant paradigms in motor behavior research. In J. J. Summers (Ed.), *Approaches to the study of motor control and learning* (pp. 3–45). Amsterdam: Elsevier.

Abernethy, B., Wood, J. M., & Parks, S. (1999). Can the anticipatory skills of experts be learned by novices? *Research Quarterly for Exercise and Sport, 70,* 313–318.

Ackerman, P. L. (1988). Determinants of individual differences during skill acquisition: Cognitive abilities and information processing. *Journal of Experimental Psychology: General, 117,* 288–318.

Ackerman, P. L. (1992). Predicting individual differences in complex skill acquisition: Dynamics of ability determinants. *Journal of Applied Psychology, 77,* 598–614.

Ada, L., O'Dwyer, N. J., & Neilson, P. D. (1993). Improvement in kinematic characteristics and coordination following stroke quantified by linear systems analysis. *Human Movement Science, 12,* 137–153.

Adams, J. A. (1986). Use of the model's knowledge of results to increase the observer's performance. *Journal of Human Movement Studies, 12,* 89–98.

Adams, J. A. (1987). Historical review and appraisal of research on the learning, retention, and transfer of human motor skills. *Psychological Bulletin, 101,* 41–74.

Adams, J. A., & Dijkstra, S. J. (1966). Short-term memory for motor responses. *Journal of Experimental Psychology, 71,* 314–318.

Allport, D. A. (1980). Attention and performance. In G. Claxton (Ed.), *Cognitive psychology: New directions* (pp. 112–153). London: Routledge & Kegan Paul.

Amazeen, E. L., Amazeen, P. G., Post, A. A., & Beek, P. J. (1999). Timing the selection of information during rhythmic catching. *Journal of Motor Behavior, 31,* 279–289.

Anderson, D. I., Magill, R. A., & Sekiya, H. (1994). A reconsideration of the trials-delay of knowledge of results paradigm in motor skill learning. *Research Quarterly for Exercise and Sport, 65,* 286–290.

Anderson, D. I., & Sidaway, B. (1994). Coordination changes associated with practice of a soccer kick. *Research Quarterly Exercise and Sport, 65,* 93–99.

Anderson, J. R. (1987). Skill acquisition: Compilation of weak-method problem solutions. *Psychological Review, 94,* 192–210.

Annesi, J. J. (1998). Effects of computer feedback on adherence to exercise. *Perceptual and Motor Skills, 87,* 723–730.

Annett, J. (1969). *Feedback and human behavior.* Baltimore, MD: Penguin.

Annett, J. (1970). The role of action feedback in the acquisition of simple motor responses. *Journal of Motor Behavior, 11,* 217–221.

Annett, J. (1959). Learning a pressure under conditions of immediate and delayed knowledge of results. *Quarterly Journal of Experimental Psychology, 11,* 3–15.

Annett, J., & Piech, J. (1985). The retention of a skill following distributed training. *Programmed Learning and Educational Technology, 22,* 182–186.

Anson, J. G. (1982). Memory drum theory: Alternative tests and explanations for the complexity effects on simple reaction time. *Journal of Motor Behavior, 14,* 228–246.

Ash, D. W., & Holding, D. H. (1990). Backward versus forward chaining in the acquisition of a keyboard skill. *Human Factors, 32,* 139–146.

Assaiante, C., Marchand, A. R., & Amblard, B. (1989). Discrete visual samples may control locomotor equilibrium and foot positioning in man. *Journal of Motor Behavior, 21,* 72–91.

Atkinson, R. C., & Shiffrin, R. M. (1968). Human memory: A proposed system and its control processes. In K. W. Spence & J. T. Spence (Eds.), *The psychology of learning and motivation: Advances in research and theory* (Vol. 2, pp. 89–197). New York: Academic Press.

Baddeley, A. D. (1986). *Working memory.* New York: Oxford University Press.

Baddeley, A. D. (1995). Working memory. In M. S. Gazzaniga (Ed.), *The cognitive neurosciences* (pp. 755–764). Cambridge, MA: MIT Press.

Baddeley, A. D., & Longman, D. J. A. (1978). The influence of length and frequency of training session on the rate of learning to type. *Ergonomics, 21,* 627–635.

Bahill, A. T., & LaRitz, T. (1984). Why can't batters keep their eyes on the ball? *American Scientist, 72,* 249–252.

Bakker, F. C., Boschker, M. S. J., & Chung, T. (1996). Changes in muscular activity while imagining weight lifting using stimulus or response propositions. *Journal of Sport & Exercise Psychology, 18,* 313–324.

Bandura, A. (1984). *Social foundations of thought and action: A social cognitive theory.* Englewood Cliffs, NJ: Prentice Hall.

Bard, C., Fleury, M., & Goulet, C. (1994). Relationship between perceptual strategies and response adequacy in sport situation. *International Journal of Sport Psychology, 25,* 266–281.

Bard, C., Paillard, J., Lajoie, Y., Fleury, M., Teasdale, N., Forget, R., & Lamarre, Y. (1992). Role of afferent information in the timing of motor commands: A comparative study with a deafferented patient. *Neuropsychologia, 30,* 201–206.

Bartlett, F. C. (1932). *Remembering: A study in experimental and social psychology.* Cambridge: Cambridge University Press.

Barton, J. W. (1921). Smaller versus larger units in learning the maze. *Journal of Experimental Psychology, 4,* 414–424.

Battig, W. F. (1979). The flexibility of human memory. In L. S. Cermak & F. I. M. Craik (Eds.), *Levels of processing in human memory* (pp. 23–44). Hillsdale, NJ: Erlbaum.

Benedetti, C., & McCullagh, P. (1987). Post-knowledge of results delay: Effects of interpolated activity on learning and performance. *Research Quarterly for Exercise and Sport, 58,* 375–381.

Bennett, S., Davids, K., & Craig, T. (1999). The effect of temporal and informational constraints on one-handed catching performance. *Research Quarterly for Exercise and Sport, 70,* 206–211.

Berg, W. P., Wade, M. G., & Greer, N. L. (1994). Visual regulation of gait in bipedal locomotion: Revisiting Lee, Lishman, & Thomson (1982). *Journal of Experimental Psychology: Human Perception and Performance, 20,* 854–863.

Berger, H. J., van Es, N. J., van Spaendonck, K. P., Teunisse, J. P., Horstink, M. W., van't Hof, M. A., & Cools, A. R. (1999). Relationship between memory strategies and motor symptoms in Parkinson's disease. *Journal of Clinical Experimental Neuropsychology, 21,* 677–684.

Bernstein, N. (1967). *The co-ordination and regulation of movement.* Oxford: Pergamon Press.

Bilodeau, E. A., Bilodeau, I. M., & Schumsky, D. A. (1959). Some effects of introducing and withdrawing knowledge of results early and late in practice. *Journal of Experimental Psychology, 58,* 142–144.

Bilodeau, I. M. (1969). Information feedback. In E. A. Bilodeau (Ed.), *Principles of skill acquisition* (pp. 225–285). New York: Academic Press.

Bizzi, E., & Polit, A. (1979). Processes controlling visually evoked movements. *Neuropsychologia, 17,* 203–213.

Blais, C. (1991). Instructions as constraints on psychomotor performance. *Journal of Human Movement Studies, 21,* 217–231.

Blouin, J., Bard, C., Teasdale, N., Paillard, J., Fleury, M., Forget, R., & Lamarre, Y. (1993). Reference systems for coding spatial information in normal subjects and a deafferented patient. *Experimental Brain Research, 93,* 324–331.

Bootsma, R. J., Marteniuk, R. G., MacKenzie, C. L., & Zaal, F. T. (1994). The speed-accuracy trade-off in manual prehension: Effects of movement amplitude, object size and object width on kinematic characteristics. *Experimental Brain Research, 98,* 535–541.

Bootsma, R. J., & Peper, C. E. (1992). Predictive visual information sources for the regulation of action with special emphasis on catching and hitting. In L. Proteau & D. Elliott (Eds.), *Vision and motor control* (pp. 285–313). Amsterdam: Elsevier.

Bootsma, R. J., & van Wieringen, P. C. W. (1990). Timing an attacking forehand drive in table tennis. *Journal of Experimental Psychology: Human Perception and Performance, 16,* 21–29.

Boulter, L. R. (1964). Evaluations of mechanisms in delay of knowledge of results. *Canadian Journal of Psychology, 18,* 281–291.

Bouzid, N., & Crawshaw, C. M. (1987). Massed versus distributed wordprocessor training. *Applied Ergonomics, 18,* 220–222.

Boyce, B. A. (1991). The effects of an instructional strategy with two schedules of augmented KP feedback upon skill acquisition of a selected shooting task. *Journal of Teaching in Physical Education, 11,* 47–58.

Brady, F. (1998). A theoretical and empirical review of the contextual interference effect and the learning of motor skills. *Quest, 50,* 266–293.

Brenner, E., & Smeets, J. B. J. (1997). Fast responses of the human hand changes in target position. *Journal of Motor Behavior, 29,* 297–310.

Brisson, T. A., & Alain, C. (1997). A comparison of two references for using knowledge of performance in learning a motor task. *Journal of Motor Behavior, 29,* 339–350.

Broadbent, D. E. (1958). *Perception and communication.* Oxford: Pergamon Press.

Brown, R. W. (1928). A comparison of the whole, part, and combination methods for learning piano music. *Journal of Experimental Psychology, 11,* 235–247.

Brown, T. G. (1911). The intrinsic factors in the act of progression in the mammal. *Proceedings of the Royal Society of London (Biology), 84,* 308–319.

Brucker, B. S., & Bulaeva, N. V. (1996). Biofeedback effect on electromyographic responses in patients with spinal cord injury. *Archives of Physical Medicine and Rehabilitation, 77,* 133–137.

Bryan, W. L., & Harter, N. (1987). Studies in the physiology and psychology of the telegraphic language. *Psychological Review, 4,* 27–53.

Buekers, M. J. A., & Magill, R. A. (1995). The role of task experience and prior knowledge for detecting invalid augmented feedback while learning a motor skill. *Quarterly Journal of Experimental Psychology, 44A,* 105–117.

Buekers, M. J. A., Magill, R. A., & Hall, K. G. (1992). The effect of erroneous knowledge of results on skill acquisition when augmented information is redundant. *Quarterly Journal of Experimental Psychology, 44A,* 105–117.

Buekers, M. J. A., Magill, R. A., & Sneyers, K. M. (1994). Resolving a conflict between sensory feedback and knowledge of results while learning a motor skill. *Journal of Motor Behavior, 26,* 27–35.

Bullock, D., & Grossberg, S. (1991). Adaptive neural networks for control of movement trajectories invariant under speed and force rescaling. *Human Movement Science, 10,* 3–53.

Butler, M. S., Reeve, T. G., & Fischman, M. G. (1996). Effects of the instructional set in the bandwidth feedback paradigm on motor skill acquisition. *Research Quarterly for Exercise and Sport, 67,* 355–359.

Campbell, K. C., & Proctor, R. W. (1993). Repetition effects with categorizable stimulus and response sets. *Journal of Experimental Psychology: Learning, Memory, and Cognition, 19,* 1345–1362.

Carlton, L. G. (1992). Visual processing time and the control of movement. In L. Proteau & D. Elliott (Eds.), *Vision and motor control* (pp. 3–31). Amsterdam: Elsevier.

Carlton, L. G., Carlton, M. J., & Newell, K. M. (1987). Reaction time and response dynamics. *Quarterly Journal of Experimental Psychology, 39A,* 337–360.

Carnahan, H., Vandervoort, A. A., & Swanson, L. R. (1996). The influence of summary knowledge of results and aging on motor learning. *Research Quarterly for Exercise and Sport, 67,* 280–287.

Carroll, W. R., & Bandura, A. (1990). Representational guidance of action production in observational learning: A causal analysis. *Journal of Motor Behavior, 22,* 85–97.

Carron, A. V. (1969). Performance and learning in a discrete motor task under massed vs. distributed practice. *Research Quarterly, 40,* 481–489.

Cauraugh, J. H., Chen, D., & Radlo, S. J. (1993). Effects of traditional and reversed bandwidth knowledge of results on motor learning. *Research Quarterly for Exercise and Sport, 64,* 413–417.

Chapman, P. R., & Underwood, G. (1998). Visual search of driving situations: Danger and experience. *Perception, 27,* 951–964.

Chase, W. G., & Ericcson, K. A. (1982). Skill and working memory. In G.H. Bower (Ed.), *The psychology of learning and motivation* (Vol. 16, pp. 1–58). New York: Academic Press.

Cherry, E. C. (1953). Some experiments on the recognition of speech, with one and two ears. *Journal of the Acoustical Society of America, 25,* 975–979.

Chieffi, S., Allport, D. A., & Woodfin, M. (1999). Hand-centred coding of target location in visuo-spatial working memory. *Neuropsychologia, 37,* 495–502.

Chieffi, S., & Gentilucci, M. (1993). Coordination between the transport and the grasp components during prehension movement. *Experimental Brain Research, 50,* 7–15.

Chollet, D., Micallef, J. P., & Rabischong, P. (1988). Biomechanical signals for external biofeedback to improve swimming techniques. In B. E. Ungerechts, K. Wilke, & K. Reichle (Eds.), *Swimming science V* (pp. 389–396). Champaign, IL: Human Kinetics.

Christina, R. W. (1973). Influence of enforced motor and sensory sets on reaction latency and movement speed. *Research Quarterly, 44,* 483–487.

Christina, R. W., Fischman, M. G., Lambert, A. L., & Moore, J. F. (1985). Simple reaction time as a function of response complexity: Christina et al. (1982) revisited. *Research Quarterly for Exercise and Sport, 56,* 316–322.

Christina, R. W., Fischman, M. G., Vercruyssen, M. J. P., & Anson, J. G. (1982). Simple reaction time as a function of response complexity: Memory drum theory revisited. *Journal of Motor Behavior, 14,* 301–321.

Christina, R. W., & Rose, D. J. (1985). Premotor and motor response time as a function of response complexity. *Research Quarterly for Exercise and Sport, 56,* 306–315.

Cockrell, D. L., Carnahan, H., & McFayden, B. J. (1995). A preliminary analysis of the coordination of reaching, grasping, and walking. *Perceptual and Motor Skills, 81,* 515–519.

Cook, T. (1936). Studies in cross education. V. Theoretical. *Psychological Review, 43,* 149–178.

Craik, R., Herman, R. H., & Finley, F. R. (1976). The human solutions for locomotion: Interlimb coordination. In R. M. Herman, S. Grillner, & P. S. G. Stein (Eds.), *Neural control of locomotion* (pp. 51–63). New York: Plenum.

Crocker, P. R. E., & Dickinson, J. (1984). Incidental psychomotor learning: The effects of number of movements, practice, and rehearsal. *Journal of Motor Behavior, 16,* 61–75.

Crossman, E. R. F. W. (1959). A theory of the acquisition of speed skill. *Ergonomics, 2,* 153–166.

Crossman, E. R. F. W., & Goodeve, P. J. (1983). Feedback control of hand movements and Fitts' law. *Quarterly Journal of Experimental Psychology, 35A,* 251–278. (Original work published in 1963.)

Cutting, J. E. (1986). *Perception with an eye for motion.* Cambridge, MA: MIT Press.

Cutting, J. E., & Kozlowski, L. T. (1977). Recognizing friends by their walk: Gait perception without familiarity cues. *Bulletin of the Psychonomic Society, 9,* 353–356.

Cutting, J. E., Vishton, P. M., & Braren, P. A. (1995). How we avoid collisions with stationary and moving objects. *Psychological Review, 102,* 627–651.

Cutton, D. M., & Landin, D. (1994). *The effects of two cognitive learning strategies on learning the tennis forehand.* Paper presented at the annual meeting of the Southern District American Alliance for Health, Physical Education, Recreation, and Dance, Nashville, TN.

Czerwinski, M., Lightfoot, N., & Shiffrin, R. A. (1992). Automatization and training in visual search. *American Journal of Psychology, 105,* 271–315.

Daniels, F. S., & Landers, D. M. (1981). Biofeedback and shooting performance: A test of disregulation and systems theory. *Journal of Sport Psychology, 3,* 271–282.

Davids, K. (1988). Developmental differences in the use of peripheral vision during catching performance. *Journal of Motor Behavior, 20,* 39–51.

Davis, R. C. (1942). The pattern of muscular action in simple voluntary movements. *Journal of Experimental Psychology, 31,* 437–466.

den Brinker, B. P. L. M., Stabler, J. R. L. W., Whiting, H. T. A., & van Wieringen, P. C. (1986). The effect of manipulating knowledge of results in the learning of slalom-ski type ski movements. *Ergonomics, 29,* 31–40.

Diedrich, F. J., & Warren, W. H., Jr. (1995). Why change gaits? Dynamics of the walk-run transition. *Journal of Experimental Psychology: Human Perception and Performance, 21,* 183–202.

Diedrich, F. J., & Warren, W. H., Jr. (1998). The dynamics of gait transitions: Effects of grade and load. *Journal of Motor Behavior, 30,* 60–78.

Diewert, G. L. (1975). Retention and coding in motor short-term memory: A comparison of storage codes for distance and location information. *Journal of Motor Behavior, 7,* 183–190.

Diewert, G. L., & Roy, E. A. (1978). Coding strategy for memory of movement extent information. *Journal of Experimental Psychology: Human Learning and Memory, 4,* 666–675.

Dishman, R. K. (1993). Exercise adherence. In R. N. Singer, M. Murphy, & L. K. Tennant (Eds.), *Handbook of research on sport psychology* (pp. 779–798). New York: Macmillan.

Docheff, D. M. (1990, November/December). The feedback sandwich. *Journal of Physical Education, Recreation, and Dance, 61,* 17–18.

Donovan, J. J., & Radosevich, D. J. (1999). A meta-analytic review of the practice distribution effect: Now you see it, now you don't. *Journal of Applied Psychology, 84,* 795–805.

Doody, S. G., Bird, A. M., & Ross, D. (1985). The effect of auditory and visual models on acquisition of a timing task. *Human Movement Science, 4,* 271–281.

Driskell, J. E., Copper, C., & Moran, A. (1994). Does mental practice enhance performance? *Journal of Applied Psychology, 79,* 481–491.

Driskell, J. E., Willis, R. P., & Copper, C. (1992). Effect of overlearning on retention. *Journal of Applied Psychology, 77,* 615–622.

Drowatzky, J. N., & Zuccato, F. C. (1967). Interrelationships between selected measures of static and dynamic balance. *Research Quarterly, 38,* 509–510.

Durand, M., Geoffroi, V., Varray, A., & Préfaut, C. (1994). Study of the energy correlates in the learning of a complex self-paced cyclical skill. *Human Movement Science, 13,* 785–799.

Eason, R. G., Beardshall, A., & Jaffee, S. (1965). Performance and physiological indicants of activation in a vigilance situation. *Perceptual and Motor Skills, 20,* 3–13.

Edwards, R. V., & Lee, A. M. (1985). The relationship of cognitive style and instructional strategy to learning and transfer of motor skills. *Research Quarterly for Exercise and Sport, 56,* 286–290.

Eghan, T. (1988). *The relation of teacher feedback to student achievement.* Unpublished doctoral dissertation. Louisiana State University.

Egeth, H. E., & Yantis, S. (1997). Visual attention: Control, representation, and time course. *Annual Review of Psychology, 48,* 269–297.

Elliott, D., & Allard, F. (1985). The utilization of visual information and feedback information during rapid pointing movements. *Quarterly Journal of Experimental Psychology, 37A,* 407–425.

Elliott, D., Zuberec, S., & Milgram, P. (1994). The effects of periodic visual occlusion on ball catching. *Journal of Motor Behavior, 26,* 113–122.

Engel, K. C., Flanders, M., & Soechting, J. F. (1997). Anticipatory and sequential motor control in piano playing. *Experimental Brain Research, 113,* 189–199.

Ericsson, K. A., & Kintsch, W. (1995). Long-term working memory. *Psychological Review, 102,* 211–245.

Ericsson, K. A., Krampe, R. T., & Tesch-Romer, C. (1993). The role of deliberate practice in the acquisition of expert performance. *Psychological Review, 100,* 363–406.

Ericsson, K. A., & Smith, J. (1991). Prospects and limits of the empirical study of expertise: An introduction. In K. A. Ericcson & J. Smith (Eds.), *Toward a general theory of expertise: Prospects and limits* (pp. 1–38). Cambridge: Cambridge University Press.

Fairweather, M. M., & Sidaway, B. (1993). Ideokinetic imagery as a postural development technique. *Research Quarterly for Exercise and Sport, 64,* 385–392.

Farrow, D., Chivers, P., Hardingham, C., & Sachse, S. (1998). The effect of video-based perceptual training on the tennis return of serve. *International Journal of Sport Psychology, 29,* 36–43.

Feltz, D. L. (1992). Understanding motivation in sport: A self-efficacy perspective. In G. C. Roberts (Ed.), *Motivation in sport and exercise* (pp. 93–127). Champaign, IL: Human Kinetics.

Fischman, M. G. (1984). Programming time as a function of number of movement parts and changes in movement direction. *Journal of Motor Behavior, 16,* 405–423.

Fischman, M. G., & Schneider, T. (1985). Skill level, vision, and proprioception in simple one-hand catching. *Journal of Motor Behavior, 17,* 219–229.

Fishman, S., & Tobey, C. (1978). Augmented feedback. In W. Anderson & G. Barrette (Eds.), *What's going on in gym: Descriptive studies of physical education classes* (pp. 51–62). *Motor Skills: Theory into Practice,* Monograph 1.

Fitts, P. M. (1954). The information capacity of the human motor system in controlling the amplitude of movement. *Journal of Experimental Psychology, 47,* 381–391.

Fitts, P. M., & Posner, M. I. (1967). *Human performance.* Belmont, CA: Brooks/Cole.

Fleishman, E. A. (1972). On the relationship between abilities, learning, and human performance. *American Psychologist, 27,* 1017–1032.

Fleishman, E. A., & Mumford, M. D. (1989). Abilities as causes of individual differences in skill acquisition. *Human Performance, 2,* 201–223.

Fleishman, E. A., & Quaintance, M. K. (1984). *Taxonomies of human performance.* Orlando, FL: Academic Press.

Flinn, N. (1995). A task-oriented approach to the treatment of a client with hemiplegia. *American Journal of Occupational Therapy, 49,* 560–569.

Franks, I. M., & Maile, L. J. (1991). The use of video in sport skill acquisition. In P. W. Dowrick (Ed.), *Practical guide to using video in the behavioral sciences* (pp. 105–124). New York: Wiley.

Franks, I. M., & Wilberg, R. B. (1982). The generation of movement patterns during the acquisition of a pursuit tracking task. *Human Movement Science, 1,* 251–272.

French, K. E., Rink, J. E., & Werner, P. H. (1990). Effects of contextual interference on retention of three volleyball skills. *Perceptual and Motor Skills, 71,* 179–186.

Gabriel, D. A., & Boucher, J. P. (1998). Practice effects on the timing and magnitude of agonist activity during ballistic elbow flexion to a target. *Research Quarterly for Exercise and Sport, 69,* 30–37.

Gallagher, J. D., & Thomas, J. R. (1980). Effects of varying post-KR intervals upon children's motor performance. *Journal of Motor Behavior, 12,* 41–46.

Gentile, A. M. (1972). A working model of skill acquisition with application to teaching. *Quest,* Monograph, *17,* 3–23.

Gentile, A. M. (1987). Skill acquisition: Action, movement, and neuromotor processes. In J. H. Carr, R. B. Shepherd, J. Gordon, A. M. Gentile, & J. M. Hinds (Eds.), *Movement science: Foundations for physical therapy in rehabilitation* (pp. 93–154). Rockville, MD: Aspen.

Gentile, A. M. (2000). Skill acquisition: Action, movement, and neuromotor processes. In J. H. Carr, & R. B. Shepherd (Eds.), *Movement science: Foundations for physical therapy* (2nd ed., pp. 111–187). Rockville, MD: Aspen.

Gentilucci, M., Chieffi, S., Scarpa, M., & Castiello, U. (1992). Temporal coupling between transport and grasp components during prehension movements: Effect of visual perturbation. *Behavioural Brain Research, 47,* 71–82.

Geurts, A. C. H., & Mulder, T. W. (1994). Attention demands in balance recovery following lower limb amputation. *Journal of Motor Behavior, 26,* 162–170.

Gibson, J. J. (1966). *The senses considered as perceptual systems.* Boston: Houghton Mifflin.

Gibson, J. J. (1979). *The ecological approach to visual perception.* Boston: Houghton Mifflin.

Gleick, J. (1987). *Chaos: Making a new science.* New York: Viking Penguin.

Goldberger, M., & Gerney, P. (1990). Effects of learner use of practice time on skill acquisition of fifth grade children. *Journal of Teaching in Physical Education, 10,* 84–95.

Goodale, M. A., & Servos, P. (1996). Visual control of prehension. In H. N. Zelaznik (Ed.), *Advances in motor learning and control* (pp. 87–121). Champaign, IL: Human Kinetics.

Goode, S. L., & Magill, R. A. (1986). The contextual interference effect in learning three badminton serves. *Research Quarterly for Exercise and Sport, 57,* 308–314.

Goodwin, J. E., & Meeuwsen, H. J. (1995). Using bandwidth knowledge of results to alter relative frequencies during motor skill acquisition. *Research Quarterly for Exercise and Sport, 66,* 99–104.

Gopher, D., Weil, M., & Siegel, D. (1989). Practice under changing priorities: An approach to the training of complex skills. *Acta Psychologica, 71,* 147–177.

Goss, S., Hall, C., Buckolz, E., & Fishburne, G. (1986). Imagery ability and the acquisition and retention of motor skills. *Memory and Cognition, 14,* 469–477.

Goulet, C., Bard, C., & Fleury, M. (1989). Expertise differences in preparing to return a tennis serve: A visual information processing approach. *Journal of Sport & Exercise Psychology, 11,* 382–398.

Green, T. D., & Flowers, J. H. (1991). Implicit versus explicit learning processes in a probabilistic, continuous fine-motor catching task. *Journal of Motor Behavior, 23,* 293–300.

Grillner, S., & Zangger, P. (1979). On the central generation of locomotion in the low spinal cat. *Experimental Brain Research, 34,* 241–261.

Guadagnoli, M. A., Dornier, L. A., & Tandy, R. D. (1996). Optimal length for summary knowledge of results: The influence of task-related experience and complexity. *Research Quarterly for Exercise and Sport, 67,* 239–248.

Guay, M., Salmoni, A., & Lajoie, Y. (1999). The effects of different knowledge of results spacing and summarizing techniques on the acquisition of a ballistic movement. *Research Quarterly for Exercise and Sport, 70,* 24–32.

Hagman, J. D. (1978). Specific-cue effects of interpolated movements on distance and location retention in short-term motor memory. *Memory and Cognition, 6,* 432–437.

Hall, C. R., & Martin, K. A. (1997). Measuring movement imagery abilities: A revision of the Movement Imagery Questionnaire. *Journal of Mental Imagery, 21,* 143–154.

Hall, C. R., & Pongrac, J. (1983). *Movement Imagery Questionnaire.* London, Ontario, Canada: University of Western Ontario.

Hall, C. R., Rodgers, W. M., & Barr, K. A. (1990). The use of imagery by athletes in selected sports. *The Sport Psychologist, 4,* 1–10.

Hall, K. G., Domingues, D. A., & Cavazos, R. (1994). Contextual interference effects with skilled baseball players. *Perceptual and Motor Skills, 78,* 835–841.

Hamilton, W. (1859). *Lectures on metaphysics and logic.* Edinburgh, Scotland: Blackwood.

Hancock, G. R., Butler, M. S., & Fischman, M. G. (1995). On the problem of two-dimensional error scores: Measures and analyses of accuracy, bias, and consistency. *Journal of Motor Behavior, 27,* 241–250.

Hand, J., & Sidaway, B. (1993). Relative frequency of modeling effects on the performance and retention of a motor skill. *Research Quarterly for Exercise and Sport, 64,* 122–126.

Haskins, M. J. (1965). Development of a response recognition training film in tennis. *Perceptual and Motor Skills, 21,* 207–211.

Hatze, H. (1976). Biomechanical aspects of successful motion optimization. In P. V. Komi (Ed.), *Biomechanics V-B* (pp. 5–12). Baltimore: University Park Press.

Hautala, R. M. (1988). Does transfer of training help children learn juggling? *Perceptual and Motor Skills, 67,* 563–567.

Hautala, R. M., & Conn, J. H. (1993). A test of Magill's closed to open continuum for skill development. *Perceptual and Motor Skills, 77,* 219–226.

Hawking, S. (1996). *The illustrated brief history of time*. New York: Bantam Books.

Healy, A. F., & McNamara, D. S. (1996). Verbal learning and memory: Does the modal model still work? *Annual Review of Psychology, 47,* 143–172.

Hebert, E. P., & Landin, D. (1994). Effects of a learning model and augmented feedback on tennis skill acquisition. *Research Quarterly for Exercise and Sport, 65,* 250–257.

Hebert, E., Landin, D., & Menickelli, J. (1998). Videotape feedback: What learners see and how they use it. *Journal of Sport Pedagogy, 4,* 12–28.

Hebert, E. P., Landin, D., & Solmon, M. A. (1996). Practice schedule effects on the performance and learning of low- and high-skilled students: An applied study. *Research Quarterly for Exercise and Sport, 67,* 52–58.

Heise, G. D. (1995). EMG changes in agonist muscles during practice of a multijoint throwing skill. *Journal of Electromyography and Kinesiology, 5,* 81–94.

Heise, G. D., & Cornwell, A. (1997). Relative contributions to the net joint moment for a planar multijoint throwing skill: Early and late in practice. *Research Quarterly for Exercise and Sport, 68,* 116–124.

Helsen, W. F., Elliott, D., Starkes, J. L., & Ricker, K. L. (1998). Temporal and spatial coupling of point of gaze and hand movements in aiming. *Journal of Motor Behavior, 30,* 249–259.

Helsen, W., & Pauwels, J. M. (1990). Analysis of visual search activity in solving tactical game problems. In D. Brogan (Ed.), *Visual search* (pp. 177–184). London: Taylor & Francis.

Helsen, W. F., Starkes, J. L., & Buekers, M. J. (1997). Effects of target eccentricity on temporal costs of point of gaze and the hand in aiming. *Motor Control, 1,* 161–177.

Henderson, J. (1996). Visual attention and the attention-action interface. In K. Akins (Ed.), *Perception* (pp. 290–316). New York: Oxford University Press.

Henry, F. M. (1960). Influence of motor and sensory sets on reaction latency and speed of discrete movements. *Research Quarterly, 31,* 459–468.

Henry, F. M. (1961). Stimulus complexity, movement complexity, age, and sex in relation to reaction latency and speed in limb movements. *Research Quarterly, 32,* 353–366.

Henry, F. M., & Rogers, D. E. (1960). Increased response latency for complicated movements and the "memory drum" theory of neuromotor reaction. *Research Quarterly, 31,* 448–458.

Heuer, H. (1991). Invariant relative timing in motor-program theory. In J. Fagard & P. H. Wolff (Eds.), *The development of timing control and temporal organization in coordinated action* (pp. 37–68). Amsterdam: Elsevier.

Hick, W. E. (1952). On the rate of gain of information. *Quarterly Journal of Experimental Psychology, 4,* 11–26.

Hicks, R. E., Gualtieri, T. C., & Schroeder, S. R. (1983). Cognitive and motor components of bilateral transfer. *American Journal of Psychology, 96,* 223–228.

Hird, J. S., Landers, D. M., Thomas, J. R., & Horan, J. J. (1991). Physical practice is superior to mental practice in enhancing cognitive and motor task performance. *Journal of Sport & Exercise Psychology, 13,* 281–293.

Hoenkamp, H. (1978). Perceptual cues that determine the labeling of human gait. *Journal of Human Movement Studies, 4,* 59–69.

Hogan, J., & Yanowitz, B. (1978). The role of verbal estimates of movement error in ballistic skill acquisition. *Journal of Motor Behavior, 10,* 133–138.

Hreljac, A. (1993). Preferred and energetically optimal gait transition speeds in human locomotion. *Medicine and Science in Sports and Exercise, 25,* 1158–1162.

Hubbard, A. W., & Seng, C. N. (1954). Visual movements of batters. *Research Quarterly, 25,* 42–57.

Ille, A., & Cadopi, M. (1999). Memory for movement sequences in gymnastics: Effects of age and skill level. *Journal of Motor Behavior, 31,* 290–300.

Intiso, D., Santilli, V., Grasso, M. G., Rossi, R., & Caruso, I. (1994). Rehabilitation of walking with electromyographic biofeedback in drop-foot after stroke. *Stroke, 25,* 1189–1192.

Jackson, G. M., Jackson, S. R., Husain, M., Harvey, M., Kramer, T., & Dow, L. (2000). The coordination of bimanual prehension movements in a centrally deafferented patient. *Brain, 123 (Part 2),* 380–393.

Jacobson, E. (1931). Electrical measurement of neuromuscular states during mental activities: VI. A note on mental activities concerning an amputated limb. *American Journal of Physiology, 43,* 122–125.

Jaegers, S. M. H. J., Peterson, R. F., Dantuma, R., Hillen, B., Geuze, R., & Schellekens, J. (1989). Kinesiologic aspects of motor learning in dart throwing. *Journal of Human Movement Studies, 16,* 161–171.

Jakobson, L. S., & Goodale, M. A. (1991). Factors influencing higher-order movement planning: A kinematic analysis of human prehension. *Experimental Brain Research, 86,* 199–208.

Jambor, E. A., & Weekes, E. M. (1995, February). Videotape feedback: Make it more effective. *Journal of Physical Education, Recreation, and Dance, 66,* 48–50.

James, W. (1890). *Principles of psychology*. New York: Holt.

Janelle, C. M., Barba, D. A., Frehlich, S. G., Tennant L. K., & Cauraugh, J. H. (1997). Maximizing performance feedback effectiveness through videotape replay and a self-controlled learning environment. *Research Quarterly for Exercise and Sport, 68,* 269–279.

Janelle, C. M., Kim, J., & Singer, R. N. (1995). Subject-controlled performance feedback and learning of a closed motor skill. *Perceptual and Motor Skills, 81,* 627–634.

Jeannerod, M. (1981). Intersegmental coordination during reaching at natural visual objects. In J. Long & A. Baddeley, (Eds.), *Attention and Performance IX* (pp. 153–168). Hillsdale, NJ: Erlbaum.

Jeannerod, M. (1984). The timing of natural prehension. *Journal of Motor Behavior, 16,* 235–254.

Jeka, J. J., Ribiero, P., Oie, K., & Lackner, J. R. (1998). The structure of somatosensory information for human postural control. *Motor Control, 2,* 13–33.

Johansson, G. (1973). Visual perception of biological motion and a model for its analysis. *Perception and Psychophysics, 14,* 201–211.

Johnson, S. H. (1998). Cerebral organization of motor imagery: Contralateral control of grip selection in mentally represented prehension. *Psychological Science, 9,* 219–222.

Jongsma, D. M., Elliott, D., & Lee, T. D. (1987). Experience and set in the running sprint start. *Perceptual and Motor Skills, 64,* 547–550.

Kahneman, D. (1973). *Attention and effort.* Englewood Cliffs, NJ: Prentice Hall.

Kamon, E., & Gormley, J. (1968). Muscular activity pattern for skilled performance and during learning of a horizontal bar exercise. *Ergonomics, 11,* 345–357.

Keele, S. W. (1968). Movement control in skilled motor performance. *Psychological Bulletin, 70,* 387–403.

Keele, S. W., & Posner, M. I. (1968). Processing of visual feedback in rapid movements. *Journal of Experimental Psychology, 77,* 153–158.

Kelso, J. A. S. (1997). Motor control mechanisms underlying human movement reproduction. *Journal of Experimental Psychology: Human Perception and Performance, 3,* 529–543.

Kelso, J. A. S. (1984). Phase transitions and critical behavior in human bimanual coordination. *American Journal of Physiology: Regulatory, Integrative, and Comparative Physiology, 15,* R1000–1004.

Kelso, J. A. S. (1997). Relative timing in brain and behavior: Some observations about the generalized motor program and self-organized coordination dynamics. *Human Movement Science, 16,* 453–460.

Kelso, J. A. S., & Holt, K. G. (1980). Exploring a vibratory systems analysis of human movement production. *Journal of Neurophysiology, 43,* 1183–1196.

Kelso, J. A. S., Holt, K. G., & Flatt, A. E. (1980). The role of proprioception in the perception and control of human movement: Toward a theoretical reassessment. *Perception and Psychophysics, 28,* 45–52.

Kelso, J. A. S., & Scholz, J. P. (1985). Cooperative phenomena in biological motion. In H. Haken (Ed.), *Complex systems: Operational approaches in neurobiology, physical systems, and computers* (pp. 124–149). Berlin: Springer-Verlag.

Kelso, J. A. S., Southard, D. L., & Goodman, D. (1979). On the coordination of two-handed movements. *Journal of Experimental Psychology: Human Perception and Performance, 5,* 229–238.

Kernodle, M. W., & Carlton, L. G. (1992). Information feedback and the learning of multiple-degree-of-freedom activities. *Journal of Motor Behavior, 24,* 187–196.

Knapp, C. G., & Dixon, W. R. (1952). Learning to juggle: II. A study of whole and part methods. *Research Quarterly, 23,* 398–401.

Laabs, G. J. (1973). Retention characteristics of different reproduction cues in motor short-term memory. *Journal of Experimental Psychology, 100,* 168–177.

Lai, Q., & Shea, C. H. (1998). Generalized motor program (GMP) learning: Effects of reduced frequency of knowledge of results and practice variability. *Journal of Motor Behavior, 30,* 51–59.

Lai, Q., & Shea, C. H. (1999a). Bandwidth knowledge of results enhances generalized motor program learning. *Research Quarterly for Exercise and Sport, 70,* 79–83.

Lai, Q., & Shea, C. H. (1999b). The role of reduced frequency of knowledge of results during constant practice. *Research Quarterly for Exercise and Sport, 70,* 33–40.

Landin, D. (1994). The role of verbal cues in skill learning. *Quest, 46,* 299–313.

Landin, D. L., & Hebert, E. P. (1997). A comparison of three practice schedules along the contextual interference continuum. *Research Quarterly for Exercise and Sport, 68,* 357–361.

Landin, D. L., & Hebert, E. P. (1999). The influence of self-talk on the performance of skilled female tennis players. *Journal of Applied Sport Psychology, 11,* 263–282.

Lange, G., Waked, W., Kirshblum, S., & DeLuca, J. (2000). Organizational strategy influence on visual memory performance after stroke: Cortical/subcortical and left/right hemisphere contrasts. *Archives of Physical Medicine and Rehabilitation, 81,* 89–94.

Langley, D. J. (1995). Student cognition in the instructional setting. *Journal of Teaching in Physical Education, 15,* 25–40.

Larish, D. D., & Stelmach, G. E. (1982). Preprogramming, programming, and reprogramming of aimed hand movements as a function of age. *Journal of Motor Behavior, 14,* 322–340.

Lashley, K. S. (1917). The accuracy of movement in the absence of excitation from the moving organ. *American Journal of Physiology, 43,* 169–194.

Lashley, K. S. (1951). The problem of serial order in behavior, In L. A. Jeffress (Ed.), *Cerebral mechanisms in behavior* (pp. 112–136). New York: Wiley.

Laszlo, J. L. (1966). The performance of a single motor task with kinesthetic sense loss. *Quarterly Journal of Experimental Psychology, 18,* 1–8.

Laszlo, J. L. (1967). Training of fast tapping with reduction of kinesthetic, tactile, visual, and auditory sensation. *Quarterly Journal of Experimental Psychology, 19,* 344–349.

Latash, M. L. (1999). Mirror writing: Learning, transfer, and implications for internal inverse models. *Journal of Motor Behavior, 31,* 107–111.

Laugier, C., & Cadopi, M. (1996). Representational guidance of dance performance in adult novices: Effect of concrete vs. abstract movement. *International Journal of Sport Psychology, 27,* 91–108.

Laurent, M., & Thomson, J. A. (1988). The role of visual information in control of a constrained locomotor task. *Journal of Motor Behavior, 20,* 17–38.

Lee, A. M., Keh, N. C., & Magill, R. A. (1993). Instructional effects of teacher feedback in physical education. *Journal of Teaching in Physical Education, 12,* 228–243.

Lee, D. N. (1974). Visual information during locomotion. In R. B. MacLeod & H. Pick (Eds.), *Perception: Essays in honor of J. J. Gibson* (pp. 250–267). Ithaca, NY: Cornell University Press.

Lee, D. N., & Aronson, E. (1974). Visual proprioceptive control of standing in human infants. *Perception and Psychophysics, 15,* 527–532.

Lee, D. N., Lishman, J. R., & Thomson, J. A. (1982). Regulation of gait in long jumping. *Journal of Experimental Psychology: Human Perception and Performance, 8,* 448–459.

Lee, T. D. (1988). Testing for motor learning: A focus on transfer-appropriate processing. In O. G. Meijer & K. Roth (Eds.), *Complex motor behaviour: "The" motor-action controversy* (pp. 210–215). Amsterdam: Elsevier.

Lee, T. D., & Genovese, E. D. (1988). Distribution of practice in motor skill acquisition: Learning and performance effects reconsidered. *Research Quarterly for Exercise and Sport, 59,* 59–67.

Lee, T. D., & Genovese, E. D. (1989). Distribution of practice in motor skill acquisition: Different effects for discrete and continuous tasks. *Research Quarterly for Exercise and Sport, 59,* 277–287.

Lee, T. D., & Hirota, T. T. (1980). Encoding specificity principle in motor short-term memory for movement extent. *Journal of Motor Behavior, 12,* 63–67.

Lee, T. D., & Magill, R. A. (1983). Activity during the post-KR interval: Effects upon performance or learning. *Research Quarterly for Exercise and Sport, 54,* 340–345.

Lee, T. D., & Magill, R. A. (1985). Can forgetting facilitate skill acquisition? In D. Goodman, R. B. Wilberg, & I. M. Franks (Eds.), *Differing perspectives in motor learning, memory and control* (pp. 3–22). Amsterdam: North-Holland.

Lee, T. D., Swinnen, S. P., & Verschueren, S. (1995). Relative phase alterations during bimanual skill acquisition. *Journal of Motor Behavior, 27,* 263–274.

Lee, T. D., White, M. A., & Carnahan, H. (1990). On the role of knowledge of results in motor learning: Exploring the guidance hypothesis. *Journal of Motor Behavior, 22,* 191–208.

Lidor, R., Tennant, K. L., & Singer, R. N. (1996). The generalizability effect of three learning strategies across motor task performances. *International Journal of Sport Psychology, 27,* 23–36.

Lindahl, L. G. (1945). Movement analysis as an industrial training method. *Journal of Applied Psychology, 29,* 420–436.

Linden, C. A., Uhley, J. E., Smith, D., & Bush, M. A. (1989). The effects of mental practice on walking balance in an elderly population. *Occupational Therapy Journal of Research, 9,* 155–169.

Lintern, G. (1991). An informational perspective on skill transfer in human-machine systems. *Human Factors, 33,* 251–266.

Lintern, G., & Roscoe, S. N. (1980). Visual cue augmentation in contact flight simulation. In S. N. Roscoe (Ed.), *Aviation psychology* (pp. 227–238). Ames, IA: Iowa State University Press.

Lintern, G., Roscoe, S. N., & Sivier, J. (1990). Display principles, control dynamics, and environmental factors in pilot training and transfer. *Human Factors, 32,* 299–317.

Little, W. S., & McCullagh, P. M. (1989). Motivation orientation and modeled instruction strategies: The effects on form and accuracy. *Journal of Sport & Exercise Psychology, 11,* 41–53.

Liu, J., & Wrisberg, C. A. (1997). The effect of knowledge of results delay and the subjective estimation of movement form on the acquisition and retention of a motor skill. *Research Quarterly for Exercise and Sport, 68,* 145–151.

Loeb, J. (1890). Untersuchungen uber die Orientirung im Fuhlraum der Hand und im Blickraum. *Pflueger Archives of General Physiology, 46,* 1–46.

Loftus, E. F. (1980). *Memory: Surprising new insights into how we remember and why we forget.* Reading, MA: Addison-Wesley.

Loftus, E. F., & Loftus, G. R. (1980). On the permanence of stored information in the human brain. *American Psychologist, 35,* 409–420.

Logan, G. D. (1985). Skill and automaticity: Relations, implications, and future directions. *Canadian Journal of Psychology, 39,* 367–386.

Logan, G. D. (1988). Toward an instance theory of automatization. *Psychological Review, 95,* 492–527.

Logan, G. D. (1998). What is learned during automatization? II. Obligatory encoding of spatial location. *Journal of Experimental Psychology: Human Perception and Performance, 24,* 1720–1736.

Loken, W. J., Thornton, A. E., Otto, R. L., & Long, C. J. (1995). Sustained attention after severe closed head injury. *Neuropsychology, 9,* 592–598.

Mackworth, N. H. (1956). Vigilance. *Nature, 178,* 1375–1377.

Magill, R. A. (1988). Activity during the post-knowledge of results interval can benefit motor skill learning. In O. G. Meijer & K. Roth (Eds.), *Complex motor behavior: "The" motor-action controversy* (pp. 231–246). Amsterdam: Elsevier.

Magill, R. A. (1998). Knowledge is more than we can talk about: Implicit learning in motor skill acquisition. *Research Quarterly for Exercise and Sport, 69,* 104–110.

Magill, R. A., Chamberlin, C. J., & Hall, K. G. (1991). Verbal knowledge of results as redundant information for learning an anticipation timing skill. *Human Movement Science, 10,* 485–507.

Magill, R. A., & Hall, K. G. (1990). A review of the contextual interference effect in motor skill acquisition. *Human Movement Science, 9,* 241–289.

Magill, R. A., & Lee, T. D. (1987). Verbal label effects on response accuracy and organization for learning limb positioning movements. *Journal of Human Movement Studies, 13,* 285–308.

Magill, R. A., & Parks, P. F. (1983). The psychophysics of kinesthesis for positioning responses: The physical stimulus-psychological response relationship. *Research Quarterly for Exercise and Sport, 54,* 346–351.

Magill, R. A., & Schoenfelder-Zohdi, B. (1996). A visual model and knowledge of performance as sources of information for learning a rhythmic gymnastics skill. *International Journal of Sport Psychology, 27,* 7–22.

Magill, R. A., & Wood, C. A. (1986). Knowledge of results precision as a learning variable in motor skill acquisition. *Research Quarterly for Exercise and Sport, 57,* 170–173.

Mahoney, M. J., & Avener, A. (1977). Psychology of the elite athlete: An exploratory study. *Cognitive Therapy and Research, 1,* 135–141.

Mané, A., & Donchin, E. (1989). The Space Fortress game. *Acta Psychologica, 71,* 17–22.

Mark, L. S., & Vogele, D. (1987). A biodynamic basis for perceived categories of action: A study of sitting and stair climbing. *Journal of Motor Behavior, 19,* 367–384.

Marotta, J. J., Kruyer, A., & Goodale, M. A. (1998). The role of head movement in the control of manual prehension. *Experimental Brain Research, 120,* 134–138.

Marteniuk, R. G. (1986). Information processes in movement learning: Capacity and structural interference. *Journal of Motor Behavior, 5,* 249–259.

Marteniuk, R. G., & Romanow, S. K. E. (1983). Human movement organization and learning as revealed by variability of movement, use of kinematic information and Fourier analysis. In R. A. Magill (Ed.), *Memory and control of action* (pp. 167–197). Amsterdam: North-Holland.

Martin, K. A., Moritz, S. A., & Hall, C. R. (1999). Imagery use in sport: A literature review and applied model. *The Sport Psychologist, 13,* 245–268.

Masser, L. S. (1993). Critical cues help first-grade students' achievement in handstands and forward rolls. *Journal of Teaching in Physical Education, 12,* 301–312.

Mathiowetz, V., & Wade, M. G. (1995). Task constraints and functional motor performance of individuals with and without multiple sclerosis. *Ecological Psychology, 7,* 99–123.

McCullagh, P. (1993). Modeling: Learning, developmental, and social psychological considerations. In R. N. Singer, M. Murphy, & L. K. Tennant (Eds.), *Handbook of research on sport psychology* (pp. 106–126). New York: Macmillan.

McCullagh, P., & Meyer, K. N. (1997). Learning versus correct models: Influence of model type on the learning of a free-weight squat lift. *Research Quarterly for Exercise and Sport, 68,* 56–61.

McCullagh, P., Stiehl, J., & Weiss, M. R. (1990). Developmental modeling effects on the quantitative and qualitative aspects of motor performance. *Research Quarterly for Exercise and Sport, 61,* 344–350.

McDonald, P. V., Oliver, S. K., & Newell, K. M. (1995). Perceptual-motor exploration as a function of biomechanical and task constraints. *Acta Psychologica, 88,* 127–165.

McIntosh, G. C., Brown, S. H., Rice, R. R., & Thaut, M. H. (1997). Rhythmic auditory-motor facilitation of gait patterns in patients with Parkinson's disease. *Journal of Neurology, Neurosurgery, and Psychiatry, 62,* 22–26.

McLeod, P., Driver, J., Dienes, Z., & Crisp, J. (1991). Filtering by movement in visual search. *Journal of Experimental Psychology: Human Perception and Performance, 17,* 55–64.

McNevin, N., Magill, R. A., & Buekers, M. J. (1994). The effects of erroneous knowledge of results on transfer of anticipation timing. *Research Quarterly for Exercise and Sport, 65,* 324–329.

McPherson, S. L., & Thomas, J. R. (1989). Relation of knowledge and performance in boy's tennis: Age and expertise. *Journal of Experimental Child Psychology, 48,* 190–211.

Meeuwsen, H., & Magill, R. A. (1987). The role of vision in gait control during gymnastics vaulting. In T. B. Hoshizaki, J. Salmela, & B. Petiot (Eds.), *Diagnostics, treatment, and analysis of gymnastic talent* (pp. 137–155). Montreal: Sport Psyche Editions.

Melnick, M. J. (1971). Effects of overlearning on the retention of a gross motor skill. *Research Quarterly, 42,* 60–69.

Meyer, D. E., Abrams, R. A., Kornblum, S., Wright, C. E., & Smith, J. E. K. (1988). Optimality in human motor performance: Ideal control of rapid aimed movements. *Psychological Review, 95,* 340–370.

Meyer, D. E., Smith, J. E. K., Kornblum, S., Abrams, R. A., & Wright, C. E. (1990). Speed-accuracy trade-offs in aimed movements: Toward a theory of rapid voluntary action. In M. Jeannerod (Ed.), *Attention and performance XIII* (pp. 173–226). Hillsdale, NJ: Erlbaum.

Miller, G. A. (1956). The magical number seven plus or minus two: Some limits on our capacity for processing information. *Psychological Review, 63,* 81–97.

Miller, G. A., Galanter, E., & Pribram, K. H. (1960). *Plans and the structure of behavior.* New York: Holt, Rinehart, and Winston.

Moore, S. P., & Marteniuk, R. G. (1986). Kinematic and electromyographic changes that occur as a function of learning a time-constrained aiming task. *Journal of Motor Behavior, 18,* 397–426.

Moreland, J., & Thomson, M. A. (1994). Efficacy of electromyographic biofeedback compared with conventional physical therapy for upper-extremity function in patients following stroke: A research overview and meta-analysis. *Physical Therapy, 74,* 534–546.

Morris, M. E., Iansek, R., Matyas, T. A., & Summers, J. J. (1994). Ability to modulate walking cadence remains intact in Parkinson's disease. *Journal of Neurology, Neurosurgery, and Psychiatry, 57,* 1532–1534.

Mourant, R. R., & Rockwell, T. H. (1972). Strategies of visual search by novice and experienced drivers. *Human Factors, 14,* 325–335.

Murphy, S. M. (1994). Imagery interventions in sport. *Medicine and Science in Sports and Exercise, 26,* 486–494.

Navon, D., & Gopher, D. (1979). On the economy of the human processing system. *Psychological Review, 86,* 214–255.

Naylor, J., & Briggs, G. (1963). Effects of task complexity and task organization on the relative efficiency of part and whole training methods. *Journal of Experimental Psychology, 65,* 217–244.

Newell, K. M. (1985). Coordination, control, and skill. In D. Goodman, R. B. Wilberg, & I. M. Franks (Eds.), *Differing perspectives in motor learning, memory, and control* (pp. 295–317). Amsterdam: North-Holland.

Newell, K. M. (1986). Constraints on the development of coordination. In M. G. Wade & H. T. A. Whiting (Eds.), *Motor development in children: Aspects of coordination and control* (pp. 341–360). The Hague, The Netherlands: Nijhoff.

Newell, K. M., & Cesari, P. (1999). On taking the grasping out of prehension. *Motor Control, 3,* 285–288.

Newell, K. M., Quinn, J. T. Jr., Sparrow, W. A., & Walter, C. B. (1983). Kinematic information feedback for learning a rapid arm movement. *Human Movement Science, 2,* 255–269.

Newell, K. M., & van Emmerik, R. E. A. (1989). The acquisition of coordination: Preliminary analysis of learning to write. *Human Movement Science, 8,* 17–32.

Nideffer, R. M. (1993). Attention control training. In R. N. Singer, M. Murphey, & L. K. Tennant (Eds.), *Handbook of research on sport psychology* (pp. 542–556). New York: Macmillan.

Norman, D. A. (1968). Toward a theory of memory and attention. *Psychological Review, 75,* 522–536.

Patla, A. E., Rietdyk, S., Martin, C., & Prentice, S. (1996). Locomotor patterns of the leading and trailing limbs as solid and fragile obstacles are stepped over: Some insights into the role of vision during locomotion. *Journal of Motor Behavior, 28,* 35–47.

Peterson, L. R., & Peterson, M. J. (1959). Short-term retention of individual verbal items. *Journal of Experimental Psychology, 58,* 193–198.

Polit, A., & Bizzi, E. (1978). Processes controlling arm movements in monkeys. *Science, 201,* 1235–1237.

Polit, A., & Bizzi, E. (1979). Characteristics of motor programs underlying arm movements in monkeys. *Journal of Neurophysiology, 42,* 183–194.

Pollock, B. J., & Lee, T. D. (1992). Effects of the model's skill level on observational learning. *Research Quarterly for Exercise and Sport, 63,* 25–29.

Poulton, E. C. (1957). On prediction in skilled movements. *Psychological Bulletin, 54,* 467–478.

Prinz, W. (1997). Perception and action planning. *European Journal of Cognitive Psychology, 9,* 129–154.

Proctor, R., & Reeve, T. G. (Eds.). (1990). *Stimulus-response compatibility: An integrated perspective.* Amsterdam: North-Holland.

Proteau, L., & Cournoyer, L. (1990). Vision of the stylus in a manual aiming task: The effects of practice. *Quarterly Journal of Experimental Psychology, 42B,* 811–828.

Proteau, L., Marteniuk, R. G., Girouard, Y., & Dugas, C. (1987). On the type of information used to control and learn an aiming movement after moderate and extensive training. *Human Movement Science, 6,* 181–199.

Raynor, A. J. (1998). Fractionated reflex and reaction times in children with developmental coordination disorder. *Motor Control, 2,* 114–124.

Rogers, C. A. (1974). Feedback precision and postfeedback interval duration. *Journal of Experimental Psychology, 102,* 604–608.

Rosenbaum, D. A. (1980). Human movement initiation: Specification of arm, direction, and extent. *Journal of Experimental Psychology: General, 109,* 444–474.

Rosenbaum, D. A. (1983). The movement precuing technique: Assumptions, applications, and extensions. In R. A. Magill (Ed.), *Memory and control of action* (pp. 251–274). Amsterdam: North-Holland.

Rosenbaum, D. A., & Jorgensen, M. J. (1992). Planning macroscopic aspects of manual control. *Human Movement Science, 11,* 61–69.

Rosenbaum, D. A., van Heutgen, C. M., & Caldwell, C. E. (1996). From cognition to biomechanics and back: The end-state comfort effect and the middle is faster effect. *Acta Psychologica, 94,* 59–85.

Rosenbaum, D. A., Vaughn, J., Jorgensen, M. J., Barnes, H. J., & Stewart, E. (1993). Plans for object manipulation. In D. E. Meyer & S. Kornblum (Eds.), *Attention and Performance XIV: Synergies in experimental psychology, artificial intelligence, and cognitive neuroscience* (pp. 803–820). Cambridge, MA: MIT Press.

Rosenberg, K. S., Pick, H. L., & von Hofsten, C. (1988). Role of visual information in catching. *Journal of Motor Behavior, 20,* 150–164.

Rothstein, A. L., & Arnold, R. K. (1976). Bridging the gap: Application of research on videotape feedback and bowling. *Motor Skills: Theory into Practice, 1,* 36–61.

Roy, E. A., & Davenport, W. G. (1972). Factors in motor short-term memory: The interference effect of interpolated activity. *Journal of Experimental Psychology, 96,* 134–137.

Saling, M., Alberts, J., Stelmach, G. E., & Bloedel, J. R. (1998). Reach-to-grasp movements during obstacle avoidance. *Experimental Brain Research, 118,* 251–258.

Salmoni, A. W., Schmidt, R. A., & Walter, C. B. (1984). Knowledge of results and motor learning: A review and reappraisal. *Psychological Bulletin, 95,* 355–386.

Savelsbergh, G. J. P., Whiting, H. T. A., Pijpers, J. R., & van Santvoord, A. A. M. (1993). The visual guidance of catching. *Experimental Brain Research, 93,* 148–156.

Schendel, J. D., & Hagman, J. D. (1982). On sustaining procedural skills over a prolonged retention interval. *Journal of Applied Psychology, 67,* 605–610.

Schmidt, R. A. (1975). A schema theory of discrete motor skill learning theory. *Psychological Review, 82,* 225–260.

Schmidt, R. A. (1985). The search for invariance in skilled movement behavior. *Research Quarterly for Exercise and Sport, 56,* 188–200.

Schmidt, R. A., & Lee, T. D. (1999). *Motor control and learning: A behavioral emphasis* (3rd ed.). Champaign, IL: Human Kinetics.

Schmidt, R. A. (1988). Motor and action perspectives on motor behavior. In O. G. Meijer & K. Roth (Eds.), *Complex motor behaviour: "The" motor-action controversy* (pp. 3–44). Amsterdam: Elsevier.

Schmidt, R. A., Lange, C., & Young, D. E. (1990). Optimizing summary knowledge of results for skill learning. *Human Movement Science, 9,* 325–348.

Schmidt, R. A., & Young, D. E. (1987). Transfer of movement control in motor skill learning. In S. M. Cormier & J. D. Hagman (Eds.), *Transfer of learning* (pp. 47–79). Orlando, FL: Academic Press.

Schmidt, R. A., Young, D. E., Swinnen, S., & Shapiro, D. C. (1989). Summary knowledge of results for skill acquisition: Support for the guidance hypothesis. *Journal of Experimental Psychology: Learning, Memory, and Cognition, 15,* 352–359.

Schmidt, R. A., Zelaznik, H. N., Hawkins, B., Frank, J. S., & Quinn, J. T. Jr. (1979). Motor output variability: A theory for the accuracy of rapid motor acts. *Psychological Review, 86,* 415–451.

Schmidt, R. C., & Turvey, M. T. (1992). Long-term consistencies in assembling coordinated rhythmic movements. *Human Movement Science, 11,* 349–376.

Schneider, K., Zernicke, R. F., Schmidt, R. A., & Hart, T. J. (1989). Changes in limb dynamics during the practice of rapid arm movement. *Journal of Biomechanics, 22,* 805–817.

Schoenfelder-Zohdi, B. G. (1992). *Investigating the informational nature of a modeled visual demonstration.* Ph.D. dissertation, Louisiana State University.

Scholz, J. P. (1990). Dynamic pattern theory: Some implications for therapeutics. *Physical Therapy, 70,* 827–843.

Scully, D. M., & Newell, K. M. (1985). Observational learning and the acquisition of motor skills: Toward a visual perception perspective. *Journal of Human Movement Studies, 11,* 169–186.

Selder, D. J., & Del Rolan, N. (1979). Knowledge of performance, skill level and performance on the balance beam. *Canadian Journal of Applied Sport Sciences, 4,* 226–229.

Servos, P. (2000). Distance estimation in the visual and visuomotor systems. *Experimental Brain Research, 130,* 35–47.

Shank, M. D., & Haywood, K. M. (1987). Eye movements while viewing a baseball pitch. *Perceptual and Motor Skills, 64,* 1191–1197.

Shapiro, D. C., Zernicke, R. F., Gregor, R. J., & Diestel, J. D. (1981). Evidence for generalized motor programs using gait-pattern analysis. *Journal of Motor Behavior, 13,* 33–47.

Shea, C. H., & Kohl, R. M. (1990). Specificity and variability of practice. *Research Quarterly for Exercise and Sport, 61,* 169–177.

Shea, C. H., & Kohl, R. M. (1991). Composition of practice: Influence on the retention of motor skills. *Research Quarterly for Exercise and Sport, 62,* 187–195.

Shea, C. H., Kohl, R., & Indermill, C. (1990). Contextual interference contributions of practice. *Acta Psychologica, 73,* 145–157.

Shea, J. B. (1977). Effects of labeling on motor short-term memory. *Journal of Experimental Psychology: Human Learning and Memory, 3,* 92–99.

Shea, J. B., & Morgan, R. L. (1979). Contextual interference effects on the acquisition, retention, and transfer of a motor skill. *Journal of Experimental Psychology: Human Learning and Memory, 5,* 179–187.

Shea, J. B., & Zimny, S. T. (1983). Context effects in memory and learning in movement information. In R. A. Magill (Ed.), *Memory and control of action* (pp. 345–366). Amsterdam: North-Holland.

Shepherd, R. B., & Gentile, A. M. (1994). Sit-to-stand: Functional relationship between upper and lower body limb segments. *Human Movement Science, 13,* 817–840.

Sheridan, M. R. (1984). Response programming, response production, and fractionated reaction time. *Psychological Research, 46,* 33–47.

Sherrington, C. S. (1906). *Integrative action of the nervous system.* New York: Scribner.

Sherwood, D. E. (1988). Effect of bandwidth knowledge of results on movement consistency. *Perceptual and Motor Skills, 66,* 535–542.

Sherwood, D. E. (1994). Hand preference, practice order, and spatial assimilation in rapid bimanual movement. *Journal of Motor Behavior, 26,* 123–134.

Shinar, D., Meir, M., & Ben-Shoham, I. (1998). How automatic is manual gear shifting? *Human Factors, 40,* 647–654.

Short, M. W., & Cauraugh, J. H. (1999). Precision hypothesis and the end-state comfort effect. *Acta Psychologica, 100,* 243–252.

Sidaway, B., Heise, G., & Schoenfelder-Zohdi, B. (1995). Quantifying the variability of angle-angle plots. *Journal of Human Movement Studies, 29,* 181–197.

Sidaway, B., McNitt-Gray, J., & Davis, G. (1989). Visual timing of muscle preactivation in preparation for landing. *Ecological Psychology, 1,* 253–264.

Sidaway, B., Moore, B., & Schoenfelder-Zohdi, B. (1991). Summary and frequency of KR presentation effects on retention of a motor skill. *Research Quarterly for Exercise and Sport, 62,* 27–32.

Sidaway, B., Sekiya, H., & Fairweather, M. (1995). Movement variability as a function of accuracy demands in programmed aiming responses. *Journal of Motor Behavior, 27,* 67–76.

Siegel, D. (1986). Movement duration, fractionated reaction time, and response programming. *Research Quarterly for Exercise and Sport, 57,* 128–131.

Silverman, S., Tyson, L. A., & Krampitz, J. (1991). *Teacher feedback and achievement in physical education: Interaction with student practice.* Paper presented at the annual meeting of the American Educational Research Association, Chicago, Illinois.

Silverman, S., Woods, A. M., & Subramaniam, P. R. (1998). Task structures, feedback to individual students, and student skill level in physical education. *Research Quarterly for Exercise and Sport, 69,* 420–424.

Silverman, S., Woods, A. M., & Subramaniam, P. R. (1999). Feedback and practice in physical education: Interrelationships with task structures and student skill level. *Journal of Human Movement Studies, 36,* 203–224.

Simmons, R. W., Smith, K., Erez, E., Burke, J. P., & Pozos, R. E. (1998). Balance retraining in a hemiparetic patient using center of gravity biofeedback: A single-case study. *Perceptual and Motor Skills, 87,* 603–609.

Singer, R. N. (1986). Sports performance: A five-step mental approach. *Journal of Physical Education and Recreation, 57,* 82–84.

Singer, R. N. (1988). Strategies and metastrategies in learning and performing self-paced athletic skills. *The Sport Psychologist, 2,* 49–68.

Singer, R. N., Cauraugh, J. H., Chen, D., Steinberg, G. M., Frehlich, S. G., & Wang, L. (1994). Training mental quickness in beginning/intermediate tennis players. *The Sport Psychologist, 8,* 305–318.

Singer, R. N., Cauraugh, J., Tennant, L. K., Murphey, M., Chen, R., & Lidor, R. (1991). Attention and distractors: Considerations for enhancing sport performances. *International Journal of Sport Psychology, 22,* 95–114.

Singer, R. N., Williams, A. M., Frehlich, S. G, Janelle, C. M., Radlo, S. J., Barba, D. A., & Bouchard, L. J. (1998). New frontiers in visual search: An exploratory study in live tennis situations. *Research Quarterly for Exercise and Sport, 69,* 290–296.

Sivak, B., & MacKenzie, C. L. (1990). Integration of visual information and motor output in reaching and grasping: The contributions of peripheral and central vision. *Neuropsychologia, 28,* 1095–1116.

Smith, W. M., & Bowen, K. F. (1980). The effects of delayed and displaced visual feedback on motor control. *Journal of Motor Behavior, 12,* 91–101.

Smyth, M. M., & Marriott, A. M. (1982). Vision and proprioception in simple catching. *Journal of Motor Behavior, 14,* 143–152.

Smyth, M. M., & Pendleton, L. R. (1990). Space and movement in working memory. *Quarterly Journal of Experimental Psychology, 42A,* 291–304.

Smyth, M. M., & Silvers, G. (1987). Functions of vision in the control of handwriting. *Acta Psychologica, 65,* 47–64.

Snoddy, G. S. (1926). Learning and stability: A psychophysical analysis of a case of motor learning with clinical applications. *Journal of Applied Psychology, 10,* 1–36.

Solmon, M. A., & Boone, J. (1993). The impact of student goal orientation in physical education classes. *Research Quarterly for Exercise and Sport, 64,* 418–424.

Solmon, M. A., & Lee, A. M. (1996). Entry characteristics, practice variables, and cognition: Student mediation of instruction. *Journal of Teaching in Physical Education, 15,* 136–150.

Southard, D., & Amos, B. (1996). Rhythmicity and preperformance ritual: Stablizing a flexible system. *Research Quarterly for Exercise and Sport, 67,* 288–296.

Southard, D., & Higgins, T. (1987). Changing movement patterns: Effects of demonstration and practice. *Research Quarterly for Exercise and Sport, 58,* 77–80.

Southard, D., & Miracle, A. (1993). Rhythmicity, ritual, and motor performance: A study of free-throw shooting in basketball. *Research Quarterly for Exercise and Sport, 64,* 284–290.

Sparrow, W. A., Donovan, E., van Emmerik, R. E. A., & Barry, E. B. (1987). Using relative motion plots to measure changes in intra-limb and inter-limb coordination. *Journal of Motor Behavior, 19,* 115–119.

Sparrow, W. A., & Irizarry-Lopez, V. W. (1987). Mechanical efficiency and metabolic cost as measures of learning a novel gross motor task. *Journal of Motor Behavior, 19,* 240–264.

Sparrow, W. A., & Newell, K. M. (1994). Energy expenditure and motor performance relationships in humans learning a motor task. *Psychophysiology, 31,* 338–346.

Sparrow, W. A., & Newell, K. M. (1998). Metabolic energy expenditure and the regulation of movement economy. *Psychonomic Bulletin & Review, 5,* 173–196.

Sparrow, W. A., & Summers, J. J. (1992). Performance on trials without knowledge of results (KR) in reduced relative frequency presentations of KR. *Journal of Motor Behavior, 24,* 197–209.

Spijkers, W. A. C., & Lochner, P. (1994). Partial visual feedback and spatial end-point accuracy of visual aiming movements. *Journal of Motor Behavior, 26,* 283–295.

Starek, J., & McCullagh, P. (1999). The effect of self-modeling on the performance of beginning swimmers. *The Sport Psychologist, 13,* 269–287.

Starkes, J. L., Deakin, J. M., Lindley, S., & Crisp, F. (1987). Motor versus verbal recall of ballet sequences by young expert dancers. *Journal of Sport Psychology, 9,* 222–230.

Staum, M. J. (1983). Music and rhythmic stimuli in the rehabilitation of gait disorders. *Journal of Music Theraphy, 20,* 69–87.

Steenbergen, B., Marteniuk, R. G., & Kalbfleisch, L. E. (1995). Achieving coordination in prehension: Joint freezing and postural contributions. *Journal of Motor Behavior, 27,* 333–348.

Stelmach, G. E. (1969). Prior positioning responses as a factor in short-term retention of a simple motor response. *Journal of Experimental Psychology, 81,* 523–526.

Summers, J. J. (1975). The role of timing in motor program representation. *Journal of Motor Behavior, 7,* 229–242.

Swinnen, S. P., (1990). Interpolated activities during the knowledge of results delay and postknowledge of results interval: Effects of performance and learning. *Journal of Experimental Psychology: Learning, Memory, and Cognition, 16,* 692–705.

Swinnen, S. P., Schmidt, R. A., Nicholson, D. E., & Shapiro, D. C. (1990). Information feedback for skill acquisition: Instantaneous knowledge of results degrades learning. *Journal of Experimental Psychology: Learning, Memory, and Cognition, 16,* 706–716.

Swinnen, S. P., Walter, C. B., Lee, T. D., & Serrien, D. J. (1993). Acquiring bimanual skills: Contrasting forms of information feedback for interlimb decoupling. *Journal of Experimental Psychology: Learning, Memory, and Cognition, 19,* 1321–1344.

Swinnen, S. P., Walter, C. B., Pauwels, J. M., Meugens, P. F., & Beirinckx, M. B. (1990). The dissociation of interlimb constraints. *Human Performance, 3,* 187–215.

Taub, E., & Berman, A. J. (1963). Avoidance conditioning in the absence of relevant proprioceptive and exteroceptive feedback. *Journal of Comparative and Physiological Psychology, 56,* 1012–1016.

Taub, E., & Berman, A. J. (1968). Movement and learning in the absence of sensory feedback. In S. J. Freedman (Ed.), *The neuropsychology of spatially oriented behavior* (pp. 173–192). Homewood, IL: Dorsey Press.

Teichner, W. H. (1954). Recent studies of simple reaction time. *Psychological Bulletin, 51,* 128–149.

Thaut, M. H., McIntosh, G. C., Rice, R. R., Miller, R. A., Rathburn, J., & Brault, J. M. (1996). Rhythmic auditory stimulation in gait training for Parkinson's disease patients. *Movement Disorders, 11,* 193–200.

Thomas, J. R., & Halliwell, W. (1976). Individual differences in motor skill acquisition. *Journal of Motor Behavior, 8,* 89–100.

Thomas, J. R., Thomas, K. T., Lee, A. M., Testerman, E., & Ashy, M. (1983). Age differences in the use of strategy for recall of movement in a large scale environment. *Research Quarterly for Exercise and Sport, 54,* 264–272.

Thorndike, E. L. (1914). *Educational psychology: Briefer course.* New York: Columbia University Press.

Treisman, A. (1988). Features and objects: The fourteenth Bartlett Memorial Lecture. *Quarterly Journal of Experimental Psychology, 40A,* 201–237.

Treisman, A., & Gelade, G. (1980). A feature integration theory of attention. *Cognitive Psychology, 12,* 97–136.

Trinity, J., & Annesi, J. J. (1996, August). Coaching with video. *Strategies, 9,* 23–25.

Trowbridge, M. H., & Cason, H. (1932). An experimental study of Thorndike's theory of learning. *Journal of General Psychology, 7,* 245–258.

Trussell, E. (1965). Prediction of success in a motor skill on the basis of early learning achievement. *Research Quarterly, 36,* 342–347.

Tulving, E. (1985). How many memory systems are there? *American Psychologist, 40,* 385–398.

Tulving, E., & Thomson, D. M. (1973). Encoding specificity and retrieval processes in episodic memory. *Psychological Review, 80,* 352–373.

Turvey, M. T. (1977). Preliminaries to a theory of action with reference to vision. In R. Shaw & J. Bransford (Eds.), *Perceiving, acting, and knowing* (pp. 211–265). Hillsdale, NJ: Erlbaum.

Turvey, M. T. (1990). Coordination. *American Psychologist, 45,* 938–953.

Turvey, M. T., Holt, K. G., LaFiandra, M. E., & Fonseca, S. T. (1999). Can the transitions to and from running and the metabolic cost of running be determined from the kinetic energy of running? *Journal of Motor Behavior, 31,* 265–278.

Twitmeyer, E. M. (1931). Visual guidance in motor learning. *American Journal of Psychology, 43,* 165–187.

van Emmerik, R. E. A., & Wagenaar, R. C. (1996). Effect of walking velocity on relative phase dynamics in the trunk in human walking. *Journal of Biomechanics, 29,* 1175–1184.

Van Gyn, G. H., Wenger, H. A., & Gaul, C. A. (1990). Imagery as a method of enhancing transfer from training to performance. *Journal of Sport & Exercise Psychology, 12,* 366–375.

Vander Linden, D. W., Cauraugh, J. H., & Greene, T. A. (1993). The effect of frequency of kinetic feedback on learning an isometric force production task in nondisabled subjects. *Physical Therapy, 73,* 79–87.

van Loon, E. M., Buekers, M. J., Helsen, W., & Magill, R. A. (1998). Temporal and spatial adaptations during the acquisition of a reversal movement. *Research Quarterly for Exercise and Sport, 69,* 38–46.

van Wieringen, P. C. W. (1996). Ecological and dynamical approaches to rehabilitation: An epilogue. *Human Movement Science, 15,* 315–323.

Vereijken, B., van Emmerik, R. E. A., Whiting, H. T. A., & Newell, K. M. (1992). Free(z)ing degrees of freedom in skill acquisition. *Journal of Motor Behavior, 24,* 133–142.

Vereijken, B., & Whiting, H. T. A. (1990). In defence of discovery learning. *Canadian Journal of Sport Science, 15,* 99–106.

Verschueren, S. M. P., Swinnen, S. P., Cordo, P. J., & Dounskaia, N. V. (1999a). Proprioceptive control of multijoint movement: Bimanual circle drawing. *Experimental Brain Research, 127,* 182–192.

Verschueren, S. M. P., Swinnen, S. P., Cordo, P. J., & Dounskaia, N. V. (1999b). Proprioceptive control of multijoint movement: Unimanual circle drawing. *Experimental Brain Research, 127,* 171–181.

Verschueren, S. M. P., Swinnen, S. P., Dom, R., & DeWeerdt, W. (1997). Interlimb coordination in patients with Parkinson's disease: Motor learning deficits and the importance of augmented information feedback. *Experimental Brain Research, 113,* 497–508.

Vickers, J. N. (1992). Gaze control in putting. *Perception, 21,* 117–132.

Vickers, J. N. (1996). Visual control when aiming at a far target. *Journal of Experimental Psychology: Human Perception and Performance, 22,* 342–354

Vishton, P. M., & Cutting, J. E. (1995). Wayfinding, displacements, and mental maps: Velocity fields are not typically used to determine one's aimpoint. *Journal of Experimental Psychology: Human Perception and Performance, 21,* 978–995.

Vorro, J., Wilson, F. R., & Dainis, A. (1978). Multivariate analysis of biomechanical profiles for the coracobrachialis and biceps brachii (caput breve) muscles in humans. *Ergonomics, 21,* 407–418.

Wagenaar, R. C., & Beek, W. J. (1992). Hemiplegic gait: A kinematic analysis using walking speed as a basis. *Journal of Biomechanics, 25,* 1007–1015.

Wagenaar, R. C., & van Emmerik, R. E. A. (1994). Dynamics of pathological gait. *Human Movement Science, 13,* 441–471.

Wallace, S. A., & Hagler, R. W. (1979). Knowledge of performance and the learning of a closed motor skill. *Research Quarterly, 50,* 265–271.

Walter, C. B. (1998). An alternative view of dynamical systems concepts in motor control and learning. *Research Quarterly for Exercise and Sport, 69,* 326–333.

Walter, C. B., & Swinnen, S. P. (1992). Adaptive tuning of interlimb attraction to facilitate bimanual coupling. *Journal of Motor Behavior, 24,* 95–104.

Walter, C. B., & Swinnen, S. P. (1994). The formulation and dissolution of "bad habits" during the acquisition of coordination skills. In S. Swinnen, H. Heuer, J. Maisson, & P. Casaer (Eds.), *Interlimb coordination: Neural, dynamical, and cognitive constraints* (pp. 491–513). San Diego, CA: Academic Press.

Wann, J. P., & Nimmo-Smith, I. (1991). The control of pen pressure in handwriting: A subtle point. *Human Movement Science, 10,* 223–246.

Warren, W. H. (1984). Perceiving affordances: Visual guidance of stair climbing. *Journal of Experimental Psychology: Human Perception and Performance, 10,* 683–703.

Warren, W. H., & Whang, S. (1987). Visual guidance of walking through apertures: Body-scaled information for affordances. *Journal of Experimental Psychology: Human Perception and Performance, 13,* 371–383.

Warren, W. H., Jr., Young, D. S., & Lee, D. N. (1986). Visual control of step length during running over irregular terrain. *Journal of Experimental Psychology: Human Perception and Performance, 12,* 259–266.

Watters, R. G. (1992). Retention of human sequenced behavior following forward chaining, backward chaining, and whole task training procedures. *Journal of Human Movement Studies, 22,* 117–129.

Weeks, D. J., & Proctor, R. W. (1990). Salient-features coding in the translation between orthogonal stimulus and response dimensions. *Journal of Experimental Psychology: General, 119,* 355–366.

Weeks, D. L., & Kordus, R. N. (1998). Relative frequency of knowledge of performance and motor skill learning. *Research Quarterly for Exercise and Sport, 68,* 224–230.

Weeks, D. L., & Sherwood, D. E. (1994). A comparison of knowledge of results scheduling methods for promoting motor skill acquisition and retention. *Research Quarterly for Exercise and Sport, 65,* 136–142.

Weeks, D. L., & Wallace, S. A. (1992). Premovement posture and focal movement velocity effects on postural responses accompanying rapid arm movement. *Human Movement Science, 11,* 717–734.

Weinberg, D. R., Guy, D. E., & Tupper, R. W. (1964). Variations of post-feedback interval in simple motor learning. *Journal of Experimental Psychology, 67,* 98–99.

Weir, P. L., & Leavitt, J. L. (1990). The effects of model's skill level and model's knowledge of results on the acquisition of an aiming task. *Human Movement Science, 9,* 369–383.

Welford, A. T. (1952). The psychological refractory period and the timing of high-speed performance—A review and a theory. *British Journal of Psychology, 43,* 2–19.

Welford, A. T. (1967). Single channel operations in the brain. *Acta Psychologica, 27,* 5–22.

Whiting, H. T. A. (Ed.). (1984). *Human movement actions: Bernstein reassessed.* Amsterdam: North-Holland.

Whiting, H. T. A. (1988). Imitation and the learning of complex cyclical actions. In O. G. Meijer & K. Roth (Eds.), *Complex motor behaviour: "The" motor-action controversy* (pp. 381–401). Amsterdam: North-Holland.

Whiting, H. T. A., Gill, E. B., & Stephenson, J. M. (1970). Critical time intervals for taking in-flight information in a ball-catching task. *Ergonomics, 13,* 265–272.

Wickens, C. D. (1980). The structure of processing resources. In R. Nickerson (Ed.), *Attention and performance VII* (pp. 239–257). Hillsdale, NJ: Erlbaum.

Wickens, C. D. (1992). *Engineering psychology and human performance* (2nd ed.). New York: HarperCollins.

Wickstrom, R. L. (1958). Comparative study of methodologies for teaching gymnastics and tumbling stunts. *Research Quarterly, 29,* 109–115.

Wiese-Bjornstal, D. M., & Weiss, M. R. (1992). Modeling effects on children's form kinematics, performance outcome, and cognitive recognition of a sport skill. *Research Quarterly for Exercise and Sport, 63,* 67–75.

Wightman, D. C., & Lintern, G. (1985). Part-task training strategies for tracking and manual control. *Human Factors, 27,* 267–283.

Wilberg, R. B., & Salmela, J. (1973). Information load and response consistency in sequential short-term memory. *Perceptual and Motor Skills, 37,* 23–29.

Williams, A. M., Davids, K., Burwitz, L., & Williams, J. G. (1994). Visual search strategies in experienced and inexperienced soccer players. *Research Quarterly for Exercise and Sport, 65,* 127–135.

Williams, J. G. (1988). Perception of a throwing action from point-light demonstrations. *Perceptual and Motor Skills, 67,* 273–274.

Williams, J. G., &. McCririe, N. (1988). Control of arm and fingers during ball catching. *Journal of Human Movement Studies, 14,* 241–247.

Wilson, P. N., Foreman, N., & Tlauka, M. (1997). Transfer of spatial information from a virtual to a real environment. *Human Factors, 39,* 526–531.

Winstein, C. J., Pohl, P. S., Cardinale, C., Green, A., Scholtz, L., Waters, C. S. (1996). Learning a partial-weight-bearing skill: Effectiveness of two forms of feedback. *Physical Therapy, 76,* 985–993.

Winstein, C. J., & Schmidt, R. A. (1990). Reduced frequency of knowledge of results enhances motor skill learning. *Journal of Experimental Psychology: Learning, Memory, and Cognition, 16,* 677–691.

Winther, K. T., & Thomas, J. R. (1981). Developmental differences in children's labeling of movement. *Journal of Motor Behavior, 13,* 77–90.

Wood, C. A., Gallagher, J. D., Martino, P. V., & Ross, M. (1992). Alternate forms of knowledge of results: Interaction of augmented feedback modality on learning. *Journal of Human Movement Studies, 22,* 213–230.

Wood, C. A., & Ging, C. A. (1991). The role of interference and task similarity on the acquisition, retention, and transfer of simple motor skills. *Research Quarterly for Exercise and Sport, 62,* 18–26.

Wood, J. M., & Abernethy, B. (1997). As assessment of the efficacy of sports vision training programs. *Optometry and Vision Science, 74,* 646–659.

Woodworth, R. S. (1899). The accuracy of voluntary movement. *Psychological Review Monographs, 3* (Whole No. 302).

Wright, D. L., Smith-Munyon, V. L., & Sidaway, B. (1997). How close is too close for precise knowledge of results? *Research Quarterly for Exercise and Sport, 68,* 172–176.

Wright, D. L., Snowden, S., & Willoughby, D. (1990). Summary KR: How much information is used from the summary? *Journal of Human Movement Studies, 19,* 119–128.

Wrisberg, C. A., & Liu, Z. (1991). The effect of contextual variety on the practice, retention, and transfer of an applied motor skill. *Research Quarterly for Exercise and Sport, 62,* 406–412.

Wrisberg, C. A., & Pein, R. L. (1992). The preshot interval and free-throw shooting accuracy: An exploratory investigation. *The Sport Psychologist, 6,* 14–23.

Wu, C., Trombly, C. A., Lin, K., & Tickle-Degnen, L. (1998). Effects of object affordances on reaching performance in persons with and without cerebrovascular accident. *American Journal of Occupational Therapy, 52,* 447–456.

Wulf, G., Hoess, M., & Prinz, W. (1998). Instructions for motor learning: Differential effects of internal versus external focus of attention. *Journal of Motor Behavior, 30,* 169–179.

Wulf, G., Lauterbach, B., & Toole, T. (1999). The learning advantages of an external focus of attention in golf. *Research Quarterly for Exercise and Sport, 70,* 120–126.

Wulf, G., & Lee, T. D. (1993). Contextual interference in movements of the same class: Differential effects on program and parameter learning. *Journal of Motor Behavior, 25,* 254–263.

Wulf, G., Lee, T. D., & Schmidt, R. A. (1994). Reducing knowledge of results about relative versus absolute timing: Differential effects on learning. *Journal of Motor Behavior, 26,* 362–369.

Wulf, G., & Schmidt, R. A. (1996). Average KR degrades parameter learning. *Journal of Motor Behavior, 28,* 371–381.

Wulf, G., Schmidt, R. A., & Deubel, H. (1993). Reduced feedback frequency enhances generalized motor program learning but not parameterization learning. *Journal of Experimental Psychology: Learning, Memory, and Cognition, 19,* 1134–1150.

Wulf, G., Shea, C. H., & Matschiner, S. (1998). Frequent feedback enhances complex skill learning. *Journal of Motor Behavior, 30,* 180–192.

Wulf, G., Shea, C. H., & Whitacre, C. A. (1998). Physical guidance benefits in learning a complex motor skill. *Journal of Motor Behavior, 30,* 367–380.

Wulf, G., & Toole, T. (1999). Physical assistance devices in complex motor skill learning: Benefits of a self-controlled practice schedule. *Research Quarterly for Exercise and Sport, 70,* 265–272.

Wulf, G., & Weigelt, C. (1997). Instructions about physical principles in learning a complex motor skill: To tell or not to tell. . . . *Research Quarterly for Exercise and Sport, 68,* 362–367.

Wuyts, I. J., & Buekers, M. J. (1995). The effects of visual and auditory models on the learning of a rhythmical synchronization dance skill. *Research Quarterly for Exercise and Sport, 66,* 105–115.

Yao, W. X., & Fischman, M. G. (1999). Kinematic characteristics of aiming movements as a function of temporal and spatial constraints. *Motor Control, 3,* 424–435.

Yao, W. X., Fischman, M. G., & Wang, Y. T. (1994). Motor skill acquisition and retention as a function of average feedback, summary feedback, and performance variability. *Journal of Motor Behavior, 26,* 273–282.

Young, D. E., & Schmidt, R. A. (1992). Augmented kinematic feedback for motor learning. *Journal of Motor Behavior, 24,* 261–273.

Zanone, P. G., & Kelso, J. A. S. (1994). The coordination dynamics of learning: Theoretical structure and experimental agenda. In S. Swinnen, H. Heuer, J. Massion, & P. Casaer (Eds.), *Interlimb coordination: Neural, dynamical, and cognitive constraints* (pp. 461–490). San Diego: Academic Press.

Zelaznik, H. N., & Franz, E. (1990). Stimulus-response compatibility and the programming of motor activity: Pitfalls and possible new directions. In R. Proctor & T. G. Reeve (Eds.), *Stimulus-response compatibility: An integrated perspective* (pp. 279–295). Amsterdam: North-Holland.

Zelaznik, H. N., Hawkins, B., & Kisselburgh, L. (1983). Rapid visual feedback processing in single-aiming movements. *Journal of Motor Behavior, 15,* 217–236.

Zelinsky, G. J., Rao, R. P. N., Hayhoe, M. M., & Ballard, D. H. (1997). Eye movements reveal the spatiotemporal dynamics of visual search. *Psychological Science, 8,* 448–453.

Zubiaur, M., Oña, A., & Delgado, J. (1999). Learning volleyball serves: A preliminary study of the effects of knowledge of performance and results, *Perceptual and Motor Skills, 89,* 223–232.

GLOSSARY

■

Ability   A general trait or capacity of an individual that is a determinant of a person's achievement potential for the performance of specific skills.

Absolute error (AE)   The unsigned deviation from the target or criterion, representing amount of error. A measure of the magnitude of an error without regard to the direction of the deviation.

Acceleration   A kinematic measure that describes change in velocity during movement. We derive it from velocity by dividing change in velocity by change in time.

Action   A goal-directed activity that consists of body and/or limb movements.

Action preparation   The activity that occurs between the intention to perform and the initiation of an action. Sometimes, the term *motor programming* is used to refer to this activity.

Arousal   The general state of excitability of a person, involving physiological, emotional, and mental systems.

Associative stage   The second stage of learning in the Fitts and Posner model. An intermediate stage on the learning stages continuum.

Asymmetric transfer   Bilateral transfer in which there is a greater amount of transfer from one limb than from the other limb.

Attention   In human performance, conscious or nonconscious engagement in perceptual, cognitive, and/or motor activities before, during, and after performing skills. The human information-processing system includes limitations to the number of these activities that can be performed simultaneously.

Attentional focus   The directing of attention to specific characteristics in a performance environment, or to action preparation activities.

Attractors   The stable behavioral steady states of systems. In terms of human coordinated movement, attractors characterize preferred behavioral states, such as the in-phase and out-of-phase states for rhythmic bimanual finger movements.

Augmented feedback   A generic term used to describe information about performing a skill that is added to sensory feedback and comes from a source external to the person performing the skill. It is sometimes referred to as extrinsic or external feedback.

Automaticity   The term used to indicate that a person performs a skill, or engages in certain information-processing activities, without requiring attention resources.

Autonomous stage   The third stage of learning in the Fitts and Posner model. The final stage on the learning continuum. Also called the *automatic stage*.

■

Bilateral transfer   Transfer of learning that occurs between two limbs.

Bimanual coordination   A motor skill that requires the simultaneous use of the two arms. The skill may require the two arms to move with the same or different spatial and/or temporal characteristics.

Biofeedback　A type of augmented feedback that provides information about physiological processes through the use of instrumentation (e.g., EMG biofeedback).

■

Central-resource theories　Attention-capacity theories that propose one central source of attention resources for which all activities requiring attention compete.

Closed-loop control system　A system of control in which during the course of an action feedback is compared against a standard or reference to enable an action to be carried out as planned.

Closed motor skill　A motor skill performed in a stable or predictable environment where the performer determines when to begin the action.

Cognitive mediation theory　A theory for explaining the benefit of a demonstration proposing that when a person observes a skilled model, the person translates the observed movement information into a cognitive code that the person stores in memory and uses when the observer performs the skill.

Cognitive stage　The first stage of learning in the Fitts and Posner model. The beginning or initial stage on the learning continuum.

Concurrent augmented feedback　Augmented feedback that is provided while a person is performing a skill or making a movement.

Constant error(CE)　The signed (+/−) deviation from the target or criterion. It represents amount and direction of error and serves as a measure of performance bias.

Contextual interference　The interference that results from practicing variations of a skill within the context of practice.

Contextual interference effect　The learning benefit resulting from practicing multiple skills in a high contextual interference practice schedule (e.g., random practice), rather than practicing the skills in a low contextual interference schedule (e.g., blocked practice).

Continuous motor skill　A motor skill with arbitrary beginning and end points. These skills usually involve repetitive movements.

Control parameters　Coordinated movement control variables (e.g., tempo, or speed, and force) that freely change according to the characteristics of an action situation. According to the dynamic pattern view of motor control when a control parameter is systematically varied (e.g., speed is increased from slow to fast), an order parameter may remain stable or change its stable state characteristic at a certain level of change of the control parameter.

Coordination　The patterning of body and limb motions relative to the patterning of environmental objects and events.

Coordinative structures　Functionally specific collectives of muscles and joints that are constrained by the nervous system to act cooperatively to produce an action.

Cost-benefit trade-off　The cost (in terms of slower RT) and benefit (in terms of faster RT) that occur as a result of biasing the preparation of an action in favor of one of several possible actions (as opposed to preparing as if each possible action is equally probable).

■

Deafferentation　A procedure that researchers use to make proprioceptive feedback unavailable (through surgically severing or removing afferent neural pathways involved in the movement). It also can result from injury or surgery to afferent neural pathways involved in proprioception.

Declarative knowledge　Knowledge about "what to do" in a situation; this knowledge typically is verbalizable.

Degrees of freedom　The number of independent elements or components in a control system and the number of ways each component can act.

Degrees-of-freedom problem　A control problem that occurs in the designing of a complex system that must produce a specific result. The design problem involves determining how to constrain the system's many degrees of freedom so that it can produce the specific result.

Descriptive KP　A verbal knowledge of performance (KP) statement that only describes the error a person has made during the performance of a skill.

Discrete motor skill　A motor skill with clearly defined beginning and end points, usually requiring a simple movement.

Displacement　A kinematic measure describing changes in the spatial positions of a limb or joint during the time course of the movement.

Distributed practice   A practice schedule in which the amount of rest between practice sessions or trials is relatively long.

Dual-task procedure   An experimental procedure used in the study of attention to determine the amount of attention required to perform an action, or a part of an action. The procedure involves assessing the degree of interference caused by one task when a person is simultaneously performing another task.

Dynamic pattern theory   An approach to describing and explaining the control of coordinated movement that emphasizes the role of information in the environment and the dynamic properties of the body and limbs. It is also known as the dynamical systems theory.

Dynamic view of modeling   A theoretical view explaining the benefit of observing a skilled model demonstrate a skill. It proposes that the visual system is capable of automatically processing the observed movement in a way that constrains the motor control system to act accordingly, so that the person does not need to engage in cognitive mediation.

■

Electromyography (EMG)   A measurement technique that records the electrical activity of a muscle or group of muscles. It indicates the onset, offset, and amount of muscle activity.

Encoding   A memory process involving the transformation of information to be remembered into a form that can be stored in memory.

Encoding specificity principle   A memory principle that indicates the close relationship between encoding and retrieval memory processes. It states that memory test performance is directly related to the amount of similarity between the practice and the test contexts, i.e., the more similarity, the better the test performance will be.

Episodic memory   A subsystem of long-term memory in which we store our knowledge about personally experienced events, along with information about the time that they were experienced.

External imagery   A form of mental practice in which a person imagines viewing himself or herself performing a skill from the perspective of an observer.

■

Fading technique   A method of decreasing the frequency of augmented feedback by systematically reducing the frequency during the course of practice so that the person is effectively "weaned" from depending on its availability.

Fine motor skill   A motor skill that requires control of small muscles to achieve the goal of the skill; typically involves eye-hand coordination and requires a high degree of precision of hand and finger movement.

Fitts' law   A human performance law specifying the movement time for an aiming action when the distance to move and the target size are known. It is quantified as MT = $a + b \log_2(2 D/W)$, where a and b are constants and W = target width, and D = distance from the starting point to the target.

Fixation/diversification   The learner's goals in the second stage of learning in Gentile's model. *Fixation* refers to the goal for learning closed skills in which learners refine movement patterns so that they can produce them correctly, consistently, and efficiently from trial to trial. *Diversification* refers to the goal for learning open skills in which learners acquire the capability to modify the movement pattern according to environmental context characteristics.

Foreperiod   In a reaction time paradigm, the time interval between a warning signal and the go signal, or stimulus.

Fractionization   A part-task training method related to bimanual skills that involves practicing each arm separately before performing with the arms together.

Freezing the degrees of freedom   A common initial strategy of beginning learners to control the many degrees of freedom associated with the coordination demands of a motor skill (e.g., the person holds some arm joints rigid, i.e., "freezes" them) while performing the skill.

■

General motor ability hypothesis   A hypothesis that maintains that the many different motor abilities that exist in an individual are highly related and can be characterized in terms of a singular, global motor ability.

Generalized motor program   The general memory representation of a class of actions that share common invariant characteristics. It provides the basis for controlling a specific action within the class of actions.

"Getting the idea of the movement"   The learner's goal in the first stage of learning in Gentile's model. It refers to the need for the learner to establish an appropriate movement coordination pattern to accomplish the goal of the skill.

Gross motor skill   A motor skill that requires the use of large musculature to achieve the goal of the skill.

Guidance hypothesis   A hypothesis indicating that the role of augmented feedback in learning is to guide performance to be correct during practice. However, if it is provided too frequently, it can cause the learner to develop a dependency on its availability and therefore to perform poorly when it is not available.

■

Hick's law   A law of human performance stating that RT will increase logarithmically as the number of stimulus-response choices increases.

■

Identical elements theory   An explanation of positive transfer proposing that transfer is due to the degree of similarity between the component parts or characteristics of two skills or two performance contexts.

Imagery ability   An individual-difference characteristic that differentiates people who can image an action with a high degree of vividness and control from people who have difficulty imaging an action.

Index of difficulty (ID)   According to Fitts' law, a quantitative measure of the difficulty of performing a skill involving both speed and accuracy requirements. It is calculated as the $\log_2(2\,D/W)$, where W = target width, and D = distance from the starting point to the target.

Internal imagery   A form of mental practice in which a person imagines being inside his or her own body while performing a skill and experiencing the sensations that are expected in the actual situation.

Intertrial variability   An environmental context characteristic in Gentile's taxonomy of motor skills. The term refers to whether the regulatory conditions that exist for the performance of a skill in one situation or for one trial are present or absent in the next situation or trial.

Invariant features   A unique set of characteristics that defines a generalized motor program and does not vary from one performance of the action to another.

■

Kinematics   The description of motion without regard to force or mass. It includes displacement, velocity, and acceleration.

Kinetics   The study of the role of force as a cause of motion.

Knowledge of performance (KP)   A category of augmented feedback that gives information about the movement characteristics that led to a performance outcome.

Knowledge of results (KR)   A category of augmented feedback that gives information about the outcome of performing a skill or about achieving the goal of the performance.

KR-delay interval   The interval of time between the completion of a movement and the presentation of augmented feedback.

■

Learning   A change in the capability of a person to perform a skill. It must be inferred from a relatively permanent improvement in performance as a result of practice or experience.

Long-term memory   A component of the structure of memory that serves as a relatively permanent storage repository for information.

■

Massed practice   A practice schedule in which the amount of rest between practice sessions or trials is very short.

Memory   (a) Our capacity to remember or be influenced by past experiences. (b) A component of the information-processing system in which information is stored and processed.

Mental practice   The cognitive rehearsal of a physical skill in the absence of overt physical movements. It usually involves imaging oneself performing a skill.

Modeling   The use of demonstration as a means of conveying information about how to perform a skill.

Motor ability   An ability that is specifically related to the performance of a motor skill.

Motor equivalence   The capability of the motor control system to enable a person to achieve an action goal in a variety of situations and conditions (e.g., writing your signature with either hand).

Motor program   A memory representation that stores information needed to perform an action.

Motor skill   A skill that requires voluntary body and/or limb movement to achieve its goal.

Movements   Behavioral characteristics of specific limbs or a combination of limbs that are component parts of an action or motor skill.

Movement time (MT)   The interval of time between the initiation of a movement and the completion of the movement.

Multiple-resource theories   Theories of attention proposing that there are several attention resource mechanisms, each of which is related to a specific information-processing activity, and is limited in how much information it can process simultaneously.

■

Negative transfer   The negative effect of prior experience on performance of a skill, so a person performs the skill less well than he or she would have without prior experience.

Nonlinear behavior   A behavior that changes in abrupt, nonlinear ways in response to systematic linear increases in the value of a specific variable (e.g., the change from smooth to turbulent water flow in a tube at a specific increase in water velocity; the change from a walking to a running gait at a specific increase in gait velocity).

■

Observational learning   Learning a skill by observing a person performing the skill. Also known as *modeling*.

Open-loop control system   A control system in which all the information needed to initiate and carry out an action as planned is contained in the initial commands to the effectors.

Open motor skill   A motor skill that involves a nonstable unpredictable environment where an object or environmental context is in motion and determines when to begin the action.

Order parameters   Functionally specific variables that define the overall behavior of a system. They enable a coordinated pattern of movement to be reproduced and distinguished from other patterns (e.g., relative phase). Known also as collective variables.

Organization   When applied to a complex motor skill, the relationship among the components of the skill.

Overlearning   Practice that continues beyond the amount needed to achieve a certain performance criterion.

■

Parameters   Features of the generalized motor program that can be varied from one performance of a skill to another. The features of a skill that must be added to the invariant features of a generalized motor program before a person can perform a skill to meet the specific demands of a situation.

Perception-action coupling   The interaction between perceptual and movement variables that result in specific movement dynamics of an action in accordance with specific characteristics of the perceptual variable (e.g., the stride-length adjustments of long jumpers during the end of the run-up according to the time to contact with the take-off board, which is specified by the perceptual variable *tau;* the specific kinematic characteristics of a reach-and-grasp action associated with specific object characteristics).

Performance   The behavioral act of performing a skill at a specific time and in a specific situation.

Performance bandwidth   In the context of providing augmented feedback, a range of acceptable performance error. Augmented feedback is given only when the amount of error is greater than this tolerance limit.

Performance curve   A line graph describing performance in which the level of achievement of a performance measure is plotted for a specific sequence of time (e.g., sec, min, days) or trials. The units of the performance measure are on the Y-axis (vertical axis) and the time units or trials are on the X-axis (horizontal axis).

Performance outcome measures   A category of motor skill performance measures that indicate the outcome or result of performing a motor skill (e.g., how far a person walked, how fast a person ran a certain distance, or how many degrees a person flexed a knee).

Performance plateau   While learning a skill, a period of time in which the learner experiences no improvement after having experienced consistent improvement. Typically, the learner then experiences further improvement with continued practice.

Performance production measures   A category of motor skill performance measures that indicate the performance of specific aspects of the motor control system during the performance of an action (e.g., limb kinematics, force, EEG, EMG, etc.)

Point-light technique   A research procedure used to determine the relative information people use to perceive and identify coordinated human actions. It involves placing LEDs or light-reflecting material on certain joints of a person, then filming or videotaping the person performing an action. When an observer views the film or video, he or she sees only the joints in action.

Positive transfer   The beneficial effect of previous experience on the learning or performance of a new skill, or on the performance of a skill in a new context.

Post-KR interval   The interval of time between the presentation of augmented feedback and the beginning of the next trial.

Power law of practice   A mathematical law describing the change in rate of performance improvement during skill learning. Large amounts of improvement occur during early practice, but smaller improvement rates characterize further practice.

Practice variability   The variety of movement and context characteristics a person experiences while practicing a skill.

Prehension   The action of reaching for and grasping an object that may be stationary or moving.

Prescriptive KP   A verbal statement of knowledge of performance (KP) that describes errors made during the performance of a skill and states (i.e., prescribes) what needs to be done to correct them.

Proactive interference   A cause of forgetting due to activity that occurs prior to the presentation of information to be remembered.

Procedural knowledge   Knowledge that enables a person to know "how to do" a skill; this knowledge typically is difficult to verbalize, or is not verbalizable.

Procedural memory   A subsystem of long-term memory that stores and provides knowledge about "how to do" a skill or activity.

Proprioception   The perception of limb, body, and head movement characteristics. Afferent neural pathways send to the central nervous system proprioceptive information about characteristics such as limb movement direction, location in space, and velocity.

Psychological refractory period (PRP)   A delay period during which a person seems to put planned action "on hold" while executing a previously initiated action.

■

Qualitative augmented feedback   Augmented feedback that is descriptive in nature (e.g., using such terms as *good, long*), and indicates the quality of performance.

Quantitative augmented feedback   Augmented feedback that includes a numeric value related to the magnitude of a performance characteristic (e.g., the speed of a pitched baseball).

■

Reaction time (RT)   The interval of time between the onset of a signal (stimulus) and the initiation of a response.

Recall test   An explicit memory test that requires a person to produce a required response with few, if any, available cues or aids.

Recognition test   An explicit memory test that requires a person to select a correct response from several alternative responses.

Regulatory conditions   Characteristics of the environmental context that determine (i.e., "regulate") the required movement characteristics needed to perform an action.

Rehearsal   A memory storage process that enables a person to transfer information from the working memory to long-term memory, and to enhance the memorability of information in long-term memory.

Relative time   The proportion of the total amount of time required by each of the various components of a skill during the performance of that skill.

Response time   The time interval involving both reaction time and movement time; that is, the time from the onset of a signal (stimulus) to the completion of a response.

Retention test   A test of a practiced skill that a learner performs following an interval of time after practice has ceased.

Retrieval   A memory process involving the search through long-term memory for information needed to perform the task at hand.

Retroactive interference   A cause of forgetting due to activity occurring during the retention interval.

Root-mean-squared error (RMSE)   An error measure used for continuous skills to indicate the amount of error between the performance curve produced and the criterion performance curve for a specific amount of time during which performance is sampled.

■

Schema   A rule or set of rules that serves to provide the basis for a decision. In Schmidt's schema theory, an abstract representation of rules governing movement.

Segmentation   A part-task training method that involves separating the skill into parts and then practicing the parts so that after one part is practiced, it is then practiced together with the next part, and so on. Also known as the progressive part method.

Self-organization   The emergence of a specific stable pattern of behavior due to certain conditions characterizing a situation rather than to a specific control mechanism organizing the behavior, e.g., in the physical world hurricanes self-organize when certain wind and water temperature conditions exist.

Semantic memory   A subsystem of long-term memory in which we store our general knowledge about the world that has developed from many experiences. This knowledge includes factual and conceptual knowledge.

Serial motor skill   A motor skill involving a series of discrete skills.

Simplification   A part-task training method that involves reducing the difficulty of specific parts or features of a skill.

Skill   (a) An action or task that has a specific goal to achieve. (b) An indicator of quality of performance.

Specificity of motor abilities hypothesis   A hypothesis that maintains that the many motor abilities in an individual are relatively independent.

Speed-accuracy trade-off   A characteristic of motor skill performance in which the speed at which a skill is performed is influenced by movement accuracy demands. The trade-off is that increasing speed yields decreasing accuracy, and vice versa.

Stability   A behavioral steady state of a system that represents a preferred behavioral state and incorporates the notion of invariance by noting that a stable system will spontaneously return to a stable state after it is slightly perturbed.

Stimulus-response compatibility   A characteristic of the spatial arrangement relationship between a stimulus and a response. This relationship will influence the amount of preparation time in a reaction time task involving stimulus and response choices.

Storage   A memory process involving the placing (i.e., storing) of information in long-term memory.

Subjective organization   A memory strategy that involves the organizing of a complex array or list of information in a way that is meaningful to the person performing the task (also referred to as *chunking, clustering, grouping*).

Summary augmented feedback   A method of reducing the frequency of augmented feedback by giving a person augmented feedback for a certain number of trials at the completion of those trials (e.g., KR for each of five trials after the completion of every fifth trial).

Superdiagonal form   A term describing the way the trial-to-trial correlations appear in a correlation matrix where all trials are correlated with each other. Trials that are closer to each other have scores more highly correlated. The correlation decreases as trials become farther apart.

Symmetric transfer   Bilateral transfer in which the amount of transfer is similar from one limb to another, no matter which limb is used first.

■

Task-intrinsic feedback   The sensory feedback that is naturally available while performing a skill.

Terminal augmented feedback   Augmented feedback that is provided after a person has completed the performance of a skill or the making of a movement.

Transfer-appropriate processing theory   An explanation of positive transfer proposing that transfer is due to the similarity in the cognitive processing characteristics required by the two skills or two performance situations.

Transfer of learning   The influence of having previously practiced or performed a skill or skills on the learning of a new skill.

Transfer test   A test in which a person performs a skill that is different from the skill that he or she practiced, or performs the practiced skill in a context or situation different from the practice context or situation.

Trials-delay procedure   An experimental procedure used in the study of augmented feedback. It involves giving augmented feedback for a trial not after a person completes that trial, but following completion of a later trial. e.g., for a two-trial delay, an experimenter gives augmented feedback for trials 1, 2, and 3 after trials 3, 4, and 5 respectively.

■

Variable error (VE)   An error score representing the variability (or conversely, the consistency) of performance.

Velocity   A kinematic measure describing the rate of change of an object's position with respect to time. It is derived by dividing displacement by time (e.g., m/sec, km/hr).

Verbal cues   Short, concise phrases that direct a performer's attention to important environmental regulatory characteristics or that prompt the person to perform key movement pattern elements while performing a skill.

Vigilance   Maintaining attention in a performance situation in which stimuli requiring a response occur infrequently.

Visual search   The process of directing visual attention to locate relevant information in the environment that will enable a person to determine how to perform a skill in a specific situation.

■

Working memory   A functional component of the structure of memory that operates to temporarily store and use recently presented information. It also serves as a temporary work space to integrate recently presented information with information retrieved from long-term memory so that problem-solving, decision-making, and action-preparation activities can be carried out as needed in a situation. It also serves as a processing center to transfer information to long-term memory.

Name Index

SUBJECT INDEX